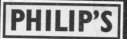

STR ATLAS

Fife & Tayside

Dundee, Dunfermline, Kirkcaldy, Perth, Stirling

www.philips-maps.co.uk

First published in 2004 by

Philip's, a division of
Octopus Publishing Group Ltd
www.octopusbooks.co.uk
2-4 Heron Quays, London E14 4JP
An Hachette Livre UK Company

Second edition 2008
First impression 2008
FATBA

ISBN-13 978-0-540-09204-8 (pocket)

© Philip's 2008

Ordnance Survey®

This product includes mapping data licensed from
Ordnance Survey® with the permission of the
Controller of Her Majesty's Stationery Office.
© Crown copyright 2008. All rights reserved.
Licence number 100011710.

Data for the speed cameras provided by
PocketGPSWorld.com Ltd.

Ordnance Survey and the OS Symbol are
registered trademarks of Ordnance Survey, the
national mapping agency of Great Britain

Post Office is a trade mark of Post Office Ltd in the
UK and other countries.

Printed by Toppan, China

Contents

II	**List of mobile speed cameras**
III	**Key to map symbols**
IV	**Key to map pages**
VI	**Route planning**
X	**Administrative and Postcode boundaries**
1	**Street maps** at 1⅓ inches to 1 mile
84	**Street maps** at 2⅔ inches to 1 mile
179	**Street map of Dundee city centre** at 5⅓ inches to 1 mile
180	**Index** of towns, villages, streets, hospitals, industrial estates, railway stations, schools, shopping centres, universities and places of interest

Digital Data

The exceptionally high-quality mapping found in this atlas is available as digital data in TIFF format, which is easily convertible to other bitmapped (raster) image formats.

The index is also available in digital form as a standard database table. It contains all the details found in the printed index together with the National Grid reference for the map square in which each entry is named.

For further information and to discuss your requirements, please contact james.mann@philips-maps.co.uk

Mobile speed cameras

The vast majority of speed cameras used on Britain's roads are operated by safety camera partnerships. These comprise local authorities, the police, Her Majesty's Court Service (HMCS) and the Highways Agency.

This table lists the sites where each safety camera partnership may enforce speed limits through the use of mobile cameras or detectors. These are usually set up on the roadside or a bridge spanning the road and operated by a police or civilian enforcement officer. The speed limit at each site (if available) is shown in red type, followed by the approximate location in black type.

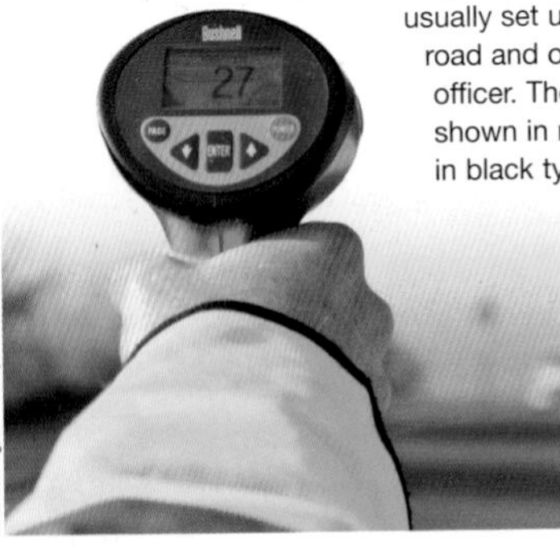

M9
70 Craigforth A84 overbridge

A9
60 Inverness to Perth road, nr Balnansteuartach

70 Perth to Inverness road, nr Inveralmond Industrial Estate

70 Stirling to Perth road, btwn Broom of Dalreoch and Upper Cairnie

70 Stirling to Perth road, Tibbermore jct

A90
70 Dundee to Perth road, Walnut Grove to Inchyra

70 Dundee to Perth road, west of Longforgan village

50 Dundee, Kingsway

50 Dundee, Swallow rdbt to Strathmartine Rd rdbt

A91
Cupar to Darsie

Deer Centre to Stratheden Jct

Guardbridge to St Andrews

Melville Lodges to St Andrews

60 Milnathort to Devon Bridge

A92
60 Arbroath to Montrose

Cadham to New Inn

Cardenden Overbridge to Chapel

Cowdenbeath to Lochgelly

Crossgates to New Inn

30 Dundee btwn Arbroath Rd and Craigie Avenue, Greendykes Rd

40 Dundee, East Dock St

Frenchie to Annsmuir

Melville Lodges to Lindifferon

New Inn to Tay Bridge

Rathillet (south) to Easter Kinnear

A93
60 Old Scone to Blairgowrie

A94
60 Scone to Coupar Angus

A822
60 Crieff to Braco

A823
Dunfermline, Queensferryroad

Dunfermline, St Margaret Drive

A907
Dunfermline, Halbeath Rd

Tullibody nr station

A908
Devonside, Alexandra St

Main St, Sanchie nr Craigview

A911
Glenrothes to Leslie

Glenrothes to Milton

A914
Dairsie to St Michaels

Edenwood to Cupar

Forgan to St Michaels

Kettlebridge

New Inn to Cupar

Pitlessie to Clushford Toll

A915
Checkbar Jct to Percival Jcts

A921
Kirkcaldy, Esplanade

Kirkcaldy, High St/Path

Kirkcaldy, Rosslyn St

Kirkcaldy, St Clair St

A923
60 Blairgowrie to Muirhead

A933
60 Colliston to Redford

A935
60 Brechin to Montrose

A955
Dysart to Coaltown of Wemyss

Methilhaven Rd, Buckhaven

Methilhaven Rd, Methil

A972
40 Dundee, Kingsway East to Pitairlie Rd

A977
Kincardine, Fere Gait

60 Kinross to Crook of Devon

A985
Culross (west) to C38 Valleyfield

Kincardine to Rosyth

Rosyth, Admiralty Rd

Waukmill to Brankholm

B914
Redcraigs to Greenknowes

B920
Crosshill to Ballingry

B942
East of Collinsburgh

B961
30 Dundee, Drumgeith Rd

B980
Rosyth, Castlandhill Rd

B981
Cowdenbeath, Broad St

Gosshill to Ballingry

Kirkcaldy, Dunnikier Way

B996
60 Kinross to Kelty

B9157
Bankhead of Pitheadle to Kirkcaldy

Orrock to East Balbairdie

Sheriff Rdbt to Kirkcaldy

White Lodge Jct to Croftgary

UNCLASSIFIED
Buckhaven, Methilhaven Rd

30 Dundee, Broughty Ferry Rd

30 Dundee, Charleston Drive

30 Dundee, Laird St

30 Dundee, Old Glamis Rd

30 Dundee, Perth Rd

30 Dundee, Strathmartine Rd

Dunfermline, Masterton Rd

Dunfermline, Townhill Rd

Glenrothes, Formonthills Rd

Glenrothes, Woodside Rd

Glenrothes, Woodside Way

Glenrothes, Woodside Rd

Kirkcaldy, Hendry Rd

Leven, Glenlyon Rd

Methil, Methilhaven Rd

Key to map symbols

III

Motorway with junction number			**Ambulance station**
Primary route – dual/single carriageway			**Coastguard station**
A road – dual/single carriageway			**Fire station**
B road – dual/single carriageway			**Police station**
Minor road – dual/single carriageway			**Accident and Emergency entrance to hospital**
Other minor road – dual/single carriageway			**Hospital**
Road under construction			**Place of worship**
Tunnel, covered road			**Information Centre** (open all year)
Speed cameras - single, multiple			**Shopping Centre**
Rural track, private road or narrow road in urban area			**Parking, Park and Ride**
Gate or obstruction to traffic (restrictions may not apply at all times or to all vehicles)			**Post Office**
Path, bridleway, byway open to all traffic, road used as a public path			**Camping site, caravan site**
Pedestrianised area			**Golf course, picnic site**
Postcode boundaries		Prim Sch	**Important buildings, schools, colleges, universities and hospitals**
County and unitary authority boundaries			**Built up area**
Railway, tunnel, railway under construction			**Woods**
Tramway, tramway under construction		River Ouse	**Tidal water, water name**
Miniature railway			**Non-tidal water** – lake, river, canal or stream
Walsall **Railway station**			**Lock, weir, tunnel**
Private railway station		Church	**Non-Roman antiquity**
South Shields **Metro station**		ROMAN FORT	**Roman antiquity**
Tram stop, tram stop under construction		87	**Adjoining page indicators and overlap bands**
Bus, coach station		237	The colour of the arrow and the band indicates the scale of the adjoining or overlapping page (see scales below)

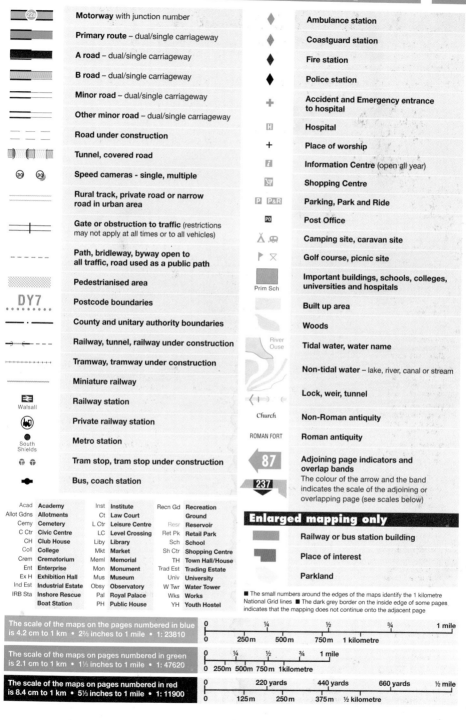

Acad	**Academy**	Inst	**Institute**	Recn Gd	**Recreation Ground**
Allot Gdns	**Allotments**	Ct	**Law Court**		
Cemy	**Cemetery**	L Ctr	**Leisure Centre**	Resr	**Reservoir**
C Ctr	**Civic Centre**	LC	**Level Crossing**	Ret Pk	**Retail Park**
CH	**Club House**	Liby	**Library**	Sch	**School**
Coll	**College**	Mkt	**Market**	Sh Ctr	**Shopping Centre**
Crem	**Crematorium**	Meml	**Memorial**	TH	**Town Hall/House**
Ent	**Enterprise**	Mon	**Monument**	Trad Est	**Trading Estate**
Ex H	**Exhibition Hall**	Mus	**Museum**	Univ	**University**
Ind Est	**Industrial Estate**	Obsy	**Observatory**	W Twr	**Water Tower**
IRB Sta	**Inshore Rescue Boat Station**	Pal	**Royal Palace**	Wks	**Works**
		PH	**Public House**	YH	**Youth Hostel**

Enlarged mapping only

	Railway or bus station building
	Place of interest
	Parkland

■ The small numbers around the edges of the maps identify the 1 kilometre National Grid lines ■ The dark grey border on the inside edge of some pages indicates that the mapping does not continue onto the adjacent page

The scale of the maps on the pages numbered in blue is 4.2 cm to 1 km • 2⅔ inches to 1 mile • 1: 23810

0   ¼   ½   ¾   1 mile
0   250m   500m   750m   1 kilometre

The scale of the maps on the pages numbered in green is 2.1 cm to 1 km • 1⅓ inches to 1 mile • 1: 47620

0   ¼   ½   ¾   1 mile
0   250m 500m 750m   1kilometre

The scale of the maps on the pages numbered in red is 8.4 cm to 1 km • 5⅓ inches to 1 mile • 1: 11900

0   220 yards   440 yards   660 yards   ½ mile
0   125m   250m   375m   ½ kilometre

IV

76	Map pages at 1⅓ inches to 1 mile
122	Map pages at 2⅔ inches to 1 mile
179	Map pages at 5⅓ inches to 1 mile

Scale

| 0 | 5 | 10 | 15 | 20 km |
| 0 | | 5 | | 10 miles |

Blairgowrie **68**
Rattray
Carsie **15**
Coupar Angus

Bankfoot
24
Stanley
Guildtown

Cargill
25
Wolfhill

Burrelton
26
Kinrossie

Buchanty
33 **34** **35**
Monzie
Gilmerton
Fowlis Wester

Harrietfield
Braegrum
Methven
Tibbermore

Luncarty
36 **37**
Almondbank
Hillyland
102 103
Perth

Balbeggie
38
Scone
Kinfauns

Kinnaird
Rait
39

Comrie
101
Crieff
The Balloch
44
Muthill

Madderty
45

Clathy
46
Aberuthven

Aberdalgie
47
Forteviot
Dunning

Friarton
48
Forgandenny

Bridge of Earn
49
Abernethy

Glencarse
Chapelhill
50
Newburgh

Braco **56**
Greenloaning

Muirton
57
Blackford

Auchterarder
104
58

59

Path of Condie
60
Duncrievie

Glenfarg
61

Auchtermuchty
62
Strathmiglo
Gateside

Kinbuck
70 **71**
Doune
Dunblane
107
Sunnylaw

Glendevon
Burnfoot
72 **73**
Yetts o' Muckhart
Crook of Devon

74 **75**
Powmill

Milnathort
108
Kinross **76**
Scotlandwell

Kinnesswood

77
Kinglassie

Thornhill
Bridge of Allan **114 115**
Menstrie **116 117**
Tullibody

Alva Tillicoultry **118 119**
Fishcross **120 121**
Blairingone

Dollar
Hill End
122 123

Cleish
Gairney Bank

Watergate
124 125
A823

Ballingry
Lochore
126 127
Kelty Lochgelly

128 129
Cardenden

Cambusbarron
Stirling
134 135
Bannockburn
Cambus
136 137
Fallin Throsk

Alloa
138 139
Clackmannan

Forest Mill
140 141
Cowstrandburn

Saline
142 143
Bowershall

144 145

Cowdenbeath
146 147
Kingseat
Crossgates

148 149
Auchtertool

153
154 155
Airth Kincardine

156 157
Oakley
158 159
Cairneyhill

160 161
Dunfermline
Crossford

Fordell
162 163

164 165
Burntisland

Denny
168 169
Culross

Crombie
170 171
Limekilns

172 173
Rosyth

174 175
Dalgety Bay
Inverkeithing

Aberdour
176 177

Kilsyth
Glasgow and West Central Scotland STREET ATLAS
Stenhousemuir
Grangemouth
Falkirk
Bo'ness
Linlithgow

North Queensferry
178
South Queensferry

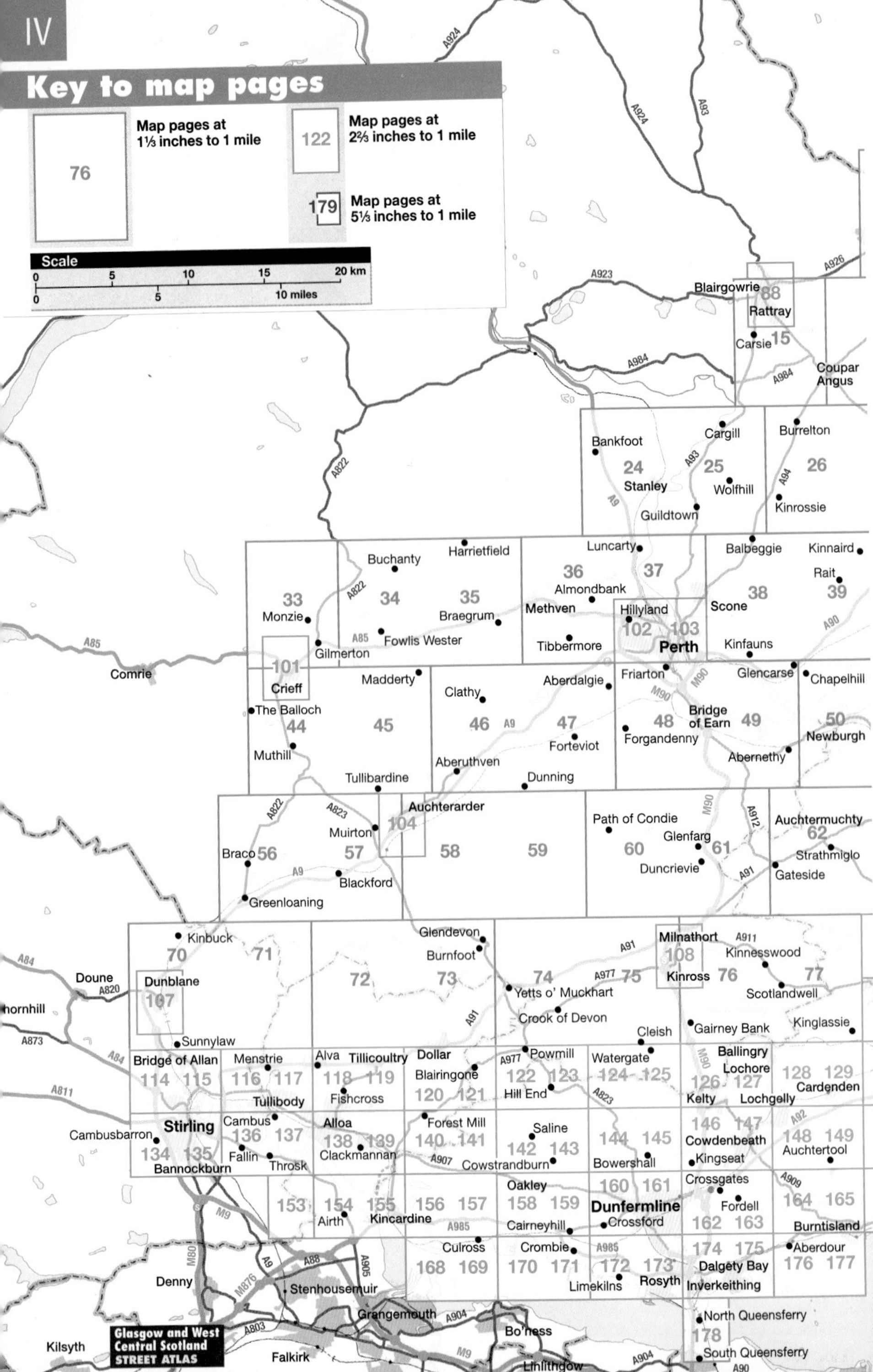

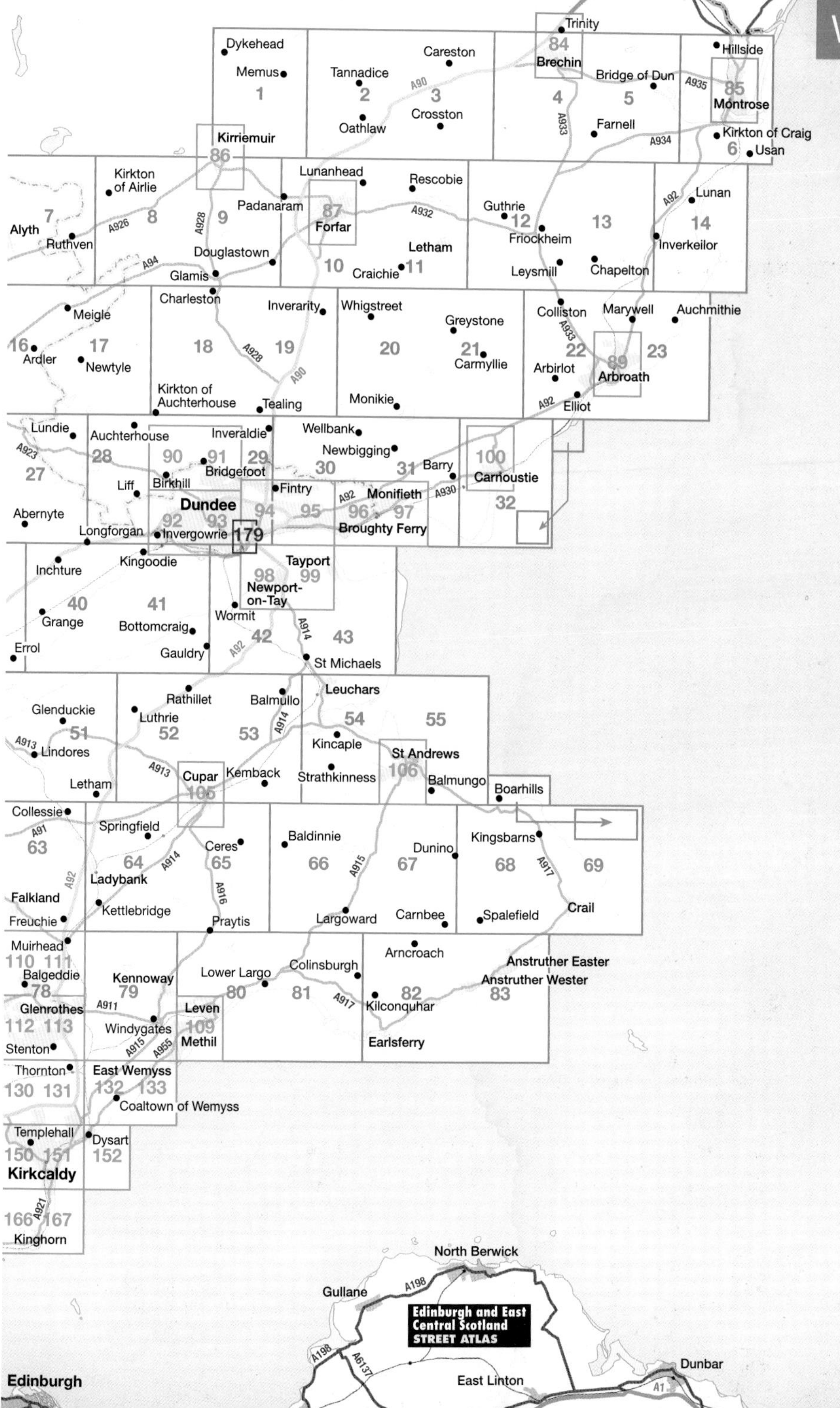

V

Dykehead
Memus
Kirriemuir
86

Tannadice
Oathlaw
1
2

Careston
Crosston
3

Trinity
Brechin
84

Bridge of Dun
Farnell
4
5

Hillside
Montrose
85

Kirkton of Craig
Usan
6

Kirkton of Airlie
Padanaram
Lunanhead
Forfar
87

Rescobie
Letham
Craichie
11

Guthrie
Friockheim
Leysmill
12

Guthrie
13

Lunan
Inverkeilor
14

Alyth
Ruthven
7
8
9

Douglastown
Glamis
Charleston
10

Meigle
16
Ardler
17
Newtyle

18
19
Inverarity
Tealing

Whigstreet
20
Monikie
Greystone
21
Carmyllie

Colliston
Arbirlot
22
Elliot

Marywell
Arbroath
89
23
Auchmithie

Lundie
27
28
Auchterhouse
90
91
29
Bridgefoot

Inveraldie
30
Newbigging
31
Barry

Wellbank
100
Carnoustie
32

Abernyte
Longforgan
Liff
Birkhill
92
93
94
179
95
96
97
Fintry
Monifieth
Broughty Ferry
Dundee

Inchture
40
Grange
Errol
41
Bottomcraig
Gauldry
42
St Michaels
43

Kingoodie
Invergowrie
98
Newport-on-Tay
Wormit
Tayport
99

Glenduckie
51
Lindores
Letham
52
Luthrie
Rathillet
53
Balmullo
Leuchars
54
Kincaple
Strathkinness
St Andrews
106
Balmungo
55
Boarhills

Collessie
63
64
Ladybank
Kettlebridge
65
Ceres
Praytis
66
Baldinnie
67
Dunino
Carnbee
68
Spalefield
69
Crail
Kingsbarns

Falkland
Freuchie
Muirhead
110 111
Balgeddie
78
Glenrothes
112 113
Stenton
Kennoway
79
Windygates
Lower Largo
80
81
82
Kilconquhar
83
Anstruther Easter
Anstruther Wester
Colinsburgh
Arncroach
Largoward
Leven
109
Methil
Earlsferry

Thornton
130 131
East Wemyss
132 133
Coaltown of Wemyss

Templehall
150 151
Kirkcaldy
Dysart
152

166 167
Kinghorn

North Berwick
Gullane
Edinburgh and East
Central Scotland
STREET ATLAS

Edinburgh
East Linton
Dunbar

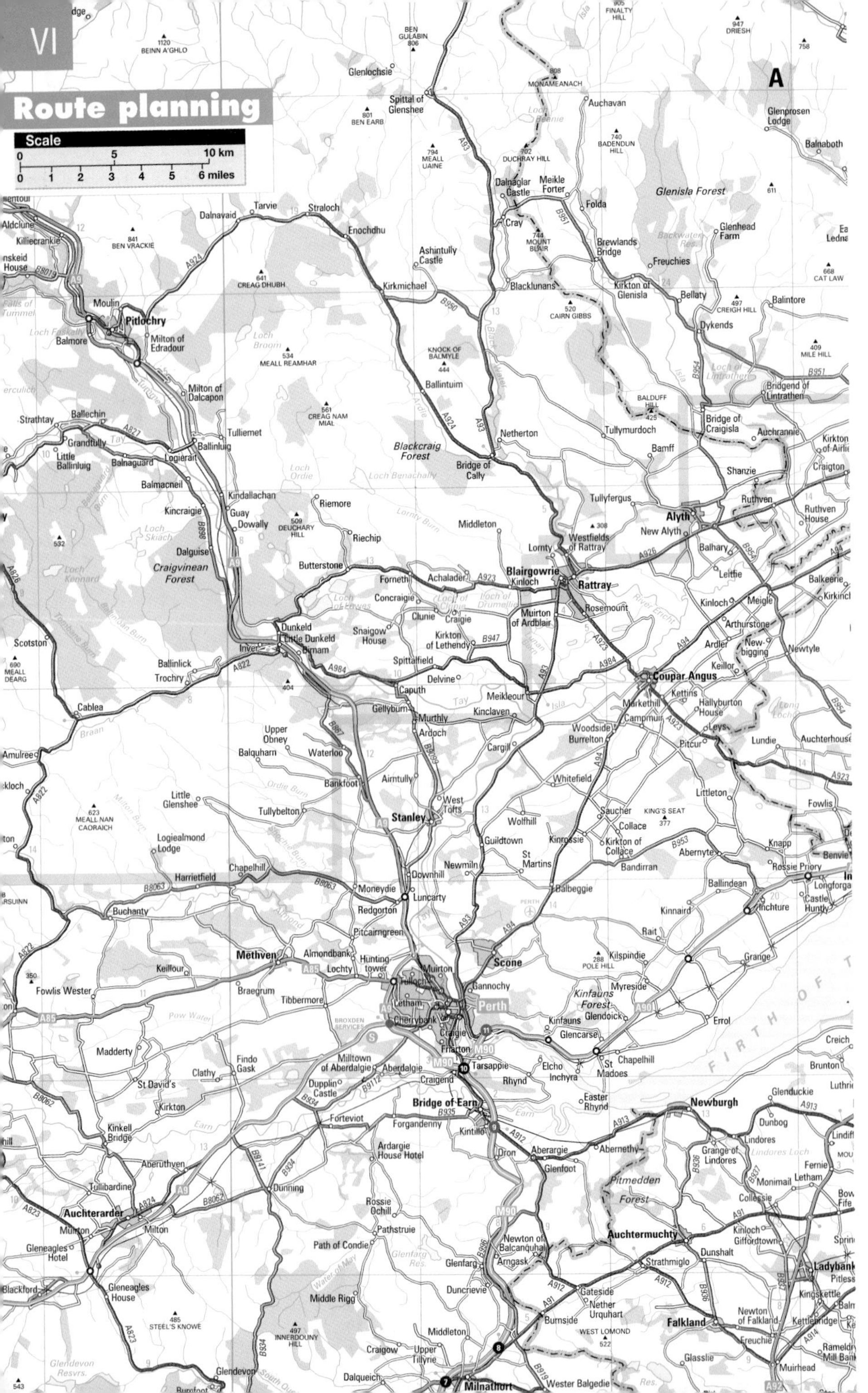

VI
Route planning
Scale
0
5
10 km
0
1
2
3
4
5
6 miles
A
BEN GULABIN 806
FINALTY HILL
947 DRIESH
758
1120 BEINN A'GHLO
Glenlochsie
Spittal of Glenshee
808 MONAMEANACH
801 BEN EARB
Auchavan
Glenprosen Lodge
Balnaboth
794 MEALL UAINE
702 DUCHRAY HILL
740 BADENDUN HILL
Dalnaglar Castle
Meikle Forter
Folda
Glenisla Forest
611
Dalnavaid
Tarvie
Straloch
Enochdhu
Cray
744 MOUNT BLAIR
Brewlands Bridge
Glenhead Farm
Aldclune
Killiecrankie
841 BEN VRACKIE
Ashintully Castle
Freuchies
Backwater Res.
668 CAT LAW
641 CREAG DHUBH
Kirkmichael
Blacklunans
Kirkton of Glenisla
Bellaty
497 CREIGH HILL
Balintore
Moulin
Pitlochry
520 CAIRN GIBBS
Dykends
Loch Faskally
Balmore
Milton of Edradour
Loch Broom
534 MEALL REAMHAR
KNOCK OF BALMYLE 444
409 MILE HILL
Loch of Lintrathen
Bridgend of Lintrathen
Milton of Dalcapon
Ballintuim
BALDUFF HILL 425
Strathtay
Ballechin
561 CREAG NAM MIAL
Bridge of Craigisla
Auchrannie
Grandtully
Tulliemet
Netherton
Tullymurdoch
Kirkton of Airlie
Little Ballinluig
Balnaguard
Logierait
Ballinluig
Blackcraig Forest
Bamff
Craigton
Balmacneil
Loch Ordie
Loch Benachally
Bridge of Cally
Shanzie
Kindallachan
Riemore
Tullyfergus
Ruthven
Kincraigie
Guay
Dowally
509 DEUCHARY HILL
Middleton
Alyth
Ruthven House
Loch Skiach
Riechip
New Alyth
308
532
Dalguise
Lornty
Westfields of Rattray
Craigvinean Forest
Butterstone
Balhary
Loch Kennard
Forneth
Achalader
Blairgowrie
Kinloch
Rattray
Leitfie
Balkeerie
Loch of Lowes
Concraigie
Loch of Clunie
Loch of Drumellie
Clunie
Craigie
Muirton of Ardblair
Rosemount
Kinloch
Meigle
River Ericht
Dunkeld
Little Dunkeld
Snaigow House
Kirkton of Lethendy
Arthurstone
Scotston
Inver
Birnam
New-bigging
Newtyle
690 MEALL DEARG
Ballinlick
Spittalfield
Ardler
Keillor
Trochry
Delvine
Coupar Angus
404
Caputh
Meikleour
Kettins
Hallyburton House
Cablea
Gellyburn
Murthly
Kinclaven
Isla
Markethill
Campmuir
Long Loch
Braan
Upper Obney
Ardoch
Woodside
Burrelton
Leys
Amulree
Balquharn
Waterloo
Cargill
Pitcur
Lundie
Auchterhouse
Airntully
Whitefield
Ordie Burn
Bankfoot
Littleton
623 MEALL NAN CAORAICH
Little Glenshee
West Tofts
Saucher
KING'S SEAT 377
Fowlis
Tullybelton
Stanley
Collace
Wolfhill
Guildtown
Kinrossie
Kirkton of Collace
Logiealmond Lodge
Abernyte
Knapp
St Martins
Benvie
Newmiln
Bandirran
Rossie Priory
Chapelhill
Harrietfield
Downhill
Ballindean
Longforgan
Balbeggie
Moneydie
Luncarty
Castle Huntly
Inchture
Kinnaird
Buchanty
Redgorton
PERTH
Pitcairngreen
Rait
Almondbank
Hunting tower
Scone
Grange
Methven
Lochty
288 POLE HILL
Kilspindie
350
Keillour
Muirton
Tulloch
Fowlis Wester
Braegrum
Gannochy
Myreside
Kinfauns Forest
Tibbermore
Letham
Perth
Glendoick
Pow Water
Cherrybank
BROXDEN SERVICES
Kinfauns
Errol
Craigie
Glencarse
Madderty
Friarton
Creich
FIRTH OF T
Fingask
Milltown of Aberdalgie
Aberdalgie
Tarsappie
Elcho
St Madoes
Chapelhill
Brunton
Clathy
Rhynd
Inchyra
St David's
Craigend
Dupplin Castle
Easter Rhynd
Luthrie
Bridge of Earn
Newburgh
Glenduckie
Kirkton
Earn
Forteviot
Forgandenny
Kintillo
Dunbog
Kinkell Bridge
Abernethy
Lindores
Lindores Loch
Aberargie
Grange of Lindores
Ardargie House Hotel
Dron
Aberuthven
Glenfoot
Fernie
Letham
Pitmedden Forest
Monimail
Tullibardine
Dunning
Auchterarder
Rossie Ochill
Collessie
Bow of Fife
Milton
Muirton
Pathstruie
Newton of Balcanquhal
Auchtermuchty
Kinloch
Giffordtown
Gleneagles Hotel
Path of Condie
Glenfarg Res.
Dunshalt
Arngask
Glenfarg
Strathmiglo
Ladybank
Pitlessie
Blackford
Water of May
Gleneagles House
Duncrievie
Gateside
Nether Urquhart
Kingskettle
Middle Rigg
Newton of Falkland
Burnside
Falkland
485 STEEL'S KNOWE
Kettlebridge
WEST LOMOND 622
497 INNERDOUNY HILL
Middleton
Freuchie
Craigow
Upper Tillyrie
Glasslie
Ramelry Mill Bank
Glendevon Resvrs.
Glendevon
Dalqueich
Milnathort
Wester Balgedie
Muirhead
543
A9
A924
A93
A827
A822
A923
A926
A94
A984
A85
A912
A913
A91
A914
A823
A824
A92
B8019
B950
B951
B954
B898
B947
B867
B9099
B8063
B953
B8062
B9112
B934
B935
B9141
B936
B937
B996
B919
M90

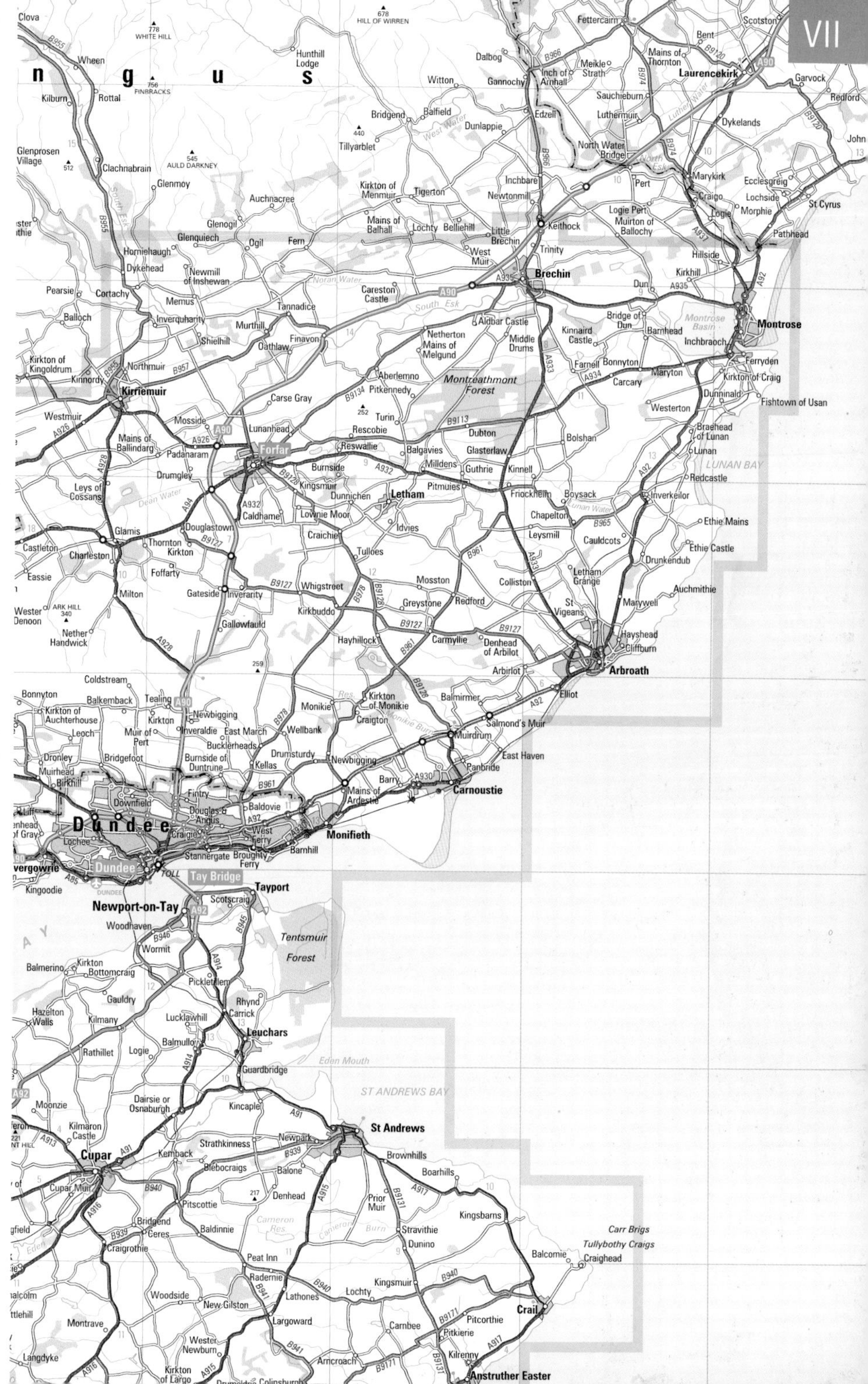
Angus
Clova
Wheen
Kilburn
Rottal
Glenprosen Village
Clachnabrain
Glenmoy
Auchnacree
Glenogil
Glenquiech
Ogil
Fern
Hornieheaugh
Dykehead
Newmill of Inshewan
Pearsie
Cortachy
Memus
Balloch
Inverquharity
Shielhill
Kirkton of Kingoldrum
Kinnordy
Northmuir
Kirriemuir
Westmuir
Mains of Ballindarg
Padanaram
Mosside
Forfar
Drumgley
Leys of Cossans
Glamis
Douglastown
Thornton
Kirkton
Castleton
Charleston
Eassie
Foffarty
Milton
Gateside
Inverarity
Wester Denoon
Nether Handwick
Gallowfauld
Coldstream
Bonnyton
Kirkton of Auchterhouse
Balkemback
Tealing
Leoch
Muir of Pert
Dronley
Bridgefoot
Muirhead
Birkhill
Downfield
Dundee
Lochee
Invergowrie
Kingoodie
Newport-on-Tay
Tay Bridge
Tayport
Scotscraig
Woodhaven
Wormit
Tentsmuir Forest
Balmerino
Kirkton
Bottomcraig
Gauldry
Pickletillem
Rhynd
Carrick
Hazelton Walls
Kilmany
Lucklawhill
Leuchars
Rathillet
Logie
Balmullo
Guardbridge
Eden Mouth
ST ANDREWS BAY
Moonzie
Dairsie or Osnaburgh
Kincaple
Kilmaron Castle
Cupar
Strathkinness
Kemback
Newpark
St Andrews
Brownhills
Blebocraigs
Balone
Cupar Muir
Pitscottie
Denhead
Boarhills
Prior Muir
Kingsbarns
Bridgend
Ceres
Baldinnie
Cameron Res
Stravithie
Dunino
Craigrothie
Peat Inn
Carr Brigs
Tullybothy Craigs
Craighead
Balcomie
Radernie
Kingsmuir
Woodside
New Gilston
Lathones
Lochty
Crail
Largoward
Carnbee
Pitcorthie
Pitkierie
Montrave
Wester Newburn
Kilrenny
Langdyke
Kirkton of Largo
Arncroach
Anstruther Easter
Colinsburgh
Hill of Wirren
White Hill
Finbracks
Hunthill Lodge
Auld Darkney
Witton
Bridgend
Balfield
Tillyarblet
Dunlappie
Kirkton of Menmuir
Tigerton
Mains of Balhall
Lochty
Belliehill
Little Brechin
West Muir
Dalbog
Gannochy
Edzell
Inch of Arnhall
Meikle Strath
Fettercairn
Mains of Thornton
Laurencekirk
Sauchieburn
Luthermuir
North Water Bridge
Inchbare
Newtonmill
Keithock
Brechin
Trinity
Scotston
Bent
Garvock
Redford
Dykelands
John
Marykirk
Pert
Ecclesgreig
Craigo
Logie
Lochside
Morphie
St Cyrus
Logie Pert
Muirton of Ballochy
Pathhead
Hillside
Kirkhill
Dun
Bridge of Dun
Montrose Basin
Montrose
Kinnaird Castle
Barnhead
Inchbraoch
Ferryden
Farnell
Bonnyton
Maryton
Kirkton of Craig
Carcary
Dunninald
Fishtown of Usan
Westerton
Careston Castle
Tannadice
Murthill
Oathlaw
Finavon
Aldbar Castle
Netherton
Mains of Melgund
Middle Drums
Aberlemno
Montreathmont Forest
Carse Gray
Pitkennedy
Turin
Lunanhead
Rescobie
Reswallie
Dubton
Balgavies
Glasterlaw
Bolshan
Braehead of Lunan
Lunan
LUNAN BAY
Redcastle
Milldens
Burnside
Guthrie
Kinnell
Kingsmuir
Pitmuies
Letham
Dunnichen
Friockheim
Boysack
Inverkeilor
Caldhame
Lownie Moor
Idvies
Chapelton
Ethie Mains
Leysmill
Cauldcots
Ethie Castle
Craichie
Tulloes
Drunkendub
Mosston
Colliston
Letham Grange
Auchmithie
Whigstreet
Greystone
Redford
St Vigeans
Marywell
Kirkbuddo
Carmyllie
Denhead of Arbilot
Hayshead
Cliffburn
Hayhillock
Arbirlot
Arbroath
Balmirmer
Elliot
Monikie
Kirkton of Monikie
Craigton
Salmond's Muir
Newbigging
Inveraldie
East March
Wellbank
Muirdrum
Bucklerheads
Burnside of Duntrune
Kellas
Drumsturdy
Newbigging
East Haven
Panbride
Barry
Carnoustie
Fintry
Baldovie
Mains of Ardestie
Douglas & Angus
Craigie
West Ferry
Monifieth
Stannergate
Broughty Ferry
Barnhill
Dundee Airport
TOLL

MEALL NAM FUARAN
Corrymuckloch
Little Glenshee
623 MEALL NAN CAORAICH
Bankfoot
Airntully
Whitefield
Newton
Logiealmond Lodge
Tullybelton
Stanley
West Tofts
Wolfhill
Guildtown
Kinrossie
931 BEN CHONZIE
648 MEALL TARSUINN
Harrietfield
Chapelhill
Moneydie
Downhill
Newmiln
St Martins
Balbeggie
Loch Turret Reservoir
Buchanty
Redgorton
Luncarty
PERTH
Pitcairngreen
Almondbank
Scone
288 POLE HILL
Methven
Hunting tower
Lochty
Muirton
Monzie
Monzie Castle
350
Fowlis Wester
Keillour
Braegrum
Tulloch
Gannochy
Kinfauns Forest
Ochtertyre
Lawers
Quoig
Hosh
Gilmerton
Tibbermore
Letham
Perth
Glendoick
Comrie
Crieff
Pow Water
BROXDEN SERVICES
Cherrybank
Craigie
Kinfauns
Glencarse
Ross
Dalginross
Lochlane
Madderty
Fındo Gask
Milltown of Aberdalgie
Aberdalgie
Friarton
Tarsappie
Elcho
St Madoes
Clathy
Inchyra
The Balloch
St David's
Dupplin Castle
Craigend
Rhynd
Easter Rhynd
Torlum Wood
Kirkton
Bridge of Earn
Culloch
Forteviot
Forgandenny
Kinkell Bridge
Kintillo
Earn
Muthill
Ochtermuthill
Ardargie House Hotel
Dron
Aberargie
Glenfoot
Aberuthven
Tullibardine
Dunning
Langside
Auchterarder
Rossie Ochill
Glenlichorn
Garrick
Muirton
Milton
Pathstruie
Path of Condie
Newton of Balcanquhal
Gleneagles Hotel
Glenfarg Res.
Glenfarg
Arngask
Braco
Blackford
Gleneagles House
Duncrievie
Gateside
Nether Urquhart
Middle Rigg
485 STEEL'S KNOWE
497 INNERDOUNY HILL
Burnside
Greenloaning
WEST LOMOND
Middleton
Craigow
Upper Tillyrie
Glendevon Resvrs.
Kinbuck
Balhaldie
Glendevon
Dalqueich
Milnathort
Wester Balgedie
Ashfield
543
Burnfoot
Castle Hill Reservoir
South Queich
Carnbo
KINROSS SERVICES
Kinross
LOCH LEVEN
Kinnesswood
611
Dunblane
Pisgah
631 BLAIRDENON HILL
721 BEN CLEUCH
Pool o' Muckhart
Yetts o' Muckhart
Drum
Crook of Devon
Coldrain
Scotlandwell
Gairney Bank
648 KING'S SEAT HILL
Rumbling Bridge
Sunnylaw
Clackmannanshire
Powmill
Cleish
Ballingry
356 BENARTY HILL
Bridge of Allan
Blairlogie
Menstrie
Tillicoultry
Dollar
Lochore
Devonside
Blairingone
Crosshill
Glencraig
Causeway-head
Alva
Tullibody
Fishcross
Coalsnaughton
Hill End
Loch Glow
Loch Ore
Kelty
Lochgelly
Raploch
Cambuskenneth
Branshill
Sauchie
Forest Mill
Keilarsbrae
Cambus
364 KNOCK HILL
Balgonar
Lassodie
Stirling
ALLOA
Torbrex
Fallin
Throsk
Clackmannan
Saline
Loch Fitty
Lumphinnans
Cowdenbeath
St Ninians
South Alloa
Kennet
Cowstrandburn
Bowershall
Kingseat
Hill of Beath
Bannockburn
Kilbagie
Comrie
Gowkhall
Wellwood
Townhill
Cowie
Dunmore
Blairhall
Oakley
Carnock
Halbeath
Crossgates
Devilla Forest
Milesmark
DUNFERMLINE
Fordell
Donibristle
Craigend
STIRLING SERVICES
Airth
Kincardine
High Valleyfield
Loch Coulter
Plean
Crossford
Cairneyhill
Letham
Culross
Low Torry
Torryburn
Kincardine Bridge
Aberdour
Torwood
Torry Bay
Dunipace
DENNY
Antonshill
Stenhousemuir
Skinflats
Charlestown
Limekilns
Rosyth
Hillend
Dalgety Bay
Bridge
Fankerton
Stoneywood
Larbert
Carron
Bainsford
GRANGEMOUTH
Inverkeithing
Head of Muir
Bonnybridge
Grangepans
Carriden
St. Margaret's Hope
Inverkeithing Bay
Dennyloanhead
FALKIRK
Laurieston
Bo'ness
Muirhouses
Forth Road Bridge
North Queensferry
Banknock
Longcroft
Greenhill
High Bonnybridge
Glen Village
Redding
Polmont
Brightons
Grougfoot
Blackness
Mannerston
Queensferry
Castlecary
Reddingmuirhead
Whitecross
Linlithgow
Newton
Dalmeny
Falkirk
Shieldhill
Maddiston
Linlithgow Bridge
Philpstoun
Old Philpstoun
Cramond
Abronhill
Jawcraig
California
Loan
Bridgend
Threemiletown
Cramond Bridge
CUMBERNAULD
Avon
Standburn
Winchburgh
Kirkliston
Turnhouse
Luggiebank
Slamannan
Crossburn
Ecclesmachan
EDINBURGH
Ingliston
Gogar
Avonbridge
Westfield
Torphichen
Broxburn
Binniehill
Uphall
Newbridge
Burnside
Ratho Station
Limerigg
312
Dechmont
Wester Dechmont
Riggend
Greengairs
Longriggend
Uphall Station
Pumpherston
Ratho
Bonnington
Wattston
Hermiston
Sighthill
Windyknowe
Bathgate
Armadale
Boghall
Deans
Wilkieston
Juniper Green
Stand
Caldercruix
LIVINGSTON
Mid Calder
East Calder
Burnwynd
Edinburgh
Currie
Plains
Westrigg
Bathville
Mayfield
Whiteside
Blackridge
Forrestfield
Oakbank
Livingston Village
Kirknewton
HARTHILL SERVICES
Blackburn
Seafield
Balerno
Malleny Mills
AIRDRIE

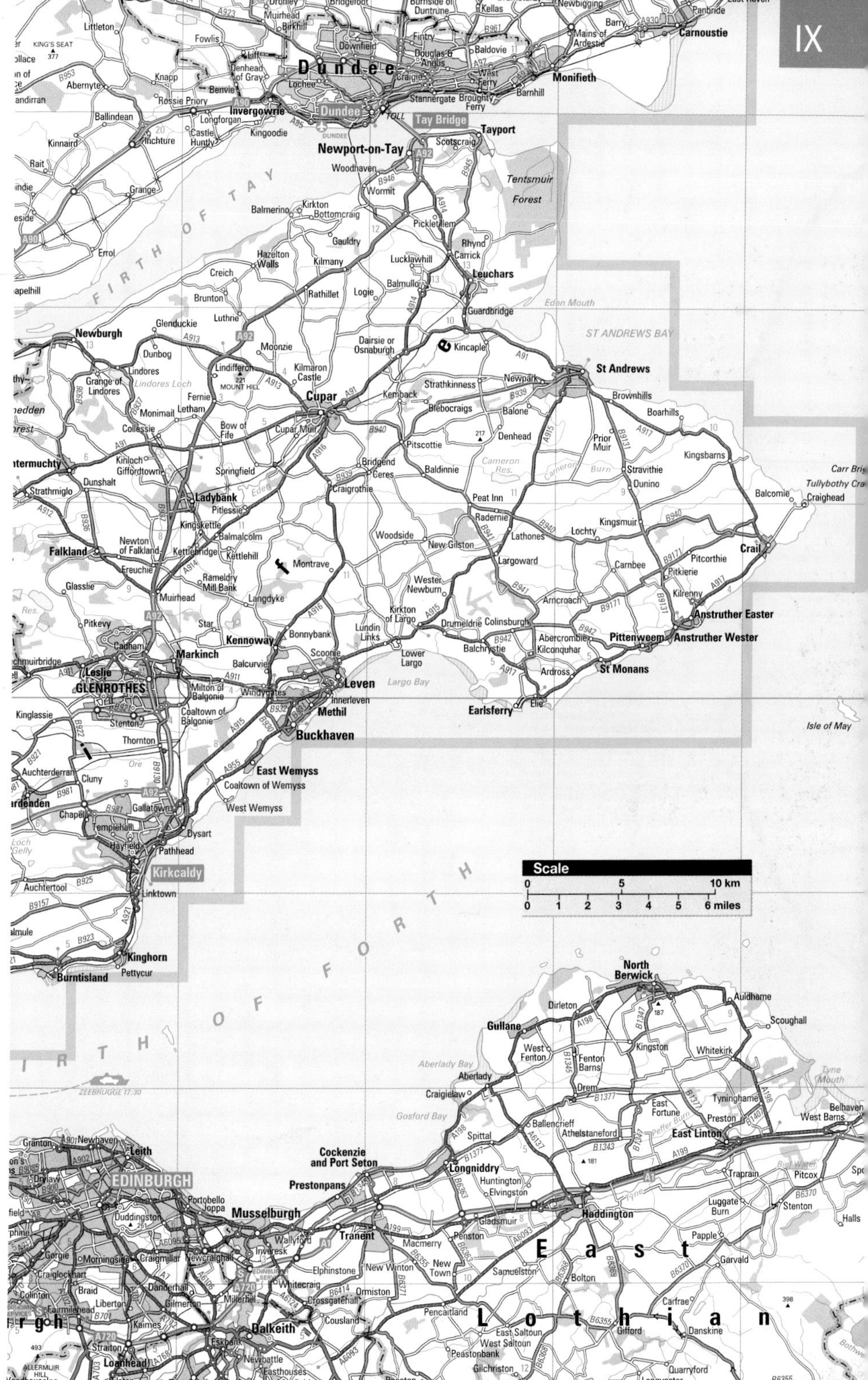

IX
Dundee
Carnoustie
Monifieth
Broughty Ferry
Invergowrie
Tay Bridge
Tayport
Newport-on-Tay
Tentsmuir Forest
FIRTH OF TAY
Leuchars
Eden Mouth
ST ANDREWS BAY
St Andrews
Newburgh
Cupar
Kincaple
Guardbridge
Balmullo
Dairsie or Osnaburgh
Kemback
Strathkinness
Brownhills
Boarhills
Kingsbarns
Crail
Cameron Res.
Peat Inn
Ceres
Pitscottie
Ladybank
Falkland
Auchtermuchty
Freuchie
Kingskettle
Kettlebridge
Markinch
Kennoway
Leslie
GLENROTHES
Leven
Methil
Buckhaven
East Wemyss
West Wemyss
Dysart
Kirkcaldy
Kinghorn
Burntisland
Pettycur
Lundin Links
Lower Largo
Largo Bay
Kirkton of Largo
Colinsburgh
Elie
Earlsferry
St Monans
Pittenweem
Anstruther Easter
Anstruther Wester
Kilrenny
Isle of May
FIRTH OF FORTH
Scale
0 5 10 km
0 1 2 3 4 5 6 miles
North Berwick
Dirleton
Gullane
Aberlady Bay
Aberlady
Gosford Bay
Longniddry
Cockenzie and Port Seton
Prestonpans
Musselburgh
Tranent
Haddington
East Linton
Tyninghame
Tyne Mouth
Belhaven
West Barns
Leith
Newhaven
Granton
EDINBURGH
Portobello
Joppa
Dalkeith
Loanhead
Gifford
East Saltoun
West Saltoun
Pencaitland
Ormiston
East Lothian
ZEEBRUGGE 17:30

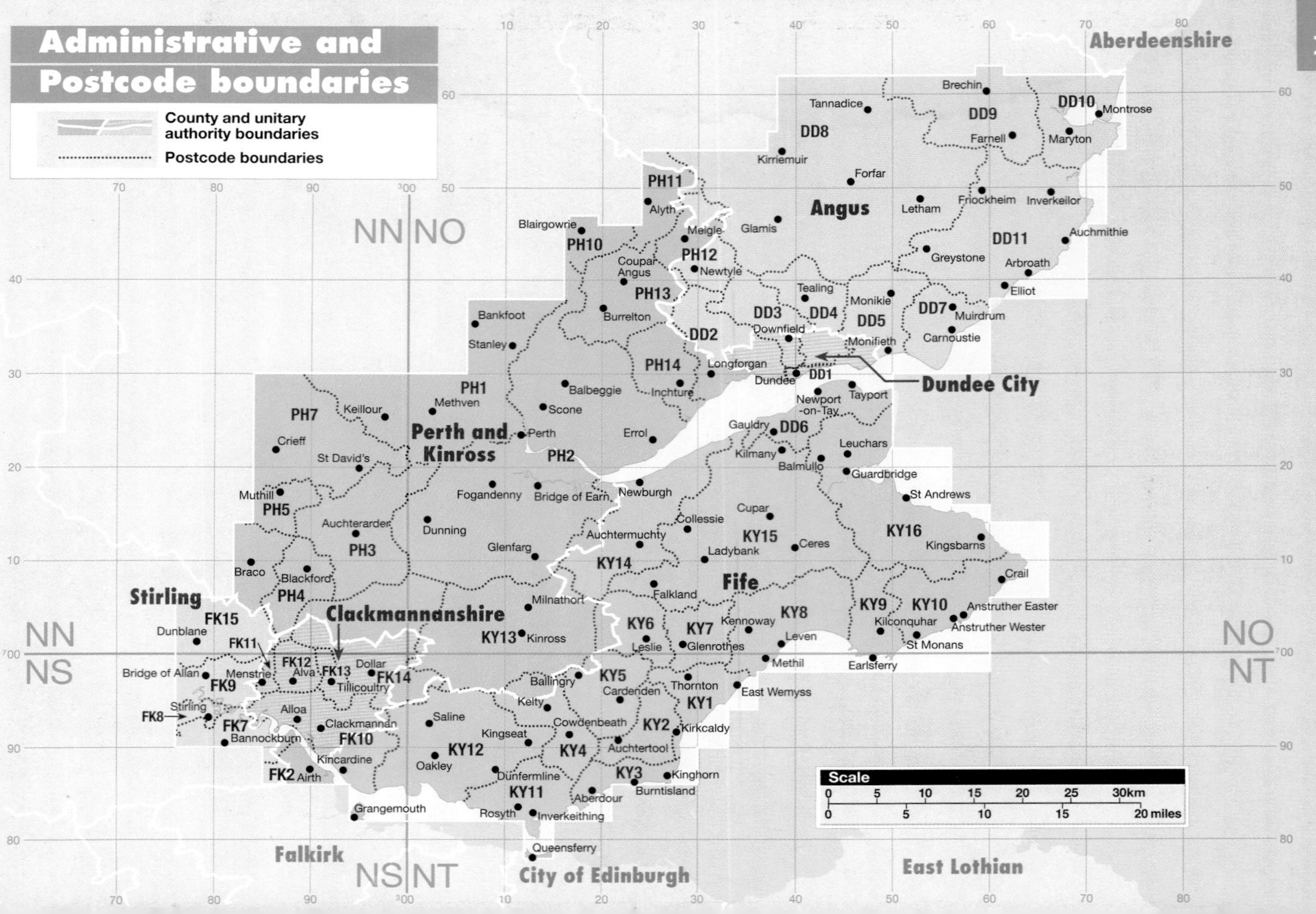

Administrative and Postcode boundaries

— County and unitary authority boundaries

⋯⋯ Postcode boundaries

Scale

0   5   10   15   20   25   30km
0   5   10   15   20 miles

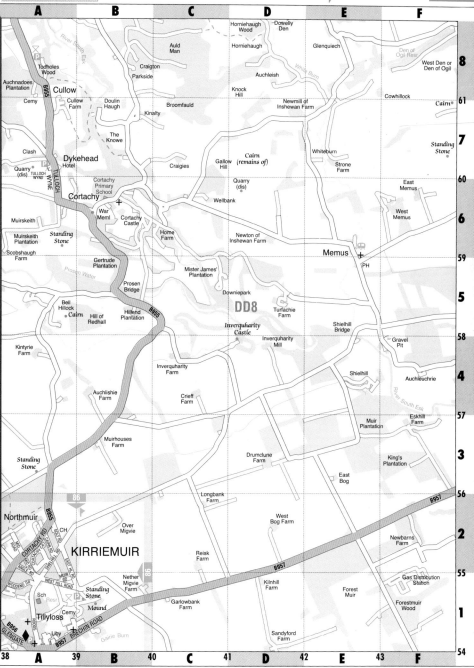

8

61

7

60

6

59

5

58

4

57

3

56

2

55

1

54

A   B   C   D   E   F

Den of Ogil Resr
West Den or Den of Ogil
Cowhillock
Cairn

Horniehaugh Wood
Dowelly Den
Horniehaugh
Glenquiech

Auld Man
Craigton
Parkside
Auchleish
Newmill of Inshewan Farm
Whiteburn
Standing Stone

Todholes Wood
Cullow
Auchnadoes Plantation
Cemy
Cullew Farm
Doulin Haugh
Broomfauld
Knock Hill
White Burn
Strone Farm
East Memus

Clash
Dykehead Hotel
The Knowe
Kinalty
Craigies
Gallow Hill
Cairn (remains of)
Quarry (dis)
West Memus

Quarry (dis)
TULLOCH WYND
Cortachy
Cortachy Primary School
War Meml
Cortachy Castle
Home Farm
Wellbank
Memus
PH

Muirskeith
Muirskeith Plantation
Standing Stone
Gertrude Plantation
Newton of Inshewan Farm

Scobshaugh Farm
Prosen Water
Prosen Bridge
Mister James' Plantation
Downiepark
DD8
Turfachie Farm
Shielhill Bridge
Gravel Pit

Bell Hillock
Cairn
Hill of Redhall
Hillend Plantation
Inverquharity Castle
Inverquharity Mill
Shielhill
Auchleuchrie

Kintyrie Farm
Inverquharity Farm
River South Esk
Eskhill Farm

Auchlishie Farm
Crieff Farm
Muir Plantation

Standing Stone
Muirhouses Farm
Drumclune Farm
King's Plantation

Longbank Farm
East Bog
B957

86
Northmuir
Over Migvie
West Bog Farm
Newbarns Farm

CORTACHY RD
KIRRIEMUIR
Reisk Farm
B957
Gas Distribution Station

Sch
Resr
Standing Stone
Nether Migvie Farm
Mound
Kilnhill Farm
Forest Muir
Forestmuir Wood

Tillyloss
Cemy
Garlowbank Farm

B956
GLENGATE
Liby
B957
BRECHIN ROAD
Gairie Burn
Sandyford Farm

River South Esk

B955

38   A   39   B   40   C   41   D   42   E   43   F

1

Scale: 1⅓ inches to 1 mile

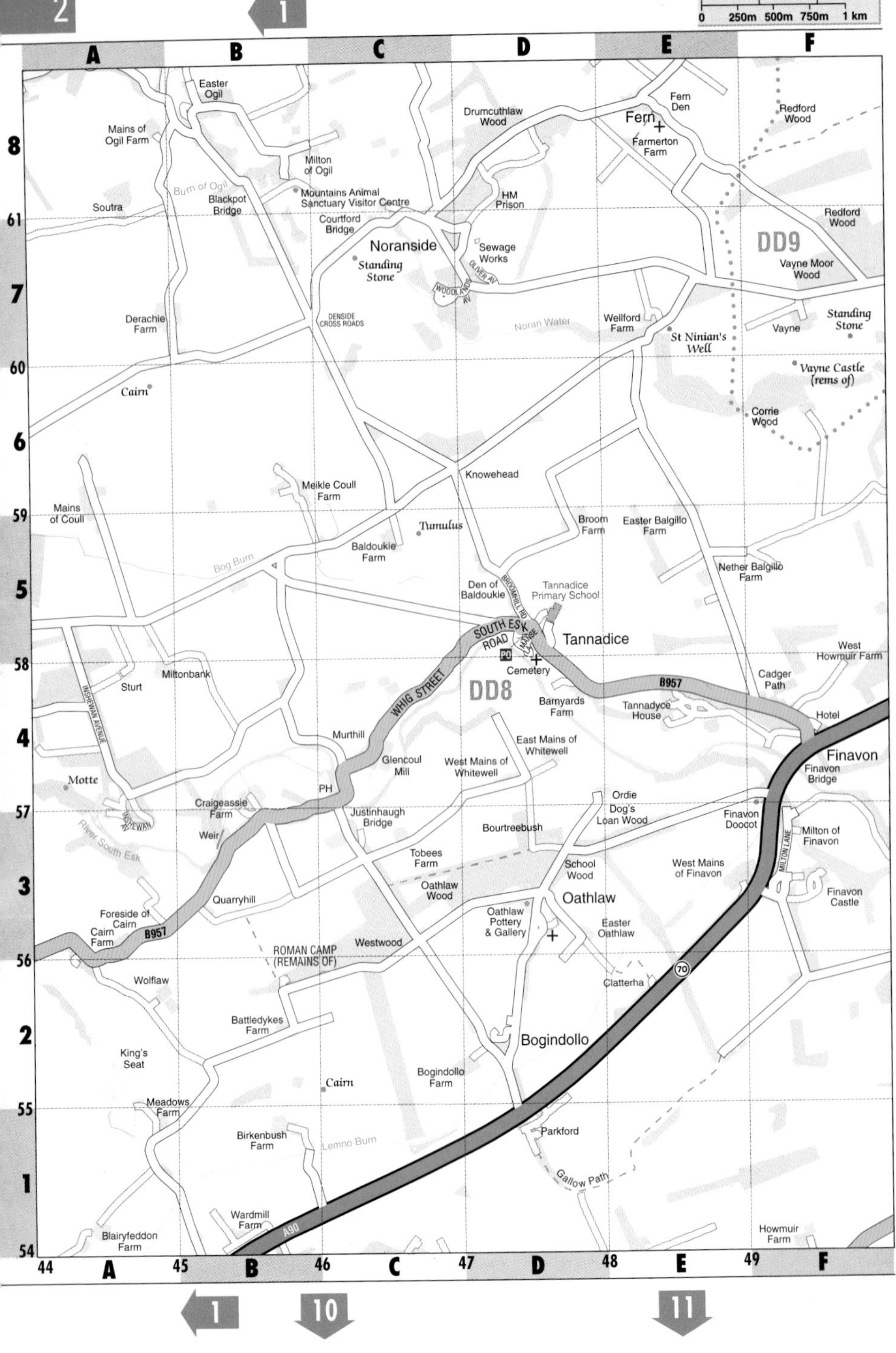
0 ¼ ½ mile
0 250m 500m 750m 1 km
A B C D E F
8 61 7 60 6 59 5 58 4 57 3 56 2 55 1 54
44 45 46 47 48 49
Easter Ogil
Mains of Ogil Farm
Milton of Ogil
Burn of Ogil
Blackpot Bridge
Soutra
Mountains Animal Sanctuary Visitor Centre
Courtford Bridge
Drumcuthlaw Wood
HM Prison
Noranside
Standing Stone
Sewage Works
OLIVER AV
WOODLANDS AV
Fern Den
Fern
Farmerton Farm
Redford Wood
Redford Wood
DD9
Vayne Moor Wood
Derachie Farm
DENSIDE CROSS ROADS
Noran Water
Wellford Farm
St Ninian's Well
Vayne
Standing Stone
Vayne Castle (rems of)
Cairn
Corrie Wood
Knowehead
Meikle Coull Farm
Mains of Coull
Tumulus
Broom Farm
Easter Balgillo Farm
Baldoukie Farm
Bog Burn
Nether Balgillo Farm
Den of Baldoukie
BROOMHILL RD
Tannadice Primary School
SOUTH ESK ROAD
MANSE LA
Tannadice
PO
Cemetery
West Howmuir Farm
Sturt
Miltonbank
INSHEWAN AVENUE
WHIG STREET
DD8
B957
Barnyards Farm
Tannadyce House
Cadger Path
Hotel
Finavon
Murthill
Glencoul Mill
West Mains of Whitewell
East Mains of Whitewell
Finavon Bridge
Motte
PH
Craigeassie Farm
INSHEWAN AV
Justinhaugh Bridge
Ordie
Dog's Loan Wood
Bourtreebush
Finavon Doocot
Milton of Finavon
Weir
River South Esk
Tobees Farm
School Wood
West Mains of Finavon
MILTON LANE
Oathlaw Wood
Oathlaw
Finavon Castle
Quarryhill
Foreside of Cairn
Cairn Farm
B957
Oathlaw Pottery & Gallery
Easter Oathlaw
Westwood
ROMAN CAMP (REMAINS OF)
Wolflaw
70
Clatterha
Battledykes Farm
Bogindollo
King's Seat
Cairn
Bogindollo Farm
Meadows Farm
Parkford
Birkenbush Farm
Lemno Burn
Gallow Path
Wardmill Farm
A90
Blairyfeddon Farm
Howmuir Farm

1 10 11

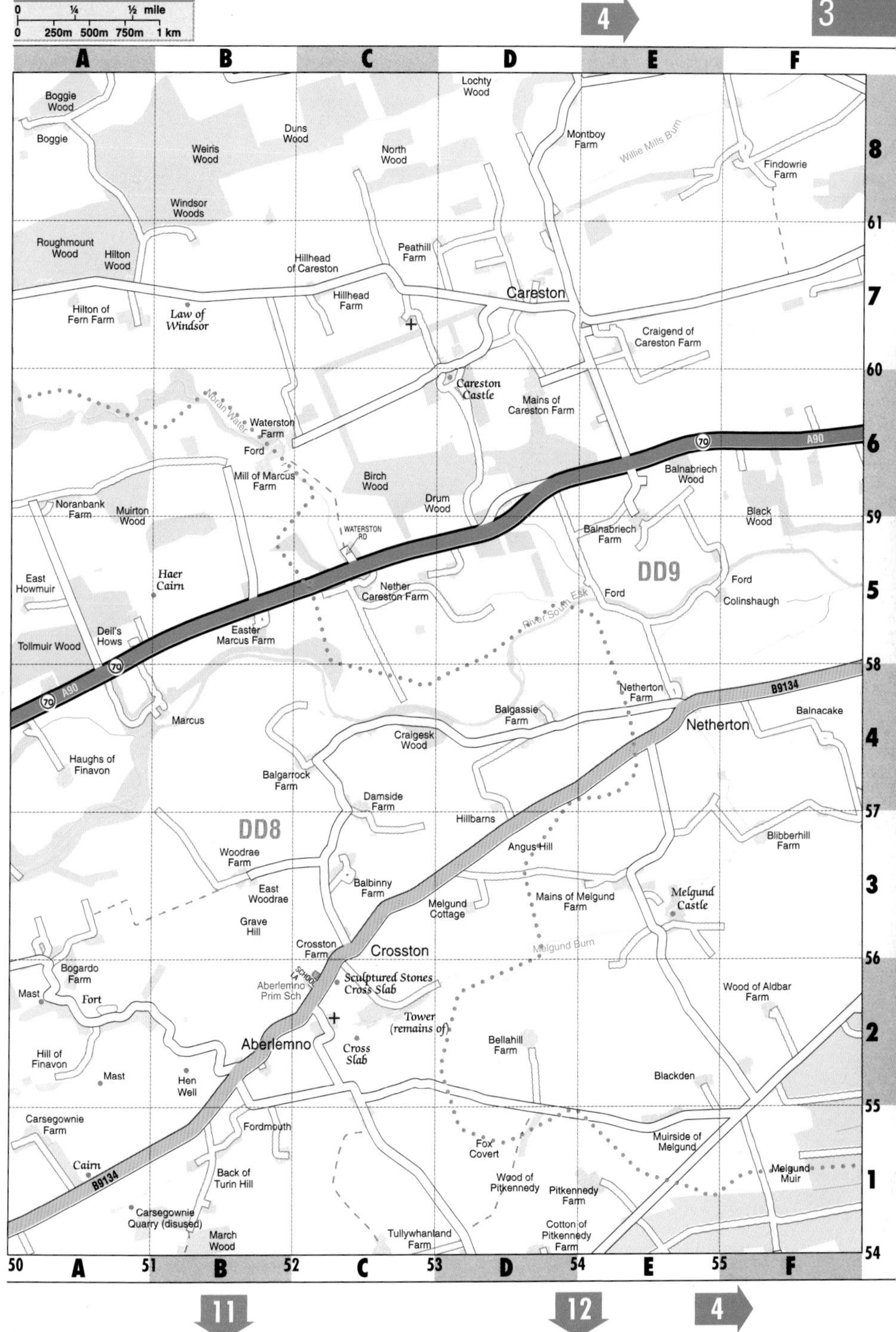

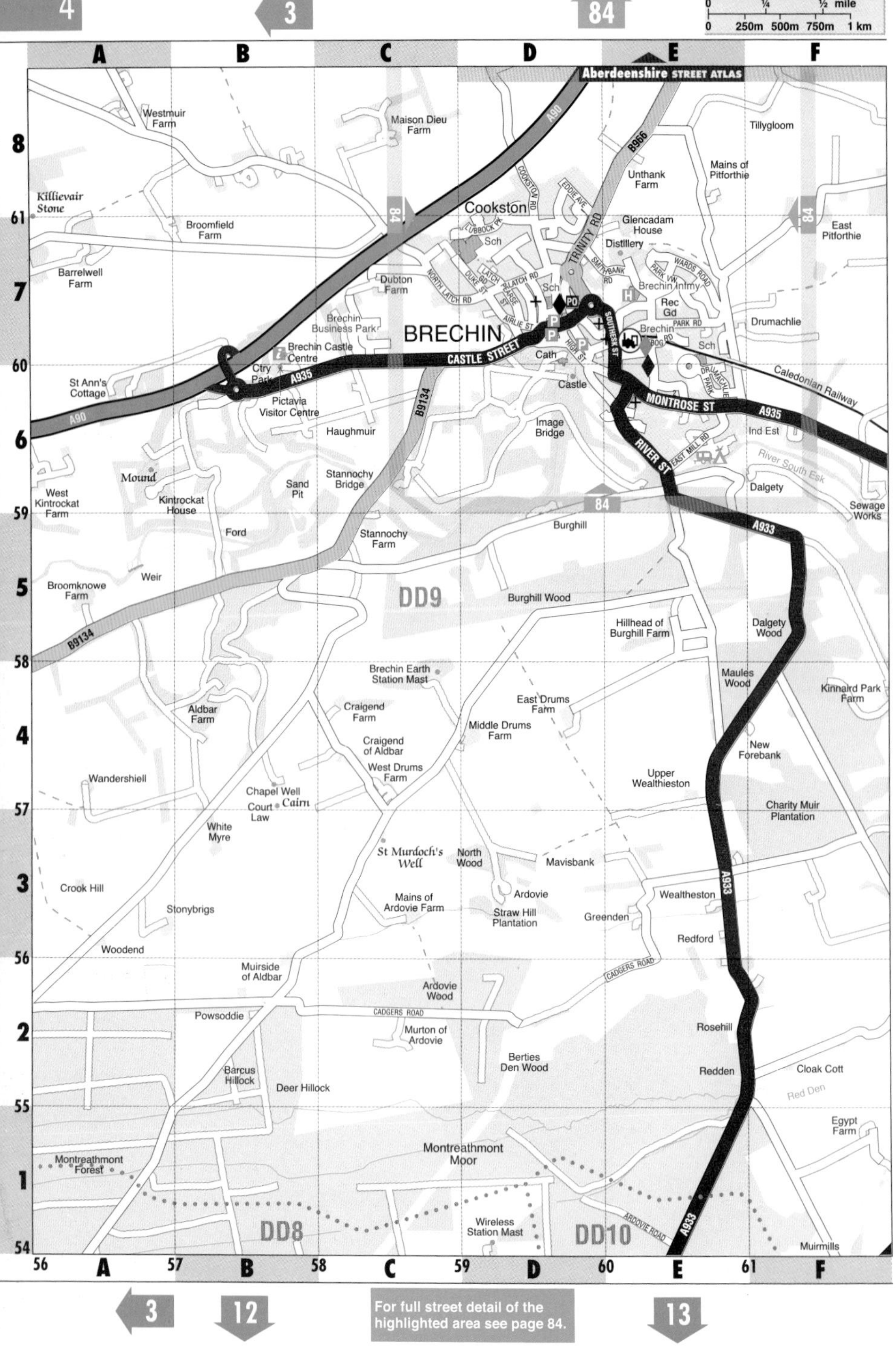

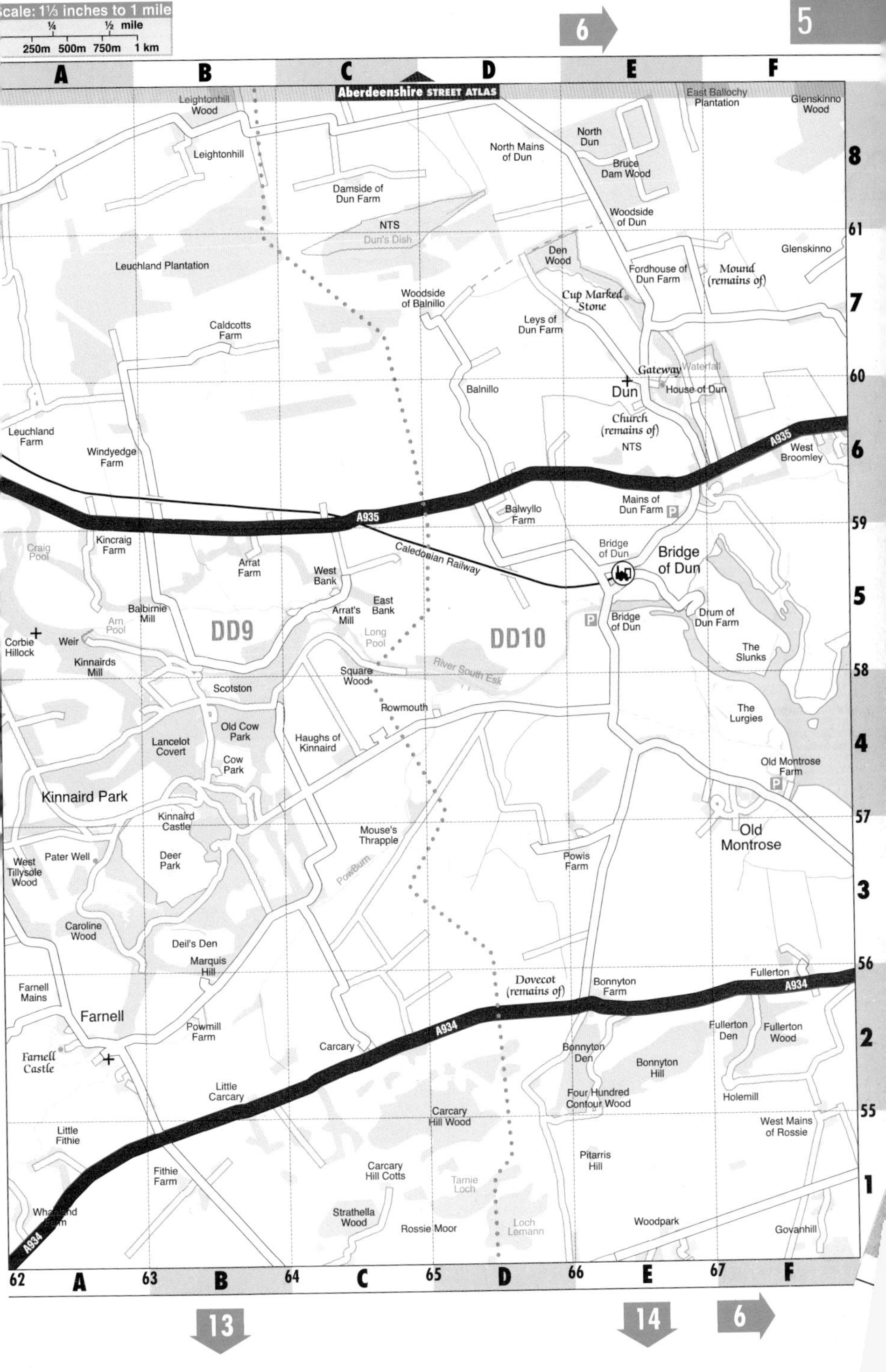

scale: 1⅓ inches to 1 mile

¼ ½ mile

250m 500m 750m 1 km

6 5

A B C D E F

Leightonhill Wood

Leightonhill

North Mains of Dun

North Dun

East Ballochy Plantation

Glenskinno Wood

8

Bruce Dam Wood

Damside of Dun Farm

Woodside of Dun

61

NTS
Dun's Dish

Leuchland Plantation

Den Wood

Glenskinno

Woodside of Balnillo

Fordhouse of Dun Farm

Mound (remains of)

7

Caldcotts Farm

Cup Marked Stone

Leys of Dun Farm

Balnillo

Gateway
Dun

Waterfall

House of Dun

60

Leuchland Farm

Church (remains of)

NTS

West Broomley

A935

6

Windyedge Farm

A935

Balwyllo Farm

Mains of Dun Farm P

59

Kincraig Farm

Craig Pool

Arrat Farm

Caledonian Railway

Bridge of Dun

Bridge of Dun

Drum of Dun Farm

5

Balbirnie Mill

Arn Pool

West Bank

Arrat's Mill

East Bank

Long Pool

DD10

P

Bridge of Dun

The Slunks

DD9

Corbie Hillock

Weir

Kinnairds Mill

Scotston

Square Wood

River South Esk

Rowmouth

58

The Lurgies

Old Cow Park

Haughs of Kinnaird

Old Montrose Farm

P

4

Lancelot Covert

Cow Park

57

Kinnaird Park

Kinnaird Castle

Deer Park

Mouse's Thrapple

Powburn

Powis Farm

Old Montrose

West Tillysole Wood

Pater Well

3

Caroline Wood

Deil's Den

Marquis Hill

Dovecot (remains of)

Bonnyton Farm

Fullerton

56

Farnell Mains

Powmill Farm

A934

Carcary

Bonnyton Den

Fullerton Den

Fullerton Wood

A934

2

Farnell

Farnell Castle

Bonnyton Hill

Little Carcary

Four Hundred Contour Wood

Holemill

55

Little Fithie

Carcary Hill Wood

Pitarris Hill

West Mains of Rossie

1

Fithie Farm

Carcary Hill Cotts

Tarnie Loch

Whappland

A934

Strathella Wood

Rossie Moor

Loch Lemann

Woodpark

Govanhill

62 A 63 B 64 C 65 D 66 E 67 F

13 14 6

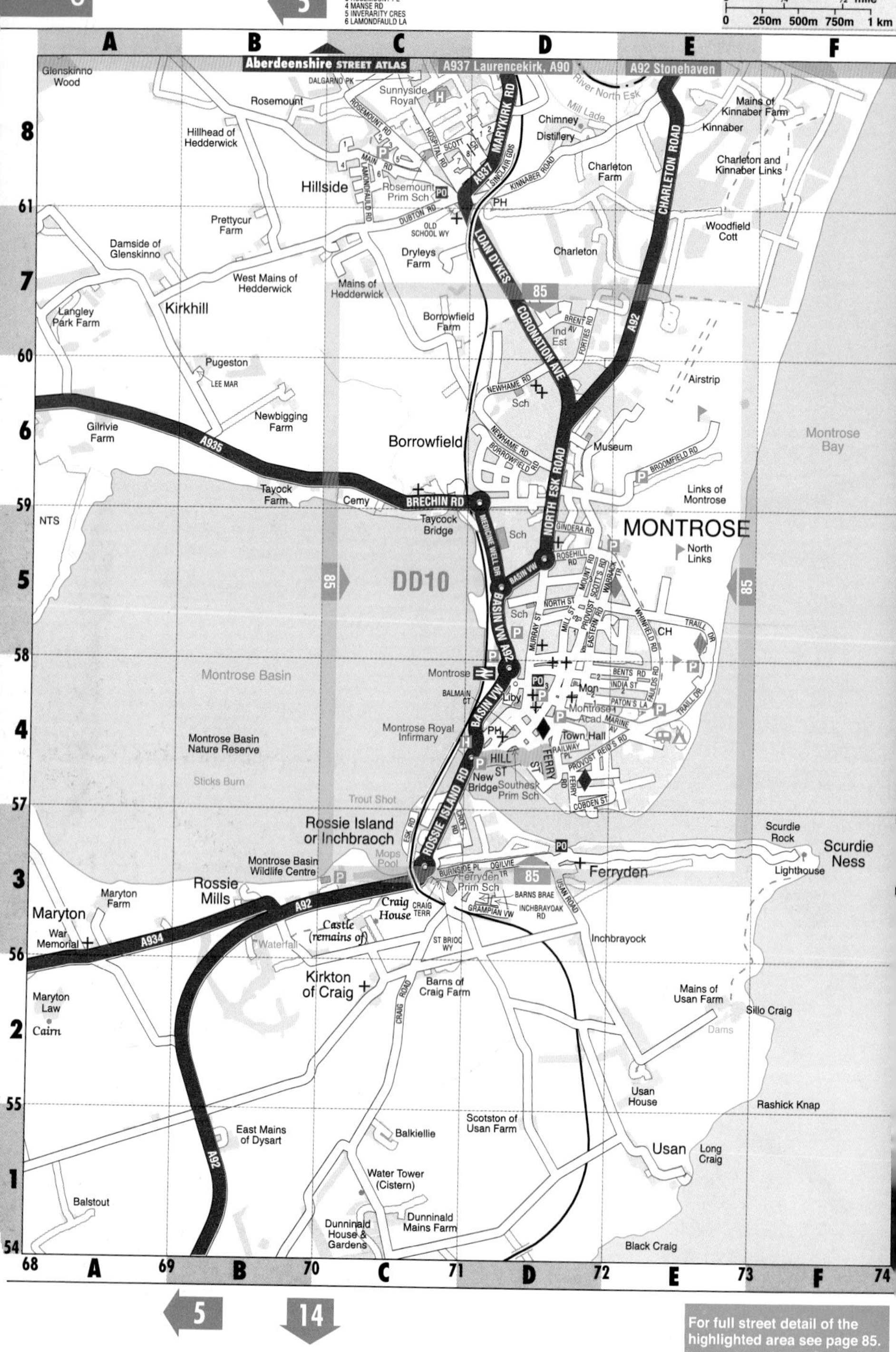

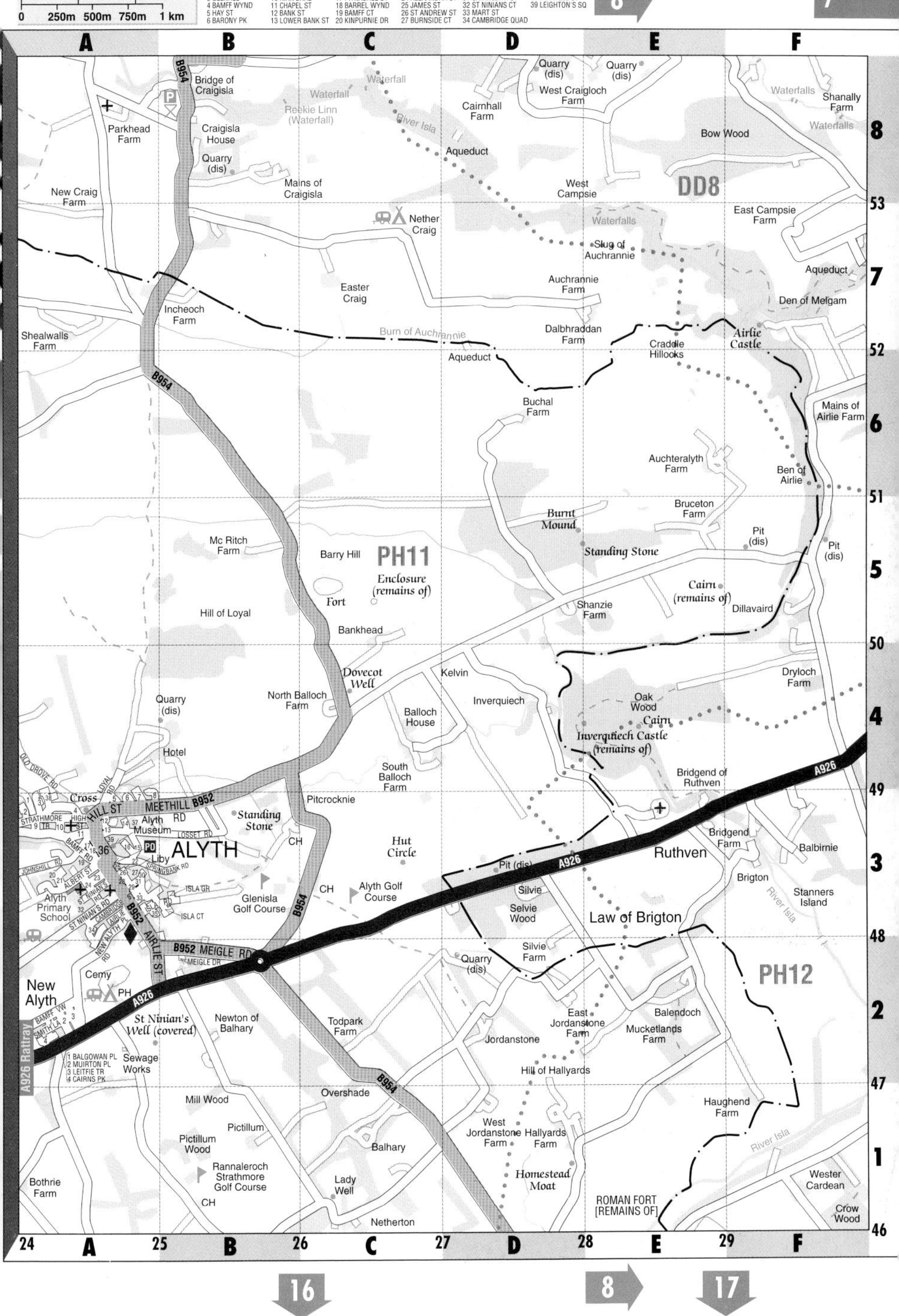

Scale: 1⅓ inches to 1 mile

0   ¼   ½ mile
0 250m 500m 750m 1 km

A3
1 OLD DROVE RD
2 STRATHMORE VW
3 GLENREE
4 BAMFF WYND
5 HAY ST
6 BARONY PK

7 AIRLIE VW
8 GLENISLA VW
9 WYLIE S BRAE
10 KIRK BRAE
11 CHAPEL ST
12 BANK ST
13 LOWER BANK ST

14 PARK VW
15 PARKSIDE RD
16 MORRISON TERR
17 PITNACREE ST
18 BARREL WYND
19 BAMFF CT
20 KINPURNIE DR

21 SIDLAW CRES
22 MILL ST
23 VICTORIA ST
24 ALEXANDRA ST
25 JAMES ST
26 ST ANDREW ST
27 BURNSIDE CT

28 MID ST
29 SMYTHE ST
30 CAIRNIE ST
31 CAIRNLEITH ST
32 ST NINIANS CT
33 MART ST
34 CAMBRIDGE QUAD

35 TAY RD
36 COMMERCIAL ST
37 LOSSET PK
38 DENWELL CT
39 LEIGHTON S SQ

7

Map grid labels: A B C D E F (top and bottom)
Row numbers: 8 53 7 52 6 51 5 50 4 49 3 48 2 47 1 46

DD8

PH11

PH12

ALYTH

16   8   17

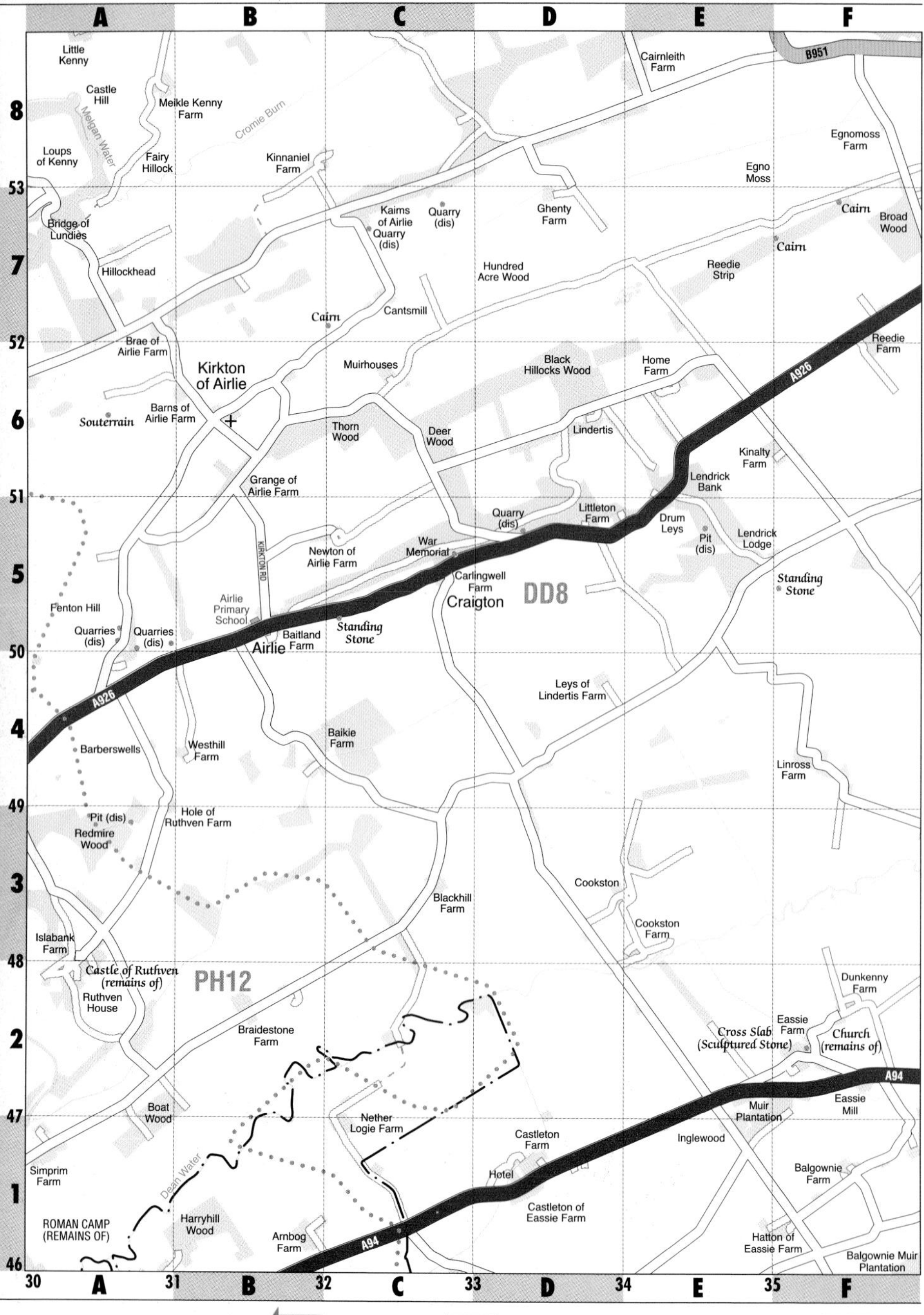

Scale: 1⅓ inches to 1 mile

0   ¼   ½ mile
0 250m 500m 750m 1 km

Little Kenny
Castle Hill
Meikle Kenny Farm
Loups of Kenny
Fairy Hillock
Kinnaniel Farm
Bridge of Lundies
Hillockhead
Morden Water
Cromie Burn

Cairnleith Farm
B951
Egnomoss Farm
Egno Moss
Reedie Strip

8

53

7

52

6

51

5

50

4

49

3

48

2

47

1

46

Kaims of Airlie Quarry (dis)
Quarry (dis)
Ghenty Farm
Cairn
Broad Wood

Brae of Airlie Farm
Cairn
Cantsmill
Hundred Acre Wood
Reedie Farm

Kirkton of Airlie
Muirhouses
Black Hillocks Wood
Home Farm
Cairn

Souterrain
Barns of Airlie Farm
Thorn Wood
Deer Wood
Lindertis
Lendrick Bank
Kinalty Farm

Grange of Airlie Farm
Quarry (dis)
Littleton Farm
Drum Leys
Lendrick Lodge

Fenton Hill
Newton of Airlie Farm
War Memorial
Carlingwell Farm
Craigton
DD8
Pit (dis)

KIRKTON RD
Airlie Primary School
Standing Stone
Leys of Lindertis Farm
Standing Stone

Quarries (dis)
Quarries (dis)
Airlie
Baitland Farm
A926

Barberswells
Westhill Farm
Baikie Farm
Linross Farm

Hole of Ruthven Farm
Pit (dis)
Redmire Wood
Blackhill Farm
Cookston
Cookston Farm

Islabank Farm
Castle of Ruthven (remains of)
Ruthven House
PH12
Dunkenny Farm

Braidestone Farm
Cross Slab (Sculptured Stone)
Eassie Farm
Church (remains of)

Boat Wood
Nether Logie Farm
Castleton Farm
Muir Plantation
Eassie Mill
A94

Simprim Farm
Hotel
Inglewood
Balgownie Farm

ROMAN CAMP (REMAINS OF)
Harryhill Wood
Arnbog Farm
A94
Castleton of Eassie Farm
Hatton of Eassie Farm
Balgownie Muir Plantation

Den Water

30   A   31   B   32   C   33   D   34   E   35   F

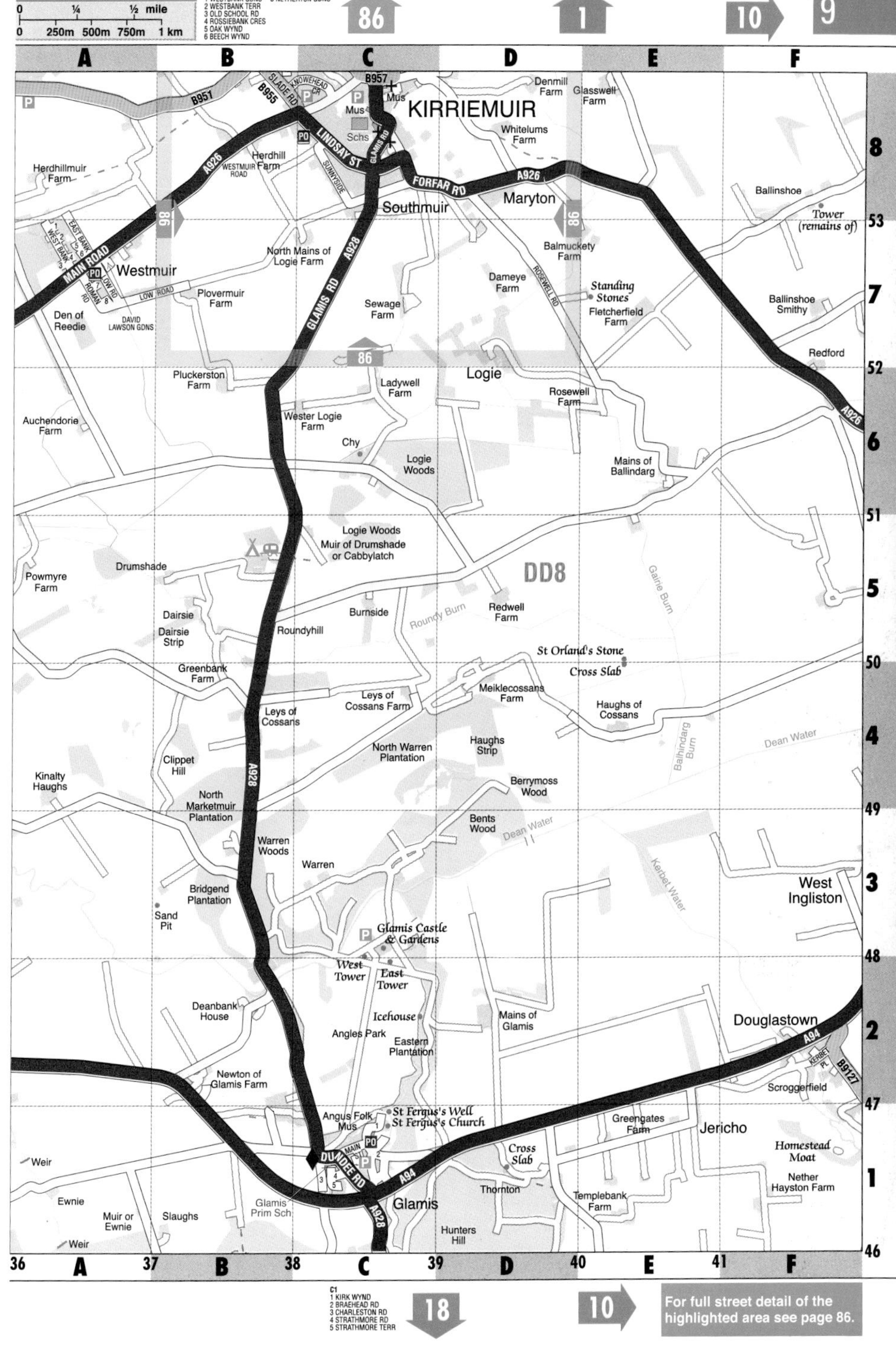
Scale: 1⅓ inches to 1 mile
0
¼
½ mile
0
250m
500m
750m
1 km
A7
1 WESTBANK GDNS
2 WESTBANK TERR
3 OLD SCHOOL RD
4 ROSSIEBANK CRES
5 OAK WYND
6 BEECH WYND
7 NETHERTON PL
8 NETHERTON GDNS
86
1
10
A
B
C
D
E
F
KIRRIEMUIR
B957
B951
B955
SLADE RD
KNOWEHEAD CR
Mus
Schs
GLAMIS RD
LINDSAY ST
SUNNYSIDE
A926
WESTMUIR ROAD
Herdhill Farm
Herdhillmuir Farm
FORFAR RD
Denmill Farm
Glasswell Farm
Whitelums Farm
Maryton
Southmuir
Ballinshoe
Tower (remains of)
EAST BANK
WEST BANK
MAIN ROAD
Westmuir
LOW RD
ROMAN RD
LOW ROAD
North Mains of Logie Farm
A928
Balmuckety Farm
Dameye Farm
ROSEWELL RD
Standing Stones
Fletcherfield Farm
Ballinshoe Smithy
Plovermuir Farm
Den of Reedie
DAVID LAWSON GDNS
GLAMIS RD
Sewage Farm
Redford
Pluckerston Farm
Logie
Ladywell Farm
Rosewell Farm
Auchendorie Farm
Wester Logie Farm
Chy
Logie Woods
Mains of Ballindarg
Logie Woods
Muir of Drumshade or Cabbylatch
Drumshade
Powmyre Farm
DD8
Gairie Burn
Dairsie
Dairsie Strip
Roundyhill
Burnside
Roundy Burn
Redwell Farm
St Orland's Stone
Cross Slab
Greenbank Farm
Leys of Cossans Farm
Meiklecossans Farm
Haughs of Cossans
Leys of Cossans
Balhindarg Burn
Dean Water
North Warren Plantation
Haughs Strip
Clippet Hill
Kinalty Haughs
Berrymoss Wood
North Marketmuir Plantation
Bents Wood
Dean Water
Warren Woods
Warren
Kerbet Water
Bridgend Plantation
West Ingliston
Sand Pit
Glamis Castle & Gardens
West Tower
East Tower
Deanbank House
Icehouse
Mains of Glamis
Douglastown
Angles Park
Eastern Plantation
A94
KERBET PL
B9127
Newton of Glamis Farm
Scroggerfield
Angus Folk Mus
St Fergus's Well
St Fergus's Church
Greengates Farm
Jericho
Weir
MAIN ST
DUNDEE RD
Cross Slab
Homestead Moat
Ewnie
Muir or Ewnie
Slaughs
Glamis Prim Sch
Glamis
Thornton
Templebank Farm
Nether Hayston Farm
Weir
Hunters Hill
36
37
38
39
40
41
46
47
48
49
50
51
52
53
1
2
3
4
5
6
7
8
C1
1 KIRK WYND
2 BRAEHEAD RD
3 CHARLESTON RD
4 STRATHMORE RD
5 STRATHMORE TERR
18
10
For full street detail of the highlighted area see page 86.

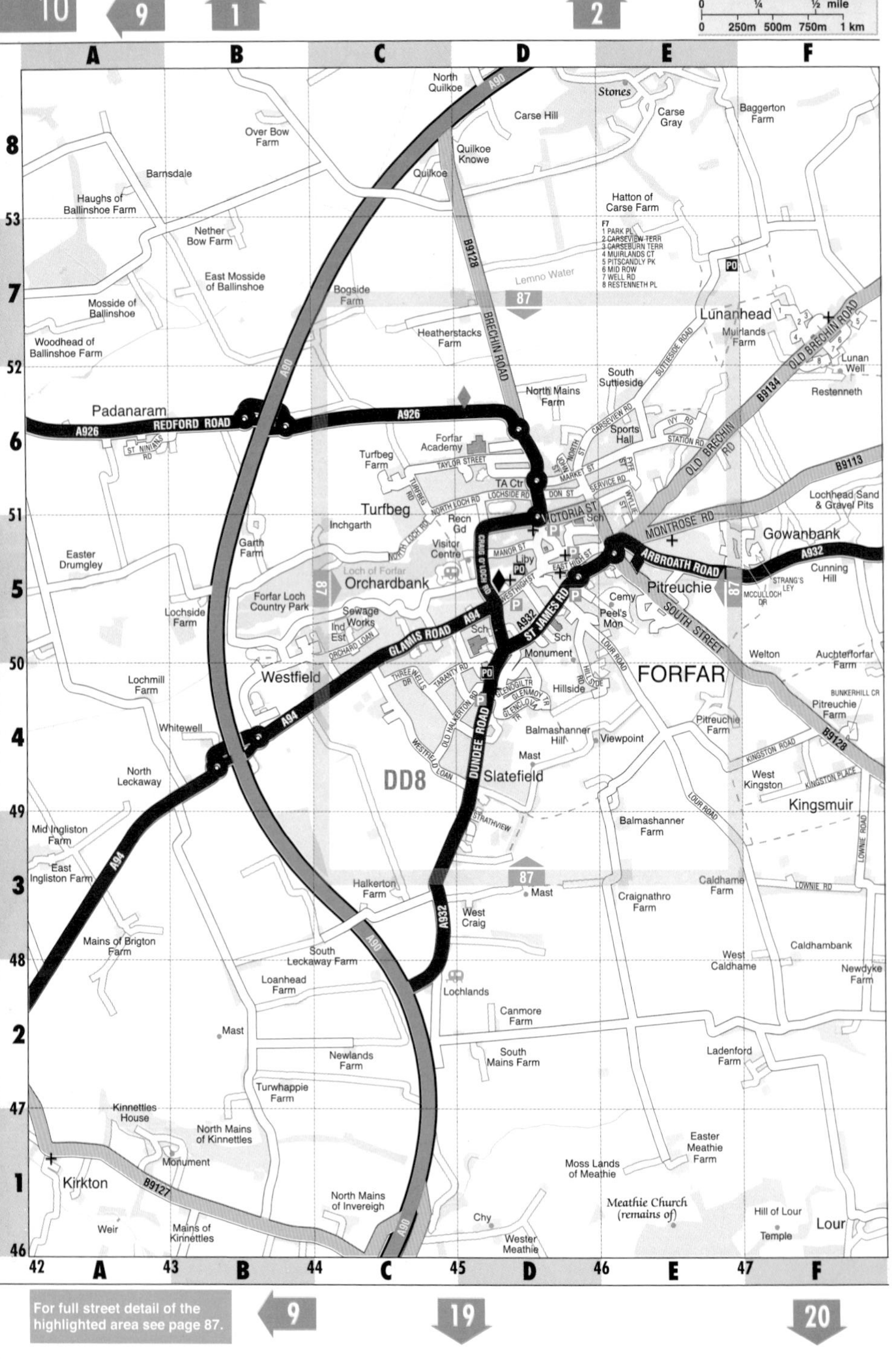

North Quilkoe
Carse Hill
Stones
Carse Gray
Baggerton Farm

Over Bow Farm
Quilkoe Knowe
Hatton of Carse Farm

Barnsdale
Quilkoe

Haughs of Ballinshoe Farm
Nether Bow Farm

F7
1 PARK PL
2 CARSEVIEW TERR
3 CARSEBURN TERR
4 MURLANDS CT
5 PITSCANDLY PK
6 MID ROW
7 WELL RD
8 RESTENNETH PL

East Mosside of Ballinshoe
Bogside Farm

Lunanhead
Muirlands Farm
Lunan Well
Restenneth

Mosside of Ballinshoe
Heatherstacks Farm
Lemno Water
87

Woodhead of Ballinshoe Farm
South Suttieside
B9134
Lochhead Sand & Gravel Pits
B9113

Padanaram
REDFORD ROAD
A926
A926
Sports Hall
Gowanbank

ST NINIAN'S RD
Forfar Academy
TAYLOR STREET
TA Ctr
Cunning Hill
A932

Turfbeg Farm
Turfbeg
Inchgarth
Recn Gd
Visitor Centre
MONTROSE RD
Pitreuchie

Easter Drumgley
Garth Farm
Loch of Forfar
Orchardbank
Libry
PO
ARBROATH ROAD
87
Welton
Auchterforfar Farm

Lochside Farm
Forfar Loch Country Park
Sewage Works
Ind Est
Cemy
Peel's Mon
SOUTH STREET
Pitreuchie Farm

Lochmill Farm
Westfield
GLAMIS ROAD
Sch
St JAMES RD
Monument
FORFAR
BUNKERHILL CR

Whitewell
A94
Hillside
West Kingston
Kingsmuir

North Leckaway
Balmashanner Hill
Viewpoint

Mid Ingliston Farm
DD8
Mast
Slatefield
Balmashanner Farm
West Caldhame

East Ingliston Farm
A932
STRATHVIEW
87
Mast
Craignathro Farm
Caldhame Farm
LOWNIE RD

Mains of Brigton Farm
Halkerton Farm
West Craig
Caldhambank

South Leckaway Farm
Lochlands
Newdyke Farm

Loanhead Farm
Canmore Farm
South Mains Farm
Ladenford Farm

Mast
Newlands Farm
Turwhappie Farm

Kinnettles House
Monument
Easter Meathie Farm

Kirkton
B9127
North Mains of Kinnettles
North Mains of Invereighty
Moss Lands of Meathie
Meathie Church (remains of)
Hill of Lour
Temple
Lour

Weir
Mains of Kinnettles
Chy
Wester Meathie

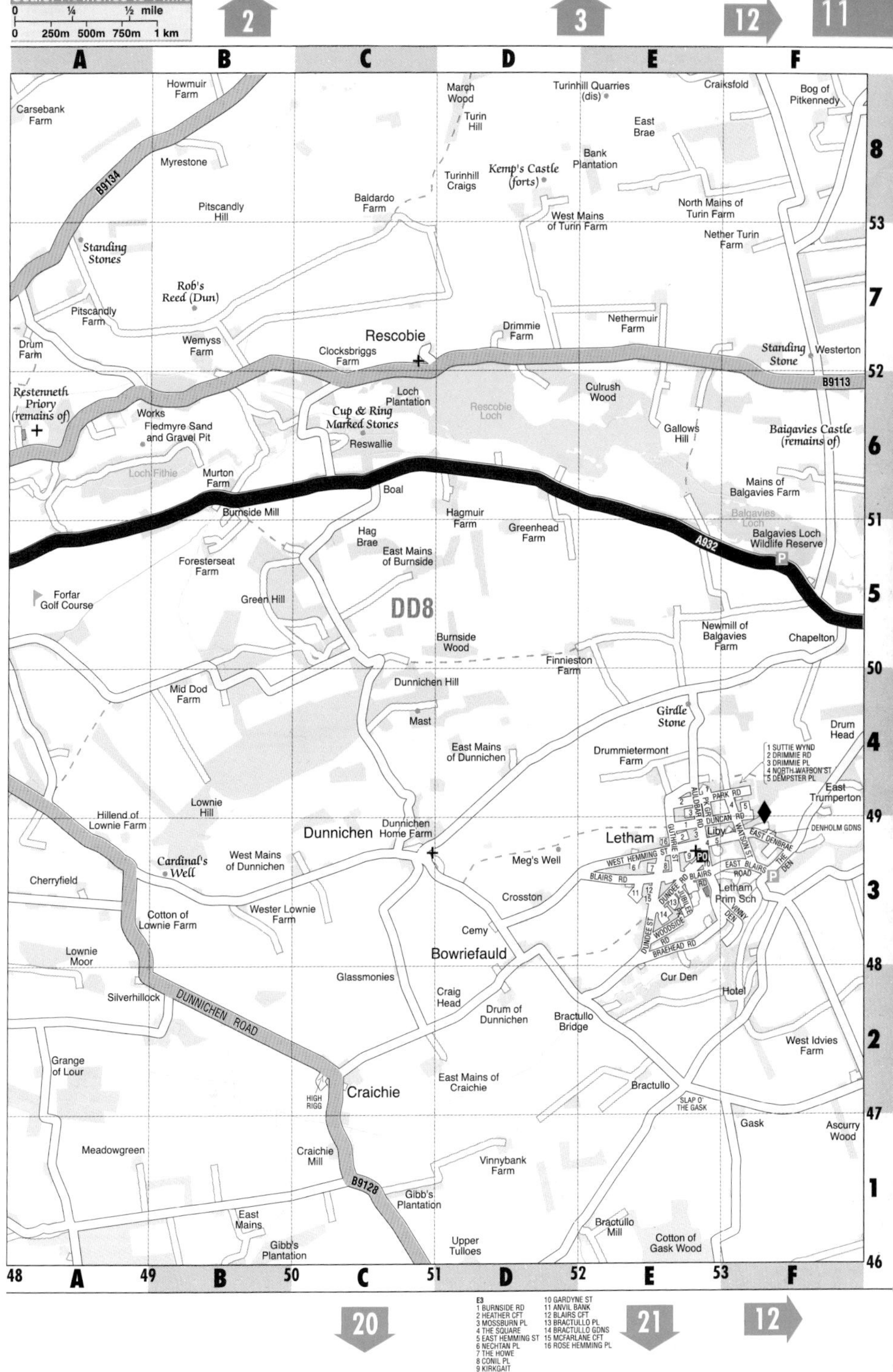

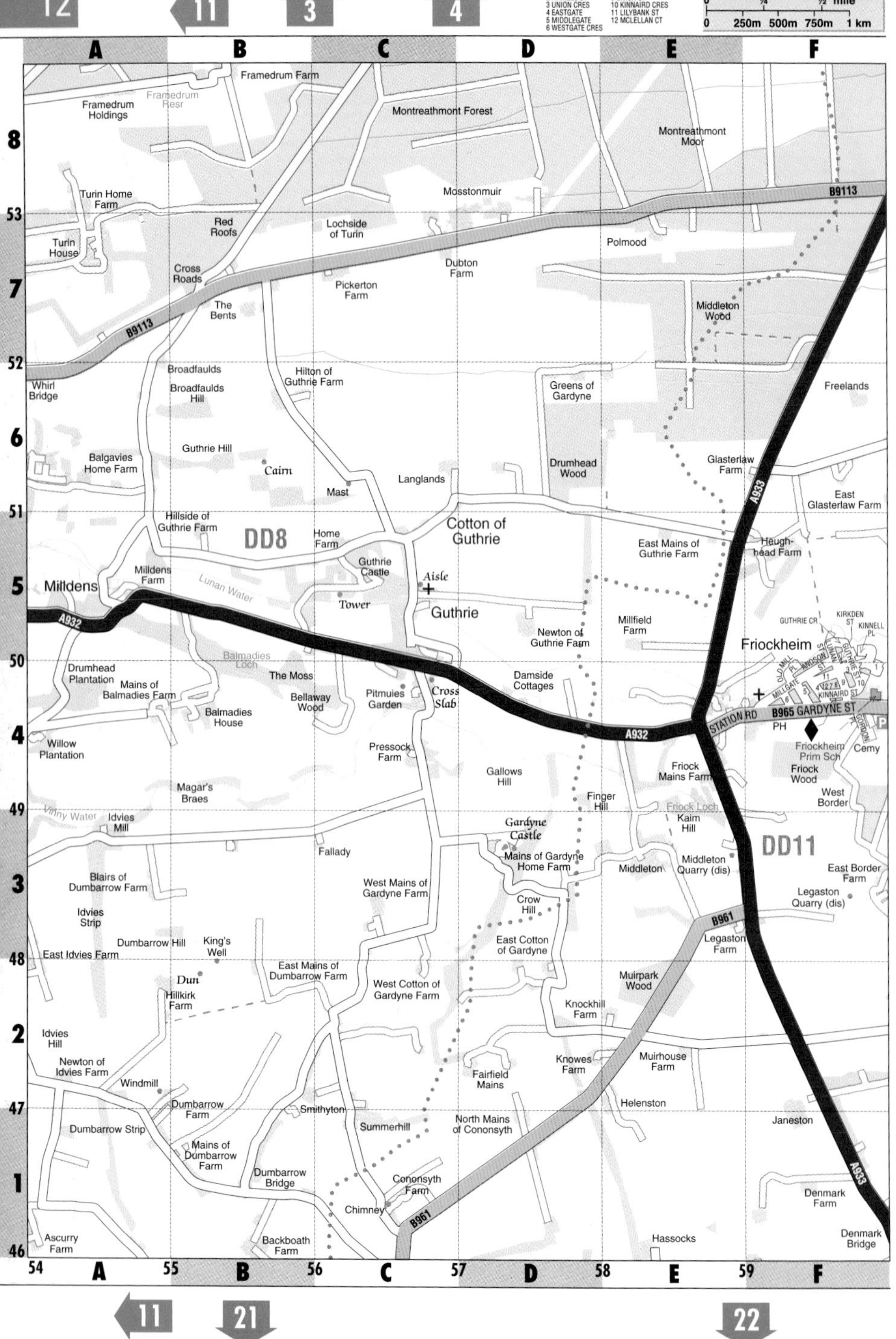

Scale: 1⅓ inches to 1 mile

F4
1 KINNELL GDNS
2 KINNELL ST
3 UNION CRES
4 EASTGATE
5 MIDDLEGATE
6 WESTGATE CRES
7 VICTORIA RD
8 CASTLE CRES
9 UNION ST
10 KINNAIRD CRES
11 LILYGATE ST
12 MCLELLAN CT

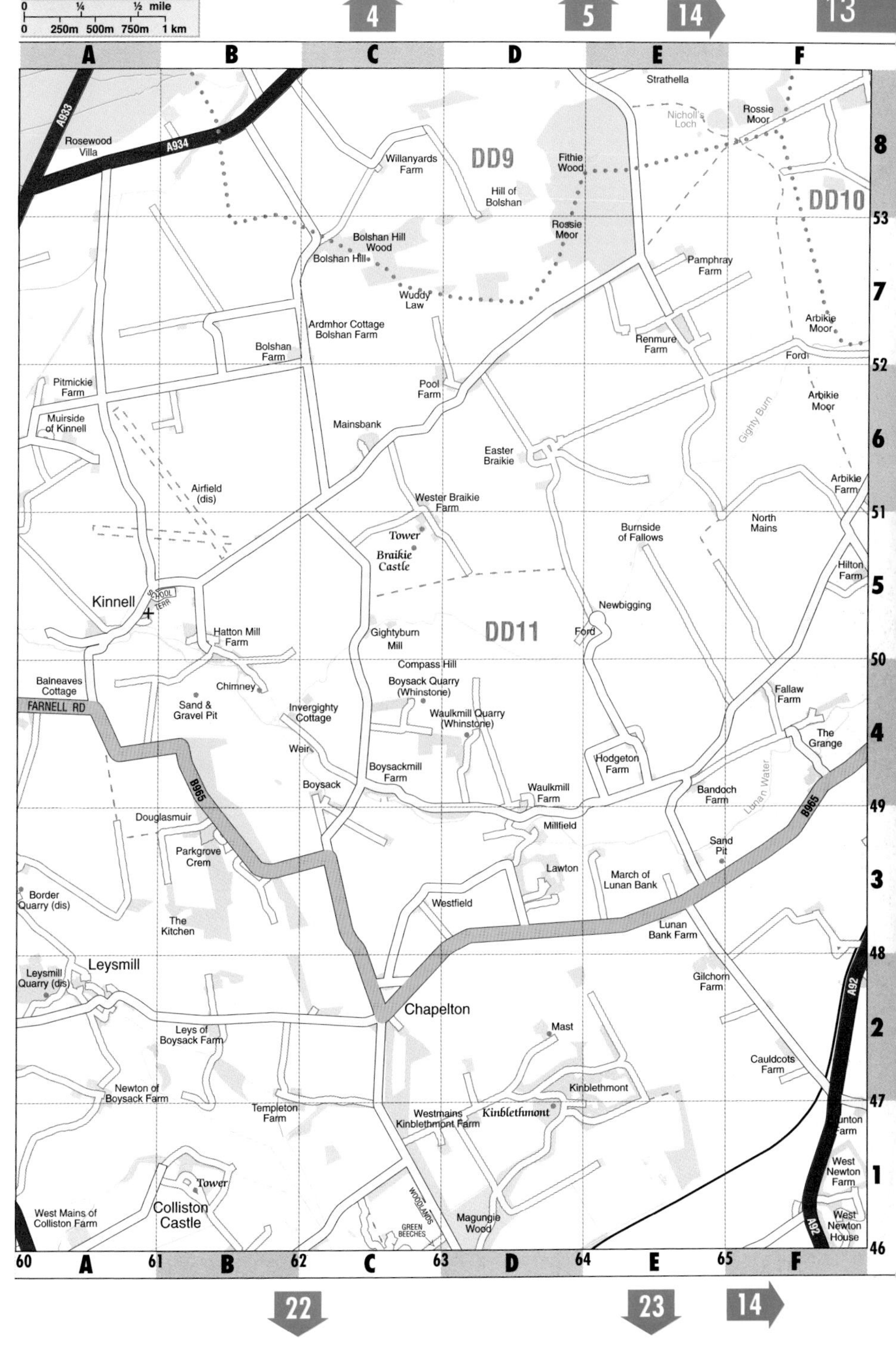
Scale: 1⅓ inches to 1 mile
0 ¼ ½ mile
0 250m 500m 750m 1 km
4
5
14
A B C D E F
Strathella
Nicholl's Loch
Rossie Moor
A933
Rosewood Villa
A934
Willanyards Farm
DD9
Fithie Wood
Hill of Bolshan
DD10
Rossie Moor
Bolshan Hill Wood
Bolshan Hill
Pamphray Farm
Wuddy Law
Ardmhor Cottage
Bolshan Farm
Arbikie Moor
Renmure Farm
Bolshan Farm
Ford
Pitmickie Farm
Pool Farm
Arbikie Moor
Muirside of Kinnell
Mainsbank
Gighty Burn
Easter Braikie
Airfield (dis)
Wester Braikie Farm
Arbikie Farm
Burnside of Fallows
North Mains
Tower
Braikie Castle
Hilton Farm
Kinnell
SCHOOL TERR
Newbigging
Hatton Mill Farm
Gightyburn Mill
DD11
Ford
Compass Hill
Balneaves Cottage
Chimney
Boysack Quarry (Whinstone)
Fallaw Farm
FARNELL RD
Sand & Gravel Pit
Invergighty Cottage
Waulkmill Quarry (Whinstone)
The Grange
Weir
Hodgeton Farm
B965
Boysackmill Farm
Boysack
Waulkmill Farm
Bandoch Farm
Lunan Water
Douglasmuir
Millfield
B965
Parkgrove Crem
Sand Pit
Lawton
March of Lunan Bank
Border Quarry (dis)
Westfield
The Kitchen
Lunan Bank Farm
Leysmill
Gilchorn Farm
Leysmill Quarry (dis)
A92
Chapelton
Leys of Boysack Farm
Mast
Cauldcots Farm
Newton of Boysack Farm
Kinblethmont
Templeton Farm
Westmains Kinblethmont Farm
Kinblethmont
Lunton Farm
Tower
West Newton Farm
West Mains of Colliston Farm
Colliston Castle
WOODLANDS
GREEN BEECHES
Magungie Wood
West Newton House
A92
8 53 7 52 6 51 5 50 4 49 3 48 2 47 1 46
60 61 62 63 64 65
22
23
14

13
5
6

Scale: 1⅓ inches to 1 mile
0 ¼ ½ mile
0 250m 500m 750m 1 km
A B C D E F
Govanhill Wood
PH
A92
LC
Todd's Hole
Dunninald Den
Boddin Farm
Mast
Reservoir
Upper Dysart
8
Gightyburn
Black Jack
Boddin Harbour
Boddin Point
DD10
Nether Dysart Farm
53
Mountboy
Drumbertnot Wood
Buckiemill
Buckie Den
7
Deil's Knap
Drumbertnot Farm
Monument
52
Quarry (dis)
Quarry (dis)
Wilkins Hole
Lunan
P
Cothill Farm
Hawkhill
6
Weir
Lunan Bridge
Courthill
Lunan Bay
Lunan Water
51
A92
Arbikie Farm
Red Castle
Gallow Hill
5
Redcastle Farm
Ironshill
50
Vault
4
LUNAN AV
Inverkeilor
DD11
B965
PO
MYRESIDE DR
MAIN RD
STATION RD
Inverkeilor Prim Sch
Newbarns
Corbie Knowe
49
Myreside Farm
Ethie Haven
Lang Craig
3
Anniston Farm
New Mill
A92
Inchock Farm
Ethie Mains
48
Kirk Loch
Raesmill Farm
North Mains
St Murdoch's Chapel (remains of)
2
Abbeythune Farm
South Mains Strip
Red Head
Comb of the Head
Brunton
East Newton Farm
Ethie Barns
47
Rosehill Farm
Cuthile Harbour
Cairnton
Ethie Castle
Prail Castle (Fort)
1
Gelly Loch
Caves
West Mains
46
Kinaldie
Boghead Farm
Fort
66 67 68 69 70 71 72

13
23

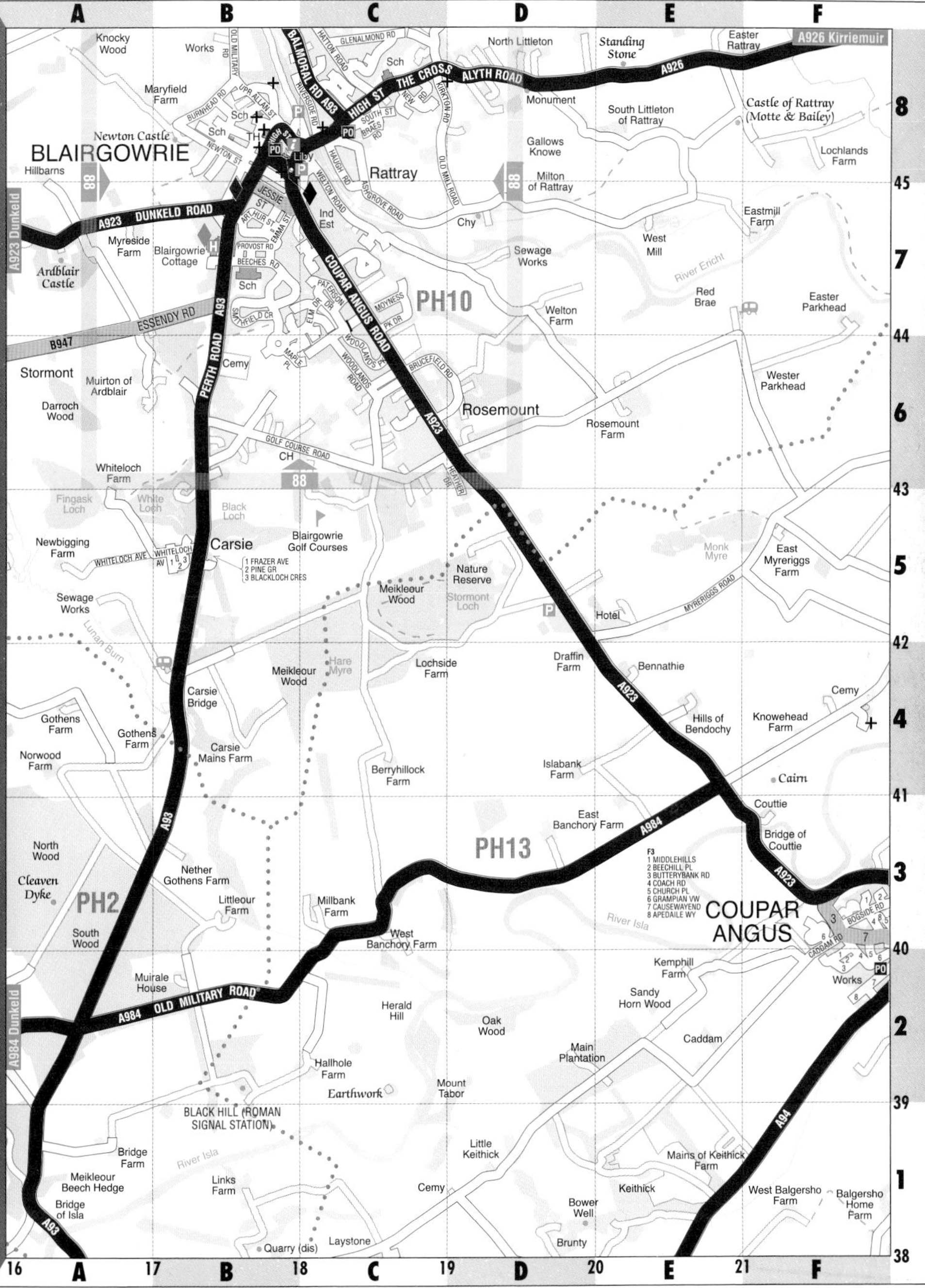

A   B   C   D   E   F

8

45

7

44

6

43

5

42

4

41

3

40

2

39

1

38

16   A   17   B   18   C   19   D   20   E   21   F

Knocky Wood
Maryfield Farm
Newton Castle
BLAIRGOWRIE
Hillbarns
Works
North Littleton
Standing Stone
Easter Rattray
A926 Kirriemuir
THE CROSS
ALYTH ROAD
Monument
South Littleton of Rattray
Castle of Rattray (Motte & Bailey)
Gallows Knowe
Lochlands Farm
Rattray
Milton of Rattray
Eastmill Farm
A923 DUNKELD ROAD
Myreside Farm
Blairgowrie Cottage
Chy
Sewage Works
West Mill
River Ericht
Red Brae
Easter Parkhead
Ardblair Castle
ESSENDY RD
PH10
Wester Parkhead
B947
Stormont
Muirton of Ardblair
Welton Farm
Darroch Wood
ROSEMOUNT
Rosemount Farm
Whiteloch Farm
Fingask Loch
White Loch
Black Loch
GOLF COURSE ROAD
CH
88
East Myreriggs Farm
Newbigging Farm
Carsie
Blairgowrie Golf Courses
1 FRAZER AVE
2 PINE GR
3 BLACKLOCH CRES
Meikleour Wood
Nature Reserve
Stormont Loch
Monk Myre
MYRERIGGS ROAD
Hotel
Sewage Works
Luran Burn
Meikleour Wood
Hare Myre
Lochside Farm
Draffin Farm
Bennathie
Carsie Bridge
Knowehead Farm
Cemy
Gothens Farm
Gothens Farm
Carsie Mains Farm
Berryhillock Farm
Islabank Farm
Hills of Bendochy
Cairn
Norwood Farm
Couttie
Bridge of Couttie
North Wood
Cleaven Dyke
PH2
Nether Gothens Farm
Littleour Farm
Millbank Farm
PH13
East Banchory Farm
A984
A923
COUPAR ANGUS
South Wood
Muirale House
A984 OLD MILITARY ROAD
West Banchory Farm
Herald Hill
Oak Wood
Main Plantation
Kemphill Farm
Sandy Horn Wood
Caddam
Works
Hallhole Farm
Earthwork
Mount Tabor
BLACK HILL (ROMAN SIGNAL STATION)
Little Keithick
Bower Well
Brunty
Mains of Keithick Farm
Keithick
West Balgersho Farm
Balgersho Home Farm
Bridge Farm
Meikleour Beech Hedge
River Isla
Links Farm
Cemy
Laystone
Quarry (dis)
Bridge of Isla
A93
A984 Dunkeld

F3
1 MIDDLEHILLS
2 BEECHILL PL
3 BUTTERYBANK RD
4 COACH RD
5 CHURCH PL
6 GRAMPIAN VW
7 CAUSEWAYEND
8 APEDAILE WY

F2
1 SIDLAW PL
2 SIDLAW GDNS
3 SIDLAW CRES
4 STRATHMORE AVE
5 KING'S RD
6 PRINCES CFT
7 GEORGE ST
8 PERTH RD

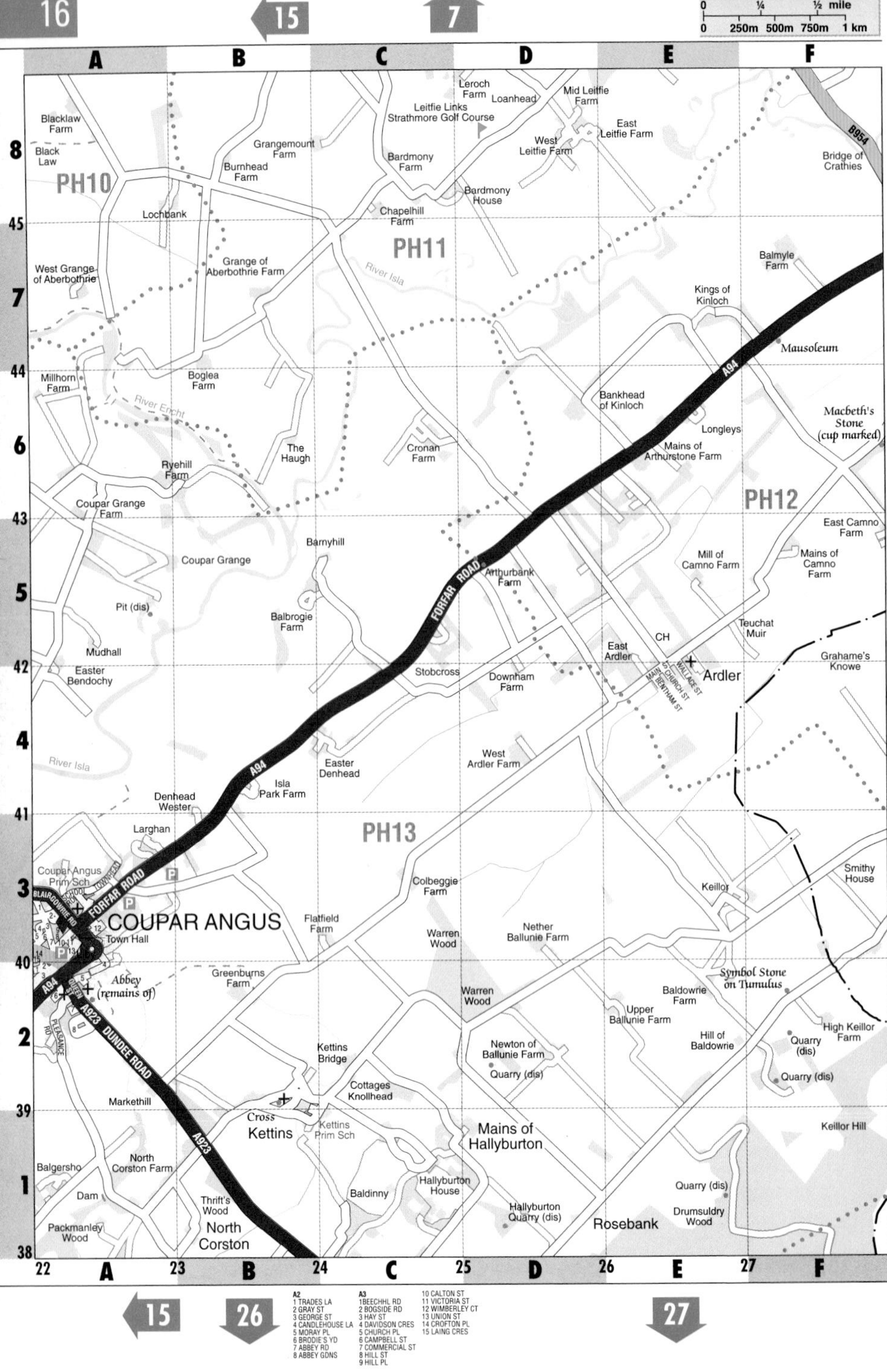

Scale: 1⅓ inches to 1 mile

| 0 | ¼ | ½ mile |
| 0 | 250m | 500m | 750m | 1 km |

PH10

Blacklaw Farm
Black Law

Burnhead Farm
Grangemount Farm

Lochbank

West Grange of Aberbothrie

Grange of Aberbothrie Farm

Millhorn Farm

Boglea Farm

Ryehill Farm

The Haugh

Coupar Grange Farm

Coupar Grange

Pit (dis)

Mudhall

Easter Bendochy

Barnyhill

Balbrogie Farm

Leroch Farm
Loanhead
Leitfie Links
Strathmore Golf Course
Bardmony Farm
Chapelhill Farm
Bardmony House

Mid Leitfie Farm
West Leitfie Farm
East Leitfie Farm

PH11

River Isla

Cronan Farm

FORFAR ROAD

Arthurbank Farm

Stobcross

Downham Farm

Bridge of Crathies
B954

Balmyle Farm

Kings of Kinloch

Mausoleum

A94

Macbeth's Stone (cup marked)

Bankhead of Kinloch

Longleys

Mains of Arthurstone Farm

PH12

East Camno Farm

Mains of Camno Farm

Mill of Camno Farm

Teuchat Muir

East Ardler

CH

Ardler

Grahame's Knowe

Easter Denhead

West Ardler Farm

A94

Isla Park Farm

Denhead Wester

Larghan

Coupar Angus Prim Sch

FORFAR ROAD

PH10

COUPAR ANGUS

Town Hall

Abbey (remains of)

A94

A923

DUNDEE ROAD

Greenburns Farm

Flatfield Farm

Kettins Bridge

Markethill

Balgersho

North Corston Farm

Dam

Packmanley Wood

Thrift's Wood

North Corston

Cross Kettins
Kettins Prim Sch

Cottages Knollhead

Baldinny

PH13

Colbeggie Farm

Warren Wood

Nether Ballunie Farm

Warren Wood

Upper Ballunie Farm

Newton of Ballunie Farm

Quarry (dis)

Mains of Hallyburton

Hallyburton House

Hallyburton Quarry (dis)

Rosebank

Keillor

Smithy House

Symbol Stone on Tumulus

Baldowrie Farm

Hill of Baldowrie

High Keillor Farm

Quarry (dis)

Quarry (dis)

Drumsuldry Wood

Quarry (dis)

Keillor Hill

River Ericht
River Isla

A2
1 TRADES LA
2 GRAY ST
3 GEORGE ST
4 CANDLEHOUSE LA
5 MORAY PL
6 BRODIE S YD
7 ABBEY RD
8 ABBEY GDNS

A3
1 BEECHHILL RD
2 BOGSIDE RD
3 HAY ST
4 DAVIDSON CRES
5 CHURCH PL
6 CAMPBELL ST
7 COMMERCIAL ST
8 HILL ST
9 HILL PL

10 CALTON ST
11 VICTORIA ST
12 WIMBERLEY CT
13 UNION ST
14 CROFTON PL
15 LAING CRES

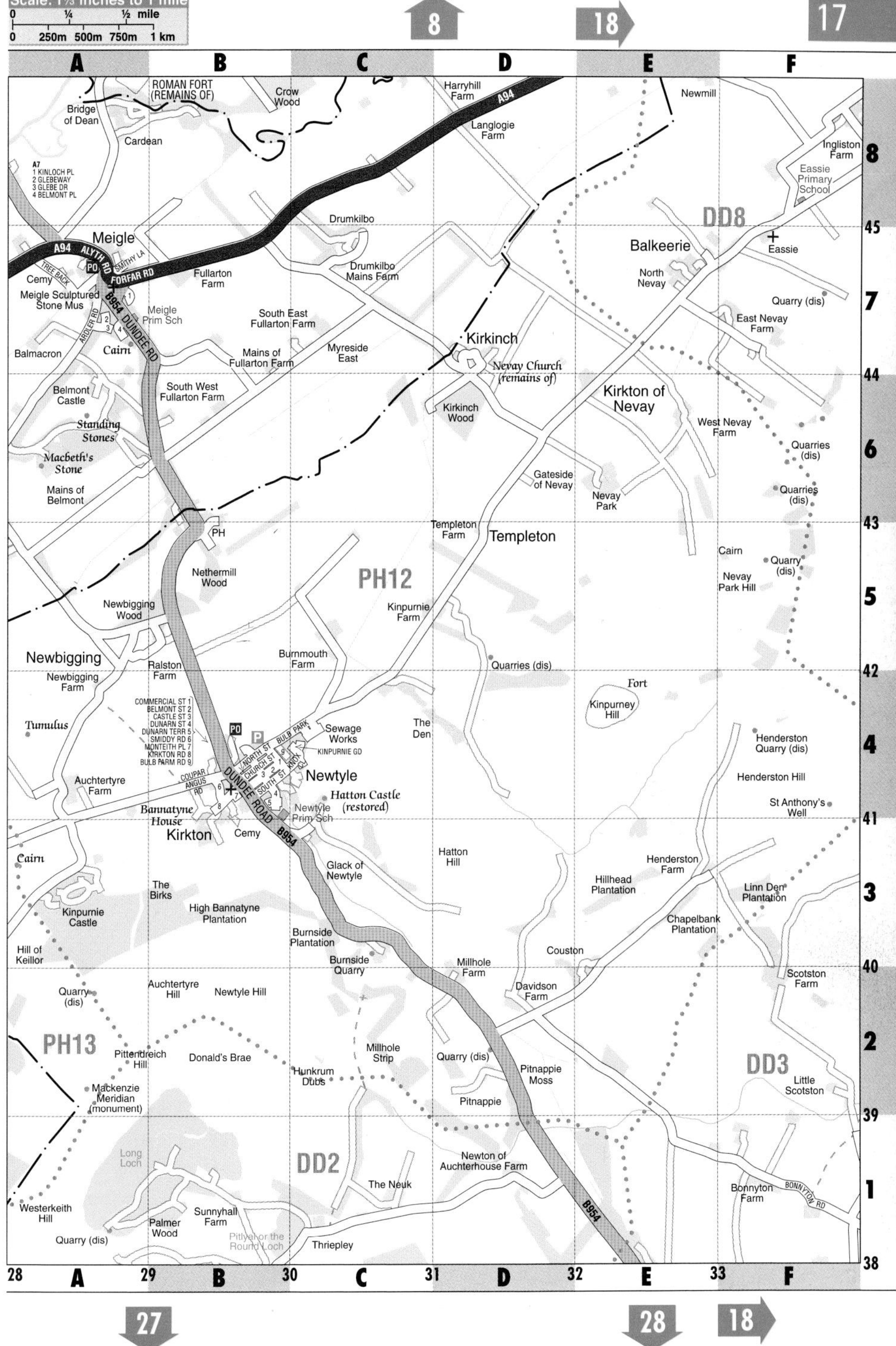
Scale: 1⅓ inches to 1 mile
0 ¼ ½ mile
0 250m 500m 750m 1 km
8
18
A B C D E F
ROMAN FORT (REMAINS OF)
Bridge of Dean
Crow Wood
Harryhill Farm
Newmill
Langlogie Farm
A94
Cardean
Ingliston Farm
Eassie Primary School
A7
1 KINLOCH PL
2 GLEBEWAY
3 GLEBE DR
4 BELMONT PL
Drumkilbo
DD8
Meigle
Balkeerie
Eassie
ALYTH RD
SMITHY LA
FORFAR RD
TREE BACK
Cemy
Fullarton Farm
Drumkilbo Mains Farm
North Nevay
Meigle Sculptured Stone Mus
B954
DUNDEE RD
Meigle Prim Sch
South East Fullarton Farm
Quarry (dis)
East Nevay Farm
ARDLER RD
Cairn
Balmacron
Mains of Fullarton Farm
Myreside East
Kirkinch
Nevay Church (remains of)
Belmont Castle
South West Fullarton Farm
Kirkinch Wood
Kirkton of Nevay
West Nevay Farm
Standing Stones
Macbeth's Stone
Quarries (dis)
Gateside of Nevay
Nevay Park
Mains of Belmont
Quarries (dis)
Templeton Farm
Templeton
PH
Cairn
Nethermill Wood
PH12
Quarry (dis)
Nevay Park Hill
Newbigging Wood
Kinpurnie Farm
Newbigging
Burnmouth Farm
Ralston Farm
Quarries (dis)
Newbigging Farm
Fort
Kinpurney Hill
COMMERCIAL ST 1
BELMONT ST 2
CASTLE ST 3
DUNARN ST 4
DUNARN TERR 5
SMIDDY RD 6
MONTEITH PL 7
KIRKTON RD 8
BULB FARM RD 9
Tumulus
PO
P
BULB PARK
Sewage Works
KINPURNIE GD
The Den
Henderston Quarry (dis)
NORTH ST
CHURCH ST
SOUTH ST
KNOX PL
Newtyle
Henderston Hill
Auchtertyre Farm
COUPAR ANGUS RD
DUNDEE ROAD
Hatton Castle (restored)
St Anthony's Well
Bannatyne House
Newtyle Prim Sch
Kirkton
Cemy
Hatton Hill
Henderston Farm
Cairn
Glack of Newtyle
The Birks
Hillhead Plantation
Linn Den Plantation
Kinpurnie Castle
High Bannatyne Plantation
Chapelbank Plantation
Burnside Plantation
Hill of Keillor
Burnside Quarry
Couston
Millhole Farm
Scotston Farm
Davidson Farm
Quarry (dis)
Auchtertyre Hill
Newtyle Hill
PH13
Pittendreich Hill
Donald's Brae
Millhole Strip
Quarry (dis)
DD3
Hunkrum Dubs
Pitnappie Moss
Little Scotston
Mackenzie Meridian (monument)
Pitnappie
Long Loch
DD2
Newton of Auchterhouse Farm
The Neuk
Bonnyton Farm
BONNYTON RD
Westerkeith Hill
Sunnyhall Farm
Palmer Wood
Quarry (dis)
Pitlyal or the Round Loch
Thriepley
8
45
7
44
6
43
5
42
4
41
3
40
2
39
1
38
28 29 30 31 32 33
27
28
18

17 8 9

Scale: 1⅓ inches to 1 mile

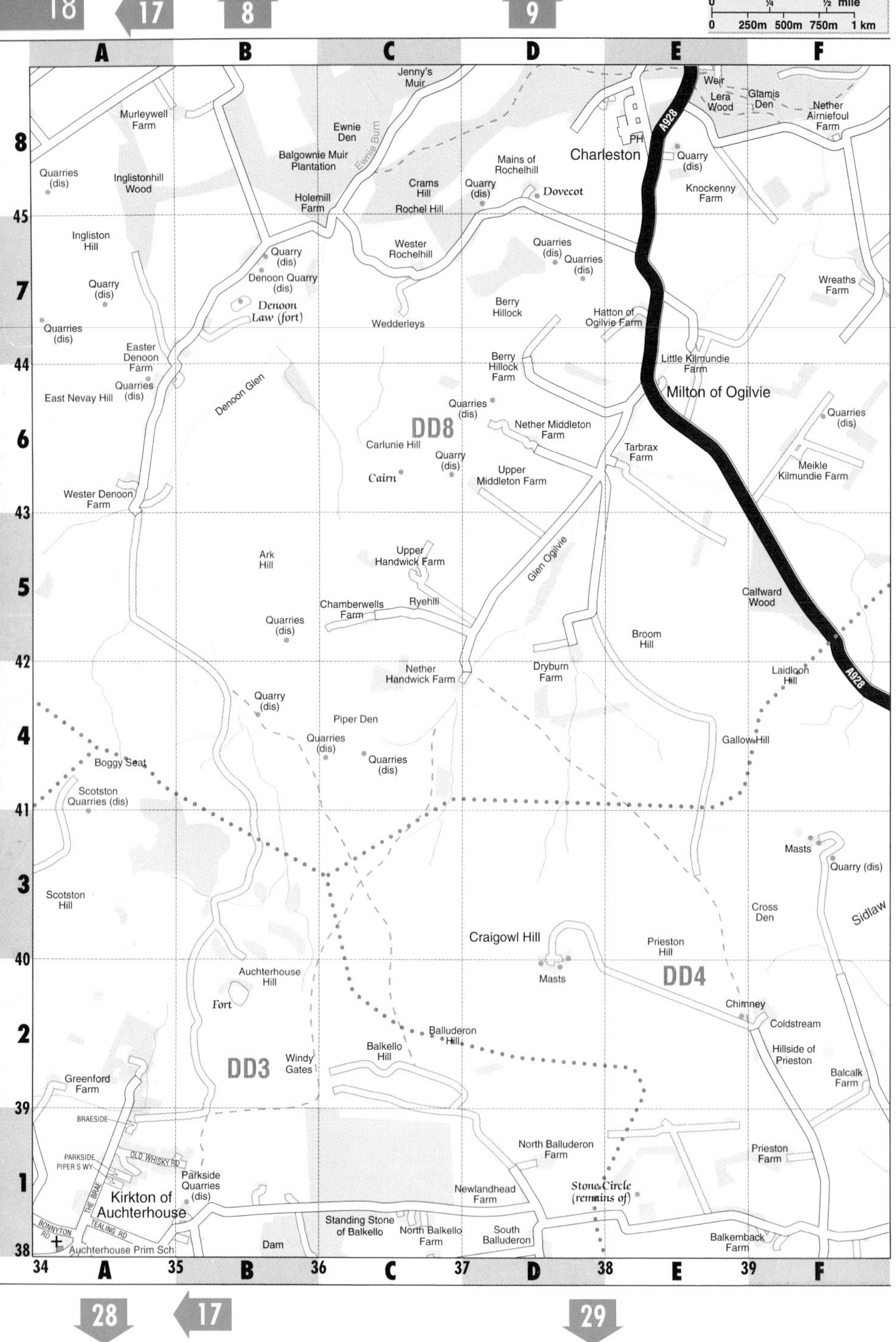

A B C D E F
8 45 7 44 6 43 5 42 4 41 3 40 2 39 1 38
34 35 36 37 38 39
Murleywell Farm
Quarries (dis)
Inglistonhill Wood
Ewnie Den
Ewnie Burn
Jenny's Muir
Balgownie Muir Plantation
Holemill Farm
Crams Hill
Rochel Hill
Mains of Rochelhill
Quarry (dis)
Dovecot
Charleston
PH
A928
Weir
Lera Wood
Glamis Den
Nether Airniefoul Farm
Quarry (dis)
Knockenny Farm
Ingliston Hill
Quarry (dis)
Denoon Quarry (dis)
Denoon Law (fort)
Wester Rochelhill
Wedderleys
Quarries (dis)
Berry Hillock
Hatton of Ogilvie Farm
Wreaths Farm
Easter Denoon Farm
East Nevay Hill
Denoon Glen
Berry Hillock Farm
Little Kilmundie Farm
Milton of Ogilvie
DD8
Carlunie Hill
Cairn
Nether Middleton Farm
Upper Middleton Farm
Tarbrax Farm
Meikle Kilmundie Farm
Wester Denoon Farm
Ark Hill
Upper Handwick Farm
Glen Ogilvie
Chamberwells Farm
Ryehill
Calfward Wood
Broom Hill
Nether Handwick Farm
Dryburn Farm
Laidloon Hill
Piper Den
Gallow Hill
Boggy Seat
Scotston Quarries (dis)
Masts
Quarry (dis)
Scotston Hill
Cross Den
Sidlaw
Craigowl Hill
Prieston Hill
DD4
Auchterhouse Hill
Fort
Chimney
Coldstream
Balluderon Hill
Balkello Hill
Hillside of Prieston
DD3
Windy Gates
Greenford Farm
Balcalk Farm
BRAESIDE
PARKSIDE
PIPER'S WY
OLD WHISKY RD
THE BRAE
North Balluderon Farm
Prieston Farm
Parkside Quarries (dis)
Kirkton of Auchterhouse
Newlandhead Farm
Stone Circle (remains of)
BONNYTON RD
TEALING RD
Standing Stone of Balkello
North Balkello Farm
South Balluderon
Balkemback Farm
Auchterhouse Prim Sch
Dam

28 17 29

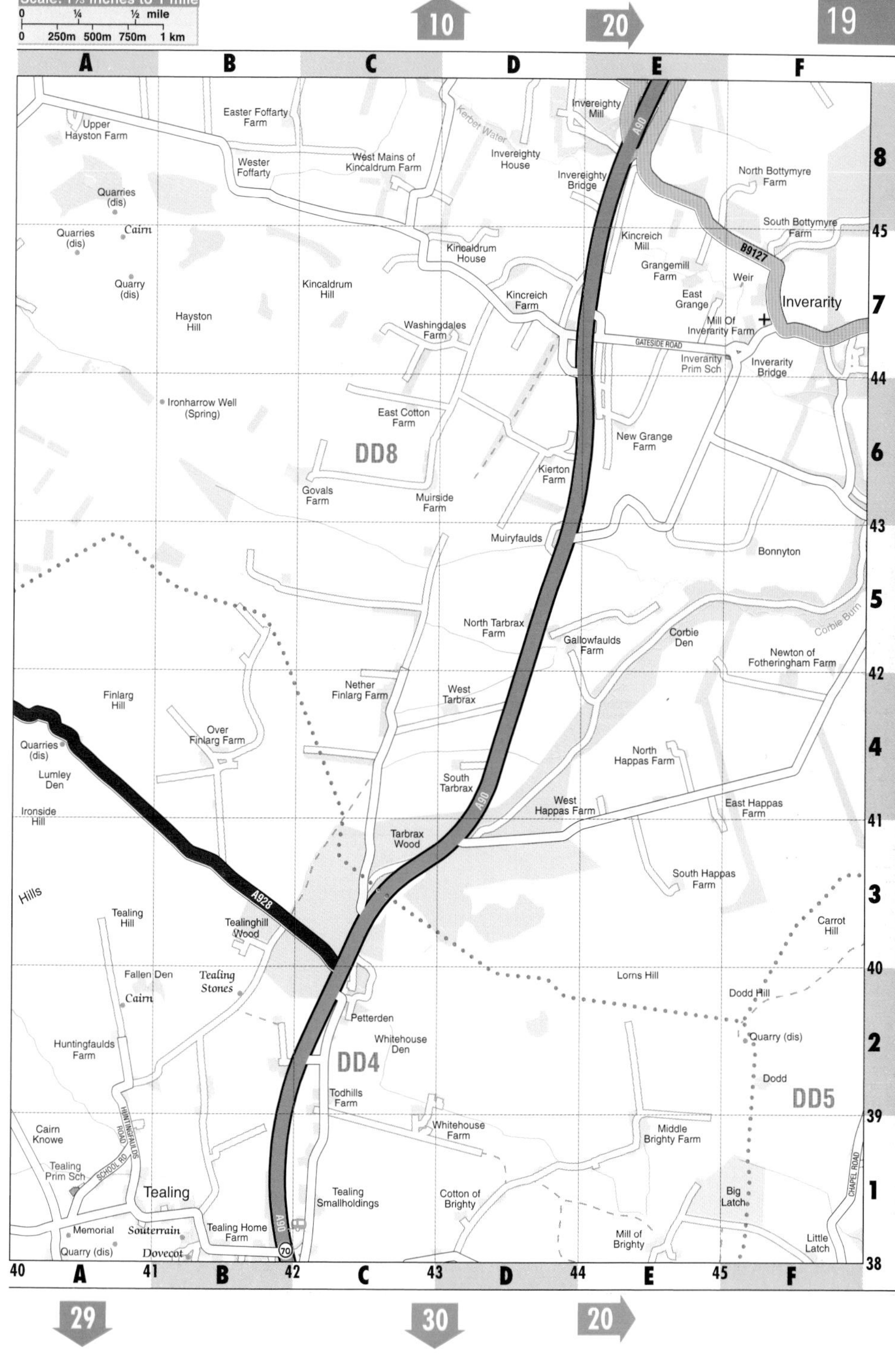

A B C D E F

Upper Hayston Farm
Easter Foffarty Farm
Wester Foffarty
West Mains of Kincaldrum Farm
Invereighty Mill
Invereighty House
Kerbet Water
A90
North Bottymyre Farm

8

Quarries (dis)
Invereighty Bridge
Invereighty Bridge
South Bottymyre Farm

45

Quarries (dis)
Cairn
Kincaldrum House
Kincreich Mill
B9127

Quarry (dis)
Kincaldrum Hill
Kincreich Farm
Grangemill Farm
East Grange
Weir
Inverarity

7

Hayston Hill
Washingdales Farm
Mill Of Inverarity Farm

Ironharrow Well (Spring)
East Cotton Farm
GATESIDE ROAD
Inverarity Prim Sch
Inverarity Bridge

44

DD8
Kierton Farm
New Grange Farm

6

Govals Farm
Muirside Farm

Muiryfaulds

43

North Tarbrax Farm
Corbie Burn

5

Gallowfaulds Farm
Corbie Den
Newton of Fotheringham Farm

Bonnyton

Finlarg Hill
Nether Finlarg Farm
West Tarbrax

42

Over Finlarg Farm
North Happas Farm

Quarries (dis)
Lumley Den

4

Ironside Hill
South Tarbrax
West Happas Farm
East Happas Farm

41

Hills
A928
Tarbrax Wood
South Happas Farm

Tealing Hill
Tealinghill Wood

3

Fallen Den
Tealing Stones
Lorns Hill
Carrot Hill

40

Cairn
Dodd Hill

Huntingfaulds Farm
Petterden
Whitehouse Den
Quarry (dis)

2

DD4
Todhills Farm
Dodd
DD5

Cairn Knowe
Whitehouse Farm

39

Tealing Prim Sch
Middle Brighty Farm

Tealing
Tealing Smallholdings
Cotton of Brighty
Big Latch

1

Memorial
Souterrain
Dovecot
Tealing Home Farm
Mill of Brighty
Little Latch

Quarry (dis)
70

38

A B C D E F
40 41 42 43 44 45

Scale: 1⅓ inches to 1 mile

| 0 | ¼ | ½ mile |
| 0 | 250m | 500m | 750m | 1 km |

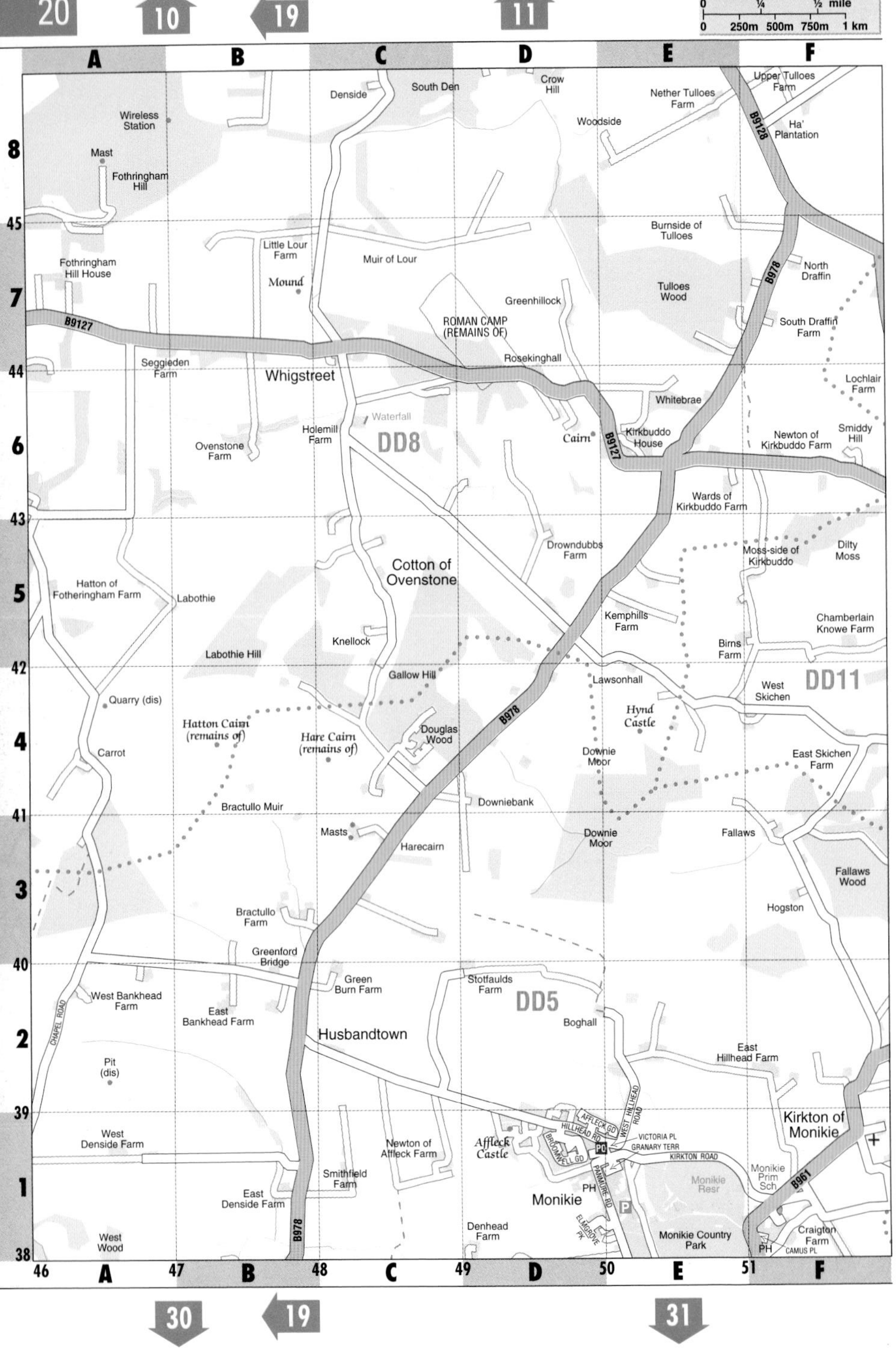

A B C D E F

8

Wireless Station

Mast

Fothringham Hill

Denside

South Den

Crow Hill

Woodside

Nether Tulloes Farm

Upper Tulloes Farm

Ha' Plantation

B9128

45

Fothringham Hill House

Little Lour Farm

Mound

Muir of Lour

Greenhillock

Burnside of Tulloes

Tulloes Wood

North Draffin

B9178

7

B9127

Seggieden Farm

Whigstreet

ROMAN CAMP (REMAINS OF)

Rosekinghall

South Draffin Farm

Lochlair Farm

44

Waterfall

DD8

Whitebrae

Kirkbuddo House

Cairn

B9127

Smiddy Hill

6

Ovenstone Farm

Holemill Farm

Drowndubbs Farm

Wards of Kirkbuddo Farm

Newton of Kirkbuddo Farm

43

Hatton of Fotheringham Farm

Labothie

Cotton of Ovenstone

Knellock

Kemphills Farm

Moss-side of Kirkbuddo

Dilty Moss

Chamberlain Knowe Farm

DD11

5

Labothie Hill

Gallow Hill

Lawsonhall

Birns Farm

West Skichen

42

Quarry (dis)

Hatton Cairn (remains of)

Hare Cairn (remains of)

Douglas Wood

B978

Hynd Castle

East Skichen Farm

4

Carrot

Bractullo Muir

Downiebank

Downie Moor

41

Masts

Harecairn

Downie Moor

Fallaws

Fallaws Wood

3

Bractullo Farm

Hogston

40

CHAPEL ROAD

Greenford Bridge

West Bankhead Farm

East Bankhead Farm

Green Burn Farm

Stotfaulds Farm

DD5

Boghall

East Hillhead Farm

2

Husbandtown

Pit (dis)

Kirkton of Monikie

39

West Denside Farm

Newton of Affleck Farm

Affleck Castle

HILLHEAD RD

AFFLECK RD

PO

VICTORIA PL

GRANARY TERR

KIRKTON ROAD

Monikie Prim Sch

B961

1

Smithfield Farm

PH

Monikie

P

Monikie Resr

ELMSIDE PK

CAMUS PL

Craigton Farm

East Denside Farm

B978

West Wood

Denhead Farm

PANMURE RD

Monikie Country Park

PH

38

46 A 47 B 48 C 49 D 50 E 51 F

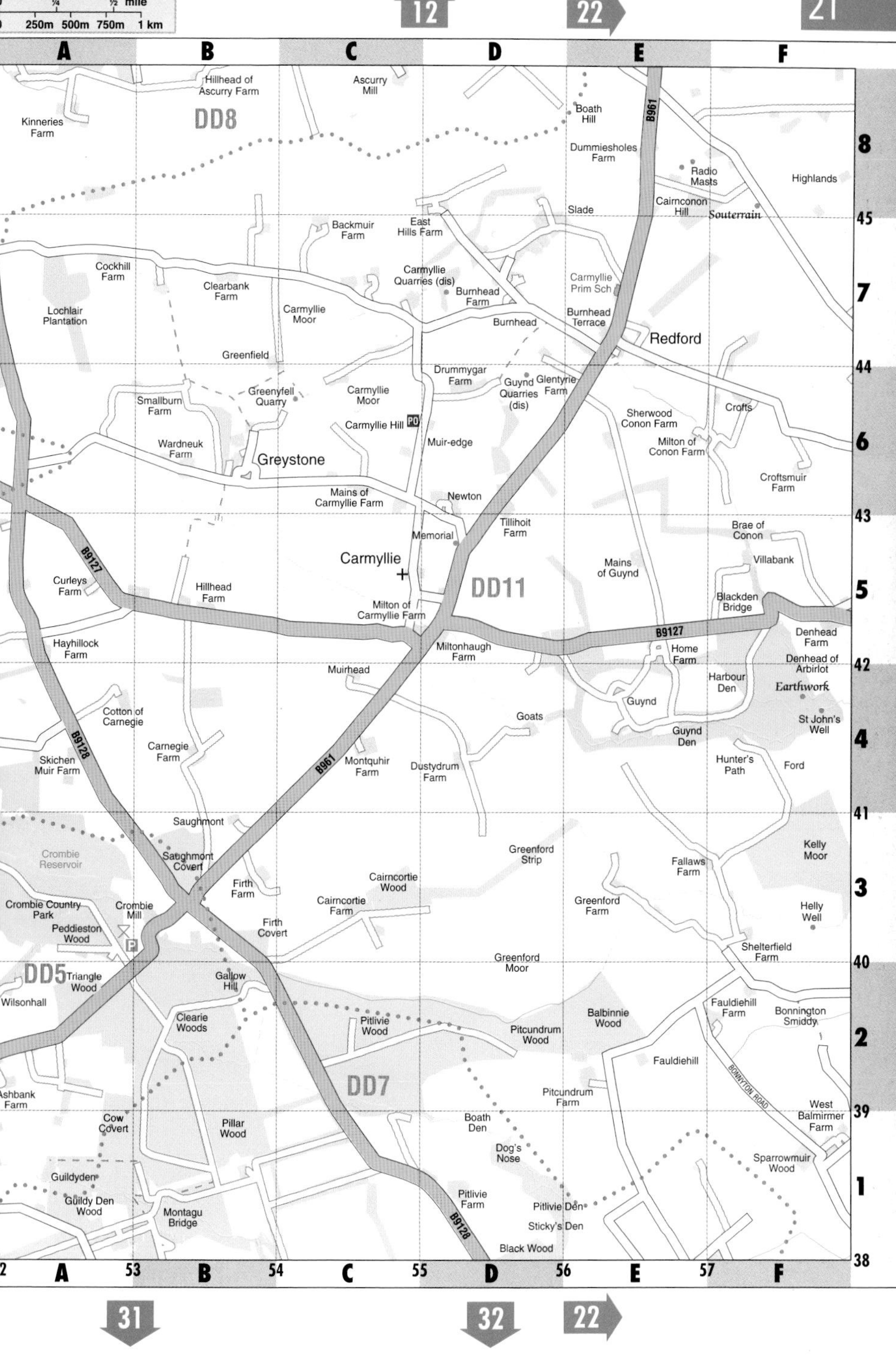

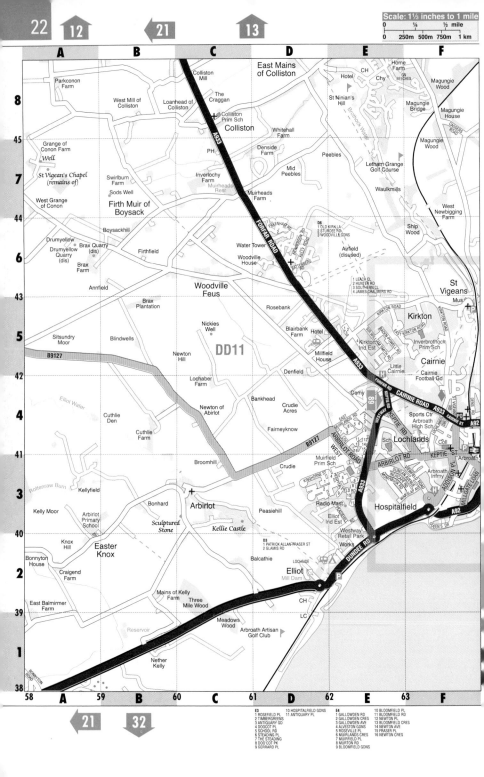

A B C D E F

8
45
7
44
6
43
5
42
4
41
3
40
2
39
1
38

Parkconon Farm
Home Farm
CH
Chy
GN BEECHES
Magungie Wood
Hotel
Magungie Bridge
Magungie House
CADGERS ROAD
West Mill of Colliston
Loanhead of Colliston
The Craggan
Colliston Mill
East Mains of Colliston
St Ninian's Hill
Magungie Wood
Colliston Prim Sch
Colliston
Whitehall Farm
Grange of Conon Farm
Well
PH
Denside Farm
Peebles
Letham Grange Golf Course
Magungie Wood
St Vigean's Chapel (remains of)
Swirlburn Farm
Sods Well
Inverlochy Farm
Muirheads Resr
Mid Peebles
Ship Wood
West Grange of Conon
Muirheads Farm
Waulkmills
West Newbigging Farm
Firth Muir of Boysack
Boysackhill
Drumyellow Quarry (dis)
Brax Quarry (dis)
Firthfield
Water Tower
Woodville House
PAKENHAM RD
D6
1 OLD KIRK LA
2 STURDZA RD
3 WOODVILLE GDNS
Airfield (disused)
St Vigeans
Mus
Drumyellow Quarry (dis)
Brax Farm
Annfield
Brax Plantation
Woodville Feus
Rosebank
1 LEACH CL
2 HUNTER RD
3 SOUTHERN CL
4 JAMES CHALMERS RD
St Vigeans
Kirkton
Sitsundry Moor
Blindwells
Nickies Well
Blairbank Farm
Hotel
KIRKTON ROAD
Kirkton Ind Est
Inverbrothock Prim Sch
B9127
Newton Hill
DD11
Millfield House
Little Cairnie
Cairnie
Cuthlie Den
Lochaber Farm
Denfield
Cairnie Football Gd
Elliot Water
Newton of Abirlot
Bankhead
Comy
CAIRNIE ROAD
Cuthlie Farm
Fairneyknow
Crudie Acres
EAST
WESTWAY
KEPTIE RD
Sports Ctr
Arbroath High Sch
A92
CAIRNIE RD
B9127
WEST
Broomhill
Crudie
ARBIRLOT ROAD
Muirfield Prim Sch
Sch
Lochlands
Coll
KEPTIE ST
Arbroath
Kellyfield
Bonhard
Arbirlot
Peasiehill
KINGHORNE RD
ARBIRLOT RD
Arbroath Infmy
Rottenraw Burn
Kelly Moor
Arbirlot Primary School
Sculptured Stone
Kellie Castle
Radio Mast
Elliot Ind Est
Hospitalfield
ADISON PL
A92
HILLGATE LOAN
Knox Hill
Easter Knox
D3
1 PATRICK ALLAN-FRASER ST
2 GLAMIS RD
Westway Retail Park
QUEEN'S DR
Bonnyton House
Craigend Farm
Balcathie
Works
LOCHSIDE
Elliot
Mill Dam
DUNDEE RD
East Balmirrer Farm
Mains of Kelly Farm
Three Mile Wood
CH
LC
Reservoir
Meadows Wood
Arbroath Artisan Golf Club
BONNYTON ROAD
Nether Kelly

58 A 59 B 60 C 61 D 62 E 63 F

E3
1 ROSEFIELD PL
2 TIMBERGREENS
3 ANTIQUARY GD
4 DOOCOT PL
5 SCHOOL RD
6 STEADING PL
7 THE STEADING
8 DOO COT PK
9 GERRARD PL
10 HOSPITALFIELD GDNS
11 ANTIQUARY PL

E4
1 GALLOWDEN RD
2 GALLOWDEN CRES
3 GALLOWDEN AVE
4 ALVESTON GDNS
5 ROSEVILLE PL
6 MUIRLANDS CRES
7 MUIRFIELD PL
8 MURTON RD
9 BLOOMFIELD GDNS
10 BLOOMFIELD PL
11 BLOOMFIELD RD
12 NEWTON PL
13 BLOOMFIELD CRES
14 NEWTON AVE
15 FRASER PL
16 NEWTON CRES

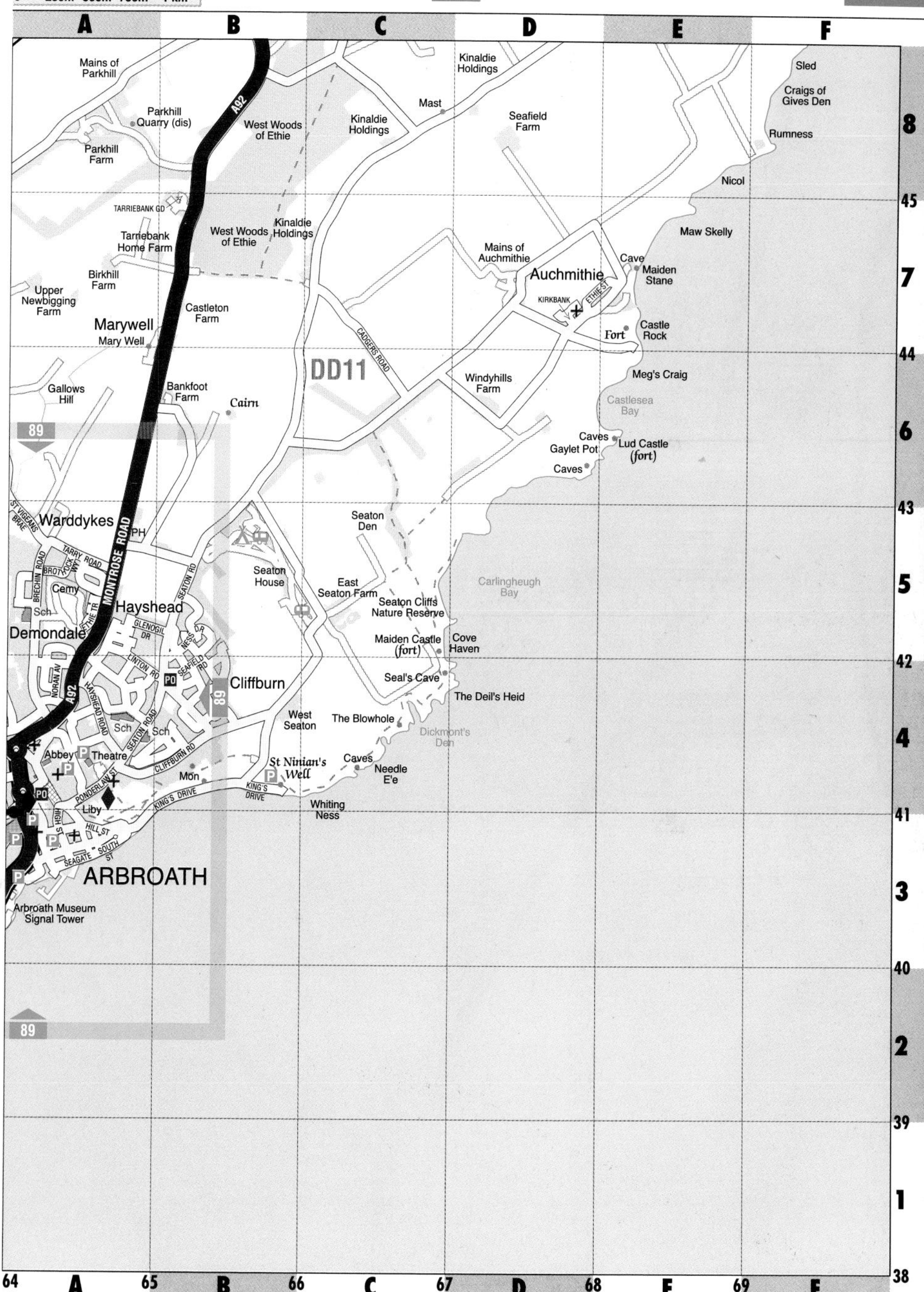

A   **B**   **C**   **D**   **E**   **F**

Mains of
Parkhill

Parkhill
Quarry (dis)

West Woods
of Ethie

Kinaldie
Holdings

Mast

Kinaldie
Holdings

Seafield
Farm

Sled

Craigs of
Gives Den

Rumness

Parkhill
Farm

TARRIEBANK GD

Tarriebank
Home Farm

West Woods
of Ethie

Kinaldie
Holdings

Nicol

8

45

Upper
Newbigging
Farm

Birkhill
Farm

Castleton
Farm

Mains of
Auchmithie

Auchmithie

KIRKBANK

Cave

Maw Skelly

Maiden
Stane

7

Marywell
Mary Well

Fort

Castle
Rock

44

Gallows
Hill

Bankfoot
Farm

Cairn

Windyhills
Farm

Meg's Craig

Castlesea
Bay

DD11

89

Caves
Gaylet Pot

Caves

Lud Castle
(fort)

6

43

Warddykes

PH

Seaton
Den

Carlingheugh
Bay

5

Seaton
House

East
Seaton Farm

Seaton Cliffs
Nature Reserve

Hayshead

Demondale

Cemy

Sch

Maiden Castle
(fort)

Cove
Haven

42

Cliffburn

89

West
Seaton

Seal's Cave

The Blowhole

The Deil's Heid

Dickmont's
Den

4

Abbey

Theatre

Mon

St Ninian's
Well

Caves

Needle
E'e

Whiting
Ness

41

Liby

PO

ARBROATH

Arbroath Museum
Signal Tower

3

40

89

2

39

1

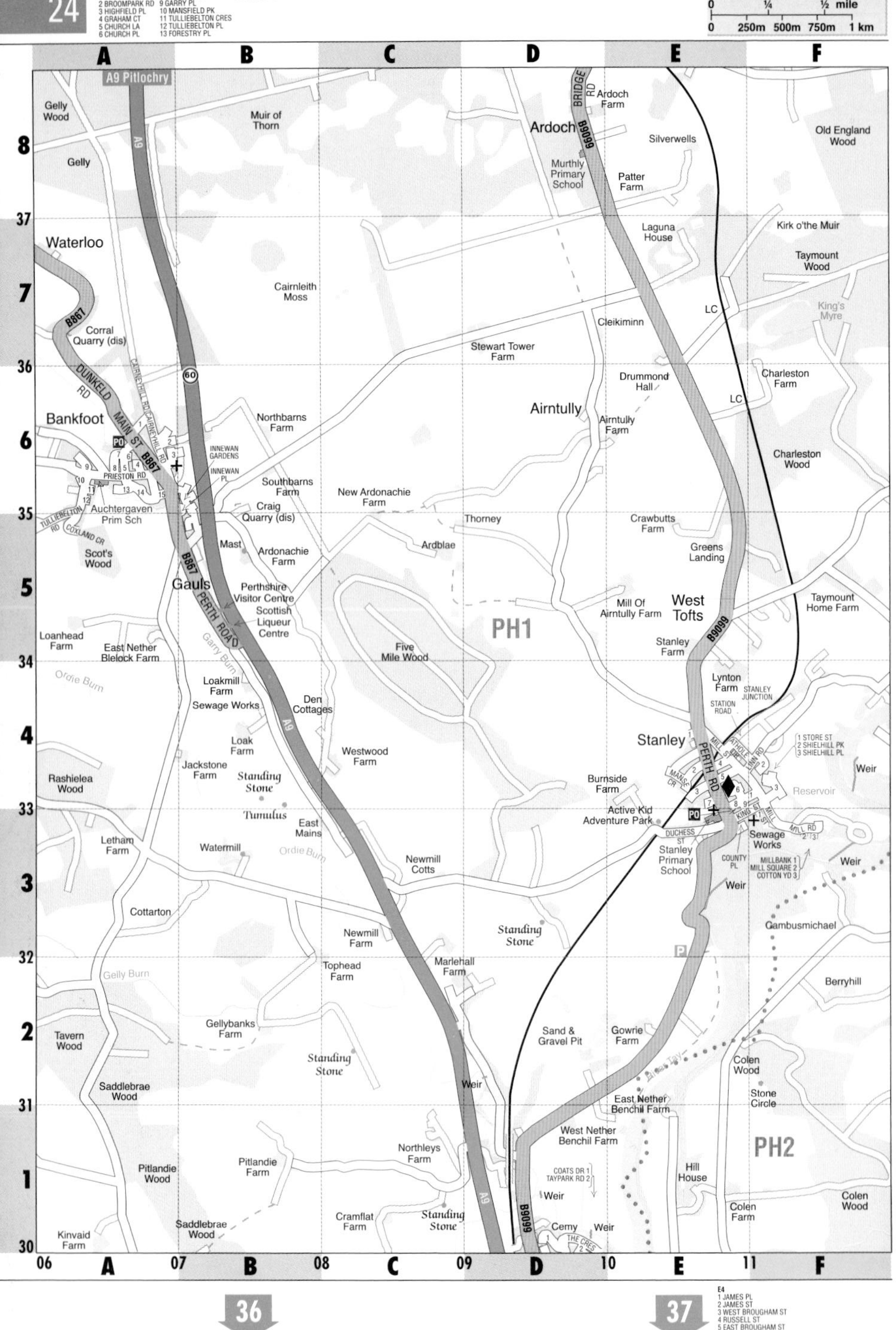

A6
1 SMITH'S BRAE
2 BROOMPARK RD
3 HIGHFIELD PL
4 GRAHAM CT
5 CHURCH LA
6 CHURCH PL

7 CROSS ST
8 NEWHALL ST
9 GARRY PL
10 MANSFIELD PK
11 TULLIEBELTON CRES
12 TULLIEBELTON PL
13 FORESTRY PL

14 NICOLL DR
15 NICOLL PL

Scale: 1⅓ inches to 1 mile

| 0 | ¼ | ½ | mile |

| 0 | 250m | 500m | 750m | 1 km |

A9 Pitlochry

Gelly Wood
Gelly

Muir of Thorn

Ardoch
Ardoch Farm

Silverwells

Old England Wood

Waterloo

Cairnleith Moss

Murthly Primary School

Patter Farm

Kirk o' the Muir

Taymount Wood

King's Myre

Corral Quarry (dis)

Stewart Tower Farm

Cleikiminn

LC

Laguna House

Charleston Farm

Charleston Wood

Bankfoot

DUNKELD RD

MAIN ST

Northbarns Farm

Airntully

Airntully Farm

Drummond Hall

LC

PO

INNEWAN GARDENS
INNEWAN PL

Southbarns Farm

New Ardonachie Farm

Thorney

Crawbutts Farm

Greens Landing

Auchtergaven Prim Sch

Craig Quarry (dis)

Ardonachie Farm

Ardblae

Taymount Home Farm

Scot's Wood

Mast

Gauls

Perthshire Visitor Centre
Scottish Liqueur Centre

Five Mile Wood

PH1

Mill Of Airntully Farm

West Tofts

Stanley Farm

Loanhead Farm

East Nether Bieleock Farm

Loakmill Farm
Sewage Works

Den Cottages

Lynton Farm

STANLEY JUNCTION

STATION ROAD

Rashielea Wood

Loak Farm

Jackstone Farm

Standing Stone

Westwood Farm

Stanley

Burnside Farm

1 STORE ST
2 SHIELHILL PK
3 SHIELHILL PL

Weir

Reservoir

Letham Farm

Watermill

Tumulus

East Mains

Active Kid Adventure Park

PO

DUCHESS ST

Weir

MILL RD

Weir

Cottarton

Ordie Burn

Newmill Cotts

Stanley Primary School

COUNTY PL

Weir

MILLBANK 1
MILL SQUARE 2
COTTON YD 3

Gelly Burn

Newmill Farm

Marlehall Farm

Standing Stone

P

Cambusmichael

Berryhill

Tavern Wood

Gellybanks Farm

Tophead Farm

Sand & Gravel Pit

Gowrie Farm

Colen Wood

Stone Circle

Saddlebrae Wood

Standing Stone

Weir

East Nether Benchil Farm

PH2

Pitlandie Wood

Pitlandie Farm

Northleys Farm

West Nether Benchil Farm

Hill House

Colen Farm

Colen Wood

Kinvaid Farm

Saddlebrae Wood

Cramflat Farm

Standing Stone

Cerny

THE CRES

COATS DR 1
TAYPARK RD 2

Weir

Weir

E4
1 JAMES PL
2 JAMES ST
3 WEST BROUGHAM ST
4 RUSSELL ST
5 EAST BROUGHAM ST
6 MURRAY PL
7 WEST PK
8 PERCY ST
9 CHARLOTTE ST

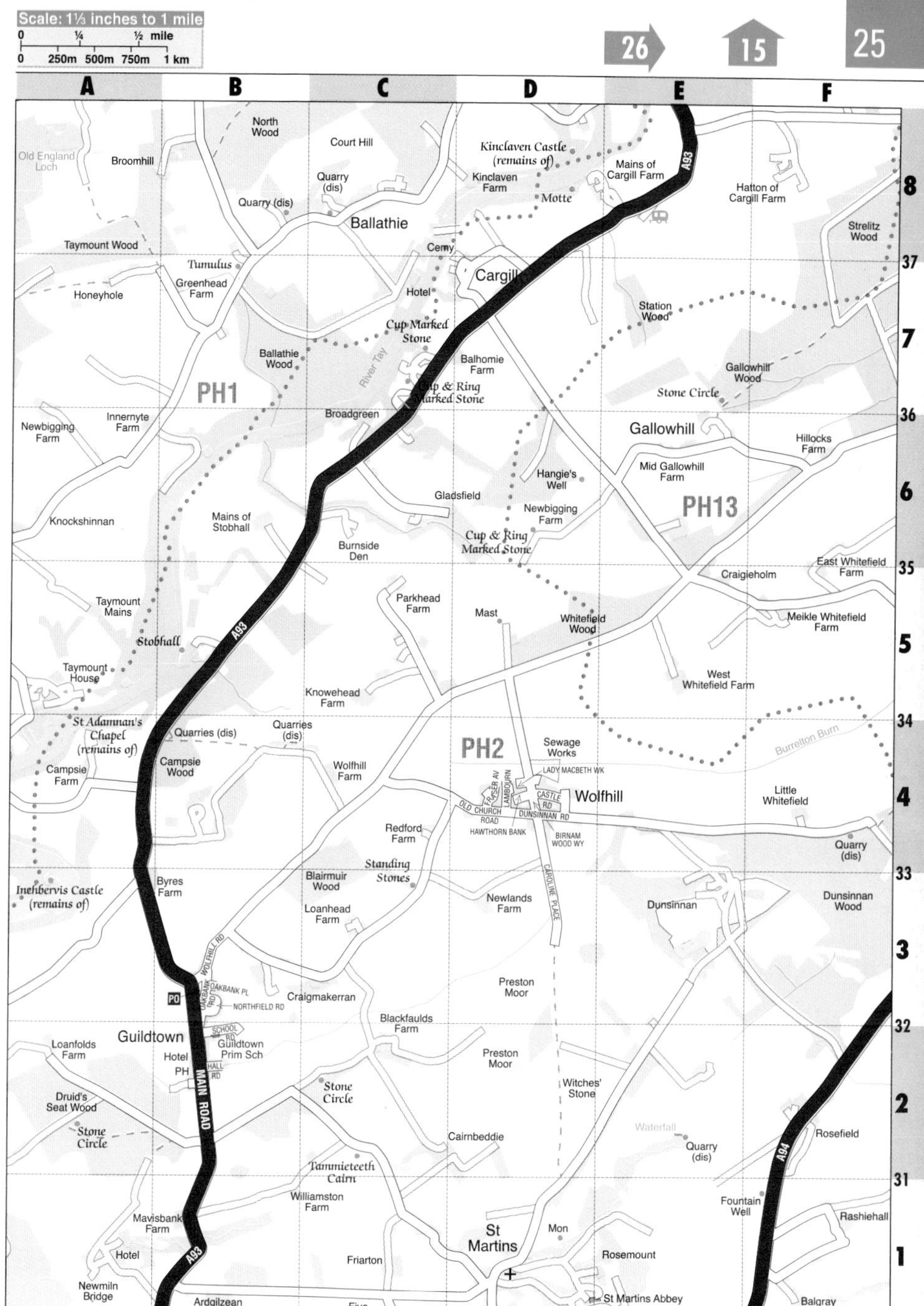
Scale: 1⅓ inches to 1 mile
0 ¼ ½ mile
0 250m 500m 750m 1 km
26
15
A B C D E F
Old England Loch
Broomhill
North Wood
Court Hill
Quarry (dis)
Quarry (dis)
Ballathie
Kinclaven Castle (remains of)
Kinclaven Farm
Motte
Mains of Cargill Farm
A93
Hatton of Cargill Farm
Strelitz Wood
Taymount Wood
Tumulus
Cemy
Cargill
Honeyhole
Greenhead Farm
Hotel
Station Wood
Cup Marked Stone
Ballathie Wood
River Tay
Balhomie Farm
Gallowhill Wood
Cup & Ring Marked Stone
Stone Circle
PH1
Broadgreen
Gallowhill
Newbigging Farm
Innernyte Farm
Hillocks Farm
Mid Gallowhill Farm
Hangie's Well
Gladsfield
PH13
Knockshinnan
Mains of Stobhall
Newbigging Farm
Cup & Ring Marked Stone
Burnside Den
East Whitefield Farm
Craigieholm
Taymount Mains
Parkhead Farm
Mast
Whitefield Wood
Meikle Whitefield Farm
Stobhall
Taymount House
West Whitefield Farm
Knowehead Farm
St Adamnan's Chapel (remains of)
Quarries (dis)
Quarries (dis)
Sewage Works
Burrelton Burn
PH2
Campsie Wood
Wolfhill Farm
Campsie Farm
LADY MACBETH WK
FRASER AV
LAMBOURN
CASTLE RD
Wolfhill
Little Whitefield
OLD CHURCH ROAD
DUNSINNAN RD
HAWTHORN BANK
BIRNAM WOOD WY
Redford Farm
Quarry (dis)
Standing Stones
Byres Farm
Blairmuir Wood
Inchbervis Castle (remains of)
Newlands Farm
CAROLINE PLACE
Dunsinnan
Dunsinnan Wood
Loanhead Farm
WOLFHILL RD
Preston Moor
PO
OAKBANK RD
OAKBANK PL
NORTHFIELD RD
Craigmakerran
SCHOOL RD
Blackfaulds Farm
Guildtown
Loanfolds Farm
Guildtown Prim Sch
Hotel
Preston Moor
PH
HALL RD
MAIN ROAD
Witches' Stone
Stone Circle
Druid's Seat Wood
Stone Circle
Waterfall
Rosefield
Cairnbeddie
Quarry (dis)
Tammieteeth Cairn
A94
Williamston Farm
Fountain Well
Rashiehall
Mavisbank Farm
St Martins
Mon
Hotel
A93
Rosemount
Friarton
Newmiln Bridge
St Martins Abbey
Balgray Farm
Ardgilzean Plantation
Five Farthings
8
37
7
36
6
35
5
34
4
33
3
32
2
31
1
30
12 A 13 B 14 C 15 D 16 E 17 F
37
38
26

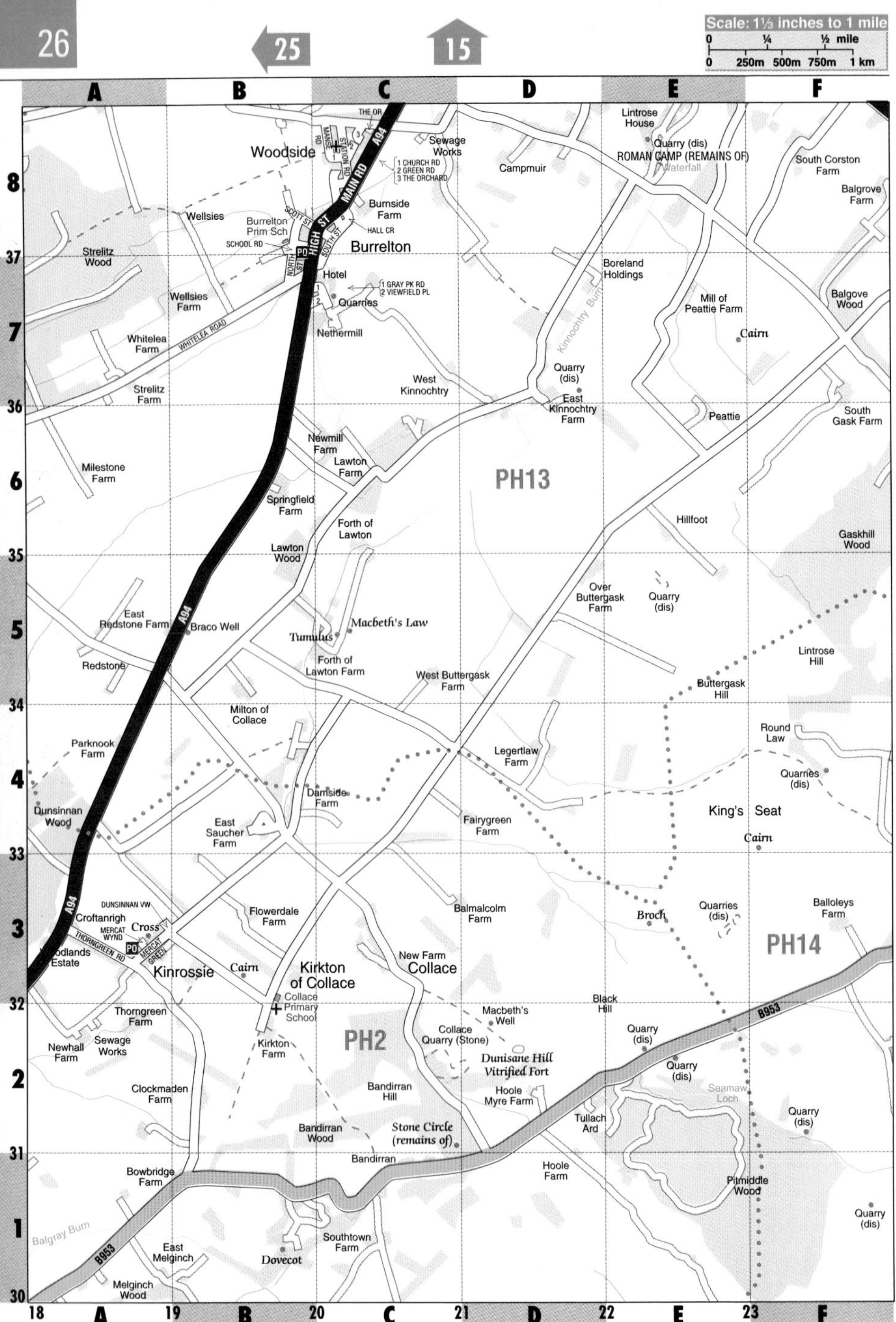

Scale: 1½ inches to 1 mile

0   ¼   ½ mile
0   250m   500m   750m   1 km

A   B   C   D   E   F

Lintrose House
Quarry (dis)
ROMAN CAMP (REMAINS OF)
Waterfall
South Corston Farm
Balgrove Farm

8

THE OR
Woodside
Sewage Works
Campmuir

1 CHURCH RD
2 GREEN RD
3 THE ORCHARD

Burnside Farm

Wellsies

Burrelton Prim Sch
SCHOOL RD
HALL CR
Burrelton

Boreland Holdings

Mill of Peattie Farm

Cairn

37

Strelitz Wood

Hotel

1 GRAY PK RD
2 VIEWFIELD PL

Balgove Wood

Wellsies Farm

Quarries

Nethermill

West Kinnochtry

Quarry (dis)

East Kinnochtry Farm

Peattie

South Gask Farm

7

Whitelea Farm

WHITELEA ROAD

Strelitz Farm

36

Newmill Farm
Lawton Farm

PH13

Milestone Farm

Springfield Farm

Forth of Lawton

Hillfoot

Gaskhill Wood

6

Lawton Wood

35

East Redstone Farm
Braco Well

Tumulus

Macbeth's Law

Forth of Lawton Farm

West Buttergask Farm

Over Buttergask Farm

Quarry (dis)

Lintrose Hill

5

Redstone

Milton of Collace

Buttergask Hill

Round Law

Quarries (dis)

34

Parknook Farm

Damside Farm

Legertlaw Farm

King's Seat
Cairn

4

Dunsinnan Wood

East Saucher Farm

Fairygreen Farm

Quarries (dis)

Balloleys Wood

33

Croftanrigh
DUNSINNAN VW
MERCAT Cross
Woodlands Estate
Kinrossie

Flowerdale Farm

Cairn

Balmalcolm Farm

Broch

PH14

3

THORNGREEN WYND

Kirkton of Collace

New Farm Collace

Black Hill

B953

32

Thorngreen Farm

Collace Primary School

Macbeth's Well

Quarry (dis)

Newhall Farm
Sewage Works

Kirkton Farm

PH2

Collace Quarry (Stone)

Dunsinane Hill Vitrified Fort

Quarry (dis)

Seamaw Loch

2

Clockmaden Farm

Bandirran Hill

Hoole Myre Farm

Tullach Ard

Quarry (dis)

Bandirran Wood

Stone Circle (remains of)

Quarry (dis)

31

Bowbridge Farm

Bandirran

Hoole Farm

Pirmiddle Wood

B953

1

Balgray Burn

East Melginch

Southtown Farm

Quarry (dis)

Dovecot

Melginch Wood

30

18   A   19   B   20   C   21   D   22   E   23   F

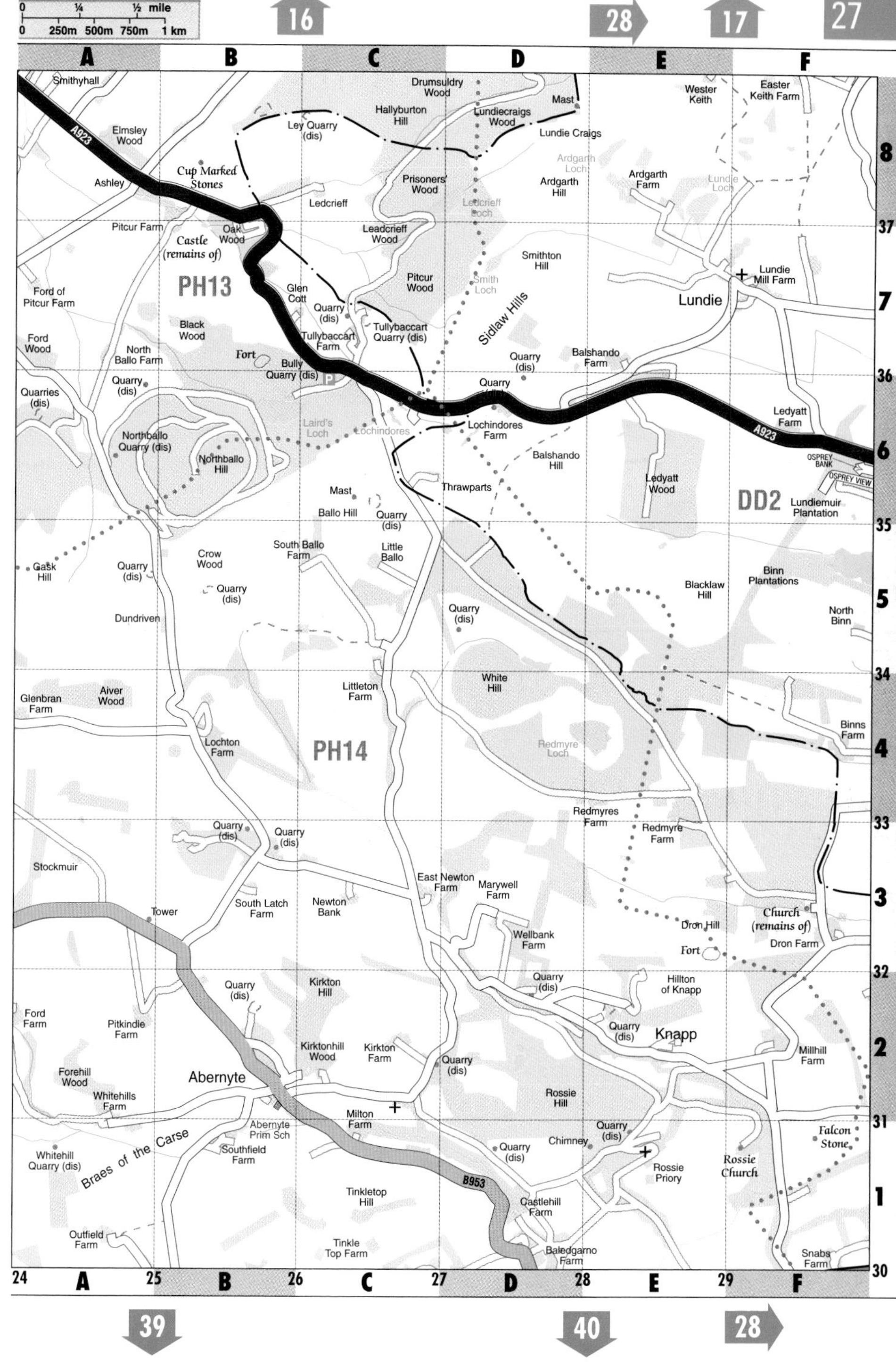
Scale: 1⅓ inches to 1 mile
16
28
17
Smithyhall
Elmsley Wood
A923
Ashley
Cup Marked Stones
Ley Quarry (dis)
Drumsuldry Wood
Hallyburton Hill
Lundiecraigs Wood
Mast
Lundie Craigs
Wester Keith
Easter Keith Farm
Ardgarth Loch
Ardgarth Hill
Ardgarth Farm
Lundie Loch
Prisoners' Wood
Ledcrieff
Ledcrieff Loch
Pitcur Farm
Oak Wood
Castle (remains of)
Leadcrieff Wood
Smithton Hill
Lundie Mill Farm
Lundie
PH13
Ford of Pitcur Farm
Pitcur Wood
Smith Loch
Glen Cott
Quarry (dis)
Sidlaw Hills
Black Wood
Tullybaccart Farm
Tullybaccart Quarry (dis)
Ford Wood
North Ballo Farm
Fort
Bully Quarry (dis)
Quarry (dis)
Balshando Farm
Quarries (dis)
Laird's Loch
Lochindores
Lochindores Farm
Ledyatt Farm
Northballo Quarry (dis)
Northballo Hill
Balshando Hill
Ledyatt Wood
Osprey Bank
Osprey View
Thrawparts
Mast
Ballo Hill
DD2
Lundiemuir Plantation
Gask Hill
Crow Wood
South Ballo Farm
Little Ballo
Blacklaw Hill
Binn Plantations
Dundriven
North Binn
Littleton Farm
White Hill
Glenbran Farm
Aiver Wood
Lochton Farm
PH14
Redmyre Loch
Binns Farm
Redmyres Farm
Redmyre Farm
Stockmuir
East Newton Farm
Marywell Farm
Tower
South Latch Farm
Newton Bank
Church (remains of)
Dron Hill
Dron Farm
Wellbank Farm
Fort
Kirkton Hill
Hillton of Knapp
Ford Farm
Pitkindie Farm
Knapp
Kirktonhill Wood
Kirkton Farm
Millhill Farm
Forehill Wood
Abernyte
Rossie Hill
Whitehills Farm
Milton Farm
Abernyte Prim Sch
Chimney
Falcon Stone
Whitehill Quarry (dis)
Braes of the Carse
Southfield Farm
Rossie Priory
Rossie Church
B953
Tinkletop Hill
Castlehill Farm
Outfield Farm
Tinkle Top Farm
Baledgarno Farm
Snabs Farm

27
17

Scale: 1⅓ inches to 1 mile

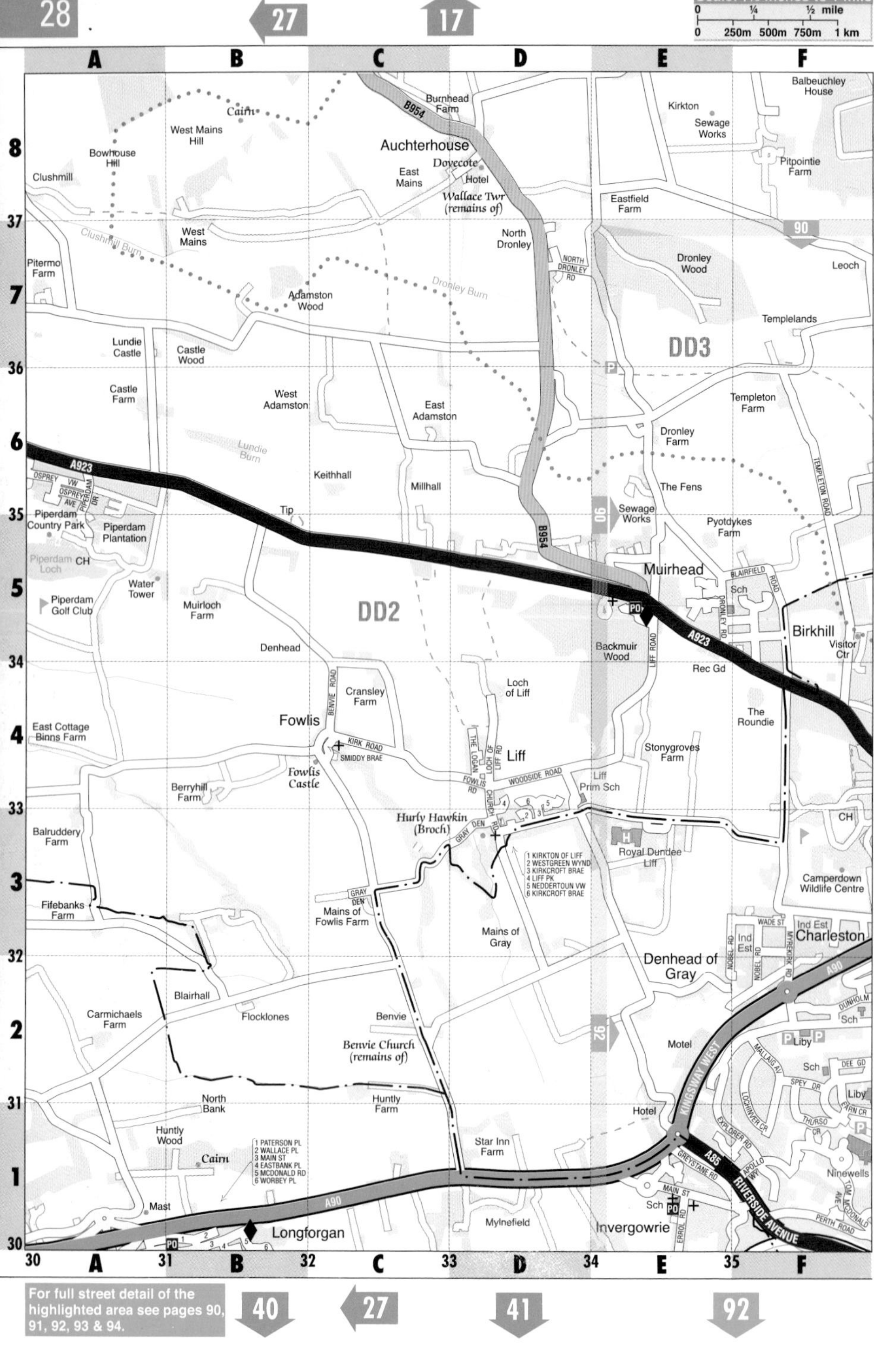

Burnhead Farm
B954
Cairn
West Mains Hill
Auchterhouse
Bowhouse Hill
Dovecote
East Mains
Hotel
Clushmill
Wallace Twr (remains of)
West Mains
North Dronley
Clushmill Burn
Pitermo Farm
Adamston Wood
Dronley Burn
NORTH DRONLEY RD
Lundie Castle
Castle Wood
Castle Farm
West Adamston
East Adamston
Lundie Burn
A923
Keithhall
Millhall
OSPREY VW
OSPREY AVE
PIPERDAM DR
Piperdam Country Park
Piperdam Plantation
Tip
Piperdam Loch
CH
Water Tower
Piperdam Golf Club
Muirloch Farm
DD2
Denhead
BENVIE ROAD
Cransley Farm
Fowlis
East Cottage Binns Farm
KIRK ROAD
SMIDDY BRAE
Fowlis Castle
Loch of Liff
THE LOGAN
LOCH OF LIFF RD
Liff
FOWLIS RD
WOODSIDE ROAD
CHURCH RD
Berryhill Farm
Hurly Hawkin (Broch)
GRAY DEN
Balruddery Farm
1 KIRKTON OF LIFF
2 WESTGREEN WYND
3 KIRKCROFT BRAE
4 LIFF PK
5 NEDDERTOUN VW
6 KIRKCROFT BRAE
Fifebanks Farm
GRAY DEN
Mains of Fowlis Farm
Mains of Gray
Blairhall
Carmichaels Farm
Flocklones
Benvie
Benvie Church (remains of)
North Bank
Huntly Farm
Huntly Wood
Cairn
1 PATERSON PL
2 WALLACE PL
3 MAIN ST
4 EASTBANK PL
5 MCDONALD RD
6 WORBEY PL
Star Inn Farm
A90
Mast
PO
Longforgan
Mylnefield
Kirkton
Sewage Works
Balbeuchley House
Pitpointie Farm
Eastfield Farm
90
Dronley Wood
Leoch
Templelands
DD3
P
Templeton Farm
Dronley Farm
The Fens
TEMPLETON ROAD
Sewage Works
90
Pyotdykes Farm
Muirhead
BLAIRFIELD ROAD
Sch
DRONLEY RD
Birkhill
Visitor Ctr
Backmuir Wood
LIFF ROAD
Rec Gd
The Roundie
Stonygroves Farm
Liff Prim Sch
CH
Royal Dundee Liff
Camperdown Wildlife Centre
WADE ST
Ind Est
Charleston
NOBEL RD
MYREKIRK RD
Denhead of Gray
DUNHOLM
Sch
92
Motel
KINGSWAY WEST
Liby
MALLAIG AV
Sch
DEE GD
SPEY DR
LOCHINVER CR
Liby
EARN CR
THURSO CR
Hotel
EXPLORER RD
A85
GREYSTANE RD
APOLLO WY
Ninewells
RIVERSIDE AVENUE
MAIN ST
Sch
ERROL RD
Invergowrie
TOM MCDONALD AVE
PERTH ROAD

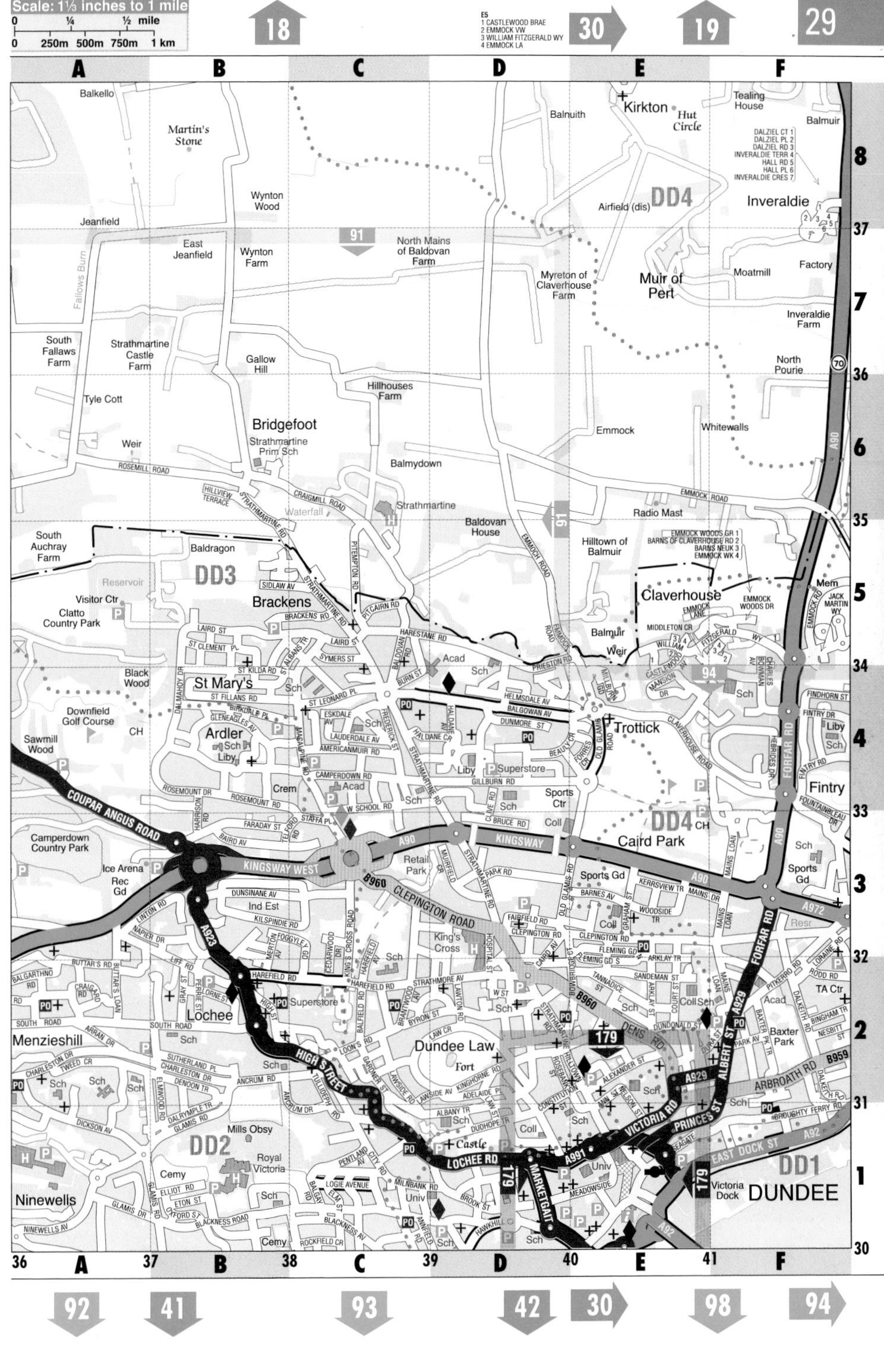

Scale: 1⅓ inches to 1 mile
0 ¼ ½ mile
0 250m 500m 750m 1 km
18
E5
1 CASTLEWOOD BRAE
2 EMMOCK VW
3 WILLIAM FITZGERALD WY
4 EMMOCK LA
30
19
Kirkton
Hut Circle
Tealing House
Balmuir
Balnuith
Balkello
Martin's Stone
DALZIEL CT 1
DALZIEL PL 2
DALZIEL RD 3
INVERALDIE TERR 4
HALL RD 5
HALL PL 6
INVERALDIE CRES 7
Inveraldie
Airfield (dis)
DD4
Wynton Wood
Jeanfield
East Jeanfield
Wynton Farm
91
North Mains of Baldovan Farm
Myreton of Claverhouse Farm
Muir of Pert
Moatmill
Factory
Inveraldie Farm
Fallows Burn
South Fallaws Farm
Strathmartine Castle Farm
Gallow Hill
Hillhouses Farm
North Pourie
Tyle Cott
Bridgefoot
Strathmartine Prim Sch
Emmock
Whitewalls
Weir
ROSEMILL ROAD
Balmydown
A90
HILLVIEW TERRACE
STRATHMARTINE RD
CRAIGMILL ROAD
Strathmartine
EMMOCK ROAD
Waterfall
Baldovan House
Radio Mast
South Auchray Farm
Baldragon
Hilltown of Balmuir
EMMOCK WOODS GR 1
BARNS OF CLAVERHOUSE RD 2
BARNS NEUK 3
EMMOCK WK 4
DD3
Reservoir
SIDLAW AV
Claverhouse
EMMOCK WOODS DR
Mem
JACK MARTIN WY
Visitor Ctr
Clatto Country Park
Brackens
BRACKENS RD
PITCAIRN RD
PITEMPTON RD
EMMOCK LANE
MIDDLETON CR
LAIRD ST
HARESTANE RD
Balmuir
FITZGERALD WY
ST CLEMENT PL
WILLIAM
Weir
Acad
Sch
PRIESTON RD
Black Wood
ST KILDA RD
SYMERS ST
BURN ST
CASTLEWOOD
MANSION AV
94
St Mary's
ST FILLANS RD
ST LEONARD PL
HELMSDALE AV
BALGOWAN AV
FINDHORN ST
Downfield Golf Course
DALMAHOY DR
GLENEAGLES AV
BIRKDALE PL
ESKDALE AV
FREDERICK ST
HALDANE AV
DUNMORE ST
Trottick
FINTRY DR
Liby
CH
Ardler
Sch
Liby
LAUDERDALE AV
HALDANE CR
CLAVERHOUSE ROAD
Sawmill Wood
AMERICANMUIR RD
BEAULY CR
FORRES CR
OLD GLAMIS ROAD
CAMPERDOWN RD
Superstore
GILLBURN RD
HEBRIDES DR
FINTRY RD
Fintry
FORFAR RD
COUPAR ANGUS ROAD
ROSEMOUNT DR
ROSEMOUNT RD
Crem
Acad
Sports Ctr
Sch
W SCHOOL RD
BRUCE RD
FOUNTAINBLEAU DR
HARRISON RD
FARADAY ST
STAFFA PL
Coll
DD4
CH
Camperdown Country Park
BAIRD AV
KINGSWAY
Caird Park
Sch
Ice Arena
Rec Gd
KINGSWAY WEST
Retail Park
MUIRFIELD CR
PARK RD
Sports Gd
Sports Gd
B960
CLEPINGTON ROAD
KERRSVIEW TR
MAINS DR
MAINS LOAN
A972
DUNSINANE AV
BARNES AV
Ind Est
KILSPINDIE RD
FAIRFIELD RD
WOODSIDE TR
LINTON RD
CLEPINGTON RD
Coll
NAPIER DR
FOGGYLEY GD
King's Cross
HOSPITAL ST
FLEMING GD
Resr
LIFE RD
CEDARWOOD DR
KING'S CROSS ROAD
HARefield RD
Sch
ARKLAY TR
LORAINE RD
BUTTAR'S RD
BUTTAR'S LOAN
TANNADICE ST
SANDEMAN ST
PITKERRO RD
RODD RD
BALGARTHNO RD
CRAIGARD RD
GRAY ST
LORNE ST
HAREFIELD RD
STRATHMORE AV
W ST
Sch
ARKLAY ST
COURT ST
Coll Sch
TA Ctr
HIGH ST
Superstore
LAWTON RD
BRANTWOOD AV
BYRON ST
B960
Sch
Acad
DALKEITH RD
BINGHAM TR
Lochee
SOUTH ROAD
LAW CR
179
DUNDONALD ST
A929
BAXTER PK TR
NESBITT ST
Baxter Park
Menzieshill
ARRAN DR
Sch
LOON'S RD
Dundee Law
Fort
ALEXANDER ST
B959
TWEED CR
SUTHERLAND PL
CHARLESTON DR
CHARLESTON DR
HIGH STREET
Sch
ARBROATH RD
Sch
Sch
DENOON TR
ANCRUM RD
GARDNER ST
LAWSIDE AV
KINGHORNE RD
ADELAIDE PL
ROSEBANK ST
A929
DALKEITH RD
VICTORIA RD
PRINCES ST
ALBERT ST
Sch
BROUGHTY FERRY RD
ELMWOOD RD
DALRYMPLE TR
GLAMIS RD
TULLIDEPH RD
CONSTITUTION ST
ANN ST
NELSON ST
DICKSON AV
ANCRUM DR
ALBANY TR
Sch
Mills Obsy
DUDHOPE TR
Sch
Coll
EAST DOCK ST
A92
DD2
Castle
SEAGATE
Royal Victoria
PENTLAND AV
CITY RD
LOCHEE RD
A991
Univ
DD1
Cemy
LOGIE AVENUE
179
MARKETGAIT
MEADOWSIDE
Victoria Dock
DUNDEE
Ninewells
ELLIOT RD
ETON ST
BALGAY ST
ELM ST
MILNBANK RD
Univ
BROOK ST
GLAMIS DR
OXFORD ST
BLACKNESS ROAD
BLACKNESS AV
NINEWELLS AV
Cemy
ROCKFIELD CR
ANNFIELD RD
HAWKHILL
Sch
Sch
A92
A B C D E F
8 7 6 5 4 3 2 1
37 36 35 34 33 32 31 30
36 37 38 39 40 41
92 41 93 42 30 98 94

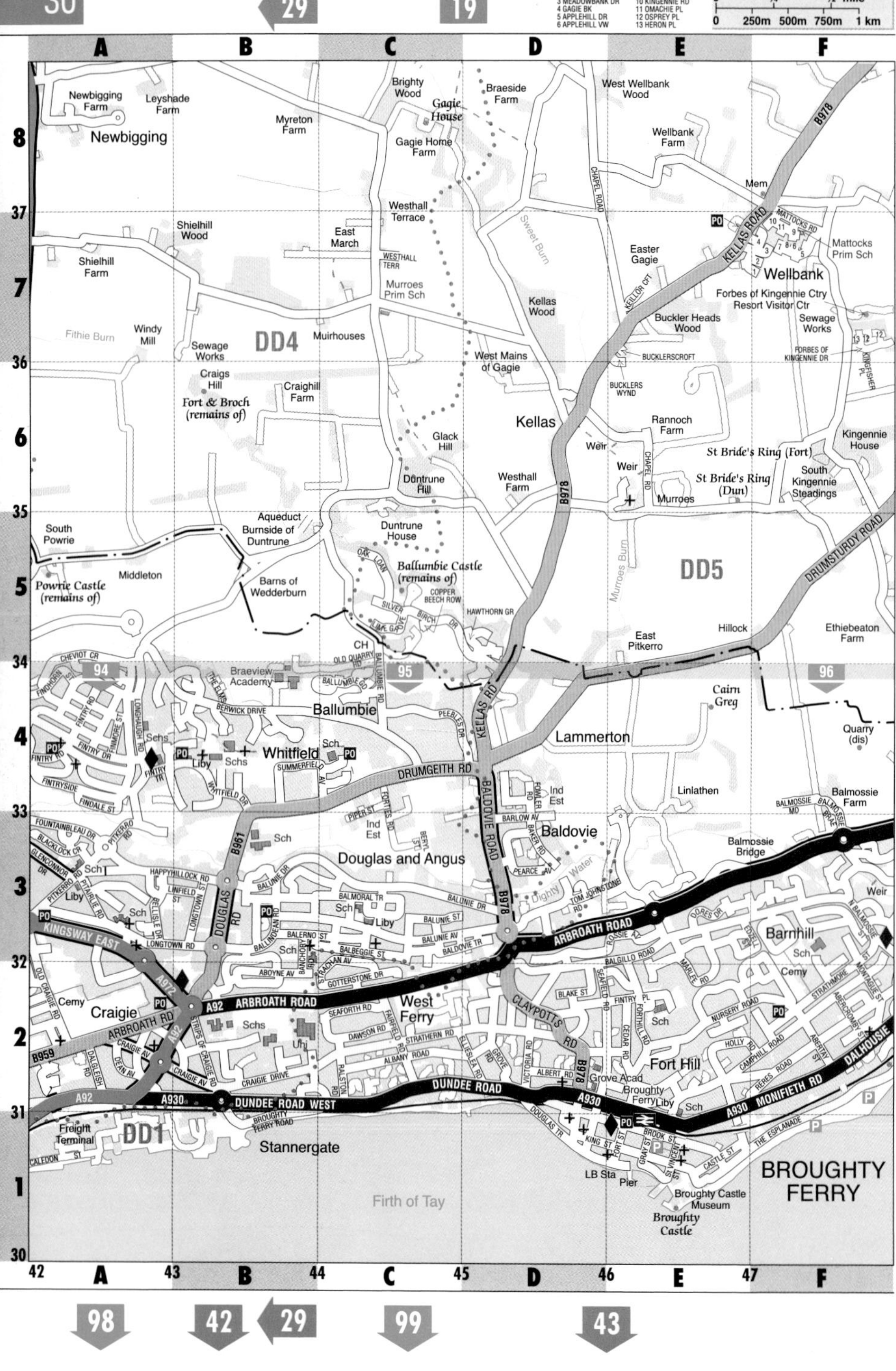

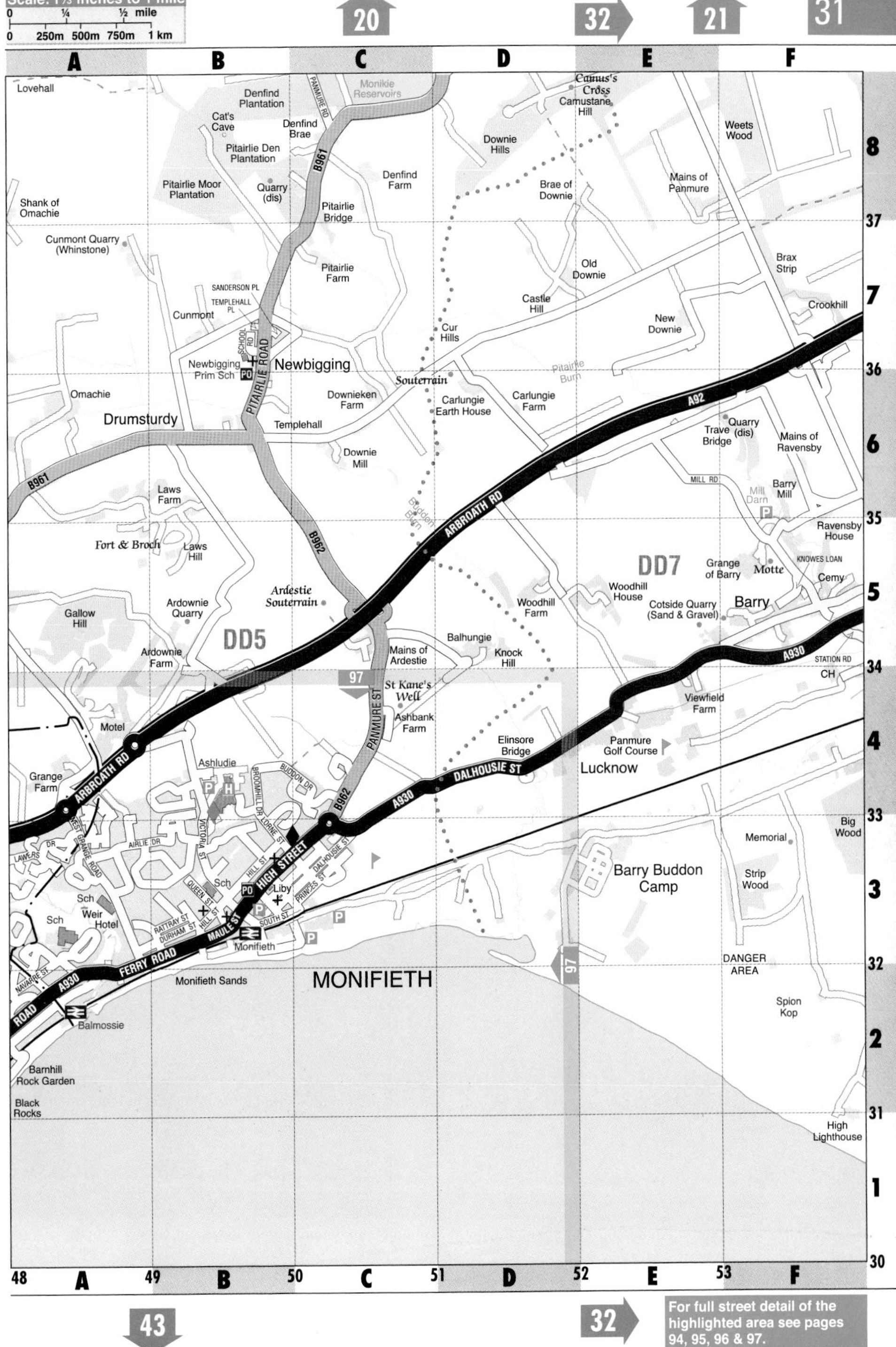

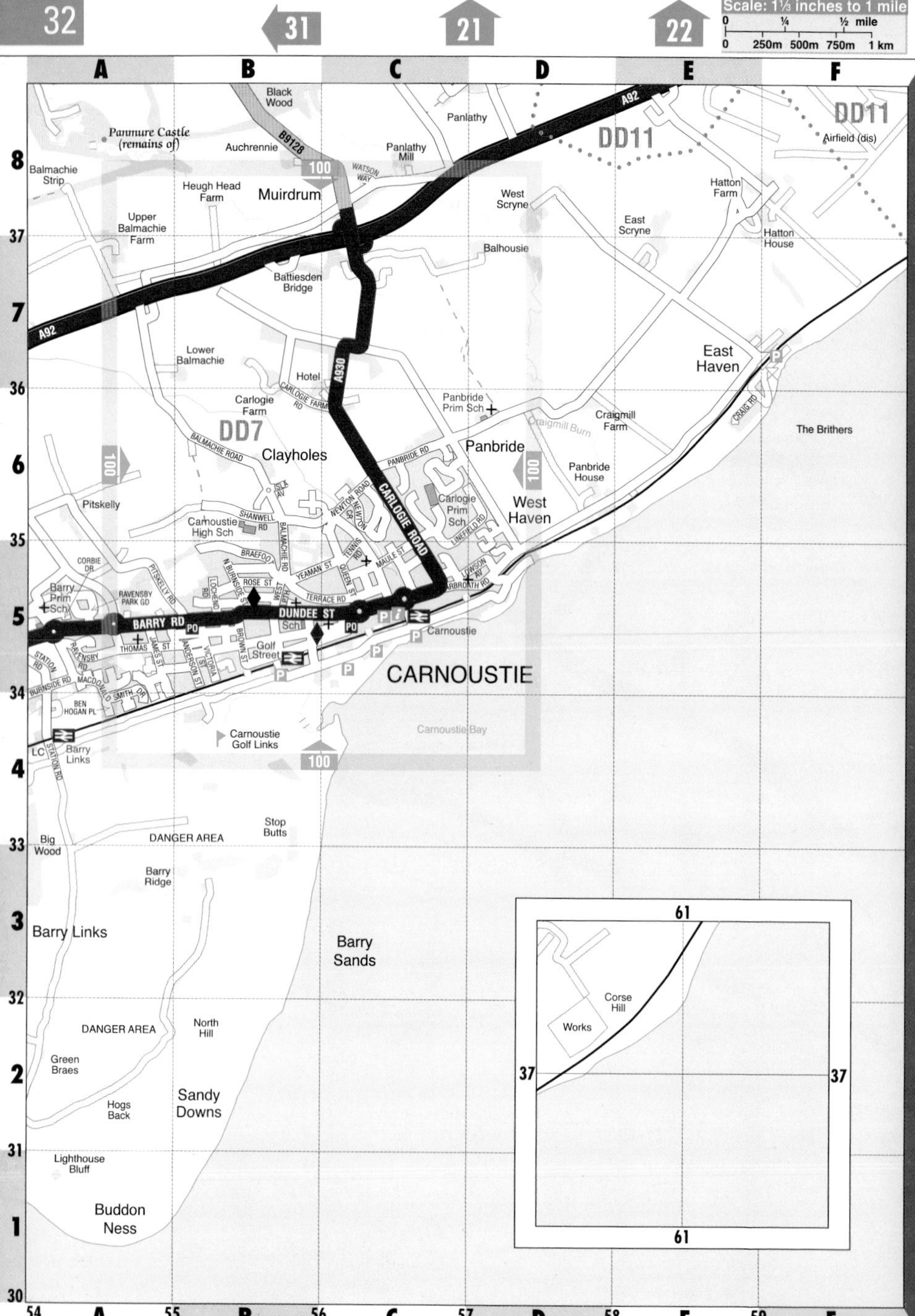

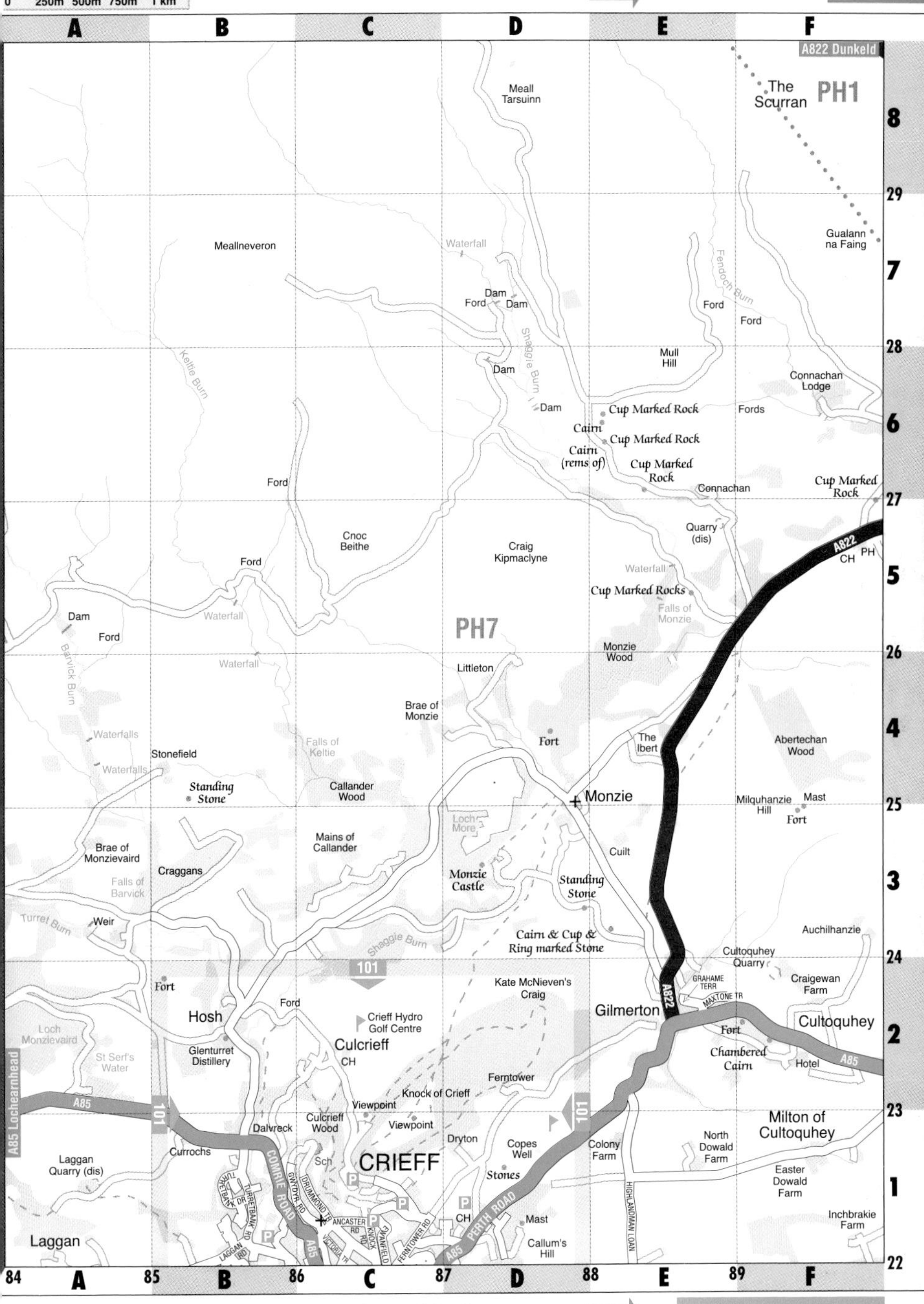

A   B   C   D   E   F

8
29
7
28
6
27
5
26
4
25
3
24
2
23
1
22

PH1

A822 Dunkeld

The Scurran

Gualann na Faing

Meall Tarsuinn

Meallneveron

Waterfall

Dam
Ford   Dam

Dam

Fendoch Burn

Ford

Ford

Mull Hill

Connachan Lodge

Fords

Cup Marked Rock

Cairn

Cup Marked Rock

Cairn (rems of)

Cup Marked Rock

Cup Marked Rock

Shaggie Burn

Dam

Connachan

Kettie Burn

Ford

Cnoc Beithe

Craig Kipmaclyne

Quarry (dis)

A822   CH   PH

Waterfall

Cup Marked Rocks

Falls of Monzie

PH7

Ford

Dam
Ford

Waterfall

Waterfall

Littleton

Brae of Monzie

Monzie Wood

Waterfalls

Stonefield

Falls of Keltie

Fort

The Ibert

Abertechan Wood

Barvick Burn

Waterfalls

Standing Stone

Callander Wood

Monzie

Milquhanzie Hill   Mast

Fort

Brae of Monzievaird

Mains of Callander

Cuilt

Craggans

Monzie Castle

Standing Stone

Auchilhanzie

Falls of Barvick

Turret Burn

Weir

Shaggie Burn

Cairn & Cup & Ring marked Stone

Cultoquhey Quarry

Craigewan Farm

A822

GRAHAME TERR

MAXTONE TR

Fort

Kate McNieven's Craig

Gilmerton

Fort

Cultoquhey

Loch Monzievaird

St Serf's Water

Hosh

Ford

Crieff Hydro Golf Centre

Chambered Cairn

Hotel

A85

A85 Lochearnhead

101

Culcrieff
CH

Glenturret Distillery

Glenturret Distillery

Knock of Crieff

Ferntower

Milton of Cultoquhey

Viewpoint

North Dowald Farm

Laggan Quarry (dis)

Currochs

Dalvreck

Culcrieff Wood

Viewpoint

Dryton

Copes Well

Colony Farm

Easter Dowald Farm

Sch

CRIEFF

Stones

Inchbrakie Farm

Laggan

LANCASTER RD

CH

Mast

Callum's Hill

HIGHLANDMAN LOAN

A85 PERTH ROAD

COMRIE ROAD

A   B   C   D   E   F

84   85   86   87   88   89

101   44

34

For full street detail of the highlighted area see page 101.

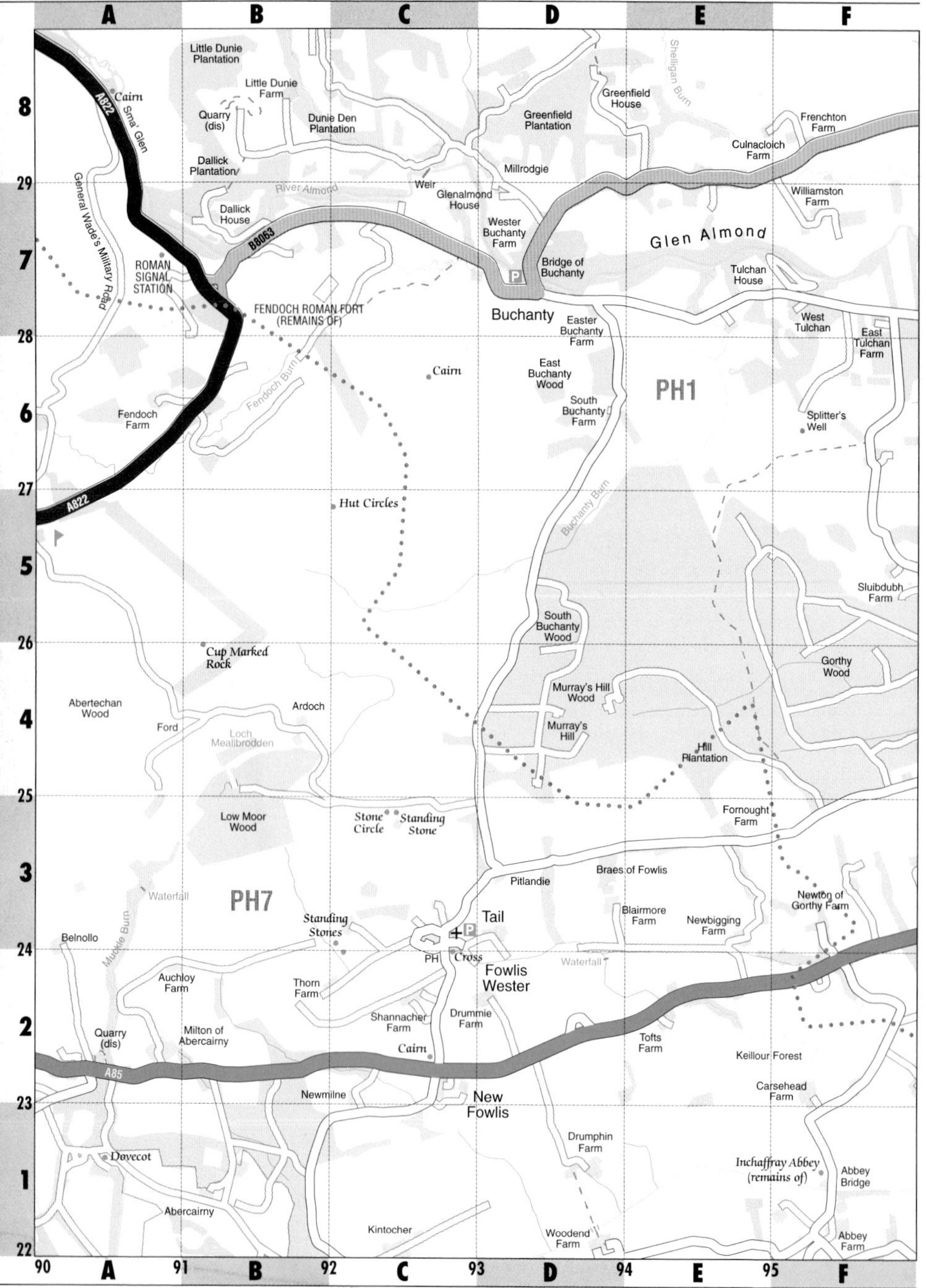

33

Scale: 1⅓ inches to 1 mile

0   ¼   ½ mile
0   250m 500m 750m   1 km

A **B** **C** **D** **E** **F**

8

Cairn

Little Dunie
Plantation

Little Dunie
Farm

Quarry
(dis)

Dunie Den
Plantation

Greenfield
Plantation

Greenfield
House

Sheilgan Burn

Frenchton
Farm

Dallick
Plantation

Culnacloich
Farm

Williamston
Farm

29

River Almond

Weir

Millrodgie

Dallick
House

Glenalmond
House

Wester
Buchanty
Farm

Glen Almond

B8063

7

Sna Glen

General Wade's Military Road

ROMAN
SIGNAL
STATION

Bridge of
Buchanty

Tulchan
House

FENDOCH ROMAN FORT
(REMAINS OF)

Buchanty

West
Tulchan

28

Easter
Buchanty
Farm

East
Tulchan
Farm

Fendoch Burn

Cairn

East
Buchanty
Wood

6

Fendoch
Farm

South
Buchanty
Farm

PH1

Splitter's
Well

27

A822

Hut Circles

Buchanty Burn

5

Sluibdubh
Farm

26

Cup Marked
Rock

South
Buchanty
Wood

Gorthy
Wood

4

Abertechan
Wood

Ford

Ardoch

Murray's Hill
Wood

Hill
Plantation

Loch
Meallbrodden

Murray's
Hill

25

Low Moor
Wood

Stone
Circle

Standing
Stone

Fornought
Farm

3

Braes of Fowlis

Pitlandie

Newton of
Gorthy Farm

Waterfall

PH7

Standing
Stones

Tail

Blairmore
Farm

Newbigging
Farm

24

Belnollo

Auchloy
Farm

Thorn
Farm

PH Cross

Fowlis
Wester

Waterfall

Muckle Burn

Keillour Forest

2

Quarry
(dis)

Milton of
Abercairny

Shannacher
Farm

Drummie
Farm

Cairn

Tofts
Farm

Carsehead
Farm

A85

Newmilne

New
Fowlis

23

Inchaffray Abbey
(remains of)

Abbey
Bridge

1

Dovecot

Drumphin
Farm

Abbey
Bridge

Abercairny

Kintocher

Woodend
Farm

22

A 90 **B** 91 92 **C** 93 **D** 94 **E** 95 **F**

33
45

A   B   C   D   E   F

8
29
7
28
6
27
5
26
4
25
3
24
2
23
1
22

Francesfield Farm
B8063
Waterfalls
Milton Farm
Drumchar Farm
Tullymoran Farm
PH
Mon
Harrietfield
Clashirgar Farm
Logiealmond Primary School
B8063
Fosten House
Millhaugh Farm
River Almond
Ford
Weir
Bridgend Wood
North Ardittie Farm

Cairnies Farm
Glenalmond College
Ford
Easter Campsie Farm
Wester Campsie Farm
Pickston Farm
South Ardittie Farm

Mains of Cairnies Farm
Pickston Wood
Drumveigh Wood

South Cairnies Farm
CH
Drumbuich Wood
Stottleburn Wood

Cogbrae Farm
Methven Reservoir
Drumbaughly Farm

North Cassochie Farm
South Cassochie Farm
Chimney
Mast

Parks of Kellour Farm
Grundcruie Farm
Cloag

Green of Keillour
Bellour Farm
Cloag Wood
Cemetery

Keillour Castle
Waterfall
PH1
Wind Pump
Linfield Farm
Whitebank Farm
MAIN STREET

Wester Keillour Farm
Craigend Farm
Braegrum
East Meckphen Farm
Sewage Works

Aldie Farm
A85
Easter Sunnyside
Forebrae Farm
Easter Backmoss
West Meckphen Farm

Wester Sunnyside
Wester Backmoss

Sparrowmuir Wood
Bachilton Farm
Methven Moss

Mains of Gorthy Farm
Burnbrae
Packhorse Cotts
Grotto Wood
Balgowan Home Farm
Greenhill Farm

Newrow Lodge
Lower Newmill

Nethermains of Gorthy Farm
Pow Water
Newmiln Farm

PH7
Redhills Farm
MUNROE AVE
EDEN SQ
MILLGLEN DR

Welltree Farm
Wind Pump
Williamston Farm
EARN DR
Balgowan
Ross Farm
Westmuir Wood

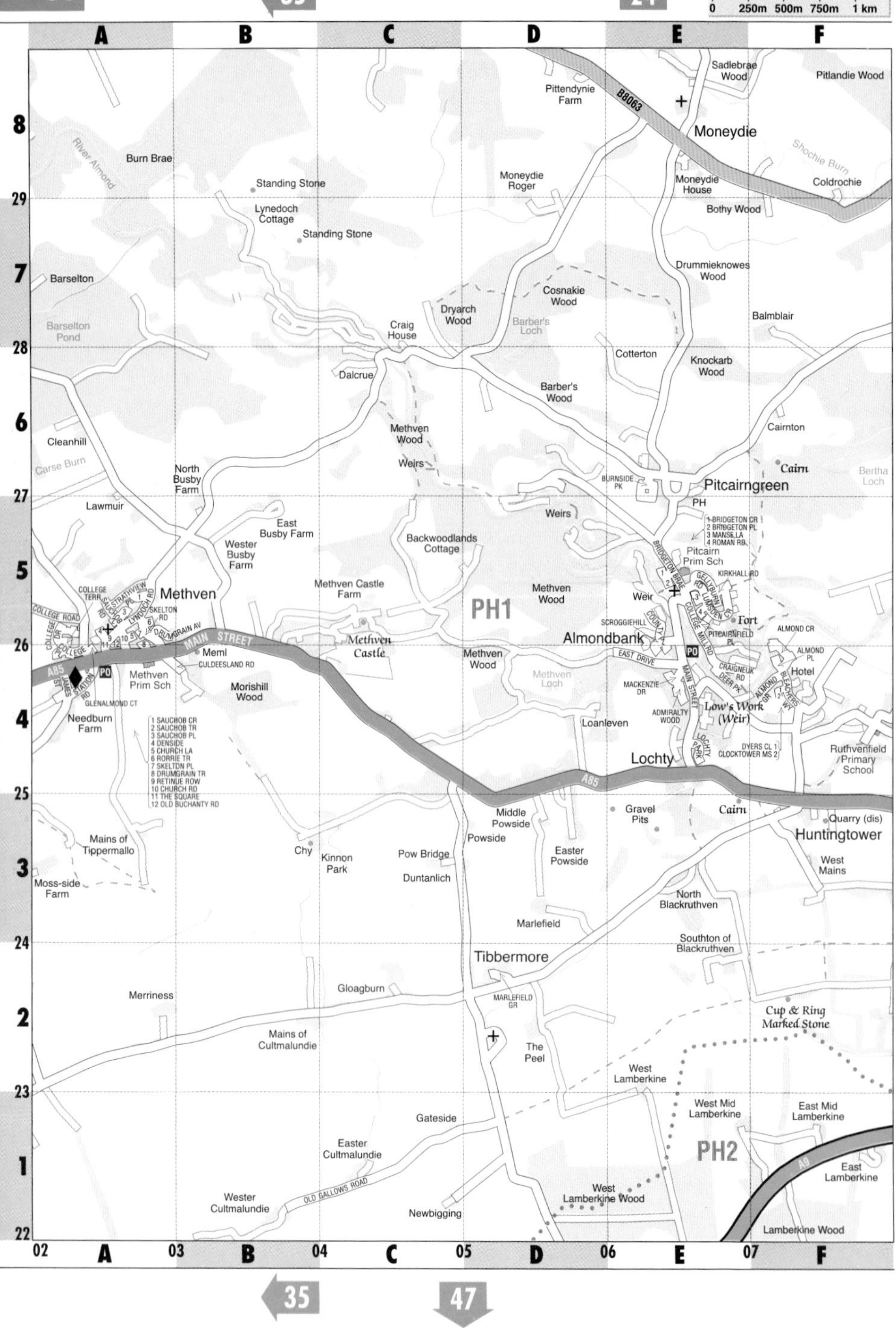
Sadlebrae Wood
Pitlandie Wood
Pittendynie Farm
B8063
Moneydie
Shochie Burn
Burn Brae
River Almond
Standing Stone
Moneydie Roger
Moneydie House
Coldrochie
Lynedoch Cottage
Bothy Wood
Standing Stone
Drummieknowes Wood
Barselton
Cosnakie Wood
Dryarch Wood
Craig House
Barber's Loch
Balmblair
Barselton Pond
Cotterton
Knockarb Wood
Dalcrue
Barber's Wood
Methven Wood
Cleanhill
Cairnton
Weirs
Carse Burn
Cairn
Bertha Loch
North Busby Farm
BURNSIDE PK
Pitcairngreen
Lawmuir
PH
Weirs
East Busby Farm
1 BRIDGETON CR
2 BRIDGETON PL
3 MANSE LA
4 ROMAN RD
Wester Busby Farm
Backwoodlands Cottage
Pitcairn Prim Sch
Methven Castle Farm
KIRKHALL RD
Methven
Methven Wood
PH1
Weir
Fort
SCROGGIEHILL
ALMOND CR
Methven Castle
Almondbank
MAIN STREET
Meml
Methven Wood
EAST DRIVE
ALMOND PL
CULDEESLAND RD
PO
Hotel
Methven Prim Sch
Methven Loch
MACKENZIE DR
Morishill Wood
GLENALMOND CT
Low's Work (Weir)
Needburn Farm
ADMIRALTY WOOD
Loanleven
1 SAUCHOB CR
2 SAUCHOB TR
3 SAUCHOB PL
4 DENSIDE
5 CHURCH LA
6 RORRIE TR
7 SKELTON PL
8 DRUMGRAIN TR
9 RETINUE ROW
10 CHURCH RD
11 THE SQUARE
12 OLD BUCHANTY RD
DYERS CL 1
CLOCKTOWER MS 2
Ruthvenfield Primary School
Lochty
A85
Middle Powside
Gravel Pits
Cairn
Quarry (dis)
Powside
Huntingtower
Mains of Tippermallo
Chy
Kinnon Park
Pow Bridge
Easter Powside
West Mains
Duntanlich
Moss-side Farm
North Blackruthven
Marlefield
Southton of Blackruthven
Tibbermore
Gloagburn
Merriness
MARLEFIELD GR
Cup & Ring Marked Stone
Mains of Cultmalundie
The Peel
West Lamberkine
West Mid Lamberkine
East Mid Lamberkine
Gateside
Easter Cultmalundie
PH2
A9
East Lamberkine
OLD GALLOWS ROAD
Wester Cultmalundie
West Lamberkine Wood
Newbigging
Lamberkine Wood

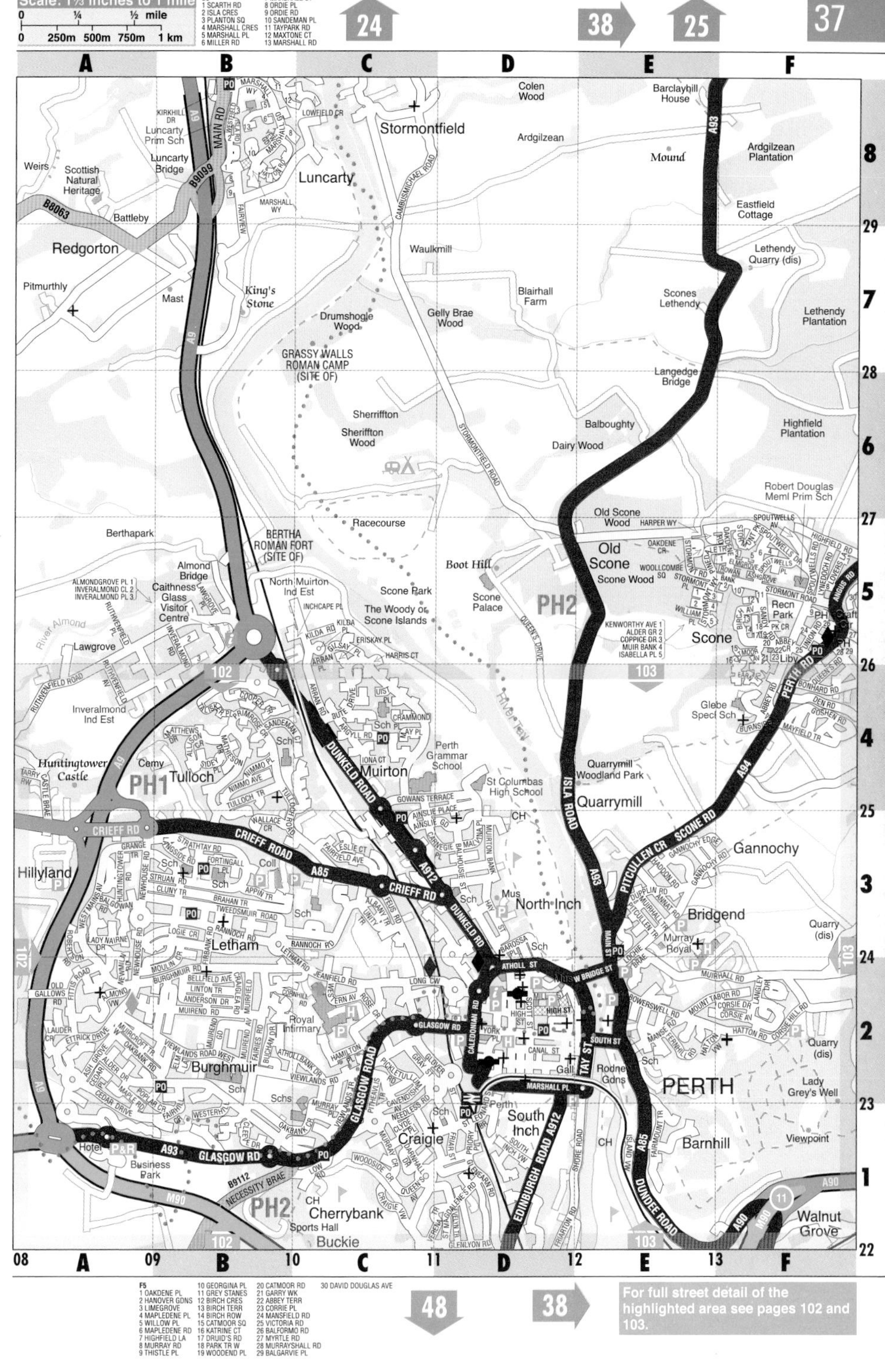

Scale: 1⅓ inches to 1 mile
0 ¼ ½ mile
0 250m 500m 750m 1 km
B8
1 SCARTH RD
2 ISLA CRES
3 PLANTON SQ
4 MARSHALL CRES
5 MARSHALL PL
6 MILLER RD
7 MARSHALL CT
8 ORDIE PL
9 ORDIE RD
10 SANDEMAN PL
11 TAYPARK RD
12 MAXTONE CT
13 MARSHALL RD
24
38
25
Stormontfield
Luncarty
Redgorton
Scone
Old Scone
Perth
Muirton
Tulloch
Letham
Burghmuir
Craigie
Cherrybank
Bridgend
Gannochy
Barnhill
Quarrymill
North Inch
South Inch
PH1
PH2
F5
1 OAKDENE PL
2 HANOVER GDNS
3 LIMEGROVE
4 MAPLEDENE PL
5 WILLOW PL
6 MAPLEDENE RD
7 HIGHFIELD LA
8 MURRAY RD
9 THISTLE PL
10 GEORGINA PL
11 GREY STANES
12 BIRCH CRES
13 BIRCH TERR
14 BIRCH ROW
15 CATMOOR SQ
16 KATRINE CT
17 DRUID'S RD
18 PARK TR W
19 WOODEND PL
20 CATMOOR RD
21 GARRY WK
22 ABBEY TERR
23 CORRIE PL
24 MANSFIELD RD
25 VICTORIA RD
26 BALFORMO RD
27 MYRTLE RD
28 MURRAYSHALL RD
29 BALGARVIE PL
30 DAVID DOUGLAS AVE
48
38
For full street detail of the highlighted area see pages 102 and 103.

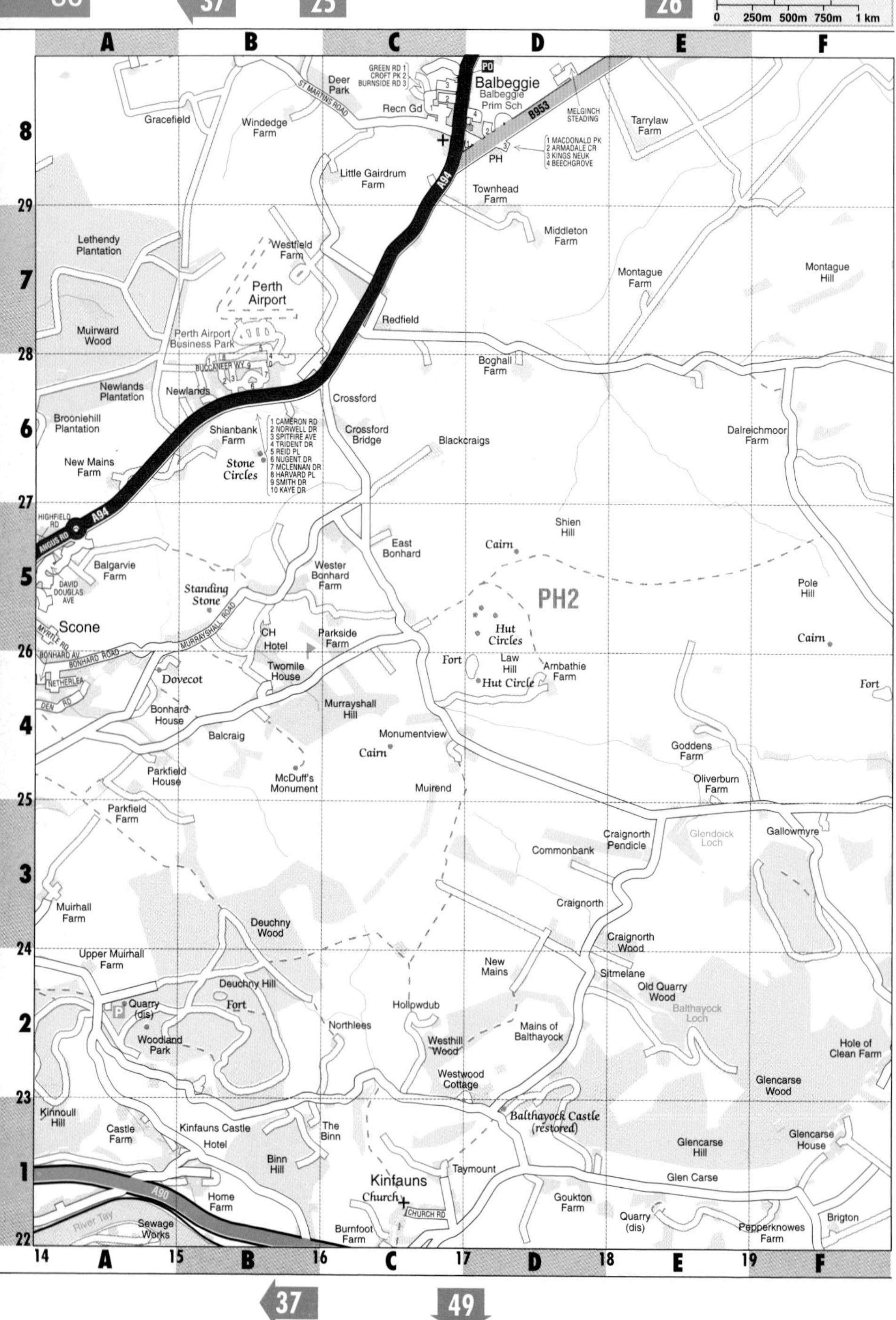

37
25
26
Scale: 1⅓ inches to 1 mile
0 ¼ ½ mile
0 250m 500m 750m 1 km
Balbeggie
Balbeggie Prim Sch
Deer Park
Recn Gd
GREEN RD 1
CROFT PK 2
BURNSIDE RD 3
ST MARTINS ROAD
B953
MELGINCH STEADING
1 MACDONALD PK
2 ARMADALE CR
3 KINGS NEUK
4 BEECHGROVE
PH
Tarrylaw Farm
Gracefield
Windedge Farm
Little Gairdrum Farm
A94
Townhead Farm
Middleton Farm
Lethendy Plantation
Westfield Farm
Perth Airport
Montague Farm
Montague Hill
Muirward Wood
Perth Airport Business Park
Redfield
BUCCANEER WY
Boghall Farm
Newlands Plantation
Newlands
Crossford
Brooniehill Plantation
Shianbank Farm
1 CAMERON RD
2 NORWELL DR
3 SPITFIRE AVE
4 TRIDENT DR
5 REID PL
6 NUGENT DR
7 MCLENNAN DR
8 HARVARD PL
9 SMITH DR
10 KAYE DR
Crossford Bridge
Blackcraigs
Dalreichmoor Farm
New Mains Farm
Stone Circles
HIGHFIELD RD
ANGUS RD
Shien Hill
Cairn
East Bonhard
Balgarvie Farm
Wester Bonhard Farm
Standing Stone
DAVID DOUGLAS AVE
MURRAYSHALL ROAD
PH2
Pole Hill
Scone
MYRTLE RD
BONHARD AV
BONHARD ROAD
CH Hotel
Parkside Farm
Hut Circles
Cairn
Fort
Law Hill
Arnbathie Farm
Dovecot
NETHERLEA
DEN RD
Twomile House
Hut Circle
Fort
Bonhard House
Murrayshall Hill
Balcraig
Monumentview
Cairn
Goddens Farm
Parkfield House
McDuff's Monument
Muirend
Oliverburn Farm
Parkfield Farm
Craignorth Pendicle
Glendoick Loch
Gallowmyre
Commonbank
Craignorth
Muirhall Farm
Deuchny Wood
Craignorth Wood
Upper Muirhall Farm
New Mains
Sitmelane
Deuchny Hill
Old Quarry Wood
Quarry (dis)
Fort
Hollowdub
Balthayock Loch
Northlees
Mains of Balthayock
Woodland Park
Westhill Wood
Hole of Clean Farm
Westwood Cottage
Glencarse Wood
Kinnoull Hill
Castle Farm
Kinfauns Castle Hotel
The Binn
Balthayock Castle (restored)
Glencarse Hill
Glencarse House
Binn Hill
Taymount
Glen Carse
Kinfauns
Church
Home Farm
A90
CHURCH RD
Goukton Farm
River Tay
Sewage Works
Burnfoot Farm
Quarry (dis)
Pepperknowes Farm
Brigton
A B C D E F
8 29 7 28 6 27 5 26 4 25 3 24 2 23 1 22
14 15 16 17 18 19
37
49

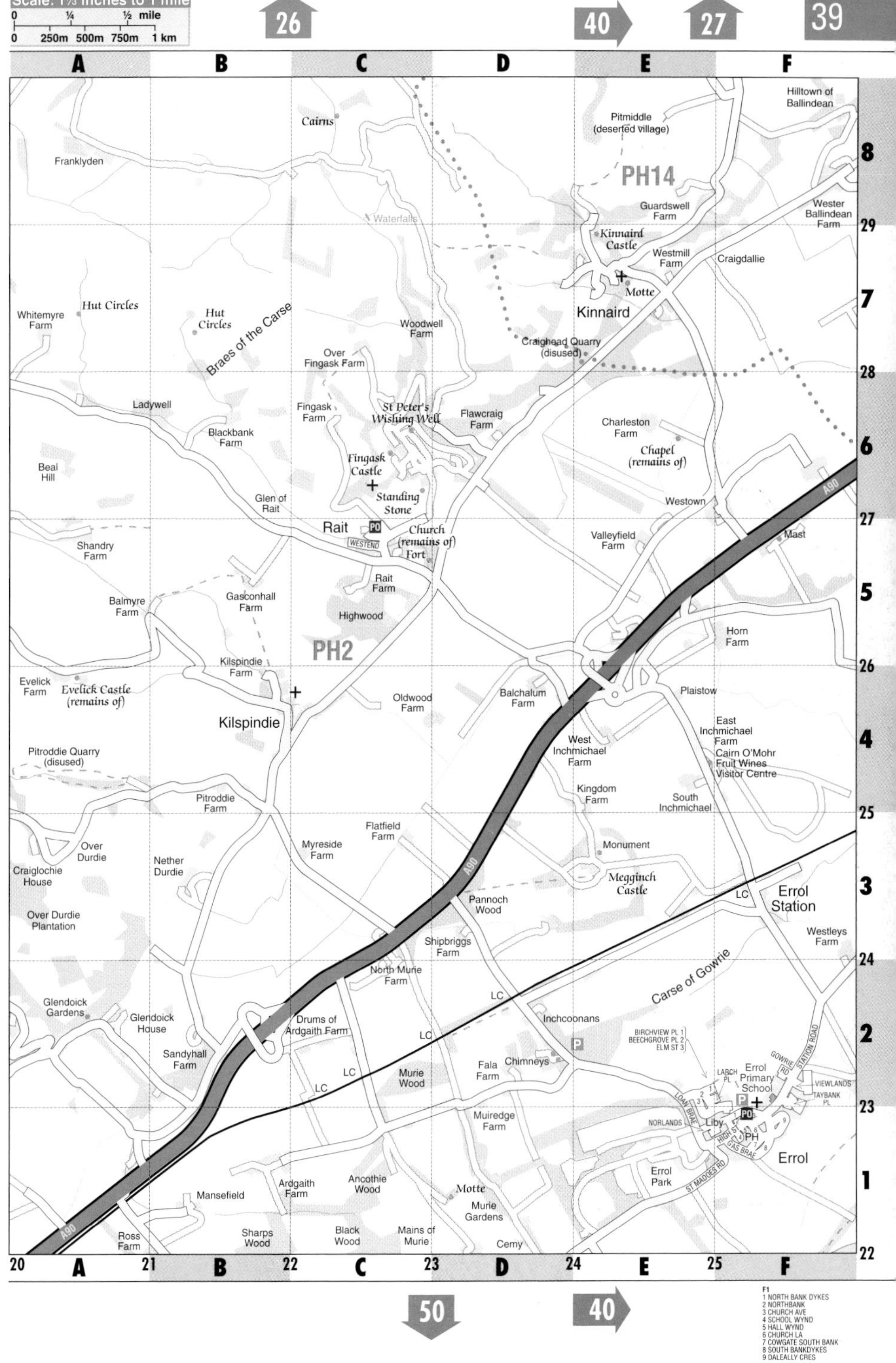

Scale: 1⅓ inches to 1 mile
0
¼
½ mile
0
250m
500m
750m
1 km
26
40
27
A
B
C
D
E
F
Hilltown of Ballindean
Pitmiddle (deserted village)
Cairns
Franklyden
PH14
8
Guardswell Farm
Wester Ballindean Farm
Waterfalls
29
Kinnaird Castle
Westmill Farm
Craigdallie
Motte
Whitemyre Farm
Hut Circles
Hut Circles
Braes of the Carse
Woodwell Farm
Kinnaird
7
Over Fingask Farm
Craighead Quarry (disused)
28
Ladywell
Fingask Farm
St Peter's Wishing Well
Flawcraig Farm
Charleston Farm
Blackbank Farm
Chapel (remains of)
6
Beal Hill
Fingask Castle
Standing Stone
Glen of Rait
Westown
A90
Rait
PO
Church (remains of)
WESTEND
Fort
Valleyfield Farm
Mast
27
Shandry Farm
Rait Farm
5
Balmyre Farm
Gasconhall Farm
Highwood
Horn Farm
PH2
Kilspindie Farm
26
Evelick Farm
Evelick Castle (remains of)
Oldwood Farm
Balchalum Farm
Plaistow
Kilspindie
East Inchmichael Farm
West Inchmichael Farm
4
Pitroddie Quarry (disused)
Cairn O'Mohr Fruit Wines Visitor Centre
Kingdom Farm
Pitroddie Farm
South Inchmichael
25
Flatfield Farm
Over Durdie
Myreside Farm
Monument
Craiglochie House
Nether Durdie
A90
Megginch Castle
3
Pannoch Wood
LC
Errol Station
Over Durdie Plantation
Westleys Farm
Shipbriggs Farm
24
North Murie Farm
Carse of Gowrie
Glendoick Gardens
LC
Glendoick House
Drums of Ardgaith Farm
Inchcoonans
2
LC
P
BIRCHVIEW PL 1
BEECHGROVE PL 2
ELM ST 3
Sandyhall Farm
Fala Farm
Chimneys
Errol Primary School
GOWRIE RD
STATION ROAD
LC
Murie Wood
LARCH PL
VIEWLANDS
LC
TAYBANK PL
LOAN BRAE
P
23
Muiredge Farm
NORLANDS
Liby
PO
HIGH ST
PH
GAS BRAE
Errol
Errol Park
1
Ardgaith Farm
Ancothie Wood
Motte
ST MADOES RD
Mansefield
Murie Gardens
Ross Farm
Sharps Wood
Black Wood
Mains of Murie
Cemy
A90
22
20
A
21
B
22
C
23
D
24
E
25
F
50
40
F1
1 NORTH BANK DYKES
2 NORTHBANK
3 CHURCH AVE
4 SCHOOL WYND
5 HALL WYND
6 CHURCH LA
7 COWGATE SOUTH BANK
8 SOUTH BANKDYKES
9 DALEALLY CRES

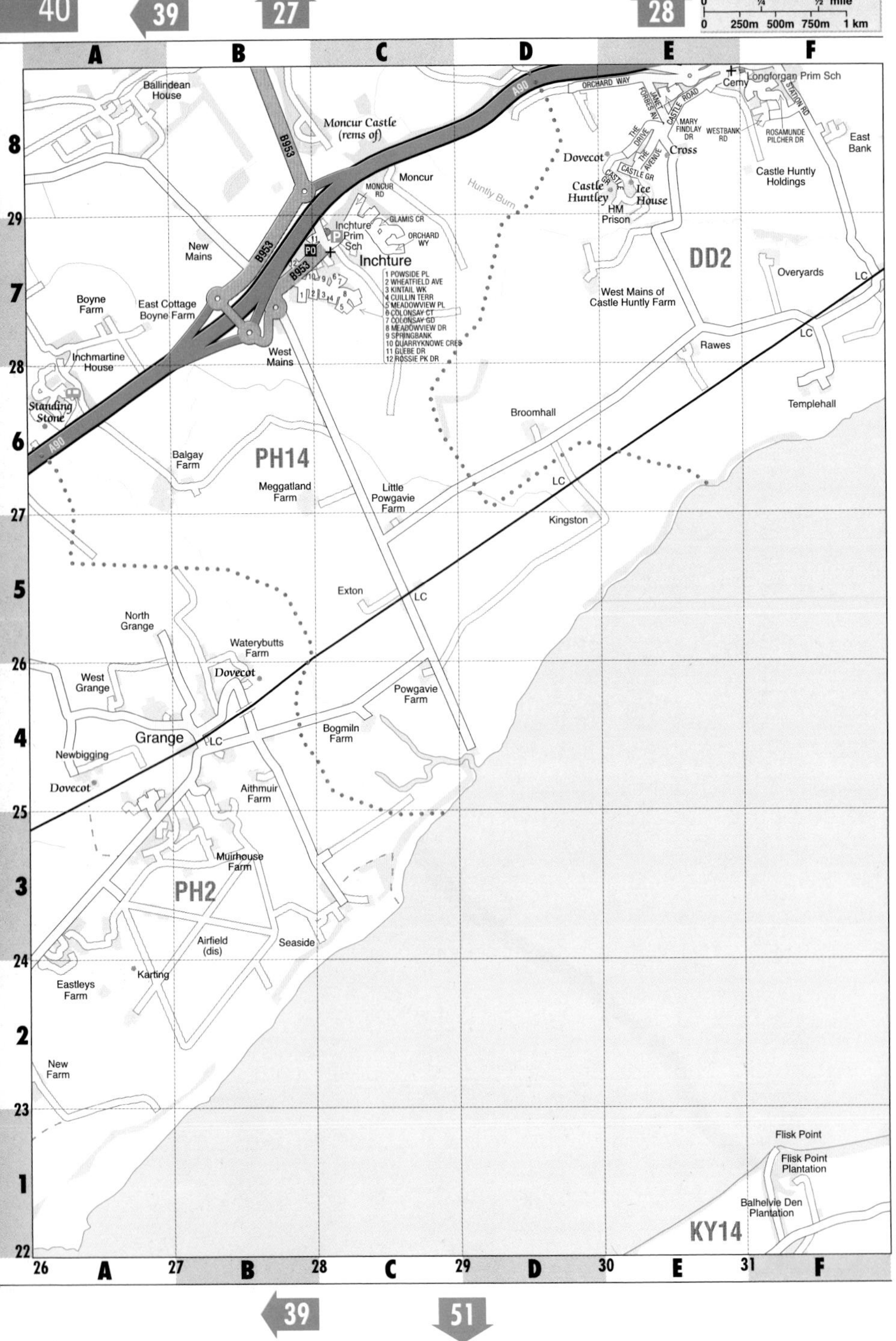

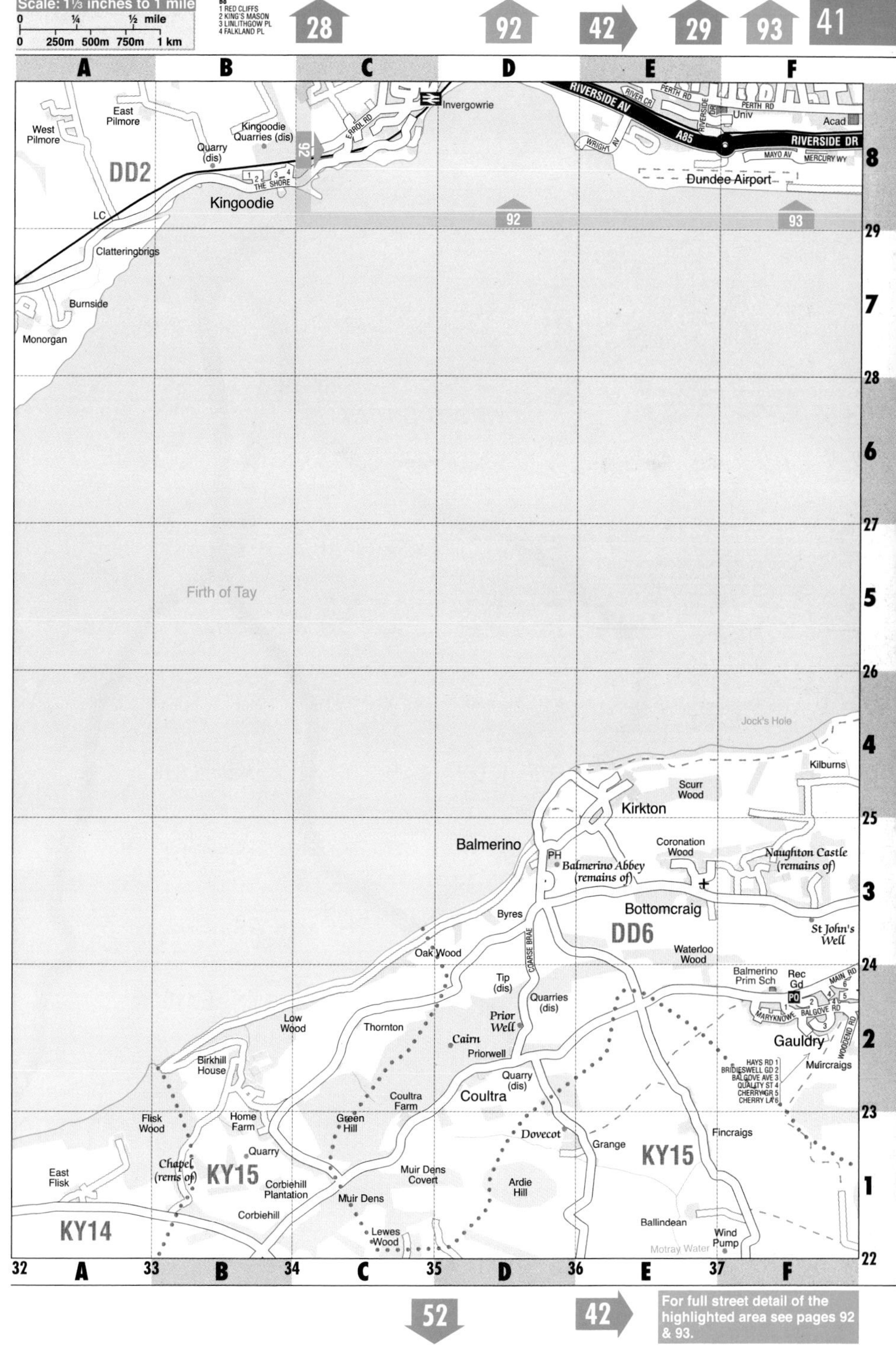

For full street detail of the highlighted area see pages 92 & 93.

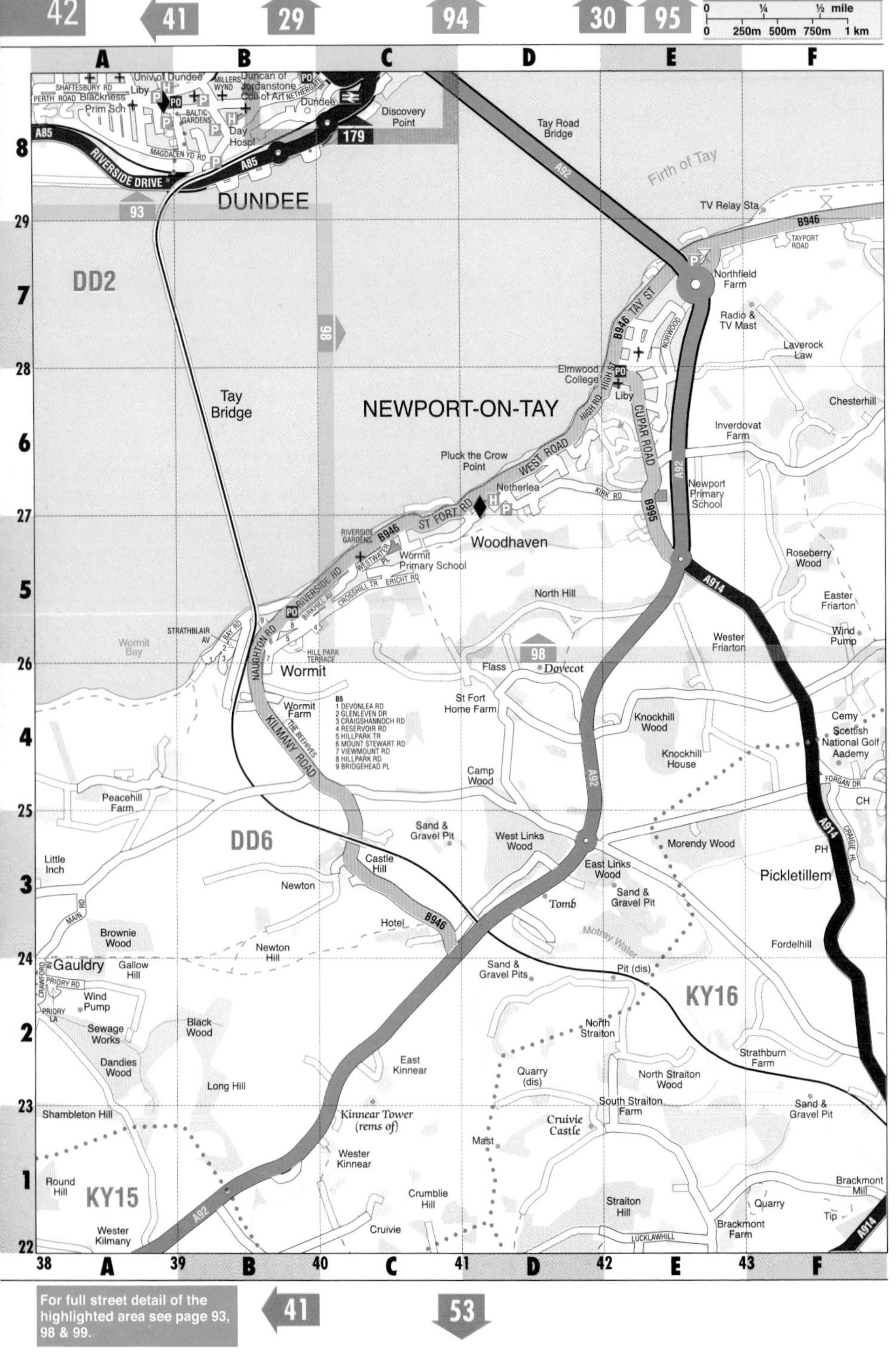

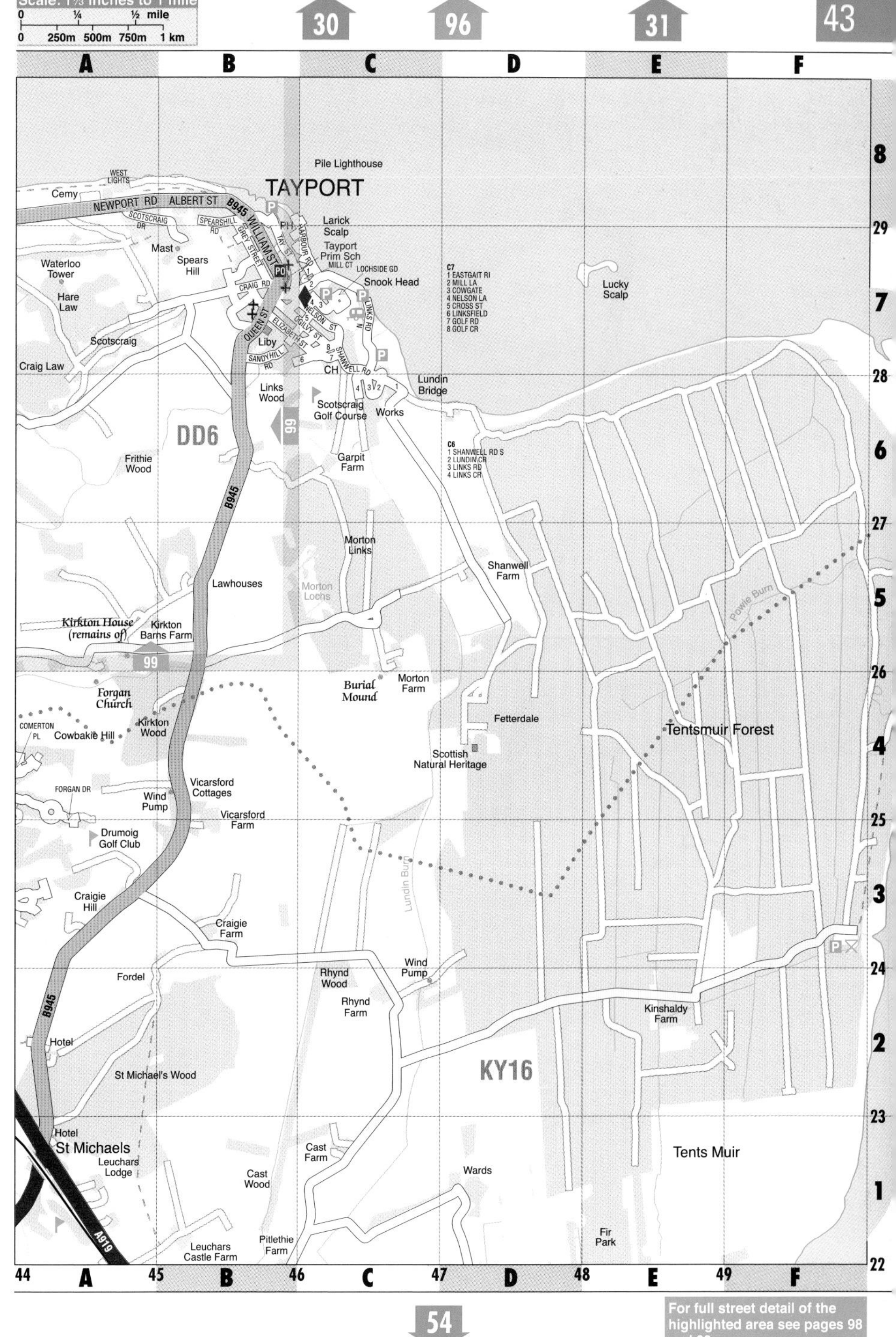

Scale: 1⅓ inches to 1 mile

| 0 | ¼ | ½ | mile |
| 0 | 250m | 500m | 750m | 1 km |

A **B** **C** **D** **E** **F**

Pile Lighthouse

TAYPORT

WEST LIGHTS
Cemy
NEWPORT RD ALBERT ST B945
SCOTSCRAIG DR
SPEARSHILL RD
Mast
Spears Hill
Waterloo Tower
Hare Law
Scotscraig
Craig Law

Larick Scalp
Tayport Prim Sch
LOCHSIDE GD
Snook Head

C7
1 EASTGAIT RI
2 MILL LA
3 COWGATE
4 NELSON LA
5 CROSS ST
6 LINKSFIELD
7 GOLF RD
8 GOLF CR

Lucky Scalp

DD6

Frithie Wood

Liby
CH
Links Wood
Scotscraig Golf Course
Works

Lundin Bridge

C6
1 SHANWELL RD S
2 LUNDIN CR
3 LINKS RD
4 LINKS CR

Garpit Farm

Lawhouses

Morton Links
Morton Lochs

Shanwell Farm

99

Kirkton House (remains of)
Kirkton Barns Farm

Forgan Church
COMERTON PL
Cowbakie Hill
Kirkton Wood

Burial Mound
Morton Farm

Fetterdale

Tentsmuir Forest

Scottish Natural Heritage

FORGAN DR
Vicarsford Cottages
Wind Pump
Vicarsford Farm

Drumoig Golf Club

Lundin Burn

Craigie Hill
Craigie Farm

Fordel

Rhynd Wood
Rhynd Farm

Wind Pump

Kinshaldy Farm

KY16

Hotel

St Michael's Wood

B945

Hotel
St Michaels
Leuchars Lodge

Cast Wood

Cast Farm

Wards

Tents Muir

Fir Park

A919

Leuchars Castle Farm
Pitlethie Farm

44 A 45 B 46 C 47 D 48 E 49 F

8 29 7 28 6 27 5 26 4 25 3 24 2 23 1 22

For full street detail of the highlighted area see pages 98 and 99.

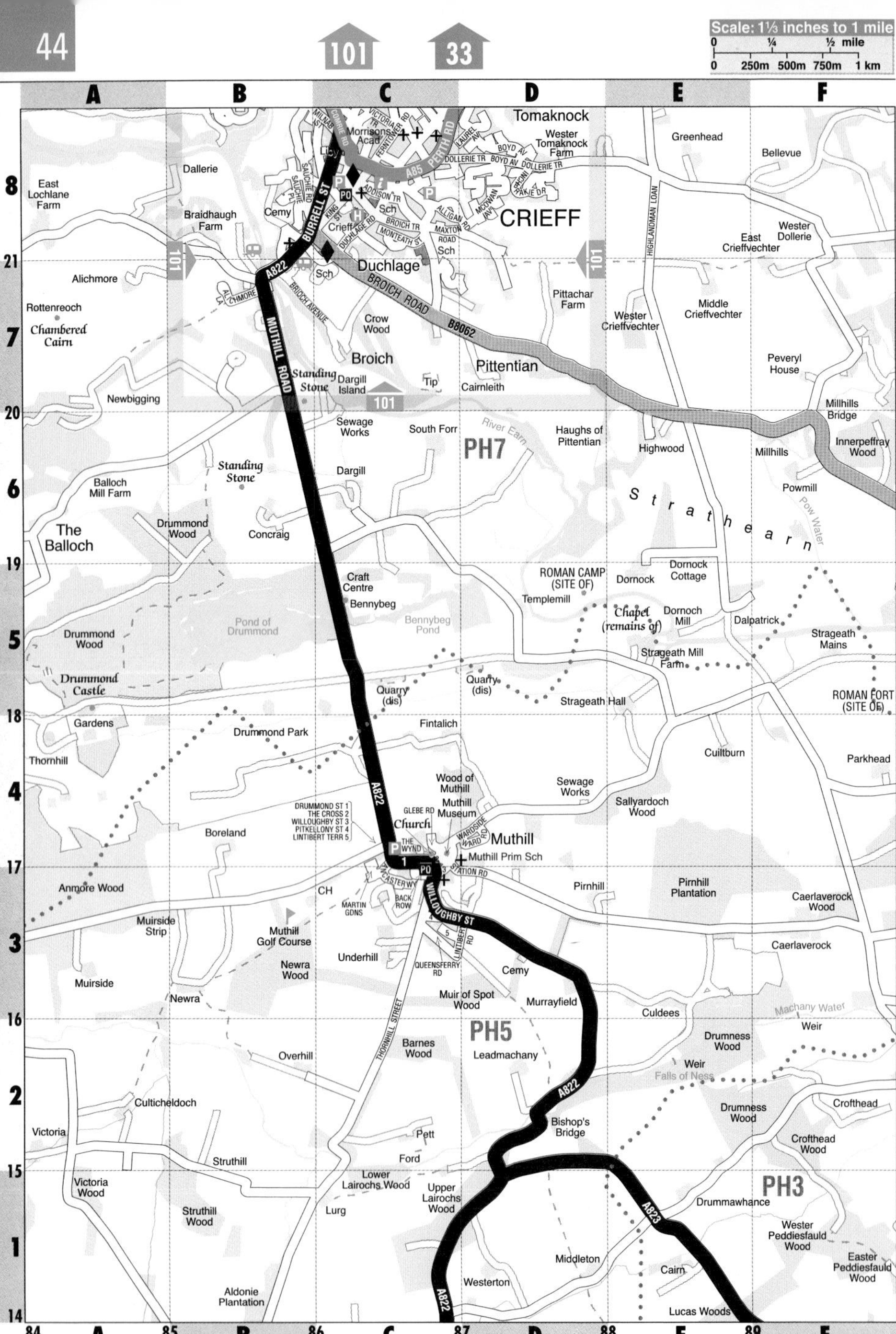

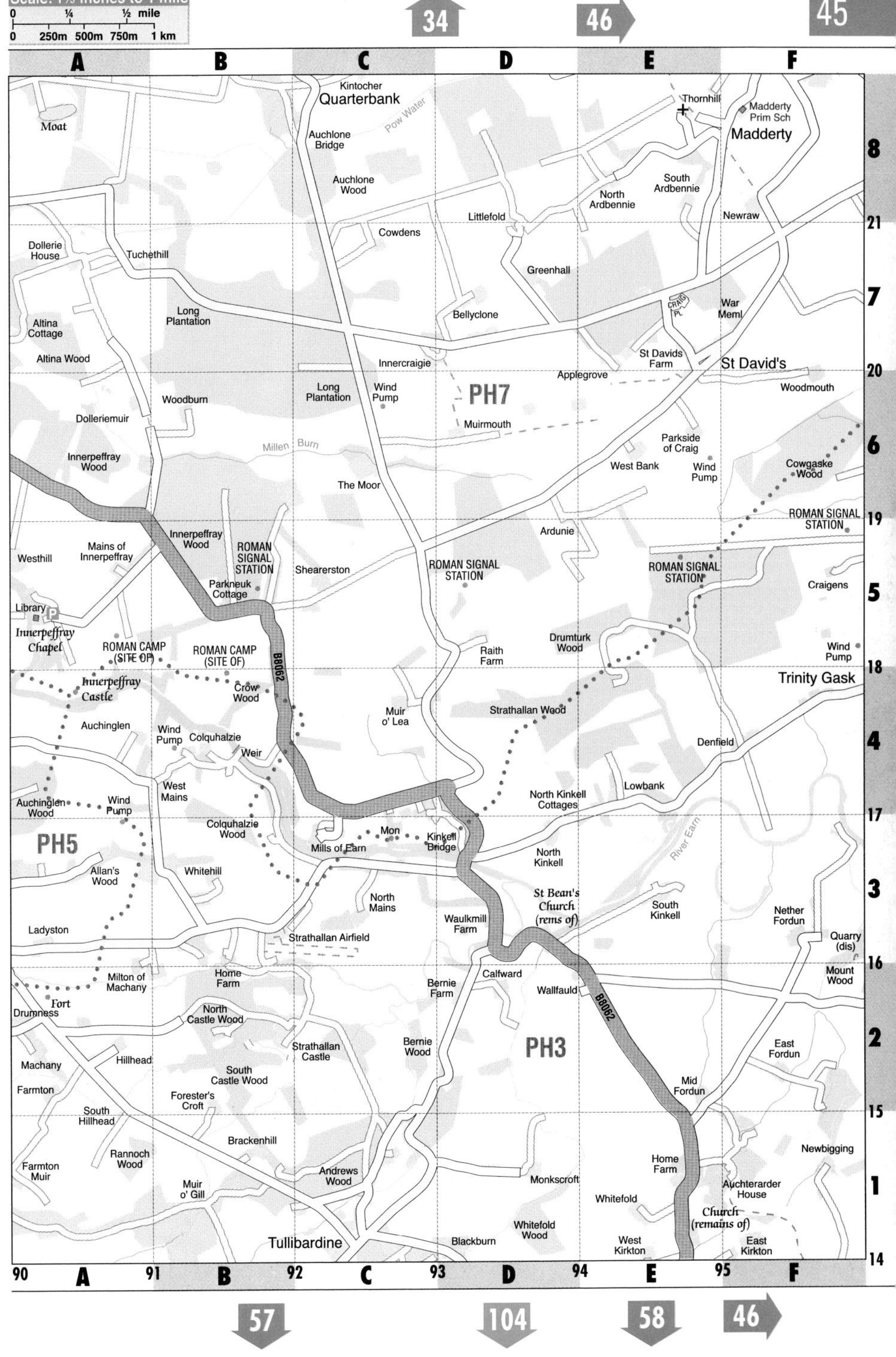

Scale: 1⅓ inches to 1 mile
0 ¼ ½ mile
0 250m 500m 750m 1 km
34
46
A B C D E F
Kintocher
Quarterbank
Pow Water
Thornhill
Madderty Prim Sch
Madderty
Moat
Auchlone Bridge
Auchlone Wood
South Ardbennie
North Ardbennie
Littlefold
Newraw
Cowdens
Dollerie House
Tuchethill
Greenhall
Long Plantation
Bellyclone
War Meml
CRAIG PL
Altina Cottage
Altina Wood
Innercraigie
St Davids Farm
St David's
Applegrove
Woodmouth
Long Plantation
Wind Pump
PH7
Woodburn
Dolleriemuir
Muirmouth
Parkside of Craig
Millen Burn
Innerpeffray Wood
West Bank
Wind Pump
Cowgaske Wood
The Moor
ROMAN SIGNAL STATION
Innerpeffray Wood
Ardunie
Mains of Innerpeffray
Westhill
ROMAN SIGNAL STATION
Shearerston
ROMAN SIGNAL STATION
ROMAN SIGNAL STATION
Parkneuk Cottage
Craigens
Library
Innerpeffray Chapel
ROMAN CAMP (SITE OF)
ROMAN CAMP (SITE OF)
B8062
Raith Farm
Drumturk Wood
Wind Pump
Trinity Gask
Innerpeffray Castle
Crow Wood
Muir o' Lea
Strathallan Wood
Auchinglen
Wind Pump
Colquhalzie
Weir
Denfield
West Mains
North Kinkell Cottages
Lowbank
Auchinglen Wood
Wind Pump
PH5
Colquhalzie Wood
Mon
Kinkell Bridge
Mills of Earn
River Earn
North Kinkell
Allan's Wood
Whitehill
St Bean's Church (rems of)
North Mains
South Kinkell
Nether Fordun
Ladyston
Waulkmill Farm
Strathallan Airfield
Quarry (dis)
Milton of Machany
Home Farm
Calfward
Bernie Farm
Wallfauld
Mount Wood
Fort
Drumness
North Castle Wood
B8062
Bernie Wood
PH3
East Fordun
Machany
Hillhead
Strathallan Castle
South Castle Wood
Farmton
Forester's Croft
Mid Fordun
South Hillhead
Brackenhill
Newbigging
Rannoch Wood
Home Farm
Farmton Muir
Muir o' Gill
Andrews Wood
Monkscroft
Whitefold
Auchterarder House
Church (remains of)
Tullibardine
Blackburn
Whitefold Wood
West Kirkton
East Kirkton
90 A 91 B 92 C 93 D 94 E 95 F
8 21 7 20 6 19 5 18 4 17 3 16 2 15 1 14
57
104
58
46

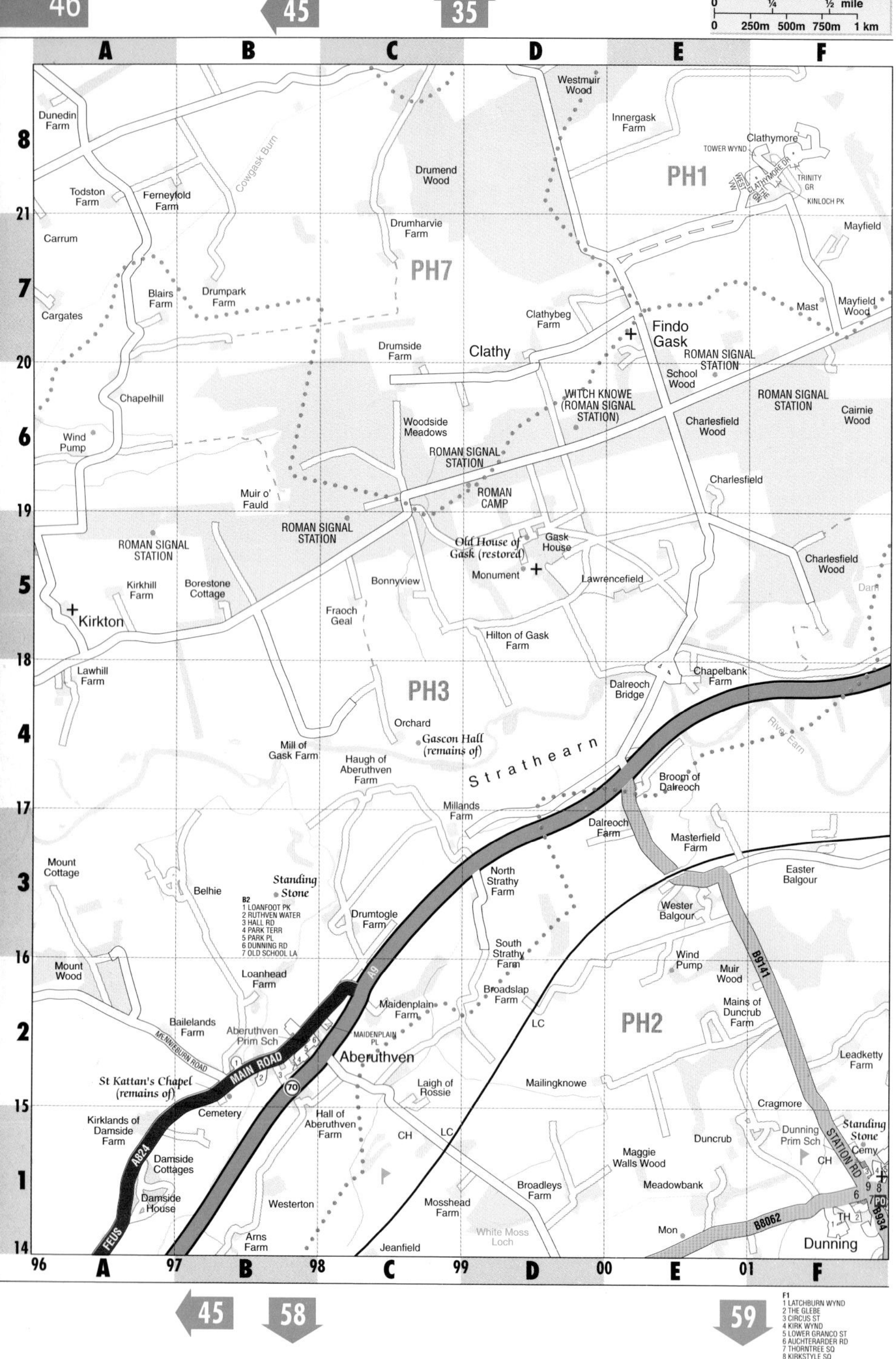

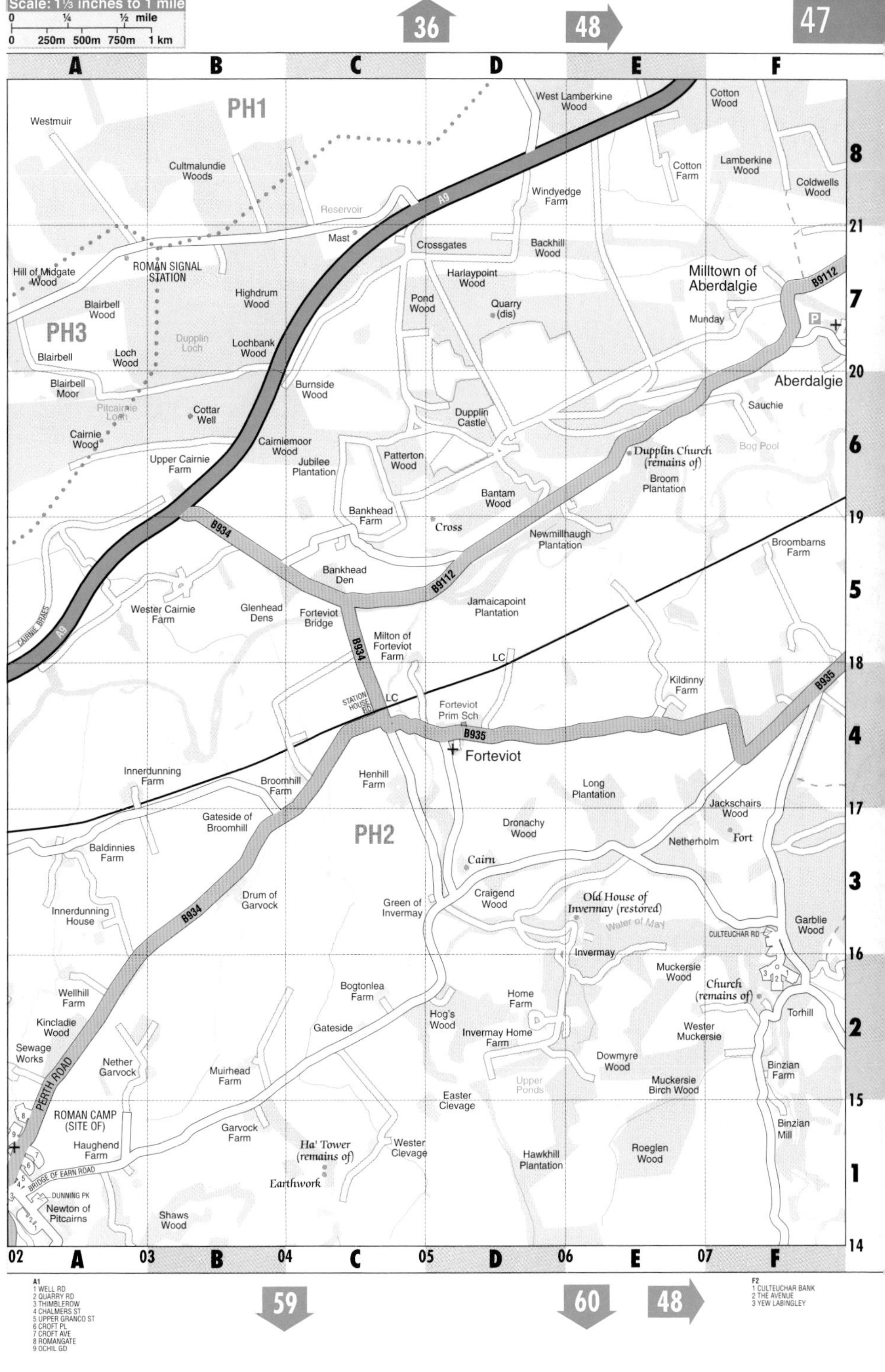

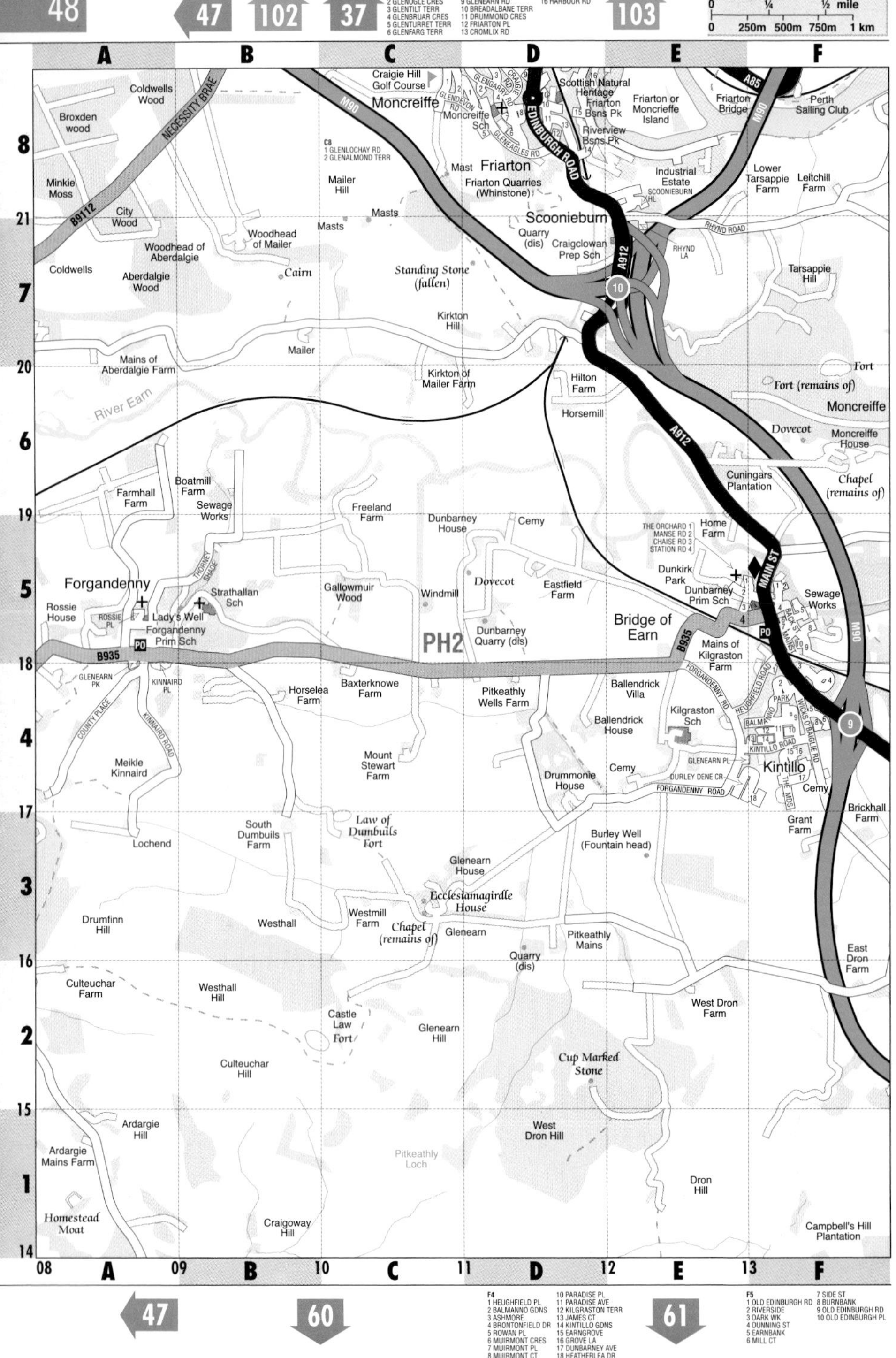

Scale: 1⅓ inches to 1 mile

0   ¼   ½ mile
0 250m 500m 750m 1 km

D8
1 GLENARTNEY TERR
2 GLENOGLE CRES
3 GLENTILT TERR
4 GLENBRUAR CRES
5 GLENTURRET TERR
6 GLENFARG TERR

C (C8)
7 GLENSHEE CRES
8 GARRY PL
9 GLENEARN RD
10 BREADALBANE CRES
11 DRUMMOND CRES
12 FRIARTON PL
13 CROMLIX RD

14 FRIARTON RD
15 FRIARTON RD
16 HARBOUR RD

C8
1 GLENLOCHAY RD
2 GLENALMOND TERR

47 60 61

F4
1 HEUGHFIELD PL
2 BALMANNO GDNS
3 ASHMORE
4 BRONTONFIELD DR
5 ROWAN PL
6 MUIRMONT CRES
7 MUIRMONT PL
8 MUIRMONT CT
9 KINTILLO PL
10 PARADISE PL
11 PARADISE AVE
12 KILGRASTON TERR
13 JAMES CT
14 KINTILLO GDNS
15 EARNGROVE
16 GROVE LA
17 DUNBARNEY AVE
18 HEATHERLEA DR

F5
1 OLD EDINBURGH RD
2 RIVERSIDE
3 DARK WK
4 DUNNING ST
5 EARNBANK
6 MILL CT
7 SIDE ST
8 BURNBANK
9 OLD EDINBURGH RD
10 OLD EDINBURGH PL

Scale: 1⅓ inches to 1 mile

38
50

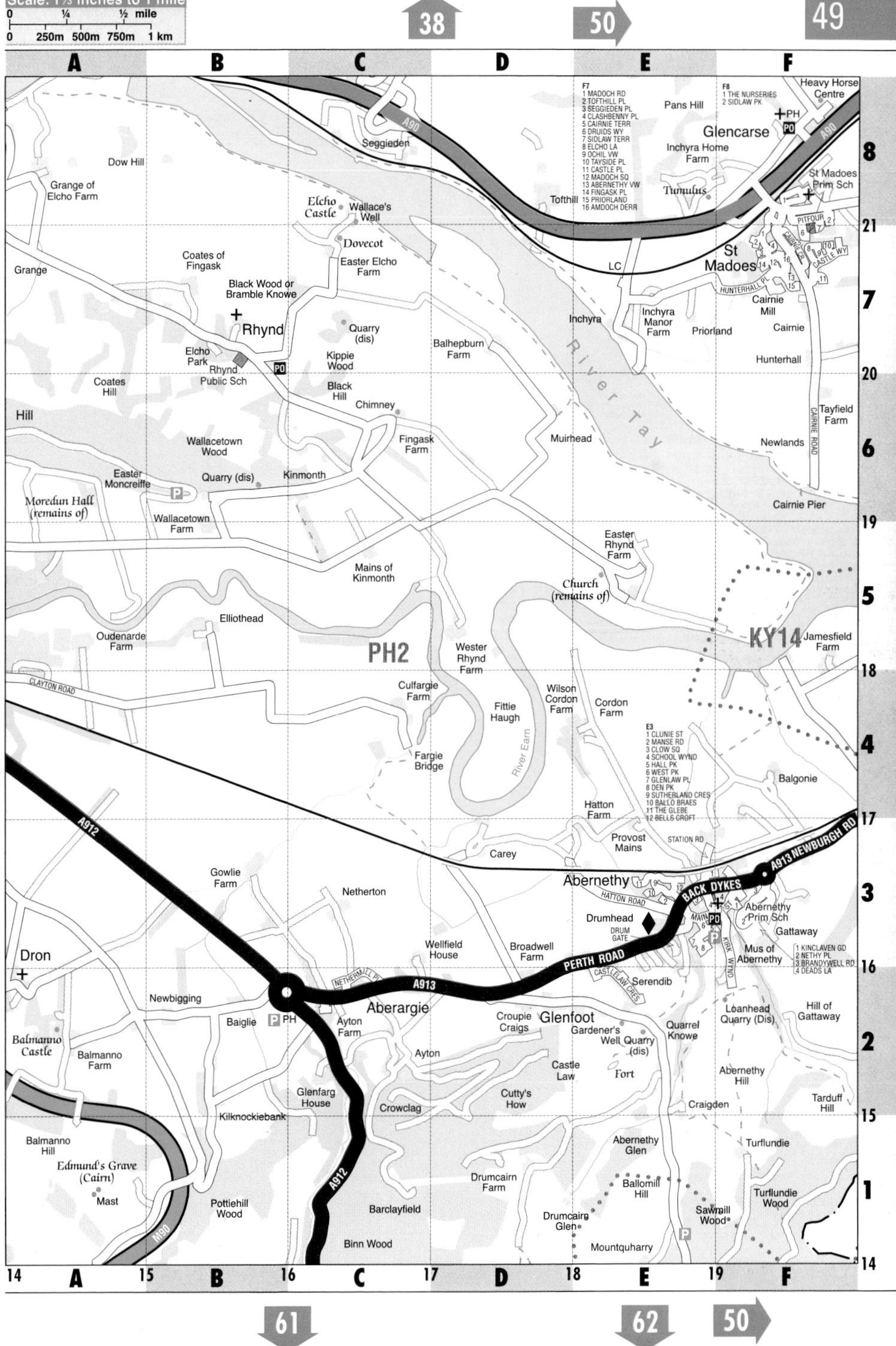
A
B
C
D
E
F
F7
1 MADOCH RD
2 TOFTHILL PL
3 SEGGIEDEN PL
4 CLASHBENNY PL
5 CAIRNIE TERR
6 DRUIDS WY
7 SIDLAW TERR
8 ELCHO LA
9 OCHIL VW
10 TAYSIDE PL
11 CASTLE PL
12 MADOCH SQ
13 ABERNETHY VW
14 FINGASK PL
15 PRIORLAND
16 AMDOCH DERR
F8
1 THE NURSERIES
2 SIDLAW PK
Heavy Horse Centre
Pans Hill
Glencarse
Inchyra Home Farm
St Madoes Prim Sch
Seggieden
Dow Hill
Grange of Elcho Farm
Elcho Castle
Wallace's Well
Dovecot
Tofthill
Tumulus
PITFOUR
Grange
Coates of Fingask
Easter Elcho Farm
LC
St Madoes
HUNTERHALL PL
CASTLE WY
Black Wood or Bramble Knowe
Rhynd
Quarry (dis)
Inchyra
Inchyra Manor Farm
Priorland
Cairnie Mill
Cairnie
Elcho Park
Rhynd Public Sch
Kippie Wood
Balhepburn Farm
Hunterhall
Coates Hill
Black Hill
River Tay
Hill
Chimney
Tayfield Farm
CAIRNIE ROAD
Wallacetown Wood
Fingask Farm
Muirhead
Newlands
Easter Moncreiffe
Quarry (dis)
Kinmonth
Moredun Hall (remains of)
Wallacetown Farm
Cairnie Pier
Easter Rhynd Farm
Mains of Kinmonth
Church (remains of)
Elliothead
Oudenarde Farm
PH2
Wester Rhynd Farm
KY14
Jamesfield Farm
CLAYTON ROAD
Culfargie Farm
Fittie Haugh
Wilson Cordon Farm
Cordon Farm
Fargie Bridge
River Earn
E3
1 CLUNIE ST
2 MANSE RD
3 CLOW SQ
4 SCHOOL WYND
5 HALL PK
6 WEST PK
7 GLENLAW PL
8 DEN PK
9 SUTHERLAND CRES
10 BALLO BRAES
11 THE GLEBE
12 BELLS CROFT
Balgonie
A912
Hatton Farm
Provost Mains
STATION RD
A913 NEWBURGH RD
Carey
Gowlie Farm
Netherton
Abernethy
HATTON ROAD
BACK DYKES
Abernethy Prim Sch
Drumhead
DRUM GATE
MAIN
KIRK WYND
Gattaway
Wellfield House
Broadwell Farm
PERTH ROAD
Mus of Abernethy
1 KINCLAVEN GD
2 NETHY PL
3 BRANDYWELL RD
4 DEADS LA
Dron
NETHERMILL PL
A913
CASTLELAW CRES
Serendib
Newbigging
Aberargie
Loanhead Quarry (Dis)
Hill of Gattaway
Baiglie
PH
Ayton Farm
Croupie Craigs
Glenfoot
Gardener's Well Quarry (dis)
Quarrel Knowe
Balmanno Castle
Balmanno Farm
Ayton
Castle Law
Fort
Abernethy Hill
Glenfarg House
Crowclag
Cutty's How
Craigden
Tarduff Hill
Kilknockiebank
Balmanno Hill
Abernethy Glen
Turflundie
Edmund's Grave (Cairn)
Drumcairn Farm
Ballomill Hill
Mast
Pottiehill Wood
Barclayfield
Turflundie Wood
Sawmill Wood
Drumcairn Glen
M90
Binn Wood
Mountquharry
8
21
7
20
6
19
5
18
4
17
3
16
2
15
1
14
14
15
16
17
18
19

61
62
50

49
39

D5
1 WEST PORT RD
2 CLINTON ST
3 MASON ST
4 MUGDRUM PL
5 HILL RD
6 WEST SHORE RD
7 YORK PL
8 CORNHILL ST
9 MID SHORE RD
10 EAST SHORE RD
11 COACH RD
12 TAY ST
13 LYALL PL
14 GUTHRIE CT
15 GUTHRIE GD
16 MITCHELL ST
17 MONCRIEFF WY

Scale: 1⅓ inches to 1 mile

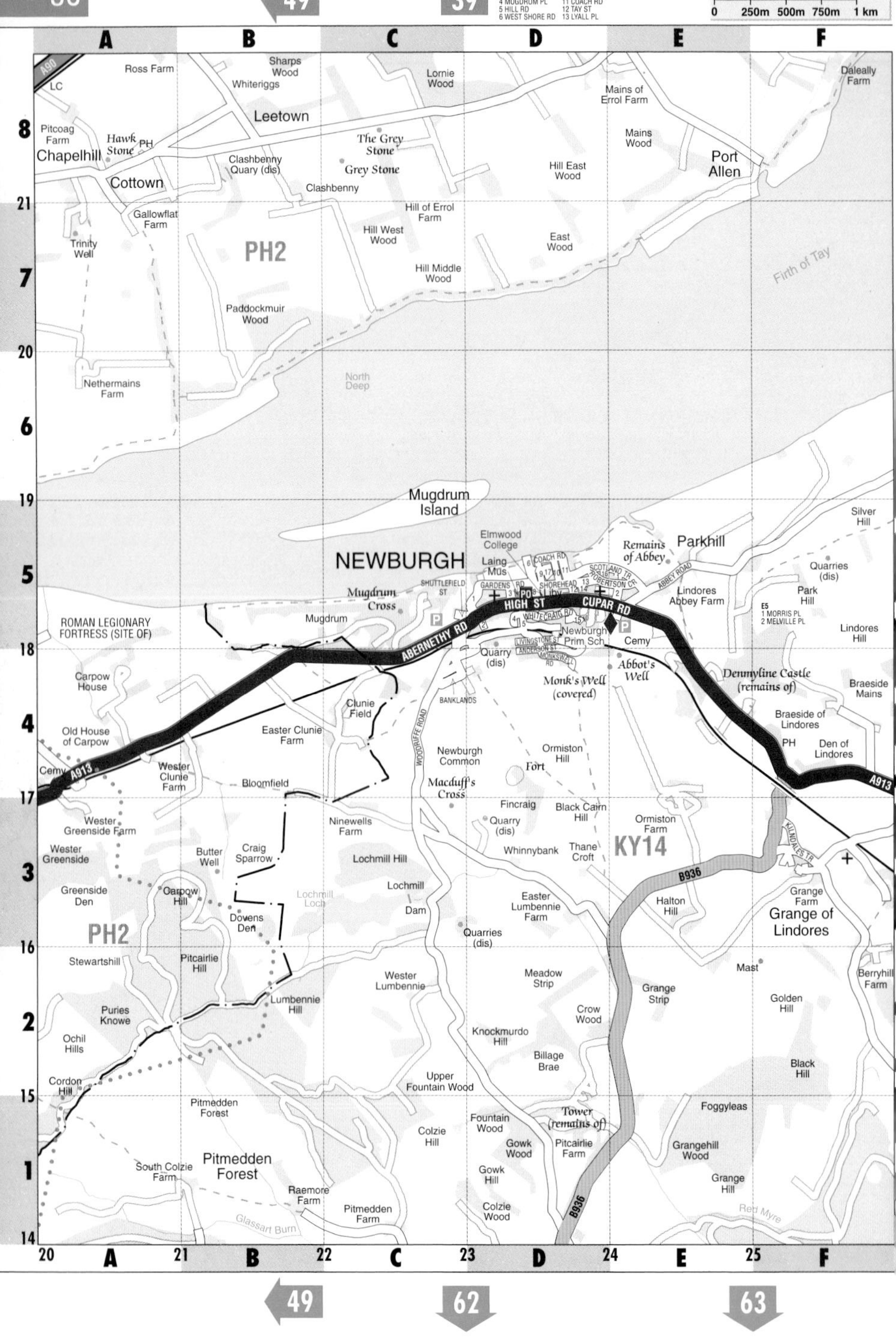

49
62
63

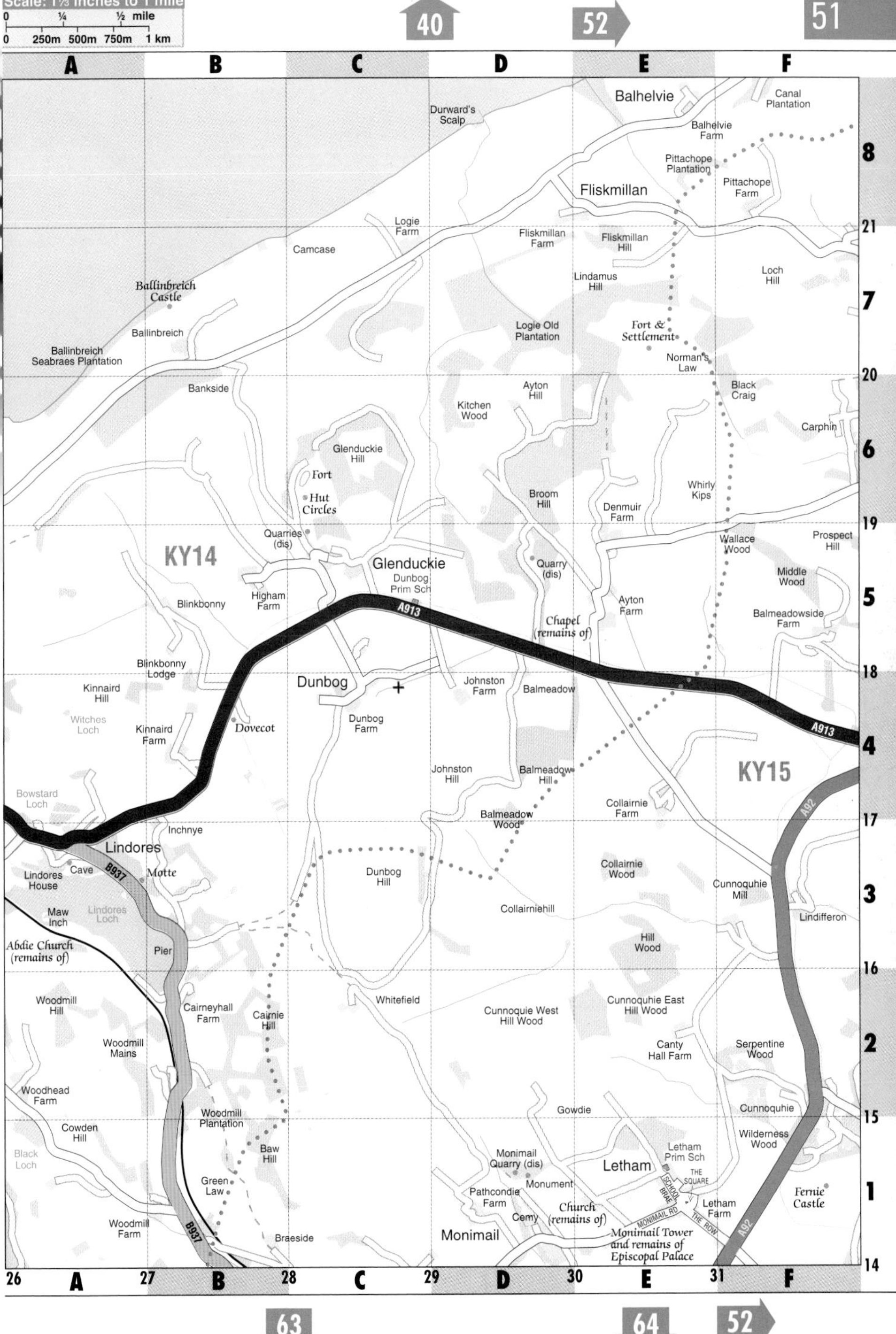
Scale: 1⅓ inches to 1 mile
40
52
Balhelvie
Canal Plantation
Durward's Scalp
Balhelvie Farm
Pittachope Plantation
Pittachope Farm
Fliskmillan
Logie Farm
Camcase
Fliskmillan Farm
Fliskmillan Hill
Loch Hill
Lindamus Hill
Ballinbreich Castle
Ballinbreich
Ballinbreich Seabraes Plantation
Logie Old Plantation
Fort & Settlement
Norman's Law
Bankside
Ayton Hill
Black Craig
Kitchen Wood
Carphin
Glenduckie Hill
Fort
Hut Circles
Broom Hill
Whirly Kips
Denmuir Farm
Quarries (dis)
Wallace Wood
Prospect Hill
KY14
Glenduckie
Quarry (dis)
Middle Wood
Dunbog Prim Sch
Higham Farm
Blinkbonny
Ayton Farm
Balmeadowside Farm
A913
Chapel (remains of)
Blinkbonny Lodge
Dunbog
Johnston Farm
Balmeadow
Kinnaird Hill
Witches Loch
Dovecot
Dunbog Farm
Kinnaird Farm
KY15
Johnston Hill
Balmeadow Hill
Bowstard Loch
Collairnie Farm
Balmeadow Wood
Inchnye
A92
Lindores
Cave
B937
Motte
Lindores House
Dunbog Hill
Collairnie Wood
Cunnoquhie Mill
Maw Inch
Lindores Loch
Collairniehill
Lindifferon
Abdie Church (remains of)
Pier
Hill Wood
Woodmill Hill
Cairneyhall Farm
Cairnie Hill
Whitefield
Cunnoquie West Hill Wood
Cunnoquhie East Hill Wood
Woodmill Mains
Canty Hall Farm
Serpentine Wood
Woodhead Farm
Woodmill Plantation
Gowdie
Cunnoquhie
Cowden Hill
Wilderness Wood
Baw Hill
Letham Prim Sch
Black Loch
Monimail Quarry (dis)
Letham
Green Law
Monument
THE SQUARE
SCHOOL BRAE
Fernie Castle
Pathcondie Farm
Church (remains of)
Letham Farm
MONIMAIL RD
THE ROW
Woodmill Farm
Cemy
Braeside
Monimail
Monimail Tower and remains of Episcopal Palace
A
B
C
D
E
F
8
21
7
20
6
19
5
18
4
17
3
16
2
15
1
14
26
27
28
29
30
31
63
64
52

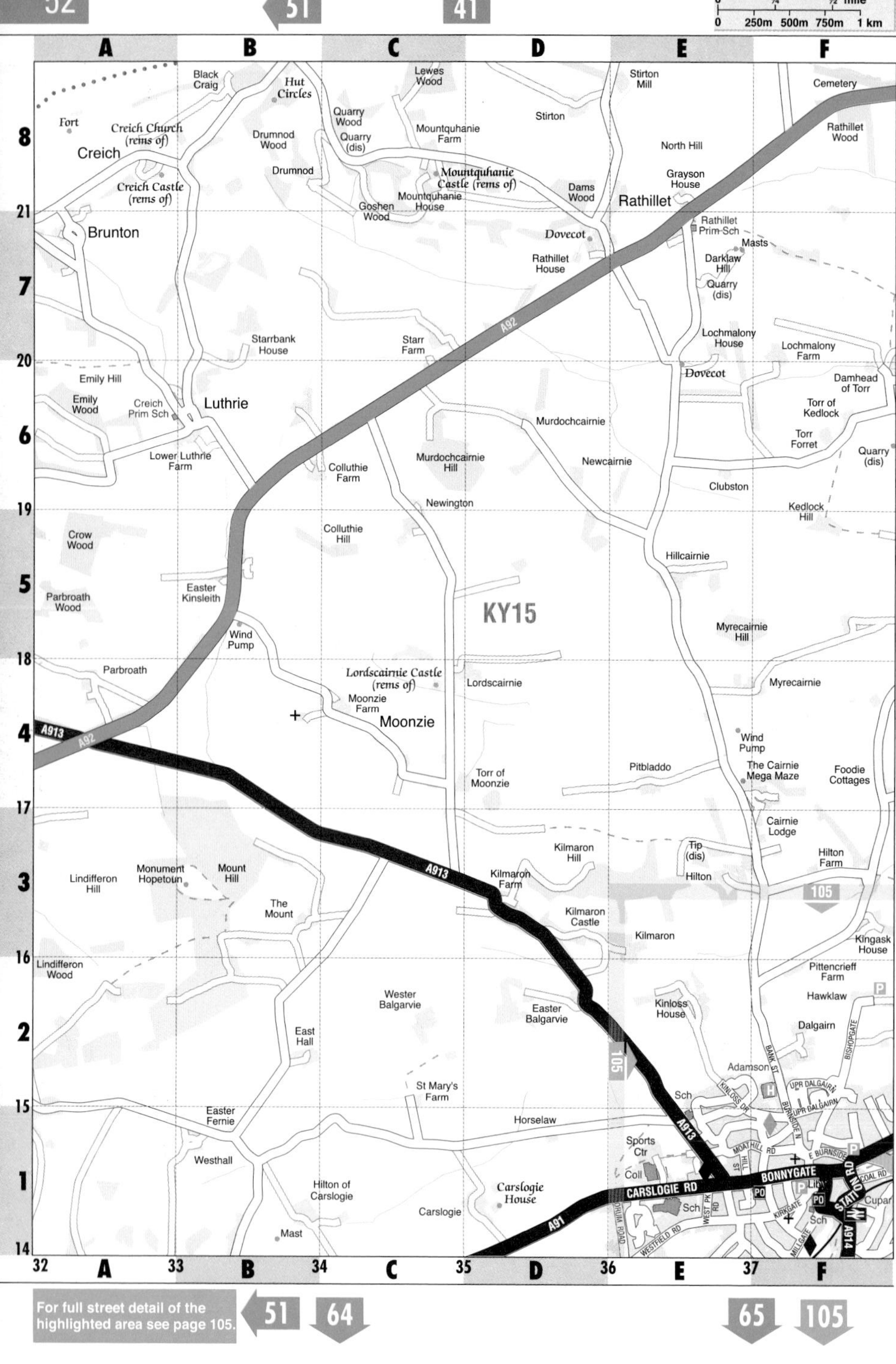

51
41

Scale: 1⅓ inches to 1 mile
0   ¼   ½   mile
0 250m 500m 750m 1 km

A **B** **C** **D** **E** **F**

Fort
Black Craig
Hut Circles
Lewes Wood
Stirton Mill
Cemetery

8
Creich Church (rems of)
Drumnod Wood
Quarry Wood
Quarry (dis)
Mountquhanie Farm
Stirton
North Hill
Rathillet Wood

Creich
Drumnod
Mountquhanie Castle (rems of)
Grayson House

21
Creich Castle (rems of)
Goshen Wood
Mountquhanie House
Dams Wood
Rathillet

Brunton
Dovecot
Rathillet Prim Sch
Masts

7
Rathillet House
Darklaw Hill
Quarry (dis)

Emily Hill
Starrbank House
Starr Farm
Lochmalony House
Lochmalony Farm

20
Emily Wood
Dovecot
Damhead of Torr

Creich Prim Sch
Luthrie
Murdochcairnie
Torr of Kedlock

6
Lower Luthrie Farm
Colluthie Farm
Murdochcairnie Hill
Newcairnie
Torr Forret

Clubston
Quarry (dis)

19
Colluthie Hill
Newington
Kedlock Hill

Crow Wood
Hillcairnie

5
Easter Kinsleith
KY15
Myrecairnie Hill

Parbroath Wood
Wind Pump

18
Parbroath
Lordscairnie Castle (rems of)
Lordscairnie
Myrecairnie

Moonzie Farm
+
Moonzie

4
A913 A92
Torr of Moonzie
Pitbladdo
Wind Pump
The Cairnie Mega Maze
Foodie Cottages

17
Cairnie Lodge
Hilton Farm

Lindifferon Hill
Monument Hopetoun
Mount Hill
Kilmaron Hill
Tip (dis)
105

3
A913
Kilmaron Farm
Hilton
Kingask House

The Mount
Kilmaron Castle
Pittencrieff Farm

16
Lindifferon Wood
Kilmaron
Hawklaw

Wester Balgarvie
Easter Balgarvie
Kinloss House
Dalgairn

2
East Hall
105
Adamson
UPR DALGAIRY

St Mary's Farm
Sch

15
Easter Fernie
Horselaw
Sports Ctr
PO

Westhall
A913
BONNYGATE
STATION RD

1
Hilton of Carslogie
Carslogie House
CARSLOGIE RD
Sch
Cupar

Mast
Carslogie
A91

14
32 **A** **33** **B** **34** **C** **35** **D** **36** **E** **37** **F**

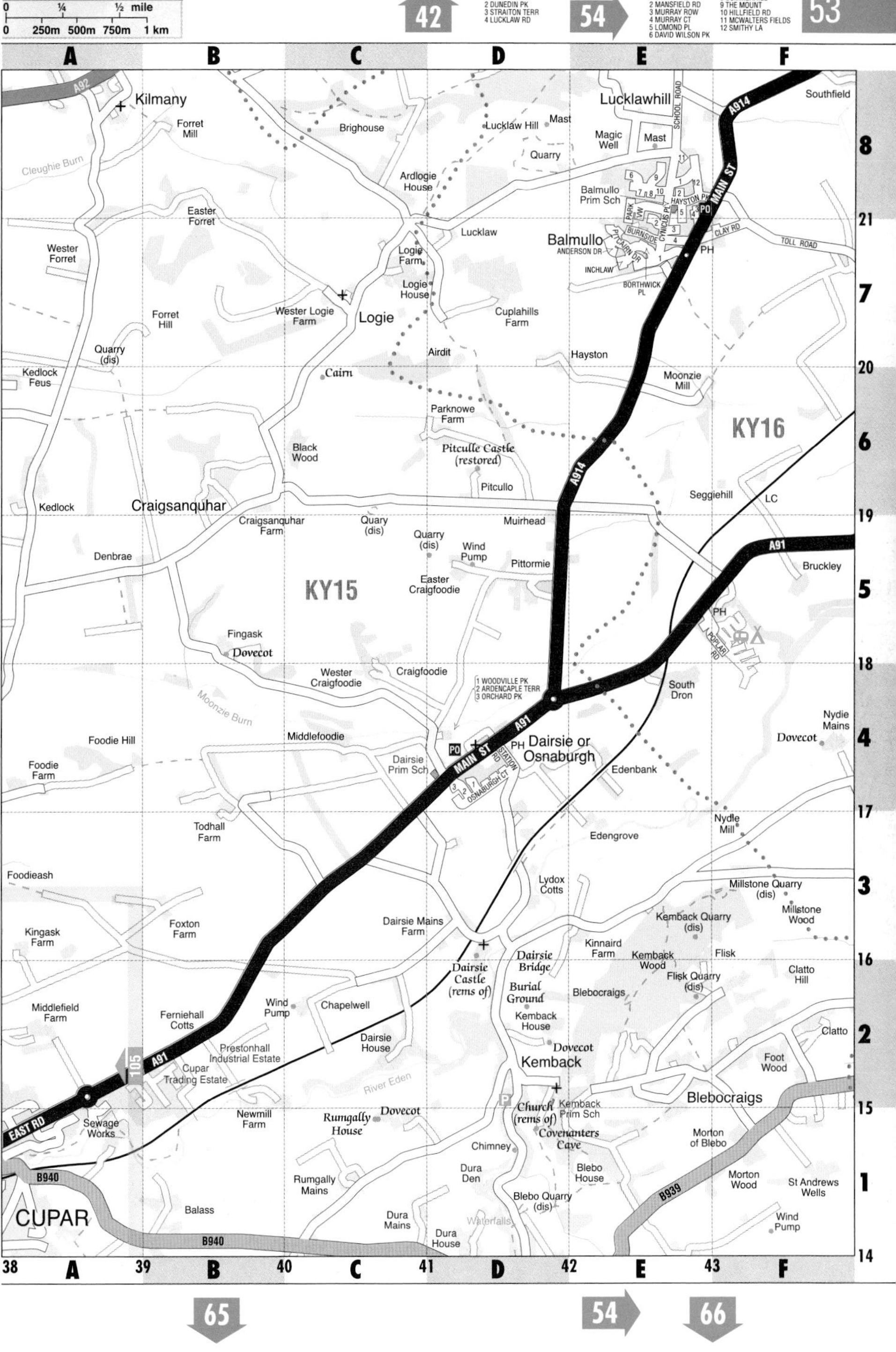
Kilmany
Forret Mill
Brighouse
Lucklaw Hill
Mast
Lucklawhill
Magic Well
Quarry
Cleughie Burn
Ardlogie House
Balmullo Prim Sch
Easter Forret
Lucklaw
Balmullo
Wester Forret
Logie Farm
Logie House
Forret Hill
Wester Logie Farm
Logie
Cuplahills Farm
Quarry (dis)
Airdit
Hayston
Kedlock Feus
Cairn
Moonzie Mill
Parknowe Farm
KY16
Black Wood
Pitculle Castle (restored)
Pitcullo
Kedlock
Craigsanquhar
Seggiehill
Craigsanquhar Farm
Quary (dis)
Muirhead
Denbrae
Wind Pump
Pittormie
Bruckley
KY15
Easter Craigfoodie
Fingask
Dovecot
Wester Craigfoodie
Craigfoodie
South Dron
1 WOODVILLE PK
2 ARDENCAPLE TERR
3 ORCHARD PK
Moonzie Burn
Nydie Mains
Foodie Hill
Middlefoodie
Dairsie or Osnaburgh
Foodie Farm
Dairsie Prim Sch
Edenbank
Todhall Farm
Nydie Mill
Edengrove
Foodieash
Lydox Cotts
Millstone Quarry (dis)
Kingask Farm
Foxton Farm
Dairsie Mains Farm
Kemback Quarry (dis)
Millstone Wood
Kinnaird Farm
Kemback Wood
Flisk
Dairsie Castle (rems of)
Dairsie Bridge
Flisk Quarry (dis)
Clatto Hill
Burial Ground
Blebocraigs
Middlefield Farm
Ferniehall Cotts
Wind Pump
Chapelwell
Kemback House
Clatto
Prestonhall Industrial Estate
Dairsie House
Dovecot
Kemback
Foot Wood
Cupar Trading Estate
River Eden
Blebocraigs
Kemback Prim Sch
Sewage Works
Newmill Farm
Rumgally House
Church (rems of)
Covenanters Cave
Morton of Blebo
Chimney
Rumgally Mains
Dura Den
Blebo House
Morton Wood
St Andrews Wells
Blebo Quarry (dis)
CUPAR
Balass
Dura Mains
Waterfalls
Dura House
Wind Pump
Southfield
MAIN ST
SCHOOL ROAD
HAYSTON PK
CLAY RD
TOLL ROAD
BURNSIDE
ANDERSON DR
INCHLAW
BORTHWICK PL
PITCAIRN DR
CYNICUS PL
PARK VW
POPLAR RD
STATION RD
OSNABURGH CT
EAST RD
LC
PH
PO
A92
A914
A91
B940
B939
105

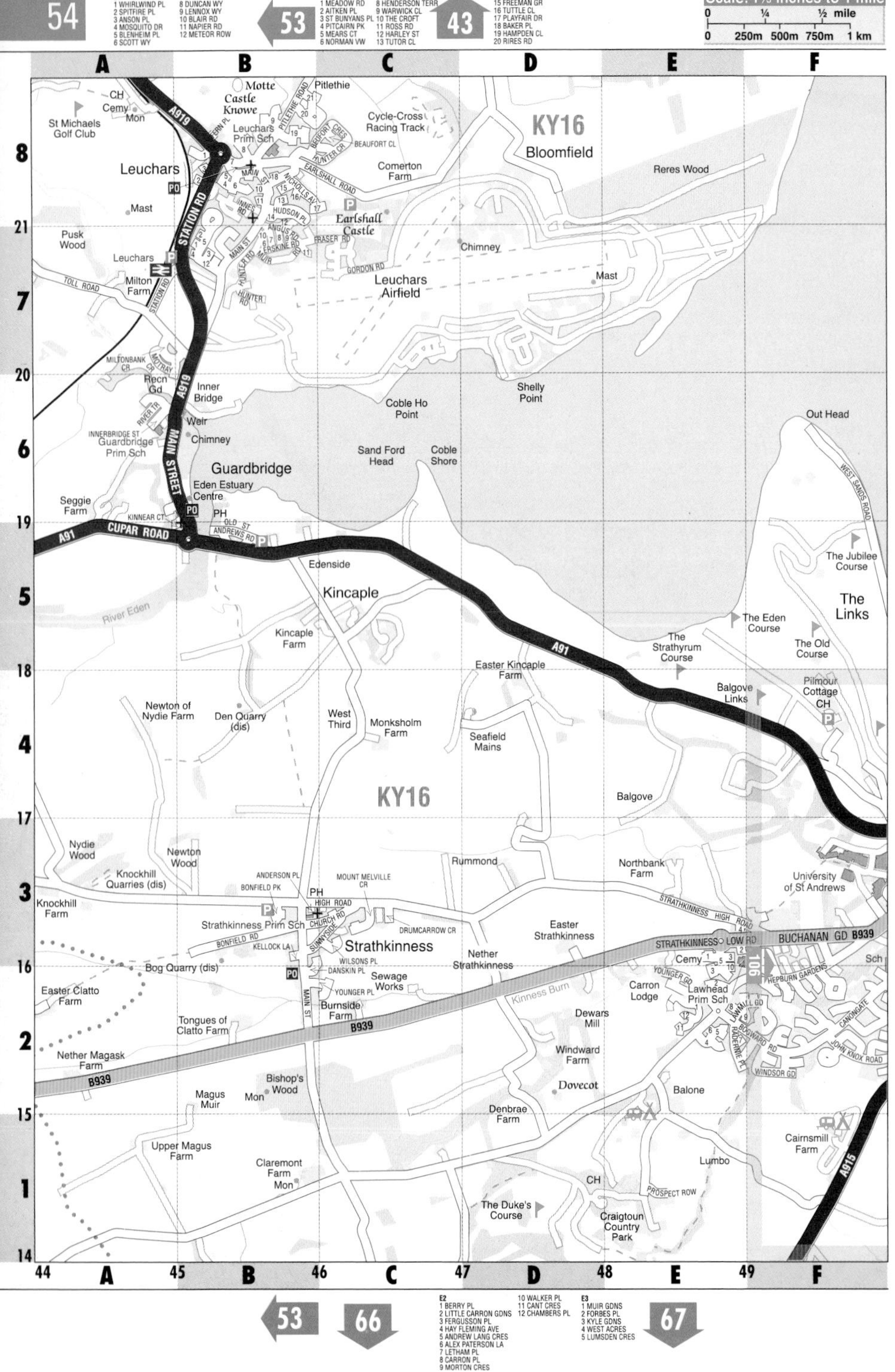
B7
1 WHIRLWIND PL
2 SPITFIRE PL
3 ANSON PL
4 MOSQUITO DR
5 BLENHEIM PL
6 SCOTT WY
7 CAMPBELL WY
8 DUNCAN WY
9 LENNOX WY
10 BLAIR RD
11 NAPIER RD
12 METEOR ROW
53
B8
1 MEADOW RD
2 AITKEN PL
3 ST BUNYANS PL
4 PITCAIRN PK
5 MEARS CT
6 NORMAN VW
7 SCHOOL HL
8 HENDERSON TERR
9 WARWICK CL
10 THE CROFT
11 ROSS RD
12 HARLEY ST
13 TUTOR CL
43
14 KEITH CRES
15 FREEMAN GR
16 TUTTLE CL
17 PLAYFAIR DR
18 BAKER PL
19 HAMPDEN CL
20 RIRES RD
21 FETTERDALE FIELDS
Scale: 1⅓ inches to 1 mile
0 ¼ ½ mile
0 250m 500m 750m 1 km
A B C D E F
8 21 7 20 6 19 5 18 4 17 3 16 2 15 1 14
CH
Cemy
Mon
St Michaels Golf Club
Motte
Castle Knowe
Pitlethie
PITLETHIE ROAD
Cycle-Cross Racing Track
KY16
Bloomfield
Leuchars
Leuchars Prim Sch
A919
BEAUFORT CRES
BEAUFORT CL
HUNTER CR
Comerton Farm
EARLSHALL ROAD
Reres Wood
PO
Mast
MAIN
NICHOLLS AV
INNES RD
HUDSON PL
Earlshall Castle
STATION RD
ANGUS RD
FRASER RD
ERSKINE RD
Chimney
Pusk Wood
Leuchars
MAIN ST
MUIR
HUNTER RD
GORDON RD
Mast
TOLL ROAD
Milton Farm
Leuchars Airfield
STATION RD
MILTONBANK CR
MOTRAY
Recn Gd
A919
Inner Bridge
Shelly Point
Coble Ho Point
RIVER TR
Weir
INNERBRIDGE ST
Guardbridge Prim Sch
Chimney
MAIN STREET
Out Head
Sand Ford Head
Coble Shore
Guardbridge
Eden Estuary Centre
WEST SANDS ROAD
Seggie Farm
PO
PH
KINNEAR CT
OLD ST ANDREWS RD
A91
CUPAR ROAD
The Jubilee Course
Edenside
Kincaple
The Links
River Eden
The Eden Course
Kincaple Farm
A91
The Strathyrum Course
The Old Course
Easter Kincaple Farm
Pilmour Cottage
CH
Balgove Links
Newton of Nydie Farm
Den Quarry (dis)
West Third
Monksholm Farm
Seafield Mains
KY16
Balgove
Nydie Wood
Newton Wood
Rummond
Northbank Farm
Knockhill Quarries (dis)
ANDERSON PL
BONFIELD PK
MOUNT MELVILLE CR
University of St Andrews
Knockhill Farm
PH
HIGH ROAD
STRATHKINNESS HIGH ROAD
Strathkinness Prim Sch
CHURCH RD
DRUMCARROW CR
Easter Strathkinness
BONFIELD RD
KELLOCK LA
SUNNYSIDE RD
Strathkinness
STRATHKINNESS LOW RD
BUCHANAN GD
B939
Nether Strathkinness
Bog Quarry (dis)
WILSONS PL
DANSKIN PL
Cemy
Sch
PO
Sewage Works
YOUNGER GD
HEPBURN GARDENS
Easter Clatto Farm
YOUNGER PL
Kinness Burn
Carron Lodge
Lawhead Prim Sch
MAIN ST
Burnside Farm
Dewars Mill
LAWMILL GD
CANONGATE
Tongues of Clatto Farm
B939
BOGWARD RD
RADERNIE PL
JOHN KNOX ROAD
Nether Magask Farm
Windward Farm
WINDSOR GD
B939
Bishop's Wood
Dovecot
Balone
Magus Muir
Mon
Denbrae Farm
Cairnsmill Farm
Upper Magus Farm
Lumbo
A915
Claremont Farm
Mon
CH
PROSPECT ROW
The Duke's Course
Craigtoun Country Park
44 45 46 47 48 49
53
66
E2
1 BERRY PL
2 LITTLE CARRON GDNS
3 FERGUSSON PL
4 HAY FLEMING AVE
5 ANDREW LANG CRES
6 ALEX PATERSON LA
7 LETHAM PL
8 CARRON PL
9 MORTON CRES
10 WALKER PL
11 CANT CRES
12 CHAMBERS PL
E3
1 MUIR GDNS
2 FORBES PL
3 KYLE GDNS
4 WEST ACRES
5 LUMSDEN CRES
67

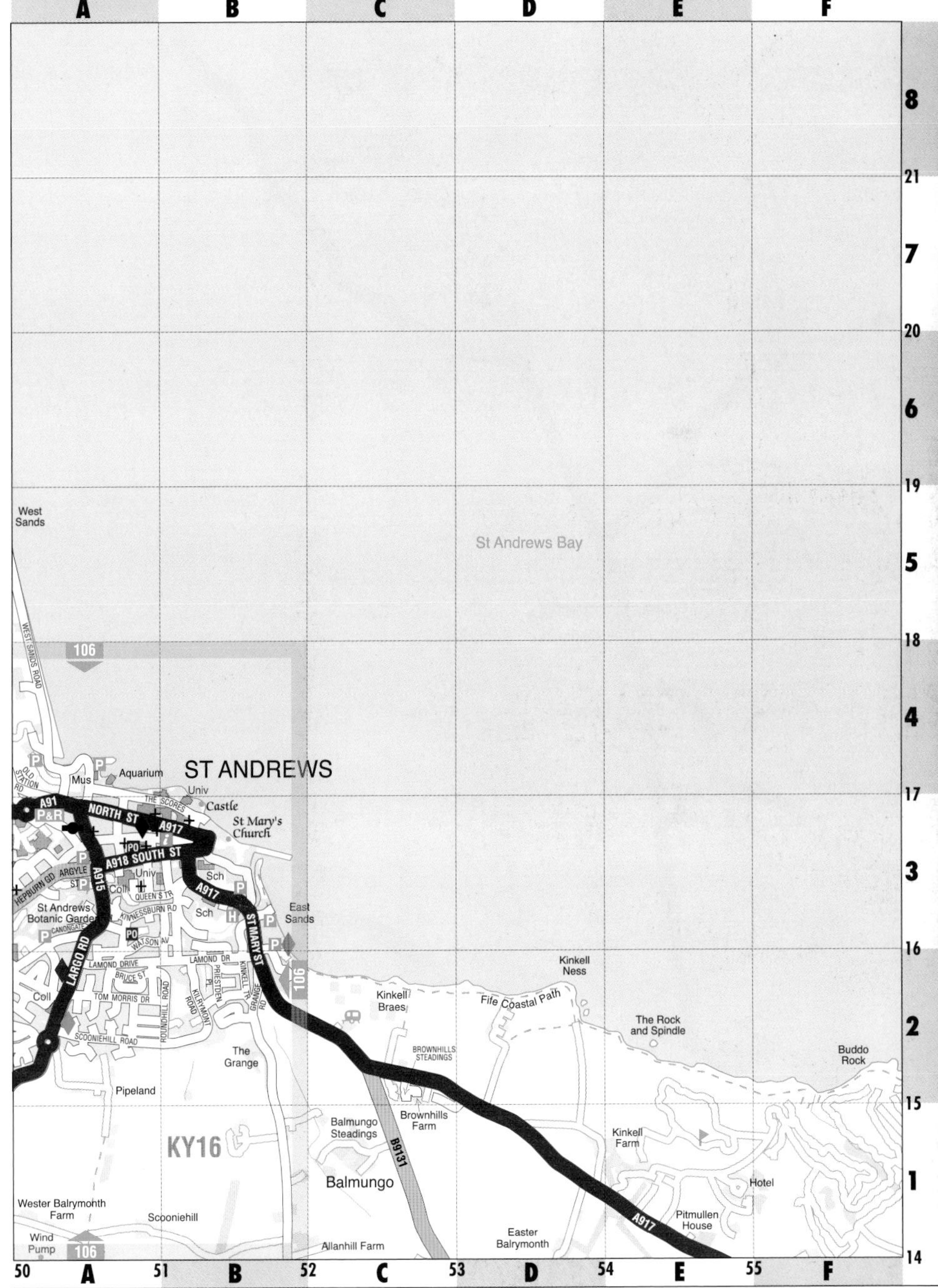

A   B   C   D   E   F

8

21

7

20

6

19

West
Sands

St Andrews Bay

5

18

4

106

17

ST ANDREWS

Mus   Aquarium

Univ

A91   Castle

P   NORTH ST   A917   St Mary's
Church

A918 SOUTH ST

3

Hepburn Gd   ARGYLE   Univ   Sch

St Andrews   Coll   Queen's Tr   A917

Botanic Garden   Sch   16

PO   H   East
Sands

Lamond Drive   St Mary St

Coll   Largo Rd   Kinnessburn Road   Preston   106

Bruce St   Kinkell   Kinkell
Ness   The Rock
and Spindle

Tom Morris Dr   Braes   File Coastal Path   2   Buddo
Rock

Sconiehill Road   BROWNHILLS
STEADINGS   15

Pipeland   The
Grange

Balmungo   Brownhills
Steadings   Farm   Kinkell
Farm

KY16   B9131   Hotel

Balmungo

Wester Balrymonth   Pitmullen
House   A917   1
Farm

Sconiehill

Wind   Allanhill Farm   Easter
Pump   106   Balrymonth   14

50   A   51   B   52   C   53   D   54   E   55   F

67   68

For full street detail of the
highlighted area see page 106.

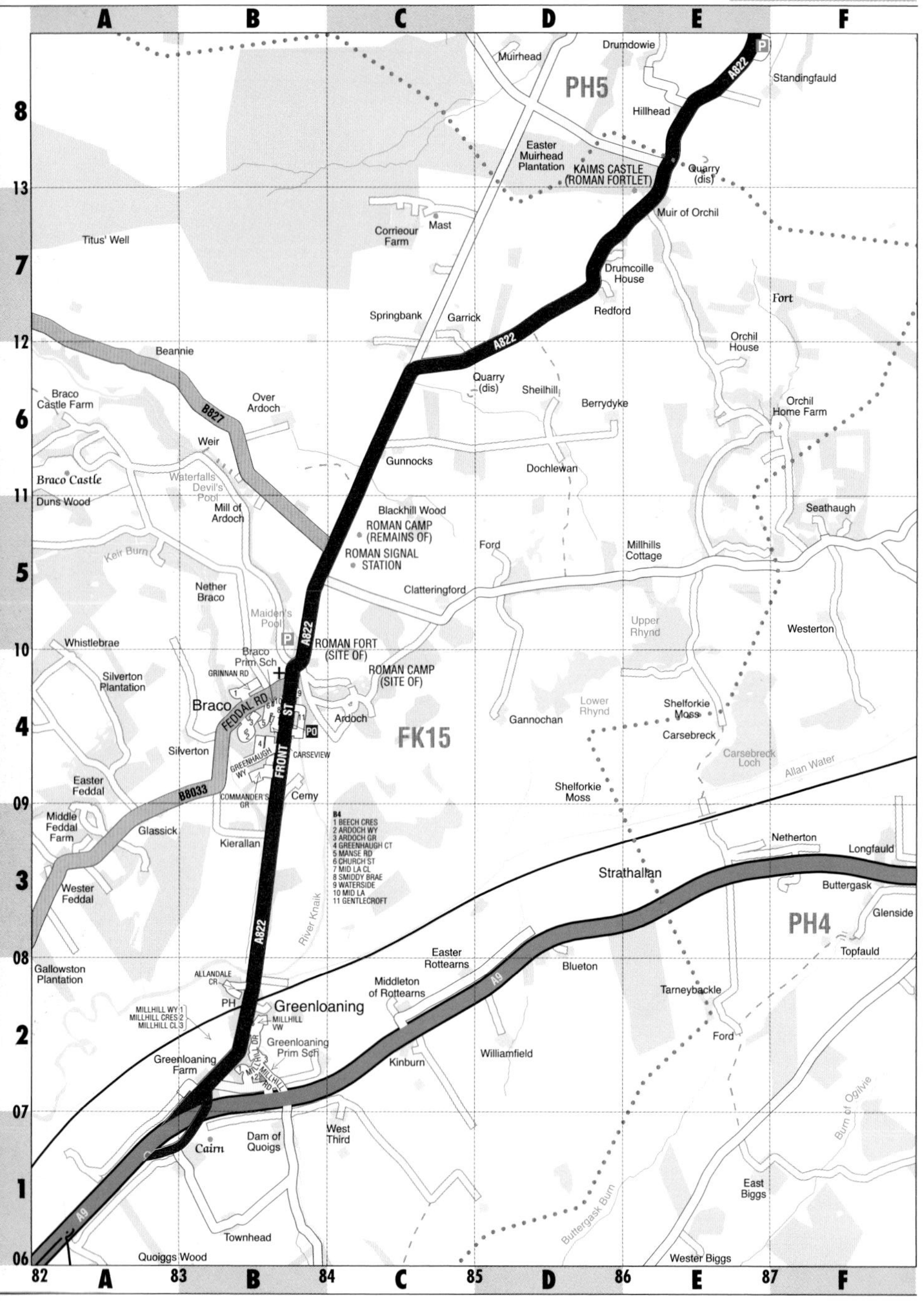

44

Scale: 1½ inches to 1 mile
0   ¼   ½   mile
0   250m 500m 750m 1 km

PH5

Drumdowie

Muirhead

Standingfauld

Hillhead

Easter
Muirhead
Plantation

KAIMS CASTLE
(ROMAN FORTLET)

Quarry
(dis)

Muir of Orchil

Titus' Well

Corrieour
Farm

Mast

Drumcoille
House

Fort

Springbank

Garrick

Redford

Orchil
House

Beannie

A822

Quarry
(dis)

Sheihill

Berrydyke

Orchil
Home Farm

Braco
Castle Farm

B827

Over
Ardoch

Weir

Gunnocks

Dochlewan

Duns Wood

Braco Castle

Waterfalls
Devil's
Pool

Mill of
Ardoch

Blackhill Wood

ROMAN CAMP
(REMAINS OF)

ROMAN SIGNAL
STATION

Ford

Millhills
Cottage

Seathaugh

Whistlebrae

Keir Burn

Nether
Braco

Maiden's
Pool

Clatteringford

Upper
Rhynd

Westerton

Silverton
Plantation

Braco
Prim Sch

GRINNAN RD

A822

Roman Fort
(SITE OF)

ROMAN CAMP
(SITE OF)

Lower
Rhynd

Shelforkie
Moss

Carsebreck

Carsebreck
Loch

Allan Water

Braco

FEDDAL RD

FRONT ST

Ardoch

Gannochan

Silverton

PO

CARSEVIEW

FK15

Easter
Feddal

B8033

GREENHAUGH
WY

COMMANDER'S
GR

Cerny

Shelforkie
Moss

Netherton

Longfauld

Middle
Feddal
Farm

Glassick

Kierallan

B4
1 BEECH CRES
2 ARDOCH WY
3 ARDOCH GR
4 GREENHAUGH CT
5 MANSE RD
6 CHURCH ST
7 MID LA CL
8 SMIDDY BRAE
9 WATERSIDE
10 MID LA
11 GENTLECROFT

Strathallan

PH4

Buttergask

Wester
Feddal

A822

Glenside

Gallowston
Plantation

ALLANDALE
CR

PH

MILLHILL WY 1
MILLHILL CRES 2
MILLHILL CL 3

MILLHILL
VW

Greenloaning

Middleton
of Rotearns

Easter
Rotearns

A9

Blueton

Topfauld

Tarneybackle

Greenloaning
Farm

Greenloaning
Prim Sch

Kinburn

Williamfield

Ford

Silverton
Plantation

River Knaik

Cairn

Dam of
Quoigs

West
Third

East
Biggs

A9

Quoiggs Wood

Townhead

Buttergask Burn

Burn of Ogilvie

Wester Biggs

71

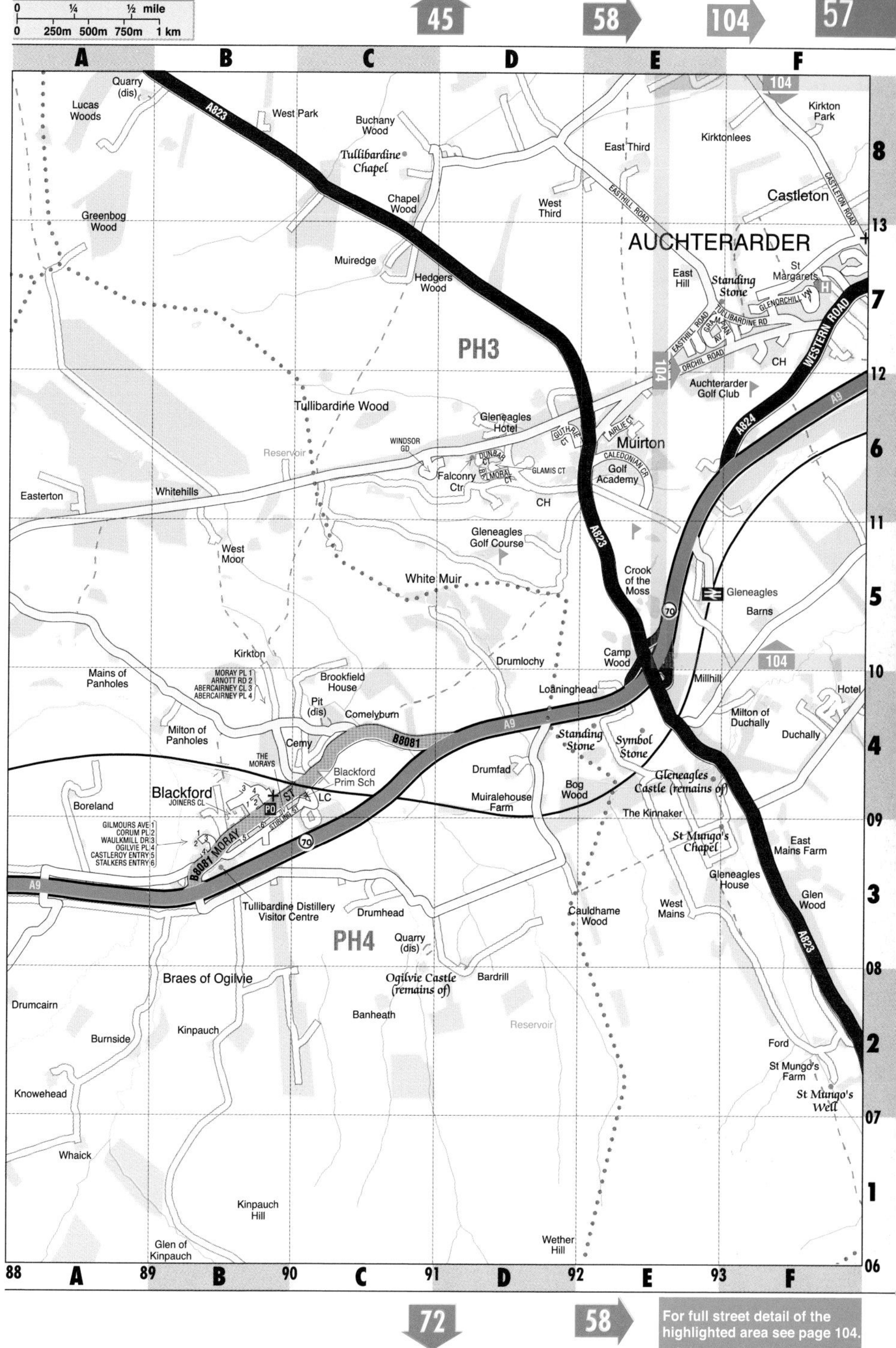

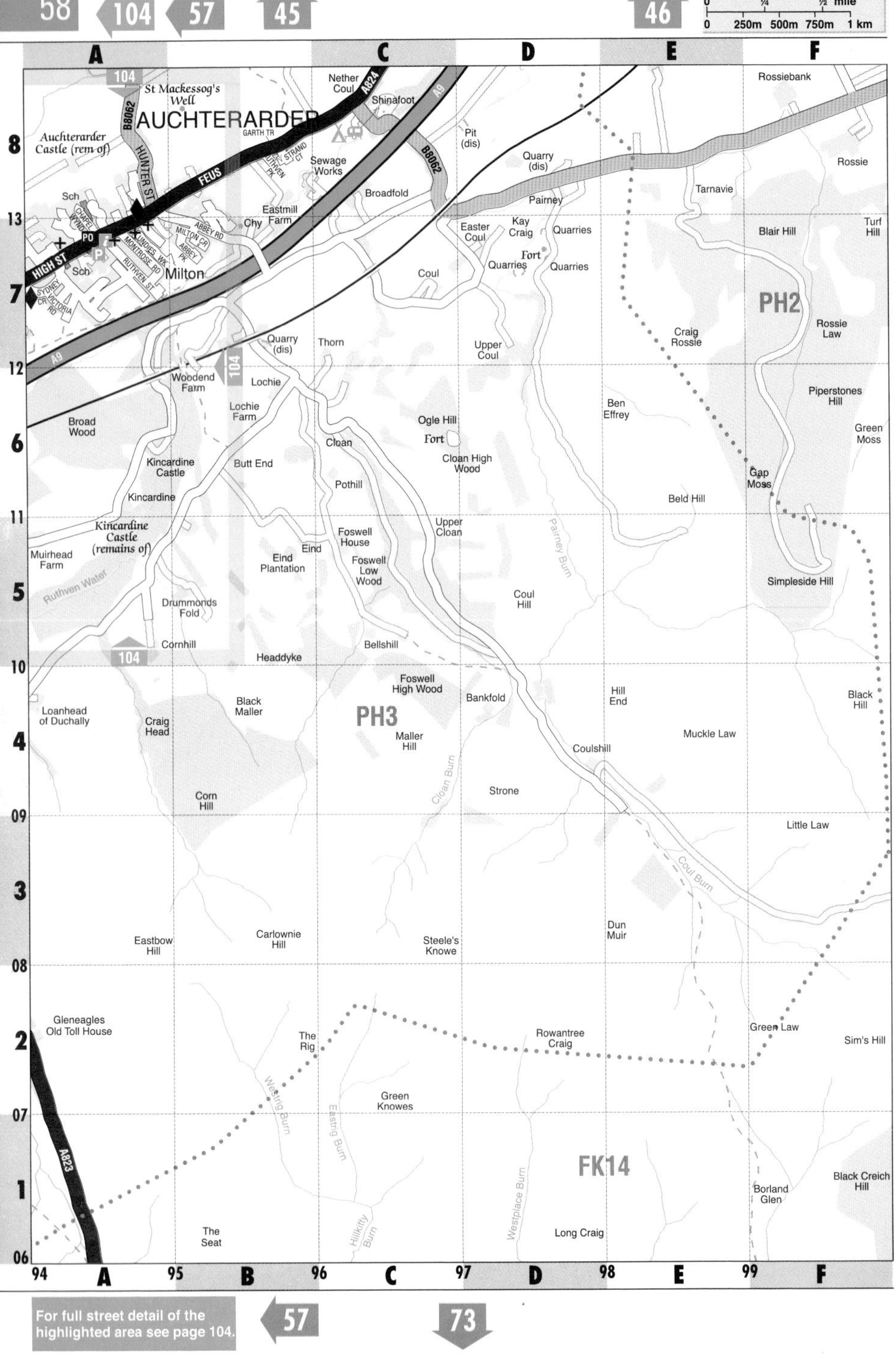

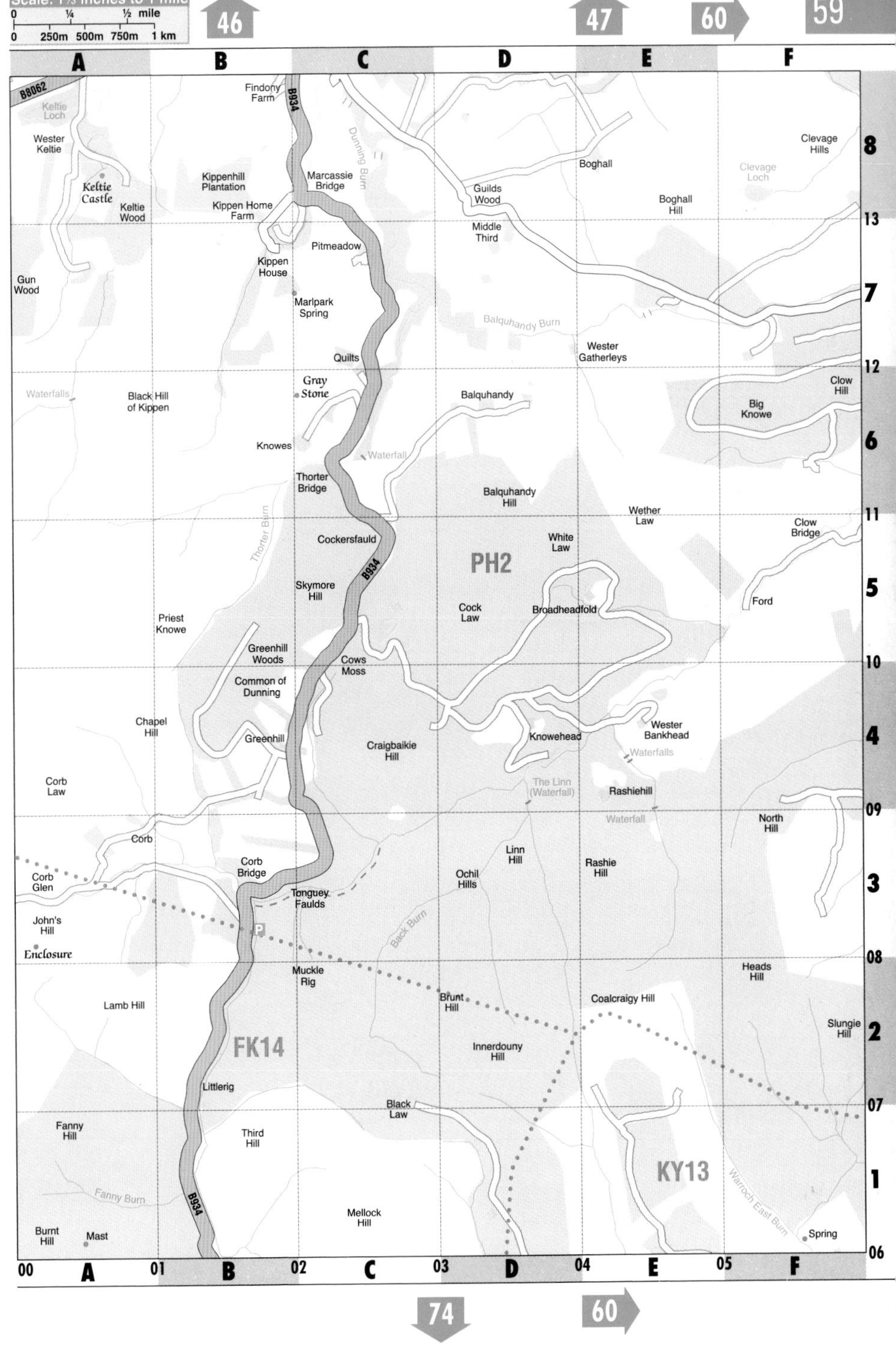
Scale: 1⅓ inches to 1 mile
0 ¼ ½ mile
0 250m 500m 750m 1 km
46
47
60
A B C D E F
B8062
Keltie Loch
Wester Keltie
Keltie Castle
Keltie Wood
Gun Wood
Findony Farm
B934
Kippenhill Plantation
Kippen Home Farm
Marcassie Bridge
Dunning Burn
Pitmeadow
Kippen House
Marlpark Spring
Quilts
Gray Stone
Waterfalls
Black Hill of Kippen
Knowes
Thorter Bridge
Thorter Burn
Cockersfauld
Skymore Hill
Priest Knowe
Greenhill Woods
Common of Dunning
Cows Moss
Chapel Hill
Greenhill
Corb Law
Corb
Corb Glen
Corb Bridge
Tonguey Faulds
John's Hill
Enclosure
Muckle Rig
Lamb Hill
FK14
Littlerig
Fanny Hill
Third Hill
Fanny Burn
Burnt Hill
Mast
Mellock Hill
Boghall
Guilds Wood
Middle Third
Clevage Hills
Clevage Loch
Boghall Hill
Balquhandy Burn
Wester Gatherleys
Balquhandy
Waterfall
Balquhandy Hill
Clow Hill
Big Knowe
Wether Law
White Law
PH2
Clow Bridge
Cock Law
Broadheadfold
Ford
Craigbaikie Hill
Knowehead
Wester Bankhead
Waterfalls
The Linn (Waterfall)
Rashiehill
Waterfall
North Hill
Linn Hill
Ochil Hills
Rashie Hill
Back Burn
Brunt Hill
Coalcraigy Hill
Heads Hill
Innerdouny Hill
Slungie Hill
Black Law
KY13
Warroch East Burn
Spring
8 13 7 12 6 11 5 10 4 09 3 08 2 07 1 06
00 01 02 03 04 05
74
60

59
47
48

Scale: 1⅓ inches to 1 mile

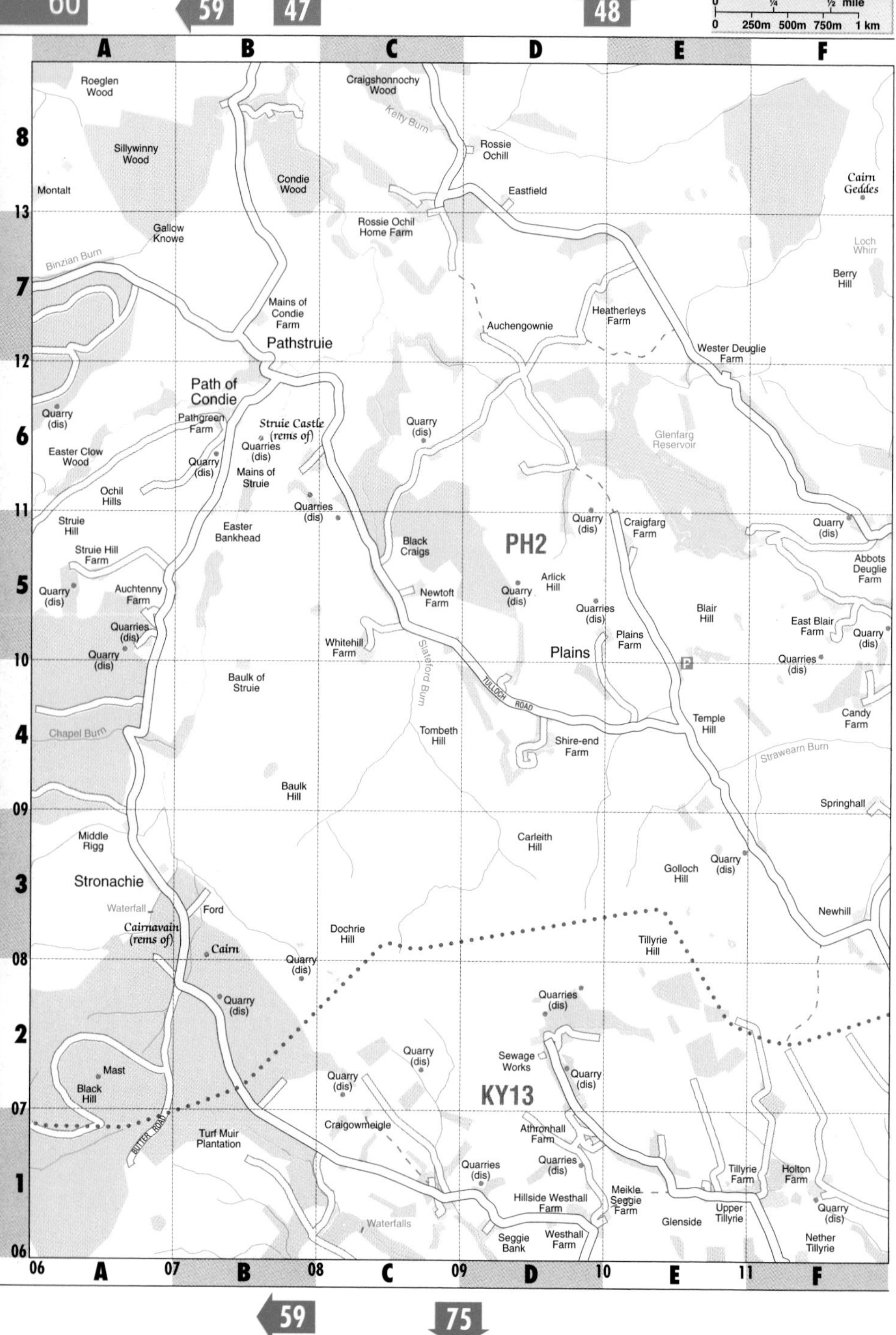
0
¼
½ mile
0
250m
500m
750m
1 km
A
B
C
D
E
F
8
7
6
5
4
3
2
1
13
12
11
10
09
08
07
06
Roeglen Wood
Sillywinny Wood
Montalt
Condie Wood
Craigshonnochy Wood
Kelty Burn
Rossie Ochill
Eastfield
Rossie Ochil Home Farm
Cairn Geddes
Loch Whirr
Berry Hill
Gallow Knowe
Binzian Burn
Mains of Condie Farm
Pathstruie
Auchengownie
Heatherleys Farm
Wester Deuglie Farm
Path of Condie
Pathgreen Farm
Struie Castle (rems of)
Quarries (dis)
Quarry (dis)
Mains of Struie
Easter Clow Wood
Ochil Hills
Glenfarg Reservoir
Struie Hill
Struie Hill Farm
Easter Bankhead
Craigfarg Farm
Black Craigs
PH2
Abbots Deuglie Farm
Auchtenny Farm
Newtoft Farm
Arlick Hill
Blair Hill
East Blair Farm
Whitehill Farm
Slateford Burn
Plains
Plains Farm
Baulk of Struie
TULLOCH ROAD
Candy Farm
Chapel Burn
Tombeth Hill
Temple Hill
Shire-end Farm
Strawearn Burn
Baulk Hill
Springhall
Middle Rigg
Carleith Hill
Golloch Hill
Stronachie
Waterfall
Ford
Newhill
Cairnavain (rems of)
Dochrie Hill
Tillyrie Hill
Cairn
Sewage Works
Mast
Black Hill
KY13
Craigowmeigle
Turf Muir Plantation
BUTTER ROAD
Athronhall Farm
Tillyrie Farm
Holton Farm
Hillside Westhall Farm
Meikle Seggie Farm
Glenside
Upper Tillyrie
Waterfalls
Seggie Bank
Westhall Farm
Nether Tillyrie
06
07
08
09
10
11

59
75

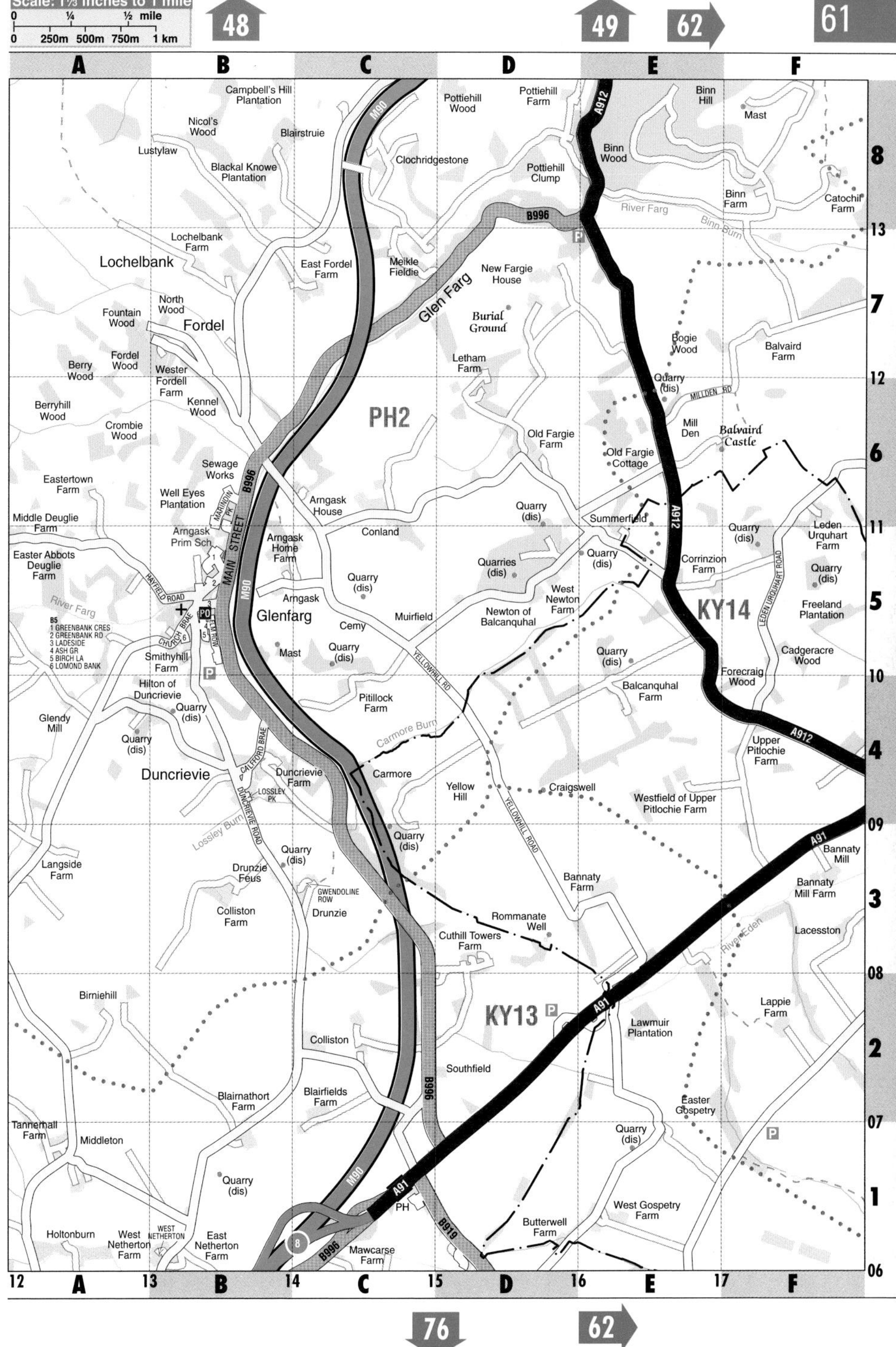
Scale: 1⅓ inches to 1 mile
0 ¼ ½ mile
0 250m 500m 750m 1 km
48
49
62
A
B
C
D
E
F
Campbell's Hill Plantation
Nicol's Wood
Lustylaw
Blairstruie
Blackal Knowe Plantation
Pottiehill Wood
Pottiehill Farm
Clochridgestone
Binn Hill
Mast
Binn Wood
Pottiehill Clump
Binn Farm
Catochil Farm
River Farg
Binn Burn
B996
Lochelbank Farm
Lochelbank
East Fordel Farm
Meikle Fieldie
New Fargie House
North Wood
Fountain Wood
Fordel
Glen Farg
Burial Ground
Bogie Wood
Balvaird Farm
Fordel Wood
Berry Wood
Wester Fordell Farm
Letham Farm
Quarry (dis)
MILLDEN RD
Kennel Wood
Berryhill Wood
Crombie Wood
PH2
Mill Den
Balvaird Castle
Old Fargie Farm
Old Fargie Cottage
Sewage Works
Eastertown Farm
Well Eyes Plantation
MAIN STREET
MAWHINDIN PK
Arngask House
Quarry (dis)
Summerfield
Middle Deuglie Farm
Arngask Prim Sch
Conland
Leden Urquhart Farm
Arngask Home Farm
Quarries (dis)
Easter Abbots Deuglie Farm
Corrinzion Farm
LEDEN URQUHART ROAD
HAYFIELD ROAD
Arngask
West Newton Farm
River Farg
Glenfarg
Muirfield
Newton of Balcanqulal
KY14
Freeland Plantation
B5
1 GREENBANK CRES
2 GREENBANK RD
3 LADESIDE
4 ASH GR
5 BIRCH LA
6 LOMOND BANK
PO
CHURCH BRAE
ELM ROW
Cemy
Mast
Cadgeracre Wood
Smithyhill Farm
YELLOWHILL RD
Forecraig Wood
Hilton of Duncrievie
Balcanqulal Farm
Pitillock Farm
Glendy Mill
Carmore Burn
A912
Upper Pitlochie Farm
CALFFORD BRAE
Duncrievie
Duncrievie Farm
Carmore
Yellow Hill
Craigswell
LOSSLEY PK
Westfield of Upper Pitlochie Farm
YELLOWHILL ROAD
DUNCRIEVIE ROAD
Lossley Burn
A91
Bannaty Mill
Langside Farm
Drunzie Feus
Bannaty Farm
Bannaty Mill Farm
GWENDOLINE ROW
Colliston Farm
Drunzie
Rommanate Well
Lacesston
Cuthill Towers Farm
River Eden
Birniehill
KY13
Lawmuir Plantation
Lappie Farm
Colliston
Southfield
Blairnathort Farm
Blairfields Farm
B996
Easter Gospetry
Tannerhall Farm
Middleton
M90
West Gospetry Farm
Butterwell Farm
PH
B919
Holtonburn
West Netherton Farm
WEST NETHERTON
East Netherton Farm
Mawcarse Farm
8
13
12
11
10
09
08
07
06
7
6
5
4
3
2
1
14
15
16
17
76
62

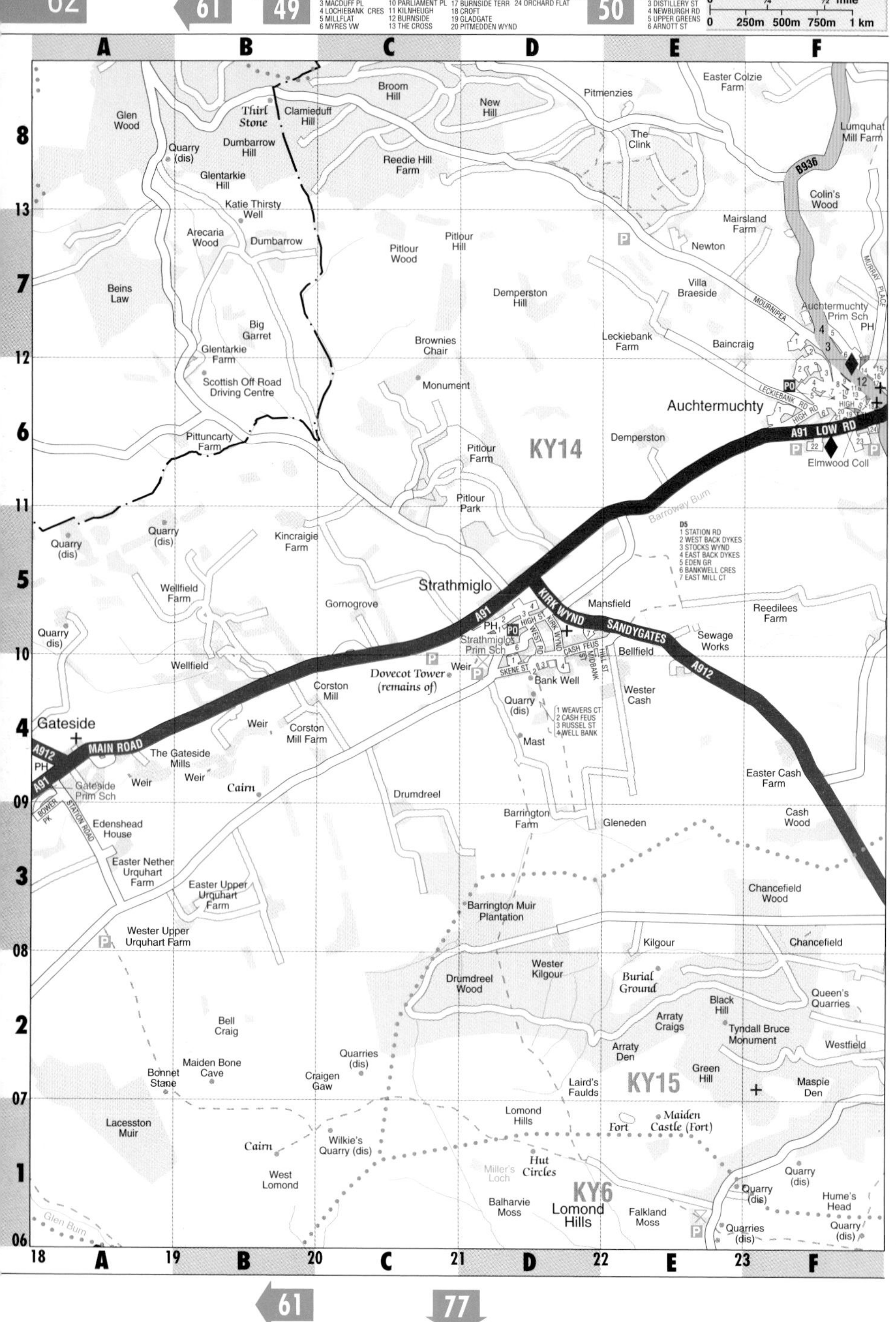

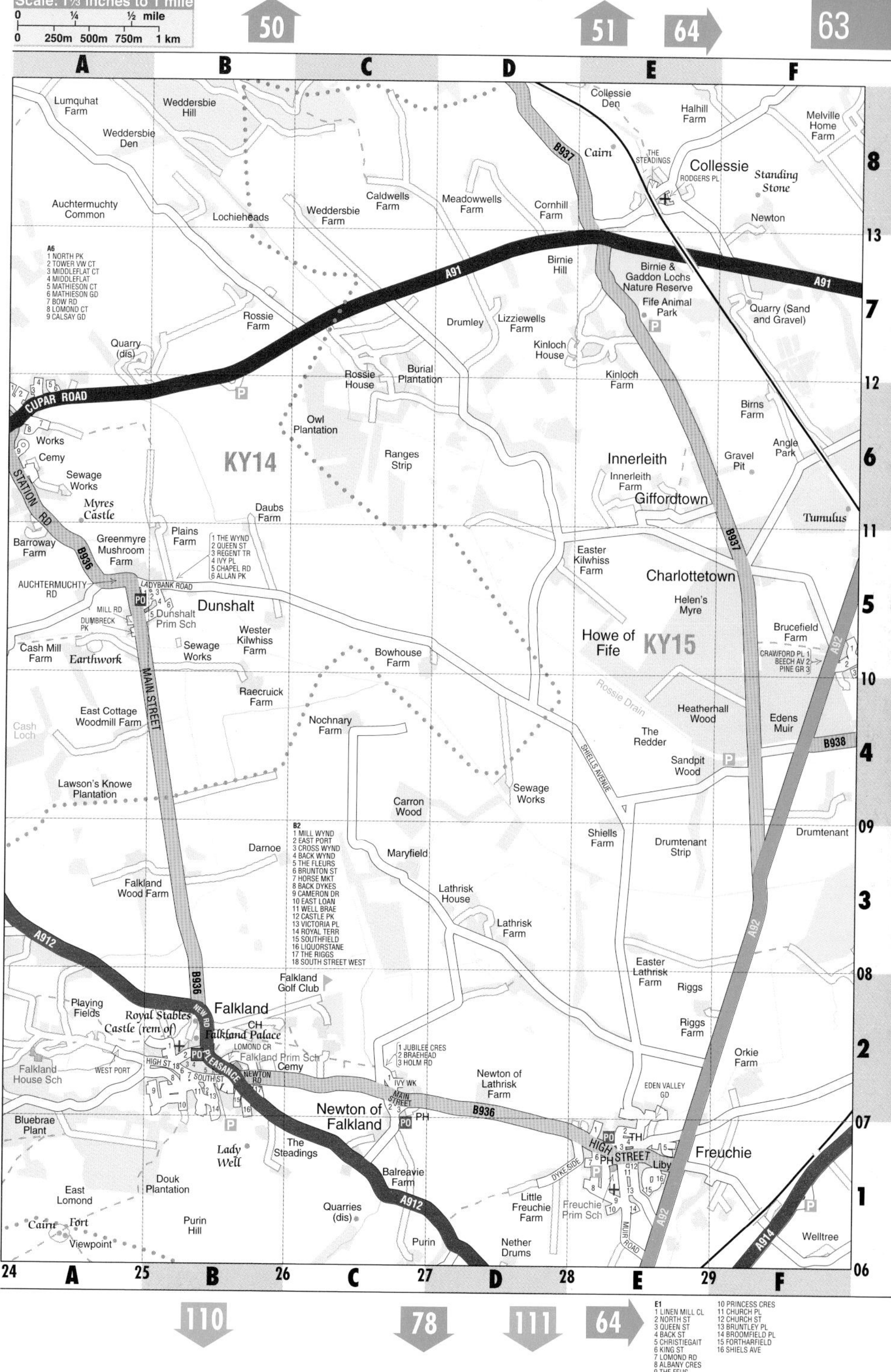

Scale: 1⅓ inches to 1 mile
0 ¼ ½ mile
0 250m 500m 750m 1 km
50
51
64
A B C D E F
Lumquhat Farm
Weddersbie Hill
Weddersbie Den
Collessie Den
Halhill Farm
Melville Home Farm
B937
Cairn
THE STEADINGS
Collessie
RODGERS PL
Standing Stone
8
Auchtermuchty Common
Lochieheads
Weddersbie Farm
Caldwells Farm
Meadowwells Farm
Cornhill Farm
Newton
13
A6
1 NORTH PK
2 TOWER VW CT
3 MIDDLEFLAT CT
4 MIDDLEFLAT
5 MATHIESON CT
6 MATHIESON GD
7 BOW RD
8 LOMOND CT
9 CALSAY GD
A91
Birnie Hill
Birnie & Gaddon Lochs Nature Reserve
Fife Animal Park
Quarry (Sand and Gravel)
7
Rossie Farm
Drumley
Lizziewells Farm
Kinloch House
Quarry (dis)
Rossie House
Burial Plantation
Kinloch Farm
CUPAR ROAD
12
Owl Plantation
Birns Farm
Works
Cemy
KY14
Ranges Strip
Angle Park
Innerleith
Innerleith Farm
Gravel Pit
6
Sewage Works
Giffordtown
STATION RD
Myres Castle
Daubs Farm
Tumulus
Barroway Farm
Greenmyre Mushroom Farm
Plains Farm
1 THE WYND
2 QUEEN ST
3 REGENT TR
4 IVY PL
5 CHAPEL RD
6 ALLAN PK
Easter Kilwhiss Farm
Charlottetown
11
B936
AUCHTERMUCHTY RD
LADYBANK ROAD
Dunshalt
Helen's Myre
5
MILL RD
DUMBRECK PK
Dunshalt Prim Sch
Wester Kilwhiss Farm
Howe of Fife
KY15
Brucefield Farm
Cash Mill Farm
Earthwork
Sewage Works
Bowhouse Farm
CRAWFORD PL 1
BEECH AV 2
PINE GR 3
A92
10
Raecruick Farm
Rossie Drain
Heatherhall Wood
East Cottage Woodmill Farm
Cash Loch
MAIN STREET
Nochnary Farm
The Redder
Edens Muir
B938
Sandpit Wood
4
Lawson's Knowe Plantation
SHIELLS AVENUE
Sewage Works
Carron Wood
Shiells Farm
Drumtenant Strip
Drumtenant
09
Darnoe
B2
1 MILL WYND
2 EAST PORT
3 CROSS WYND
4 BACK WYND
5 THE FLEURS
6 BRUNTON ST
7 HORSE MKT
8 BACK DYKES
9 CAMERON DR
10 EAST LOAN
11 WELL BRAE
12 CASTLE PK
13 VICTORIA PL
14 ROYAL TERR
15 SOUTHFIELD
16 LIQUORSTANE
17 THE RIGGS
18 SOUTH STREET WEST
Maryfield
Falkland Wood Farm
Lathrisk House
3
A912
Lathrisk Farm
Easter Lathrisk Farm
Riggs
08
Falkland Golf Club
Playing Fields
Falkland
Royal Stables
NEW RD
Castle (rem of)
CH
Falkland Palace
Riggs Farm
LOMOND CR
Orkie Farm
2
Falkland House Sch
WEST PORT
HIGH ST
PLEASANCE
Falkland Prim Sch
Cemy
1 JUBILEE CRES
2 BRAEHEAD
3 HOLM RD
SOUTH ST
NEWTON RD
IVY WK
Newton of Lathrisk Farm
EDEN VALLEY GD
MAIN STREET
Newton of Falkland
PH
B936
Bluebrae Plant
07
TH
HIGH STREET
Freuchie
The Steadings
Lady Well
PH
Liby
Balreavie Farm
DYKESIDE
East Lomond
Douk Plantation
Little Freuchie Farm
Freuchie Prim Sch
1
Quarries (dis)
Cairn
Fort
Purin Hill
MUIR ROAD
Viewpoint
Purin
Nether Drums
A914
Welltree
24 A 25 B 26 C 27 D 28 E 29 F 06
110
78
111
64
E1
1 LINEN MILL CL
2 NORTH ST
3 QUEEN ST
4 BACK ST
5 CHRISTIEGAIT
6 KING ST
7 LOMOND RD
8 ALBANY CRES
9 THE FEUS
10 PRINCESS CRES
11 CHURCH PL
12 CHURCH ST
13 BRUNTLEY PL
14 BROOMFIELD PL
15 FORTHARFIELD
16 SHIELS AVE

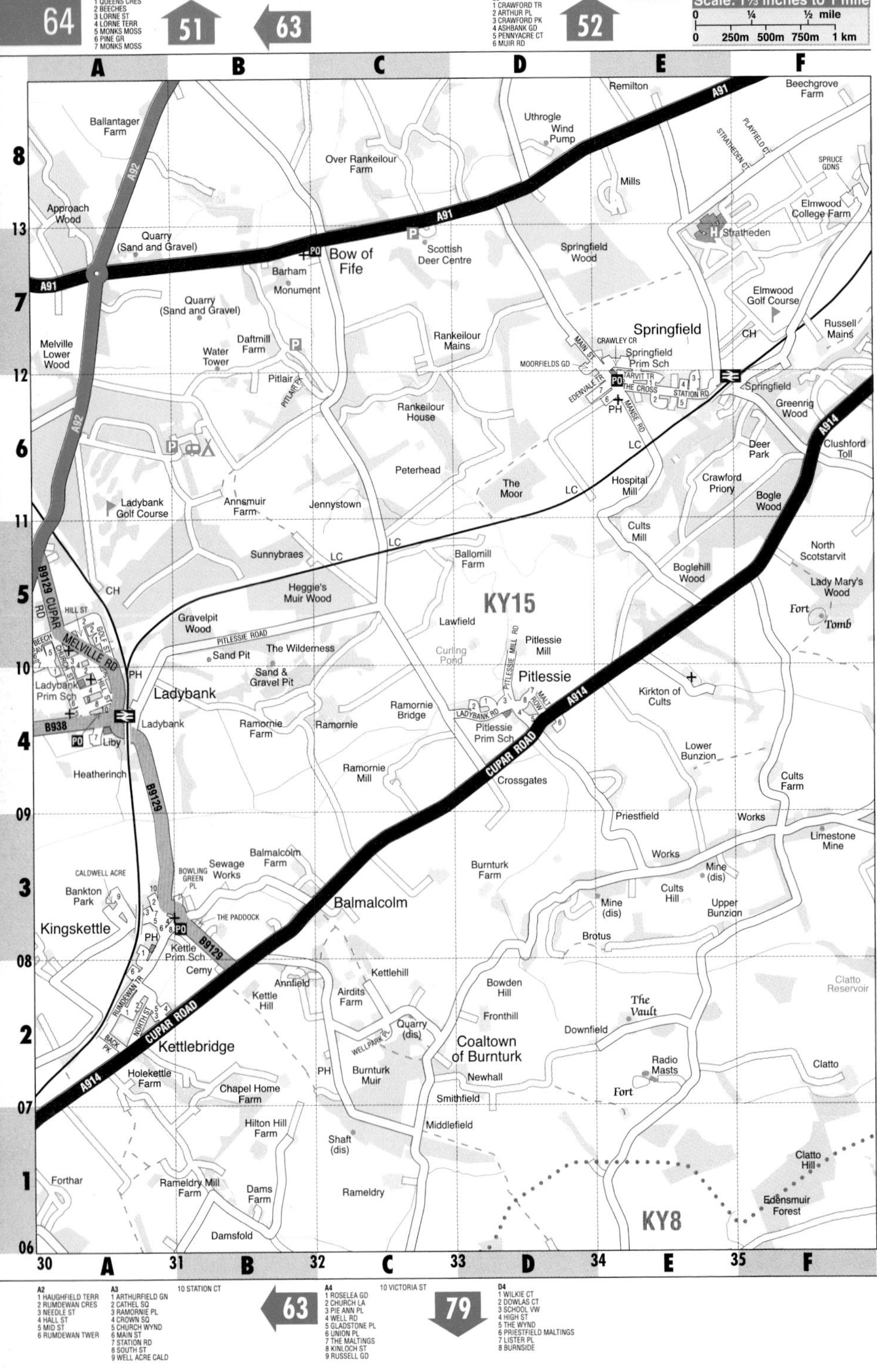
Ballantager Farm
Approach Wood
Quarry (Sand and Gravel)
Over Rankeilour Farm
Uthrogle Wind Pump
Remilton
Beechgrove Farm
Mills
Bow of Fife
Barham
Monument
Scottish Deer Centre
Springfield Wood
Stratheden
Elmwood College Farm
Melville Lower Wood
Water Tower
Daftmill Farm
Pitlair
Rankeilour Mains
Springfield
Springfield Prim Sch
Elmwood Golf Course
Russell Mains
Rankeilour House
Greenrig Wood
Peterhead
The Moor
Hospital Mill
Deer Park
Crawford Priory
Clushford Toll
Ladybank Golf Course
Annsmuir Farm
Jennystown
Bogle Wood
Cults Mill
Sunnybraes
Heggie's Muir Wood
Ballomill Farm
Boglehill Wood
North Scotstarvit
Lady Mary's Wood
KY15
Gravelpit Wood
Lawfield
Fort
Tomb
Sand Pit
The Wilderness
Curling Pond
Pitlessie Mill
Pitlessie
Sand & Gravel Pit
Ladybank
Ladybank Prim Sch
Ramornie Bridge
Pitlessie Prim Sch
Kirkton of Cults
Ramornie Farm
Ramornie
Lower Bunzion
Heatherinch
Ramornie Mill
Crossgates
Cults Farm
Priestfield
Works
Limestone Mine
Balmalcolm Farm
Sewage Works
Burnturk Farm
Mine (dis)
Bankton Park
Balmalcolm
Cults Hill
Upper Bunzion
Kingskettle
Kettle Prim Sch
Brotus
Cemy
Kettlehill
Bowden Hill
Clatto Reservoir
Annfield
Airdits Farm
Kettle Hill
Fronthill
The Vault
Quarry (dis)
Downfield
Kettlebridge
Coaltown of Burnturk
Radio Masts
Clatto
Holekettle Farm
Burnturk Muir
Newhall
Chapel Home Farm
Smithfield
Hilton Hill Farm
Middlefield
Shaft (dis)
Clatto Hill
Forthar
Rameldry Mill Farm
Dams Farm
Rameldry
Edensmuir Forest
KY8
Damsfold
A91
A92
A914
B9129
B938
CUPAR ROAD
PITLESSIE ROAD
MELVILLE RD
STATION RD
MANSE RD
THE CROSS
MAIN ST
THE PADDOCK
CALDWELL ACRE
BOWLING GREEN PL
LADYBANK RD
PITLESSIE MILL RD
RUMDEWAN TR
NORTH ST
BACK PK
WELLPARK PL
STRATHEDEN CT
PLAYFIELD CT
SPRUCE GDNS
CRAWLEY CR
MOORFIELDS GD
EDENVALE TR
TARVIT TR
HILL ST
GOLF ST
CHURCH ST
PH
PO
LC
CH

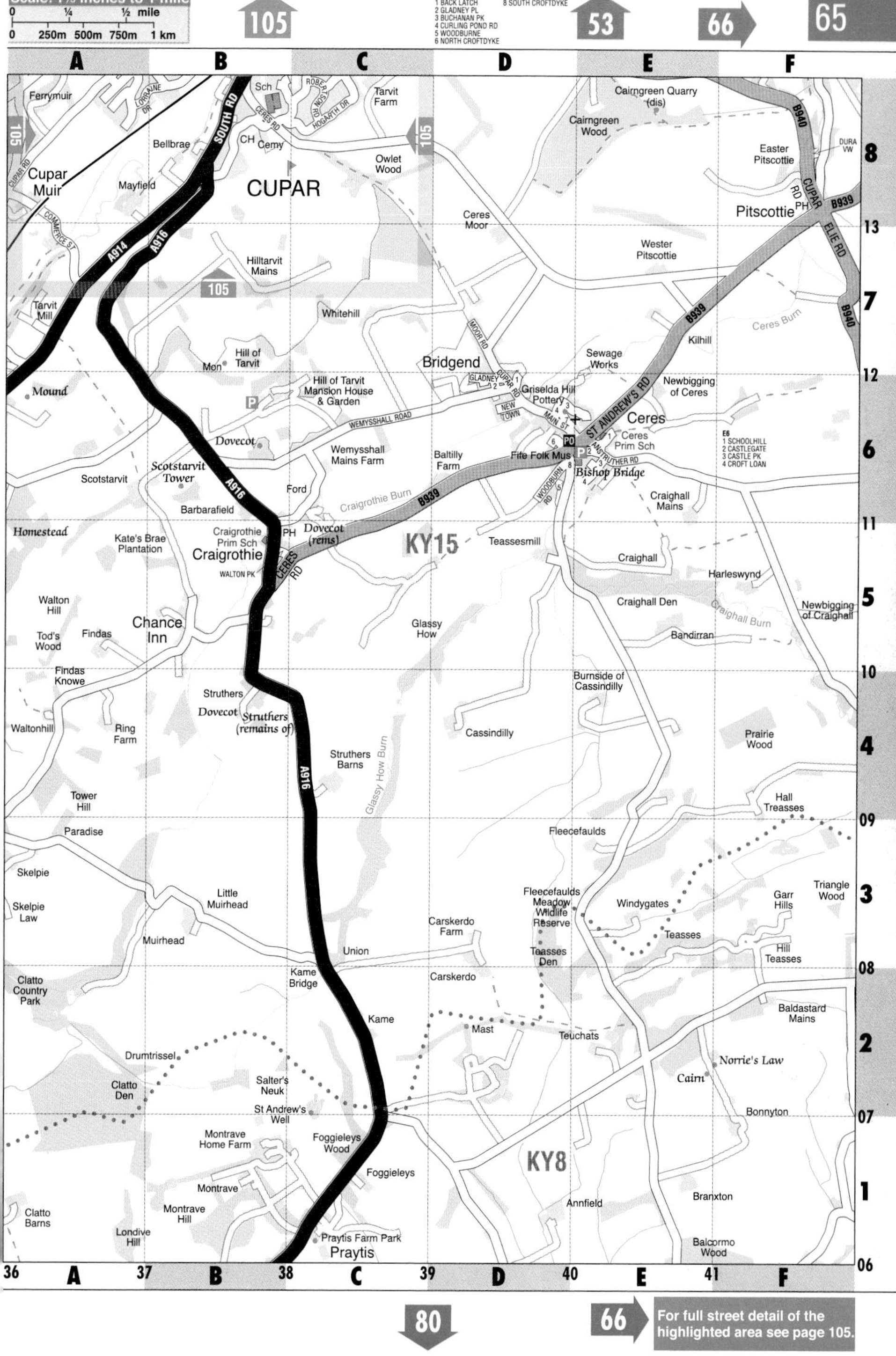

53 65 54

Scale: 1⅓ inches to 1 mile

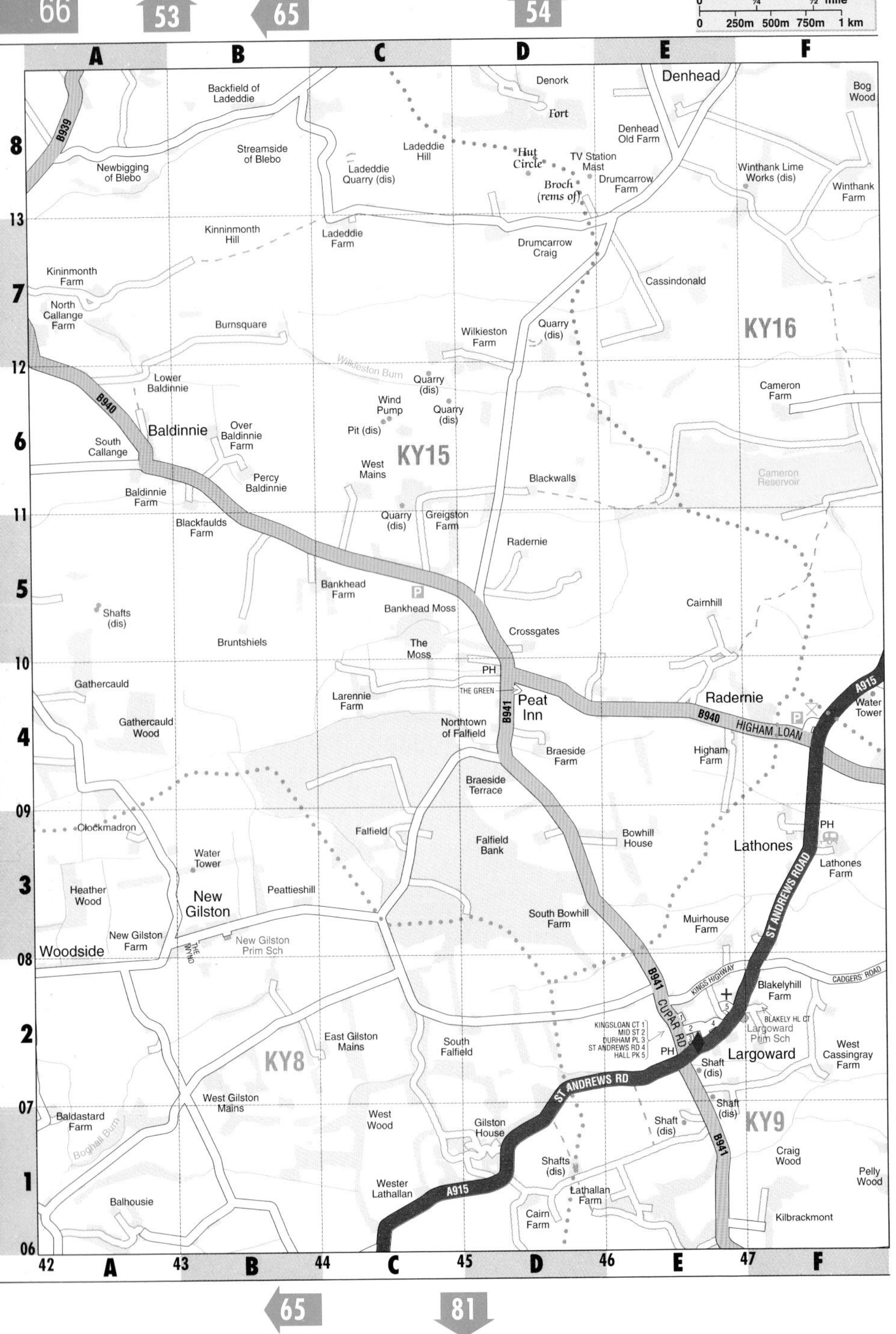

A
B
C
D
E
F
8
13
7
12
6
11
5
10
4
09
3
08
2
07
1
06
42
43
44
45
46
47
B939
Backfield of Ladeddie
Newbigging of Blebo
Streamside of Blebo
Ladeddie Quarry (dis)
Ladeddie Hill
Denork
Fort
Hut Circle
Broch (rems of)
TV Station Mast
Denhead
Denhead Old Farm
Drumcarrow Farm
Bog Wood
Winthank Lime Works (dis)
Winthank Farm
Kinninmonth Hill
Ladeddie Farm
Drumcarrow Craig
Kininmonth Farm
North Callange Farm
Cassindonald
Burnsquare
Wilkieston Farm
Quarry (dis)
KY16
Wilkieston Burn
Lower Baldinnie
B940
Quarry (dis)
Wind Pump
Quarry (dis)
Cameron Farm
Baldinnie
Over Baldinnie Farm
Pit (dis)
South Callange
KY15
West Mains
Percy Baldinnie
Blackwalls
Cameron Reservoir
Baldinnie Farm
Blackfaulds Farm
Quarry (dis)
Greigston Farm
Radernie
Bankhead Farm
Bankhead Moss
Shafts (dis)
Cairnhill
Bruntshiels
Crossgates
The Moss
Gathercauld
PH
THE GREEN
Larennie Farm
Peat Inn
Radernie
A915
Water Tower
B941
B940
HIGHAM LOAN
Gathercauld Wood
Northtown of Falfield
Braeside Farm
Higham Farm
Braeside Terrace
Clockmadron
Falfield
Falfield Bank
Bowhill House
PH
Lathones
Water Tower
Lathones Farm
ST ANDREWS ROAD
Heather Wood
New Gilston
Peattieshill
South Bowhill Farm
Muirhouse Farm
New Gilston Farm
Woodside
THE WYND
New Gilston Prim Sch
B941
CUPAR RD
KINGS HIGHWAY
CADGERS' ROAD
Blakelyhill Farm
BLAKELY HL CT
Largoward Prim Sch
KINGSLOAN CT 1
MID ST 2
DURHAM PL 3
ST ANDREWS RD 4
HALL PK 5
East Gilston Mains
South Falfield
PH
Largoward
West Cassingray Farm
KY8
Shaft (dis)
ST ANDREWS RD
West Gilston Mains
Shaft (dis)
Baldastard Farm
West Wood
Gilston House
Shaft (dis)
KY9
Boghall Burn
B941
Craig Wood
Shafts (dis)
Pelly Wood
Wester Lathallan
A915
Lathallan Farm
Balhousie
Cairn Farm
Kilbrackmont

65 81

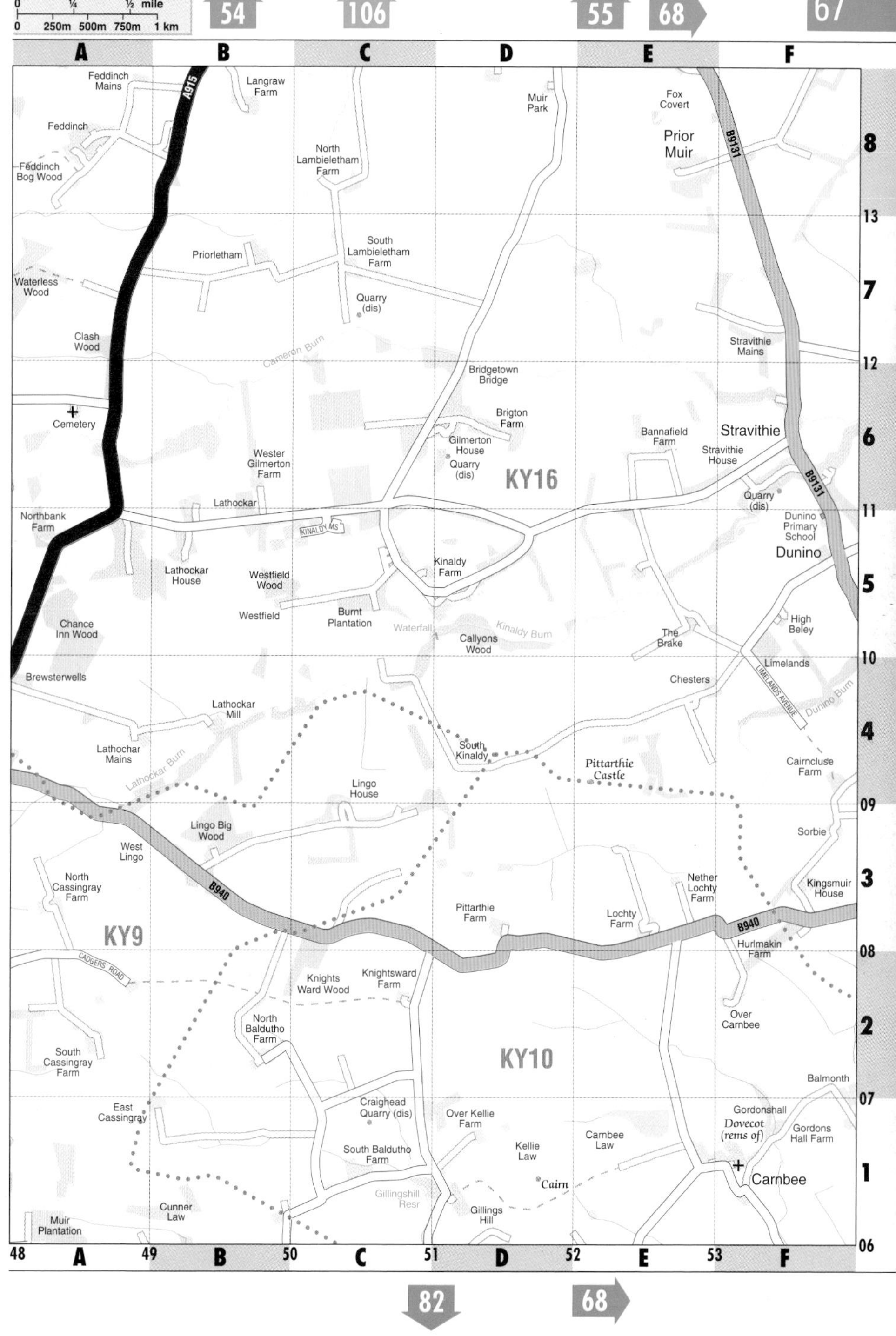

Scale: 1⅓ inches to 1 mile
0 ¼ ½ mile
0 250m 500m 750m 1 km
54
106
55
68
A B C D E F
8
13
7
12
6
11
5
10
4
09
3
08
2
07
1
06
48 49 50 51 52 53
Feddinch Mains
Langraw Farm
Muir Park
Fox Covert
Prior Muir
Feddinch
Feddinch Bog Wood
North Lambieletham Farm
A915
B9131
Priorletham
South Lambieletham Farm
Waterless Wood
Quarry (dis)
Clash Wood
Cameron Burn
Stravithie Mains
Bridgetown Bridge
Cemetery
Brigton Farm
Gilmerton House
Quarry (dis)
Bannafield Farm
Stravithie
Stravithie House
Wester Gilmerton Farm
KY16
Lathockar
Quarry (dis)
Northbank Farm
KINALDY MS
Dunino Primary School
Dunino
Lathockar House
Westfield Wood
Kinaldy Farm
Westfield
Burnt Plantation
Chance Inn Wood
Waterfall
Kinaldy Burn
Callyons Wood
The Brake
High Beley
Limelands
Brewsterwells
Chesters
LIMELANDS AVENUE
Dunino Burn
Lathockar Mill
South Kinaldy
Lathochar Mains
Lathockar Burn
Pittarthie Castle
Cairncluse Farm
Lingo House
Lingo Big Wood
Sorbie
West Lingo
North Cassingray Farm
B940
Nether Lochty Farm
Kingsmuir House
Pittarthie Farm
Lochty Farm
KY9
Hurlmakin Farm
CADGERS ROAD
Knights Ward Wood
Knightsward Farm
North Baldutho Farm
Over Carnbee
KY10
South Cassingray Farm
Balmonth
Craighead Quarry (dis)
Gordonshall
East Cassingray
Over Kellie Farm
Dovecot (rems of)
Gordons Hall Farm
Carnbee Law
Kellie Law
South Baldutho Farm
Cairn
Carnbee
Gillingshill Resr
Cunner Law
Gillings Hill
Muir Plantation
82
68

55
67

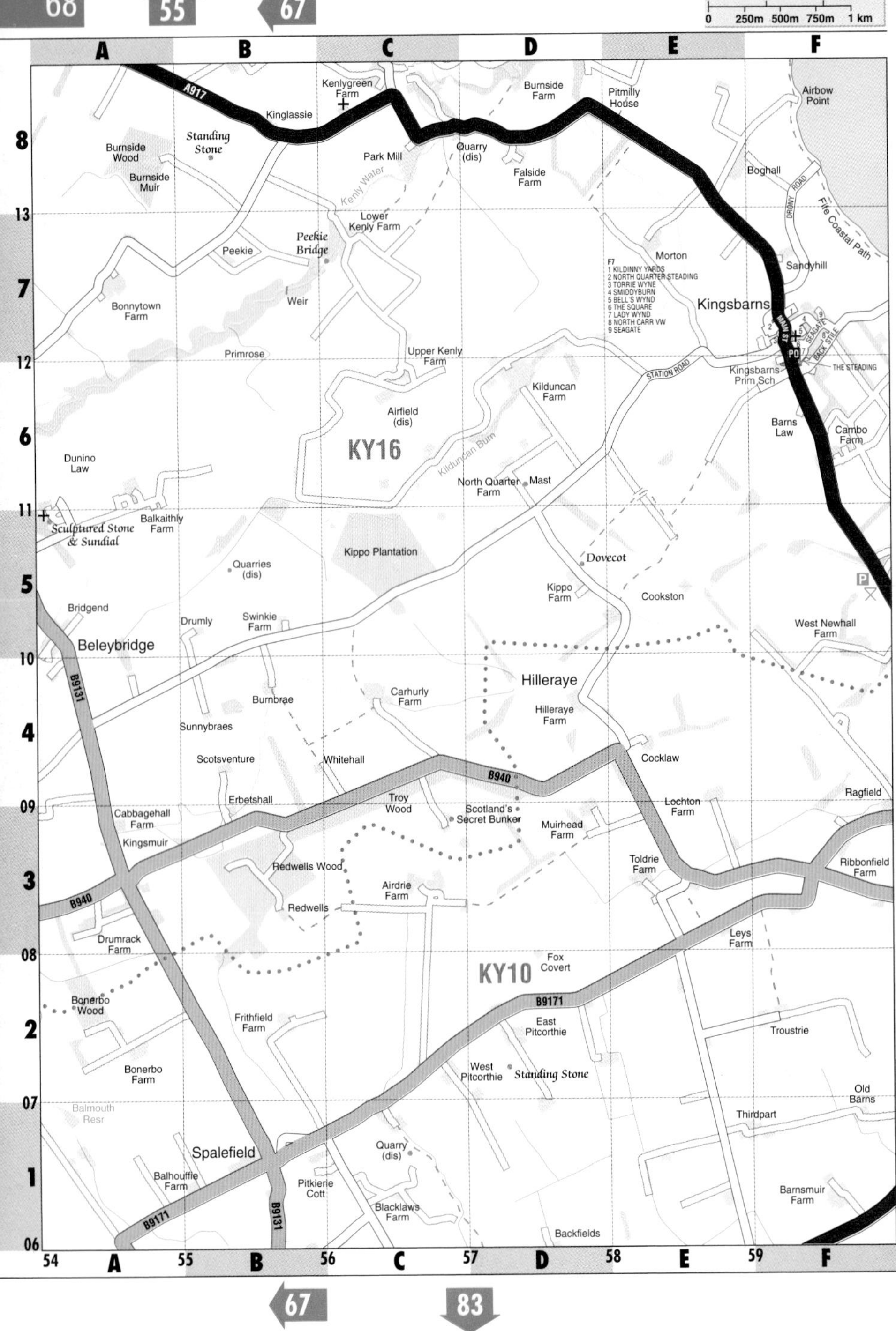
Scale: 1⅓ inches to 1 mile
0 ¼ ½ mile
0 250m 500m 750m 1 km
A B C D E F
8 13 7 12 6 11 5 10 4 09 3 08 2 07 1 06
54 55 56 57 58 59
A917
Kinglassie
Kenlygreen Farm
Burnside Farm
Pitmilly House
Airbow Point
Standing Stone
Burnside Wood
Burnside Muir
Park Mill
Quarry (dis)
Falside Farm
Boghall
ORONY ROAD
Fife Coastal Path
Kenly Water
Lower Kenly Farm
Peekie
Peekie Bridge
Morton
Sandyhill
Weir
Bonnytown Farm
F7
1 KILDINNY YARDS
2 NORTH QUARTER STEADING
3 TORRIE WYNE
4 SMIDDYBURN
5 BELL'S WYND
6 THE SQUARE
7 LADY WYND
8 NORTH CARR VW
9 SEAGATE
Kingsbarns
MAIN ST
SEAGATE
BACK STILE
PO
THE STEADING
Primrose
Upper Kenly Farm
STATION ROAD
Kingsbarns Prim Sch
Kilduncan Farm
Airfield (dis)
KY16
Kilduncan Burn
Barns Law
Cambo Farm
Dunino Law
North Quarter Farm
Mast
Sculptured Stone & Sundial
Balkaithly Farm
Kippo Plantation
Quarries (dis)
Dovecot
Kippo Farm
Cookston
Bridgend
Drumly
Swinkie Farm
Beleybridge
West Newhall Farm
B9131
Hilleraye
Burnbrae
Carhurly Farm
Hilleraye Farm
Sunnybraes
Scotsventure
Whitehall
Cocklaw
B940
Erbetshall
Troy Wood
Scotland's Secret Bunker
Lochton Farm
Ragfield
Cabbagehall Farm
Muirhead Farm
Kingsmuir
Toldrie Farm
Ribbonfield Farm
Redwells Wood
Airdrie Farm
Redwells
Drumrack Farm
Leys Farm
Fox Covert
KY10
B9171
Bonerbo Wood
Frithfield Farm
East Pitcorthie
Troustrie
West Pitcorthie
Standing Stone
Bonerbo Farm
Old Barns
Balmouth Resr
Thirdpart
Quarry (dis)
Spalefield
Balhouffie Farm
Pitkierie Cott
Barnsmuir Farm
Blacklaws Farm
Backfields

67
83

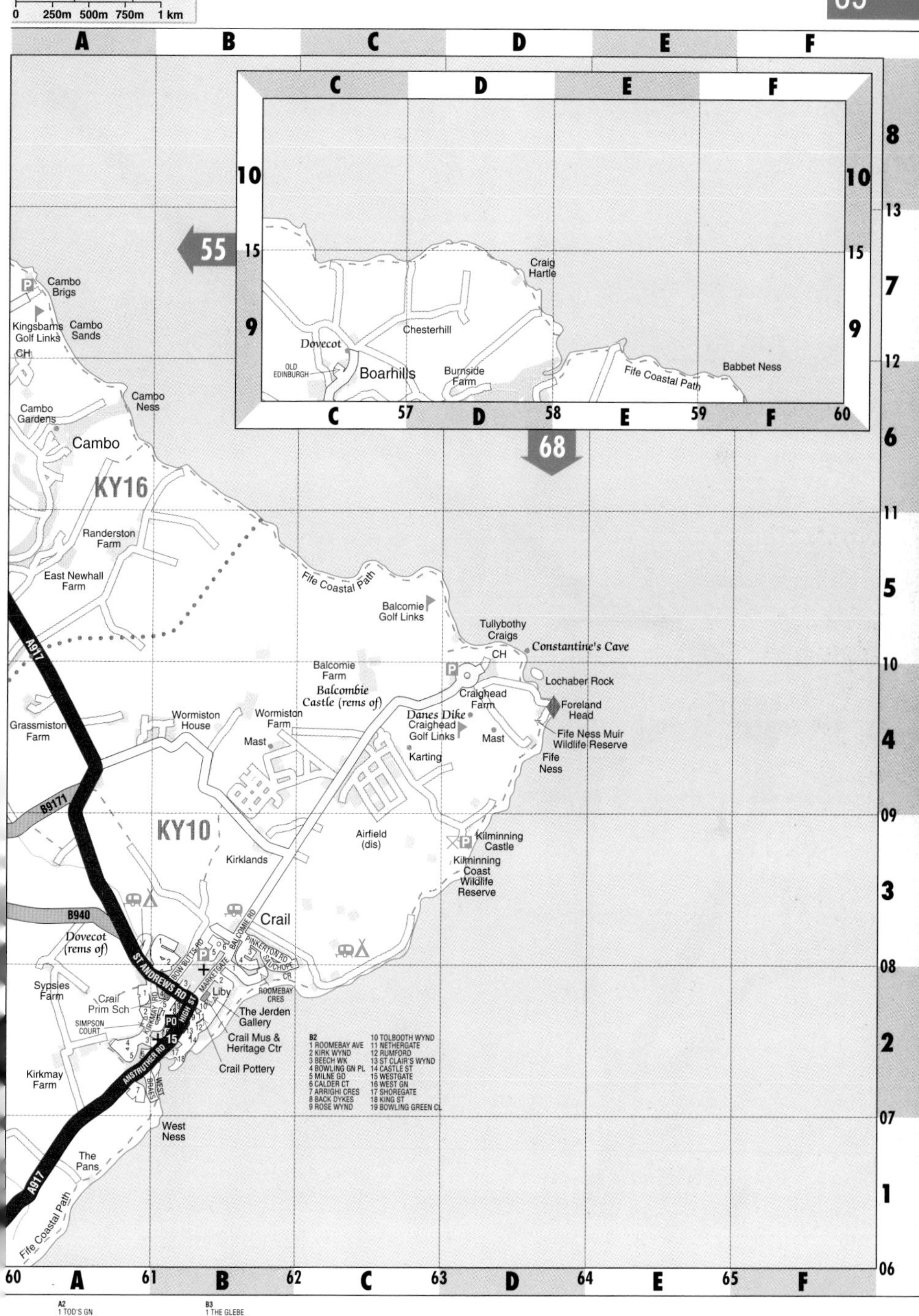

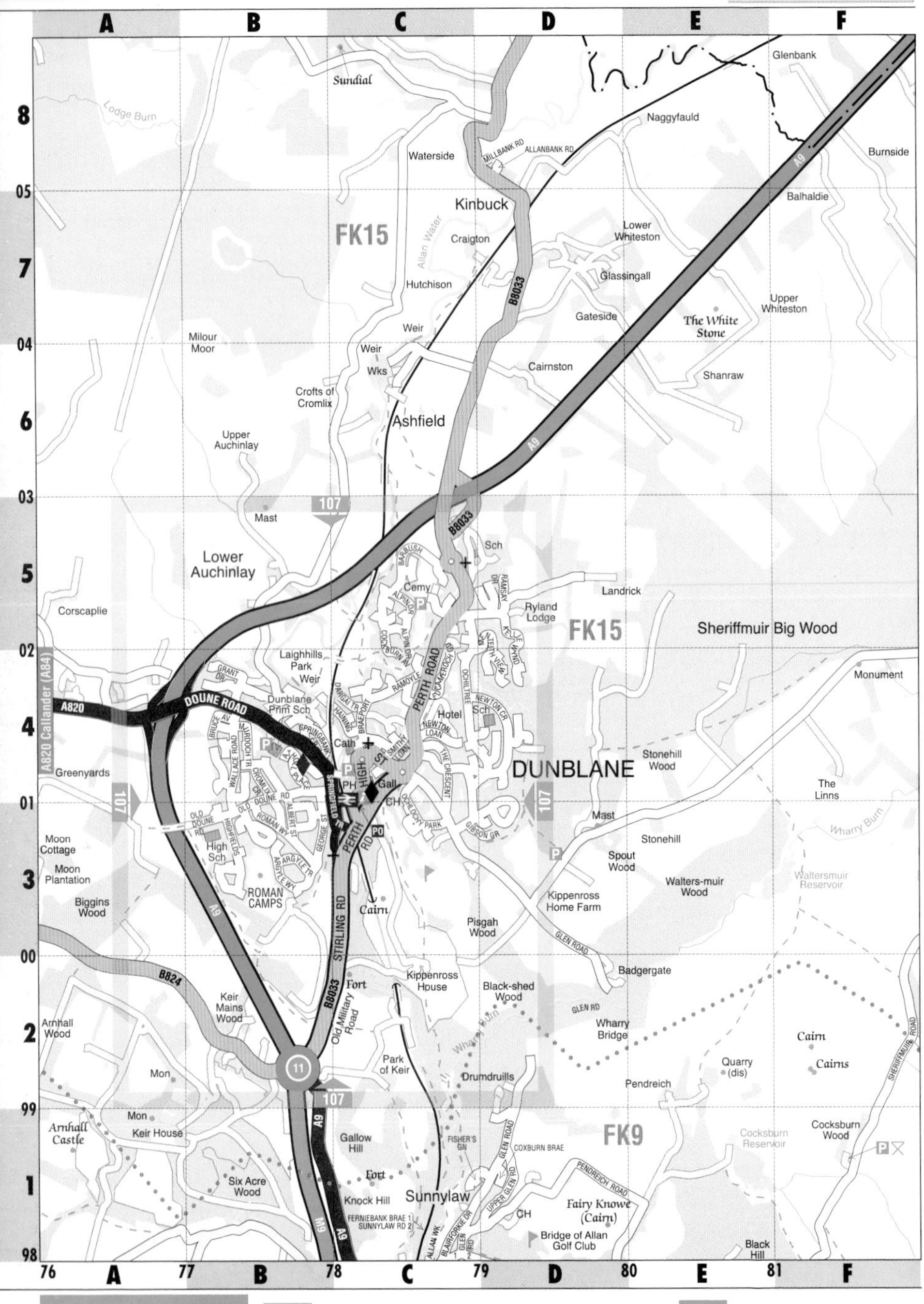

A   B   C   D   E   F

8

Sundial

Glenbank

Lodge Burn

Naggyfauld

Burnside

Waterside

MILLBANK RD

ALLANBANK RD

05

Kinbuck

Balhaldie

FK15

Craigton

Lower
Whiteston

7

Allan Water

Upper
Whiteston

Hutchison

Glassingall

04

Weir

B8033

Gateside

The White
Stone

Weir

Milour
Moor

Wks

Cairnston

Shanraw

6

Crofts of
Cromlix

Ashfield

Upper
Auchinlay

03

Mast

107

B8033

Sch

Landrick

Lower
Auchinlay

Cemy

Sheriffmuir Big Wood

5

Corscaplie

Ryland
Lodge

FK15

Monument

02

Laighhills
Park
Weir

A820 Callander (A84)

DOUNE ROAD

Dunblane
Prim Sch

Hotel

PERTH ROAD

A820

DUNBLANE

Stonehill
Wood

The
Linns

4

Greenyards

Cath

Gall

107

Mast

Wharry Burn

01

Moon
Cottage

PH

Stonehill

Waltersmuir
Reservoir

High Sch

Spout
Wood

Walters-muir
Wood

3

Moon
Plantation

**ROMAN
CAMPS**

STIRLING RD

Cairn

Kippenross
Home Farm

Biggins
Wood

Pisgah
Wood

GLEN ROAD

00

B824

Fort

Kippenross
House

Black-shed
Wood

Badgergate

A9

Keir
Mains
Wood

B8033

Old Military Road

GLEN RD

Wharry
Bridge

Cairn

2

Arnhall
Wood

Park
of Keir

Drumdruills

Pendreich

Quarry
(dis)

Cairns

SHERIFFMUIR ROAD

Mon

FISHER'S
GN

COXBURN BRAE

99

Arnhall
Castle

Mon

Keir House

107

Gallow
Hill

FK9

Cocksburn
Reservoir

Cocksburn
Wood

A9

Fort

PENDREICH ROAD

Six Acre
Wood

Knock Hill

Sunnylaw

CH

Fairy Knowe
(Cairn)

Black
Hill

1

FERNIBANK BRAE 1
SUNNYLAW RD 2

M9

Bridge of Allan
Golf Club

98

A   B   C   D   E   F

76   77   78   79   80   81

11

For full street detail of the
highlighted area see page 107.

114

115

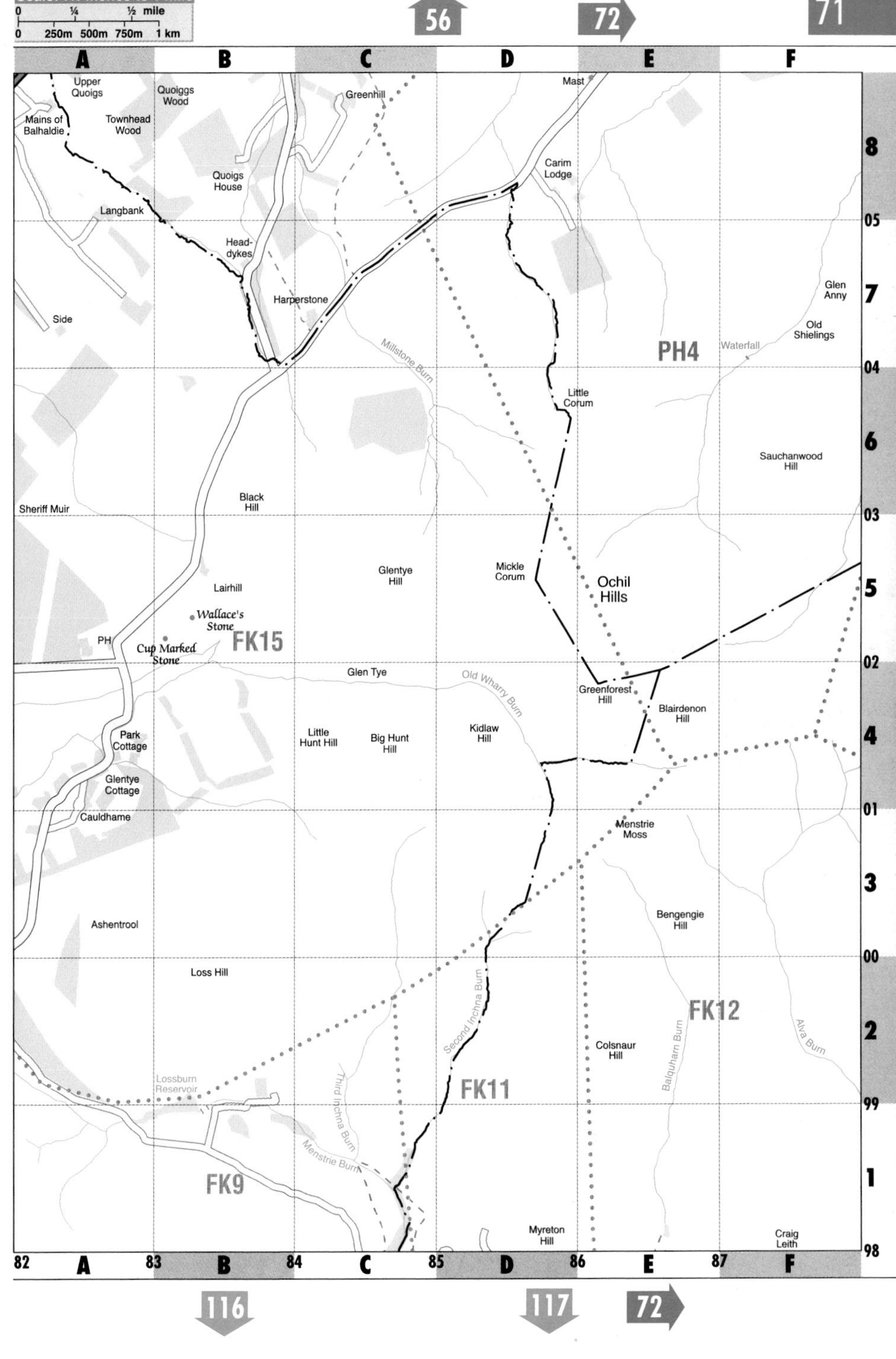

8
7
6
5
4
3
2
1

05
04
03
02
01
00
99
98

Upper Quoigs
Mains of Balhaldie
Townhead Wood
Quoiggs Wood
Greenhill
Mast
Langbank
Quoigs House
Carim Lodge
Head-dykes
Harperstone
Side
Millstone Burn
PH4
Glen Anny
Waterfall
Old Shielings
Little Corum
Sauchanwood Hill
Sheriff Muir
Black Hill
Glentye Hill
Mickle Corum
Ochil Hills
Lairhill
Wallace's Stone
FK15
Cup Marked Stone
PH
Glen Tye
Old Wharry Burn
Greenforest Hill
Blairdenon Hill
Park Cottage
Little Hunt Hill
Big Hunt Hill
Kidlaw Hill
Glentye Cottage
Cauldhame
Menstrie Moss
Ashentrool
Bengengie Hill
Loss Hill
FK12
Second Inchna Burn
Colsnaur Hill
Balquhan Burn
Alva Burn
Lossburn Reservoir
FK11
Third Inchna Burn
Menstrie Burn
FK9
Myreton Hill
Craig Leith

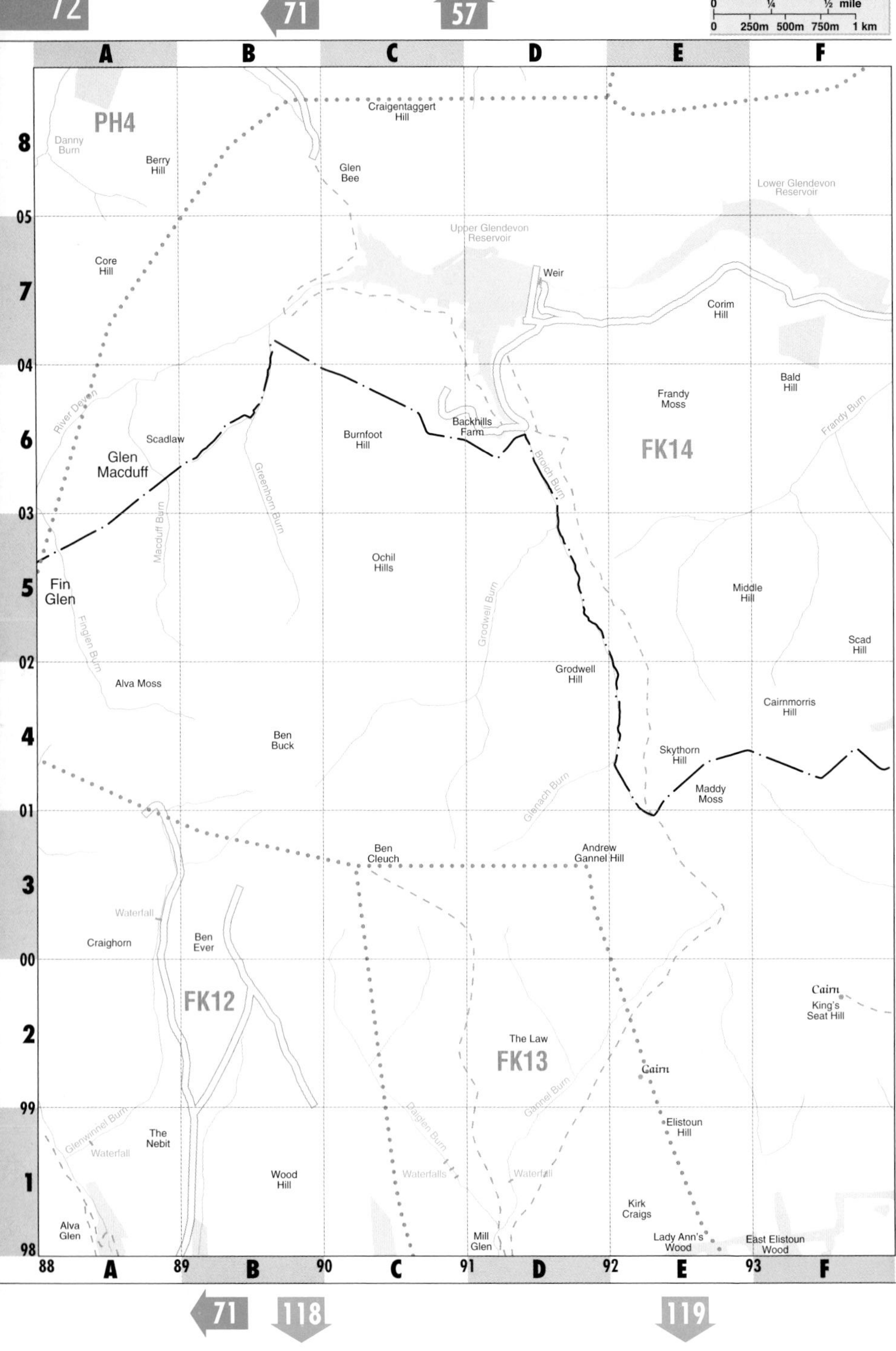

Scale: 1⅓ inches to 1 mile

0   ¼   ½   mile
0   250m 500m 750m 1 km

A   **B**   **C**   **D**   **E**   **F**

PH4

Danny Burn

Berry Hill

Craigentaggert Hill

Glen Bee

Lower Glendevon Reservoir

Core Hill

Upper Glendevon Reservoir

Weir

Corim Hill

Bald Hill

Scadlaw

Burnfoot Hill

Backhills Farm

Frandy Moss

FK14

Glen Macduff

River Devon

Greenhorn Burn

Macduff Burn

Beich Burn

Frandy Burn

Fin Glen

Finglen Burn

Ochil Hills

Middle Hill

Scad Hill

Alva Moss

Grodwell Burn

Grodwell Hill

Cairnmorris Hill

Ben Buck

Skythorn Hill

Maddy Moss

Glenach Burn

Ben Cleuch

Andrew Gannel Hill

Waterfall

Craighorn

Ben Ever

FK12

Cairn

King's Seat Hill

The Law

FK13

Cairn

Gannel Burn

Daiglen Burn

Elistoun Hill

Glenwinnel Burn

Waterfall

The Nebit

Wood Hill

Waterfalls

Waterfall

Kirk Craigs

Alva Glen

Mill Glen

Lady Ann's Wood

East Elistoun Wood

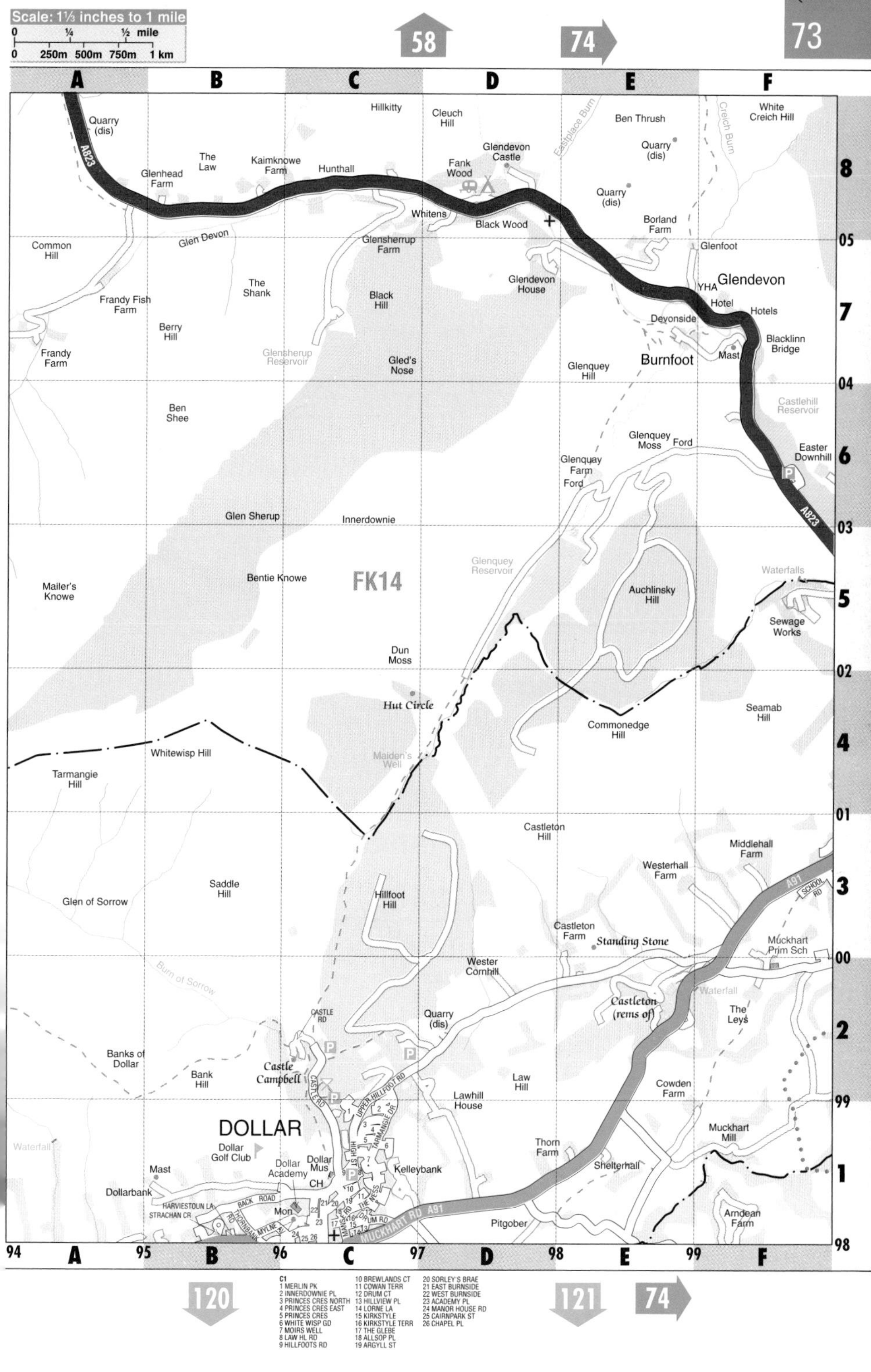

Scale: 1⅓ inches to 1 mile
0 ¼ ½ mile
0 250m 500m 750m 1 km
58
74
Quarry (dis)
Hillkitty
Cleuch Hill
Ben Thrush
White Creich Hill
Eastplace Burn
Creich Burn
A823
The Law
Kaimknowe Farm
Hunthall
Glendevon Castle
Fank Wood
Quarry (dis)
Glenhead Farm
Whitens
Black Wood
Quarry (dis)
Borland Farm
Common Hill
Glen Devon
Glensherrup Farm
Glenfoot
Glendevon House
YHA
Glendevon
Hotel
Hotels
The Shank
Black Hill
Frandy Fish Farm
Devonside
Berry Hill
Blacklinn Bridge
Mast
Frandy Farm
Glensherup Reservoir
Gled's Nose
Glenquey Hill
Burnfoot
Ben Shee
Castlehill Reservoir
Glenquey Moss
Ford
Easter Downhill
Glenquay Farm
Ford
Glen Sherup
Innerdownie
Glenquey Reservoir
Waterfalls
Mailer's Knowe
Bentie Knowe
FK14
Auchlinsky Hill
Sewage Works
Dun Moss
Hut Circle
Seamab Hill
Commonedge Hill
Whitewisp Hill
Maiden's Well
Tarmangie Hill
Castleton Hill
Middlehall Farm
Westerhall Farm
A91
SCHOOL RD
Saddle Hill
Glen of Sorrow
Hillfoot Hill
Castleton Farm
Standing Stone
Muckhart Prim Sch
Wester Cornhill
Burn of Sorrow
Waterfall
Castleton (rems of)
CASTLE RD
Quarry (dis)
The Leys
Banks of Dollar
Castle Campbell
Bank Hill
Law Hill
Cowden Farm
Lawhill House
UPPER HILLFOOT RD
CASTLE RD
TARMANGIE DR
HIGH ST
DOLLAR
Waterfall
Thorn Farm
Muckhart Mill
Dollar Golf Club
Dollar Mus
Kelleybank
Shelterhall
Dollar Academy
Mast
CH
Dollarbank
HARVIESTOUN LA
BACK ROAD
STRACHAN CR
RD
HORNBANK
MYLNE AV
Mon
MANSE RD
THE NESS
DRUM RD
MUCKHART RD A91
Pitgober
Arndean Farm
A B C D E F
8 05 7 04 6 03 5 02 4 01 3 00 2 99 1 98
94 A 95 B 96 C 97 D 98 E 99 F 98
120
121
74
C1
1 MERLIN PK
2 INNERDOWNIE PL
3 PRINCES CRES NORTH
4 PRINCES CRES EAST
5 PRINCES CRES
6 WHITE WISP GD
7 MOIRS WELL
8 LAW HL RD
9 HILLFOOTS RD
10 BREWLANDS CT
11 COWAN TERR
12 DRUM CT
13 HILLVIEW PL
14 LORNE LA
15 KIRKSTYLE
16 KIRKSTYLE TERR
17 THE GLEBE
18 ALLSOP PL
19 ARGYLL ST
20 SORLEY'S BRAE
21 EAST BURNSIDE
22 WEST BURNSIDE
23 ACADEMY PL
24 MANOR HOUSE RD
25 CAIRNPARK ST
26 CHAPEL PL

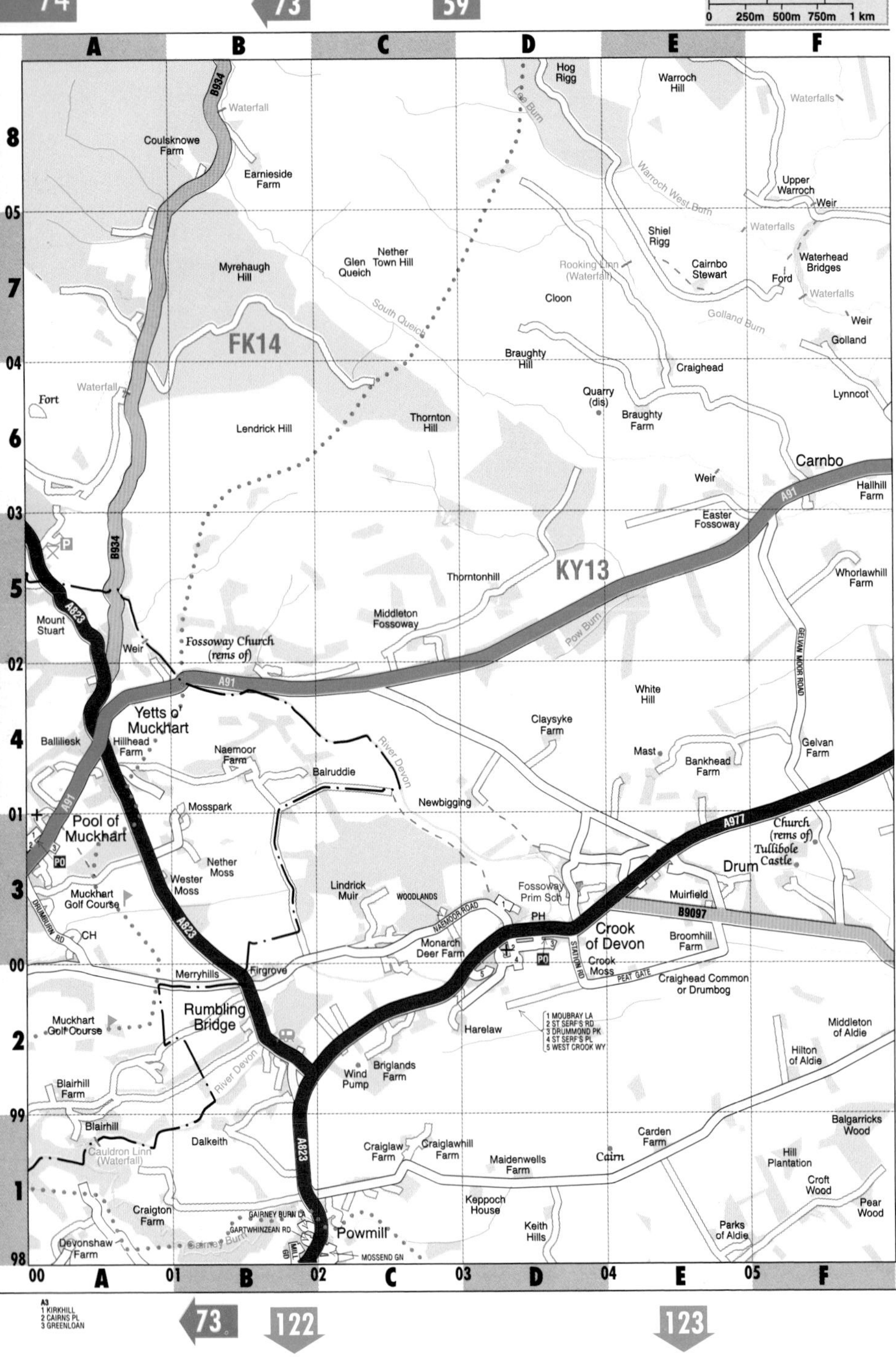

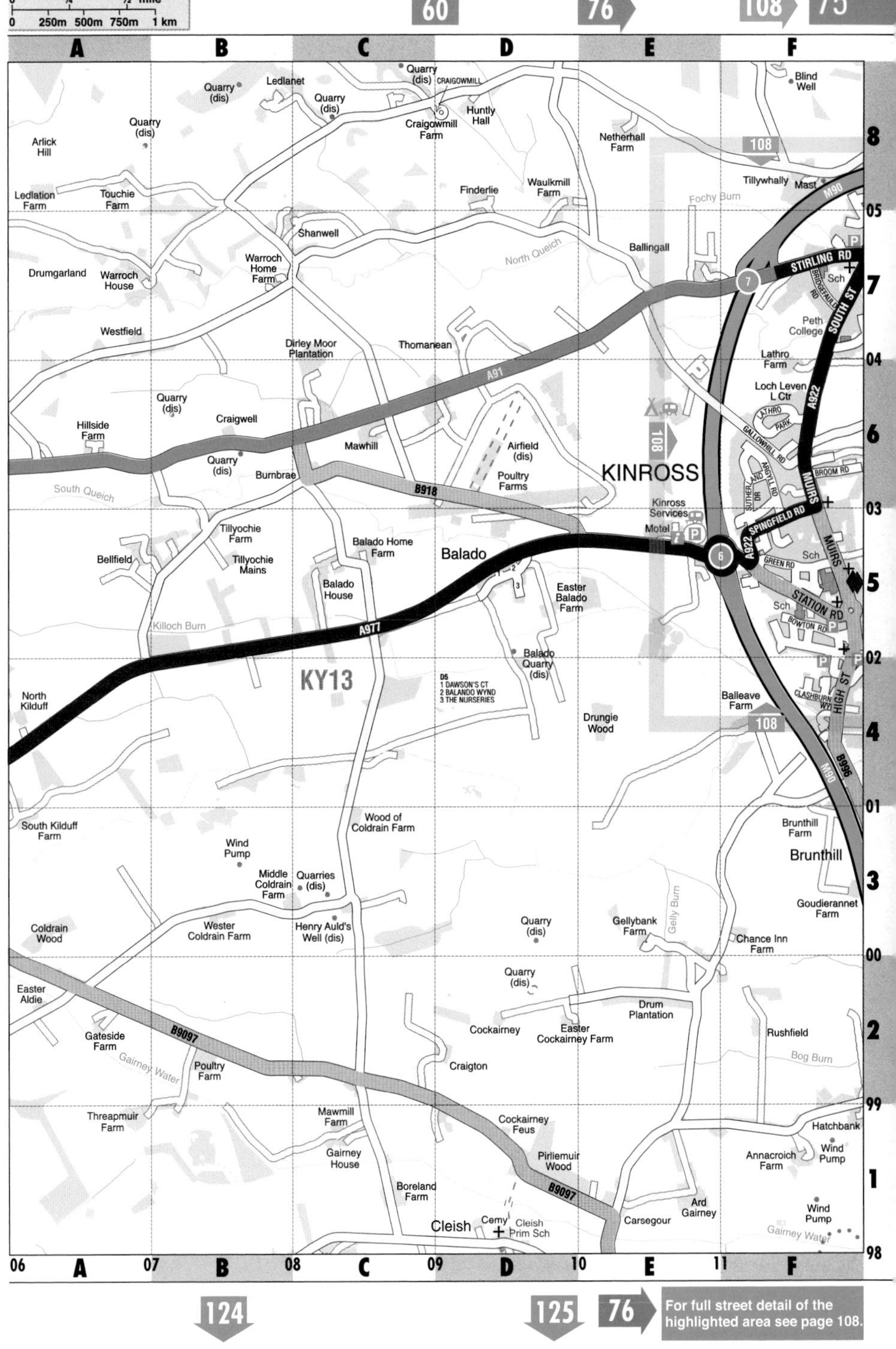

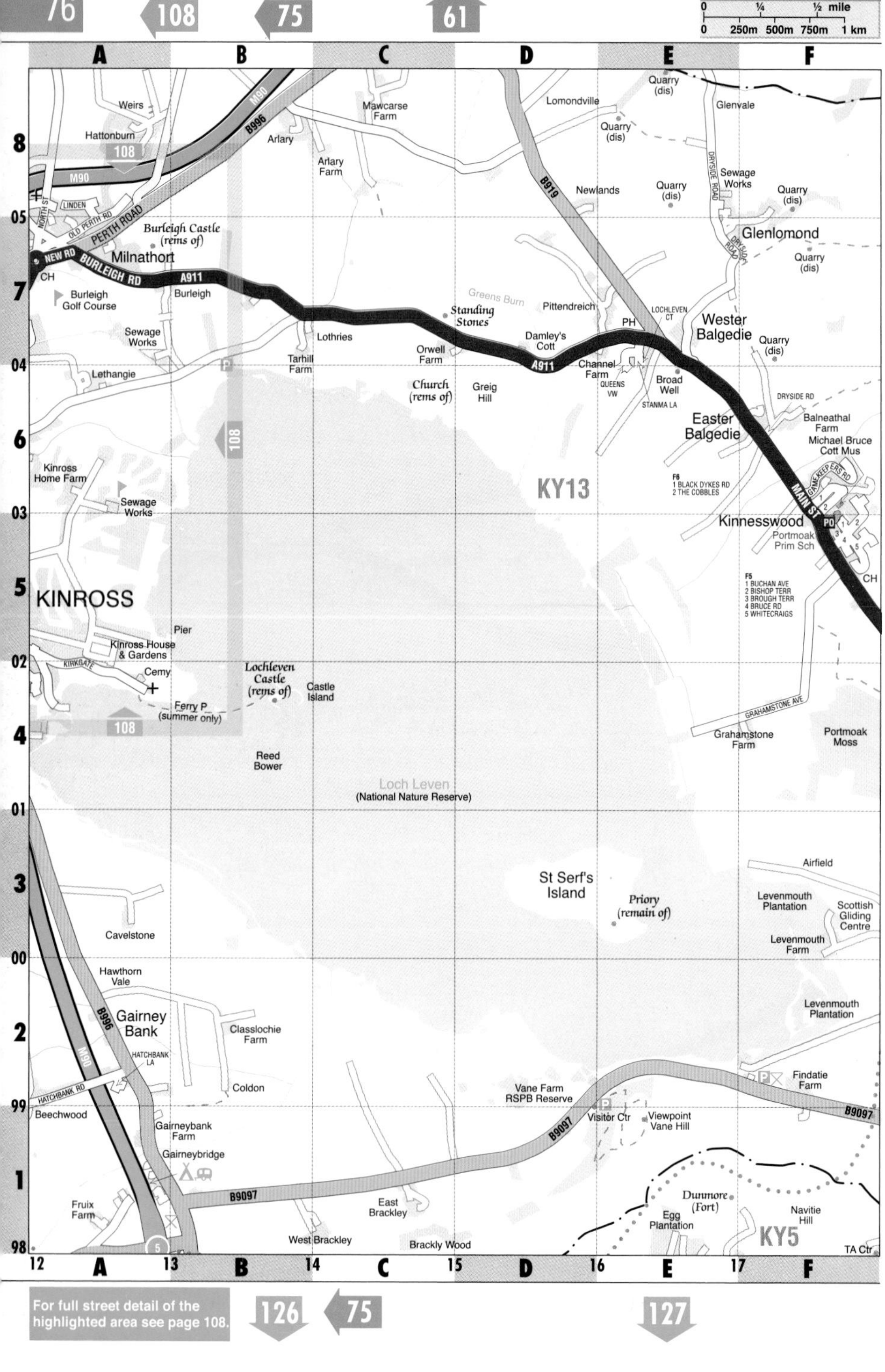

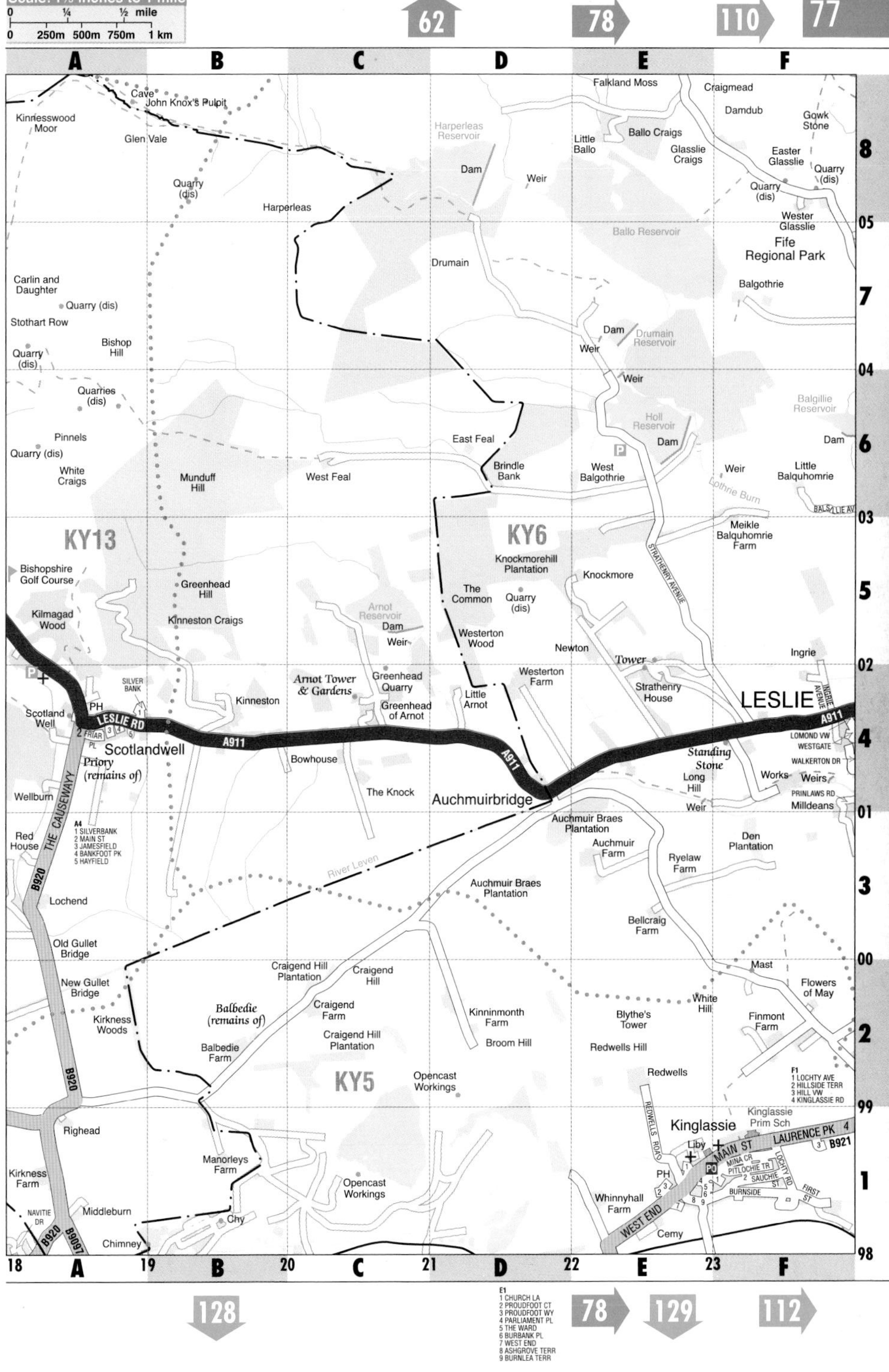
Scale: 1⅓ inches to 1 mile
0 ¼ ½ mile
0 250m 500m 750m 1 km
62
78
110
A B C D E F
Falkland Moss
Craigmead
Cave
John Knox's Pulpit
Kinnesswood Moor
Glen Vale
Harperleas Reservoir
Little Ballo
Ballo Craigs
Damdub
Gowk Stone
Glasslie Craigs
Easter Glasslie
Quarry (dis)
Dam
Weir
Quarry (dis)
Harperleas
Wester Glasslie
Ballo Reservoir
Fife Regional Park
Drumain
Balgothrie
Carlin and Daughter
Quarry (dis)
Stothart Row
Bishop Hill
Dam
Drumain Reservoir
Weir
Weir
Quarries (dis)
Balgillie Reservoir
Holl Reservoir
Pinnels
East Feal
Dam
Dam
Quarry (dis)
White Craigs
Munduff Hill
West Feal
Brindle Bank
West Balgothrie
Weir
Little Balquhomrie
Lothrie Burn
BALSILLIE AV
KY13
KY6
Meikle Balquhomrie Farm
Bishopshire Golf Course
Knockmorehill Plantation
Knockmore
STRATHENRY AVENUE
Greenhead Hill
The Common
Quarry (dis)
Arnot Reservoir
Kilmagad Wood
Kinneston Craigs
Dam
Westerton Wood
Weir
Newton
Ingrie
Tower
Arnot Tower & Gardens
Greenhead Quarry
Westerton Farm
Strathenry House
SILVER BANK
LESLIE
INGRIE AVENUE
Scotland Well
PH
Kinneston
Greenhead of Arnot
Little Arnot
A911
LESLIE RD
FRIAR PL
Scotlandwell
A911
A911
LOMOND VW
WESTGATE
Priory (remains of)
Bowhouse
Standing Stone
WALKERTON DR
Works
Weirs
Long Hill
Wellburn
The Knock
Auchmuirbridge
PRINLAWS RD
Weir
Milldeans
A4
1 SILVERBANK
2 MAIN ST
3 JAMESFIELD
4 BANKFOOT PK
5 HAYFIELD
Auchmuir Braes Plantation
Red House
THE CAUSEWAY
Auchmuir Farm
Den Plantation
Ryelaw Farm
River Leven
B920
Lochend
Auchmuir Braes Plantation
Bellcraig Farm
Old Gullet Bridge
Craigend Hill Plantation
Craigend Hill
Mast
New Gullet Bridge
Flowers of May
Balbedie (remains of)
Craigend Farm
Kinninmonth Farm
White Hill
Kirkness Woods
Blythe's Tower
Finmont Farm
Craigend Hill Plantation
Broom Hill
Balbedie Farm
Redwells Hill
Redwells
KY5
Opencast Workings
B920
F1
1 LOCHTY AVE
2 HILLSIDE TERR
3 HILL VW
4 KINGLASSIE RD
Righead
Kinglassie Prim Sch
REDWELLS ROAD
Kinglassie
LAURENCE PK
B921
Manorleys Farm
Liby
MAIN ST
MINA CR
PITLOCHIE TR
LOCHTY RD
Kirkness Farm
PH
PO
SAUCHIE ST
Opencast Workings
BURNSIDE
FIRST ST
Whinnyhall Farm
NAVITIE DR
Middleburn
WEST END
Chy
Cemy
B920
B9097
Chimney
18 A 19 B 20 C 21 D 22 E 23 F
98
8
05
7
04
6
03
5
02
4
01
3
00
2
99
1
128
E1
1 CHURCH LA
2 PROUDFOOT CT
3 PROUDFOOT WY
4 PARLIAMENT PL
5 THE WARD
6 BURBANK PL
7 WEST END
8 ASHGROVE TERR
9 BURNLEA TERR
78
129
112

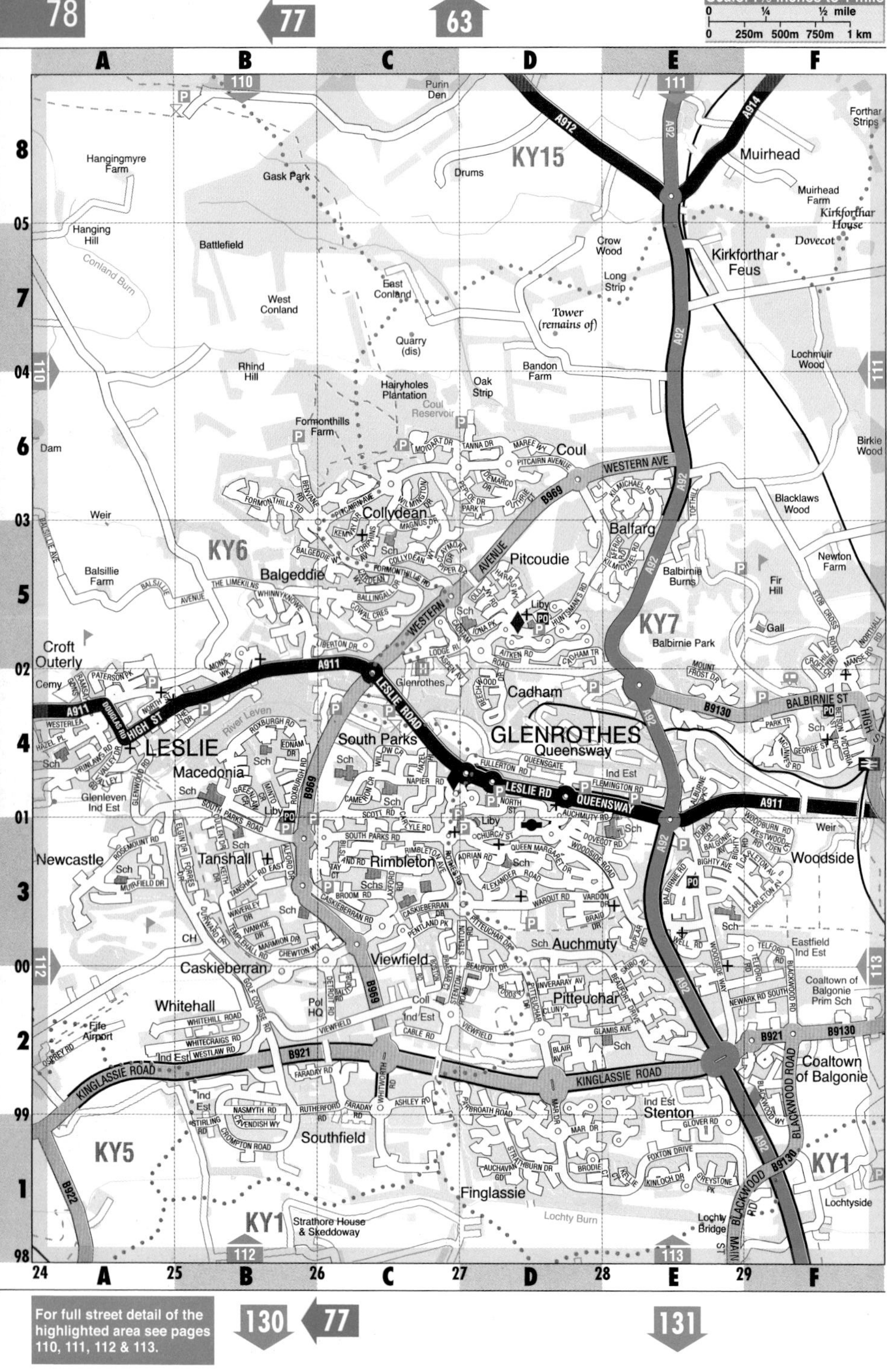

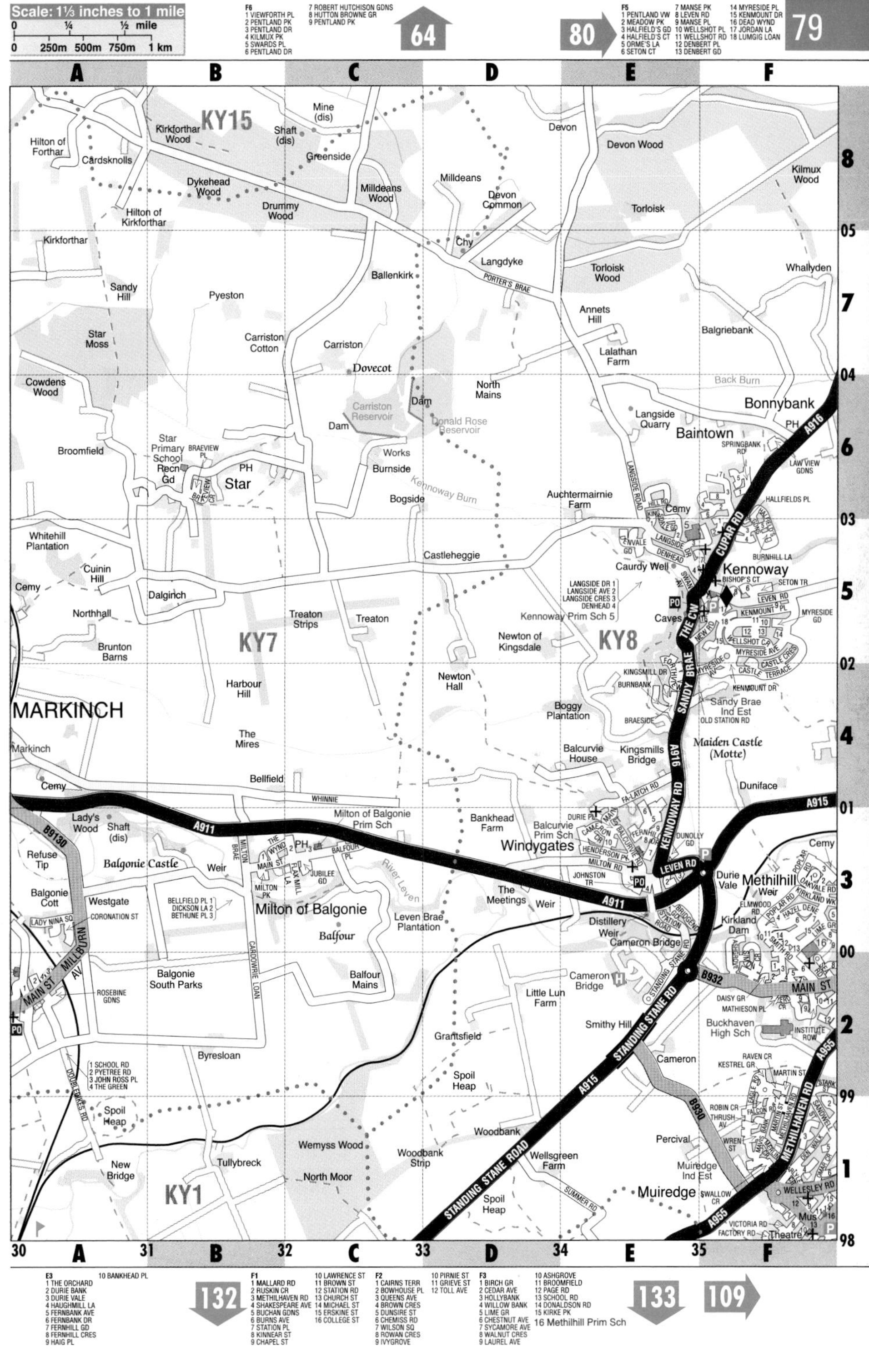

Scale: 1⅓ inches to 1 mile
0
¼
½ mile
0
250m
500m
750m
1 km
F6
1 VIEWFORTH PL
2 PENTLAND PK
3 PENTLAND DR
4 KILMUX PK
5 SWARDS PL
6 PENTLAND DR
7 ROBERT HUTCHISON GDNS
8 HUTTON BROWNE GR
9 PENTLAND PK
64
80
F5
1 PENTLAND VW
2 MEADOW PK
3 HALFIELD'S GD
4 HALFIELD'S CT
5 ORME'S LA
6 SETON CT
7 MANSE PK
8 LEVEN RD
9 MANSE PL
10 WELLSHOT PL
11 WELLSHOT RD
12 DENBERT PL
13 DENBERT GD
14 MYRESIDE PL
15 KENMOUNT DR
16 DEAD WYND
17 JORDAN LA
18 LUMGIG LOAN
79
A
B
C
D
E
F
KY15
Mine (dis)
Shaft (dis)
Greenside
Hilton of Forthar
Kirkforthar Wood
Cardsknolls
Dykehead Wood
Hilton of Kirkforthar
Drummy Wood
Milldeans Wood
Milldeans
Devon Common
Devon
Devon Wood
Kilmux Wood
Torloisk
Kirkforthar
Chy
Langdyke
PORTER'S BRAE
Torloisk Wood
Whallyden
Ballenkirk
Sandy Hill
Pyeston
Annets Hill
Balgriebank
Star Moss
Carriston Cotton
Carriston
Lalathan Farm
Dovecot
Back Burn
Cowdens Wood
Carriston Reservoir
Dam
North Mains
Bonnybank
Donald Rose Reservoir
Langside Quarry
Baintown
PH
A916
Broomfield
Star Primary School
Recn Gd
BRAEVIEW PL
PH
Star
Works
Burnside
SPRINGBANK RD
LAW VIEW GDNS
Kennoway Burn
Bogside
Auchtermairnie Farm
LANGSIDE ROAD
HALLFIELDS PL
Cemy
CUPAR RD
Whitehill Plantation
Castleheggie
LANGSIDE DR
DENHEAD
BURNHILL LA
Cuinin Hill
Caurdy Well
Kennoway
BISHOP'S CT
SETON TR
Cemy
Dalginch
LANGSIDE DR 1
LANGSIDE AVE 2
LANGSIDE CRES 3
DENHEAD 4
Kennoway Prim Sch 5
LEVEN RD
KENMOUNT PL
MYRESIDE GD
Northhall
Treaton Strips
Treaton
Caves
THE CW
NEW RD
Brunton Barns
KY7
Newton of Kingsdale
KY8
WELLSHOT CR
MYRESIDE AVE
CASTLE CRES
CASTLE TERRACE
KENMOUNT DR
KINGSMILL DR
BURNBANK
SANDY BRAE
Harbour Hill
Newton Hall
MARKINCH
Boggy Plantation
Sandy Brae Ind Est
OLD STATION RD
BRAESIDE
Markinch
The Mires
Balcurvie House
Kingsmills Bridge
Maiden Castle (Motte)
Bellfield
Cemy
WHINNIE
FA-LATCH RD
KENNOWAY RD
Duniface
A915
Lady's Wood
Shaft (dis)
A911
Milton of Balgonie Prim Sch
Bankhead Farm
DURIE PL
Balcurvie Prim Sch
Windygates
DUNOLLY GD
Cemy
B9130
Refuse Tip
Balgonie Castle
Weir
MILTON BRAE
THE WYND
MAIN ST
FLAX MILL
JUBILEE GD
BALFOUR PL
River Leven
HENDERSON PK
MILTON RD
JOHNSTON TR
LEVEN RD
Durie Vale
Methilhill
Weir
Balgonie Cott
Westgate
MILTON PK
Milton of Balgonie
The Meetings
Weir
ELMWOOD RD
POPLAR RD
HAZEL DENE
LADY NINA SQ
CORONATION ST
BELLFIELD PL 1
DICKSON LA 2
BETHUNE PL 3
Balfour
Leven Brae Plantation
Distillery
Weir
Cameron Bridge
BRIDGEND
STATION RD
Kirkland Dam
MILLBURN AV
MAIN ST
CARDOWRIE LOAN
Balgonie South Parks
Balfour Mains
Cameron Bridge
STANDING STANE RD
B932
MAIN ST
ROSEBINE GDNS
Little Lun Farm
DAISY GR
MATHIESON PL
PO
Smithy Hill
Buckhaven High Sch
INSTITUTE ROW
Grantsfield
Byresloan
Cameron
RAVEN CR
KESTREL GR
MARTIN ST
1 SCHOOL RD
2 PYETREE RD
3 JOHN ROSS PL
4 THE GREEN
DOUBLEDYKES RD
Spoil Heap
A915
B930
Spoil Heap
Woodbank
ROBIN CR
FALCON RD
THRUSH AV
Percival
WREN ST
METHILHAVEN RD
Wemyss Wood
Woodbank Strip
Wellsgreen Farm
New Bridge
Tullybreck
STANDING STANE ROAD
Muiredge Ind Est
North Moor
KY1
Spoil Heap
SUMMER RD
Muiredge
SWALLOW CR
WELLESLEY RD
A955
VICTORIA RD
FACTORY RD
Mus
Theatre
30
31
32
33
34
35
05
04
03
02
01
00
99
98
8
7
6
5
4
3
2
1
E3
1 THE ORCHARD
2 DURIE BANK
3 DURIE VALE
4 HAUGHMILL LA
5 FERNBANK AVE
6 FERNBANK DR
7 FERNHILL GD
8 FERNHILL CRES
9 HAIG PL
10 BANKHEAD PL
132
F1
1 MALLARD RD
2 RUSKIN CR
3 METHILHAVEN RD
4 SHAKESPEARE AVE
5 BUCHAN GDNS
6 BURNS AVE
7 STATION PL
8 KINNEAR ST
9 CHAPEL ST
10 LAWRENCE ST
11 BROWN ST
12 STATION RD
13 CHURCH ST
14 MICHAEL ST
15 ERSKINE ST
16 COLLEGE ST
F2
1 CAIRNS TERR
2 BOWHOUSE PL
3 QUEENS AVE
4 BROWN CRES
5 DUNSIRE ST
6 CHEMISS RD
7 WILSON SQ
8 ROWAN CRES
9 IVYGROVE
10 PIRNIE ST
11 GRIEVE ST
12 TOLL AVE
F3
1 BIRCH GR
2 CEDAR AVE
3 HOLLYBANK
4 WILLOW BANK
5 LIME GR
6 CHESTNUT AVE
7 SYCAMORE AVE
8 WALNUT CRES
9 LAUREL AVE
10 ASHGROVE
11 BROOMFIELD
12 PAGE RD
13 SCHOOL RD
14 DONALDSON RD
15 KIRKE PK
16 Methilhill Prim Sch
133
109

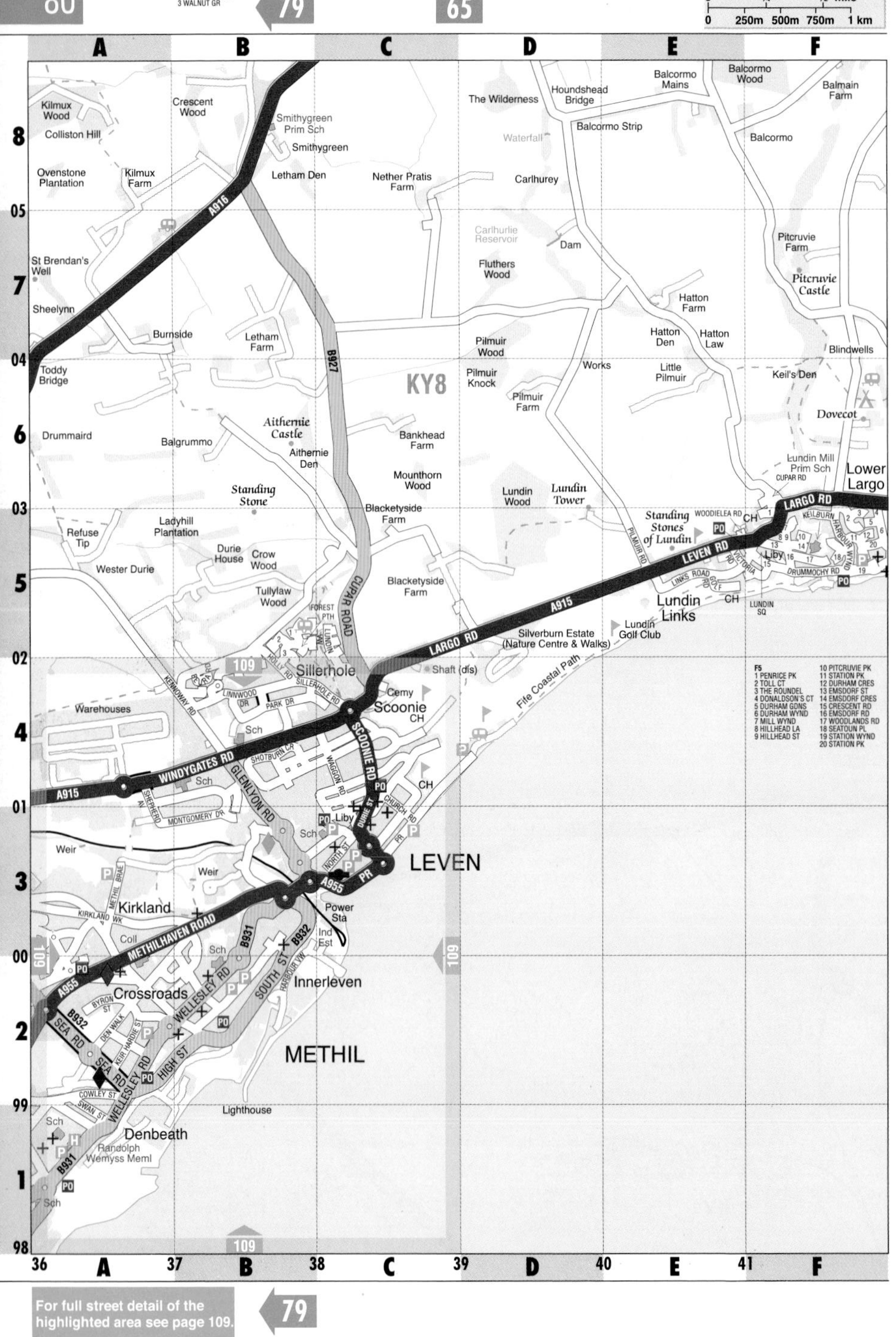

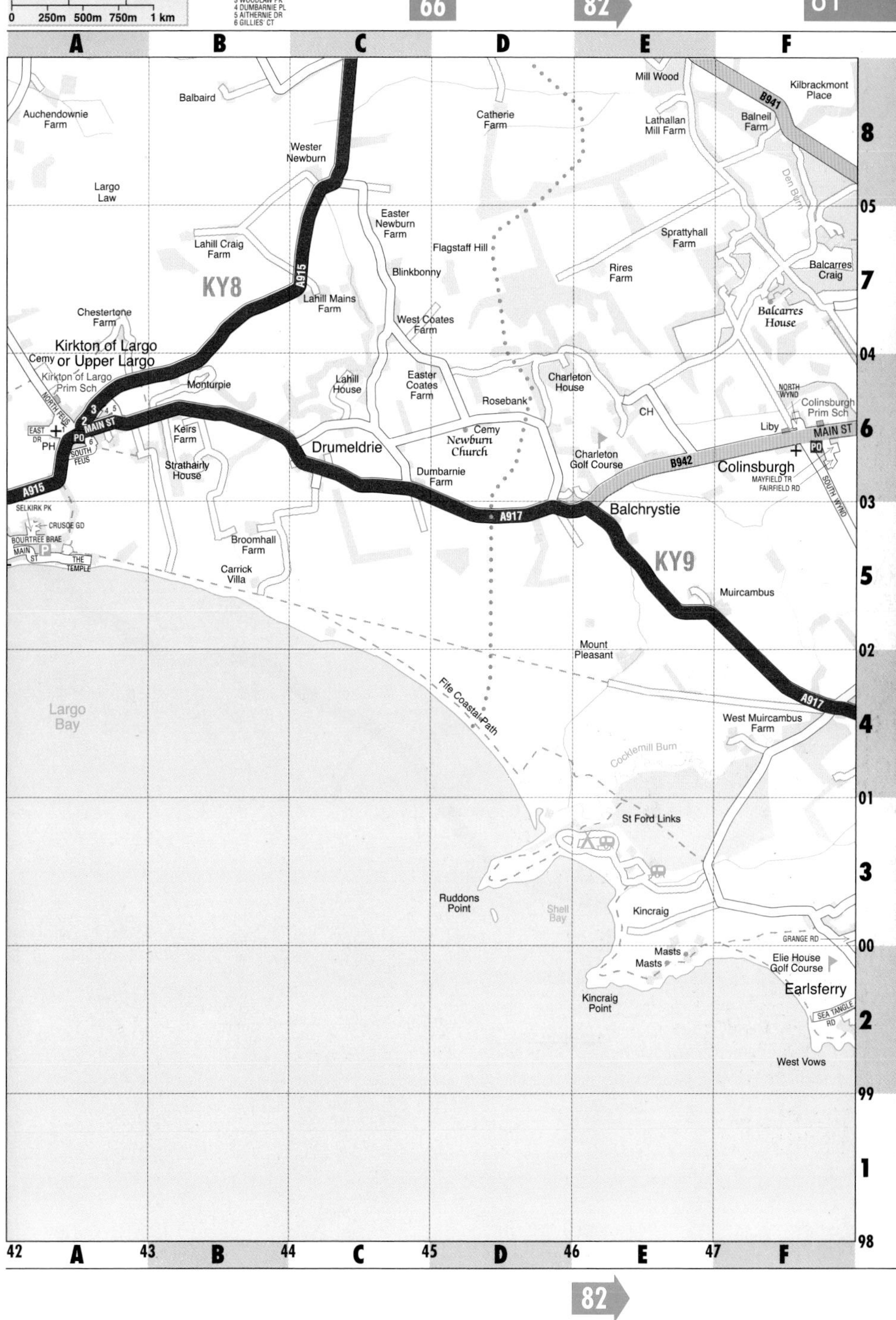

81

67

Scale: 1⅓ inches to 1 mile

0   ¼   ½   mile
0 250m 500m 750m 1 km

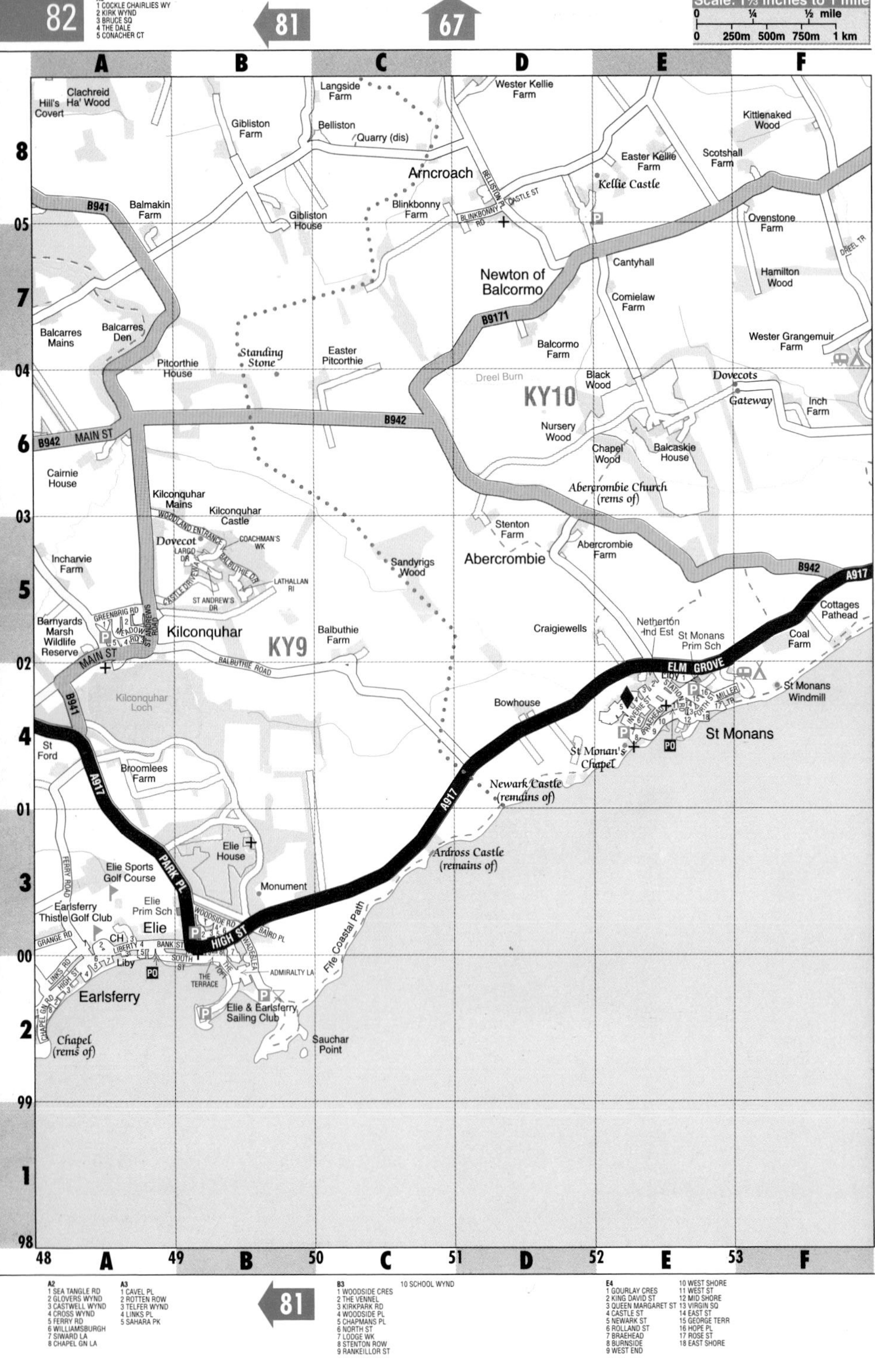

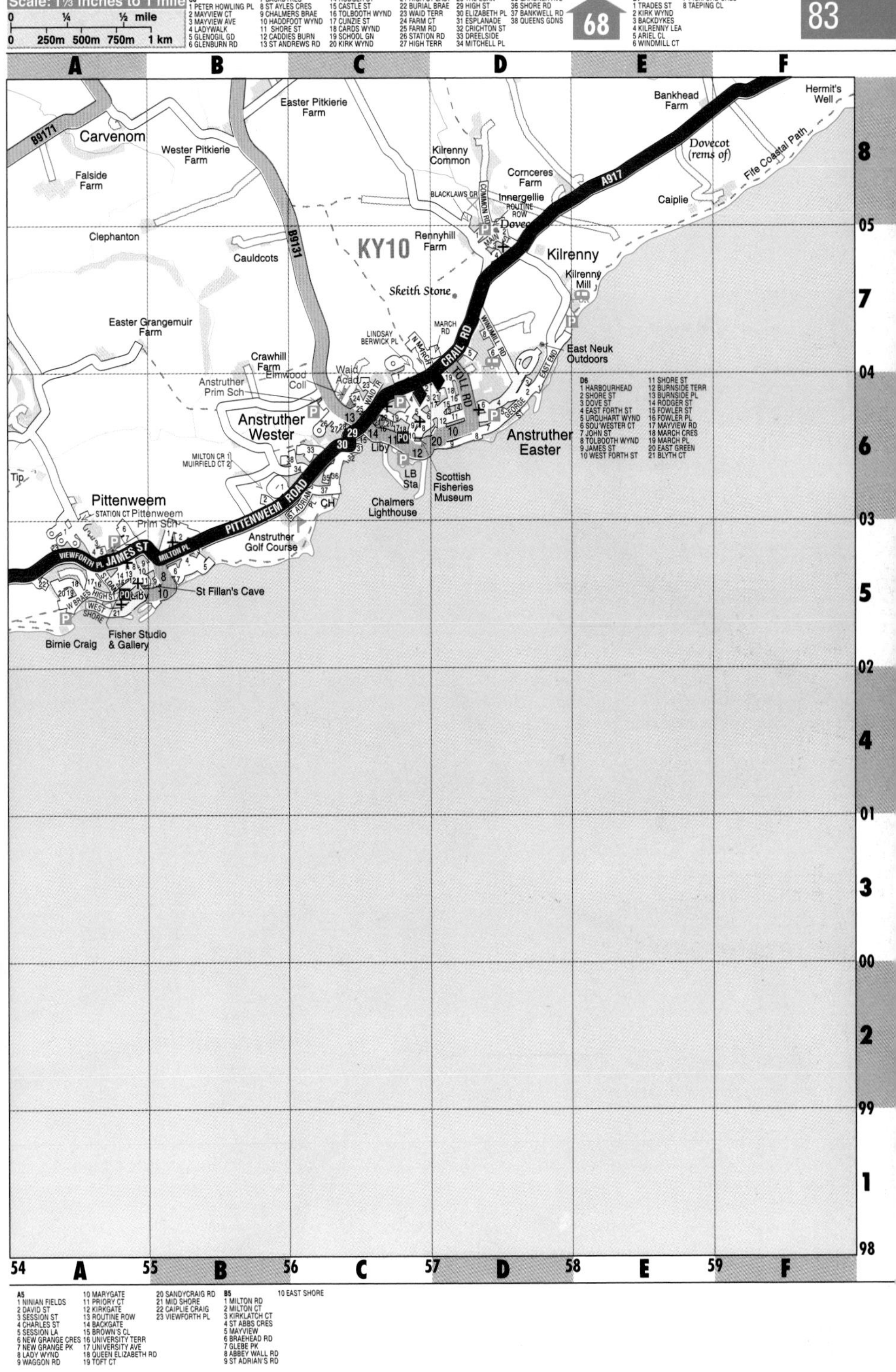
Scale: 1⅓ inches to 1 mile
0 ¼ ½ mile
0 250m 500m 750m 1 km
C6
1 PETER HOWLING PL
2 MAYVIEW CT
3 MAYVIEW AVE
4 LADYWALK
5 GLENOGIL GD
6 GLENBURN RD
7 BACKDYKES
8 ST AYLES CRES
9 CHALMERS BRAE
10 HADDFOOT WYND
11 SHORE ST
12 CADDIES BURN
13 ST ANDREWS RD
14 RODGER ST
15 CASTLE ST
16 TOLBOOTH WYND
17 CUNZIE ST
18 CARDS WYND
19 SCHOOL GN
20 KIRK WYND
21 HIGH ST EAST
22 BURIAL BRAE
23 WAID TERR
24 FARM CT
25 FARM RD
26 STATION RD
27 HIGH TERR
28 THE LOAN
29 HIGH ST
30 ELIZABETH PL
31 ESPLANADE
32 CRICHTON ST
33 DREELSIDE
34 MITCHELL PL
35 GARDNER AVE
36 SHORE RD
37 BANKWELL RD
38 QUEENS GDNS
68
D7
1 TRADES ST
2 KIRK WYND
3 BACKDYKES
4 KILRENNY LEA
5 ARIEL CL
6 WINDMILL CT
7 PICKFORD CRES
8 TAEPING CL
A B C D E F
Carvenom
B9171
Falside Farm
Wester Pitkierie Farm
Easter Pitkierie Farm
Kilrenny Common
Bankhead Farm
Hermit's Well
Dovecot (rems of)
Fife Coastal Path
A917
Cornceres Farm
BLACKLAWS CR
Innergellie
ROUTINE ROW
COMMON RD
Caiplie
Clephanton
Cauldcots
B9131
KY10
Rennyhill Farm
Kilrenny
Kilrenny Mill
Skeith Stone
Easter Grangemuir Farm
LINDSAY BERWICK PL
MARCH RD
CRAIL RD
WINDMILL RD
East Neuk Outdoors
Crawhill Farm
Elmwood Coll
Waid Acad
Anstruther Prim Sch
TOLL RD
EAST END
D6
1 HARBOURHEAD
2 SHORE ST
3 DOVE ST
4 EAST FORTH ST
5 URQUHART WYND
6 SOU'WESTER CT
7 JOHN ST
8 TOLBOOTH WYND
9 JAMES ST
10 WEST FORTH ST
11 SHORE ST
12 BURNSIDE TERR
13 BURNSIDE PL
14 RODGER ST
15 FOWLER ST
16 FOWLER PL
17 MAYVIEW RD
18 MARCH CRES
19 MARCH PL
20 EAST GREEN
21 BLYTH CT
Anstruther Wester
WAID TR
Anstruther Easter
GEORGE ST
Liby
PO
LB Sta
Scottish Fisheries Museum
MILTON CR 1
MUIRFIELD CT 2
Tip
Pittenweem
STATION CT
Pittenweem Prim Sch
PITTENWEEM ROAD
ST ADRIAN'S PL
CH
Chalmers Lighthouse
Anstruther Golf Course
VIEWFORTH PL
JAMES ST
MILTON PL
St Fillan's Cave
W BRAES
HIGH ST
WEST SHORE
Birnie Craig
Fisher Studio & Gallery
8
05
7
04
6
03
5
02
4
01
3
00
2
99
1
98
54 A 55 B 56 C 57 D 58 E 59 F
A5
1 NINIAN FIELDS
2 DAVID ST
3 SESSION ST
4 CHARLES ST
5 SESSION LA
6 NEW GRANGE CRES
7 NEW GRANGE PK
8 LADY WYND
9 WAGGON RD
10 MARYGATE
11 PRIORY CT
12 KIRKGATE
13 ROUTINE ROW
14 BACKGATE
15 BROWN'S CL
16 UNIVERSITY TERR
17 UNIVERSITY AVE
18 QUEEN ELIZABETH RD
19 TOFT CT
20 SANDYCRAIG RD
21 MID SHORE
22 CAIPLIE CRAIG
23 VIEWFORTH PL
B5
1 MILTON RD
2 MILTON CT
3 KIRKLATCH CT
4 ST ABBS CRES
5 MAYVIEW
6 BRAEHEAD RD
7 GLEBE PK
8 ABBEY WALL RD
9 ST ADRIAN'S RD
10 EAST SHORE

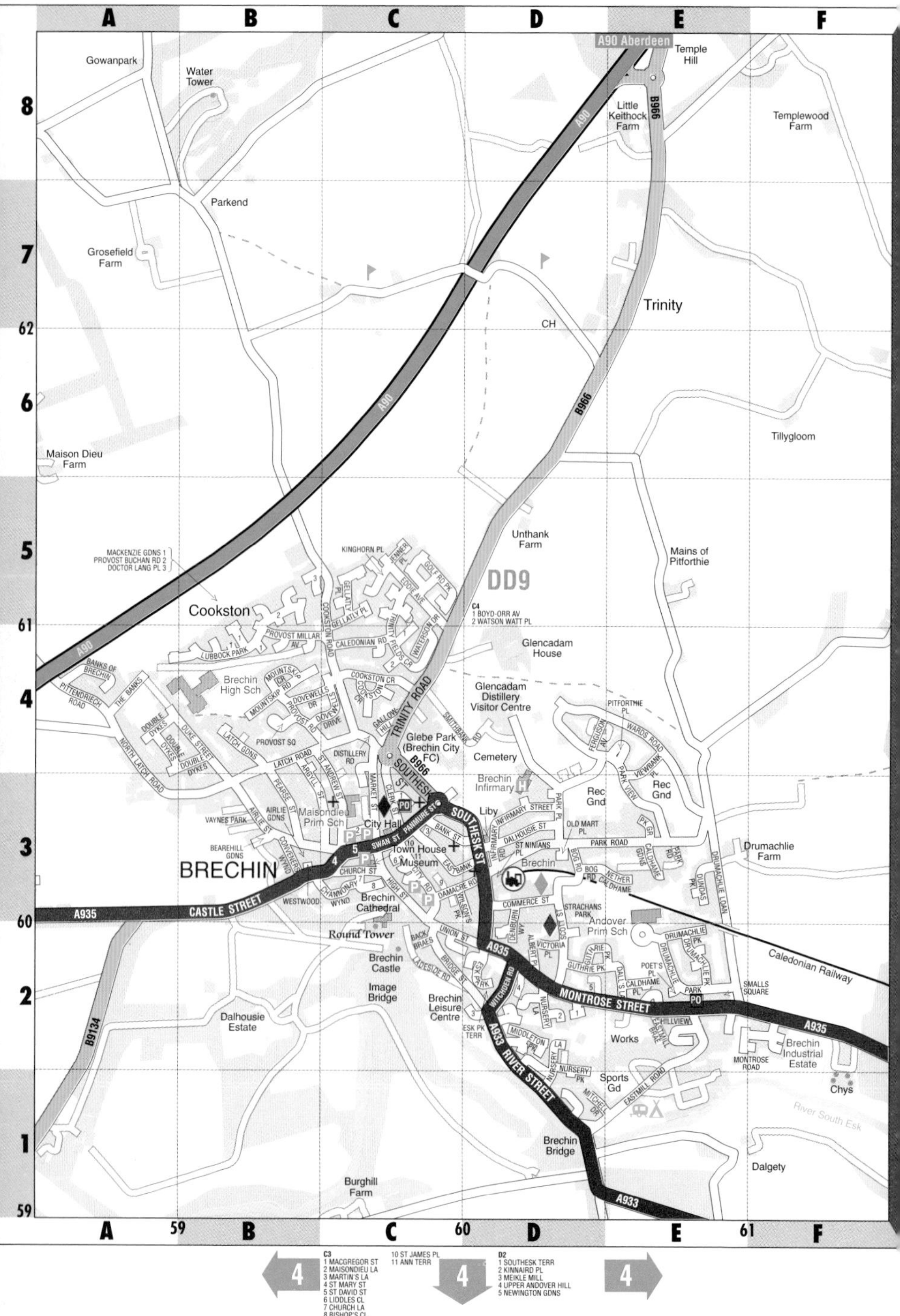

BRECHIN

◄ 4

C3
1 MACGREGOR ST
2 MAISONDIEU LA
3 MARTIN'S LA
4 ST MARY ST
5 ST DAVID ST
6 LIDDLES CL
7 CHURCH LA
8 BISHOP'S CL
9 MATHERS PK

10 ST JAMES PL
11 ANN TERR

4

D2
1 SOUTHESK TERR
2 KINNAIRD PL
3 MEIKLE MILL
4 UPPER ANDOVER HILL
5 NEWINGTON GDNS

4 ►

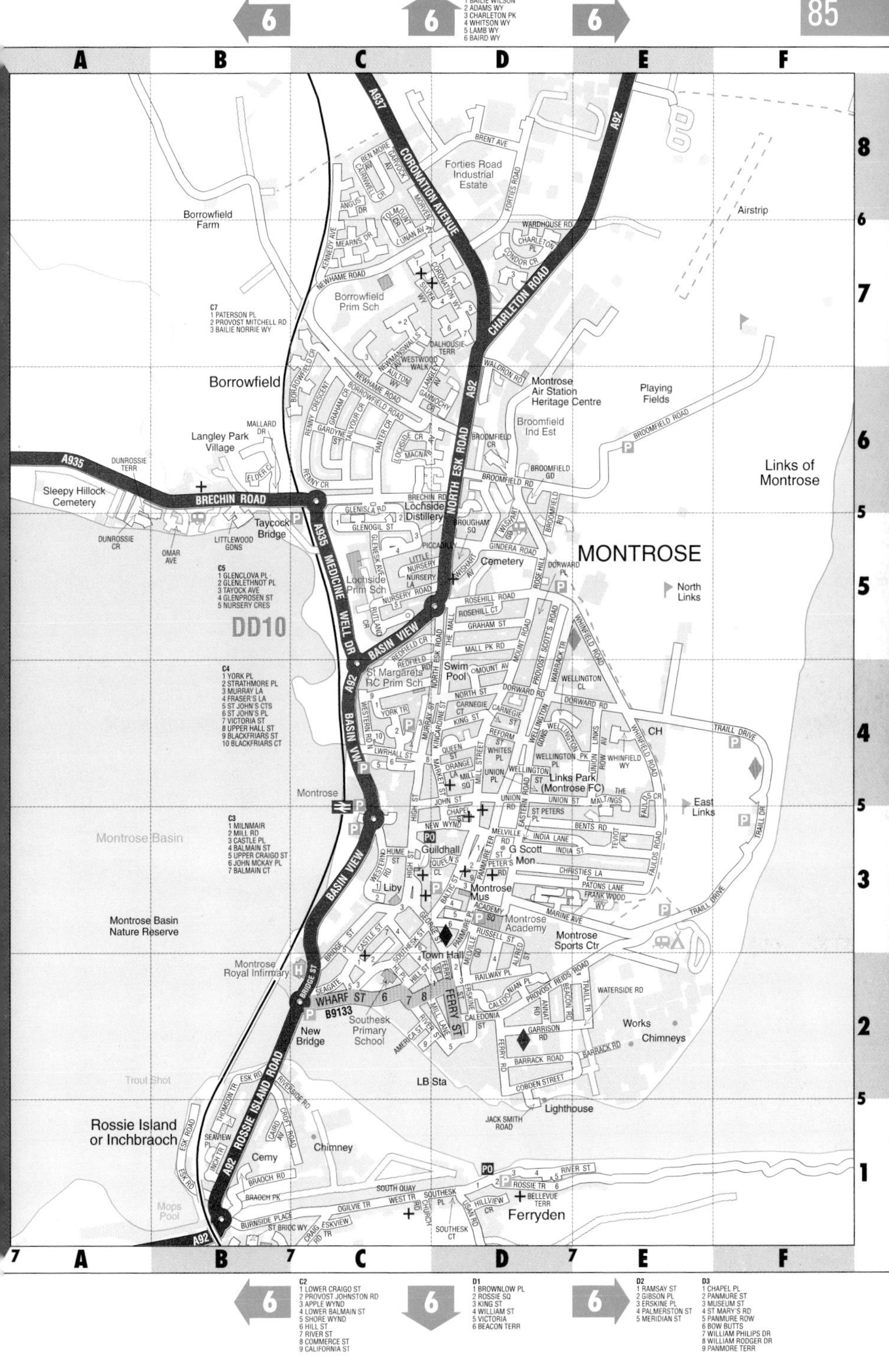

6 ←   6   6 →

D7
1 BAILIE WILSON
2 ADAMS WY
3 CHARLETON PK
4 WHITSON WY
5 LAMB WY
6 BAIRD WY

7 FETTES WY

A   B   C   D   E   F

MONTROSE

DD10

Borrowfield Farm

Borrowfield

C7
1 PATERSON PL
2 PROVOST MITCHELL RD
3 BAILIE NORRIE WY

Borrowfield Prim Sch

Langley Park Village

Sleepy Hillock Cemetery

A935

DUNROSSIE TERR

DUNROSSIE CR

OMAR AVE

C6
1 GLENCLOVA PL
2 GLENLETHNOT PL
3 TAYOCK AVE
4 GLENPROSEN ST
5 NURSERY CRES

BRECHIN ROAD

Taycock Bridge

LITTLEWOOD GDNS

Lochside Distillery

Lochside Prim Sch

Montrose Air Station Heritage Centre

Broomfield Ind Est

Broomfield GD

Playing Fields

Links of Montrose

Cemetery

MONTROSE

North Links

C4
1 YORK PL
2 STRATHMORE PL
3 MURRAY LA
4 FRASER'S LA
5 ST JOHN'S CTS
6 ST JOHN'S PL
7 VICTORIA ST
8 UPPER HALL ST
9 BLACKFRIARS ST
10 BLACKFRIARS CT

St Margarets RC Prim Sch

Swim Pool

Montrose Basin

Montrose

C3
1 MILNMAIR
2 MILL RD
3 CASTLE PL
4 BALMAIN ST
5 UPPER CRAIGO ST
6 JOHN MCKAY PL
7 BALMAIN CT

Montrose Basin Nature Reserve

Troul Shot

Links Park (Montrose FC)

CH

East Links

Guildhall

G Scott Mon

Christies La

Montrose Mus

Montrose Academy

Montrose Sports Ctr

Liby

Montrose Royal Infirmary

Town Hall

WHARF ST

B9133

New Bridge

Southesk Primary School

Railway

Works

Chimneys

Waterside Rd

Garrison

Barrack Road

Cowden Street

LB Sta

Lighthouse

Rossie Island or Inchbraoch

Cemy

Chimney

Mops Pool

BRAOCH RD

BRAOCH PK

SOUTH QUAY

WEST TR

SOUTHESK PL

HILLVIEW

BELLEVUE TERR

Ferryden

JACK SMITH ROAD

RIVER ST

ROSSIE TR

SOUTHESK CT

A   B   C   D   E   F

6 ←   6   6 →

C2
1 LOWER CRAIGO ST
2 PROVOST JOHNSTON RD
3 APPLE WYND
4 LOWER BALMAIN ST
5 SHORE WYND
6 HILL ST
7 RIVER ST
8 COMMERCE ST
9 CALIFORNIA ST

D1
1 BROWNLOW PL
2 ROSSIE SQ
3 KING ST
4 WILLIAM ST
5 VICTORIA
6 BEACON TERR

D2
1 RAMSAY ST
2 GIBSON PL
3 MUSEUM ST
4 ERSKINE PL
5 PALMERSTON ST
6 MERIDIAN ST

D3
1 CHAPEL PL
2 PANMURE ST
3 MUSEUM ST
4 ST MARY'S RD
5 PANMURE ROW
6 BOW BUTTS
7 WILLIAM PHILIPS DR
8 WILLIAM RODGER DR
9 PANMURE TERR

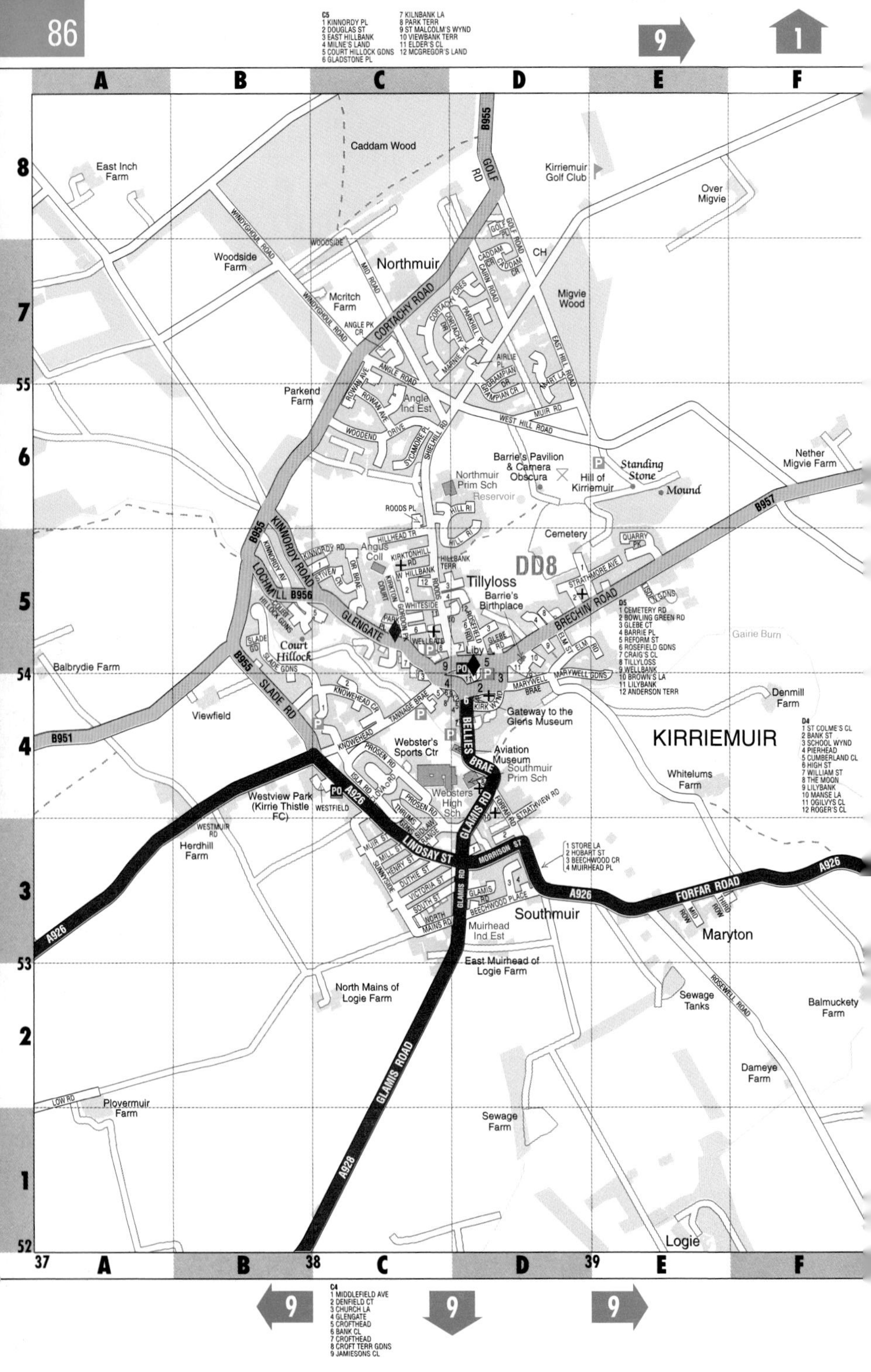

C5
1 KINNORDY PL
2 DOUGLAS ST
3 EAST HILLBANK
4 MILNE'S LAND
5 COURT HILLOCK GDNS
6 GLADSTONE PL

7 KILNBANK LA
8 PARK TERR
9 ST MALCOLM'S WYND
10 VIEWBANK TERR
11 ELDER'S CL
12 MCGREGOR'S LAND

Caddam Wood

B955
GOLF RD

East Inch Farm

Kirriemuir Golf Club

Over Migvie

Woodside Farm

Northmuir

CH

Migvie Wood

Mcritch Farm

CORTACHY ROAD

Parkend Farm

Angle Ind Est

WEST HILL ROAD
MUIR RD

Nether Migvie Farm

B957

Standing Stone

Barrie's Pavilion & Camera Obscura

Hill of Kirriemuir

Mound

Northmuir Prim Sch

Reservoir

Cemetery

QUARRY PK

DD8

Balbrydie Farm

KINNORDY ROAD

Angus Coll

Tillyloss

Barrie's Birthplace

BRECHIN ROAD

Gairie Burn

LOCHMILL

B956

GLENGATE

SLADE RD

D5
1 CEMETERY RD
2 BOWLING GREEN RD
3 GLEBE CT
4 BARRIE PL
5 REFORM ST
6 ROSEFIELD GDNS
7 CRAIG'S CL
8 TILLYLOSS
9 WELLBANK
10 BROWN'S LA
11 LILYBANK
12 ANDERSON TERR

Court Hillock

Libry

Denmill Farm

B951

Viewfield

Herdhill Farm

Westview Park (Kirrie Thistle FC)

Gateway to the Glens Museum

KIRRIEMUIR

D4
1 ST COLME'S CL
2 BANK ST
3 SCHOOL WYND
4 PIERHEAD
5 CUMBERLAND CL
6 HIGH ST
7 WILLIAM ST
8 THE MOON
9 LILYBANK
10 MANSE LA
11 OGILVY'S CL
12 ROGER'S CL

Westview Park (Kirrie Thistle FC)

WESTFIELD

Webster's Sports Ctr

Aviation Museum
Southmuir Prim Sch

Whitelums Farm

Webster's High Sch

GLAMIS RD

BELLIES BRAE

A926

FORFAR ROAD

Maryton

WESTMAIN

LINDSAY ST

MORRISON ST

1 STORE LA
2 HOBART ST
3 BEECHWOOD CR
4 MUIRHEAD PL

Southmuir

North Mains of Logie Farm

Muirhead Ind Est

GLAMIS ROAD

East Muirhead of Logie Farm

Sewage Tanks

Balmuckety Farm

Plovermuir Farm

A926

Dameye Farm

Sewage Farm

Logie

C4
1 MIDDLEFIELD AVE
2 DENFIELD CT
3 CHURCH LA
4 GLENGATE
5 CROFTHEAD
6 BANK CL
7 CROFTHEAD
8 CROFT TERR GDNS
9 JAMIESONS CL

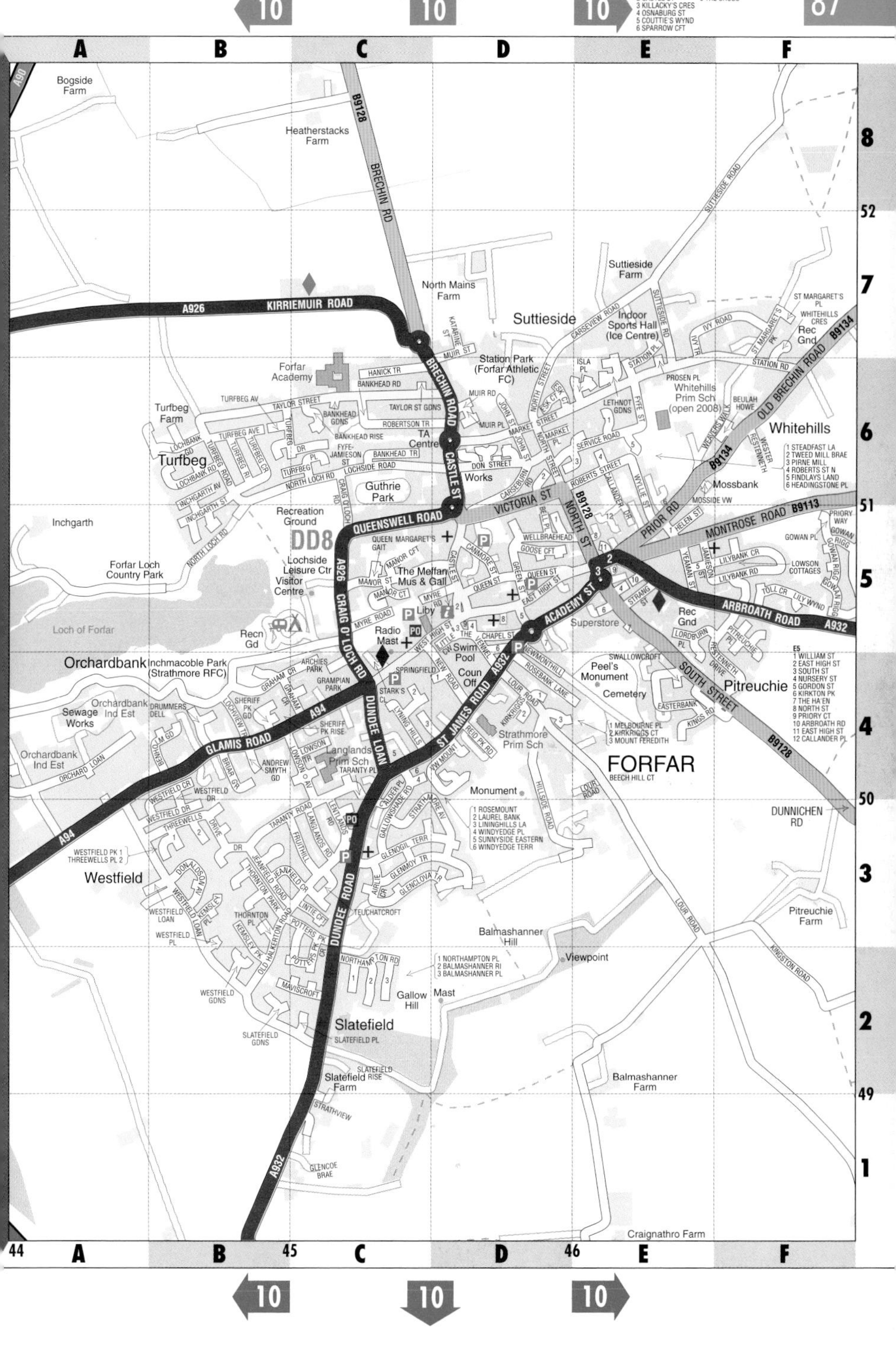

D5
1 PEFFER'S PL
2 CASTLE ST
3 KILLACKY'S CRES
4 OSNABURG ST
5 COUTTIE'S WYND
6 SPARROW CFT
7 NEWMONTHILL
8 ALBION PL
9 THE CROSS

10   10   10   10   10   10

A   B   C   D   E   F

8
52
7
6
51
5
4
50
3
2
49
1

Bogside Farm
Heatherstacks Farm
B9128
BRECHIN RD
North Mains Farm
Suttieside Farm
ST MARGARET'S LA
WHITEHILLS CRES
Rec Gnd
B9134
OLD BRECHIN ROAD
STATION RD
A926 KIRRIEMUIR ROAD
Suttieside
Indoor Sports Hall (Ice Centre)
PROSEN PL
Whitehills Prim Sch (open 2008)
BEULAH HOWE
Whitehills
Turfbeg Farm
Forfar Academy
Station Park (Forfar Athletic FC)
Mossbank
MOSSIDE VW
1 STEADFAST LA
2 TWEED MILL BRAE
3 PIRNE MILL
4 ROBERTS ST N
5 FINDLAYS LAND
6 HEADINGSTONE PL
TURFBEG AV
TAYLOR ST GONS
HANICK TR
BANKHEAD RD
TAYLOR ST
TAYLOR ST GONS
MUIR ST
ROBERTSON TR
MARKET STREET
SERVICE STREET
TA Centre
BANKHEAD RISE
FYFE-JAMIESON
BANKHEAD TR
MUIR PL
ROBERTS STREET
PRIOR RD
MONTROSE ROAD B9113
GOWAN PL
GOWAN
PRIORY WAY
Turfbeg Farm
Turfbeg
LOCHSIDE ROAD
DON STREET
Works
CARSEVIEW
LILYBANK CR
LILYBANK RD
LOWSON COTTAGES
TOLL CR
LILY WYND
NORTH LOCH RD
Guthrie Park
Recreation Ground
Inchgarth
DD8
QUEENSWELL ROAD
VICTORIA ST
B9128
NORTH ST
HELEN ST
ARBROATH ROAD A932
Rec Gnd
Forfar Loch Country Park
Lochside Leisure Ctr
Visitor Centre
QUEEN MARGARET'S GAIT
The Meffan Mus & Gall
MANOR CFT
MYRE
QUEEN ST
EAST HIGH ST
STRANG
CRAIG O' LOCH RD
A926
Loch of Forfar
Recn Gd
Radio Mast
ACADEMY ST
A932
Superstore
E5
1 WILLIAM ST
2 EAST HIGH ST
3 SOUTH ST
4 NURSERY ST
5 GORDON ST
6 KIRKTON PK
7 THE HA'EN
8 NORTH ST
9 PRIORY CT
10 ARBROATH RD
11 EAST HIGH ST
12 CALLANDER PL
Orchardbank
Inchmacoble Park (Strathmore RFC)
GRAHAM
GRAMPIAN PARK
SPRINGFIELD
Swim Pool
Coun Off
CHAPEL ST
SWALLOWCROFT
Peel's Monument
Cemetery
EASTERBANK
SOUTH STREET
Pitreuchie
Sewage Works
Orchardbank Ind Est
ARCHIES
SHERIFF
DRUMMERS DELL
ANDREW SMYTH GD
LONDON ST
DUNDEE LOAN
ST JAMES ROAD A932
ROSEMAN LANE
Strathmore Prim Sch
1 MELBOURNE PL
2 KIRKRIGGS CT
3 MOUNT FEREDITH
FORFAR
BEECH HILL CT
Orchardbank Ind Est
ORCHARD LOAN
A94
GLAMIS ROAD
SHERIFF PK RISE
TARANTY PL
Langlands Prim Sch
Monument
1 ROSEMOUNT
2 LAUREL BANK
3 LININGHILLS LA
4 WINDYEDGE PL
5 SUNNYSIDE EASTERN
6 WINDYEDGE TERR
DUNNICHEN RD
A94
WESTFIELD DR
WESTFIELD PK 1
THREEWELLS PL 2
THREEWELLS
DUNDEE ROAD A932
GLENGOIL TERR
GLENMAY TR
GLENOLIVA TR
Pitreuchie Farm
Westfield
WESTFIELD LOAN
WESTFIELD PL
THORNTON PL
TEUCHATCROFT
NORTHAMPTON RD
LOCH RD
KINGSTON ROAD
WESTFIELD GDNS
Balmashanner Hill
Viewpoint
1 NORTHAMPTON PL
2 BALMASHANNER RI
3 BALMASHANNER PL
MAINSCROFT
Gallow Hill
Mast
Balmashanner Farm
Slatefield
SLATEFIELD GDNS
SLATEFIELD PL
SLATEFIELD RISE
Slatefield Farm
STRATHVIEW
A932
GLENCOE BRAE
Craignathro Farm

44   45   46
A   B   C   D   E   F
10   10   10

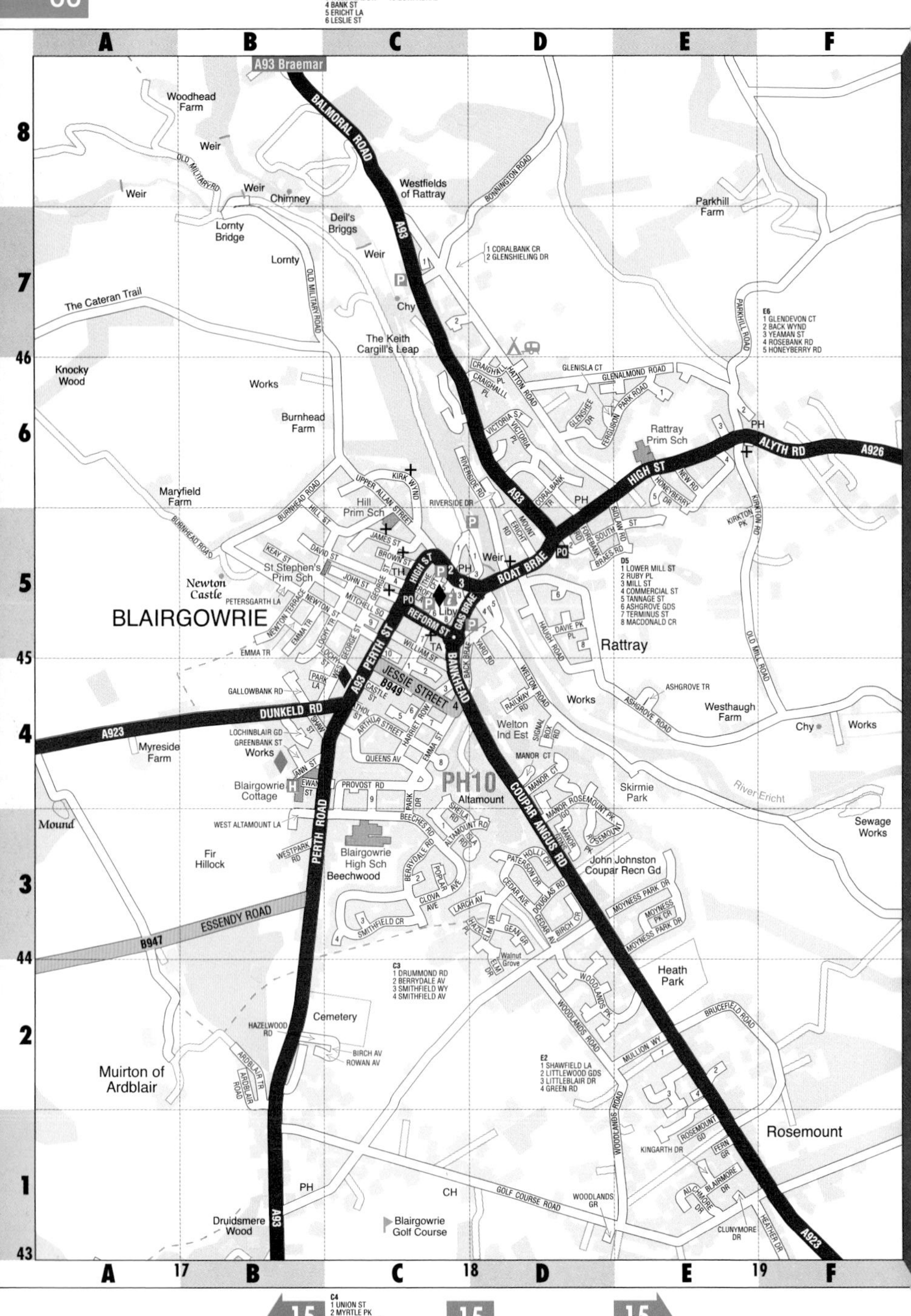

BLAIRGOWRIE

Rattray

PH10
Altamount

Rosemount

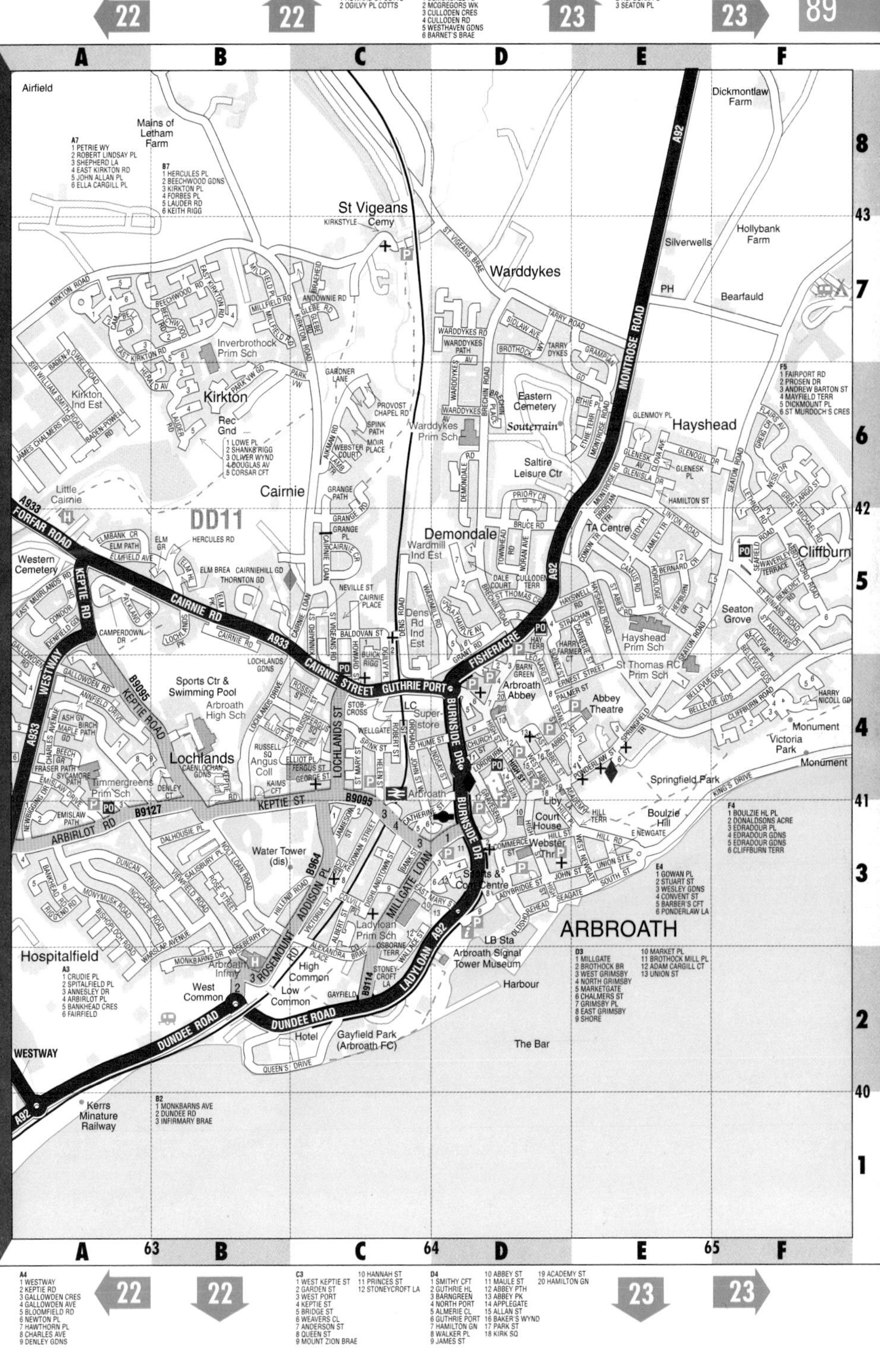

89
22
22
23
23
C5
1 HOWARD ST COTTS
2 OGILVY PL COTTS
D5
1 DEMONDALE PL
2 MCGREGORS WK
3 CULLODEN CRES
4 CULLODEN RD
5 WESTHAVEN GDNS
6 BARNET'S BRAE
7 ANDREW WELSH WAY
E5
1 NECTAN TERR
2 HEPBURN PL
3 SEATON PL
A
B
C
D
E
F
Airfield
Mains of Letham Farm
A7
1 PETRIE WY
2 ROBERT LINDSAY PL
3 SHEPHERD LA
4 EAST KIRKTON RD
5 JOHN ALLAN PL
6 ELLA CARGILL PL
B7
1 HERCULES PL
2 BEECHWOOD GDNS
3 KIRKTON PL
4 FORBES PL
5 LAUDER RD
6 KEITH RIGG
Dickmontlaw Farm
A92
8
43
St Vigeans Cemy
KIRKSTYLE
Hollybank Farm
Silverwells
Warddykes
PH
Bearfauld
7
KIRKTON ROAD
MONTROSE ROAD
TARRY ROAD
Inverbrothock Prim Sch
Kirkton Ind Est
Kirkton
Rec Gnd
Eastern Cemetery
Souterrain
F5
1 FAIRPORT RD
2 PROSEN DR
3 ANDREW BARTON ST
4 MAYFIELD TERR
5 DICKMOUNT PL
6 ST MURDOCH'S CRES
Warddykes Prim Sch
Hayshead
6
1 LOWE PL
2 SHANKS RIGG
3 OLIVER WYND
4 DOUGLAS AV
5 CORSAR CFT
Saltire Leisure Ctr
Little Cairnie
Cairnie
A933
FORFAR ROAD
DD11
42
Demondale
TA Centre
Wardmill Ind Est
Western Cemetery
Cliffburn
5
CAIRNIE RD
Dens Rd Ind Est
FISHERACRE
Seaton Grove
Hayshead Prim Sch
St Thomas RC Prim Sch
Sports Ctr & Swimming Pool
Arbroath High Sch
CAIRNIE STREET
GUTHRIE PORT
Arbroath Abbey
Abbey Theatre
WESTWAY
KEPTIE ROAD
Super-store
LC
BURNSIDE DR
4
Monument
Victoria Park
Monument
Lochlands
Angus Coll
Springfield Park
Timmergreens Prim Sch
KEPTIE ST
B9095
B9127
ARBIRLOT RD
Arbroath
Liby
Court House
Boulzie Hill
KING'S DRIVE
41
F4
1 BOULZIE HL PL
2 DONALDSONS ACRE
3 EDRADOUR PL
4 EDRADOUR GDNS
5 EDRADOUR GDNS
6 CLIFFBURN TERR
Water Tower (dis)
Webster Thr
3
E4
1 GOWAN PL
2 STUART ST
3 WESLEY GDNS
4 CONVENT ST
5 BARBER'S CFT
6 PONDERLAW LA
Sports & Com Centre
Ladyloan Prim Sch
ARBROATH
LB Sta
Hospitalfield
Arbroath Signal Tower Museum
D3
1 MILLGATE
2 BROTHOCK BR
3 WEST GRIMSBY
4 NORTH GRIMSBY
5 MARKETGATE
6 CHALMERS ST
7 GRIMSBY PL
8 EAST GRIMSBY
9 SHORE
10 MARKET PL
11 BROTHOCK MILL PL
12 ADAM CARGILL CT
13 UNION ST
A3
1 CRUDIE PL
2 SPITALFIELD PL
3 ANNESLEY DR
4 ARBIRLOT PL
5 BANKHEAD CRES
6 FAIRFIELD
Arbroath Infmy
High Common
Low Common
West Common
Harbour
2
DUNDEE ROAD
LADYLOAN
Hotel
Gayfield Park (Arbroath FC)
The Bar
WESTWAY
40
Kerrs Minature Railway
B2
1 MONKBARNS AVE
2 DUNDEE RD
3 INFIRMARY BRAE
1
63
64
65
A4
1 WESTWAY
2 KEPTIE RD
3 GALLOWDEN CRES
4 GALLOWDEN AVE
5 BLOOMFIELD RD
6 NEWTON PL
7 HAWTHORN PL
8 CHARLES AVE
9 DENLEY GDNS
C3
1 WEST KEPTIE ST
2 GARDEN ST
3 WEST PORT
4 KEPTIE ST
5 BRIDGE ST
6 WEAVERS CL
7 ANDERSON ST
8 QUEEN ST
9 MOUNT ZION BRAE
10 HANNAH ST
11 PRINCES ST
12 STONEYCROFT LA
D4
1 SMITHY CFT
2 GUTHRIE HL
3 BARNGREEN
4 NORTH PORT
5 ALMERIE CL
6 GUTHRIE PORT
7 HAMILTON GN
8 WALKER PL
9 JAMES ST
10 ABBEY ST
11 MAULE ST
12 ABBEY PTH
13 ABBEY PK
14 APPLEGATE
15 ALLAN ST
16 BAKER'S WYND
17 PARK ST
18 KIRK SQ
19 ACADEMY ST
20 HAMILTON GN

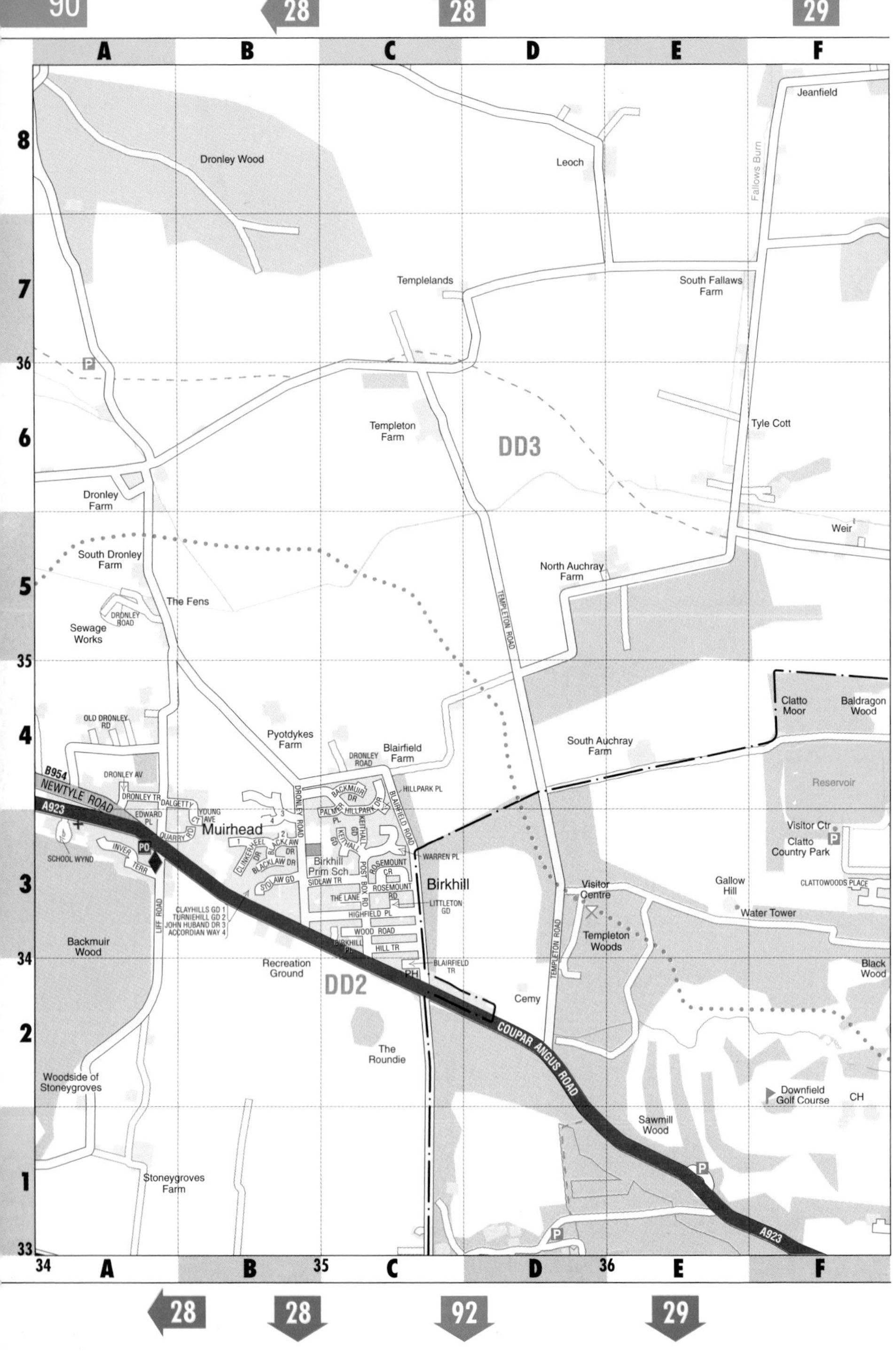
28
28
29
A
B
C
D
E
F
8
7
36
6
5
35
4
3
34
2
1
33
Jeanfield
Dronley Wood
Leoch
Fallows Burn
Templelands
South Fallaws
Farm
Templeton
Farm
DD3
Tyle Cott
Dronley
Farm
Weir
South Dronley
Farm
North Auchray
Farm
The Fens
DRONLEY
ROAD
Sewage
Works
TEMPLETON ROAD
Clatto
Moor
Baldragon
Wood
OLD DRONLEY
RD
Pyotdykes
Farm
Blairfield
Farm
South Auchray
Farm
DRONLEY
ROAD
B954
DRONLEY AV
NEWTYLE ROAD
HILLPARK PL
Reservoir
A923
DRONLEY TR
DALGETTY
YOUNG
AVE
EDWARD
PL
QUARRY RD
Muirhead
Visitor Ctr
Clatto
Country Park
SCHOOL WYND
INVER
TERR
PD
WARREN PL
Birkhill
Prim Sch
SIDLAW TR
Birkhill
Visitor
Centre
Gallow
Hill
CLATTOWOODS PLACE
Water Tower
THE LANE
HIGHFIELD PL
LITTLETON
GD
CLAYHILLS GD 1
TURNIEHILL GD 2
JOHN HUBAND DR 3
ACCORDIAN WAY 4
LIFF ROAD
WOOD ROAD
Templeton
Woods
Backmuir
Wood
HILL TR
Recreation
Ground
BLAIRFIELD
TR
PH
DD2
Cemy
Black
Wood
COUPAR ANGUS ROAD
The
Roundie
Woodside of
Stoneygroves
Downfield
Golf Course
CH
Sawmill
Wood
Stoneygroves
Farm
A923
34
35
36

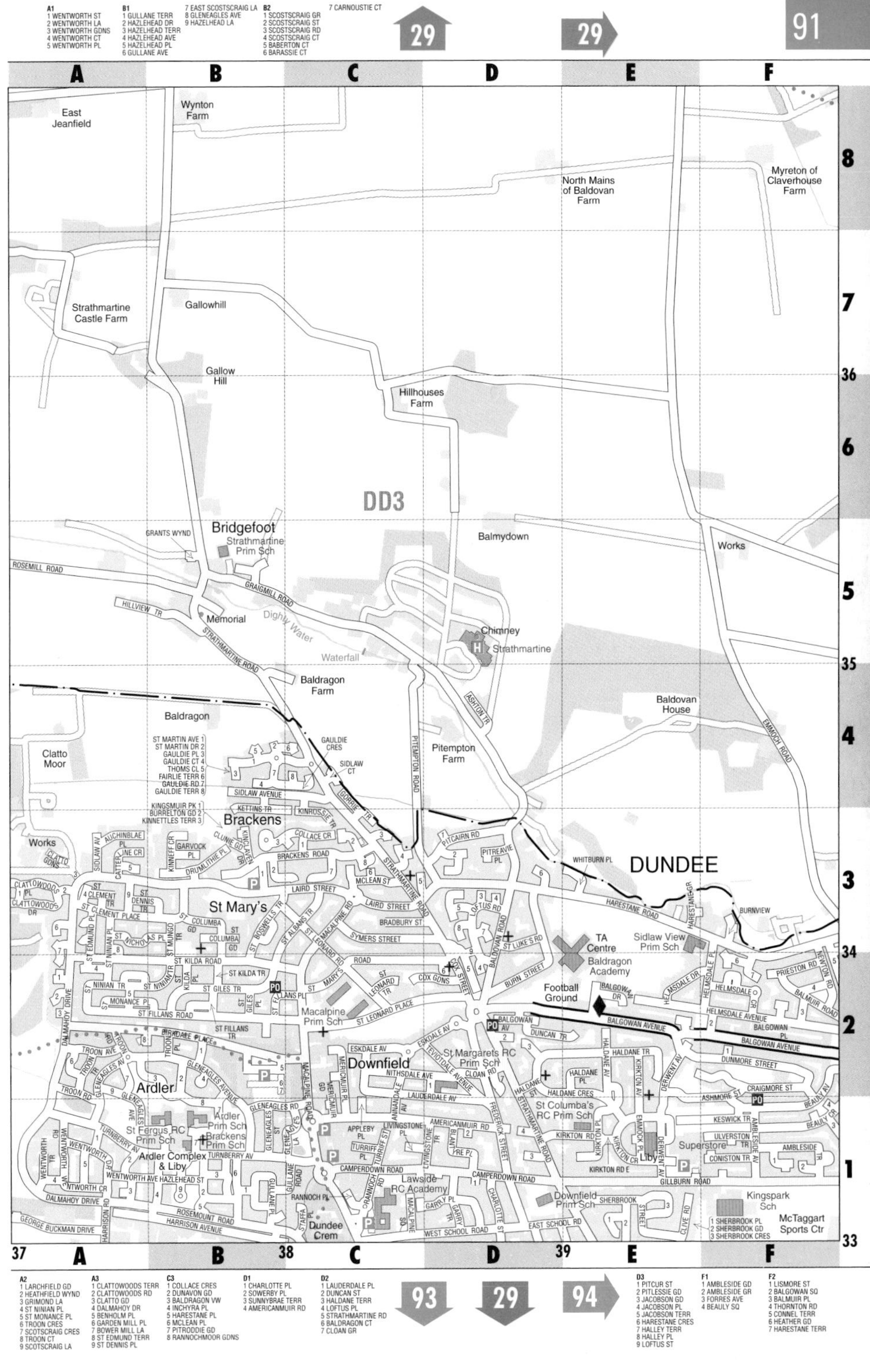

A1
1 WENTWORTH ST
2 WENTWORTH LA
3 WENTWORTH GDNS
4 WENTWORTH CT
5 WENTWORTH PL

B1
1 GULLANE TERR
2 HAZELHEAD DR
3 HAZELHEAD TERR
4 HAZELHEAD AVER
5 HAZELHEAD PL
6 GULLANE AVE

7 EAST SCOTSCRAIG LA
8 GLENEAGLES AVE
9 HAZELHEAD LA

B2
1 SCOTSCRAIG GR
2 SCOTSCRAIG GR
3 SCOTSCRAIG RD
4 SCOTSCRAIG CT
5 BABERTON CT
6 BARASSIE CT

7 CARNOUSTIE CT

29   29

A   **B**   **C**   **D**   **E**   **F**

East Jeanfield

Wynton Farm

8

Myreton of Claverhouse Farm

North Mains of Baldovan Farm

7

Strathmartine Castle Farm

Gallowhill

36

Gallow Hill

Hillhouses Farm

6

DD3

Bridgefoot

Balmydown

Works

5

GRANTS WYND

Strathmartine Prim Sch

ROSEMILL ROAD

HILLVIEW TR

Memorial

Dighty Water

Waterfall

Chimney

Strathmartine

35

Baldragon Farm

Baldovan House

4

Clatto Moor

Baldragon

ST MARTIN AVE 1
ST MARTIN DR 2
GAULDIE PL 3
GAULDIE CT 4
THOMS CL 5
FAIRLIE TERR 6
GAULDIE RD 7
GAULDIE TERR 8

GAULDIE CRES

SIDLAW CT

SIDLAW AVENUE

KETTINS TR

Pitempton Farm

Works

KINGSMUIR PK 1
BURRELTON GD 2
KINNETTLES TERR 3

KINROSSIE TR

Brackens

CALLACE CR

BRACKENS ROAD

PITCAIRN RD

PITREAVIE PL

WHITBURN PL

DUNDEE

3

CLATTOWOODS
DR

AUCHINBLAE

CLUNE CRES

GARVOCK PL

DRUMLITHIE PL

KINNEFF CR

LAIRD STREET

McLEAN ST

HARESTANE ROAD

BURNVIEW

34

Works

ST CLEMENT
GD

ST DENNIS
ST

DALMAHOY DR

ST EDMUND
ST

ST COLUMBA
GD

St Mary's

ST COLUMBA
GD

LAIRD STREET

BRADBURY ST

SYMERS STREET

ST LUKE'S RD

HARESTANE RD

TA Centre

Baldragon Academy

Sidlaw View Prim Sch

PRIESTON RD

BALFUIR RD

CLATTOWOOD
DR

ST
CLEMENT PLACE

NICHOLS

ST KILDA ROAD

ST KILDA TR

ST GILES TR

ROAD

ST MARY

COX GDNS

BURN STREET

Football Ground

BALGOWAN
DR

HELMSDALE GD

HELMSDALE AV

BALGOWAN

NINIAN TR

ST FILLANS ROAD

MONANCE
ST

MACALPINE

ST LEONARD PLACE

LANS PL

Macalpine Prim Sch

ESKDALE AV

ST LEONARD PLACE

NITHSDALE AVE

St Margarets RC Prim Sch

DUNCAN TR

BALGOWAN AV

BALGOWAN AVENUE

DUNMORE STREET

ULVERSTON

BALGOWAN AVENUE

2

TROON AVE

BRIDE PLACE

GLENEAGLES TERR

Downfield

LAUDERDALE AV

CLOAN

HALDANE TR

HALDANE TR

ASHMORE

CRAIGMORE ST

KESWICK RD

Ardler

St Fergus RC Prim Sch

Ardler Prim Sch

Brackens Prim Sch

GLENEAGLES TERR

APPLEBY

LIVINGSTONE

AMERICANMUIR RD

FIFE PL

HALDANE CRES

St Columba's RC Prim Sch

KIRKTON AV

DERWENT AV

Superstore

CONISTON TR

AMBLESIDE

1

WENTWORTH
TR

GARBURN
TERR

Ardler Complex & Liby

HAZELHEAD ST

TURNBERRY AV

TURRIFF

CAMPERDOWN ROAD

LAUDERDALE AV

KIRKTON AV

KIRKTON
RD

Liby

GILLBURN ROAD

Kingspark Sch

DALMAHOY DRIVE

RANNOCH PL

ROSEMOUNT ROAD

HARRISON ROAD

Lawside RC Academy

CAMPERDOWN ROAD

WEST SCHOOL ROAD

EAST SCHOOL RD

Downfield Prim Sch

SHERBROOK

1 SHERBROOK GD
2 SHERBROOK GD
3 SHERBROOK CRES

McTaggart Sports Ctr

GEORGE BUCKMAN DRIVE

Dundee Crem

33

37   **A**   **B**   38   **C**   **D**   39   **E**   **F**

A2
1 LARCHFIELD GD
2 HEATHFIELD WYND
3 GRIMOND LA
4 ST NINIAN PL
5 ST MONANCE PL
6 TROON CRES
7 SCOTSCRAIG CRES
8 TROON CT
9 SCOTSCRAIG LA

A3
1 CLATTOWOODS TERR
2 CLATTOWOODS RD
3 CLATTO GD
4 DALMAHOY DR
5 BENHOLM PL
6 GARDEN MILL PL
7 BOWER MILL LA
8 ST EDMUND TERR
9 ST DENNIS PL

C3
1 COLLACE CRES
2 DUNAVON GD
3 BALDRAGON VW
4 INCHYRA PL
5 HARESTANE PL
6 McLEAN PL
7 PITRODDIE GD
8 RANNOCHMOOR GDNS

D1
1 CHARLOTTE PL
2 SOWERBY PL
3 SUNNYBRAE TERR
4 AMERICANMUIR RD

D2
1 LAUDERDALE PL
2 DUNCAN ST
3 HALDANE TERR
4 LOFTUS GD
5 STRATHMARTINE RD
6 BALDRAGON CT
7 CLOAN GR

D3
1 PITCUR ST
2 PITLESSIE GD
3 JACOBSON GD
4 JACOBSON PL
5 JACOBSON TERR
6 HARESTANE CRES
7 HALLEY TERR
8 HALLEY PL
9 LOFTUS ST

F1
1 AMBLESIDE GD
2 AMBLESIDE GR
3 FORRES AVE
4 BEAULY SQ

F2
1 LISMORE ST
2 BALGOWAN SQ
3 BALMUIR PL
4 THORNTON RD
5 CONNEL TERR
6 HEATHER GD
7 HARESTANE TERR

93   29   94

28 28 90 29

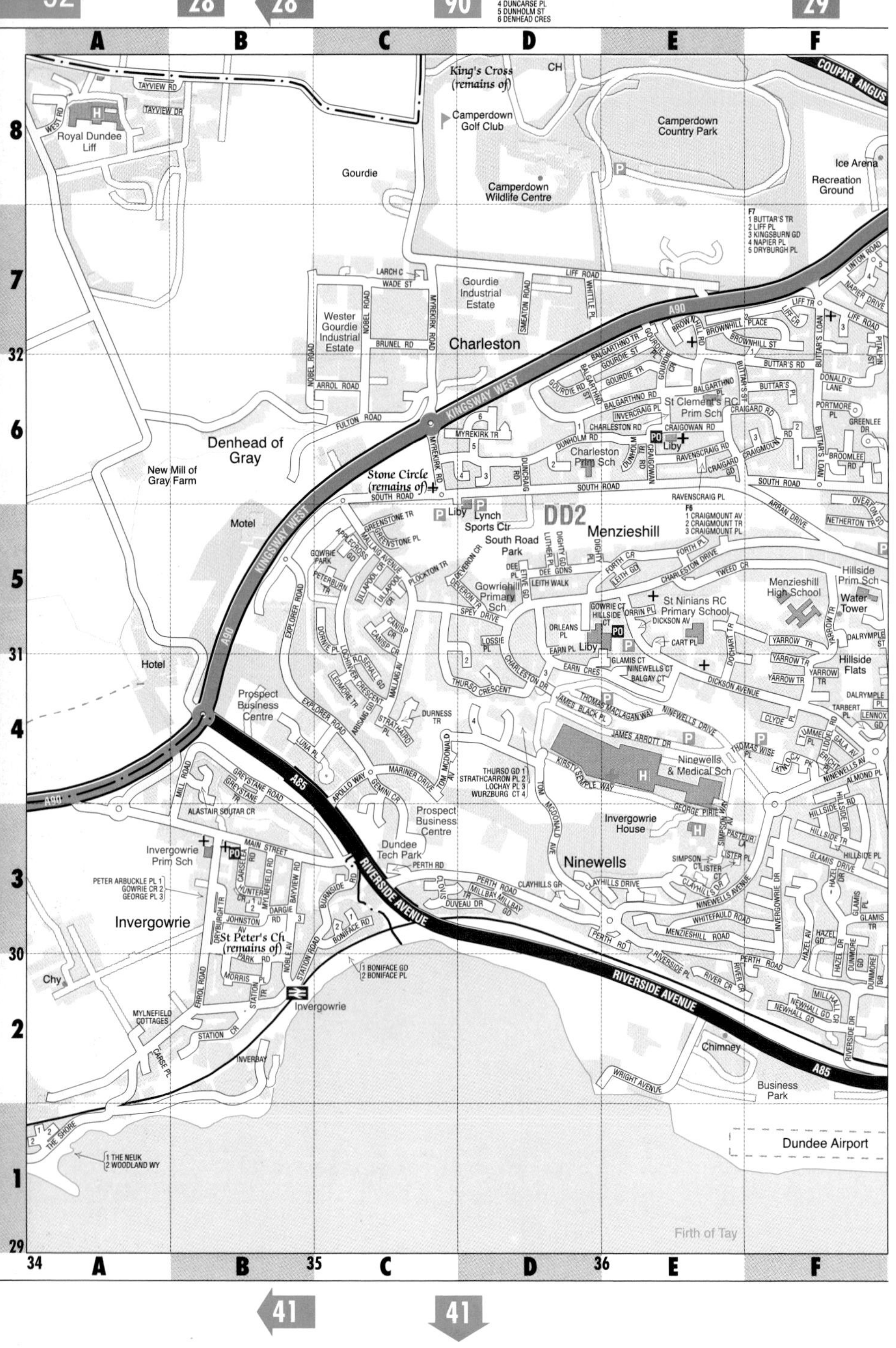
D6
1 CHARLESTON ST
2 DUNHOLM PL
3 DUNCARSE RD
4 DUNCARSE PL
5 DUNHOLM ST
6 DENHEAD CRES
A
B
C
D
E
F
8
7
32
6
5
31
4
3
30
2
1
29
34
35
36
King's Cross (remains of)
CH
COUPAR ANGUS
Camperdown Golf Club
Camperdown Country Park
Royal Dundee Liff
TAYVIEW RD
TAYVIEW DR
WEST RD
Gourdie
Camperdown Wildlife Centre
Ice Arena
Recreation Ground
F7
1 BUTTAR'S TR
2 LIFF PL
3 KINGSBURN GD
4 NAPIER PL
5 DRYBURGH PL
LARCH C
WADE ST
Gourdie Industrial Estate
LIFF ROAD
WHITTLE PL
SMEATON ROAD
Wester Gourdie Industrial Estate
NOBEL ROAD
BRUNEL RD
ARROL ROAD
MYREKIRK ROAD
Charleston
A90
KINGSWAY WEST
FULTON ROAD
Denhead of Gray
New Mill of Gray Farm
Stone Circle (remains of)
SOUTH ROAD
Liby
Lynch Sports Ctr
South Road Park
DD2
Menzieshill
Motel
St Clement's RC Prim Sch
Charleston Prim Sch
Menzieshill High School
Hillside Prim Sch
Water Tower
Hillside Flats
Gowriehill Primary Sch
St Ninians RC Primary School
Hotel
Prospect Business Centre
EXPLORER ROAD
DICKSON AVENUE
NINEWELLS DRIVE
JAMES ARROTT DR
Ninewells & Medical Sch
Invergowrie House
Ninewells
A85
RIVERSIDE AVENUE
PERTH ROAD
Dundee Tech Park
Invergowrie Prim Sch
Invergowrie
St Peter's Ch (remains of)
Chy
MYLNEFIELD COTTAGES
STATION CR
INVERBAY
1 BONIFACE GD
2 BONIFACE PL
1 THE NEUK
2 WOODLAND WY
THE SHORE
PETER ARBUCKLE PL 1
GOWRIE CR 2
GEORGE PL 3
THURSO GD 1
STRATHCARRON PL 2
LOCHAY PL 3
WURZBURG CT 4
F6
1 CRAIGMOUNT AV
2 CRAIGMOUNT TR
3 CRAIGMOUNT PL
Chimney
Business Park
WRIGHT AVENUE
Dundee Airport
Firth of Tay

41 41

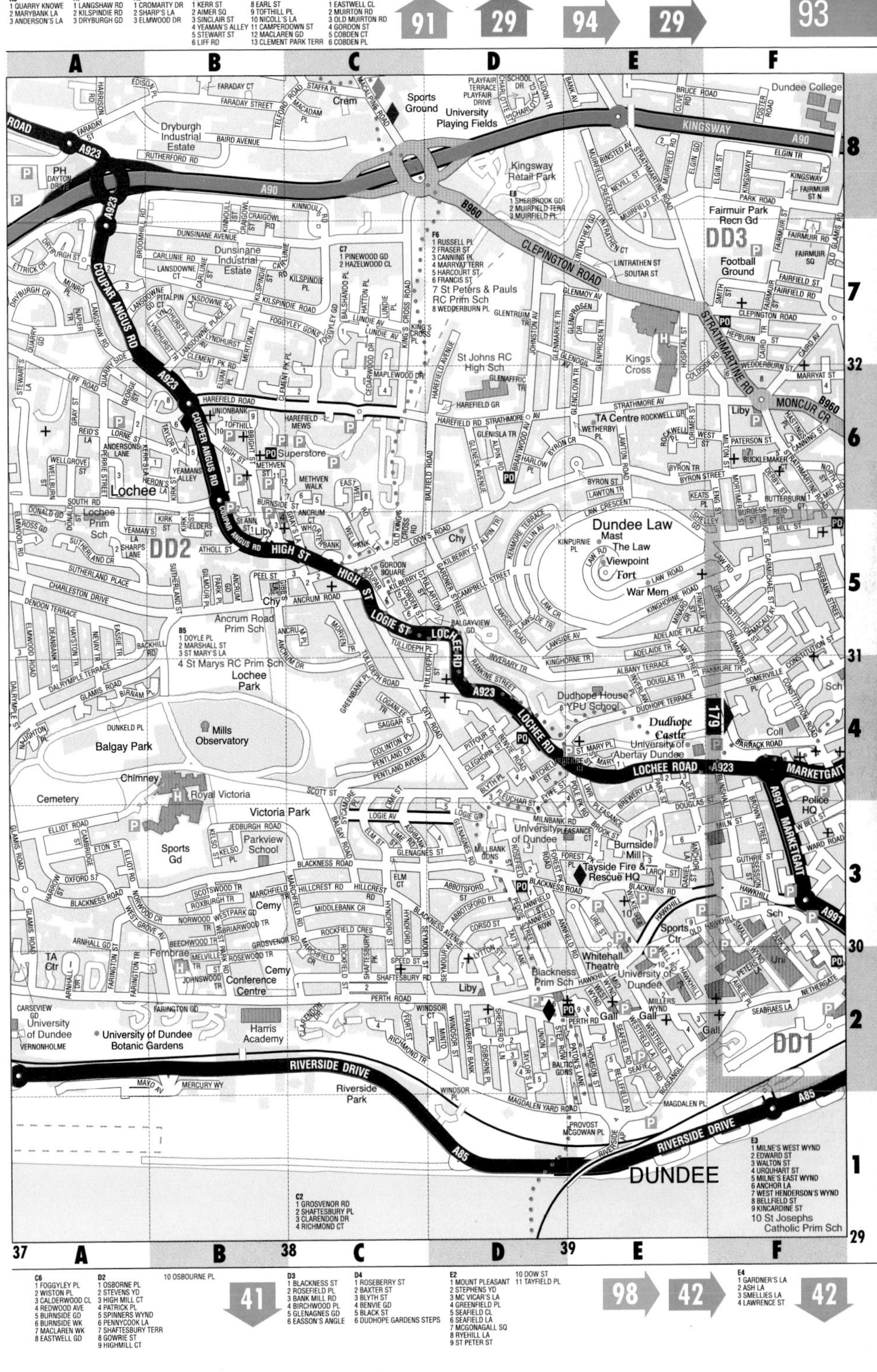

93
91
29
94
29
A6
1 QUARRY KNOWE
2 MARYBANK LA
3 ANDERSON'S LA
A7
1 LANGSHAW RD
2 KILSPINDIE RD
3 DRYBURGH GD
A5
1 CROMARTY DR
2 SHARP'S LA
3 ELMWOOD DR
B6
1 KERR ST
2 AIMER SQ
3 SINCLAIR ST
4 YEAMAN'S ALLEY
5 STEWART ST
6 LIFF RD
7 ANGUS ST
8 EARL ST
9 TOFTHILL PL
10 NICOLL'S LA
11 CAMPERDOWN ST
12 MACLAREN GD
13 CLEMENT PARK TERR
C5
1 EASTWELL CL
2 MUIRTON RD
3 OLD MUIRTON RD
4 GORDON ST
5 COBDEN CT
6 COBDEN ST
A
B
C
D
E
F
8
7
32
6
5
31
4
3
30
2
1
29
37
38
39
Dryburgh Industrial Estate
Sports Ground
Crem
University Playing Fields
Kingsway Retail Park
KINGSWAY
A90
A923
B960
Dundee College
E8
1 SHERBROOK GD
2 MUIRFIELD TERR
3 MUIRFIELD PL
F6
1 RUSSELL PL
2 FRASER ST
3 CANNING PL
4 MARRYAT TERR
5 HARCOURT ST
6 FRANCIS ST
7 St Peters & Pauls RC Prim Sch
8 WEDDERBURN PL
C7
1 PINEWOOD GD
2 HAZELWOOD CL
Dunsinane Industrial Estate
Fairmuir Park Recn Gd
DD3
Football Ground
CLEPINGTON ROAD
COUPAR ANGUS RD
St Johns RC High Sch
Kings Cross
STRATHMARTINE RD
MONCUR CR
TA Centre
Liby
Superstore
Lochee
Lochee Prim Sch
DD2
HIGH ST
Dundee Law
Mast
The Law
Viewpoint
Fort
War Mem
Chy
LOGIE ST
LOCHEE RD
Ancrum Road Prim Sch
B5
1 DOYLE PL
2 MARSHALL ST
3 ST MARY'S LA
4 St Marys RC Prim Sch
Lochee Park
Dudhope House YPU School
Dudhope Castle
University of Abertay Dundee
Balgay Park
Mills Observatory
Chimney
Royal Victoria
Cemetery
Victoria Park
LOCHEE ROAD
MARKETGAIT
A991
Police HQ
Coll
Sch
Sports Gd
Parkview School
University of Dundee
Burnside Mill
Tayside Fire & Rescue HQ
Sports Ctr
Whitehall Theatre
Cemy
TA Ctr
Fernbrae
Conference Centre
Blackness Prim Sch
Gall
Uni
DD1
University of Dundee
University of Dundee Botanic Gardens
Harris Academy
RIVERSIDE DRIVE
Riverside Park
A85
DUNDEE
E3
1 MILNE'S WEST WYND
2 EDWARD ST
3 WALTON ST
4 URQUHART ST
5 MILNE'S EAST WYND
6 ANCHOR LA
7 WEST HENDERSON'S WYND
8 BELLFIELD ST
9 KINCARDINE ST
10 St Josephs Catholic Prim Sch
C2
1 GROSVENOR RD
2 SHAFTESBURY PL
3 CLARENDON DR
4 RICHMOND CT
C6
1 FOGGYLEY PL
2 WISTON PL
3 CALDERWOOD CL
4 REDWOOD AVE
5 BURNSIDE GD
6 BURNSIDE WK
7 MACLAREN WK
8 EASTWELL GD
D2
1 OSBORNE PL
2 STEVENS YD
3 HIGH MILL CT
4 PATRICK PL
5 SPINNERS WYND
6 PENNYCOOK LA
7 SHAFTESBURY TERR
8 GOWRIE ST
9 HIGHMILL CT
10 OSBOURNE PL
41
D3
1 BLACKNESS ST
2 ROSEFIELD PL
3 BANK MILL RD
4 BIRCHWOOD PL
5 GLENAGNES GD
6 EASSON'S ANGLE
D4
1 ROSEBERRY ST
2 BAXTER ST
3 BLYTH ST
4 BENVIE GD
5 BLACK ST
6 DUDHOPE GARDENS STEPS
E2
1 MOUNT PLEASANT
2 STEPHENS YD
3 MC VICAR'S LA
4 GREENFIELD PL
5 SEAFIELD CL
6 SEAFIELD LA
7 MCGONAGALL SQ
8 RYEHILL LA
9 ST PETER ST
10 DOW ST
11 TAYFIELD PL
98
42
E4
1 GARDNER'S LA
2 ASH LA
3 SMELLIES LA
4 LAWRENCE ST
42

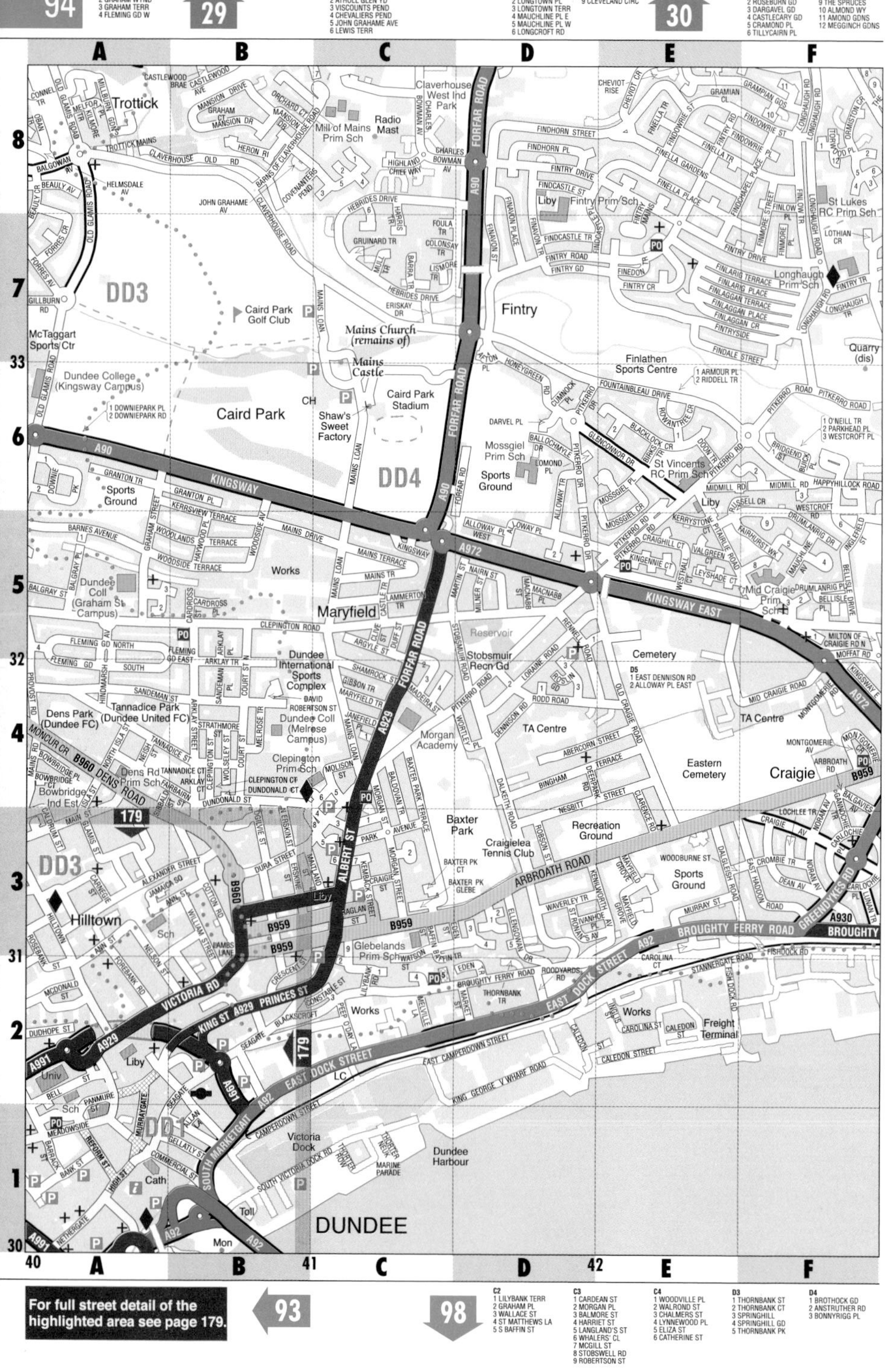

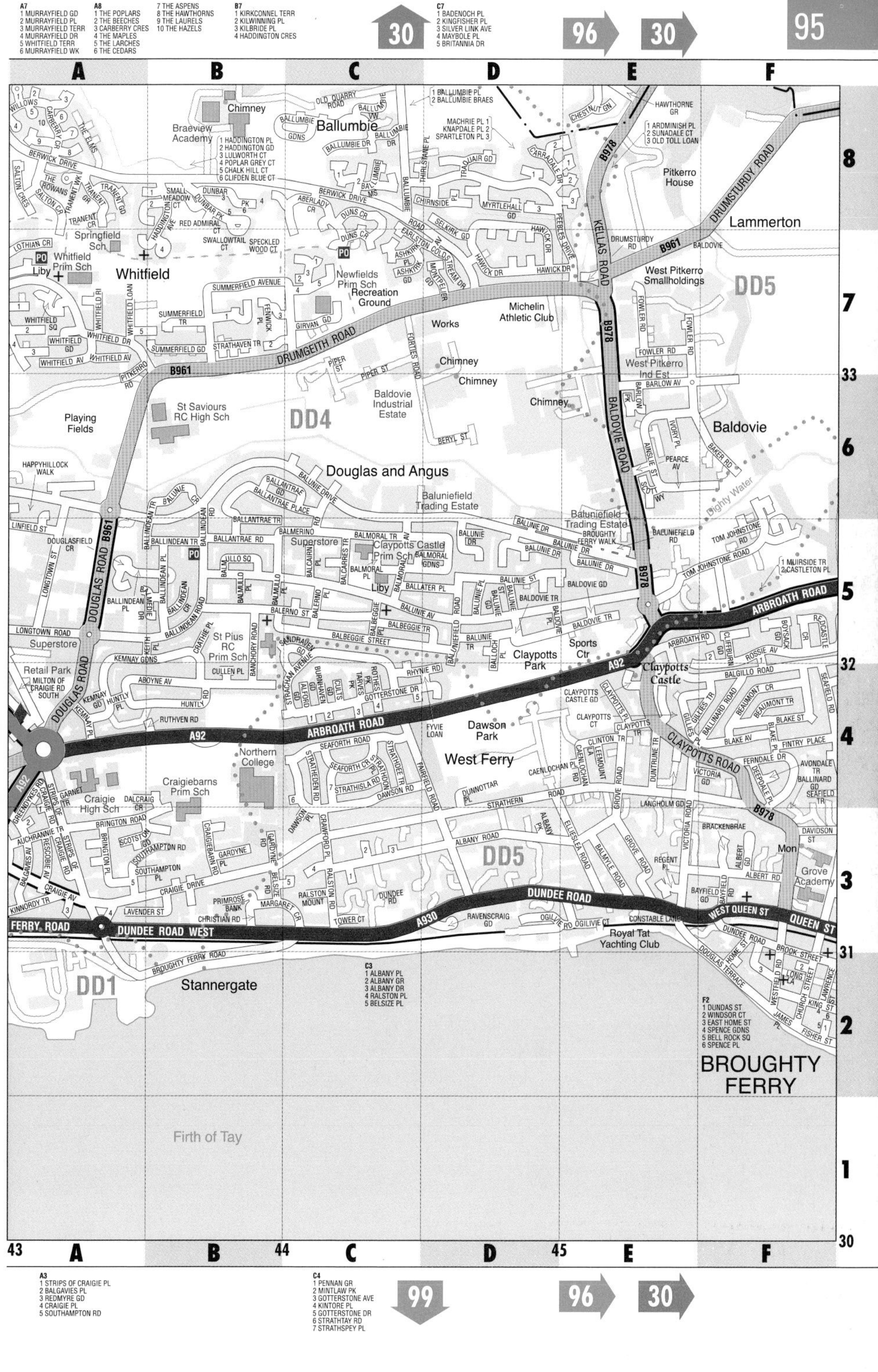
A7
1 MURRAYFIELD GD
2 MURRAYFIELD PL
3 MURRAYFIELD TERR
4 MURRAYFIELD DR
5 WHITFIELD TERR
6 MURRAYFIELD WK
A8
1 THE POPLARS
2 THE BEECHES
3 CARBERRY CRES
4 THE MAPLES
5 THE LARCHES
6 THE CEDARS
7 THE ASPENS
8 THE HAWTHORNS
9 THE LAURELS
10 THE HAZELS
B7
1 KIRKCONNEL TERR
2 KILWINNING PL
3 KILBRIDE PL
4 HADDINGTON CRES
30
C7
1 BADENOCH PL
2 KINGFISHER PL
3 SILVER LINK AVE
4 MAYBOLE PL
5 BRITANNIA DR
96
30
A
B
C
D
E
F
8
7
33
6
5
32
4
3
31
2
1
30
43
44
45
Chimney
Braeview Academy
Ballumbie
1 HADDINGTON PL
2 HADDINGTON GD
3 LULWORTH CT
4 POPLAR GREY CT
5 CHALK HILL CT
6 CLIFDEN BLUE CT
1 BALLUMBIE PL
2 BALLUMBIE BRAES
MACHRIE PL 1
KNAPDALE PL 2
SPARTLETON PL 3
HAWTHORNE GR
1 ARDMINISH PL
2 SUNADALE CT
3 OLD TOLL LOAN
Pitkerro House
DRUMSTURDY ROAD
Lammerton
BERWICK DRIVE
BERWICK DRIVE
Springfield Sch
Whitfield Prim Sch
Liby
Whitfield
Newfields Prim Sch
Recreation Ground
KELLAS ROAD
B978
B961
West Pitkerro Smallholdings
DD5
Works
Michelin Athletic Club
DRUMGEITH ROAD
Chimney
Chimney
West Pitkerro Ind Est
B961
St Saviours RC High Sch
Playing Fields
Baldovie Industrial Estate
DD4
Chimney
BALDOVIE ROAD
Baldovie
Douglas and Angus
Baluniefield Trading Estate
Baluniefield Trading Estate
Dighty Water
Superstore
Claypotts Castle Prim Sch
Liby
DOUGLAS ROAD
1 MUIRSIDE TR
2 CASTLETON PL
ARBROATH ROAD
Superstore
St Pius RC Prim Sch
Claypotts Park
Sports Ctr
Retail Park
A92
Claypotts Castle
DOUGLAS ROAD
ARBROATH ROAD
A92
Dawson Park
Northern College
West Ferry
CLAYPOTTS ROAD
Craigiebarns Prim Sch
Craigie High Sch
B978
DD5
Mon
Grove Academy
DUNDEE ROAD
A930
FERRY ROAD
DUNDEE ROAD WEST
WEST QUEEN ST
QUEEN ST
Royal Tat Yachting Club
BROUGHTY FERRY ROAD
DD1
Stannergate
C3
1 ALBANY PL
2 ALBANY GR
3 ALBANY DR
4 RALSTON PL
5 BELSIZE PL
F2
1 DUNDAS ST
2 WINDSOR CT
3 EAST HOME ST
4 SPENCE GDNS
5 BELL ROCK SQ
6 SPENCE PL
BROUGHTY FERRY
Firth of Tay
A3
1 STRIPS OF CRAIGIE PL
2 BALGAVIES PL
3 REDMYRE GD
4 CRAIGIE PL
5 SOUTHAMPTON RD
C4
1 PENNAN GR
2 MINTLAW PK
3 GOTTERSTONE AVE
4 KINTORE PL
5 GOTTERSTONE AVE
6 STRATHTAY RD
7 STRATHSPEY PL
99
96
30

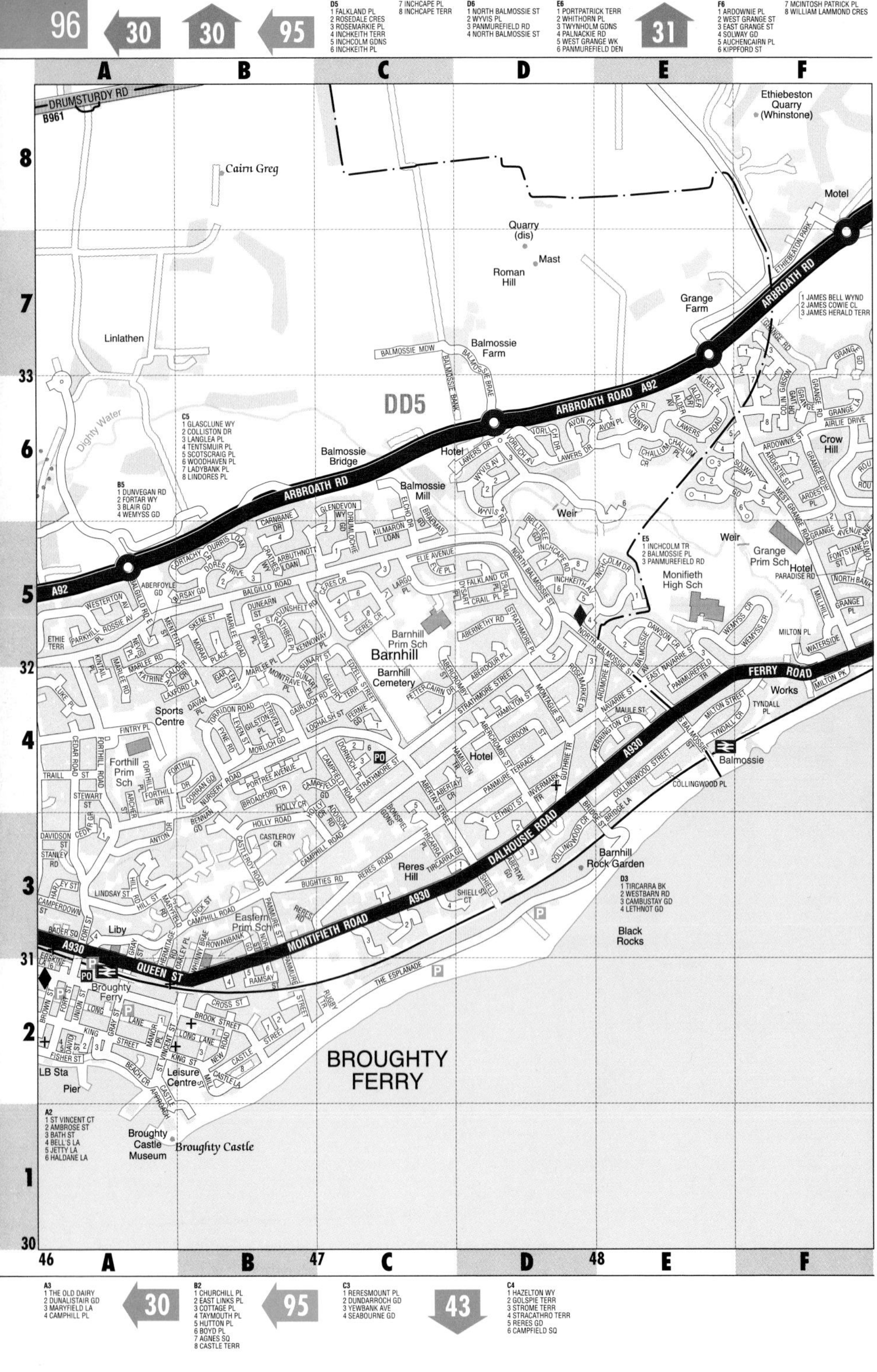

D5
1 FALKLAND PL
2 ROSEDALE CRES
3 ROSEMARKIE PL
4 INCHKEITH TERR
5 INCHCOLM GDNS
6 INCHKEITH PL

7 INCHCAPE PL
8 INCHCAPE TERR

D6
1 NORTH BALMOSSIE ST
2 WYVIS PL
3 PANMUREFIELD RD
4 NORTH BALMOSSIE ST

E6
1 PORTPATRICK TERR
2 WHITHORN PL
3 TWYNHOLM GDNS
4 PALNACKIE RD
5 WEST GRANGE WK
6 PANMUREFIELD DEN

F6
1 ARDOWNIE PL
2 WEST GRANGE ST
3 EAST GRANGE ST
4 SOLWAY GD
5 AUCHENCAIRN PL
6 KIPPFORD ST

7 MCINTOSH PATRICK PL
8 WILLIAM LAMMOND CRES

DRUMSTURDY RD
B961

Cairn Greg

Linlathen

DD5

Ethiebeston
Quarry
(Whinstone)

Motel

Quarry
(dis)

Roman
Hill

Mast

Balmossie
Farm

Grange
Farm

ARBROATH ROAD A92

F7
1 JAMES BELL WYND
2 JAMES COWIE CL
3 JAMES HERALD TERR

Crow
Hill

Airlie PL

C5
1 GLASCLUNE WY
2 COLLISTON DR
3 LANGLEA PL
4 TENTSMUIR PL
5 SCOTSCRAIG PL
6 WOODHAVEN PL
7 LADYBANK PL
8 LINDORES PL

B5
1 DUNVEGAN RD
2 FORTAR WY
3 BLAIR GD
4 WEMYSS GD

Balmossie
Bridge

Hotel

Balmossie
Mill

ARBROATH RD

Weir

Balmossie
Farm

E5
1 INCHCOLM TR
2 BALMOSSIE PL
3 PANMUREFIELD RD

Weir

Grange
Prim Sch

Hotel
PARADISE RD

Monifieth
High Sch

Grange
PL

A92

Barnhill
Prim Sch
Barnhill

Barnhill
Cemetery

FERRY ROAD

Works

Sports
Centre

Forthill
Prim
Sch

Hotel

PO

Balmossie

TYNDALL

Collingwood PL

Barnhill
Rock Garden

D3
1 TIRCARRA BK
2 WESTBARN RD
3 CAMBUSTAY GD
4 LETHNOT GD

Reres
Hill

Eastern
Prim Sch

DALHOUSIE ROAD

P

Black
Rocks

Liby

A930

MONIFIETH ROAD

QUEEN ST

A930

PO

Broughty
Ferry

The Esplanade

P

BROUGHTY
FERRY

LB Sta
Pier

Leisure
Centre

A2
1 ST VINCENT CT
2 AMBROSE ST
3 BATH ST
4 BELL'S LA
5 JETTY LA
6 HALDANE LA

Broughty
Castle
Museum

Broughty Castle

46   47   48

A3
1 THE OLD DAIRY
2 DUNALISTAIR GD
3 MARYFIELD LA
4 CAMPHILL PL

← 30

B2
1 CHURCHILL PL
2 EAST LINKS PL
3 COTTAGE PL
4 TAYMOUTH PL
5 HUTTON PL
6 BOYD PL
7 AGNES SQ
8 CASTLE TERR

95

C3
1 RERESMOUNT PL
2 DUNDARROCH GD
3 YEWBANK AVE
4 SEABOURNE GD

43

C4
1 HAZELTON WY
2 GOLSPIE TERR
3 STROME TERR
4 STRACATHRO TERR
5 RERES GD
6 CAMPIELD SQ

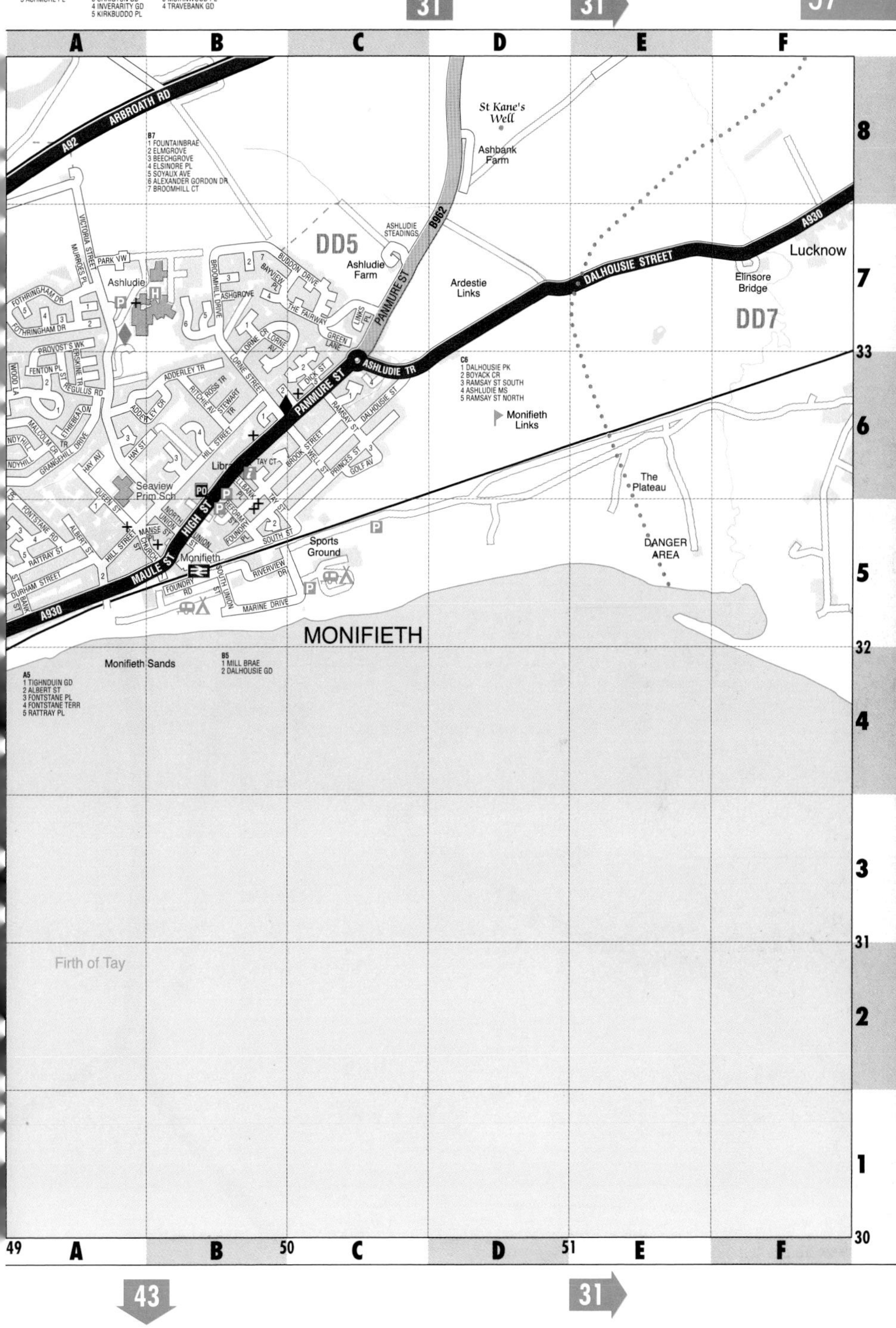

A6
1 CORTACHY CIRC
2 LAWS PL
3 ACHMORE PL

A7
1 REDFORD PL
2 CARMYLLIE PL
3 CRAIGTON GD
4 INVERARITY GD
5 KIRKBUDDO PL

B6
1 GREENBOURNE GD
2 LAIRD ST
3 MUIRNWOOD PL
4 TRAVEBANK GD

B7
1 FOUNTAINBRAE
2 ELMGROVE
3 BEECHGROVE
4 ELSINORE PL
5 SOYAUX AVE
6 ALEXANDER GORDON DR
7 BROOMHILL CT

C6
1 DALHOUSIE PK
2 BOYACK CR
3 RAMSAY ST SOUTH
4 ASHLUDIE MS
5 RAMSAY ST NORTH

A5
1 TIGHNDUIN GD
2 ALBERT ST
3 FONTSTANE PL
4 FONTSTANE TERR
5 RATTRAY PL

B5
1 MILL BRAE
2 DALHOUSIE GD

ARBROATH RD
A92

St Kane's Well
Ashbank Farm

DD5
Ashludie Farm
ASHLUDIE STEADINGS
Ardestie Links

DALHOUSIE STREET
Lucknow
Elinsore Bridge
DD7

Monifieth Links

PANMURE ST
ASHLUDIE TR
Seaview Prim Sch
Library
Monifieth
Sports Ground
HIGH ST
MAULE ST
A930
MARINE DRIVE
RIVERVIEW DR

The Plateau
DANGER AREA

MONIFIETH

Monifieth Sands

Firth of Tay

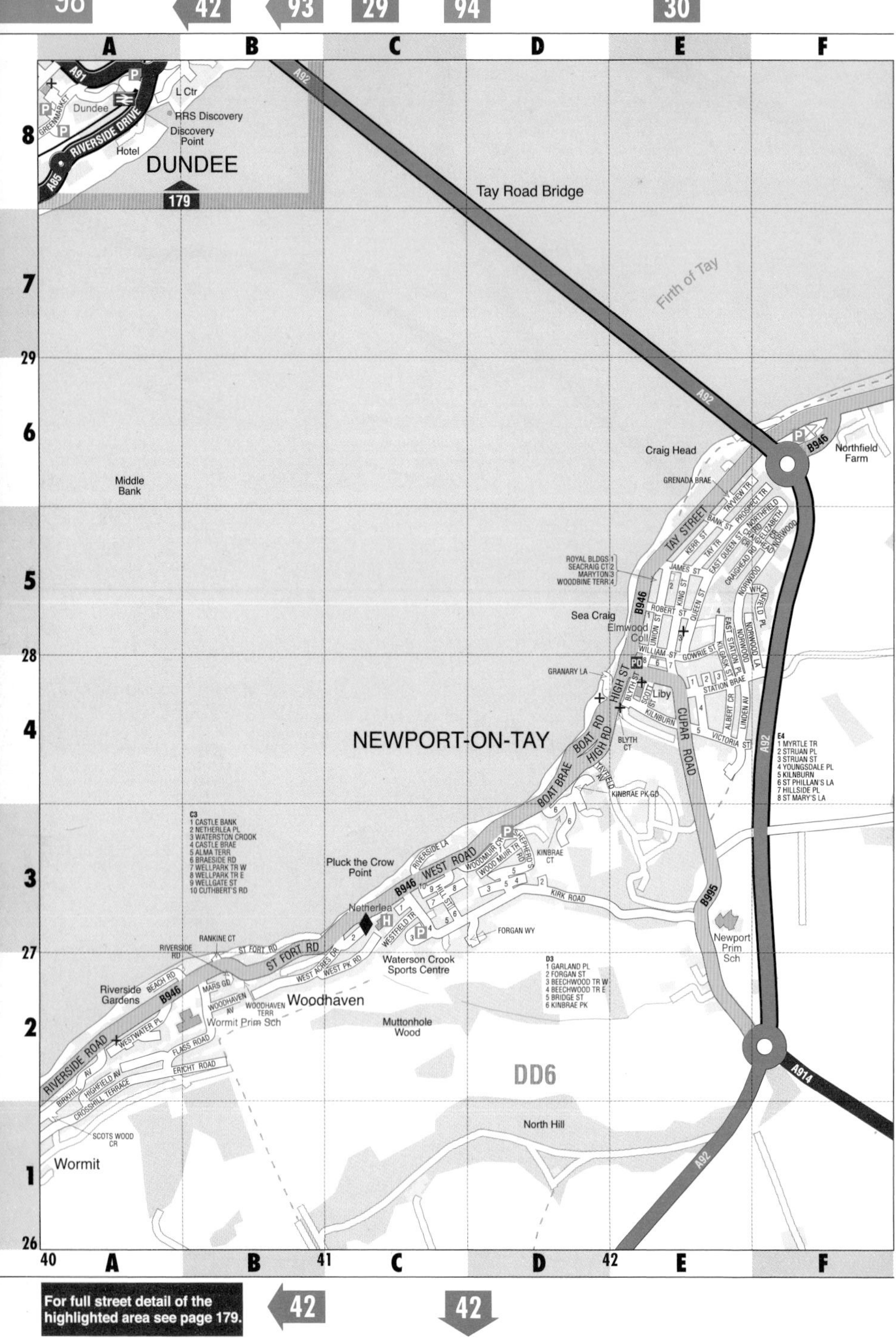

42 93 29 94 30

Tay Road Bridge

DUNDEE

179

Firth of Tay

Middle Bank

Craig Head

Northfield Farm

GRENADA BRAE

TAY STREET

ROYAL BLDGS 1
SEACRAIG CT 2
MARYTON 3
WOODBINE TERR 4

Sea Craig

Elmwood Coll

GRANARY LA

Liby

NEWPORT-ON-TAY

E4
1 MYRTLE TR
2 STRUAN PL
3 STRUAN ST
4 YOUNGSDALE PL
5 KILNBURN
6 ST PHILLAN S LA
7 HILLSIDE PL
8 ST MARY S LA

BLYTH CT

CUPAR ROAD

KINBRAE PK GD

C3
1 CASTLE BANK
2 NETHERLEA PL
3 WATERSTON CROOK
4 CASTLE BRAE
5 ALMA TERR
6 BRAESIDE RD
7 WELLPARK TR W
8 WELLPARK TR E
9 WELLGATE ST
10 CUTHBERT S RD

Pluck the Crow Point

RIVERSIDE LA

WEST ROAD

KINBRAE CT

KIRK ROAD

Netherlea

B946

FORGAN WY

Newport Prim Sch

RANKINE CT

ST FORT RD

Waterson Crook Sports Centre

D3
1 GARLAND PL
2 FORGAN ST
3 BEECHWOOD TR W
4 BEECHWOOD TR E
5 BRIDGE ST
6 KINBRAE PK

RIVERSIDE RD

MARS GD

Riverside Gardens

B946

WOODHAVEN TERR

Woodhaven

Muttonhole Wood

DD6

Wormit Prim Sch

KLAES ROAD

ERICHT ROAD

RIVERSIDE ROAD

CROSSHILL TERRACE

HIGHFIELD AV

SCOTS WOOD CR

North Hill

Wormit

A914

A92

For full street detail of the highlighted area see page 179.
42 42

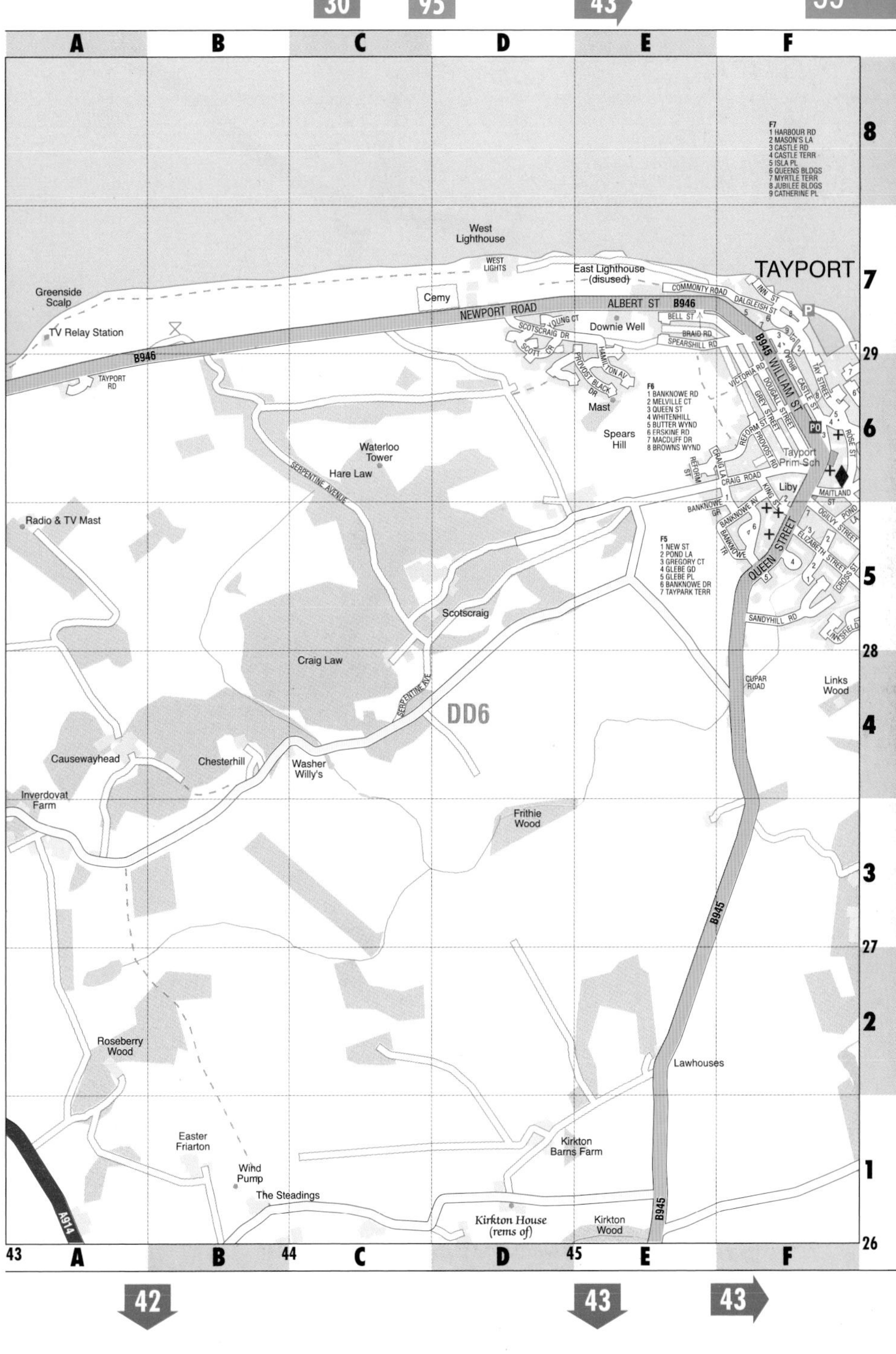

A   B   C   D   E   F

8

F7
1 HARBOUR RD
2 MASON'S LA
3 CASTLE RD
4 CASTLE TERR
5 ISLA PL
6 QUEENS BLDGS
7 MYRTLE TERR
8 JUBILEE BLDGS
9 CATHERINE PL

West
Lighthouse

TAYPORT   7

WEST
LIGHTS

East Lighthouse
—(disused)

COMMONTY ROAD

Greenside
Scalp

Cemy

NEWPORT ROAD   ALBERT ST   B946

DALGLEISH ST

LINN ST

TV Relay Station

B946

SCOTSCRAIG DR

SCOTT ST

QUNG CT

Downie Well

BELL ST

BRAID RD

SPEARSHILL RD

B946 WILLIAM ST

29

TAYPORT
RD

HAMILTON AV

KINGS BLACK
DR

Mast

Spears
Hill

F6
1 BANKNOWE RD
2 MELVILLE CT
3 QUEEN ST
4 WHITENHILL
5 BUTTER WYND
6 ERSKINE RD
7 MACDUFF DR
8 BROWNS WYND

P
PO

Tayport
Prim Sch

MAITLAND ST

6

Waterloo
Tower

Hare Law

SERPENTINE AVENUE

CRAIG ROAD

Liby

Radio & TV Mast

BANKNOWE DR

BANKNOWE PL

QUEEN STREET

ELIZABETH STREET

SHANWELL RD

F5
1 NEW ST
2 POND LA
3 GREGORY CT
4 GLEBE GD
5 GLEBE PL
6 BANKNOWE DR
7 TAYPARK TERR

5

Scotscraig

SANDYHILL RD

28

Craig Law

SERPENTINE RD

CUPAR
ROAD

Links
Wood

DD6

4

Causewayhead

Chesterhill

Washer
Willy's

Frithie
Wood

Inverdovat
Farm

B945

3

27

Roseberry
Wood

2

Lawhouses

Easter
Friarton

Kirkton
Barns Farm

Wind
Pump

The Steadings

Kirkton House
(rems of)

Kirkton
Wood

B945

1

A914

32 32 32

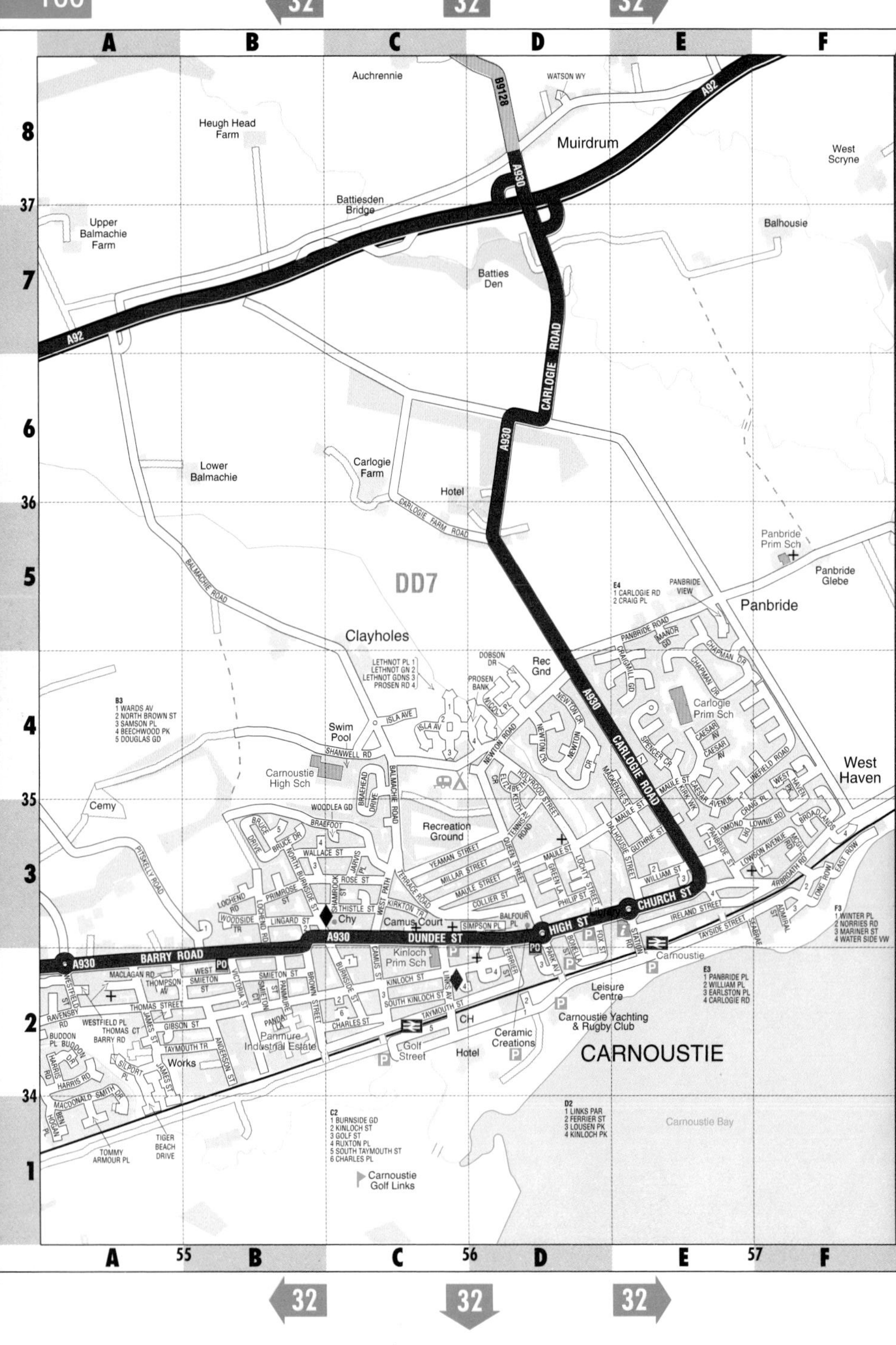

Auchrennie
WATSON WY
B9128
A92
Heugh Head Farm
Muirdrum
West Scryne
A930
Battiesden Bridge
Upper Balmachie Farm
Balhousie
Batties Den
CARLOGIE ROAD
Lower Balmachie
Carlogie Farm
Hotel
CARLOGIE FARM ROAD
Panbride Prim Sch
Panbride Glebe
BALMACHIE ROAD
DD7
E4 1 CARLOGIE RD 2 CRAIG PL
PANBRIDE VIEW
Panbride
PANBRIDE ROAD
MANOR GD
Clayholes
LETHNOT PL 1 LETHNOT GN 2 LETHNOT GDNS 3 PROSEN RD 4
DOBSON DR
PROSEN BANK
Rec Gnd
CHAPMAN DR
Carlogie Prim Sch
B3 1 WARDS AV 2 NORTH BROWN ST 3 SAMSON PL 4 BEECHWOOD PK 5 DOUGLAS GD
ISLA AVE
Swim Pool
SHANWELL RD
NEWTON ROAD
NEWTON CR
SPENCER CR
CAESAR AV
LINEFIELD ROAD
Carnoustie High Sch
BRAEHEAD DRIVE
HOLYROOD STREET
MACKENZIE ST
MAULE ST
KIRK WK
CAESAR AVENUE
CRAIG PL
WEST PK
West Haven
Cemy
WOODLEA GD
BRAEFOOT
Recreation Ground
TENNIS ROAD
MAULE ST
GUTHRIE ST
LOMOND
LOWNIE RD
BROADLANDS
BRUCE DRIVE
BRUCE DR
WALLACE ST
JARVIS PL
YEAMAN STREET
QUEEN STREET
DALHOUSIE STREET
PANBRIDE ST
LOWSON AVENUE
ARBROATH RD
EAST ROW
PITSKELLY ROAD
NORTH BURNSIDE ST
ROSE ST
MILLAR STREET
GREEN LA
LOCHTY STREET
WILLIAM ST
LONG ROW
LOCHEND RD
PRIMROSE ST
SHAMROCK ST
THISTLE ST
WEST PATH
KIRKTON TR
TERRACE ROAD
MAULE STREET
COLLIER ST
PHILIP ST
CHURCH ST
WOODSIDE TR
LINGARD ST
Chy
Camus Court
SIMPSON PL
BALFOUR PL
HIGH ST
Library
IRELAND STREET
F3 1 WINTER PL 2 NORRIES RD 3 MARINER ST 4 WATER SIDE VW
A930
DUNDEE ST
FOX ST
STATION RD
TAYSIDE STREET
SEABRAE ST
ADMIRAL ST
BARRY ROAD
PO
Kinloch Prim Sch
FERRIER ST
PARK AV
BONELLA ST
Carnoustie
WESTFIELD RD
MACLAGAN RD
THOMPSON AV
WEST SMIETON ST
VICTORIA ST
SMIETON ST
PANMURE ST
BROWN STREET
BURNSIDE ST
CAMUS ST
KINLOCH ST
LINKS AV
E3 1 PANBRIDE PL 2 WILLIAM PL 3 EARLSTON PL 4 CARLOGIE RD
Leisure Centre
RAVENSBY RD
THOMAS STREET
SOUTH KINLOCH ST
TAYMOUTH ST
CH
Carnoustie Yachting & Rugby Club
WESTFIELD PL
THOMAS CT
GIBSON ST
PANDA LA
CHARLES ST
BUDDON PL
BUDDON DR
BARRY RD
Panmure Industrial Estate
Ceramic Creations
HARRIS RD
SILPORT PL
TAYMOUTH TR
ANDERSON ST
Works
Golf Street
Hotel
CARNOUSTIE
HARRIS RD
JAMES ST
MACDONALD SMITH DR
BEN HOGAN PL
TOMMY ARMOUR PL
TIGER BEACH DRIVE
C2 1 BURNSIDE GD 2 KINLOCH ST 3 GOLF ST 4 RUXTON PL 5 SOUTH TAYMOUTH ST 6 CHARLES PL
D2 1 LINKS PAR 2 FERRIER ST 3 LOUSEN PK 4 KINLOCH PK
Carnoustie Bay
Carnoustie Golf Links
A B C D E F
8 37 7 6 36 5 4 35 3 2 34 1
55 56 57

32 32 32

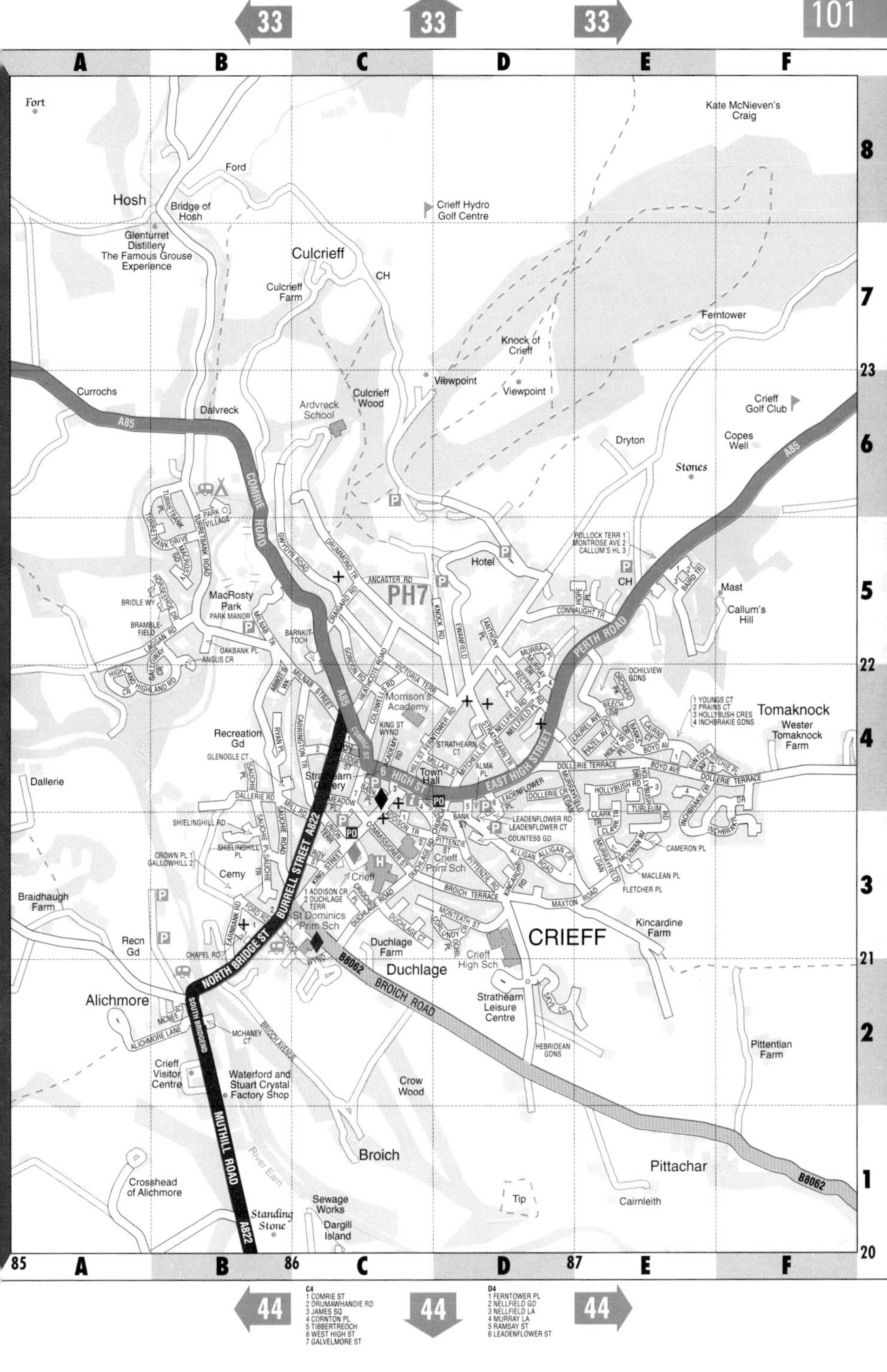

33 33 33

8

7

23

6

5

22

4

3

21

2

1

20

A B C D E F

Fort

Hosh

Kate McNieven's
Craig

Ford

Bridge of
Hosh

Glenturret
Distillery
The Famous Grouse
Experience

Crieff Hydro
Golf Centre

Culcrieff

CH

Ferntower

Culcrieff
Farm

Knock of
Crieff

Currochs

Dalvreck

A85

Viewpoint

Viewpoint

Dryton

Crieff
Golf Club

Culcrieff
Wood

Ardvreck
School

Copes
Well

Stones

Mast

COMRIE ROAD

Hotel

POLLOCK TERR 1
MONTROSE AVE 2
CALLUM'S HL 3

Callum's
Hill

CH

A85

PERTH ROAD

ANCASTER RD

PH7

MacRosty
Park
PARK MANOR

OCHILVIEW
GDNS

Tomaknock

Wester
Tomaknock
Farm

Morrison's
Academy

Dallerie

Recreation
Gd

1 YOUNGS CT
2 PRAWNS CT
3 HOLLYBUSH CRES
4 INCHBRAKIE GDNS

EAST HIGH STREET

DOLLERIE TERRACE

Strathearn
Gallery

Town
Hall

PO

DOLLERIE TERRACE

HIGH ST

LEADENFLOWER RD
LEADENFLOWER CT
COUNTESS GD

Crieff

Crieff
Prim Sch

MACLEAN PL

FLETCHER PL

Braidhaugh
Farm

BURRELL STREET A822

NORTH BRIDGE ST

1 ADDISON CR
2 DUCHLAGE
   TERR

St Dominics
Prim Sch

BROICH TERRACE

Kincardine
Farm

MAXTON

Recn
Gd

Duchlage
Farm

CRIEFF

CHAPEL RD

B8062

Crieff
High Sch

Alichmore

SOUTH BRIDGEND

Duchlage

BROICH ROAD

Strathearn
Leisure
Centre

Pittentian
Farm

Crieff
Visitor
Centre

Waterford and
Stuart Crystal
Factory Shop

HEBRIDEAN
GDNS

Crow
Wood

MUTHILL ROAD

A822

Crosshead
of Alichmore

River Earn

Broich

Pittachar

B8062

Standing
Stone

Sewage
Works

Dargill
Island

Tip

Cairnleith

85 A 86 C D 87 E F

44 44 44

C4
1 COMRIE ST
2 DRUMAWHANDIE RD
3 JAMES SQ
4 CORNTON PL
5 TIBBERTREOCH
6 WEST HIGH ST
7 GALVELMORE ST

D4
1 FERNTOWER PL
2 NELLFIELD GD
3 NELLFIELD LA
4 MURRAY LA
5 RAMSAY ST
6 LEADENFLOWER ST

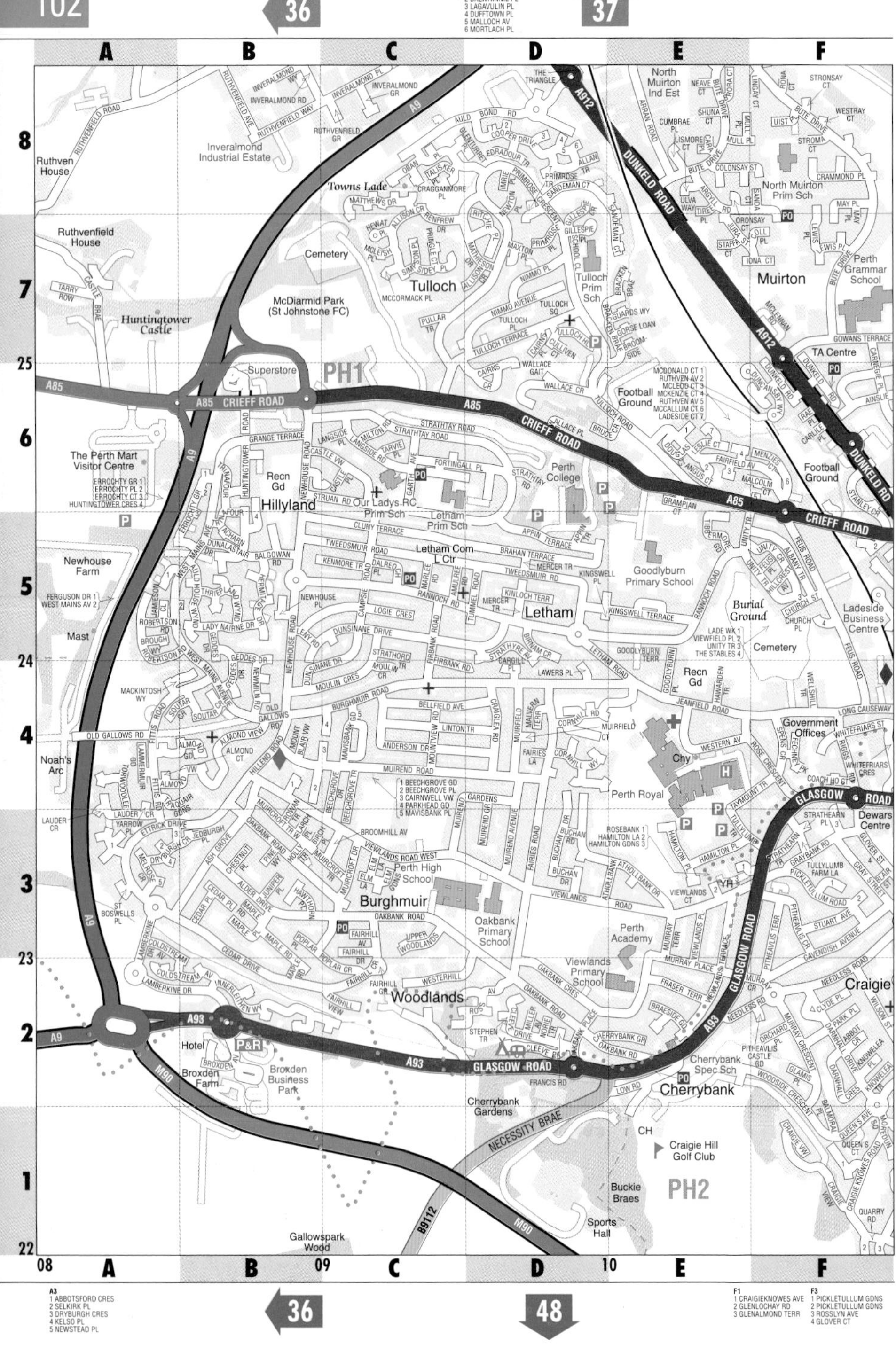

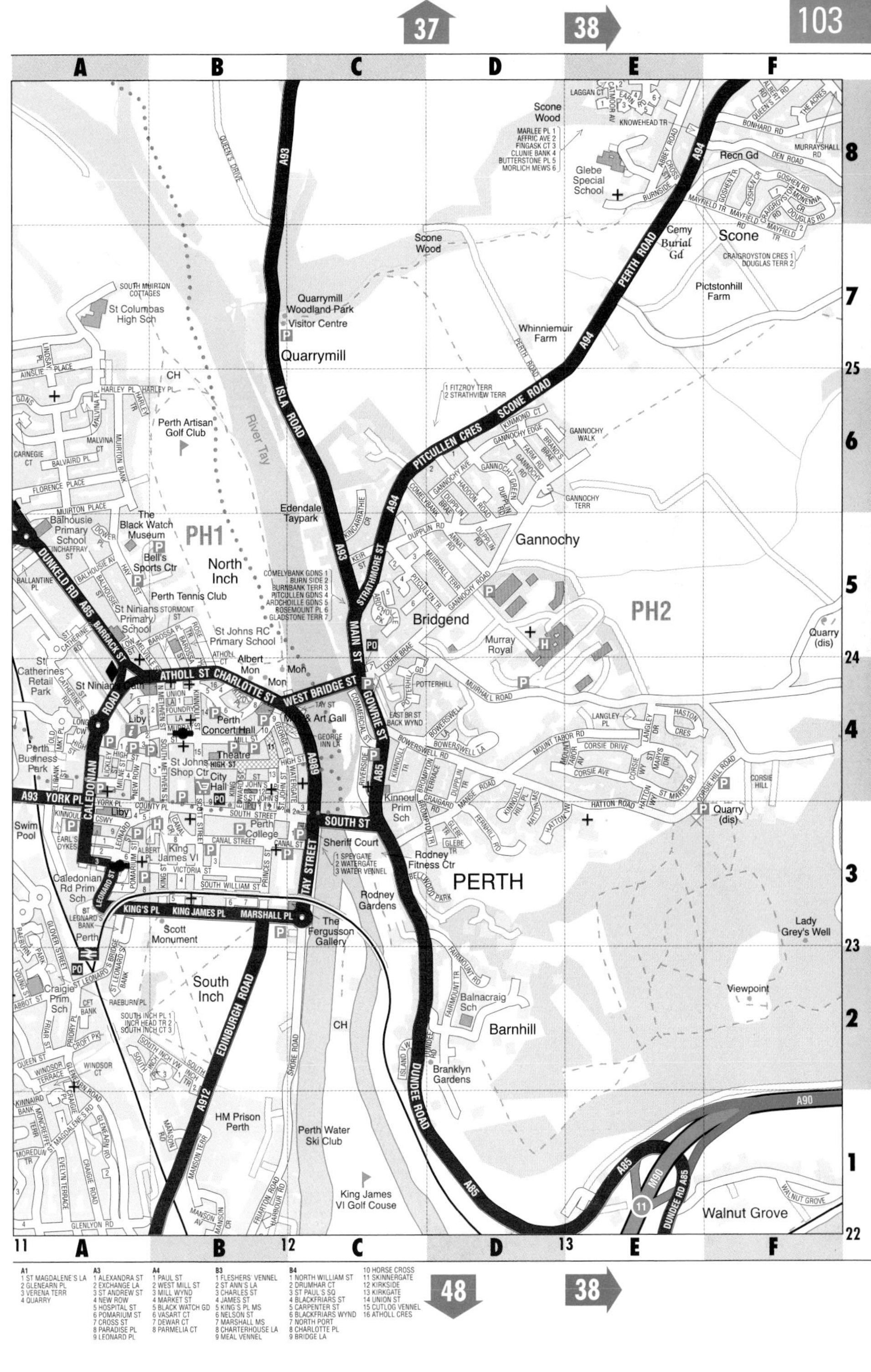

37
38
A
B
C
D
E
F
8
7
25
6
5
24
4
3
23
2
1
22
11
12
13
Scone Wood
Glebe Special School
Recn Gd
Scone
Cemy Burial Gd
Pictstonhill Farm
Whinniemuir Farm
Quarrymill Woodland Park Visitor Centre
Quarrymill
St Columbas High Sch
SOUTH MUIRTON COTTAGES
Perth Artisan Golf Club
River Tay
Edendale Taypark
Balhousie Primary School
The Black Watch Museum
PH1
North Inch
Bell's Sports Ctr
Perth Tennis Club
St Ninians Primary School
St Johns RC Primary School
Albert Mon
Mon
St Catherines Retail Park
St Ninians Cath
Gannochy
PH2
Bridgend
Murray Royal
Quarry (dis)
Perth Concert Hall
Mus & Art Gall
Theatre
St Johns Shop Ctr
City Hall
Perth Business Park
Swim Pool
Liby
Perth College
Sheriff Court
King James VI
Kinnoull Prim Sch
Rodney Fitness Ctr
PERTH
Caledonian Rd Prim Sch
Scott Monument
The Fergusson Gallery
Rodney Gardens
Lady Grey's Well
Viewpoint
South Inch
Craigie Prim Sch
Balnacraig Sch
Barnhill
Branklyn Gardens
HM Prison Perth
Perth Water Ski Club
King James VI Golf Couse
Walnut Grove
A93
A94
A85
A989
A912
A90
M90
PERTH ROAD
SCONE ROAD
PITCULLEN CRES
ISLA ROAD
MAIN ST
STRATHMORE ST
GOWRIE ST
DUNKELD RD
BARRACK ST
ATHOLL ST
CHARLOTTE ST
WEST BRIDGE ST
CALEDONIAN ROAD
YORK PL
SOUTH ST
TAY STREET
KING'S PL
KING JAMES PL
MARSHALL PL
EDINBURGH ROAD
DUNDEE ROAD
MUIRHALL ROAD
HATTON ROAD
BOWERSWELL RD
CORSIE DRIVE
MOUNT TABOR RD
MANSE ROAD
KNOWEHEAD TR
BONHARD RD
MAYFIELD TR
DEN ROAD
MARLEE PL 1
AFFRIC AVE 2
FINGASK CT 3
CLUNIE BANK 4
BUTTERSTONE PL 5
MORLICH MEWS 6
CRAIGROYSTON CRES 1
DOUGLAS TERR 2
1 FITZROY TERR
2 STRATHVIEW TERR
COMELYBANK GDNS 1
BURN SIDE 2
BURNBANK TERR 3
PITCULLEN GDNS 4
ARDCHOILLE GDNS 5
ROSEMOUNT PL 6
GLADSTONE TERR 7
1 SPEYGATE
2 WATERGATE
3 WATER VENNEL
SOUTH INCH PL 1
INCH HEAD TR 2
SOUTH INCH CT 3
A1
1 ST MAGDALENE'S LA
2 GLENEARN PL
3 VERENA TERR
4 QUARRY
A3
1 ALEXANDRA ST
2 EXCHANGE LA
3 ST ANDREW ST
4 NEW ROW
5 HOSPITAL ST
6 POMARIUM ST
7 CROSS ST
8 PARADISE PL
9 LEONARD PL
A4
1 PAUL ST
2 WEST MILL ST
3 MILL WYND
4 MARKET ST
5 BLACK WATCH GD
6 VASART CT
7 DEWAR CT
8 PARMELIA CT
B3
1 FLESHERS' VENNEL
2 ST ANN'S LA
3 CHARLES ST
4 JAMES ST
5 KING'S PL MS
6 NELSON ST
7 MARSHALL MS
8 CHARTERHOUSE LA
9 MEAL VENNEL
B4
1 NORTH WILLIAM ST
2 DRUMHAR CT
3 ST PAUL'S SQ
4 BLACKFRIARS ST
5 CARPENTER ST
6 BLACKFRIARS WYND
7 NORTH PORT
8 CHARLOTTE PL
9 BRIDGE LA
10 HORSE CROSS
11 SKINNERGATE
12 KIRKSIDE
13 KIRKGATE
14 UNION ST
15 CUTLOG VENNEL
16 ATHOLL CRES
48
38

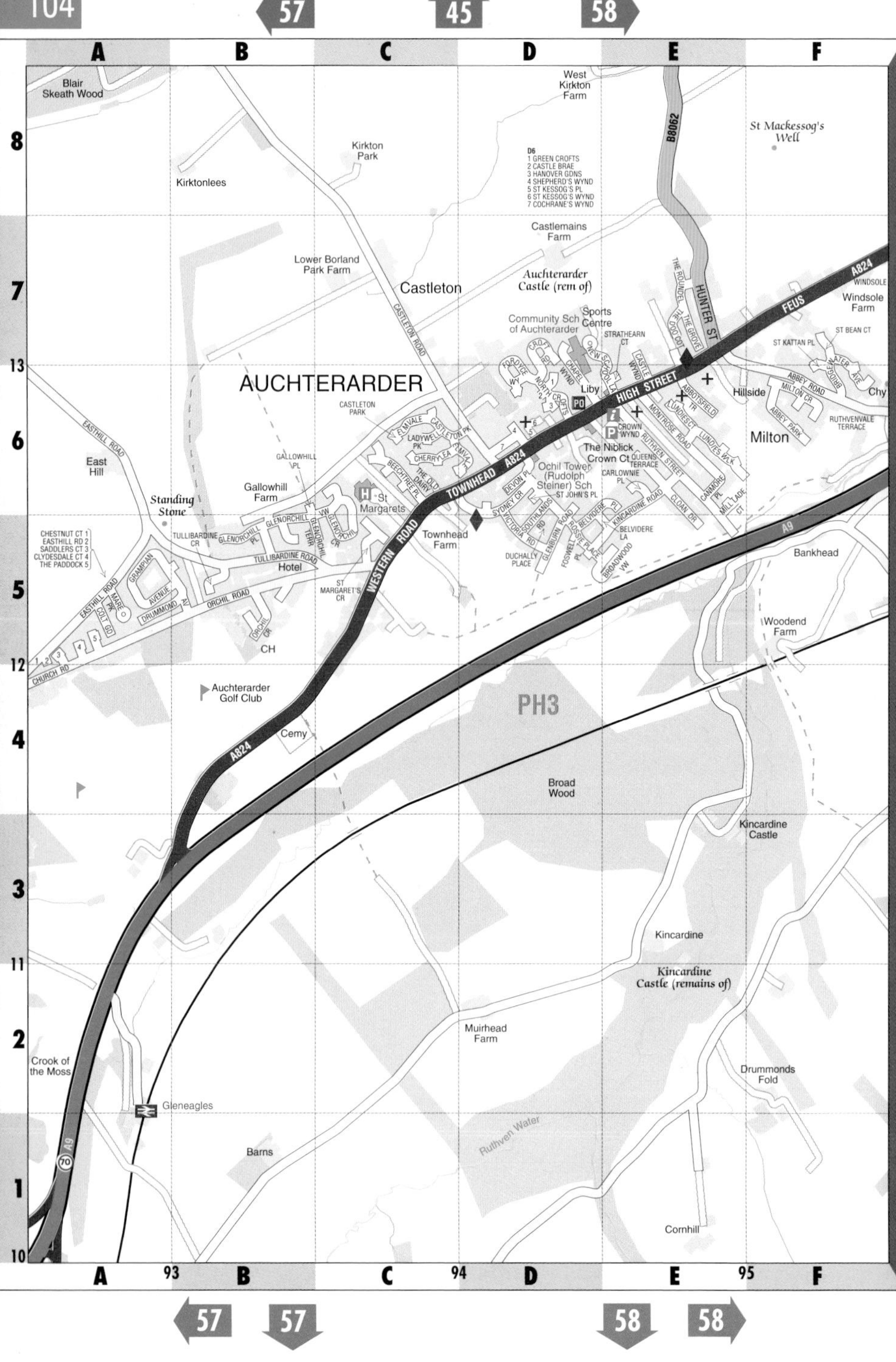

8

Blair
Skeath Wood

West
Kirkton
Farm

St Mackessog's
Well

Kirkton
Park

Kirktonlees

D6
1 GREEN CROFTS
2 CASTLE BRAE
3 HANOVER GDNS
4 SHEPHERD'S WYND
5 ST KESSOG'S PL
6 ST KESSOG'S WYND
7 COCHRANE'S WYND

7

Lower Borland
Park Farm

Castlemains
Farm

Auchterarder
Castle (rem of)

Castleton

Windsole
Farm

A824

FEUS

HUNTER ST

B8062

THE ROUND OF THE CROSS

ST KATTAN PL

ST BEAN CT

13

Sports
Centre

Community Sch
of Auchterarder

STRATHEARN
CT

ABBEY ROAD

MILTON CT

Chy

AUCHTERARDER

Liby

PO

HIGH STREET

Hillside

Milton

ABBEY PARK

RUTHVENVALE
TERRACE

Castleton
Park

6

East
Hill

GALLOWHILL
PL

GLENVALE

LADYWEL

CHERRY LEA

The Niblick
Crown Ct

Ochil Tower
(Rudolph
Steiner) Sch
ST JOHN'S PL

CARLOWNIE
TERRACE

CARLOWNIE

QUEEN'S
WYND

RUTHIE'S STREET

EASTHILL ROAD

Standing
Stone

Gallowhill
Farm

GLENORCHIL

GLENORCHIL
CR

ST
Margarets

BEECHFIELD

A824

TOWNHEAD

WESTERN ROAD

KINCARDINE ROAD

BELVIDERE
LA

BELVIDERE

CLERK CR

CAMBDALE

MILL LADE

A9

CHESTNUT CT 1
EASTHILL RD 2
SADDLERS CT 3
CLYDESDALE CT 4
THE PADDOCK 5

TULLIBARDINE
CR

DRUMMOND

ORCHIL ROAD

TULLIBARDINE ROAD

Hotel

ST
MARGARET'S
CR

Townhead
Farm

DUCHALLY
PLACE

BRAMWOOD
VW

Bankhead

5

EASTHILL ROAD

CHURCH RD

CH

CEMY

Woodend
Farm

12

Auchterarder
Golf Club

Cemy

PH3

Kincardine
Castle

4

A824

Broad
Wood

Kincardine

3

Kincardine
Castle (remains of)

11

Crook of
the Moss

Muirhead
Farm

Drummonds
Fold

2

A9

70

Gleneagles

Barns

Ruthven Water

Cornhill

1

A9

10

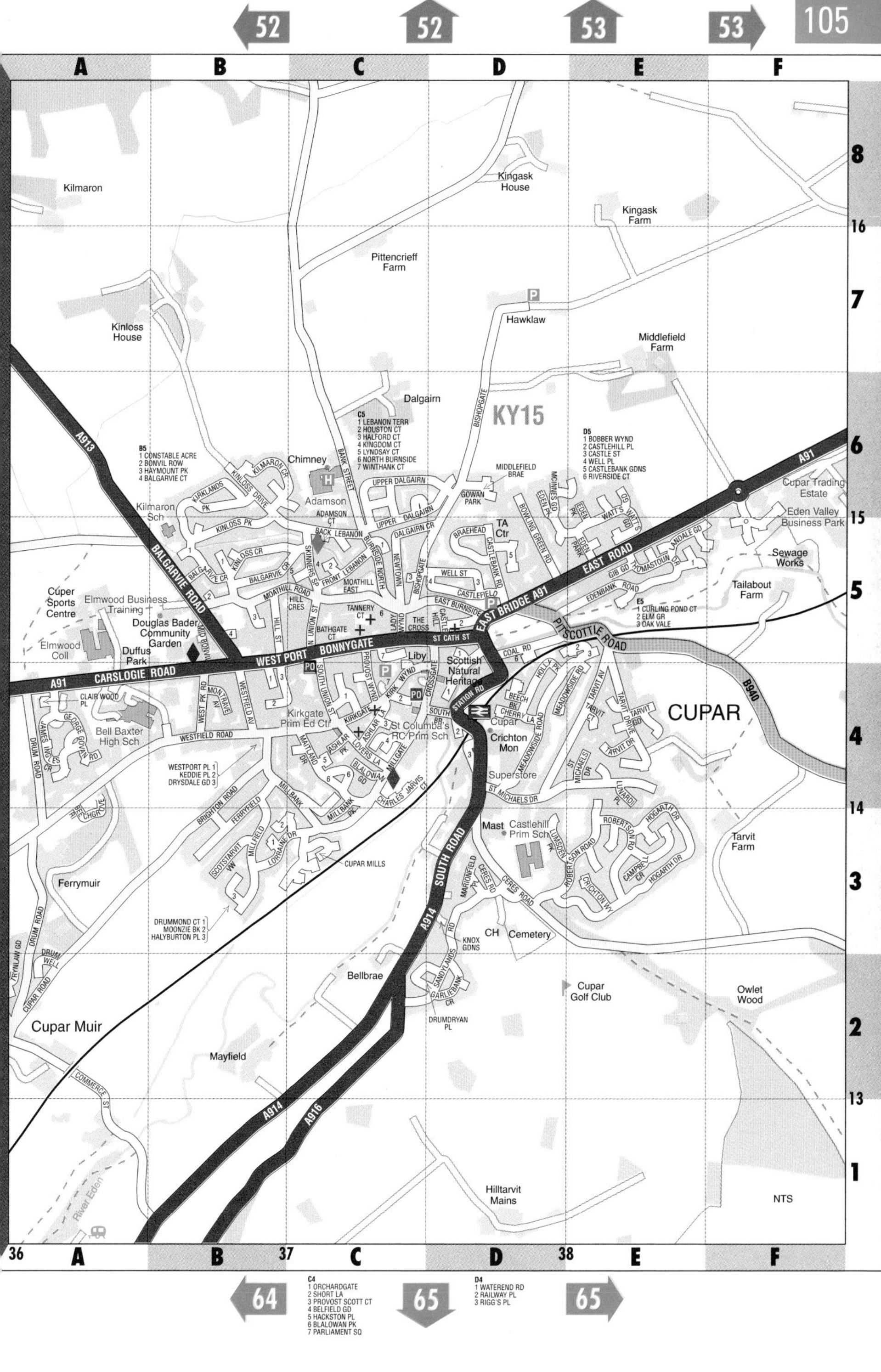

A B C D E F

8

16

7

Kilmaron

Kingask
House

Kingask
Farm

Pittencrieff
Farm

P

Hawklaw

Middlefield
Farm

Kinloss
House

Dalgairn

KY15

A91

Cupar Trading
Estate

B5
1 CONSTABLE ACRE
2 BONVIL ROW
3 HAYMOUNT PK
4 BALGARVIE CT

C5
1 LEBANON TERR
2 HOUSTON CT
3 HALFORD CT
4 KINGDOM CT
5 LYNDSAY CT
6 NORTH BURNSIDE
7 WINTHANK CT

D5
1 BOBBER WYND
2 CASTLEHILL PL
3 CASTLE ST
4 WELL PL
5 CASTLEBANK GDNS
6 RIVERSIDE CT

6

15

Eden Valley
Business Park

Chimney

Kilmaron
Sch

Adamson

MIDDLEFIELD
BRAE

GOWAN
PARK

TA
Ctr

Sewage
Works

Elmwood Business
Training

Cupar
Sports
Centre

Douglas Bader
Community
Garden

Duffus
Park

WEST PORT BONNYGATE

Liby

St CATH ST

Scottish
Natural
Heritage

EAST BRIDGE A91

EAST ROAD

Tailabout
Farm

5

E5
1 CURLING POND CT
2 ELM GR
3 OAK VALE

Elmwood
Coll

A91 CARSLOGIE ROAD

P

PO

PITSCOTTIE ROAD

CUPAR

14

WESTPORT PL 1
KEDDIE PL 2
DRYSDALE GD 3

Kirkgate
Prim Ed Ctr

St Columba's
RC Prim Sch

Crichton
Mon

Superstore

Cupar

Mast Castlehill
Prim Sch

Tarvit
Farm

B904

Clair Wood
PL

Bell Baxter
High Sch

Westfield Road

Ferrymuir

4

3

DRUMMOND CT 1
MOONZIE BK 2
HALYBURTON PL 3

Cupar Mills

SOUTH ROAD

A914

KNOX
GDNS

CH

Cemetery

Cupar
Golf Club

Owlet
Wood

Cupar Muir

Bellbrae

2

13

Mayfield

DRUMDRYAN
PL

A914

A916

Hilltarvit
Mains

NTS

1

River Eden

36 A B 37 C D 38 E F

C4
1 ORCHARDGATE
2 SHORT LA
3 PROVOST SCOTT CT
4 BELFIELD GD
5 HACKSTON PL
6 BLALOWAN PK
7 PARLIAMENT SQ

D4
1 WATEREND RD
2 RAILWAY PL
3 RIGG'S PL

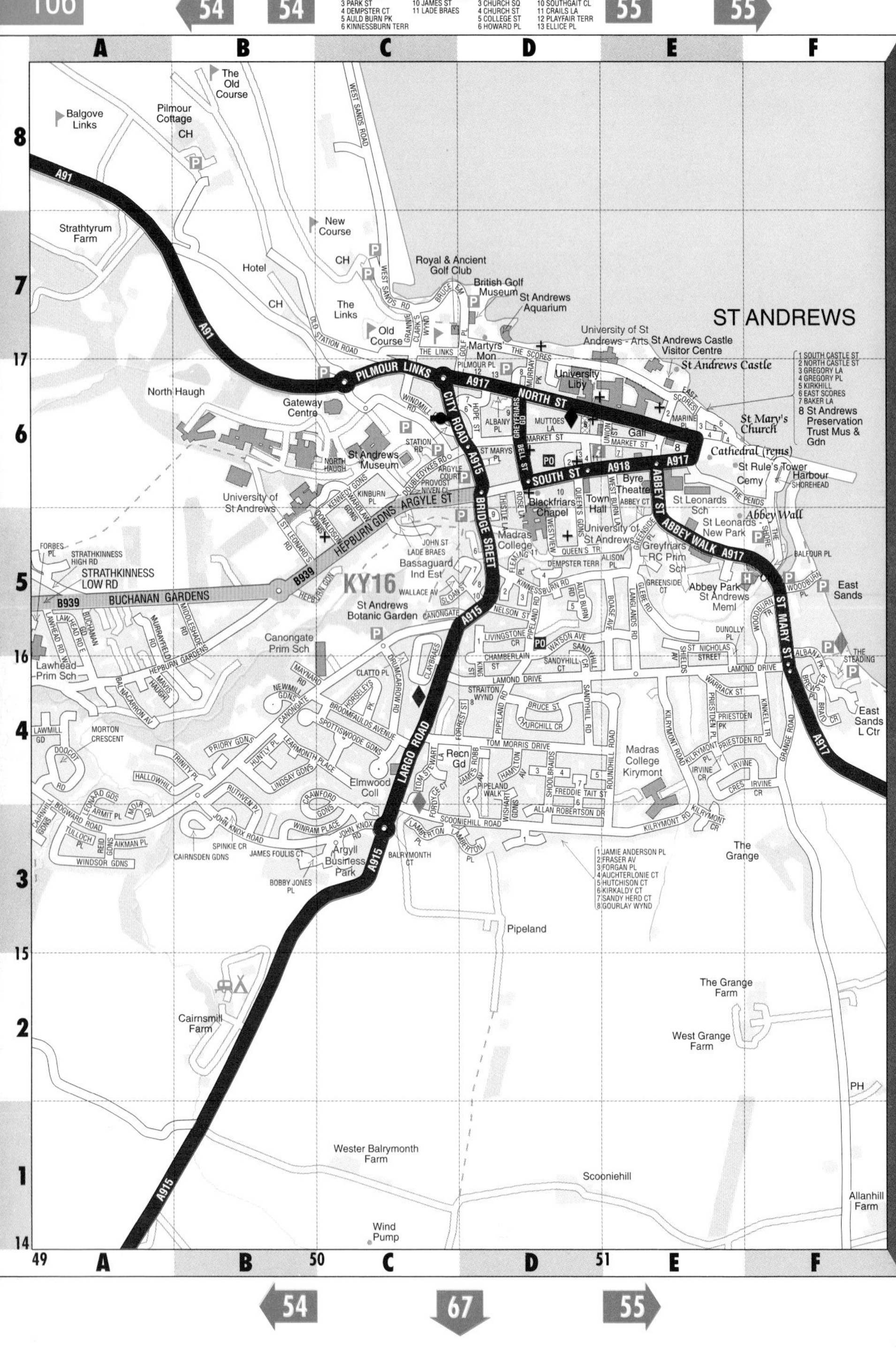

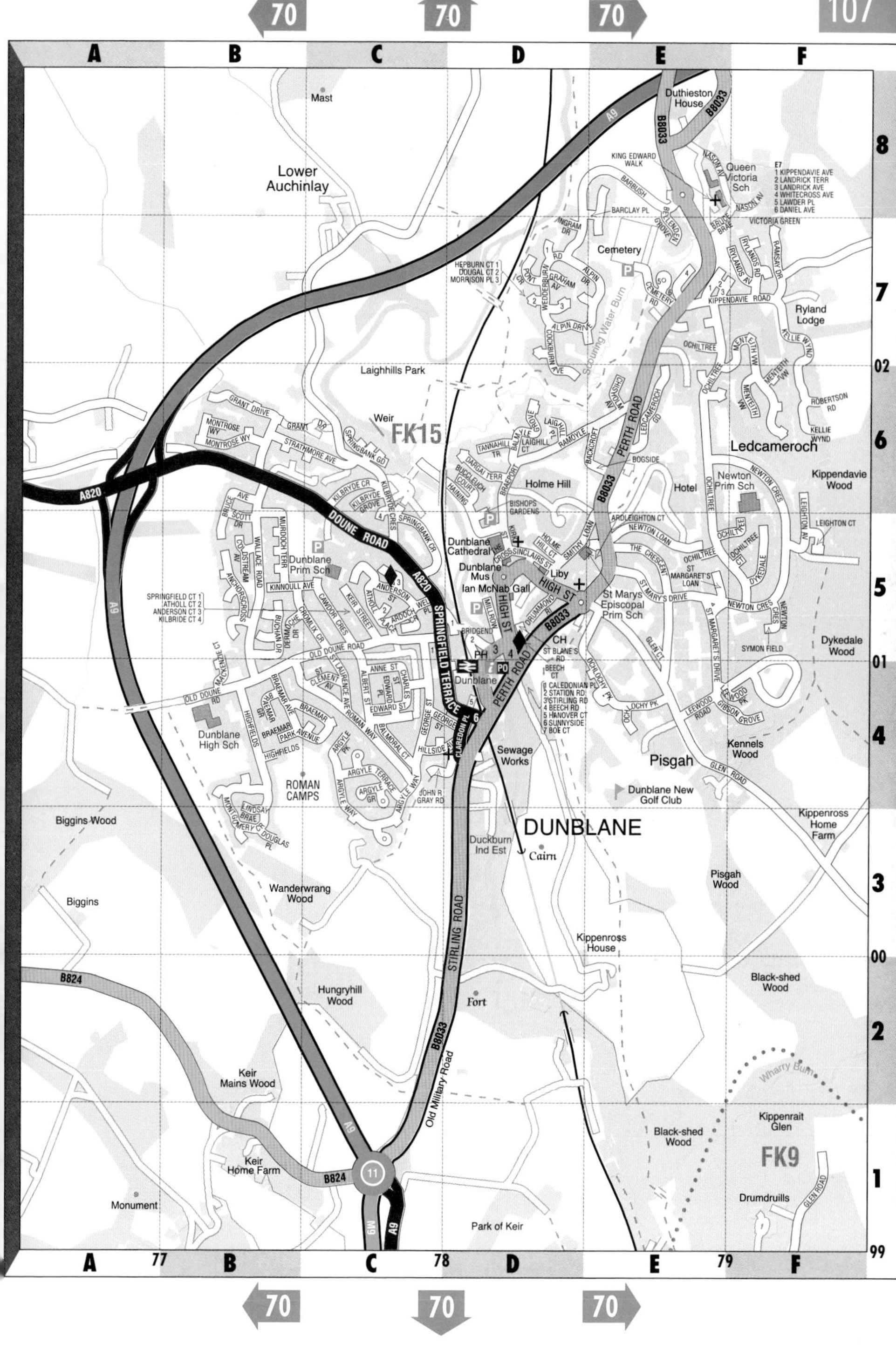
70
70
70
A
B
C
D
E
F
8
7
02
6
5
01
4
3
00
2
1
99
77
78
79
Mast
Lower Auchinlay
Duthieston House
B8033
A9
KING EDWARD WALK
Queen Victoria Sch
E7
1 KIPPENDAVIE AVE
2 LANDRICK TERR
3 LANDRICK AVE
4 WHITECROSS AVE
5 LAWDER PL
6 DANIEL AVE
VICTORIA GREEN
Cemetery
HEPBURN CT 1
DOUGAL CT 2
MORRISON PL 3
Ryland Lodge
KIPPENDAVIE ROAD
Laighhills Park
Weir
FK15
PERTH ROAD
Ledcameroch
Holme Hill
Hotel
Newton Prim Sch
Kippendavie Wood
A820
DOUNE ROAD
Dunblane Cathedral
Dunblane Prim Sch
Dunblane Mus
Ian McNab Gall
Liby
HIGH ST
St Marys Episcopal Prim Sch
SPRINGFIELD CT 1
ATHOLL CT 2
ANDERSON CT 3
KILBRIDE CT 4
SPRINGFIELD TERRACE
Dykedale Wood
SYMON FIELD
PH
Dunblane
1 CALEDONIAN PL
2 STATION RD
3 STIRLING RD
4 BEECH RD
5 HANOVER CT
6 SUNNYSIDE
7 BOE CT
OLD DOUNE ROAD
Dunblane High Sch
Sewage Works
Kennels Wood
Pisgah
Dunblane New Golf Club
ROMAN CAMPS
Biggins Wood
DUNBLANE
Kippenross Home Farm
Duckburn Ind Est
Cairn
Wanderwrang Wood
Biggins
STIRLING ROAD
Pisgah Wood
Kippenross House
Black-shed Wood
B824
Hungryhill Wood
Fort
Old Military Road
Wharry Burn
Keir Mains Wood
Black-shed Wood
Kippenrait Glen
FK9
Keir Home Farm
11
Monument
Drumdruills
Park of Keir
M9

70
70
70

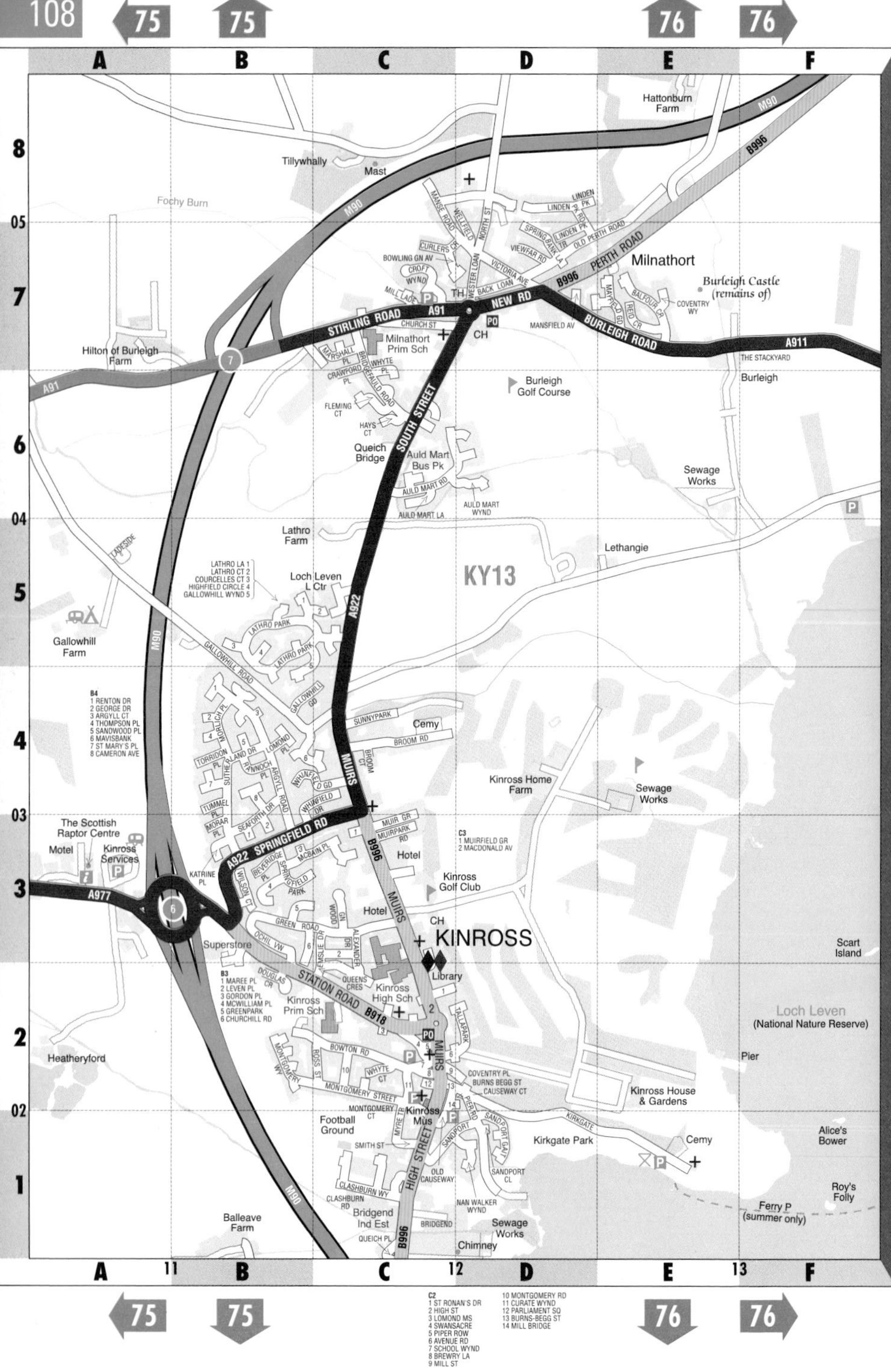

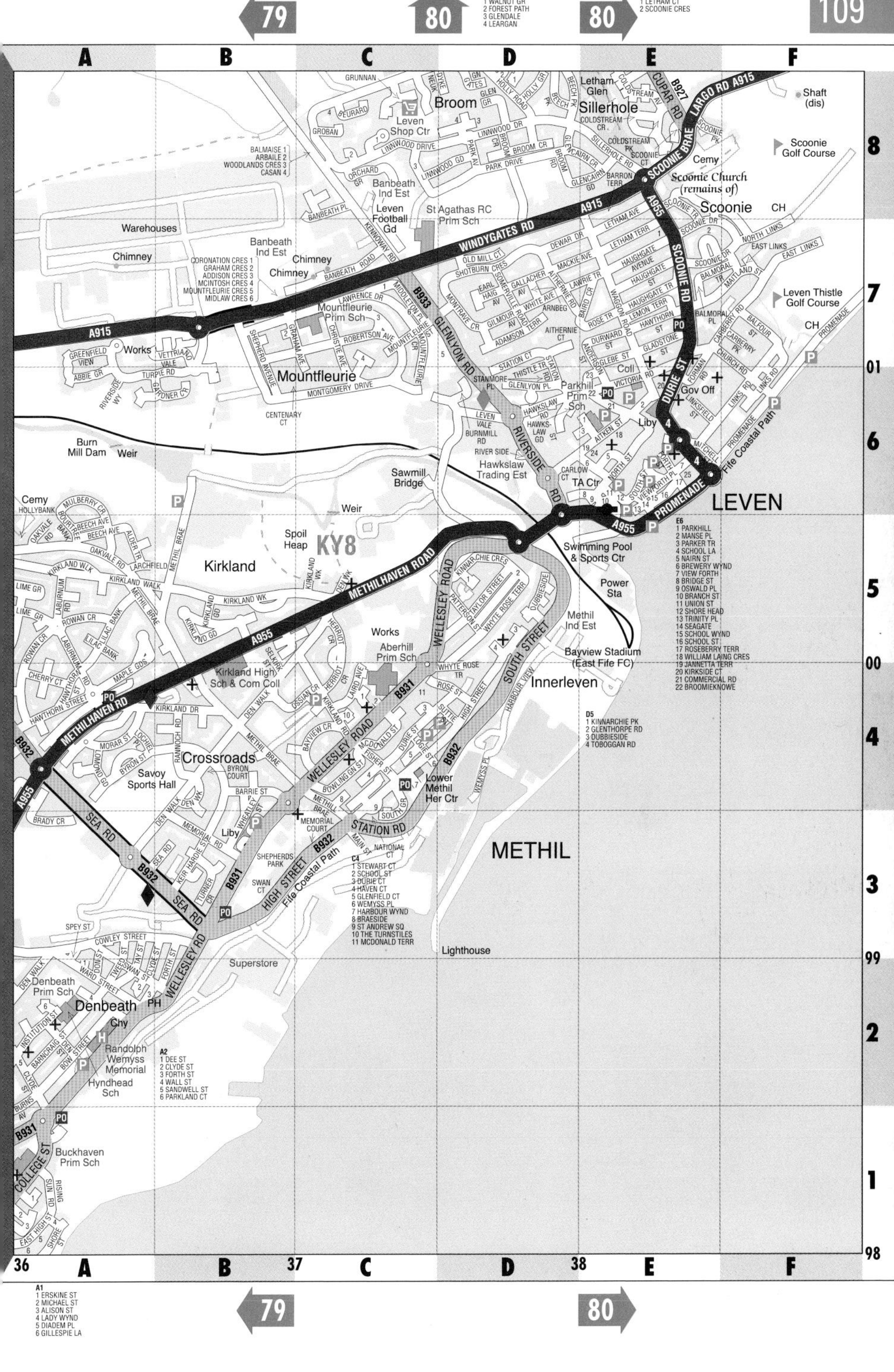
79
80
D8
1 WALNUT GR
2 FOREST PATH
3 GLENDALE
4 LEARGAN
80
E7
1 LETHAM CT
2 SCOONIE CRES
A
B
C
D
E
F
8
7
01
6
5
00
4
3
99
2
1
98
36
37
38
Broom
Leven Shop Ctr
Letham Glen
Sillerhole
Shaft (dis)
Scoonie Golf Course
Cemy
Scoonie Church (remains of)
Scoonie
CH
BALMAISE 1
ARBAILE 2
WOODLANDS CRES 3
CASAN 4
Banbeath Ind Est
Leven Football Gd
St Agathas RC Prim Sch
Warehouses
Chimney
CORONATION CRES 1
GRAHAM CRES 2
ADDISON CRES 3
MCINTOSH CRES 4
MOUNTFLEURIE CRES 5
MIDLAW CRES 6
WINDYGATES RD
A915
LARGO RD A915
CUPAR RD
B927
SCOONIE BRAE
SCOONIE RD
A955
Mountfleurie Prim Sch
Mountfleurie
Works
GLENLYON RD
B933
Leven Thistle Golf Course
CH
Parkhill Prim Sch
Coll
Gov Off
Liby
DURIE ST
Burn Mill Dam
Weir
Sawmill Bridge
Hawkslaw Trading Est
RIVERSIDE RD
TA Ctr
PROMENADE
Fife Coastal Path
LEVEN
Cemy
Weir
Spoil Heap
KY8
Kirkland
METHILHAVEN ROAD
Swimming Pool & Sports Ctr
Power Sta
E6
1 PARKHILL
2 MANSE PL
3 PARKER TR
4 SCHOOL LA
5 NAIRN ST
6 BREWERY WYND
7 VIEW FORTH
8 BRIDGE ST
9 OSWALD PL
10 BRANCH ST
11 UNION ST
12 SHORE HEAD
13 TRINITY PL
14 SEAGATE
15 SCHOOL WYND
16 SCHOOL ST
17 ROSEBERRY TERR
18 WILLIAM LAING CRES
19 JANNETTA TERR
20 KIRKSIDE CT
21 COMMERCIAL RD
22 BROOMIEKNOWE
Methil Ind Est
Works
Aberhill Prim Sch
WELLESLEY ROAD
SOUTH STREET
Bayview Stadium (East Fife FC)
Innerleven
Kirkland High Sch & Com Coll
D5
1 KINNARCHIE PK
2 GLENTHORPE RD
3 DUBBIESIDE
4 TOBOGGAN RD
Crossroads
Savoy Sports Hall
Lower Methil Her Ctr
B931
B932
SEA RD
Liby
STATION RD
HIGH STREET
METHIL
C4
1 STEWART CT
2 SCHOOL ST
3 DURIE CT
4 HAVEN CT
5 GLENFIELD CT
6 WEMYSS PL
7 HARBOUR WYND
8 BRAESIDE
9 ST ANDREW SQ
10 THE TURNSTILES
11 MCDONALD TERR
Lighthouse
Superstore
Denbeath Prim Sch
Denbeath
Chy
Randolph Wemyss Memorial
Hyndhead Sch
A2
1 DEE ST
2 CLYDE ST
3 FORTH ST
4 WALL ST
5 SANDWELL ST
6 PARKLAND CT
Buckhaven Prim Sch
COLLEGE ST
79
80
A1
1 ERSKINE ST
2 MICHAEL ST
3 ALISON ST
4 LADY WYND
5 DIADEM PL
6 GILLESPIE LA

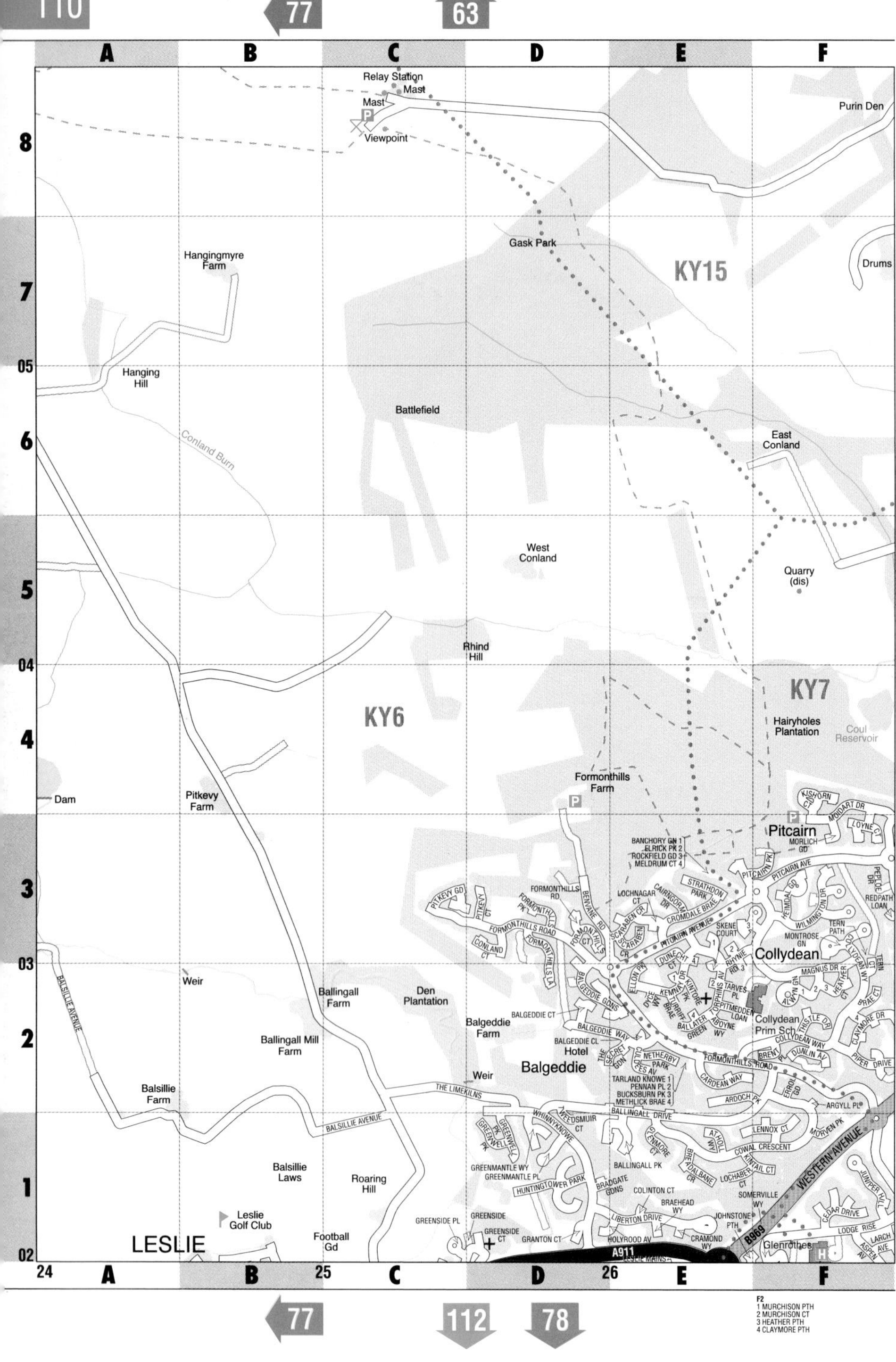

77
63

KY15

KY6

KY7

Purin Den

Drums

Gask Park

East Conland

Hanging Hill

Hangingmyre Farm

Battlefield

West Conland

Quarry (dis)

Conland Burn

Rhind Hill

Hairyholes Plantation

Coul Reservoir

Formonthills Farm

Pitcairn

Collydean

Dam

Pitkevy Farm

BANCHORY GN 1
ELRICK PK 2
ROCKFIELD GD 3
MELDRUM CT 4

Collydean Prim Sch

Weir

Ballingall Farm

Den Plantation

Balgeddie Farm

Ballingall Mill Farm

Balgeddie Hotel

Balgeddie

Weir

Balsillie Farm

Balsillie Laws

Roaring Hill

Football Gd

Leslie Golf Club

LESLIE

Glenrothes

F2
1 MURCHISON PTH
2 MURCHISON CT
3 HEATHER PTH
4 CLAYMORE PTH

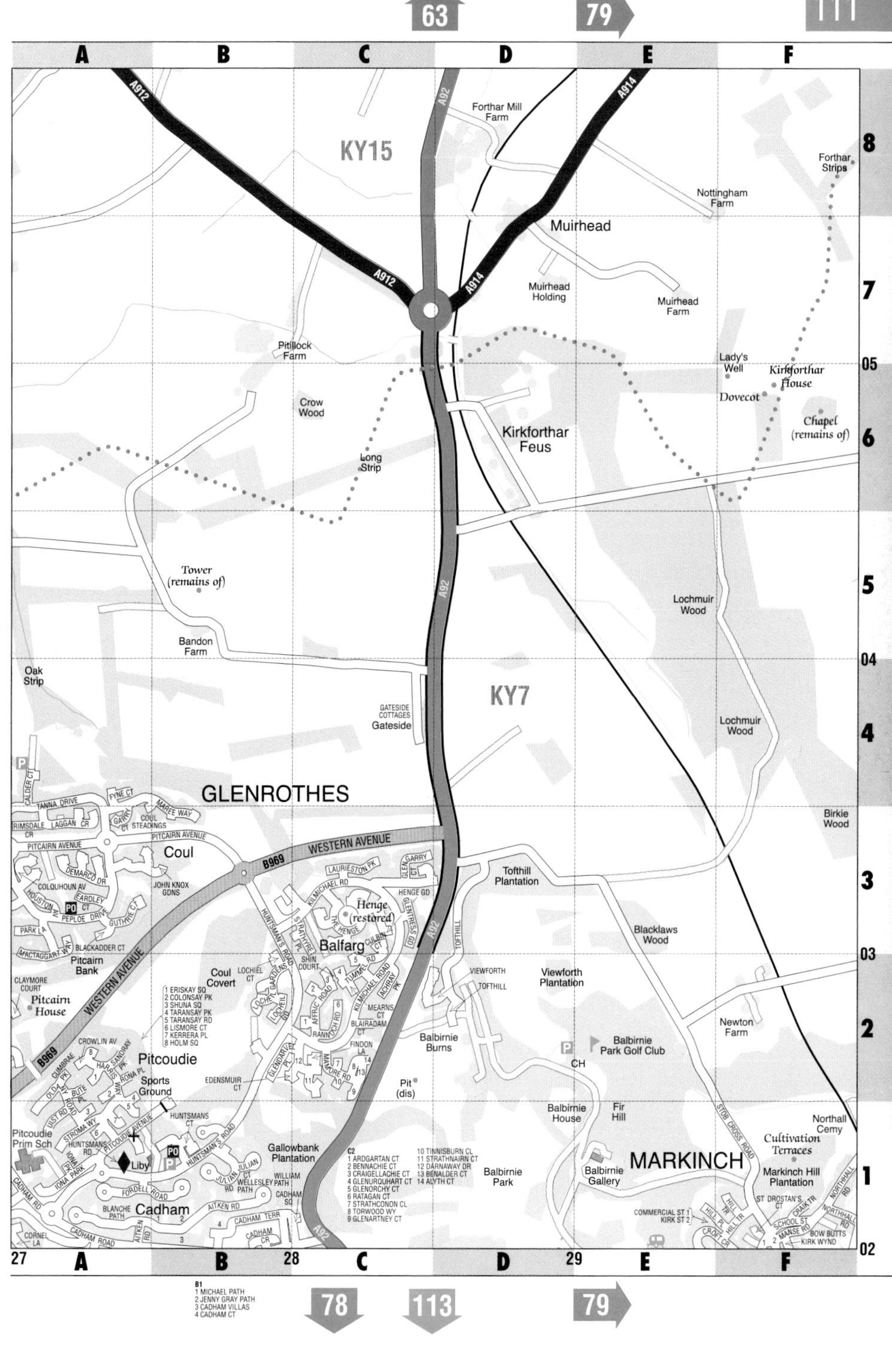

A   B   C   D   E   F

A912

A92

A914

Forthar Mill Farm

KY15

8

Forthar Strips

Nottingham Farm

Muirhead

7

Muirhead Holding

Muirhead Farm

A912

A914

05

Lady's Well

Kirkforthar House

Pitillock Farm

Dovecot

Crow Wood

Kirkforthar Feus

Chapel (remains of)

6

Long Strip

Tower (remains of)

5

Lochmuir Wood

Bandon Farm

Oak Strip

04

Lochmuir Wood

KY7

4

GATESIDE COTTAGES
Gateside

A92

GLENROTHES

Birkie Wood

Coul

WESTERN AVENUE

B969

LAURIESTON PK

3

Tofthill Plantation

JOHN KNOX GDNS

PITCAIRN AVENUE

DEMARCO DR
LAGGAN CR

RIMSDALE

TANNA DRIVE

PINE CT

MAREE WAY
GDNS
STEADINGS

PITCAIRN AVENUE

HOUSTON CT

COLQUHOUN AV

PEPLOE DRIV

EARDLEY

GARRY

HENGE GD

03

PARK L

MACTAGGART ST

BLACKADDER CT

Pitcairn Bank

GUTHRIE CT

KILMICHAEL RD

Henge (restored)

HENGE

Balfarg

Blacklaws Wood

Viewforth Plantation

CLAYMORE COURT

Pitcairn House

B969

WESTERN AVENUE

CROWLIN AV

Coul Covert

LOCHIEL CT

Coul Covert

SHIN COURT

MEARNS CT

VIEWFORTH

TOFTHILL

Newton Farm

Balbirnie Park Golf Club

2

OMBRIE

STRONA

Pitcoudie

1 ERISKAY SQ
2 COLONSAY PK
3 SHUNA SQ
4 TARANSAY PK
5 TARANSAY RD
6 LISMORE CT
7 KERRERA PL
8 HOLM SQ

BLAIRADAM

RANN

FINDON

Balbirnie Burns

CH

Fir Hill

Northall Cemy

LOIRSTON

Pitcoudie Prim Sch

Sports Ground

EDENSMUIR CT

Pit (dis)

Balbirnie House

Balbirnie Gallery

Cultivation Terraces

Gallowbank Plantation

HUNTSMANS CT

WILLIAM

Balbirnie Park

Markinch Hill Plantation

Liby

CADHAM

MARKINCH

LONG CROSS RD

CADHAM ROAD

Blanche Path

Cadham

AITKEN RD

CADHAM TERR

CADHAM SQ

CADHAM CR

C2
1 ARDGARTAN CT
2 BENNACHIE CT
3 CRAIGELLACHIE CT
4 GLENURQUHART CT
5 GLENORCHY CT
6 RATAGAN CT
7 STRATHCONON CL
8 TORWOOD WY
9 GLENARTNEY CT

10 TINNISBURN CL
11 STRATHNAIRN CT
12 DARNAWAY DR
13 BENALDER CT
14 ALYTH CT

COMMERCIAL ST
KIRK ST

St Drostan's

BOW BUTTS
KIRK WYND

FORTHAR RD
SCHOOL ST

MANSE RD

1

27   A   B   28   C   D   29   E   F

02

B1
1 MICHAEL PATH
2 JENNY GRAY PATH
3 CADHAM VILLAS
4 CADHAM CT

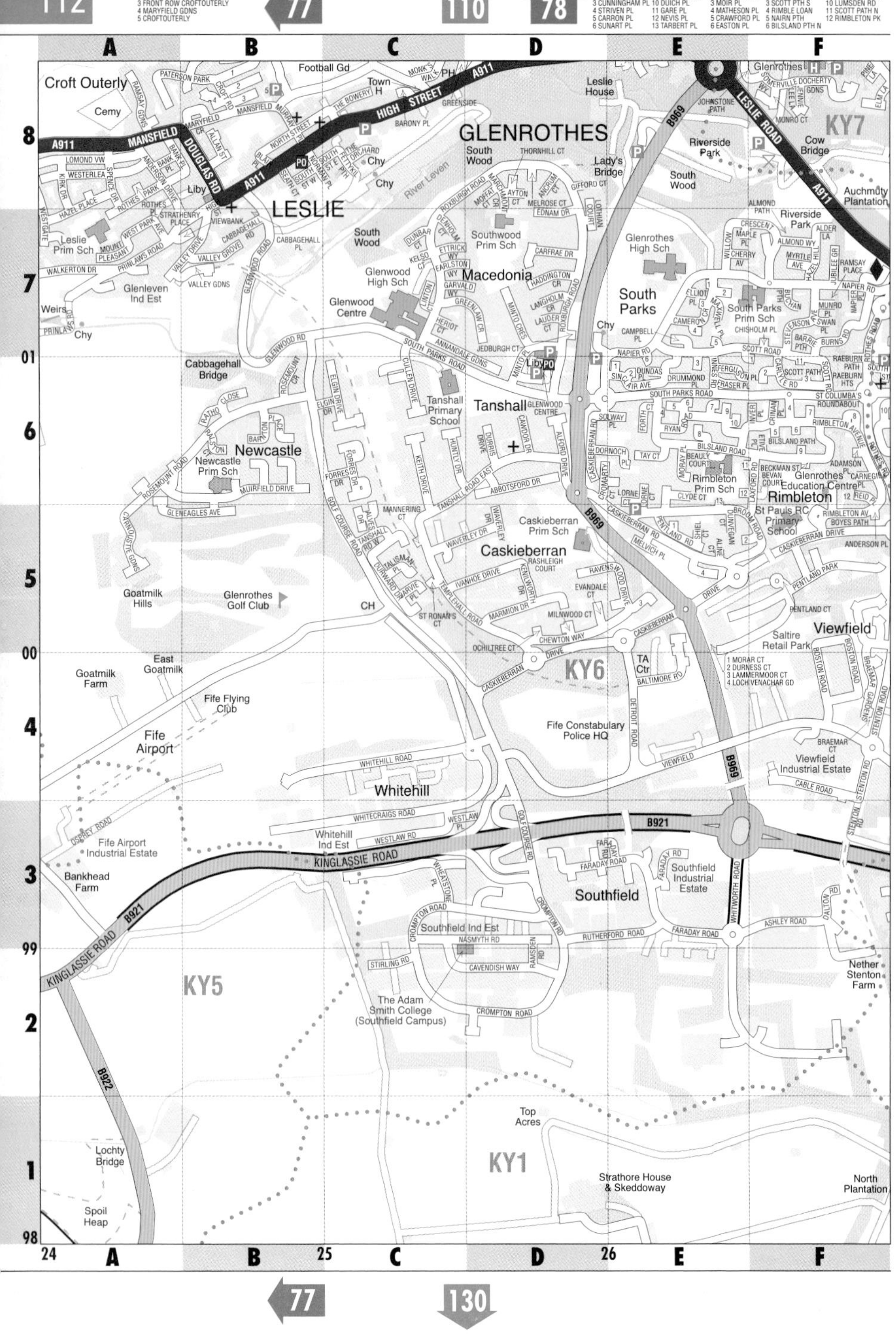

112
B8
1 BACK ROW CROFTOUTERLY
2 MID ROW CROFTOUTERLY
3 FRONT ROW CROFTOUTERLY
4 MARYFIELD GDNS
5 CROFTOUTERLY
77
110
78
E6
1 DOUGLAS PL
2 DAVIDSON PL
3 CUNNINGHAM PL
4 STRIVEN PL
5 CARRON PL
6 SUNART PL
7 MELFORD PL
8 AILORT PL
9 TORRIDON PL
10 DUICH PL
11 GARE PL
12 NEVIS PL
13 TARBERT PL
E7
1 MURDOCH PL
2 MORRISON PL
3 MOIR PL
4 MATHESON PL
5 CRAWFORD PL
6 EASTON PL
F6
1 CADZOW PL
2 HAMILTON PL
3 SCOTT PTH S
4 RIMBLE LOAN
5 NAIRN PTH
6 BILSLAND PTH N
7 RIMBLE PTH
8 RIMBLE SQ
9 BILSLAND PTH S
10 LUMSDEN RD
11 SCOTT PATH N
12 RIMBLETON PK
A
B
C
D
E
F
8
7
01
6
5
00
4
3
99
2
1
98
24
25
26
Croft Outerly
Cemy
Football Gd
Town H
HIGH STREET
A911
MANSFIELD
DOUGLAS RD
Leslie House
GLENROTHES
LESLIE
Liby
Leslie Prim Sch
Glenleven Ind Est
Weirs
Chy
South Wood
River Leven
Lady's Bridge
Riverside Park
Cow Bridge
KY7
Auchmuty Plantation
Glenrothes
Glenrothes High Sch
South Parks
South Parks Prim Sch
Southwood Prim Sch
Macedonia
Glenwood High Sch
Glenwood Centre
Cabbagehall Bridge
Newcastle
Newcastle Prim Sch
Tanshall
Tanshall Primary School
Rimbleton
Rimbleton Prim Sch
Glenrothes Education Centre
St Pauls RC Primary School
Caskieberran
Caskieberran Prim Sch
B969
Goatmilk Hills
Glenrothes Golf Club
CH
Viewfield
Saltire Retail Park
1 MORAR CT
2 DURNESS CT
3 LAMMERMOOR CT
4 LOCH VENACHAR GD
KY6
TA Ctr
Goatmilk Farm
East Goatmilk
Fife Flying Club
Fife Airport
Fife Constabulary Police HQ
Viewfield Industrial Estate
Whitehill
Whitehill Ind Est
Fife Airport Industrial Estate
Bankhead Farm
B921
KINGLASSIE ROAD
Southfield
Southfield Industrial Estate
Southfield Ind Est
The Adam Smith College (Southfield Campus)
KY5
Nether Stenton Farm
B922
Top Acres
KY1
Lochty Bridge
Spoil Heap
Strathore House & Skeddoway
North Plantation
130

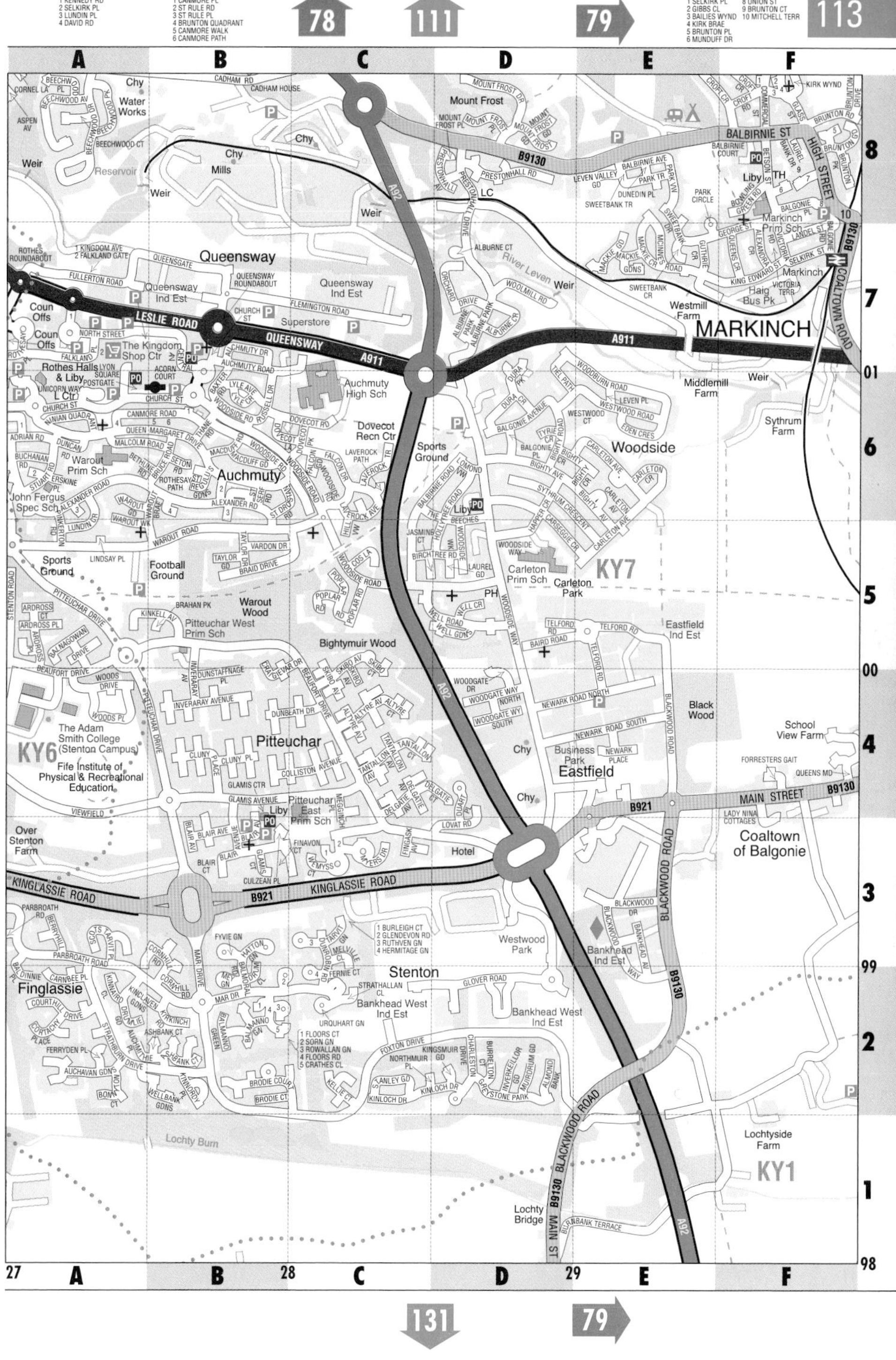
A6
1 KENNEDY RD
2 SELKIRK PL
3 LUNDIN PL
4 DAVID RD
B6
1 CANMORE PL
2 ST RULE RD
3 ST RULE PL
4 BRUNTON QUADRANT
5 CANMORE WALK
6 CANMORE PATH
78
111
79
F8
1 SELKIRK PL
2 GIBBS CL
3 BAILIES WYND
4 KIRK BRAE
5 BRUNTON PL
6 MUNDUFF DR
7 HOWIEGATE GD
8 UNION ST
9 BRUNTON CT
10 MITCHELL TERR
A
B
C
D
E
F
Mount Frost
Water Works
Reservoir
Weir
Chy
Mills
CADHAM RD
CADHAM HOUSE
BEECHWOOD CT
BALBIRNIE ST
B9130
HIGH STREET
PRESTONHALL RD
LC
Liby
TH
Markinch Prim Sch
Markinch
Haig Bus Pk
Westmill Farm
MARKINCH
COALTOWN ROAD
River Leven
Queensway
Queensway Ind Est
QUEENSWAY ROUNDABOUT
ROTHES ROUNDABOUT
FULLERTON ROAD
FLEMINGTON ROAD
Superstore
LESLIE ROAD
QUEENSWAY
A911
A92
Coun Offs
The Kingdom Shop Ctr
Rothes Halls & Liby
L Ctr
Auchmuty High Sch
Dovecot Recn Ctr
Sports Ground
Woodside
Middlemill Farm
Sythrum Farm
Auchmuty
Warout Prim Sch
John Fergus Spec Sch
Carleton Prim Sch
Carleton Park
KY7
Football Ground
Warout Wood
Pitteuchar West Prim Sch
Bightymuir Wood
Eastfield Ind Est
Black Wood
School View Farm
KY6
The Adam Smith College (Stenton Campus)
Fife Institute of Physical & Recreational Education
Pitteuchar
Pitteuchar East Prim Sch
Business Park
Eastfield
MAIN STREET
B921
Coaltown of Balgonie
Over Stenton Farm
Hotel
KINGLASSIE ROAD
BLACKWOOD ROAD
Westwood Park
Bankhead Ind Est
Stenton
Bankhead West Ind Est
Finglassie
Lochty Burn
Lochtyside Farm
KY1
Lochty Bridge
BURNBANK TERRACE
MAIN ST
1 BURLEIGH CT
2 GLENDEVON RD
3 RUTHVEN GN
4 HERMITAGE GN
1 FLOORS CT
2 SORN GN
3 ROWALLAN GN
4 FLOORS RD
5 CRATHES CL
8
7
01
6
5
00
4
3
99
2
1
98
27
28
29
131
79

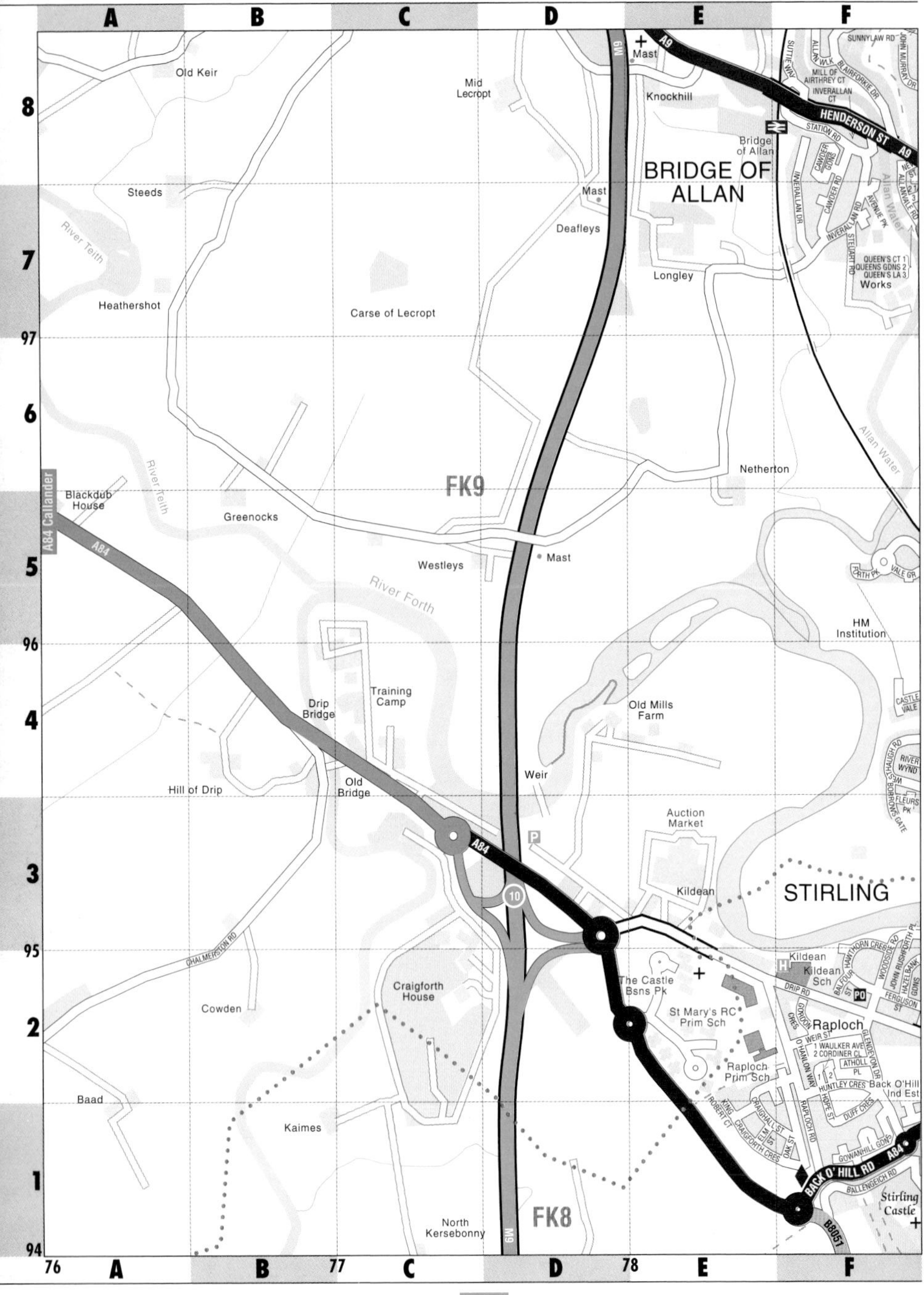
Old Keir
Mid Lecropt
Mast
Knockhill
Bridge of Allan
BRIDGE OF ALLAN
HENDERSON ST
Steeds
River Teith
Mast
Deafleys
Longley
Heathershot
Carse of Lecropt
Works
Netherton
Allan Water
Blackdub House
Greenocks
FK9
River Teith
A84 Callander
Westleys
Mast
River Forth
HM Institution
Training Camp
Drip Bridge
Old Mills Farm
Weir
Hill of Drip
Old Bridge
Auction Market
Kildean
STIRLING
CHALMERSTON RD
Kildean
Kildean Sch
The Castle Bsns Pk
Craigforth House
St Mary's RC Prim Sch
Raploch
Cowden
Raploch Prim Sch
Back O'Hill Ind Est
Baad
Kaimes
BACK O' HILL RD
North Kersebonny
FK8
Stirling Castle
M9
A9
A84
B8057

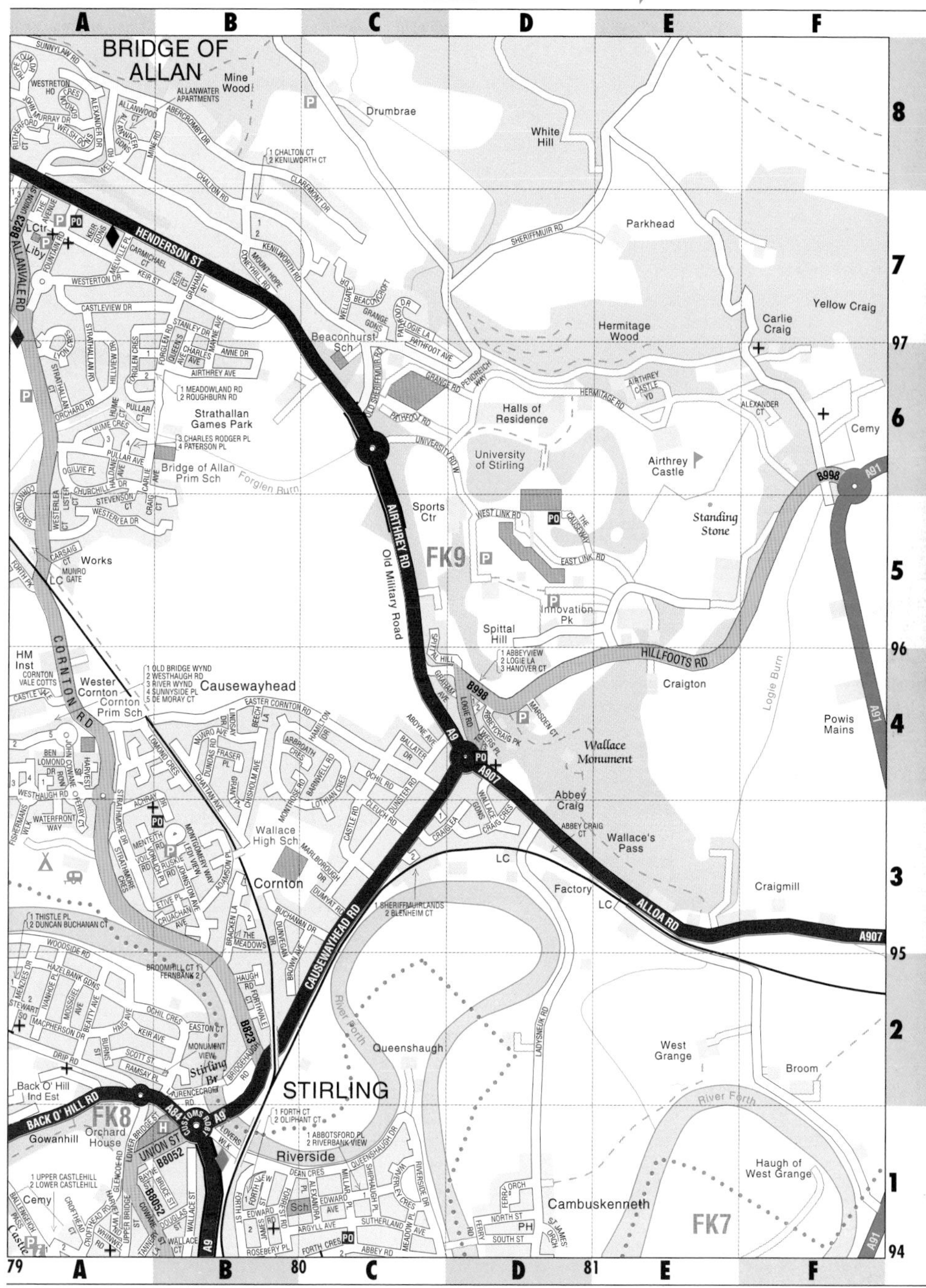

BRIDGE OF ALLAN

STIRLING

115
71

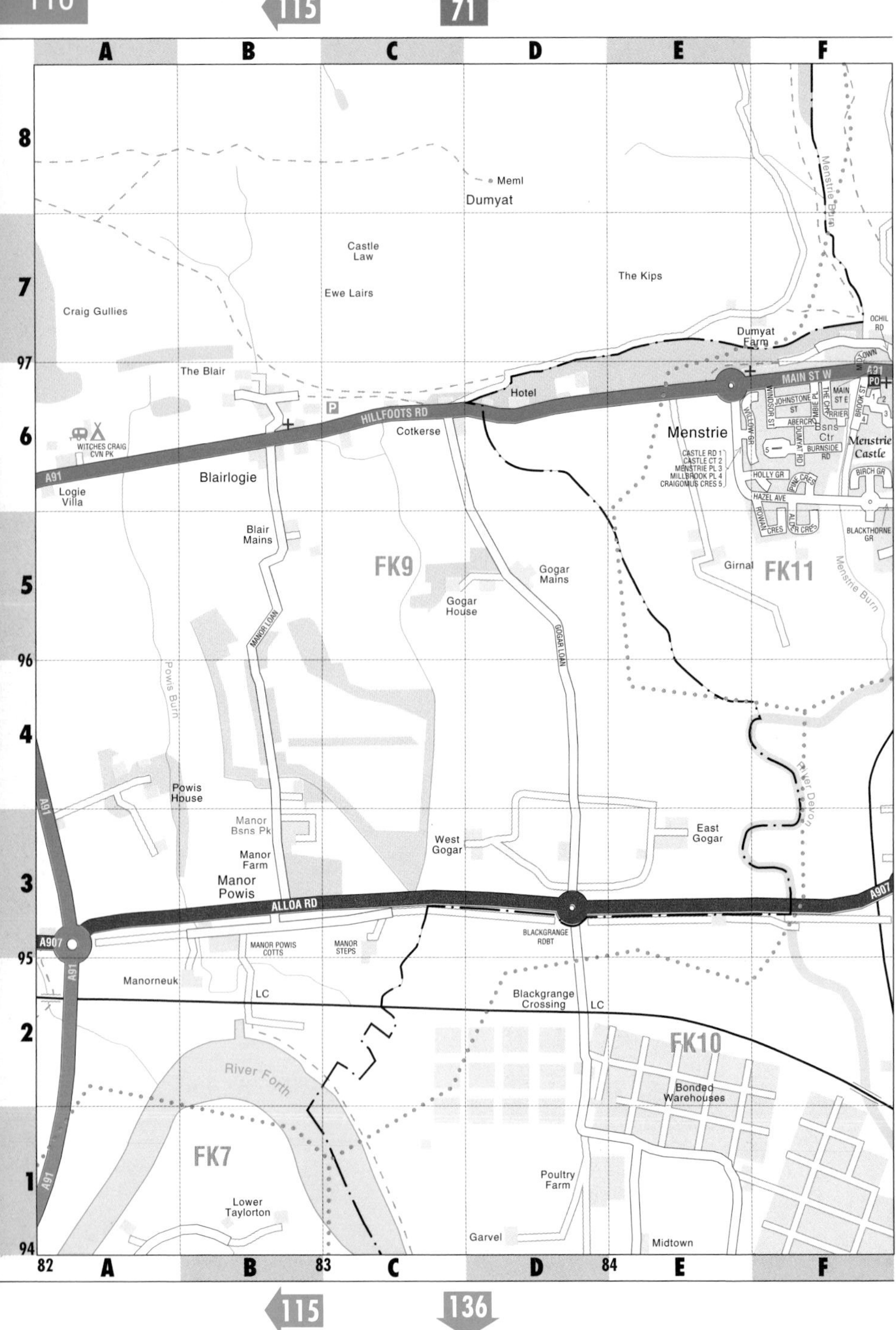
A
B
C
D
E
F
8
7
97
6
5
96
4
3
95
2
1
94
82
83
84
Meml
Dumyat
Castle
Law
Ewe Lairs
The Kips
Craig Gullies
Dumyat
Farm
OCHIL
RD
MIDTOWN
The Blair
Hotel
MAIN ST W
A91
PO
HILLFOOTS RD
Cotkerse
Menstrie
WITCHES CRAIG
CVN PK
A91
Blairlogie
Logie
Villa
CASTLE RD 1
CASTLE CT 2
MENSTRIE PL 3
MILLBROOK PL 4
CRAIGOMUS CRES 5
Menstrie
Castle
WINDSOR ST
JOHNSTONE
ST
ABERCR
DUMYAT RD
MAIN
ST E
BROOK ST
Bsns
Ctr
BURNSIDE
RD
HOLLY GR
PINE CRES
BIRCH GR
HAZEL AVE
ROWAN CRES
ALDER CRES
BLACKTHORNE
GR
Menstrie Burn
Blair
Mains
FK9
Gogar
Mains
Girnal
FK11
Gogar
House
MANOR LOAN
GOGAR LOAN
Powis Burn
River Devon
A91
Powis
House
Manor
Bsns Pk
West
Gogar
East
Gogar
Manor
Farm
Manor
Powis
ALLOA RD
A907
A907
BLACKGRANGE
RDBT
MANOR POWIS
COTTS
MANOR
STEPS
A91
Manorneuk
LC
Blackgrange
Crossing
LC
River Forth
FK10
Bonded
Warehouses
FK7
A91
Poultry
Farm
Lower
Taylorton
Garvel
Midtown

115
136

71
118

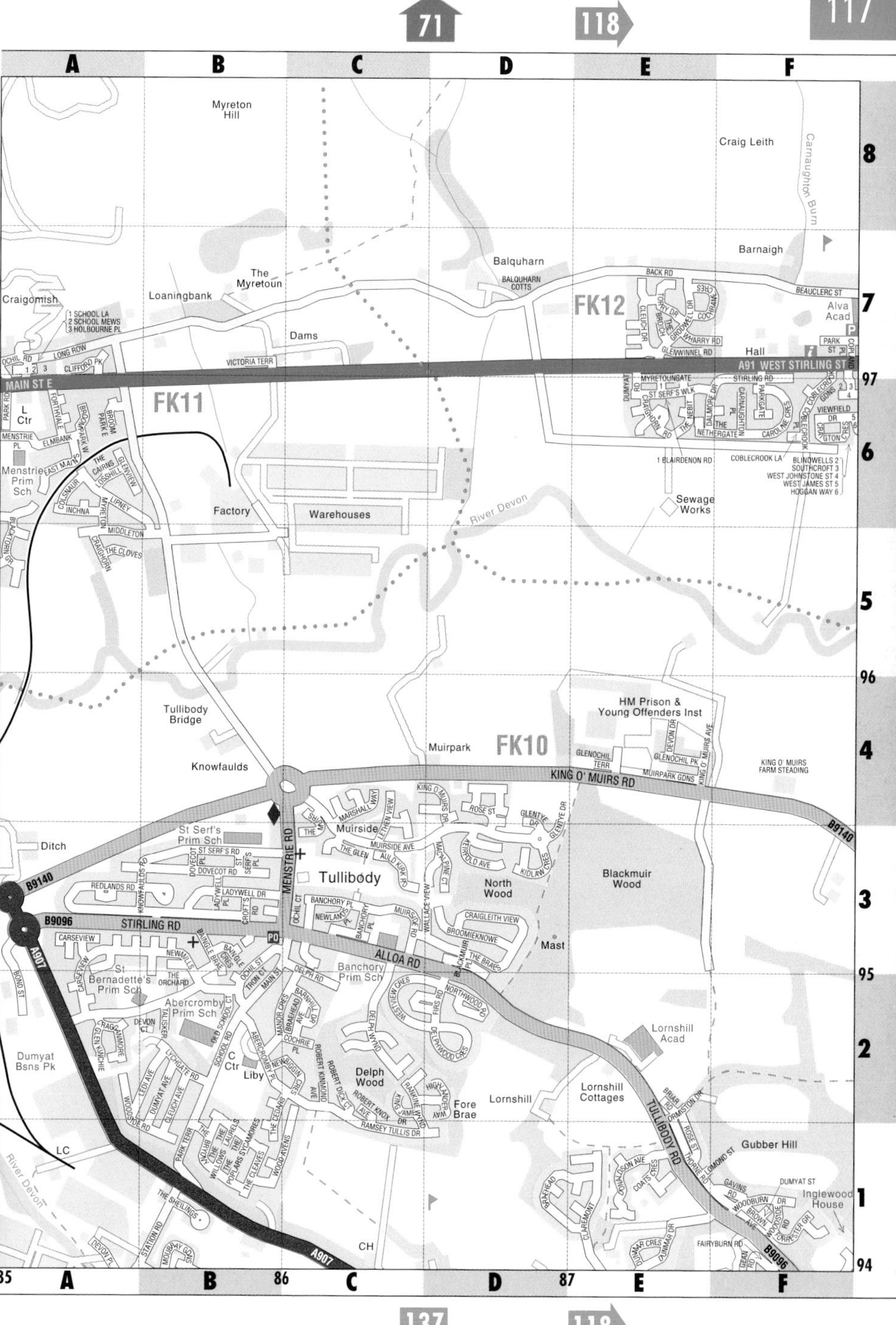
Myreton Hill
Craig Leith
Carnaughton Burn
Barnaigh
Balquharn
The Myretoun
Loaningbank
Craigomish
FK12
FK11
FK10
Dams
Alva Acad
Hall
A91 WEST STIRLING ST
MAIN ST E
Menstrie Prim Sch
Factory
Warehouses
River Devon
Sewage Works
Tullibody Bridge
HM Prison & Young Offenders Inst
Muirpark
Knowfaulds
KING O' MUIRS RD
KING O' MUIRS FARM STEADING
St Serf's Prim Sch
Ditch
Muirside
Tullibody
North Wood
Blackmuir Wood
MENSTRIE RD
STIRLING RD
ALLOA RD
B9140
B9096
A907
Mast
Banchory Prim Sch
St Bernadette's Prim Sch
Abercromby Prim Sch
Lornshill Acad
Dumyat Bsns Pk
Delph Wood
Fore Brae
Lornshill
Lornshill Cottages
TULLIBODY RD
Gubber Hill
Inglewood House
CH
LC
1 SCHOOL LA
2 SCHOOL MEWS
3 HOLBOURNE PL
1 BLAIRDENON RD
BLINDWELLS 2
SOUTHCROFT 3
WEST JOHNSTONE ST 4
WEST JAMES ST 5
HOGGAN WAY 6
A B C D E F
8 7 6 5 4 3 2 1
97 96 95 94
85 86 87

137
118

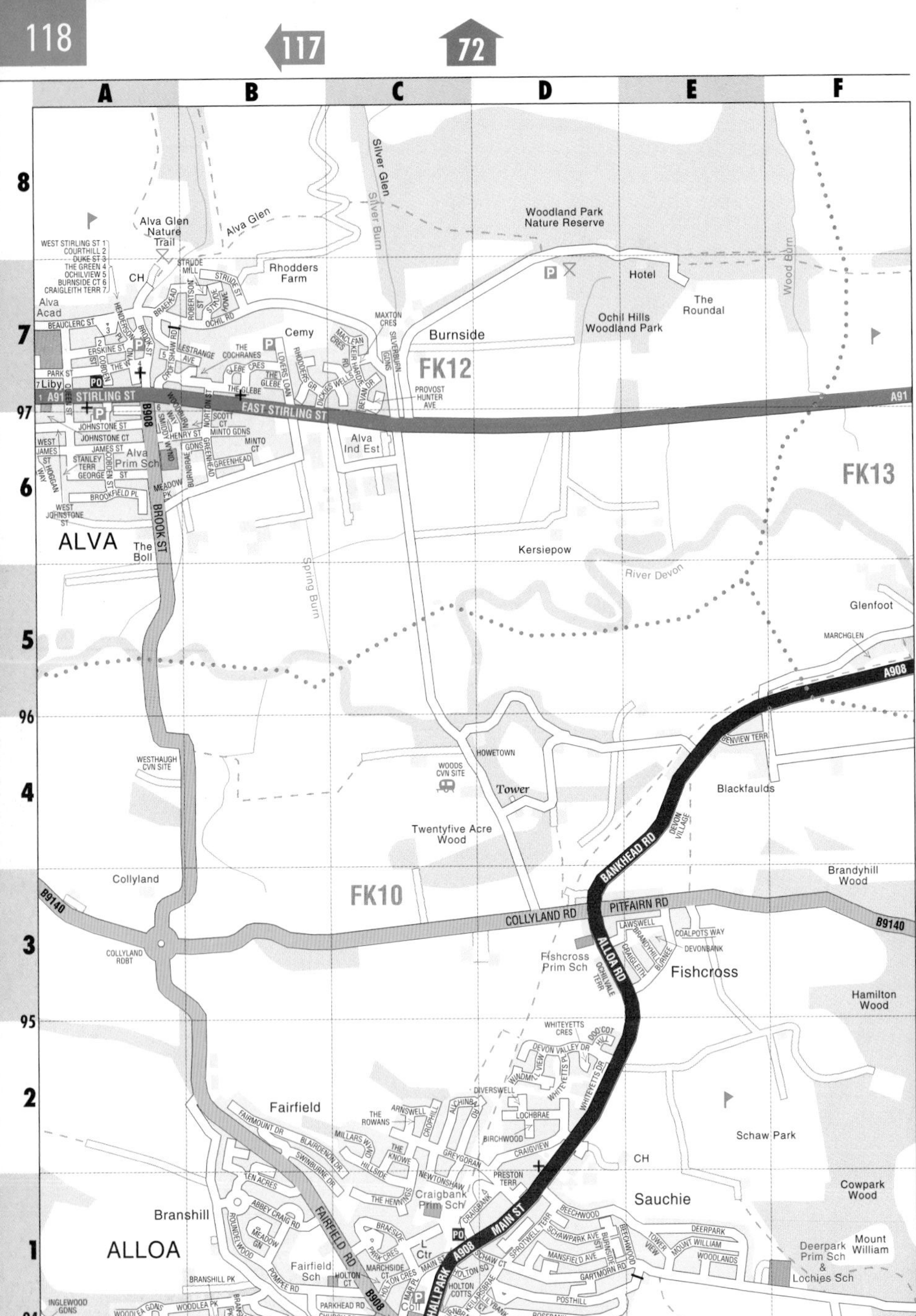

A **B** **C** **D** **E** **F**

8

WEST STIRLING ST 1
COURTHILL 2
DUKE ST 3
THE GREEN 4
OCHILVIEW 5
BURNSIDE CT 6
CRAIGLEITH TERR 7.

Alva Glen
Nature Trail

Alva Glen

Rhodders Farm

Silver Glen

Silver Burn

Woodland Park
Nature Reserve

CH

STRUDE MILL

Cemy

Alva
Acad

Beauclerc St

ERSKINE ST

PARK ST

7 Libry

P

97 A91 STIRLING ST

EAST STIRLING ST

MAXTON CRES

Burnside

FK12

Hotel

The
Roundal

Ochil Hills
Woodland Park

P

PROVOST HUNTER AVE

A91

7

JOHNSTONE ST

JAMES ST

STANLEY TERR

GEORGE ST

Alva
Prim Sch

BROOKFIELD PL

MEADOW

GREENHEAD

MINTO GDNS

MINTO CT

SCOTT CT

Alva
Ind Est

FK13

6

WEST
JAMES
ST

MORGAN
WAY

WEST
JOHNSTONE
ST

ALVA

BROOK ST

The
Boll

Spring Burn

Kersiepow

River Devon

Glenfoot

MARCHGLEN

5

96

WESTHAUGH
CVN SITE

WOODS
CVN SITE

HOWETOWN

Tower

DEVONVIEW TERR

A908

Blackfaulds

Brandyhill
Wood

4

Twentyfive Acre
Wood

BANKHEAD RD

DEVON
VILLAGE

Collyland

B9140

FK10

COLLYLAND RD

PITFAIRN RD

LAWSWELL

COALPOTS WAY

DEVONBANK

B9140

3

Collyland
RDBT

Fishcross
Prim Sch

ALLOA RD

CRAIGVIEW TERRACE

Fishcross

Hamilton
Wood

95

WHITEYETTS
CRES

LOG COT

DEVON VALLEY DR

WHITEYETTS DR

2

Fairfield

FAIRMOUNT DR

BLAIRDENON DR

SWINBURNE DR

MILLARS AV

HILLSIDE

THE KNOWE

ARNSWELL

CHAPELLE

CHINES

THE
ROWANS

DIVERSWELL

WOODMYN

LOCHBRAE

BIRCHWOOD

Schaw Park

Cowpark
Wood

1

Branshill

ALLOA

TEN ACRES

ABBEY CRAIG RD

BRANSHILL RD

BIRKENWOOD

Fairfield
Sch

BRANSHILL PK

MARCHSIDE

BRAESIDE

THE HENRYS

HOLTON

FAIRFIELD RD

POFFLE RD

CHURCH RD

PARKHEAD RD

Ctr

P

HOLTON COTTS

NEWTONSHAW

Craigbank
Prim Sch

GREYFRIARS

PRESTON TERR

HALLPARK RD

MAIN ST

ALLOA RD

B908

SCHAWPARK AVE

BEECHWOOD

SANDYWELL

MANSFIELD AVE

GARTMORN RD

POSTHILL

ROSEBANK

CH

DEERPARK

MOUNT WILLIAM

WOODLANDS

Sauchie

Deerpark
Prim Sch
&
Lochies Sch

Mount
William

94

INGLEWOOD
GDNS

WOODLEA GDNS

WOODLEA PK

88 **A** 89 **B** **C** 90 **D** **E** **F**

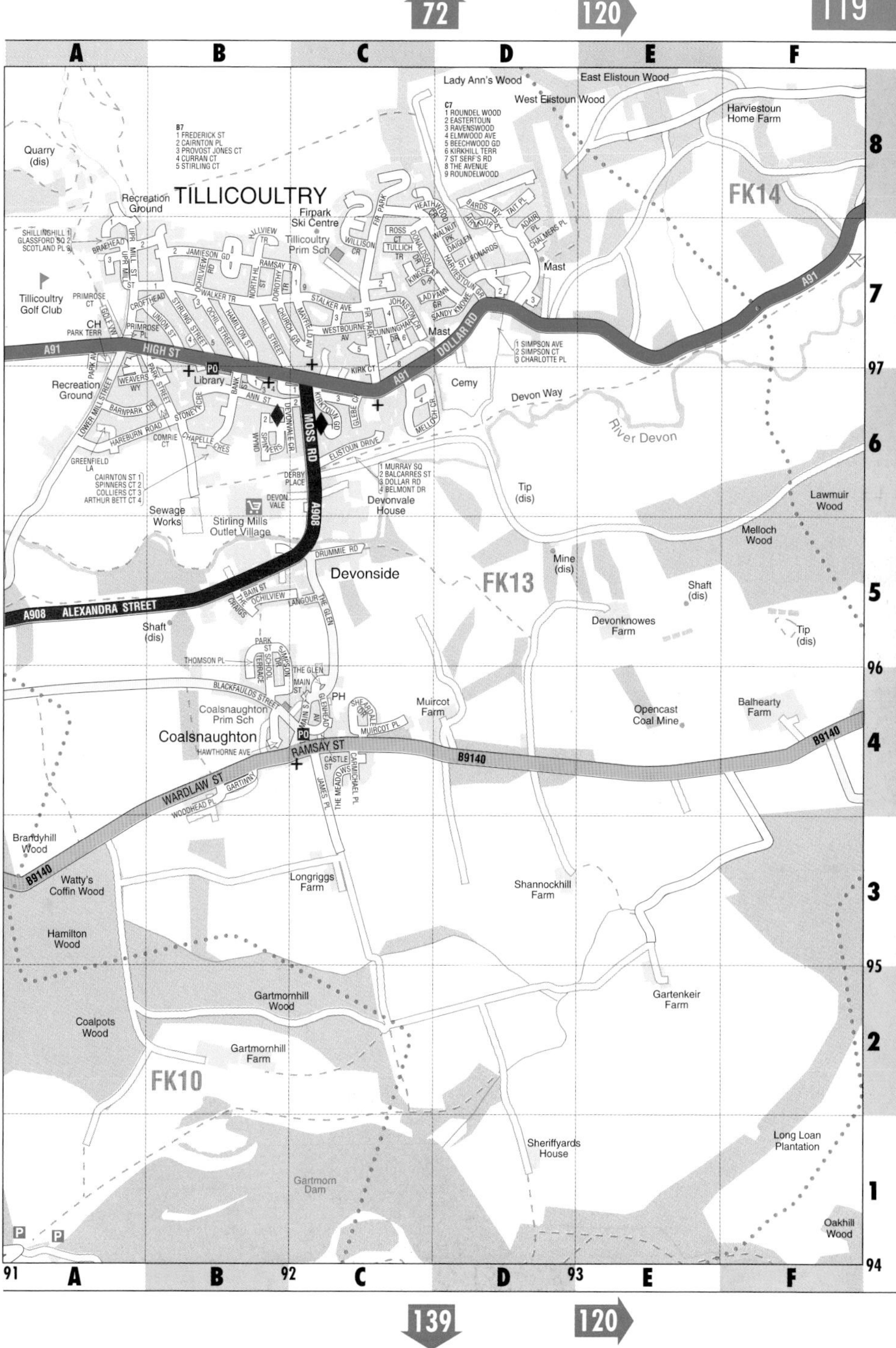
TILLICOULTRY
Devonside
Coalsnaughton
FK14
FK13
FK10
Quarry (dis)
Recreation Ground
Tillicoultry Golf Club
Firpark Ski Centre
Tillicoultry Prim Sch
Library
Sewage Works
Stirling Mills Outlet Village
Devonvale House
Cemy
Devon Way
River Devon
Lady Ann's Wood
East Elistoun Wood
West Elistoun Wood
Harviestoun Home Farm
Mast
Tip (dis)
Mine (dis)
Shaft (dis)
Melloch Wood
Lawmuir Wood
Devonknowes Farm
Opencast Coal Mine
Balhearty Farm
Muircot Farm
Coalsnaughton Prim Sch
Brandyhill Wood
Watty's Coffin Wood
Hamilton Wood
Coalpots Wood
Longriggs Farm
Shannockhill Farm
Gartenkeir Farm
Gartmornhill Wood
Gartmornhill Farm
Sheriffyards House
Gartmorn Dam
Long Loan Plantation
Oakhill Wood
A91
A908
B9140
HIGH ST
DOLLAR RD
MOSS RD
ALEXANDRA STREET
RAMSAY ST
WARDLAW ST
B7
1 FREDERICK ST
2 CAIRNTON PL
3 PROVOST JONES CT
4 CURRAN CT
5 STIRLING CT
C7
1 ROUNDEL WOOD
2 EASTERTOUN
3 RAVENSWOOD
4 ELMWOOD AVE
5 BEECHWOOD GD
6 KIRKHILL TERR
7 ST SERF'S RD
8 THE AVENUE
9 ROUNDELWOOD
1 SHILLINGHILL
2 GLASSFORD SQ
3 SCOTLAND PL
1 SIMPSON AVE
2 SIMPSON CT
3 CHARLOTTE PL
1 MURRAY SQ
2 BALCARRES ST
3 DOLLAR RD
4 BELMONT DR
CAIRNTON ST 1
SPINNERS CT 2
COLLIERS CT 3
ARTHUR BETT CT 4
A B C D E F
8 7 97 6 5 96 4 3 95 2 1 94
91 92 93

119
73

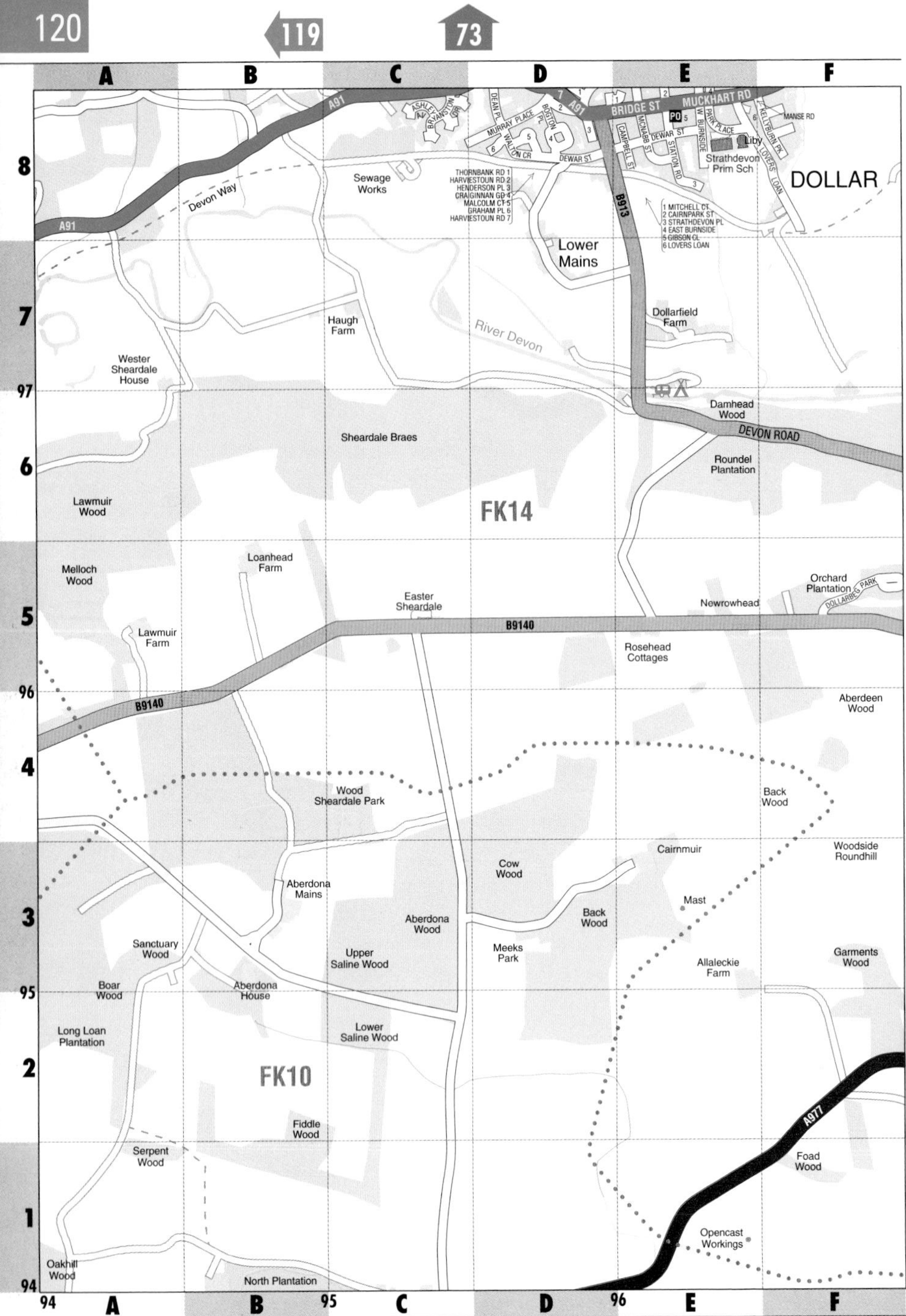
A
B
C
D
E
F
8
7
97
6
5
96
4
3
95
2
1
94
A91
Devon Way
Sewage Works
ASHLEY AV
BRYANSTON DR
DEAN PL
MURRAY PLACE
BOGTON PL
WALTON CR
DEWAR ST
BRIDGE ST
MUCKHART RD
CAMPBELL ST
MCNABB ST
DEWAR ST
STATION RD
W BURNSIDE
PARK PLACE
KELLYBURN PK
MANSE RD
LOVERS LOAN
PO
Liby
Strathdevon Prim Sch
DOLLAR
THORNBANK RD 1
HARVIESTOUN RD 2
HENDERSON PL 3
CRAIGINNAN GD 4
MALCOLM CT 5
GRAHAM PL 6
HARVIESTOUN RD 7
1 MITCHELL CT
2 CAIRNPARK ST
3 STRATHDEVON PL
4 EAST BURNSIDE
5 GIBSON CL
6 LOVERS LOAN
B913
Lower Mains
Dollarfield Farm
Haugh Farm
River Devon
Wester Sheardale House
Damhead Wood
DEVON ROAD
Sheardale Braes
Roundel Plantation
FK14
Lawmuir Wood
Melloch Wood
Loanhead Farm
Easter Sheardale
Orchard Plantation
DOLLARBEG PARK
Newrowhead
B9140
Lawmuir Farm
Rosehead Cottages
Aberdeen Wood
B9140
Wood Sheardale Park
Back Wood
Cairnmuir
Woodside Roundhill
Cow Wood
Aberdona Mains
Mast
Aberdona Wood
Back Wood
Sanctuary Wood
Upper Saline Wood
Meeks Park
Allaleckie Farm
Garments Wood
Boar Wood
Aberdona House
Lower Saline Wood
Long Loan Plantation
FK10
A977
Fiddle Wood
Serpent Wood
Foad Wood
Opencast Workings
Oakhill Wood
North Plantation
94
95
96

119
140

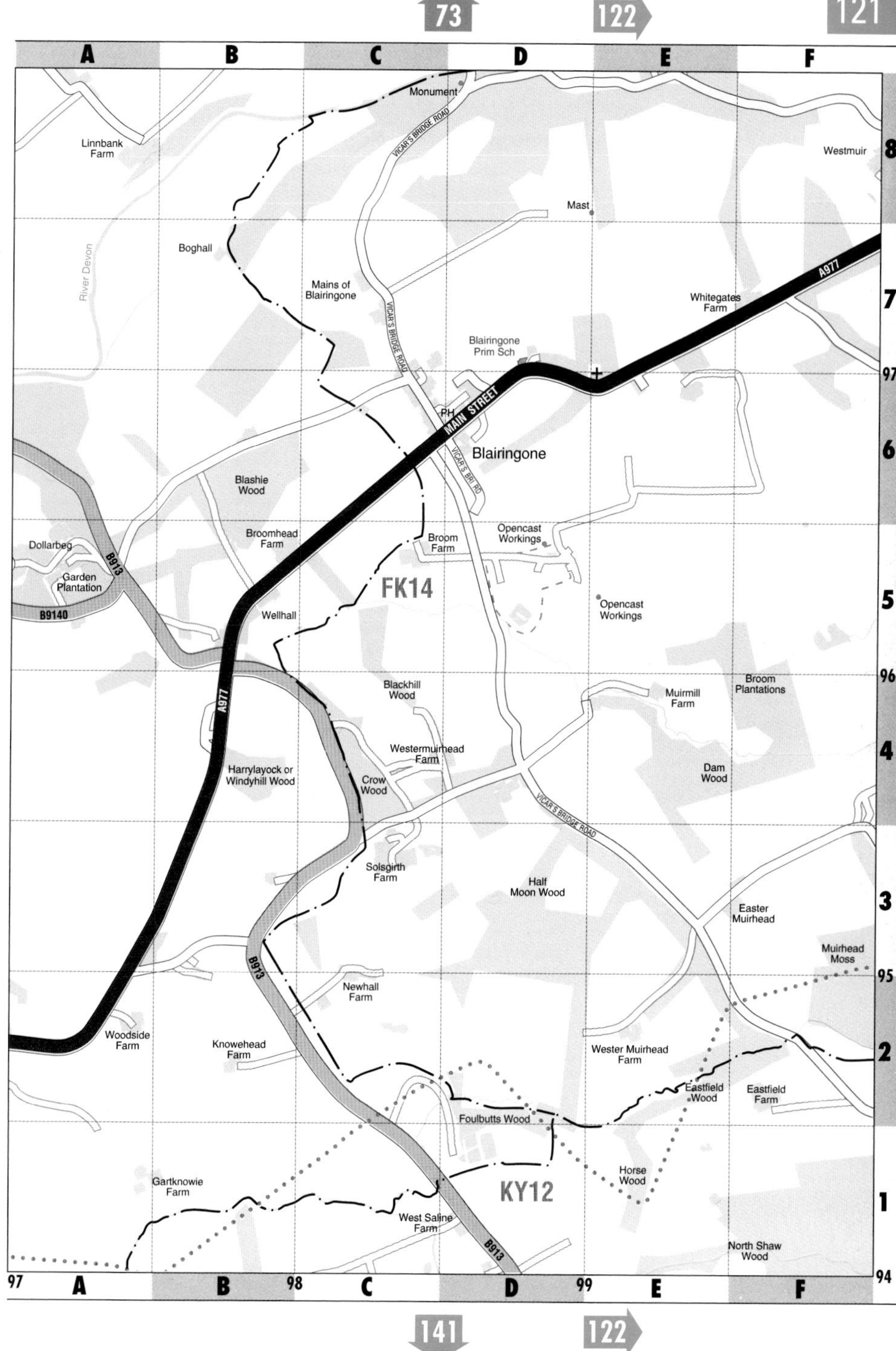

A B C D E F

Monument

Linnbank
Farm

8

Westmuir

River Devon

Boghall

Mains of
Blairingone

Mast

A9971

7

Whitegates
Farm

Blairingone
Prim Sch

97

Blairingone

Blashie
Wood

6

Dollarbeg

Broomhead
Farm

Broom
Farm

Opencast
Workings

B913

Garden
Plantation

FK14

Wellhall

B9140

Opencast
Workings

5

96

Blackhill
Wood

Muirmill
Farm

Broom
Plantations

4

Westermuirhead
Farm

Harrylayock or
Windyhill Wood

A9977

Crow
Wood

Dam
Wood

Solsgirth
Farm

Half
Moon Wood

Easter
Muirhead

3

Muirhead
Moss

95

Newhall
Farm

B913

Woodside
Farm

Knowehead
Farm

Wester Muirhead
Farm

2

Eastfield
Wood

Eastfield
Farm

Foulbutts Wood

Gartknowie
Farm

KY12

Horse
Wood

1

West Saline
Farm

B913

North Shaw
Wood

94

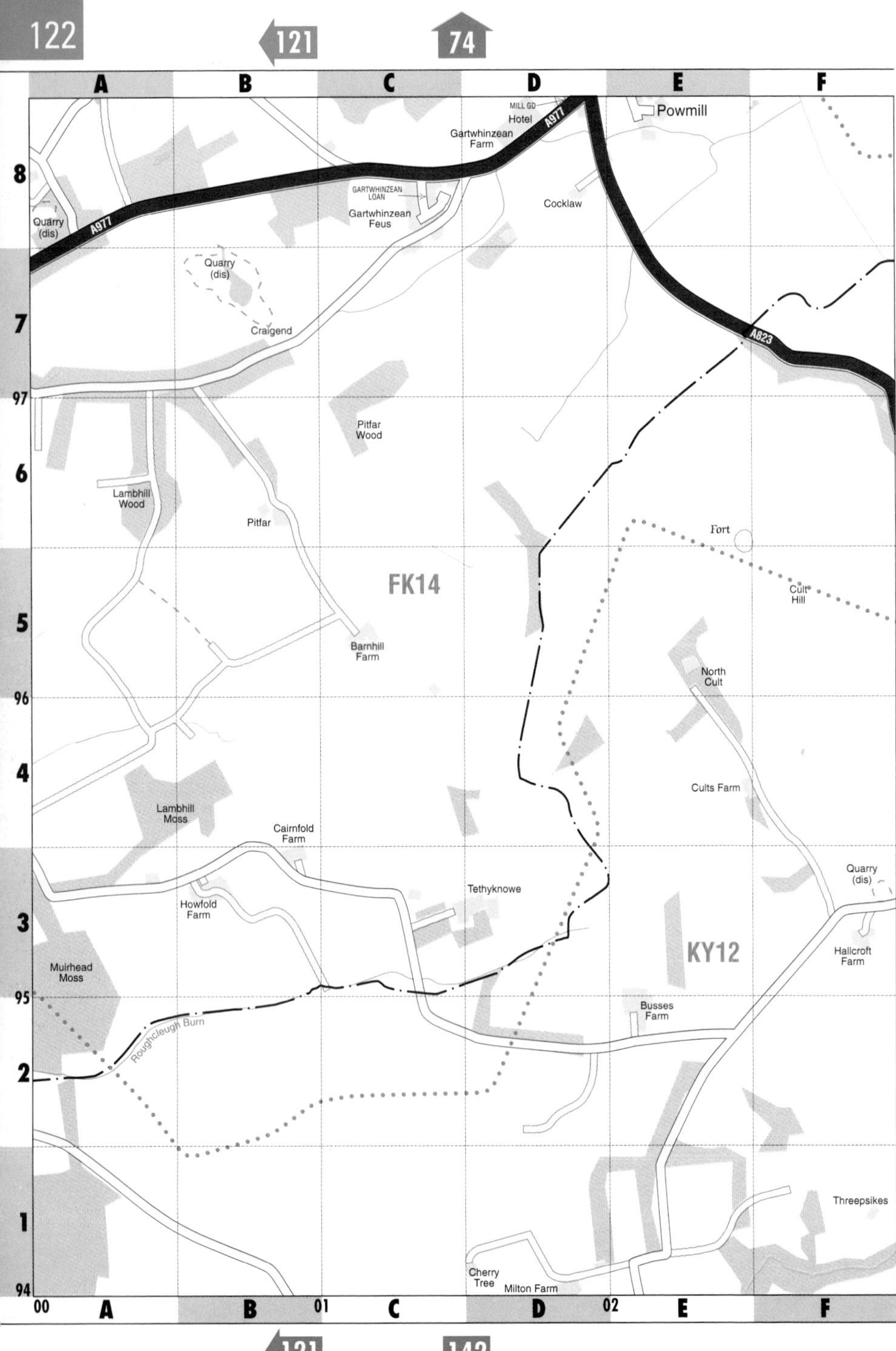

Powmill

MILL GD
Hotel

Gartwhinzean
Farm

GARTWHINZEAN
LOAN

Gartwhinzean
Feus

Cocklaw

Quarry
(dis)

A977

A977

A823

Quarry
(dis)

Craigend

Pitfar
Wood

Fort

Cult
Hill

Lambhill
Wood

Pitfar

FK14

North
Cult

Barnhill
Farm

Cults Farm

Lambhill
Moss

Cairnfold
Farm

Quarry
(dis)

Tethyknowe

KY12

Howfold
Farm

Hallcroft
Farm

Muirhead
Moss

Roughcleugh Burn

Busses
Farm

Threepsikes

Cherry
Tree

Milton Farm

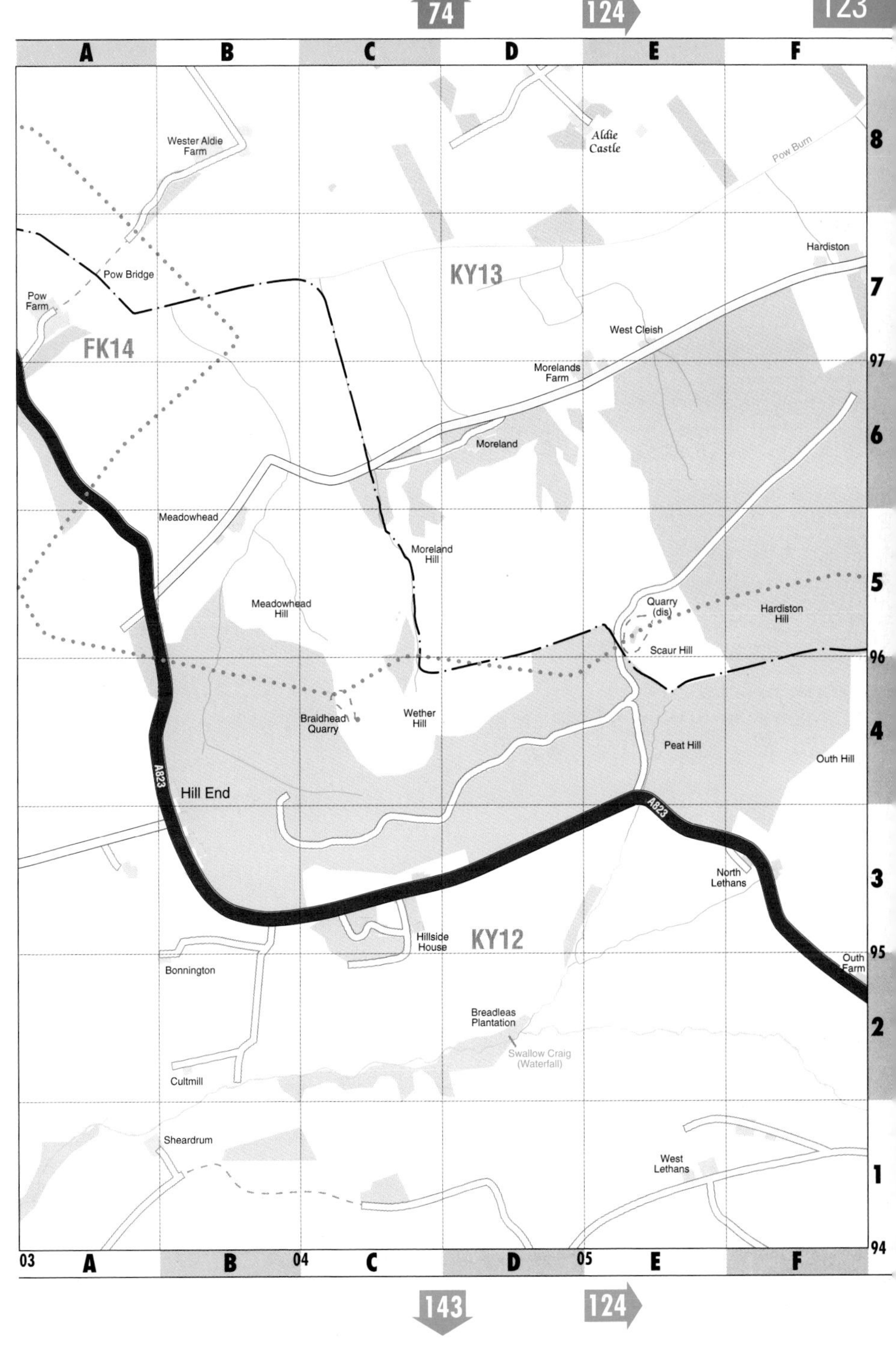
A
B
C
D
E
F
Wester Aldie Farm
Aldie Castle
Pow Burn
8
Hardiston
Pow Bridge
KY13
Pow Farm
7
West Cleish
FK14
97
Morelands Farm
Moreland
6
Meadowhead
Moreland Hill
5
Meadowhead Hill
Quarry (dis)
Hardiston Hill
Scaur Hill
96
Braidhead Quarry
Wether Hill
4
Peat Hill
Outh Hill
A823
Hill End
A823
North Lethans
3
Hillside House
KY12
95
Bonnington
Outh Farm
Breadleas Plantation
2
Swallow Craig (Waterfall)
Cultmill
Sheardrum
West Lethans
1
94
03
A
B
04
C
D
05
E
F

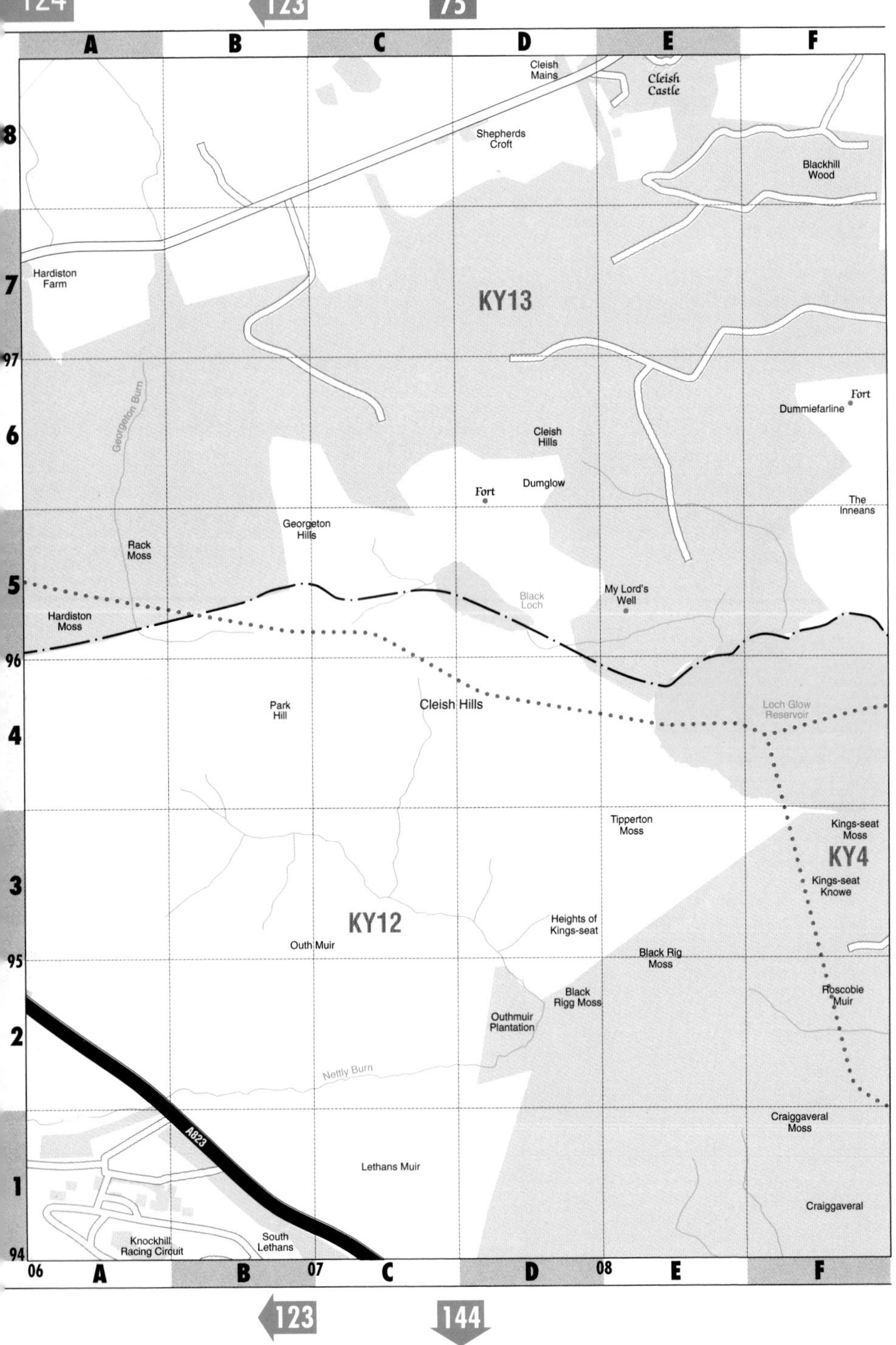

8

Cleish
Mains

*Cleish
Castle*

Shepherds
Croft

Blackhill
Wood

7 Hardiston
Farm

KY13

97

Georgeton Burn

Fort
Dummiefarline •

6

Cleish
Hills

Dumglow

Fort •

The
Inneans

Georgeton
Hills

Rack
Moss

Black
Loch

My Lord's
Well •

5

Hardiston
Moss

96

Park
Hill

Cleish Hills

Loch Glow
Reservoir

4

Tipperton
Moss

Kings-seat
Moss

KY4

3

KY12

Outh Muir

Heights of
Kings-seat

Kings-seat
Knowe

95

Black Rig
Moss

Roscobie
Muir

2

Outhmuir
Plantation

Black
Rigg Moss

Nettly Burn

Craiggaveral
Moss

A823

1

Lethans Muir

Craiggaveral

94

Knockhill
Racing Circuit

South
Lethans

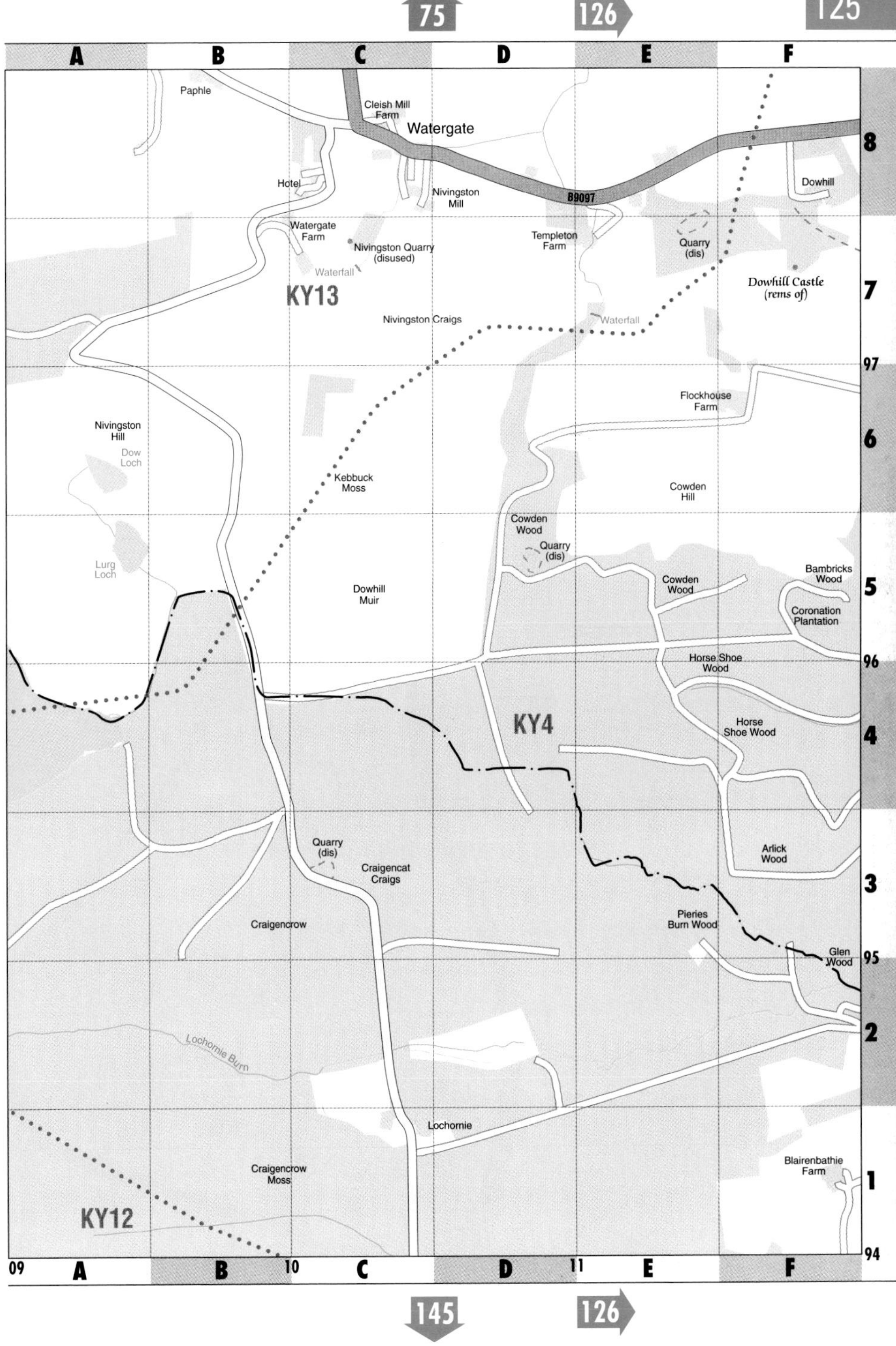

Paphle

Cleish Mill Farm

Watergate

Hotel

Nivingston Mill

B9097

Dowhill

Watergate Farm

Nivingston Quarry (disused)

Templeton Farm

Quarry (dis)

Dowhill Castle (rems of)

Waterfall

KY13

Nivingston Craigs

Waterfall

Flockhouse Farm

Nivingston Hill

Dow Loch

Kebbuck Moss

Cowden Hill

Lurg Loch

Dowhill Muir

Cowden Wood

Quarry (dis)

Cowden Wood

Bambricks Wood

Coronation Plantation

Horse Shoe Wood

KY4

Horse Shoe Wood

Quarry (dis)

Craigencat Craigs

Arlick Wood

Craigencrow

Pieries Burn Wood

Glen Wood

Lochornie Burn

Lochornie

Craigencrow Moss

Blairenbathie Farm

KY12

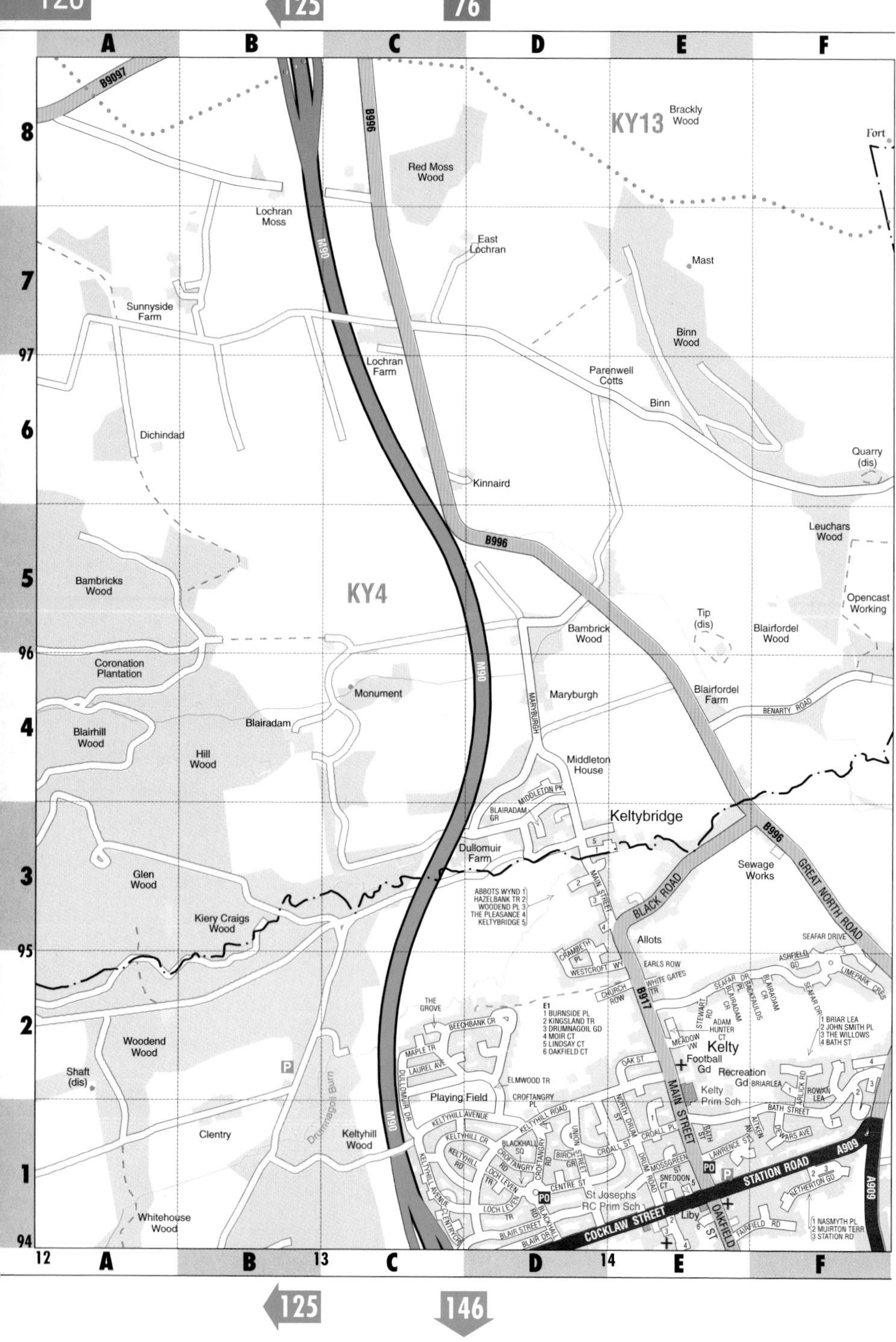

125
76

KY13

Brackly
Wood

Fort

Red Moss
Wood

B9097

Lochran
Moss

East
Lochran

Mast

B996

Sunnyside
Farm

Binn
Wood

Lochran
Farm

Parenwell
Cotts

Binn

Dichindad

Quarry
(dis)

Kinnaird

Leuchars
Wood

B996

Bambricks
Wood

KY4

Opencast
Working

Bambrick
Wood

Tip
(dis)

Blairfordel
Wood

Coronation
Plantation

Maryburgh

Blairfordel
Farm

BENARTY ROAD

Monument

Blairhill
Wood

Blairadam

Hill
Wood

Middleton
House

BLAIRADAM
GR

Keltybridge

Dullomuir
Farm

B996

Sewage
Works

GREAT NORTH ROAD

ABBOTS WYND 1
HAZELBANK TR 2
WOODEND PL 3
THE PLEASANCE 4
KELTYBRIDGE 5

BLACK ROAD

Glen
Wood

Allots

SEAFAR DRIVE

Kiery Craigs
Wood

EARLS ROW

ASHFIELD
RD

LIMEPARK CRES

WHITE GATES

THE
GROVE

WESTCROFT WY

MEADOW
VW

ADAM
HUNTER
TER

BLAIRADAM
CR

SEAFAR RD

1 BRIAR LEA
2 JOHN SMITH PL
3 THE WILLOWS
4 BATH ST

E1
1 BURNSIDE PL
2 KINGSLAND TR
3 DRUMMAGOIL GD
4 MOIR CT
5 LINDSAY CT
6 OAKFIELD CT

BEECHBANK DR

MAPLE TR

LAUREL AV

Woodend
Wood

ELMWOOD TR

Kelty
Football
Gd

Recreation
Gd

BRIARLEA

ROWAN
LEA

Shaft
(dis)

CROFTANGRY
PL

BATH STREET

BATH
STREET

Kelty
Prim Sch

PARS AVE

KELTYHILL AVENUE

Keltyhill
Wood

KELTYHILL CR

KELTYHILL RD

BLACKHALL
SQ

BIRCH
PL

St Josephs
RC Prim Sch

MOSSGREEN

SNEDDON
PL

CROALL PL

STATION ROAD

A909

Clentry

LOCH LEVEN
CT

B917

MAIN STREET

LAWRENCE ST

GLEN
AVEN

NETHERTON RD

A909

Whitehouse
Wood

BLAIR STREET

BLAIR ST

COCKLAW STREET

Liby

OAKFIELD ST

YARDFIELD RD

1 NASMYTH PL
2 MUIRTON TERR
3 STATION RD

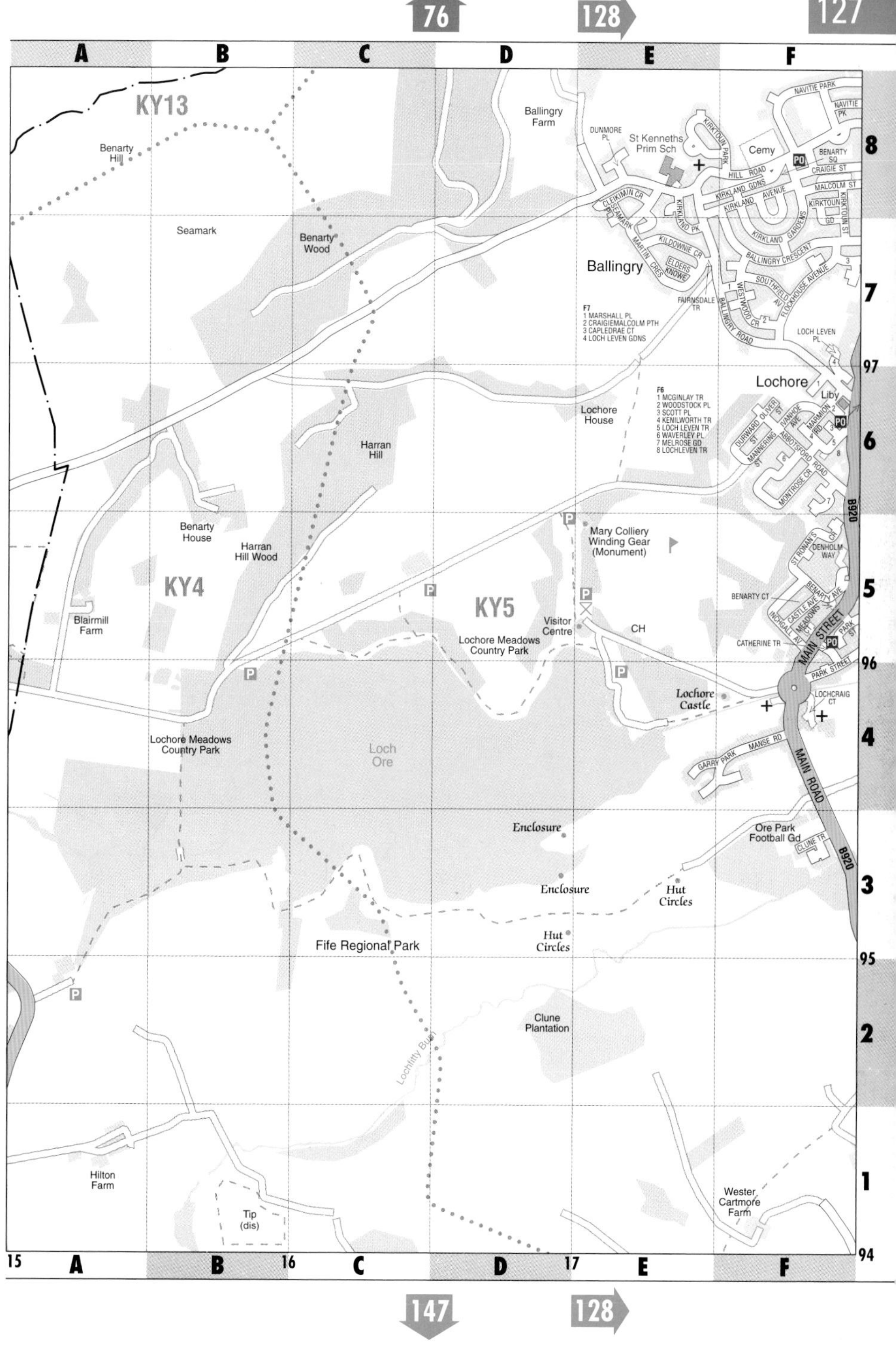

A B C D E F

KY13

Benarty Hill

Seamark

Benarty Wood

Ballingry Farm

DUNMORE PL

St Kenneths Prim Sch

Cemy

NAVITIE PARK

NAVITIE PK

BENARTY SQ

CRAIGIE CR

MALCOLM ST

KIRKTOUN

HILL ROAD

CLACKMANNAN CR

CAMDEN LN

MAIN ST

KILDONNIE CR

ELDERS KNOWE

KIRKLAND AVENUE

KIRKLAND GARDENS

KIRKLAND CRESCENT

Ballingry

F7
1 MARSHALL PL
2 CRAIGIEMALCOLM PTH
3 CAPLEDRAE CT
4 LOCH LEVEN GDNS

FAIRNSDALE TR

SOUTHWOOD CR

WESTWOOD CR

BALLINGRY ROAD

SOUTHWOOD AVENUE

ELLDERSHOUSE AVENUE

LOCH LEVEN PL

97

Lochore

Lby

PO

Harran Hill

Lochore House

F8
1 MCGINLAY TR
2 WOODSTOCK PL
3 SCOTT PL
4 KENILWORTH TR
5 LOCH LEVEN TR
6 WAVERLEY PL
7 MELROSE GD
8 LOCHLEVEN TR

DURWARD PL

MANNERING

ST COLUMBA'S

SANQUHAR PL

HANNOK

MANN

6

B920

Benarty House

Harran Hill Wood

KY4

Mary Colliery Winding Gear (Monument)

P

MORTHOUSE CR

MONTROSE DR

DENHOLM WAY

5

Blairmill Farm

P

Visitor Centre

KY5

Lochore Meadows Country Park

P

CH

BENARTY CT

ST DUNSTAN'S

CASTLE AVE

BENARTY AVE

MCGINN PL

MAIN STREET

PO

Lochore Meadows Country Park

P

Lochore Castle

CATHERINE TR

PARK STREET

96

LOCHCRAIG CT

Loch Ore

MANSE RD

CARNY PARK

MAIN ROAD

Ore Park Football Gd

CLUNE TR

4

Enclosure

Enclosure

Hut Circles

3

B920

Fife Regional Park

Hut Circles

95

Clune Plantation

2

P

Lochty Burn

Hilton Farm

Wester Cartmore Farm

1

Tip (dis)

94

15 16 17

8 7 6 5 4 3 2 1

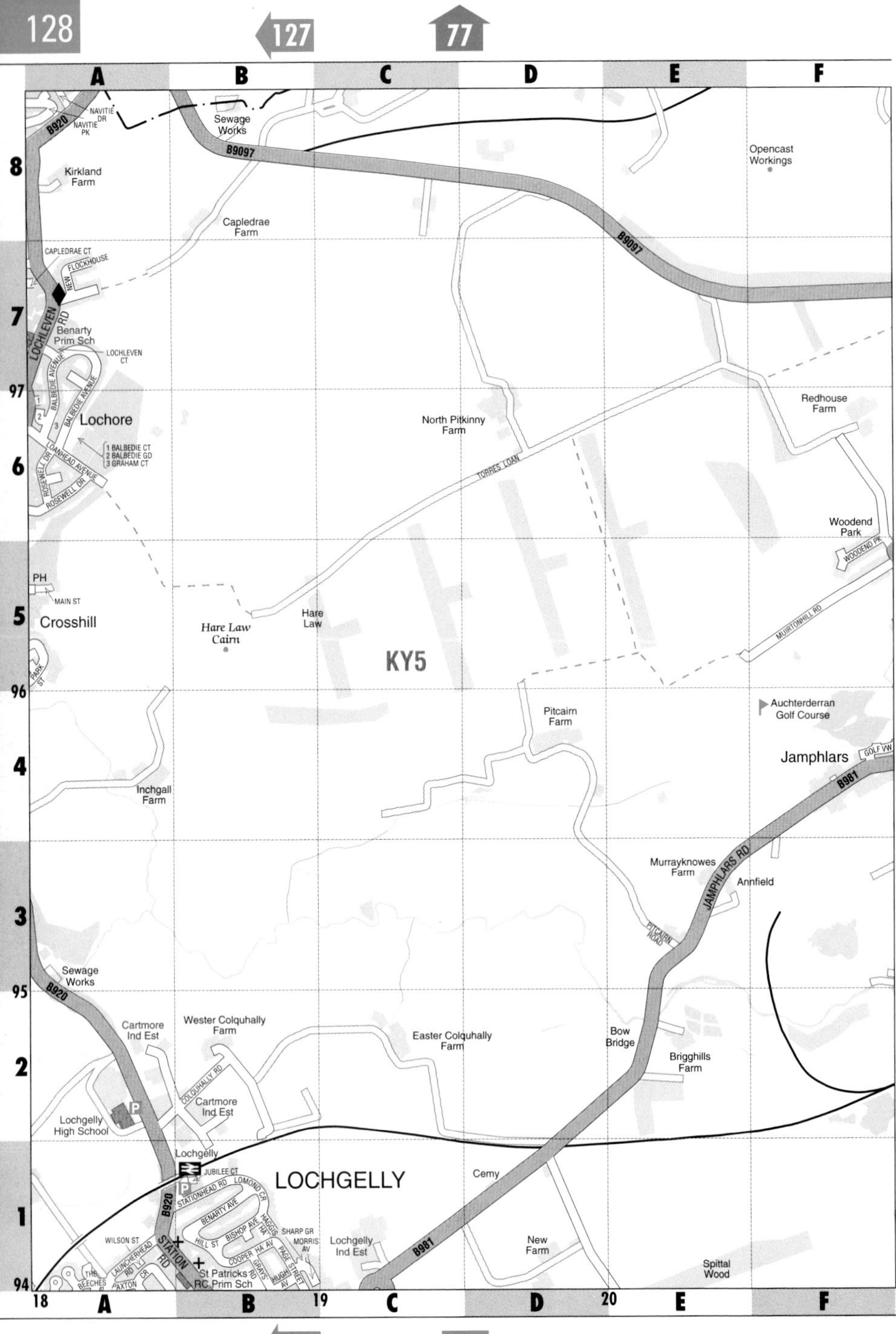
A
B
C
D
E
F
8
7
97
6
5
96
4
3
95
2
1
94
18
19
20
Kirkland Farm
Sewage Works
B9097
B920
NAVITIE DR
NAVITIE PK
Capledrae Farm
CAPLEDRAE CT
NEW FLOCKHOUSE
LOCHLEVEN RD
Benarty Prim Sch
LOCHLEVEN CT
BALBEDIE AVENUE
Lochore
1 BALBEDIE CT
2 BALBEDIE GD
3 GRAHAM CT
LOANHEAD AVENUE
ROSEWELL DR
Opencast Workings
North Pitkinny Farm
TORRES LOAN
Redhouse Farm
Woodend Park
WOODEND PK
PH
MAIN ST
Crosshill
Hare Law Cairn
Hare Law
KY5
MUIRTONHILL RD
PARK ST
Pitcairn Farm
Auchterderran Golf Course
Jamphlars
GOLF VW
B981
Inchgall Farm
Murrayknowes Farm
JAMPHLARS RD
Annfield
PITCAIRN ROAD
Sewage Works
B920
Cartmore Ind Est
Wester Colquhally Farm
Easter Colquhally Farm
Bow Bridge
Brigghills Farm
COLQUHALLY RD
Cartmore Ind Est
Lochgelly High School
Lochgelly
JUBILEE CT
LOCHGELLY
Cemy
STATIONHEAD RD
LOMOND CR
BENARTY AVE
HAGGIS HA
BISHOP AVE
HILL ST
SHARP GR
MORRIS AV
WILSON ST
COOPER HA AV
PAGE STREET
GRAYS RD
HUGH AV
Lochgelly Ind Est
New Farm
Spittal Wood
LAUNCHERHEAD RD
THE BEECHES
PAXTON CR
STATION RD
St Patricks RC Prim Sch

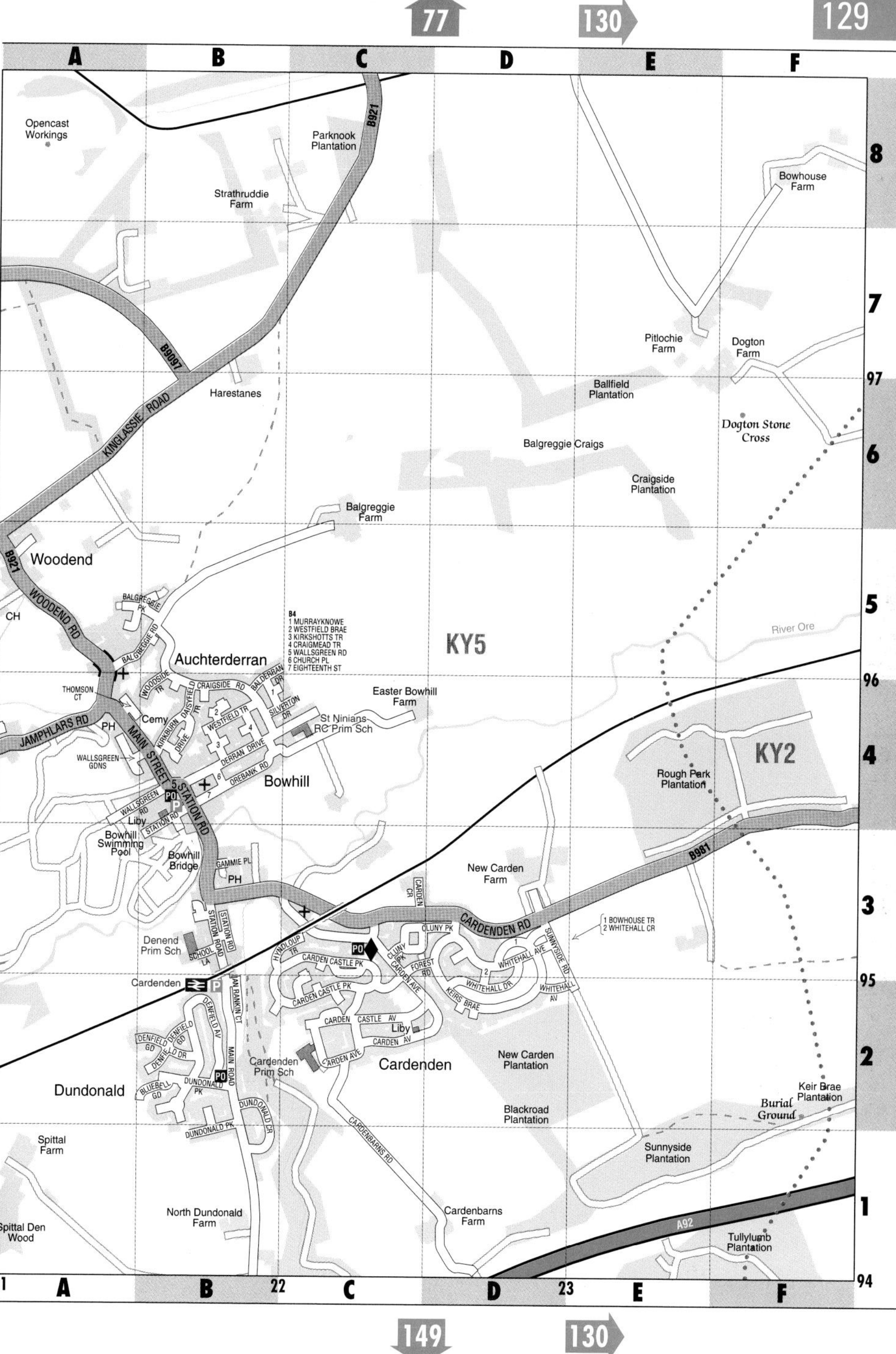

A   B   C   D   E   F

Opencast
Workings

Parknook
Plantation

B921

Bowhouse
Farm

8

Strathruddie
Farm

7

B981

KINGLASSIE ROAD

Harestanes

Pitlochie
Farm

Dogton
Farm

97

Ballfield
Plantation

*Dogton Stone
Cross*

B921

Balgreggie Craigs

Craigside
Plantation

6

Woodend

Balgreggie
Farm

5

WOODEND RD

CH

84
1 MURRAYKNOWE
2 WESTFIELD BRAE
3 KIRKSHOTTS TR
4 CRAIGMEAD TR
5 WALLSGREEN RD
6 CHURCH PL
7 EIGHTEENTH ST

KY5

River Ore

BALGREGGIE
PK

Auchterderran

THOMSON
CT

CRAIGSIDE RD

BALGREGGIE

Easter Bowhill
Farm

96

JAMPHLARS RD

PH

Cemy

WESTFIELD

SILVERTON
DR

KY2

Rough Park
Plantation

4

WALLSGREEN
GDNS

WOODSIDE
TR

MAIN STREET

DERBAN DRIVE

St Ninians
RC Prim Sch

Bowhill

B981

PO

Liby

STATION RD

WALLSGREEN
RD

Bowhill
Swimming
Pool

Bowhill
Bridge

GAMMIE PL

PH

New Carden
Farm

3

1 BOWHOUSE TR
2 WHITEHALL CR

Denend
Prim Sch

STATION ROAD

SCHOOL RD

CARDEN

CARDENDEN RD

OLUNY PK

SUNNYSIDE RD

95

Cardenden

FITZROY CLUP
PK

PO

CARDEN CASTLE PK

CARDEN CASTLE AV

FOREST
RD

LUN

CLUNY PL

WHITEHALL AVE

WHITEHALL PK

2
1

WHITEHALL
AV

Dundonald

DENFIELD
GD

DENFIELD
GD

CLAREFIELD
GD

MAIN ROAD

BLUEBELL
GD

DUNDONALD
PK

Cardenden
Prim Sch

CARDEN
AV

CARDEN CASTLE AV

CARDEN AV

Liby

KING BRAE

New Carden
Plantation

Keir Brae
Plantation

2

*Burial
Ground*

Spittal
Farm

DUNDONALD PK

CARDENBARNS RD

Blackroad
Plantation

Sunnyside
Plantation

Spittal Den
Wood

North Dundonald
Farm

Cardenbarns
Farm

A92

Tullylumb
Plantation

1

94

A   B   22   C   D   23   E   F

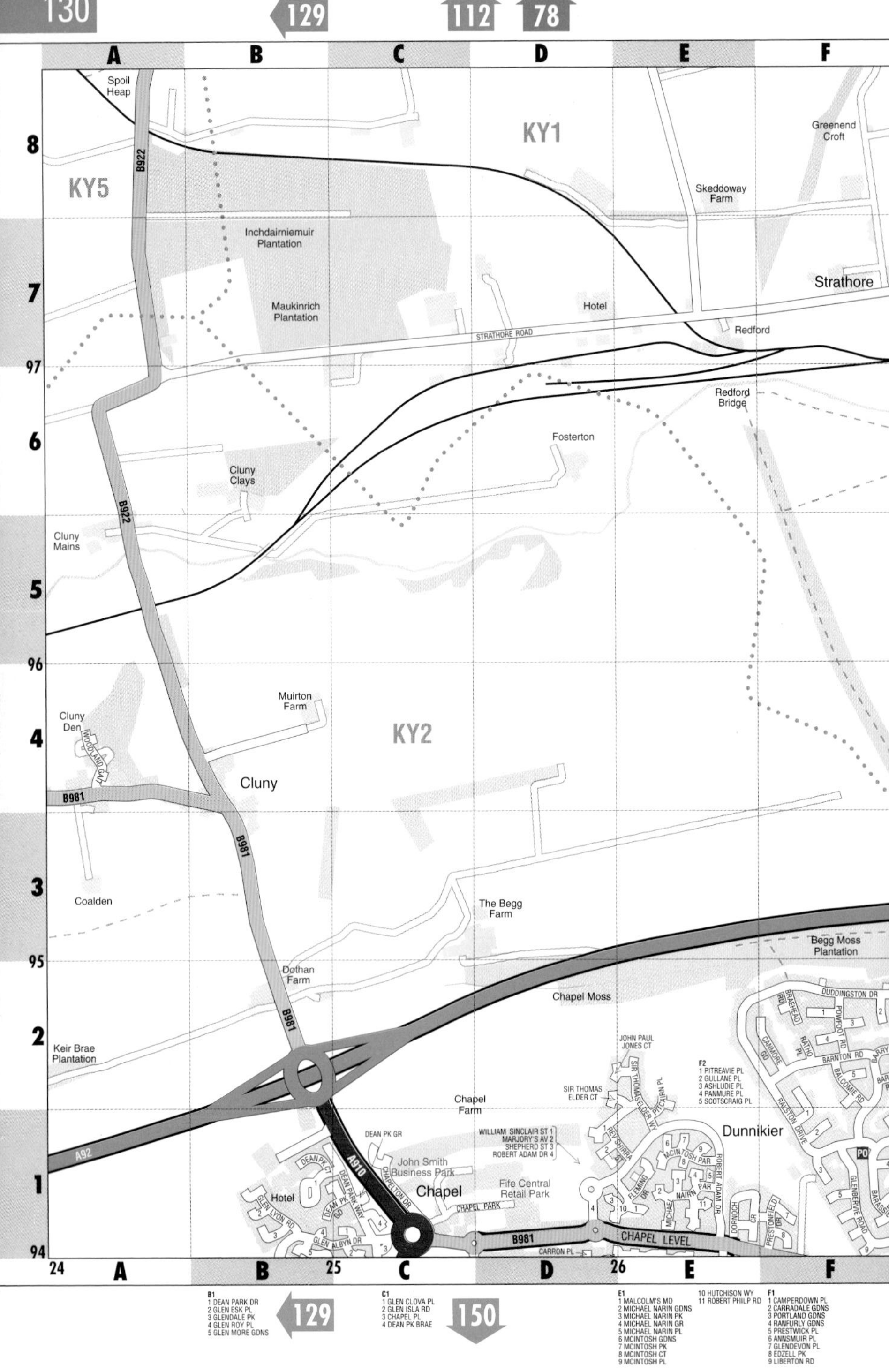

KY1

Spoil Heap

KY5

B922

Greenend Croft

Skeddoway Farm

Strathore

Inchdairniemuir Plantation

Maukinrich Plantation

STRATHORE ROAD

Hotel

Redford

Redford Bridge

Fosterton

B922

Cluny Clays

Cluny Mains

Muirton Farm

KY2

Cluny Den

ROUSLAND GAIT

B981

Cluny

B981

Coalden

The Begg Farm

Begg Moss Plantation

Dothan Farm

Keir Brae Plantation

A92

Chapel Moss

Chapel Farm

JOHN PAUL JONES CT

SIR THOMAS ELDER CT

DUDDINGSTON DR

BARNTON RD

F2
1 PITREAVIE PL
2 GULLANE PL
3 ASHLUDIE PL
4 PANMURE PL
5 SCOTSCRAIG PL

Dunnikier

DEAN PK GR

John Smith Business Park

A910

DEAN PARK

WILLIAM SINCLAIR ST 1
MARJORY S AV 2
SHEPHERD ST 3
ROBERT ADAM DR 4

Fife Central Retail Park

PO

Hotel

GLEN LYON RD

GLEN ALBYN DR

Chapel

CHAPEL PARK

CHAPEL LEVEL

B981

CARRON PL

CHAPEL LEVEL

24   25   26

129 150

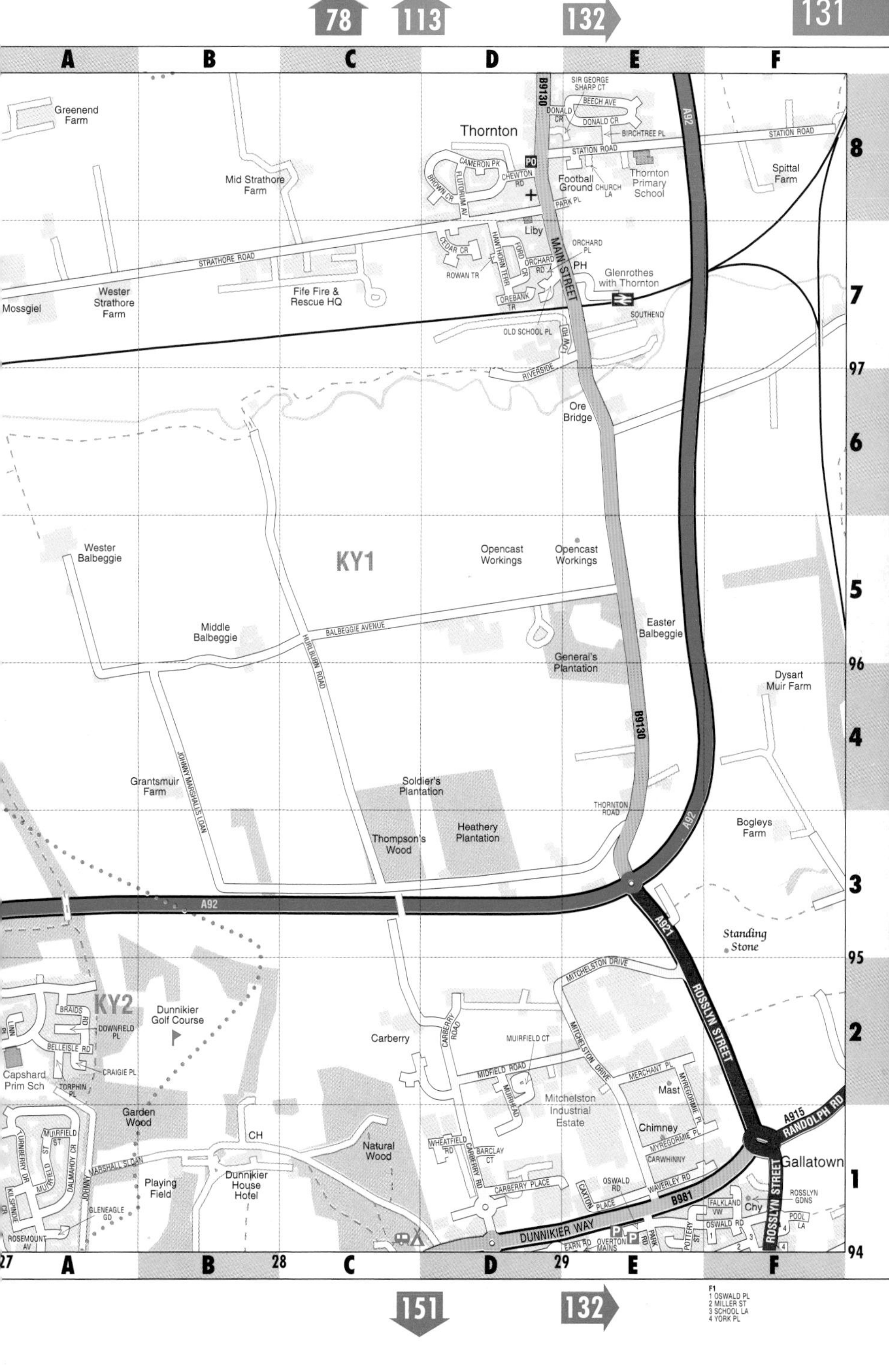

	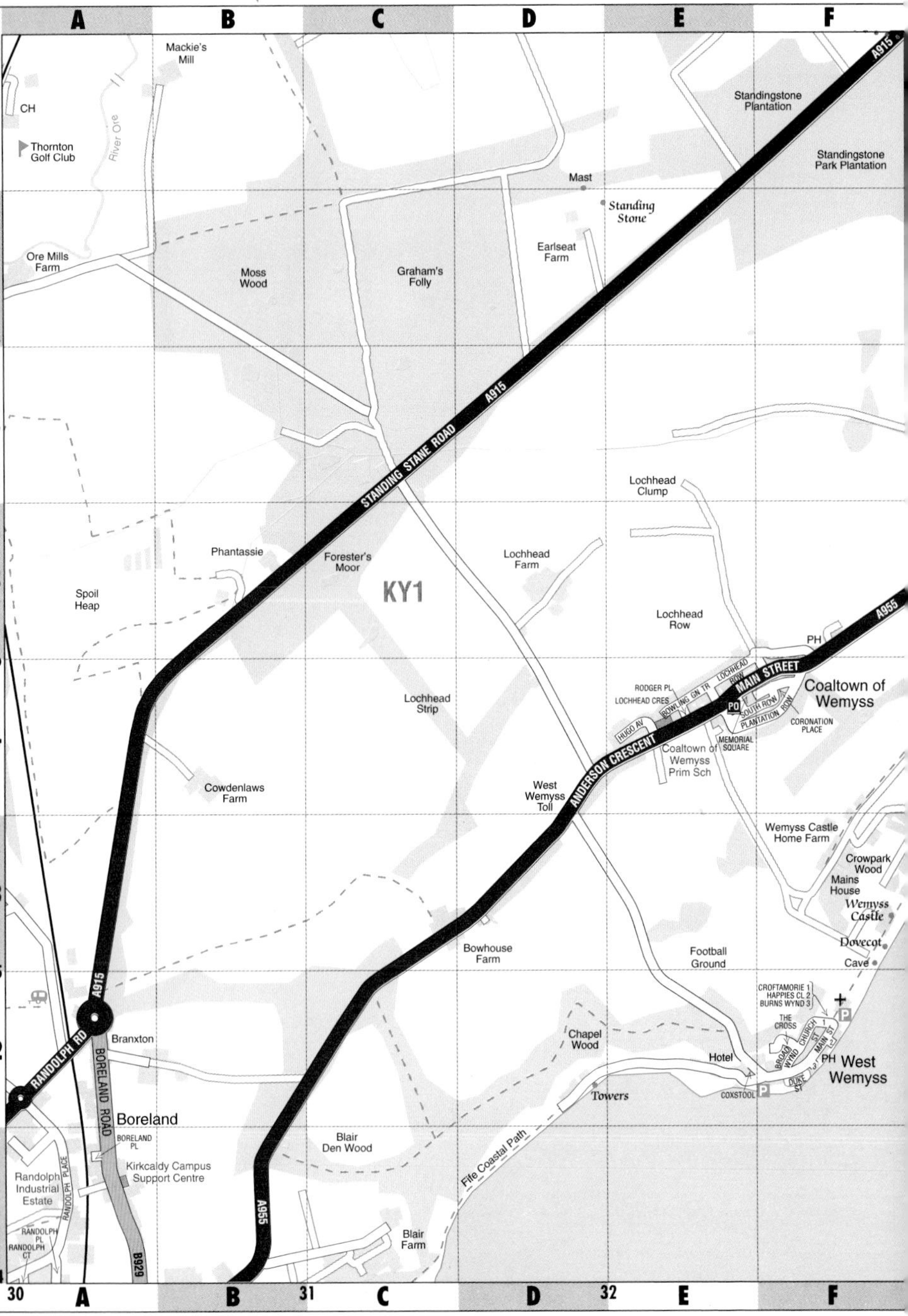 A	B	C	D	E	F

8

CH

Mackie's Mill

Thornton Golf Club

River Ore

Standingstone Plantation

Standingstone Park Plantation

A915

Mast

Standing Stone

7

Ore Mills Farm

Moss Wood

Graham's Folly

Earlseat Farm

97

6

STANDING STANE ROAD

A915

Lochhead Clump

5

Spoil Heap

Phantassie

Forester's Moor

Lochhead Farm

KY1

Lochhead Row

PH

A955

MAIN STREET

Coaltown of Wemyss

96

Lochhead Strip

LOCHHEAD

Rodger Pl.
Lochhead Cres.

PO

Coronation Place

4

Cowdenlaws Farm

West Wemyss Toll

ANDERSON CRESCENT

Coaltown of Wemyss Prim Sch

Memorial Square

Wemyss Castle Home Farm

Crowpark Wood

3

Mains House

Wemyss Castle

Dovecot Cave

Bowhouse Farm

Football Ground

95

CROFTAMORIE 1
HAPPIES CL 2
BURNS WYND 3

THE CROSS

Chapel Wood

2

Branxton

A915

RANDOLPH RD

BORELAND ROAD

Hotel

Towers

COXSTOOL

DUKE ST

PH West Wemyss

Boreland

BORELAND PL

Fife Coastal Path

1

Randolph Industrial Estate

Kirkcaldy Campus Support Centre

A955

Blair Den Wood

RANDOLPH PL
RANDOLPH CT

Blair Farm

94

B923

79

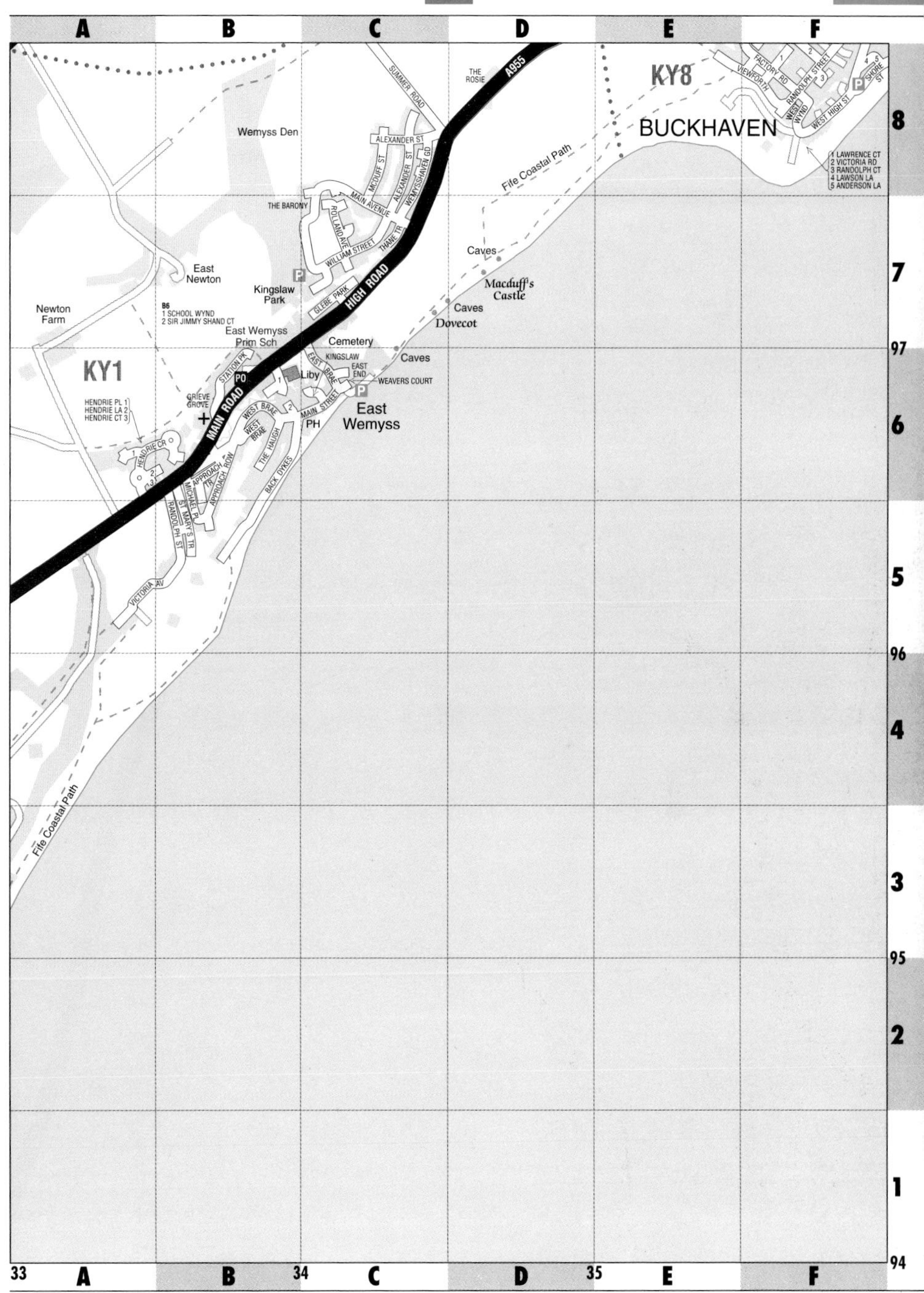
A
B
C
D
E
F
KY8
BUCKHAVEN
THE ROSIE
A955
SUMMER ROAD
FACTORY RD
VIEWFORTH
RANDOLPH STREET
WEST WYND
WEST HIGH ST
SHORE ST
1 LAWRENCE CT
2 VICTORIA RD
3 RANDOLPH CT
4 LAWSON LA
5 ANDERSON LA
Wemyss Den
ALEXANDER ST
MCDUFF ST
ALEXANDER ST
WEMYSSHAVEN GD
MAIN AVENUE
THE BARONY
ROLLAND AVE
WILLIAM STREET
THANE TR
Fife Coastal Path
Caves
Macduff's Castle
Caves
Dovecot
East Newton
Kingslaw Park
GLEBE PARK
HIGH ROAD
Newton Farm
B6
1 SCHOOL WYND
2 SIR JIMMY SHAND CT
East Wemyss Prim Sch
Cemetery
KINGSLAW
Caves
KY1
STATION PK
PO
Liby
EAST BRAE
EAST END
WEAVERS COURT
East Wemyss
HENDRIE PL 1
HENDRIE LA 2
HENDRIE CT 3
GRIEVE GROVE
MAIN ROAD
WEST BRAE
MAIN STREET
PH
HENDRIE CR
WEST BRAE
THE HAUGH
APPROACH ROW
APPROACH TR
MICHAEL PL
BACK DYKES
RANDOLPH ST
ST MARY'S TR
VICTORIA AV
Fife Coastal Path
8
7
97
6
5
96
4
3
95
2
1
94
33
34
35

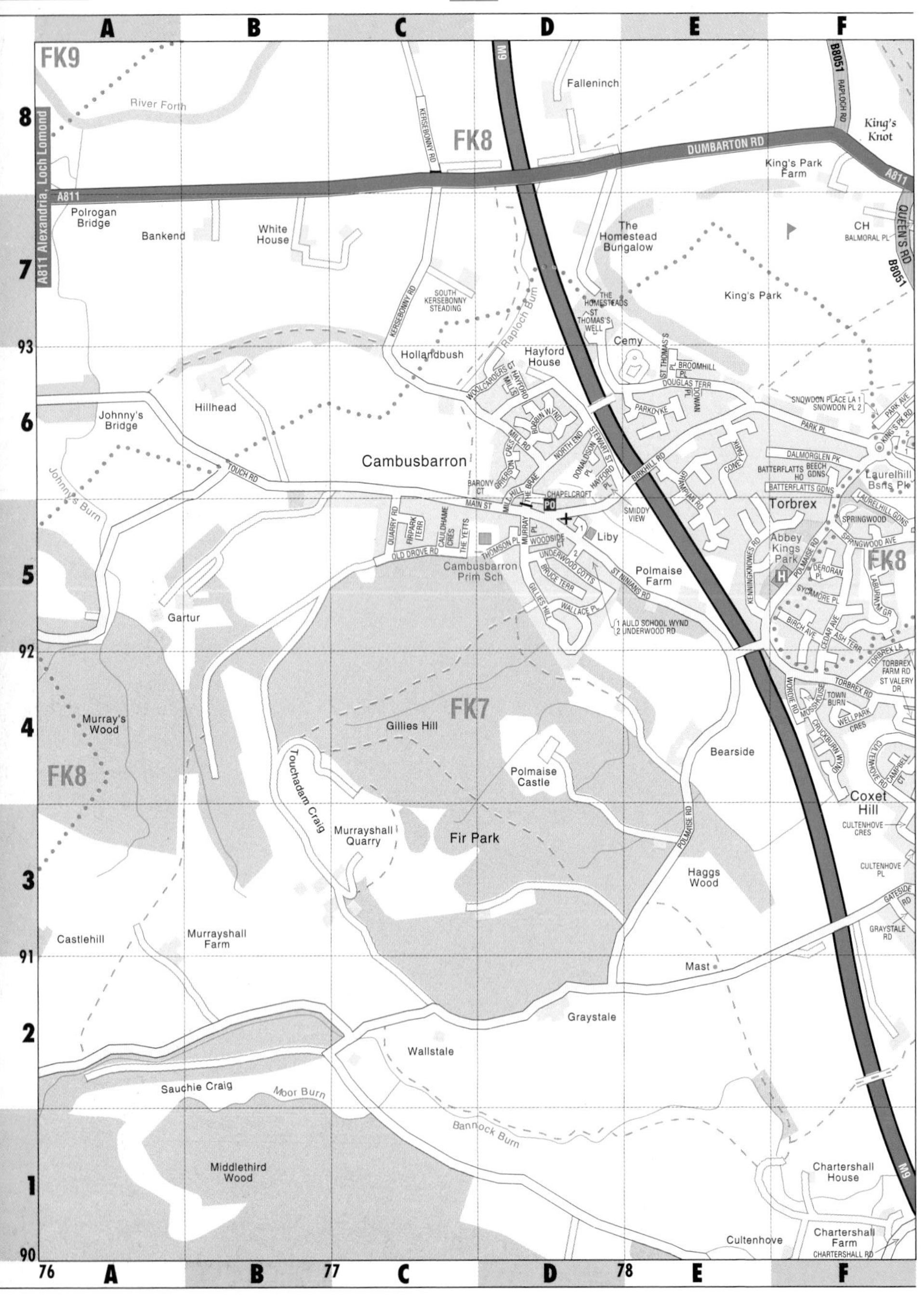

FK9

River Forth

FK8

Falleninch

DUMBARTON RD

King's Knot

King's Park Farm

CH
BALMORAL PL

QUEEN'S RD

B8051

A811

A811 Alexandria, Loch Lomond

A811

Polrogan Bridge

Bankend

White House

The Homestead Bungalow

King's Park

SOUTH KERSEBONNY STEADING

THE HOMESTEADS

ST THOMAS'S WELL

Cemy

BROOMHILL PL

DOUGLAS TERR

SNOWDON PLACE LA 1
SNOWDON PL 2

PARK AVE

Johnny's Bridge

Hillhead

Hollandbush

Hayford House

PARKDYKE

DALMORGLEN PK

BATTERFLATTS
BEECH
GDNS
BATTERFLATTS GDNS

Laurelhill
Bsns Pk

Johnny's Burn

TOUCH RD

Cambusbarron

NORTH END

Torbrex

Abbey Kings Park

SPRINGWOOD

SPRINGWOOD AVE

FK8

CHAPELCROFT

PO

Liby

SMIDDY VIEW

H

DEROBA

FK8

Gartur

QUARRY RD

OLD DROVE RD

LUDGATE
DRIVE
THE YETTS

Cambusbarron Prim Sch

BRUCE TERR

WALLACE PL

Polmaise Farm

1 AULD SCHOOL WYND
2 UNDERWOOD RD

TORBREX
FARM RD
ST VALERY DR

TOWN
WELLPARK CRES

Murray's Wood

FK7

Gillies Hill

Polmaise Castle

Bearside

Coxet Hill

CULTENHOVE CRES

Touchadam Craig

Murrayshall Quarry

Fir Park

CULTENHOVE PL

Haggs Wood

GATESIDE RD

GRAYSTALE RD

Castlehill

Murrayshall Farm

Mast

Sauchie Craig

Moor Burn

Wallstale

Graystale

Middlethird Wood

Bannock Burn

Chartershall House

Chartershall Farm
CHARTERSHALL RD

Cultenhove

M9

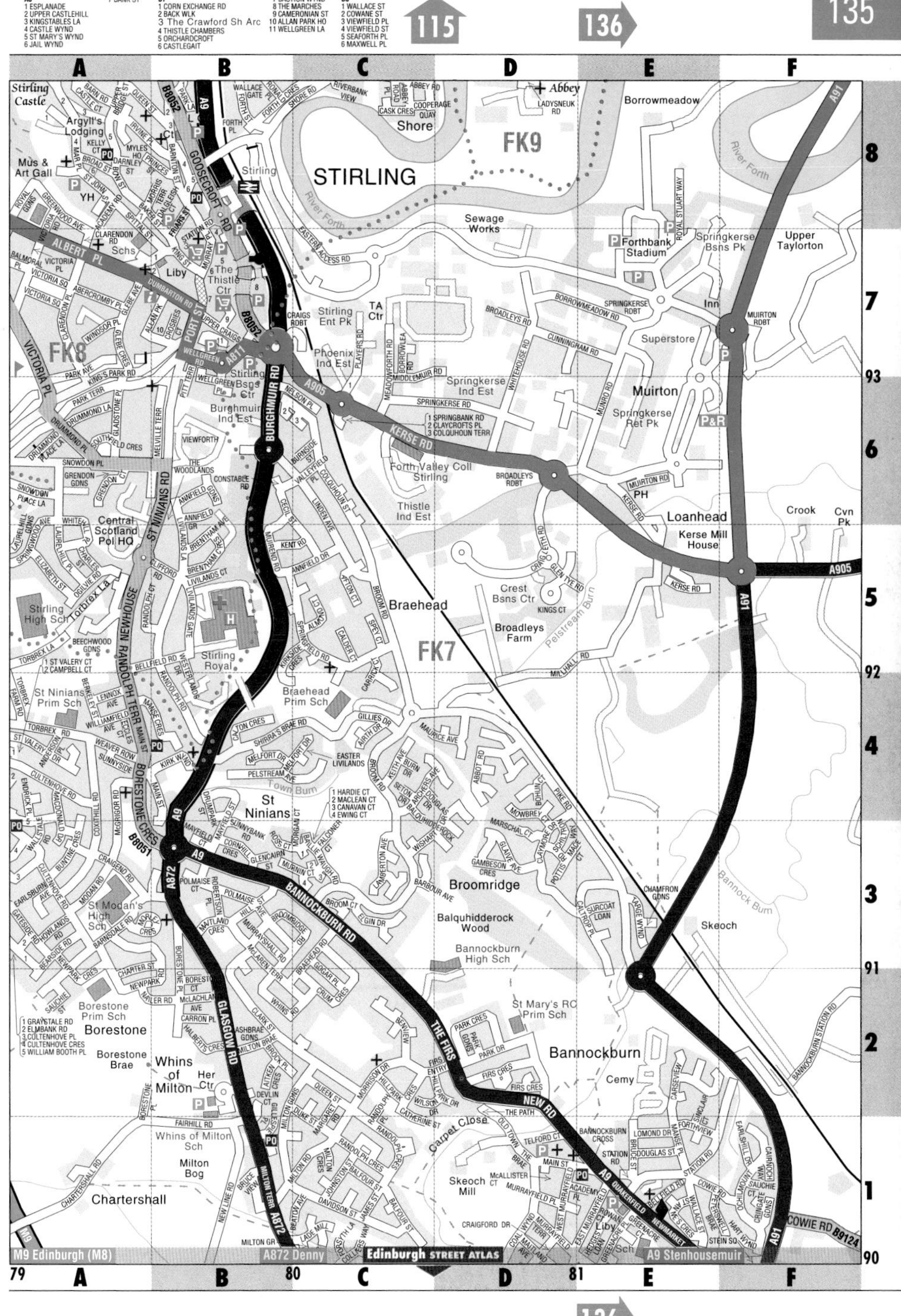

A8
1 ESPLANADE
2 UPPER CASTLEHILL
3 KINGSTABLES LA
4 CASTLE WYND
5 ST MARY'S WYND
6 JAIL WYND

7 BANK ST

B7
1 CORN EXCHANGE RD
2 BACK WLK
3 The Crawford Sh Arc
4 THISTLE CHAMBERS
5 ORCHARDCROFT
6 CASTLEGAIT

7 BASTION WYND
8 THE MARCHES
9 CAMERONIAN ST
10 ALLAN PARK HO
11 WELLGREEN LA

B8
1 WALLACE ST
2 COWANE ST
3 VIEWFIELD PL
4 VIEWFIELD ST
5 SEAFORTH ST
6 MAXWELL PL

115

136

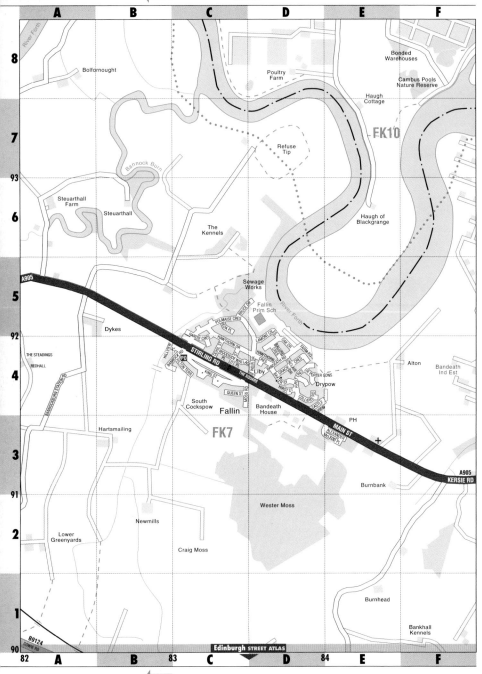

135
116
135

8

7

93

6

5

92

4

3

91

2

1

90

A   B   C   D   E   F

82   83   84

River Forth

Bolfornought

Poultry
Farm

Bonded
Warehouses

Cambus Pools
Nature Reserve

Haugh
Cottage

FK10

Refuse
Tip

Bannock Burn

Steuarthall
Farm

Steuarthall

The
Kennels

Haugh of
Blackgrange

A905

Sewage
Works

Dykes

Fallin
Prim Sch

River Forth

THE STEADINGS

REDHALL

POLMAISE CRES

HARDIE CRES

STIRLING RD

HAWTHORN DR

BRECK DR

WALLACE

AMONT CRES

OAK DR

FARM RD

HAWTHORN

MOODIESIDE

HILLVIEW

BANNOCK RD

PO

KING ST

QUEEN ST

THE SQUARE

MOSS RD

LYON TERR

Liby

BANDEATH RD

GRACE CRES

HURST CT

CRES

PORTER GDNS

Alton

Bandeath
Ind Est

South
Cockspow

Fallin

Bandeath
House

Drypow

CASTLE

VIEW

Hartsmailing

FK7

MAIN ST

PH

ALEXANDER
MCLEOD PL

+

A905

KERSIE RD

Burnbank

Newmills

Wester Moss

Lower
Greenyards

Craig Moss

Burnhead

B9124

COWIE RD

Burnhall
Kennels

Bankhall
Kennels

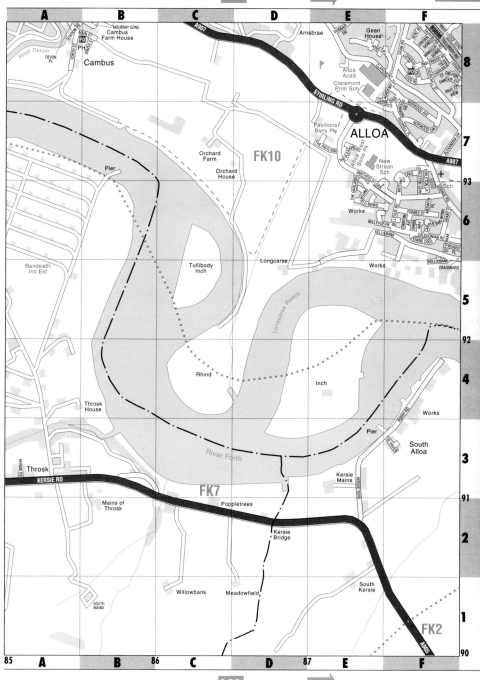

A B C D E F

8 7 93 6 5 92 4 3 91 2 1 90

River Devon
DEVON PL
STATION RD
MAIN ST
PH
MOUBRAY GDNS
Cambus
Farm House
Cambus

A907
Arnsbrae
Gean House
Alloa Acad
Claremont Prim Sch
STIRLING RD
CLAREMONT

ALLOA
Pavilions Bsns Pk
THE PAVILIONS
Alloa West Bsns Pk
New Strean Sch
A907

FK10
Orchard Farm
Orchard House

Pier

Works
OLD MDWS
BELLEVUE PK
KELLIEBANK
Works
KELLIEBANK
CRAIGWARD

Bandeath Ind Est

Tullibody Inch
Longcarse

Longcarse Reach

Rhind
Inch

Throsk House
Pier
Works
South Alloa

KERSIE RD
Throsk
KERSIE RD
River Forth
FK7
Kersie Mains
KERSIE TER

Mains of Throsk
Poppletrees
Kersie Bridge

SOUTH MAINS
Willowbank
Meadowfield
South Kersie

A905
FK2

85 86 87

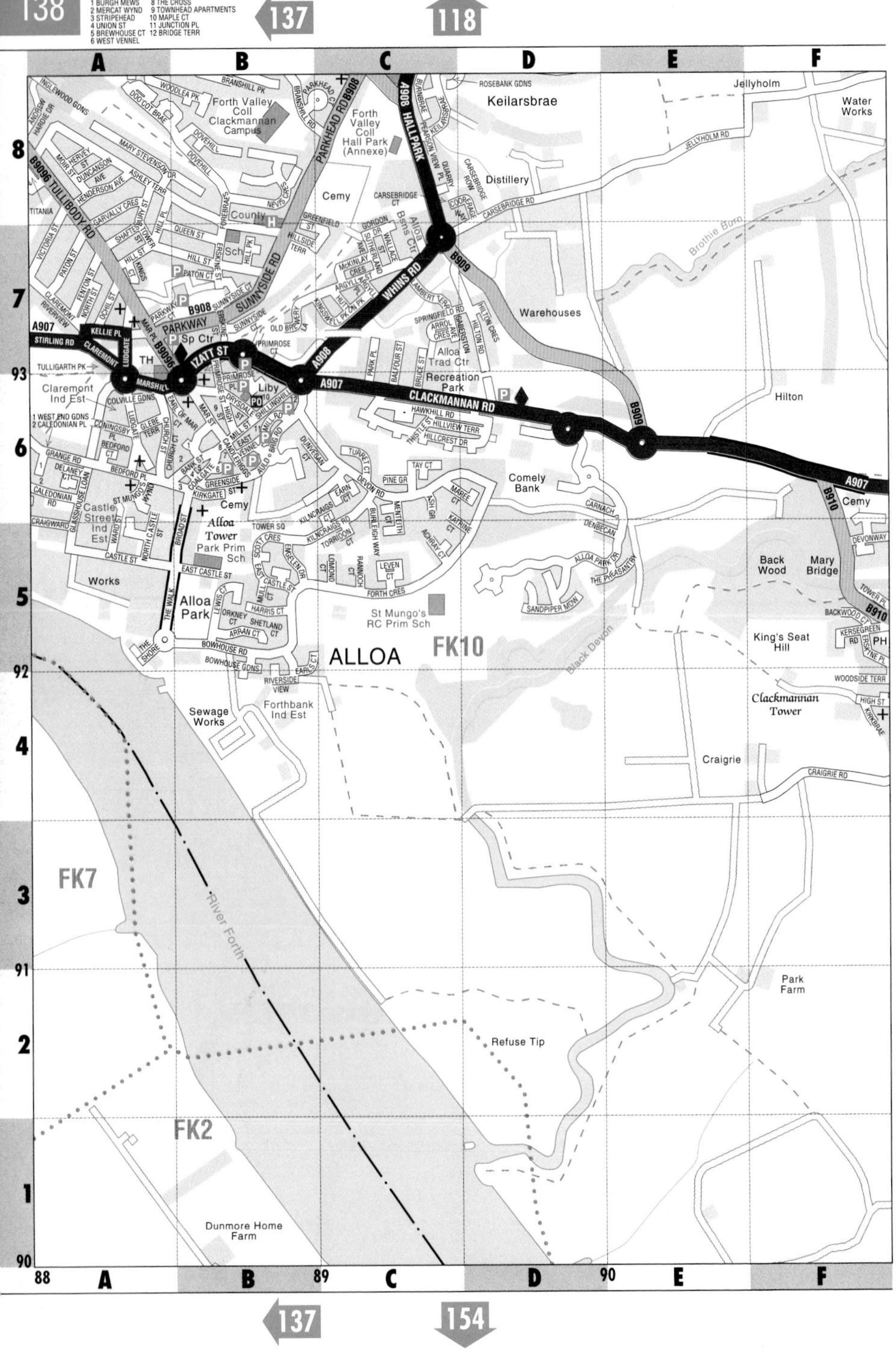

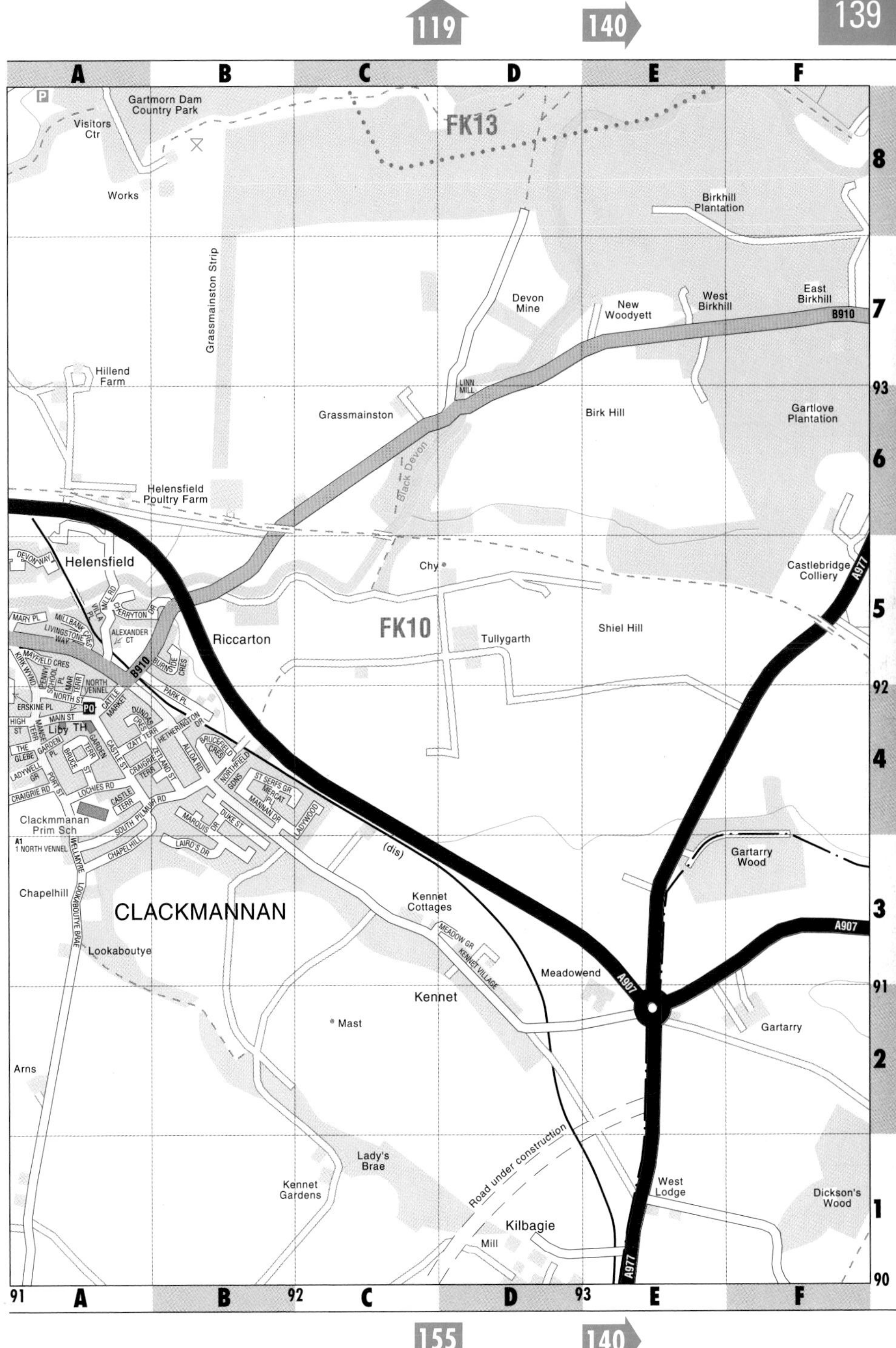

A   B   C   D   E   F

8

Gartmorn Dam
Country Park

Visitors
Ctr

P

FK13

Works

Birkhill
Plantation

7

Devon
Mine

New
Woodyett

West
Birkhill

East
Birkhill

B910

Grassmainston Strip

Hillend
Farm

Grassmainston

LINN
MILL

Birk Hill

Gartlove
Plantation

93

Black Devon

6

Helensfield
Poultry Farm

Castlebridge
Colliery

A977

DEVON WAY

Helensfield

Chy

5

MARY PL
MILLBANK CRES
SKERRYTON DR
LIVINGSTONE CRES
ALEXANDER CT

Riccarton

FK10

Tullygarth

Shiel Hill

92

MAYFIELD CRES
NORTH ST
NORTH VENNEL
ERSKINE PL

PARK PL

B910

DUNCAN CRES
HEATHERSTON

4

HIGH ST
MAIN ST
Liby TH
THE GLEBE
LADYWELL GR
CRAIGIE RD
PO
CASTLE ST
MATT CRES
CASTLE TERR
CRAIGDEN
MARKET
SOUTH PRIMROSE RD
LOCHIES RD

ST SERFS GR
MANNAN DR

LAIRD'S DR

LADYWOOD

Clackmmanan
Prim Sch

CHAPELHILL

MANOR

DYKE ST

(dis)

A1
1 NORTH VENNEL

3

Chapelhill

MAIN STREET

CLACKMANNAN

LOOKABOUTYE BRAE

Lookaboutye

Kennet
Cottages

Gartarry
Wood

A907

Meadowend

MEADOW GR
KENNET VILLAGE

91

Arns

Kennet

Mast

Gartarry

2

Lady's
Brae

Road under construction

West
Lodge

Dickson's
Wood

1

Kennet
Gardens

Kilbagie

Mill

90

91   A   B   92   C   D   93   E   F

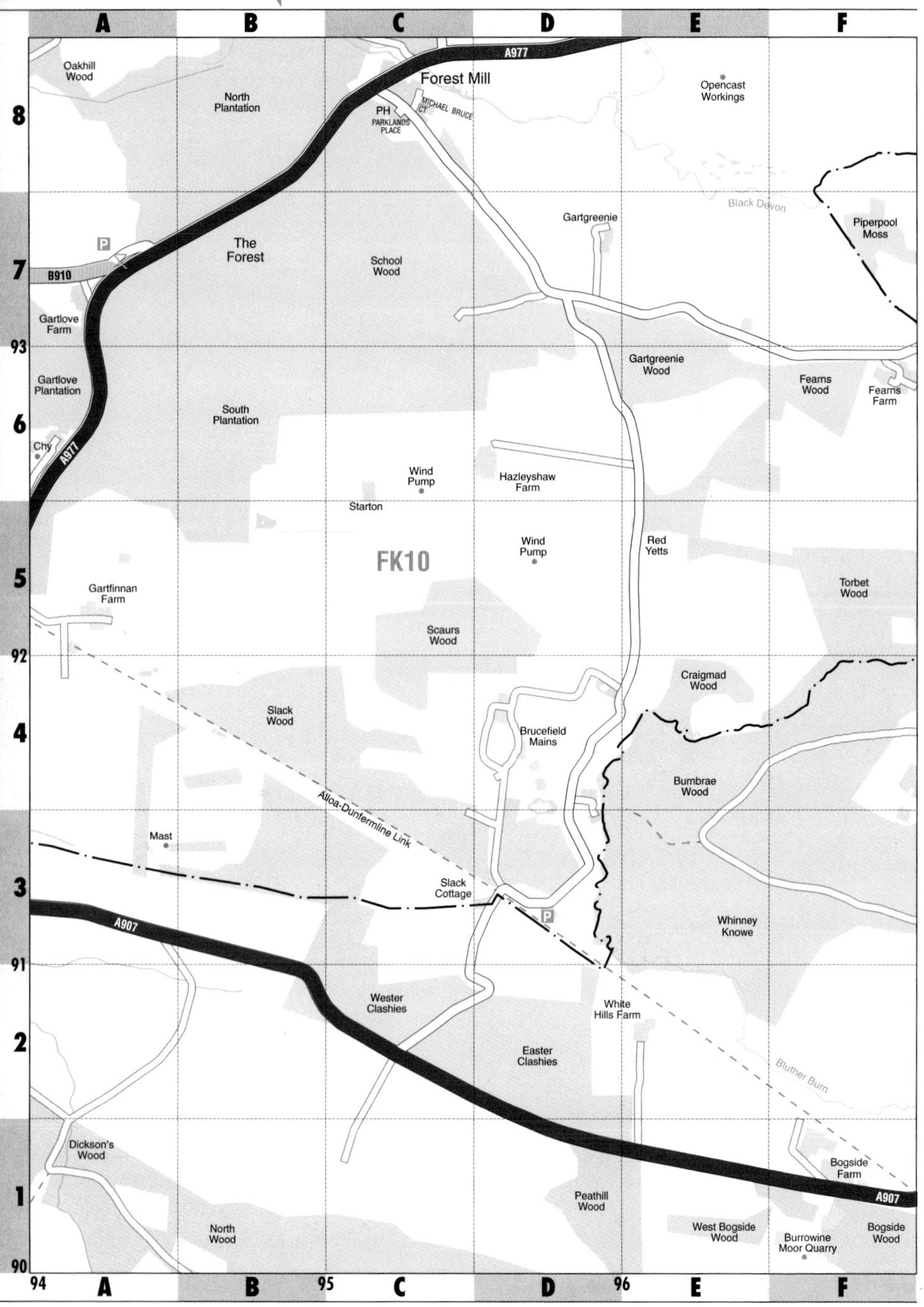

Map grid references (columns): A B C D E F

Oakhill Wood

Forest Mill

North Plantation

PH PARKLANDS PLACE

MICHAEL BRUCE CT

A977

Opencast Workings

The Forest

School Wood

Gartgreenie

Black Devon

Piperpool Moss

B910

P

Gartlove Farm

93

Gartlove Plantation

Gartgreenie Wood

Fearns Wood

Fearns Farm

Chy

A977

South Plantation

Wind Pump

Starton

Hazleyshaw Farm

Red Yetts

Torbet Wood

FK10

Wind Pump

Gartfinnan Farm

Scaurs Wood

Craigmad Wood

92

Slack Wood

Brucefield Mains

Burnbrae Wood

Alloa-Dunfermline Link

Mast

Slack Cottage

P

Whinney Knowe

A907

91

Wester Clashies

White Hills Farm

Easter Clashies

Bluther Burn

Dickson's Wood

Bogside Farm

Peathill Wood

A907

North Wood

West Bogside Wood

Burrowine Moor Quarry

Bogside Wood

90

94   A   B   95   C   D   96   E   F

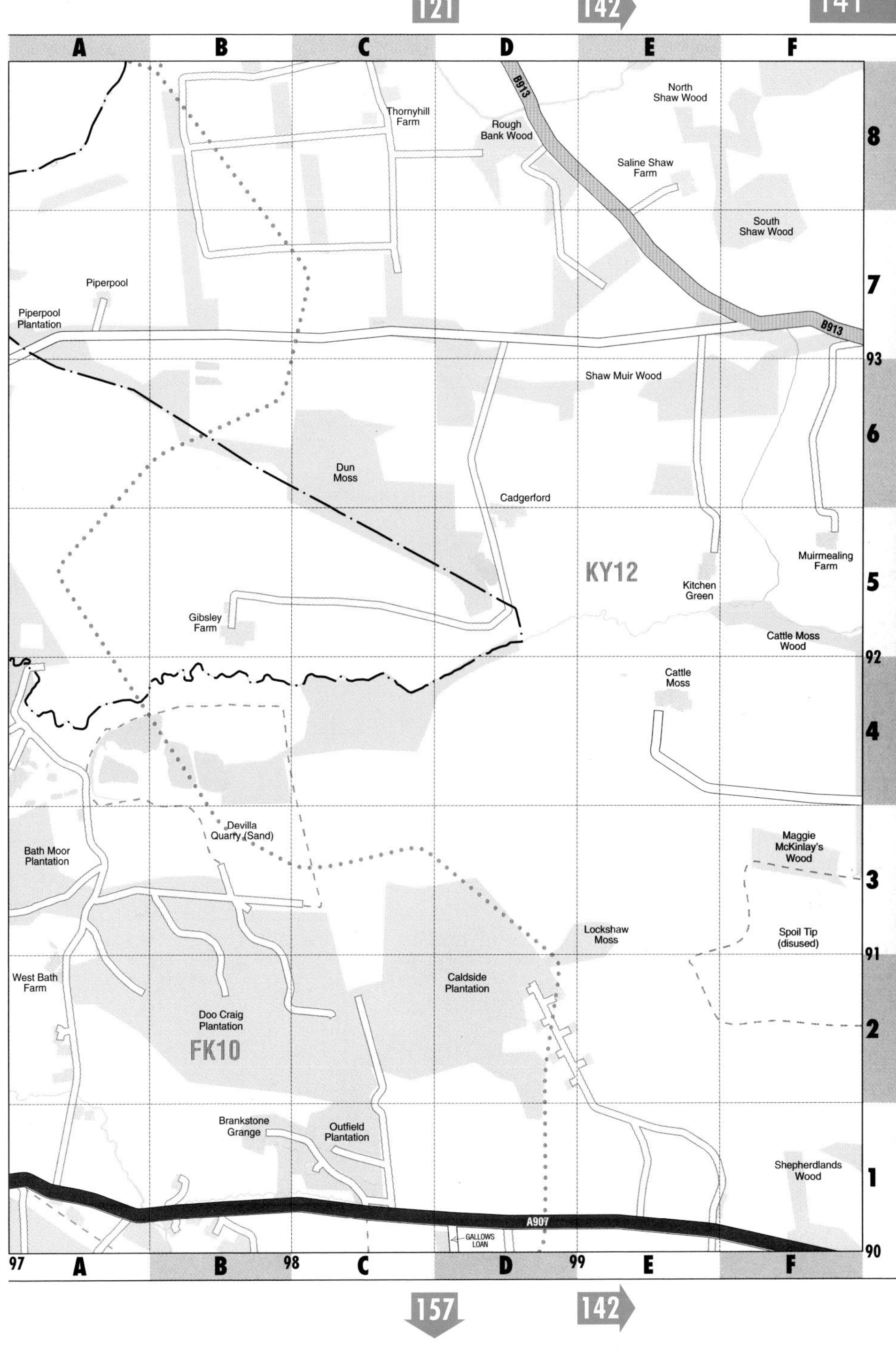

A B C D E F

North
Shaw Wood

Thornyhill
Farm

Rough
Bank Wood

B913

Saline Shaw
Farm

South
Shaw Wood

Piperpool

Piperpool
Plantation

B913

Shaw Muir Wood

Dun
Moss

Cadgerford

KY12

Muirmealing
Farm

Kitchen
Green

Cattle Moss
Wood

Gibsley
Farm

Cattle
Moss

Bath Moor
Plantation

Devilla
Quarry (Sand)

Maggie
McKinlay's
Wood

Spoil Tip
(disused)

West Bath
Farm

Lockshaw
Moss

Caldside
Plantation

Doo Craig
Plantation

FK10

Brankstone
Grange

Outfield
Plantation

Shepherdlands
Wood

A907

GALLOWS
LOAN

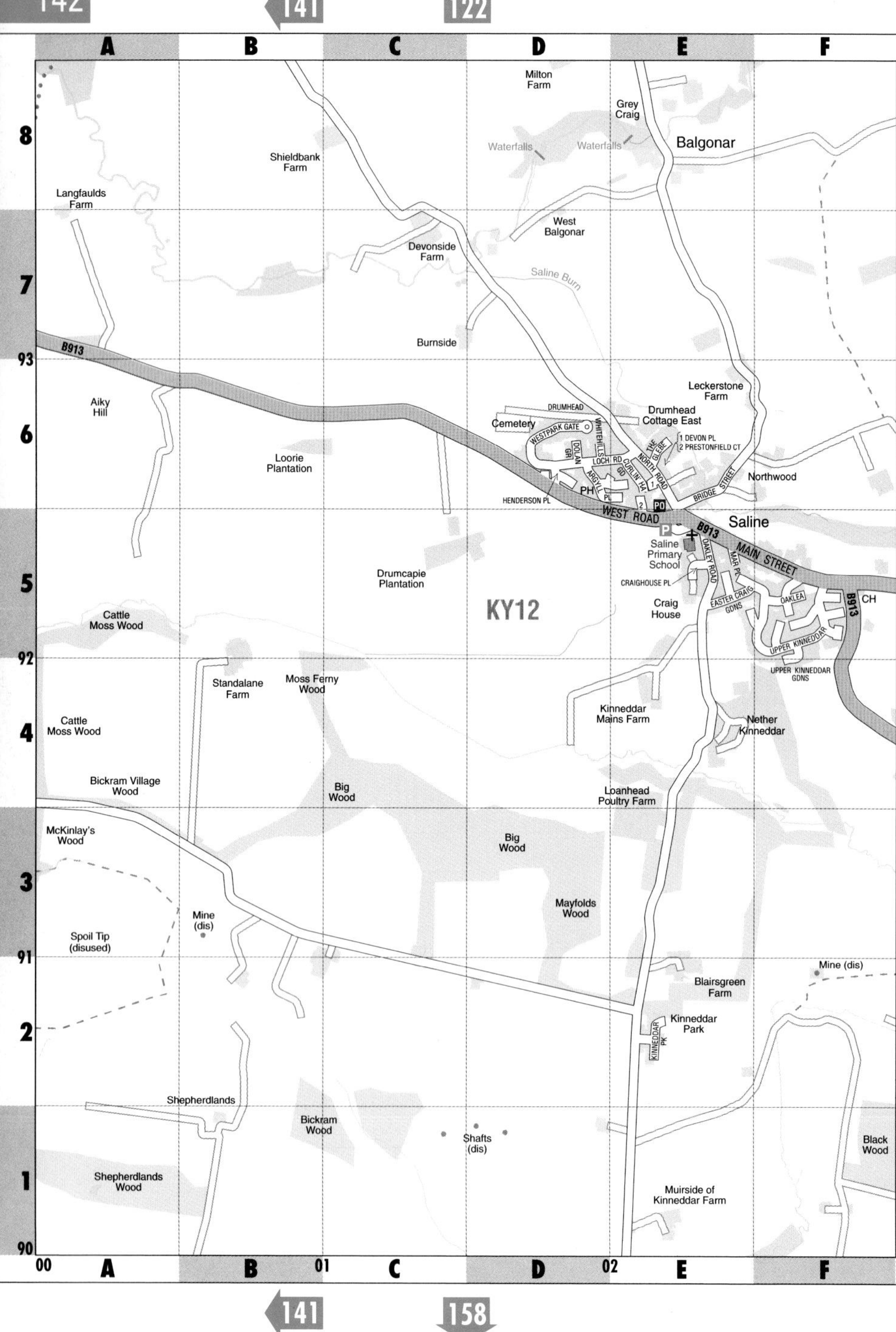

| | A | B | C | D | E | F |

8

Milton Farm

Grey Craig

Balgonar

Shieldbank Farm

Waterfalls   Waterfalls

Langfaulds Farm

West Balgonar

7

Devonside Farm

Saline Burn

Burnside

93

B913

Leckerstone Farm

Aiky Hill

Drumhead Cottage East

DRUMHEAD

Cemetery

1 DEVON PL
2 PRESTONFIELD CT

6

Loorie Plantation

Northwood

WESTPARK GATE

LOCH. RD

DOLAN GDN

WHITEHILLS

NORTH ROW

THE GLEN

THE GLEN

BRIDGE STREET

PH

HENDERSON PL

WEST ROAD

PO

Saline

Saline Primary School

5

Drumcapie Plantation

KY12

CRAIGHOUSE PL

Craig House

EASTER CRAIG GDNS

OAKLEA

GREEN ROAD

B913

CH

Cattle Moss Wood

UPPER KINNEDDAR

UPPER KINNEDDAR GDNS

92

Standalane Farm

Moss Ferny Wood

Kinneddar Mains Farm

Nether Kinneddar

4

Cattle Moss Wood

Big Wood

Loanhead Poultry Farm

Bickram Village Wood

3

McKinlay's Wood

Big Wood

Big Wood

Mayfolds Wood

Mine (dis)

Spoil Tip (disused)

91

Mine (dis)

Blairsgreen Farm

2

Kinneddar Park

KINNEDDAR PK

Shepherdlands

Bickram Wood

1

Shepherdlands Wood

Shafts (dis)

Black Wood

Muirside of Kinneddar Farm

90

| 00 | A | | B | 01 | C | | D | 02 | E | | F |

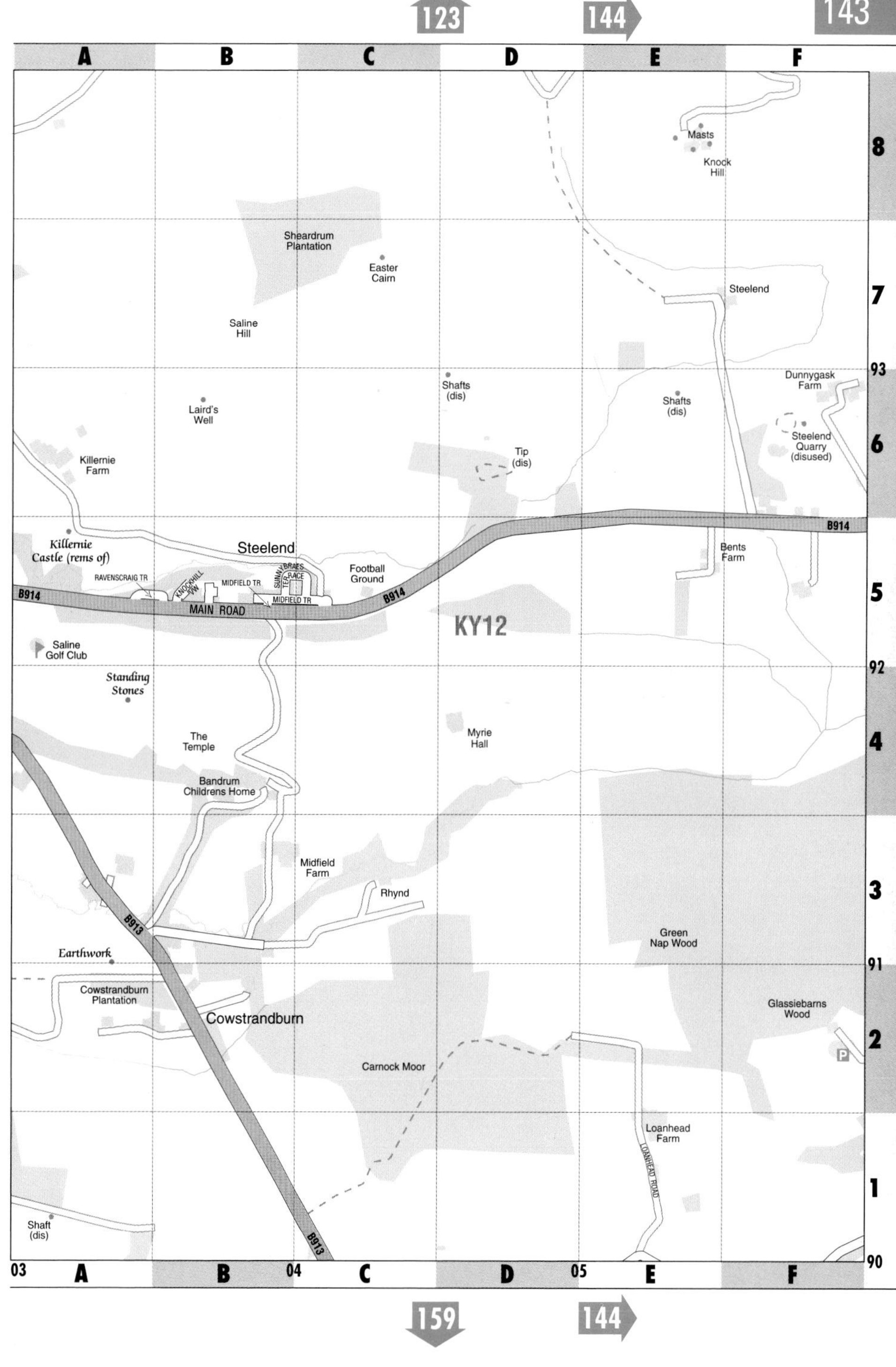

8

Masts
Knock
Hill

Sheardrum
Plantation

Easter
Cairn

7

Steelend

Saline
Hill

93

Shafts
(dis)

Shafts
(dis)

Dunnygask
Farm

6

Laird's
Well

Tip
(dis)

Steelend
Quarry
(disused)

Killernie
Farm

Killernie
Castle (rems of)

Steelend

B914

5

RAVENSCRAIG TR

MIDFIELD TR

Football
Ground

Bents
Farm

SUNNYSIDE
BRAES
TERRACE

KNOCKHILL
VIEW

MIDFIELD TR

B914

B914

MAIN ROAD

KY12

Saline
Golf Club

92

Standing
Stones

Myrie
Hall

4

The
Temple

Bandrum
Childrens Home

Midfield
Farm

Rhynd

Green
Nap Wood

3

B913

91

Earthwork

Cowstrandburn
Plantation

Cowstrandburn

Glassiebarns
Wood

2

Carnock Moor

P

Loanhead
Farm

LOANHEAD ROAD

1

Shaft
(dis)

B913

03

04

05

90

A   B   C   D   E   F

143
124

A   B   C   D   E   F

A823

Mast
Mast

Waterfall

8

Knockhill
Racing
Circuit

Din Moss

7

Tarry Well

93

Quarry
(dis)

Roscobie
Farm

6

Hilltop
Farm

Quarry (dis)

Roscobie Hills

Lylowan

B914

Lielowan
Meadow
Reserve

Lynn
Farm

Quarry
(dis)

Quarry
(dis)

5

KY12

Quarry
(dis)

Loanhead
Cott

Quarry
(dis)

92

Dolly Farm

Shaft
(dis)

4

Quarry
(dis)

A823

Dunduff
Farm

Thornyhill

3

Black
Loch

Hillhead

Craigluscar
Hill

91

Craigs Wood

Craigluscar
Farm

2

Lochhead

Craigluscar West
Reservoir

Craigluscar East
Reservoir

CRAIGLUSCAR ROAD

Quarry

Craigluscar
Nature
Reserve

Spoil
Heap

1

Craigluscar
Compensation
Reservoir

Dam
Wood

A823

90

06 A   B 07 C   D 08 E   F

143
160

125
146

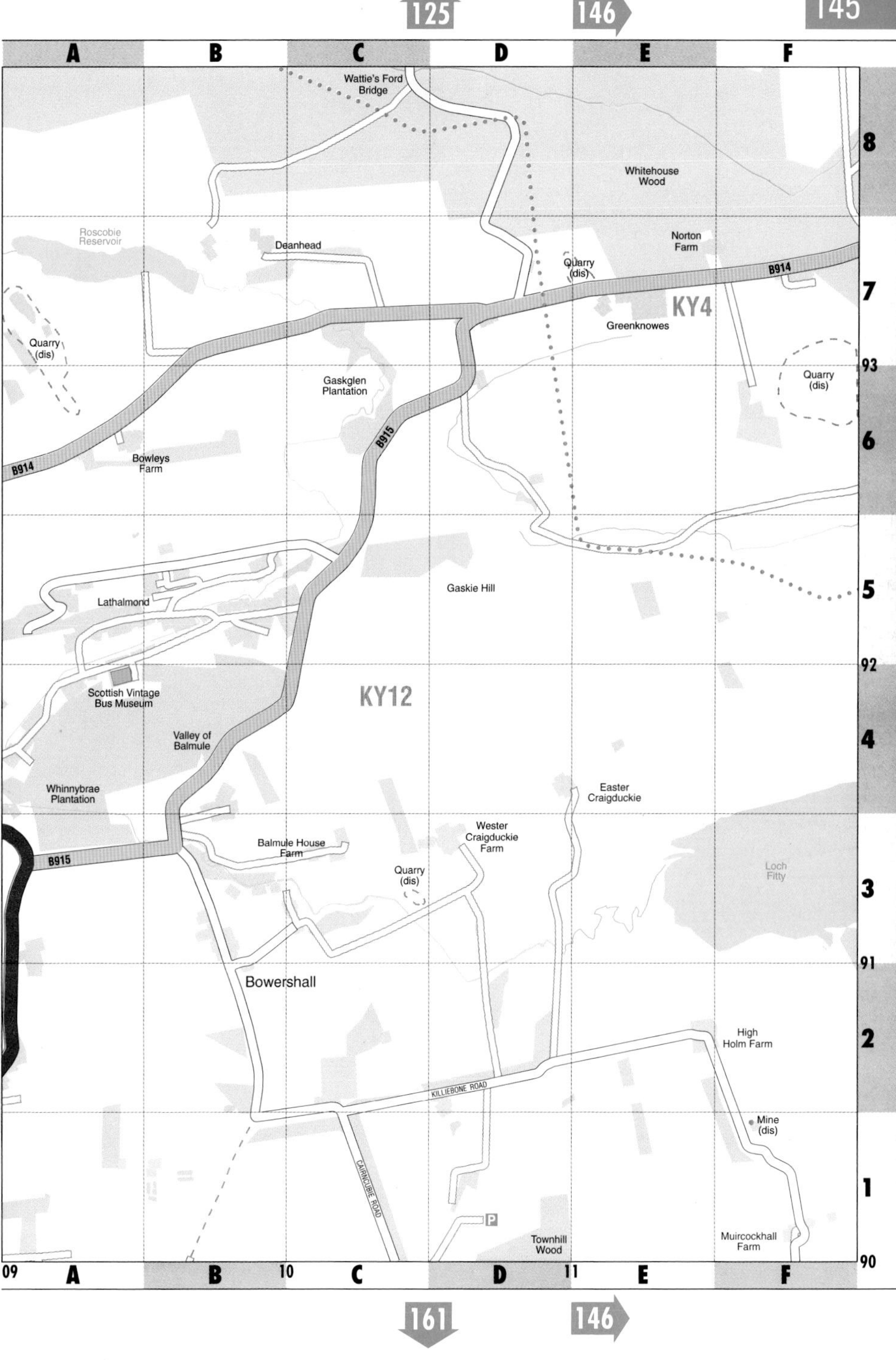
A
B
C
D
E
F
Wattie's Ford Bridge
Whitehouse Wood
8
Roscobie Reservoir
Deanhead
Norton Farm
Quarry (dis)
B914
7
KY4
Greenknowes
Quarry (dis)
93
Gaskglen Plantation
Quarry (dis)
B915
6
B914
Bowleys Farm
5
Lathalmond
Gaskie Hill
92
Scottish Vintage Bus Museum
KY12
4
Valley of Balmule
Easter Craigduckie
Whinnybrae Plantation
Wester Craigduckie Farm
Balmule House Farm
B915
Quarry (dis)
Loch Fitty
3
91
Bowershall
High Holm Farm
2
KILLIEBONE ROAD
Mine (dis)
1
CAIRNCUBIE ROAD
P
Townhill Wood
Muircockhall Farm
90
09
10
11
A
B
C
D
E
F

161
146

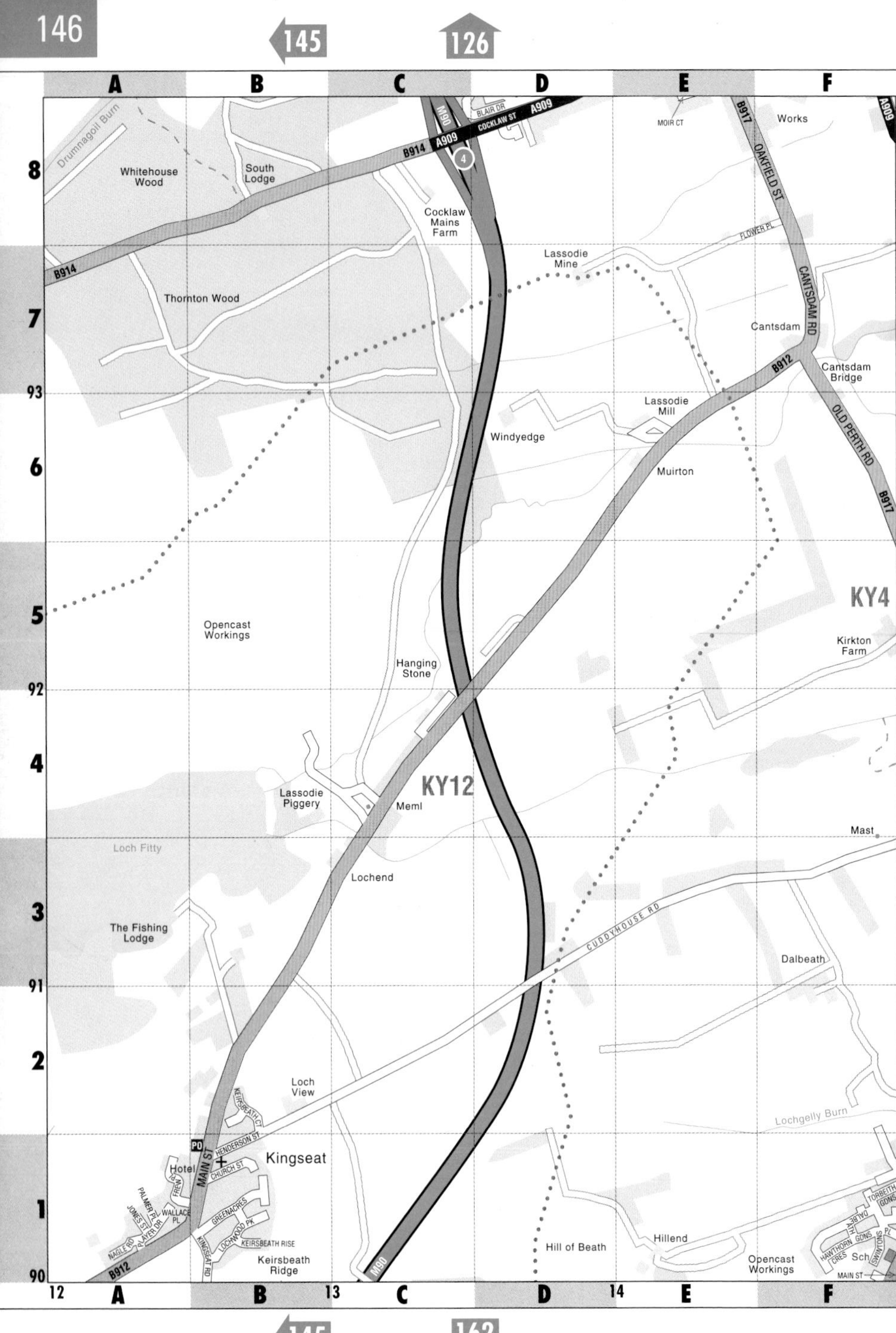

145
126

A B C D E F

8

7

93

6

5

92

4

3

91

2

1

90

12 A B 13 C D 14 E F

Drumnagoil Burn

Whitehouse Wood

South Lodge

B914

B914

A90

A909

COCKLAW ST

BLAIR DR

A909

4

MOIR CT

Works

B917

OAKFIELD ST

Cocklaw Mains Farm

FLOWER PL

Lassodie Mine

CANTSDAM RD

Cantsdam

B812

Cantsdam Bridge

Thornton Wood

Windyedge

Lassodie Mill

OLD PERTH RD

B917

Muirton

KY4

Opencast Workings

Hanging Stone

Kirkton Farm

KY12

Lassodie Piggery

Meml

Loch Fitty

Lochend

Mast

The Fishing Lodge

CUDDYHOUSE RD

Dalbeath

Loch View

Lochgelly Burn

PO

Hotel

MAIN ST

CHURCH ST

HENDERSON ST

KINGSKAVIL CT

Kingseat

PALMERSTON PL

JONES TER

BRAMBLE DR

WALLACE PL

RAITH PL

GREENACRES

LOCHWOOD PK

KEIRSBEATH CT

Keirsbeath Rise

Keirsbeath Ridge

A90

Hill of Beath

Hillend

Opencast Workings

Sch

MAIN ST

HAWTHORN GDNS

ORBEITH GDNS

DALBEATH CRES

145
162

127
148

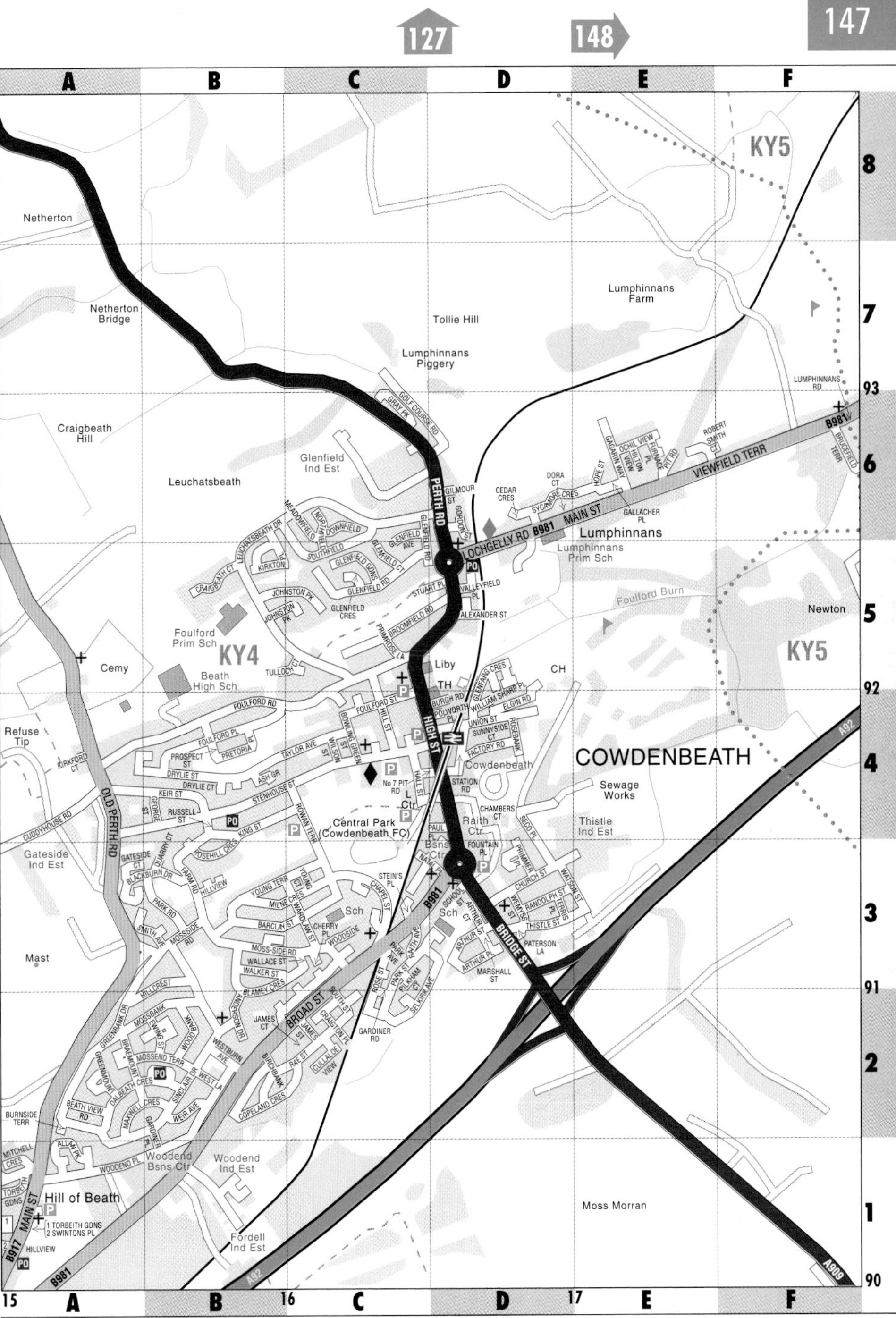
Netherton
Netherton Bridge
Tollie Hill
Lumphinnans Piggery
Lumphinnans Farm
KY5
Craigbeath Hill
Leuchatsbeath
Glenfield Ind Est
Lumphinnans
Lumphinnans Prim Sch
Foulford Burn
Newton
Foulford Prim Sch
KY4
Cemy
Beath High Sch
Liby
TH
CH
Refuse Tip
COWDENBEATH
Sewage Works
Central Park (Cowdenbeath FC)
Thistle Ind Est
Gateside Ind Est
Mast
Hill of Beath
Woodend Bsns Ctr
Woodend Ind Est
Fordell Ind Est
Moss Morran
PERTH RD
HIGH ST
BRIDGE ST
OLD PERTH RD
LOCHGELLY RD
MAIN ST
VIEWFIELD TERR
BROAD ST
B981
A92
A909
B917
1 TORBEITH GDNS
2 SWINTONS PL

163
148

147
128

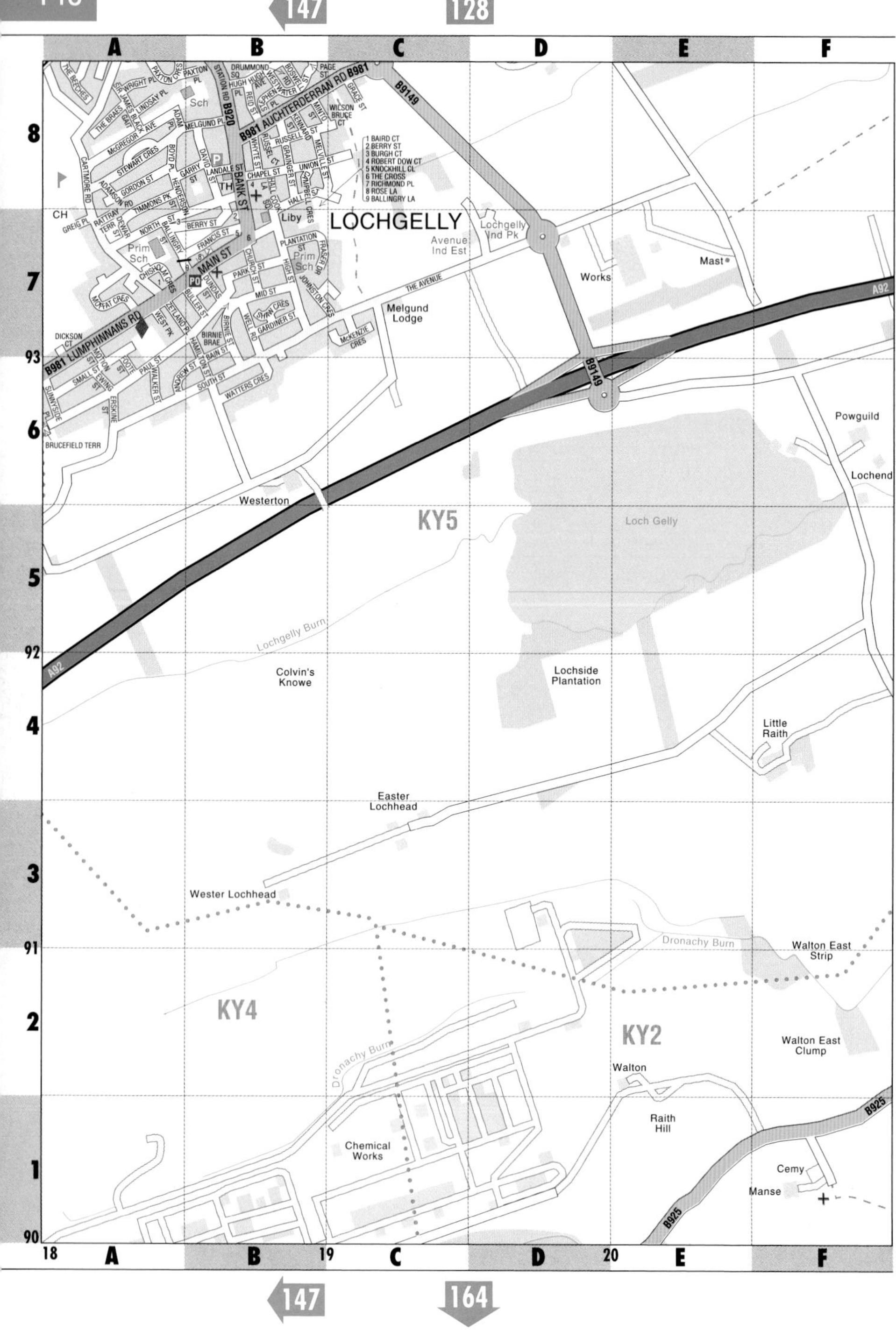
LOCHGELLY
KY5
KY4
KY2
Loch Gelly
Lochside Plantation
Colvin's Knowe
Westerton
Melgund Lodge
Avenue Ind Est
Lochgelly Ind Pk
Works
Mast
Powguild
Lochend
Little Raith
Easter Lochhead
Wester Lochhead
Dronachy Burn
Walton East Strip
Walton East Clump
Walton
Raith Hill
Chemical Works
Cemy
Manse
Lochgelly Burn
A92
B9149
B925
B981 AUCHTERDERRAN RD
B981 LUMPHINNANS RD
B920
MAIN ST
BANK ST
THE AVENUE
1 BAIRD CT
2 BERRY ST
3 BURGH CT
4 ROBERT DOW CT
5 KNOCKHILL CL
6 THE CROSS
7 RICHMOND PL
8 ROSE LA
9 BALLINGRY LA
BRUCEFIELD TERR
A B C D E F
8 7 6 5 4 3 2 1
93 92 91 90
18 19 20

147
164

129
150

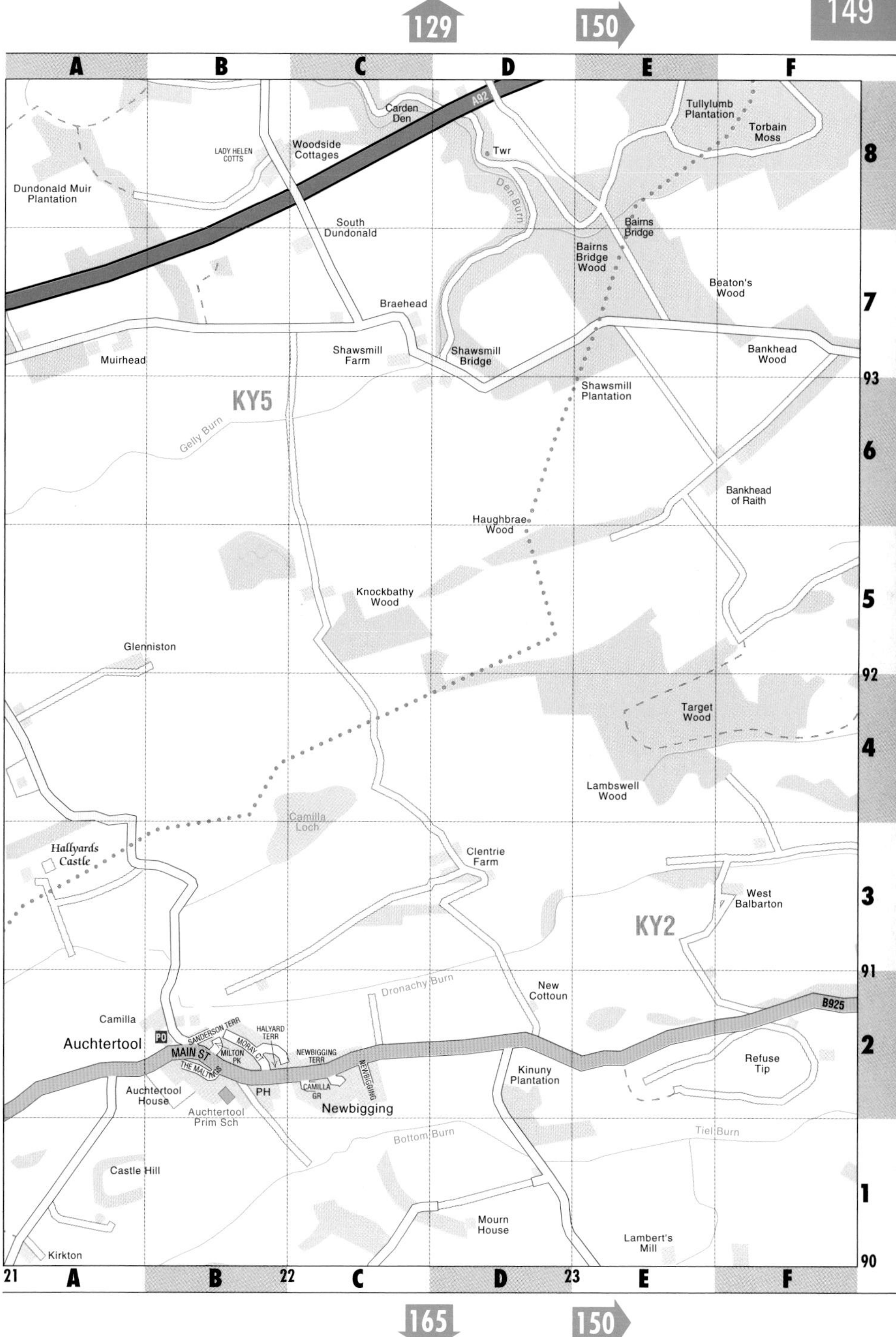
A
B
C
D
E
F
A92
Carden Den
Tullylumb Plantation
Torbain Moss
Woodside Cottages
LADY HELEN COTTS
Twr
Dundonald Muir Plantation
Den Burn
South Dundonald
Bairns Bridge
Bairns Bridge Wood
Beaton's Wood
Braehead
Shawsmill Farm
Shawsmill Bridge
Bankhead Wood
Muirhead
Shawsmill Plantation
KY5
Gelly Burn
Bankhead of Raith
Haughbrae Wood
Knockbathy Wood
Glenniston
Target Wood
Lambswell Wood
Camilla Loch
Hallyards Castle
Clentrie Farm
West Balbarton
KY2
Dronachy Burn
New Cottoun
B925
Camilla
Auchtertool
PO
SANDERSON TERR
HALYARD TERR
MORAY CT
MAIN ST
MILTON PK
THE MALTINGS
NEWBIGGING TERR
NEWBIGGING
CAMILLA GR
Kinuny Plantation
Refuse Tip
Auchtertool House
PH
Auchtertool Prim Sch
Newbigging
Bottom Burn
Tiel Burn
Castle Hill
Mourn House
Lambert's Mill
Kirkton
8
7
93
6
5
92
4
3
91
2
1
90
21
22
23

165
150

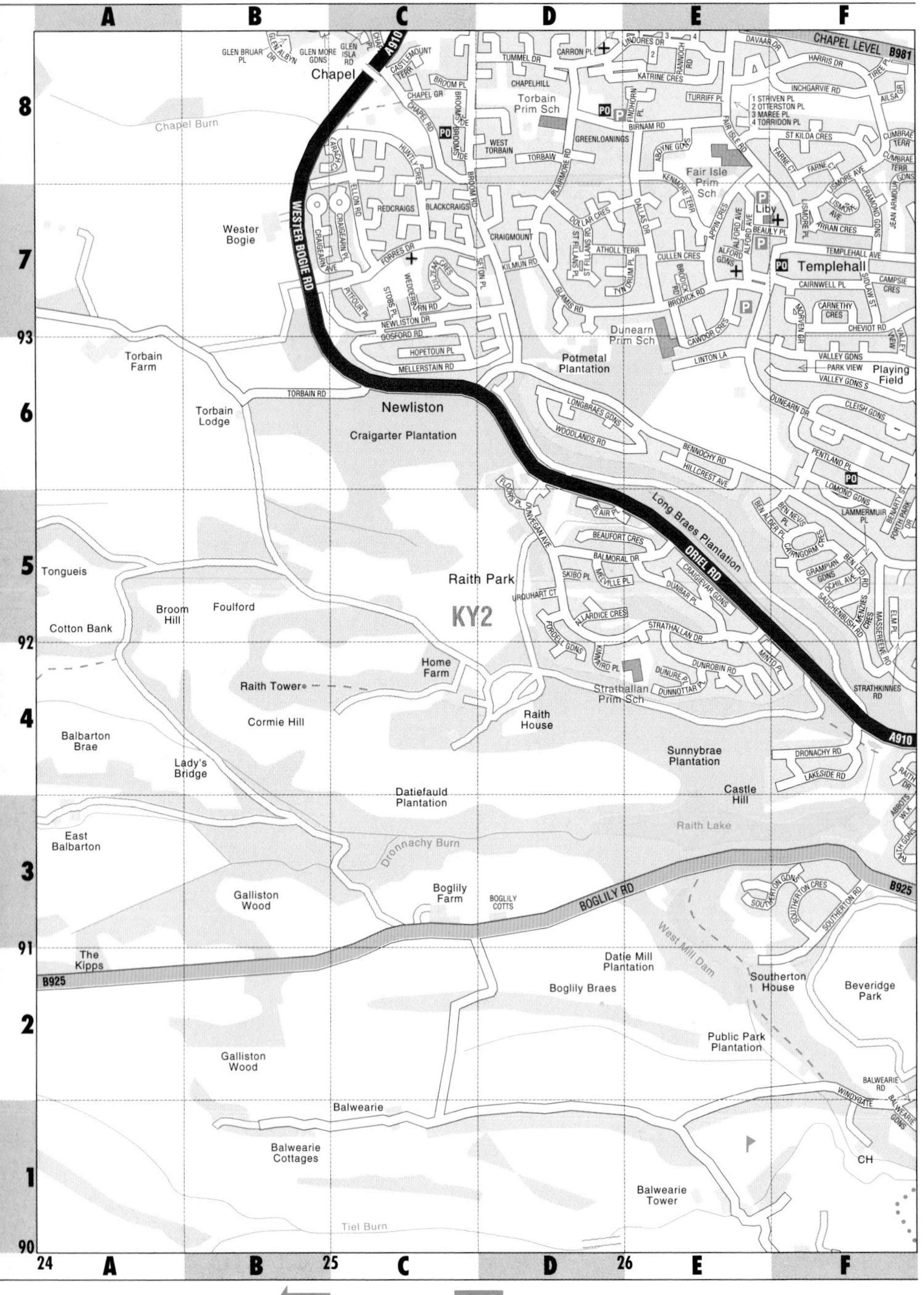

	A		B		C		D		E		F

8

7

93

6

5

92

4

3

91

2

1

90

CHAPEL LEVEL B981

Chapel
Chapel Burn
Wester Bogie
Torbain Farm
WESTER BOGIE RD
A910
Torbain Lodge
TORBAIN RD
Newliston
Craigarter Plantation

Torbain Prim Sch
WEST TORBAIN
GREENLOANINGS
Fair Isle Prim Sch
Libly
Templehall
PO
1 STRIVEN PL
2 OTTERSTON PL
3 MAREE PL
4 TORRIDON PL
Dunearn Prim Sch
Playing Field
Potmetal Plantation
LONGBRAES GDNS
WOODLANDS RD
HILLCREST AVE
BENNOCHY RD
Long Braes Plantation
ORIEL RD

Tongueis
Cotton Bank
Broom Hill
Foulford
Raith Park
KY2
Home Farm
Raith Towers
Cormie Hill
Balbarton Brae
Lady's Bridge
Raith House
Strathallan Prim Sch
BEAUFORT CRES
BALMORAL DR
Sunnybrae Plantation
Castle Hill
DRONACHY RD
LAKESIDE RD
STRATHKINNESS RD
A910

East Balbarton
Dronnachy Burn
Raith Lake
Galliston Wood
Boglily Farm
BOGLILY COTTS
BOGLILY RD
West Mill Dam
B925
The Kipps
B925
Datie Mill Plantation
Boglily Braes
Southerton House
Beveridge Park
Galliston Wood
Public Park Plantation
BALWEARIE
WINDYGATE
Balwearie
Balwearie Cottages
Balwearie Tower
CH
Tiel Burn

A B C D E F

8 7 93 6 5 92 4 3 91 2 1 90

Crem
Rosemount Ave
Barassie Dr
Chapel Level
Kirkcaldy High Sch
Dunnikier Park Playing Field
Smeaton
B981
Dunnikier Way
St Andrew's RC High Sch
Earn Rd
St Marie's RC Prim Sch
Gallatown
South Row
Miller St
Doctor's Row
Seaforth Pl
Randolph Pl
York Pl
Playing Field
Rosslyn St
A921
B928
Windmill Rd
Overton Mains
Napier St
Tweed Ave
Westwood Ave
Lawson St
Cumbrae Terr
Cumbrae Ct
1 Jean Armour Gdns
2 Tarbolton Ct
Den Burn
Middle Den
Whytemans Brae
Veronica Cres
Oaktree Sq
Sycamore Ave
Oaktree Ct
Almond Pl
Cedar Ave
Lilac Cres
Laburnum Rd
Willow Dr
Chestnut Ave
Holly Pl
Hayfield Rd
Hayfield Pl
Hayfield Ind Est
Cemy
H
P
Macindoe Cres
Pathhead Prim Sch
Kilgour Ave
Wright Pl
Beatty Cres
Haig Ave
Overton Rd
Lansbury St
Dunsire St
Cairns Street E
Cairns Street W
East March St
McKenzie St
Sinclairtown
Cemy
Sinclairtown Prim Sch
1 Birrell's La
2 Caithness Ct
3 Sutherland Pl
Lochlea Terr
Templehall Ave
Frederick Wilson Pk
Jute Pl
Rosin Ct
Linum Gr
Calender Ave
Smeaton Ind Site
Pannie Rd
East Burn Ct
Beatty Ct
Christie Pl
West March St
Ross Gdns
Cromarty Pl
Orkney Pl
Shetland Pl
Aitken St
Rosabelle St
Union St
Loughborough Rd
Viewforth Gdns
Viewforth High Sch
Liby
Poplar Gdns
Myrtle
Poplar Cres
Maple St
Laurel Cres
Edward St
Victoria
Works
KY1
Kidd St
Orne St
Rutherford Ct
Junction Rd
Institution St
Bank St
Smeaton Rd
Anderson St
Lady Nairn Ave
Spencer Pl
A955
Valley Prim Sch
Valley Gdns
Hayfield
Adamson Ave
Wilson Ave
1 Patterson Pl
2 Nelson St
3 Mariners St
4 Murray Terr
Lauder Rd
Kennedy Cres
Walker St
Denend Cres
Kelso Pl
Thornhill Cres
Thornhill Rd
Dunnikier Dr
Pathhead
Nairn St
Millie St
B925
Factory Rd
Church St
Ravenscraig
Harriet St
Dysart Rd
Briarcliff St
Wishart Pl
Ravenscraig Park Nature Trail
Ravenscraig Park
Cleish Gdns
Winifred St
Winifred Cres
Grieve St
King St
Loom Rd
Patterson St
Nile St
Matthew St
Denburn Pl
Provost Kay Pk
Canon Byrne Glebe
Rymalton
Commercial St
Mid St
Nether St
The Kyles
Brae Head Lodge
Braehead Hd
The Path
Ravenscraig Castle
Loanhead Pl
Baldwin Cres
Forth Park Dr
Forth Park Gns
Meldrum Rd
Harcourt Rd
Elgin St
Viceroy St
Montgomery St
Whytebank Gdns
Victoria Rd
St Mary's Glebe
St Mary's Pl
Adam Smith Coll (Priory Campus)
Forth Park
Bennochy Rd
Bennochy Ct
Dunnikier Prim Sch
Rosebery Ct
Maria St
Berwick Pl
Bennochy Ave
Cemy
Ollerton Ct
Stanley Pk
Alexandra St
Townsend Cres
Maryhall St
Malcolm's Wynd
High St
Lord Gambier Wharf
Pathhead Sands
Percival St
Strathkinnes Rd
Gourlay St
Duncan St
Dean Rd
Massereene Rd
Victoria Gdns
West Albert Rd
Mitchell St
Ind Est
Coal Wynd
Deas Wharf
Harbour
Williamson's Quay
East Pier
South Pier
KY2
Kirkcaldy
Liby Mus & Gall
Univ
Oriel Rd
Oriel Road Rdbt
Forth Ave
Bennochy Rd
Carlyle Rd
Adam Smith Coll
Townsend Pl
Church St
Oswald's Wynd
Hill Pl
Kirk Wynd
John Hunter Ct
TA HQ
St Brycedale Ave
Brycedale Ct
Redburn Wynd
Adam Smith Ct
Adam Smith Cl
Port Brae
Abbots Wlk
Forth Ave Ind Est
Osborne Ho
Abbotshall Rd
East Fergus Pl
Wemyssfield
Hunter Pl
Tolbooth St
George Burn Wynd
The Mercat
TH
Fife Coastal Path
KIRKCALDY
Kirkcaldy Sands
Raith Gdns
Arbots Mill
West Fergus Pl
Whytescauseway
Whytehouse Ave
Park Pl
South Fergus Pl
Swan Rd
Beveridge Rd
Ct
Fallodon Cres
Boglily Rd
Nicol St
A910
Sandford Gate
Olympia Arc
Douglas St
David St
Volunteer's Gn
Thistle St
1 The Postings
2 Charlotte St
3 Glasswork St
Asquith St
B9157
Abbotshall Rd
Boating Lake
Lady Helen St
Munro St
Halley's Ct
School Wynd
Gas Wynd
Esplanade
Beveridge Park
Novar Cres
Milton Rd
Sch
James Gr
4 Gladney Sq
5 Purves Ct
6 Bute Wynd
7 Aitken Ct
8 Hendry's Wynd
9 Buchanan Ct
Linktown
William St
Methven Rd
Links St
Alison St
Scott St
Saunders St
Marion St
Balwearie Rd
Balwearie Cres
Kininmonth St
Ramsay Rd
Liby
Links Sands
Balwearie High Sch
Balwearie Gdns
Stark's Park (Raith Rovers FC)
Pratt St
Barnet Cres
Heggie's Wynd
Fergus Wynd
Invertiel Bank
Tiel Burn
Invertiel Terr
Bridge St
Mill St

C5
1 Russel Pl
2 Young's Terr
3 Smith's Terr

D6
1 Pathhead Ct
2 Mitchell Pl
3 Hawksmuir
4 Citron Glebe
5 Birrell Street Wynd
6 Birrell Cl
7 Chief's Cl
8 Broad Wynd
9 Branning Ct
10 Bogies Wynd
11 Ravens Craig
12 Flesh Wynd
13 West Wynd

27 A B 28 C D 29 E F

167 152

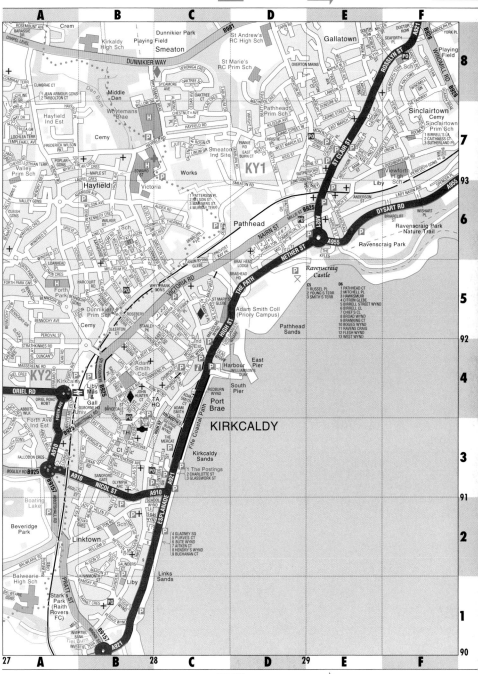

151 132

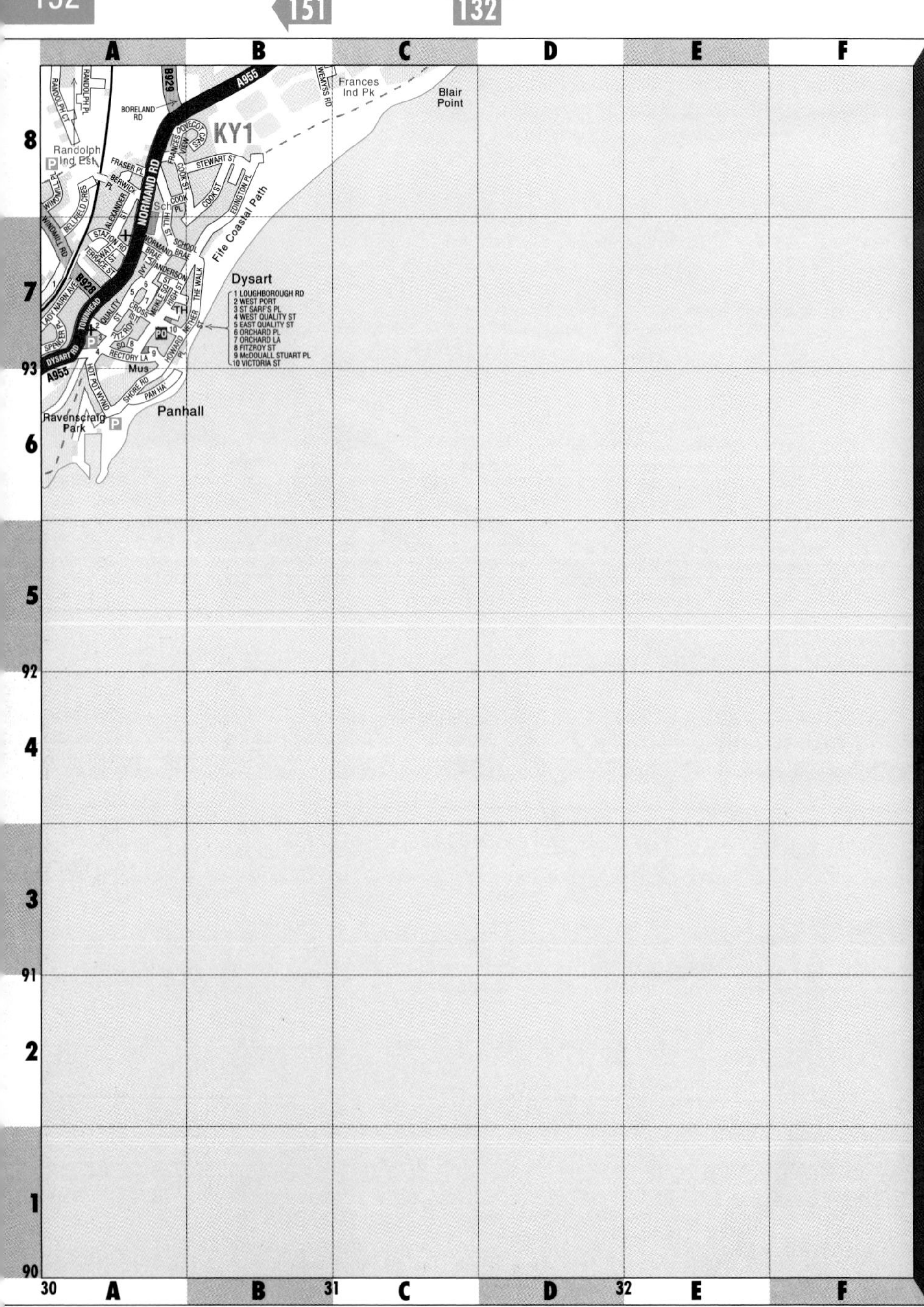

KY1

Frances Ind Pk

Blair Point

Fife Coastal Path

Dysart
1 LOUGHBOROUGH RD
2 WEST PORT
3 ST SARF'S PL
4 WEST QUALITY ST
5 EAST QUALITY ST
6 ORCHARD PL
7 ORCHARD LA
8 FITZROY ST
9 McDOUALL STUART PL
10 VICTORIA ST

Mus

Panhall

Ravenscraig Park

BORELAND RD
NORMAND RD
A955
B924
Randolph Ind Est

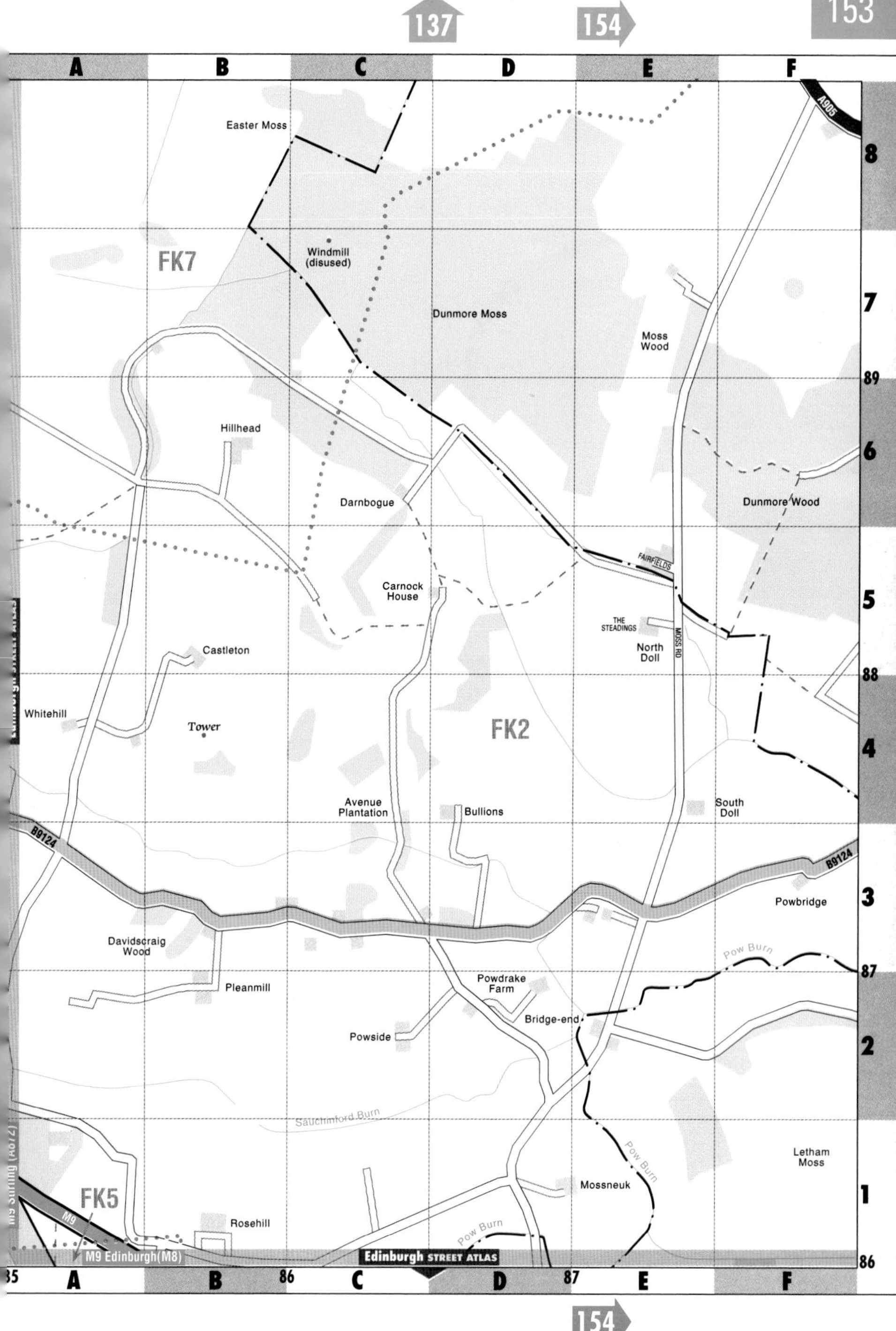

A B C D E F

8

FK7

Easter Moss

Windmill (disused)

Dunmore Moss

Moss Wood

89

7

Hillhead

Darnbogue

Dunmore Wood

6

FAIRFIELDS

Carnock House

THE STEADINGS

North Doll

5

Castleton

88

Whitehill

Tower

FK2

4

Avenue Plantation

Bullions

South Doll

B8124

B8124

Powbridge

3

Davidscraig Wood

Pow Burn

87

Pleanmill

Powdrake Farm

Powside

Bridge-end

2

Sauchinford Burn

Pow Burn

Letham Moss

FK5

Mossneuk

1

Rosehill

Pow Burn

85 A B 86 C D 87 E F 86

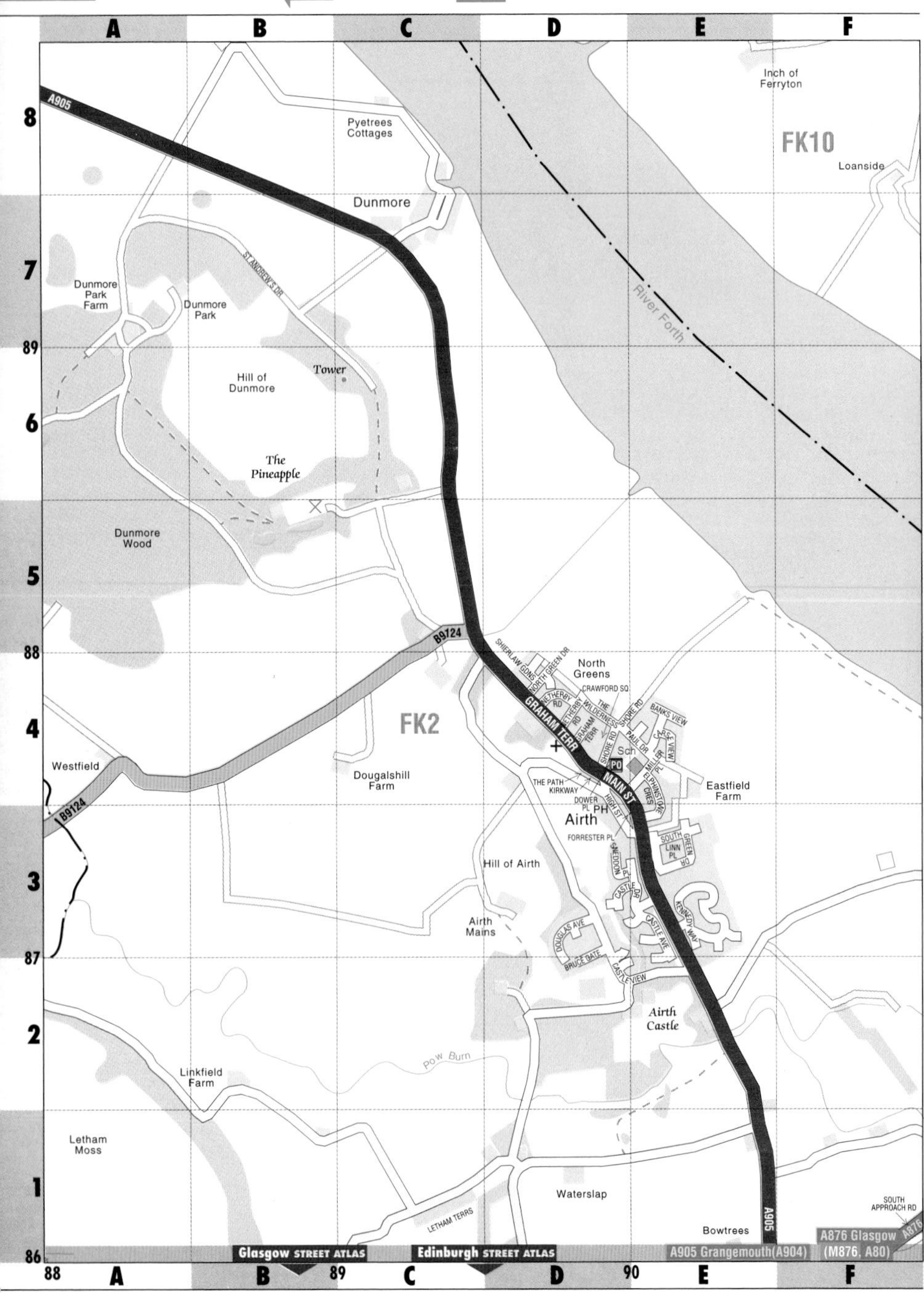

FK10

Inch of
Ferryton

Loanside

A905

8

Pyetrees
Cottages

Dunmore

7

ST ANDREW'S DR

River Forth

Dunmore
Park
Farm

Dunmore
Park

89

Hill of
Dunmore

Tower

6

The
Pineapple

X

Dunmore
Wood

5

B9124

88

SHIRLAW EDINS LN

North
Greens

SHERIFF RD
GREEN RD

CRAWFORD SQ

BANK'S VIEW

FK2

4

GRAHAM TERR

Sch

VIEW LNY

Westfield

Dougalshill
Farm

B9124

THE PATH
KIRKWAY

DOWER
PL

Airth

MAIN ST

PO

PH

Eastfield
Farm

SOUTH
LINN PL

GREEN PL

B9124

FORRESTER PL

3

Hill of Airth

Airth
Mains

DOUGLAS AVE

BRUCE GATE

CASTLE AVE

CASTLE AVE

KINGS WAY

87

EAST VIEW

2

POW BURN

Airth
Castle

Linkfield
Farm

1

Letham
Moss

Waterslap

LETHAM TERRS

Bowtrees

A905

SOUTH
APPROACH RD

A876

86

A905 Grangemouth(A904)

A876 Glasgow
(M876, A80)

88

A

B

89

C

D

90

E

F

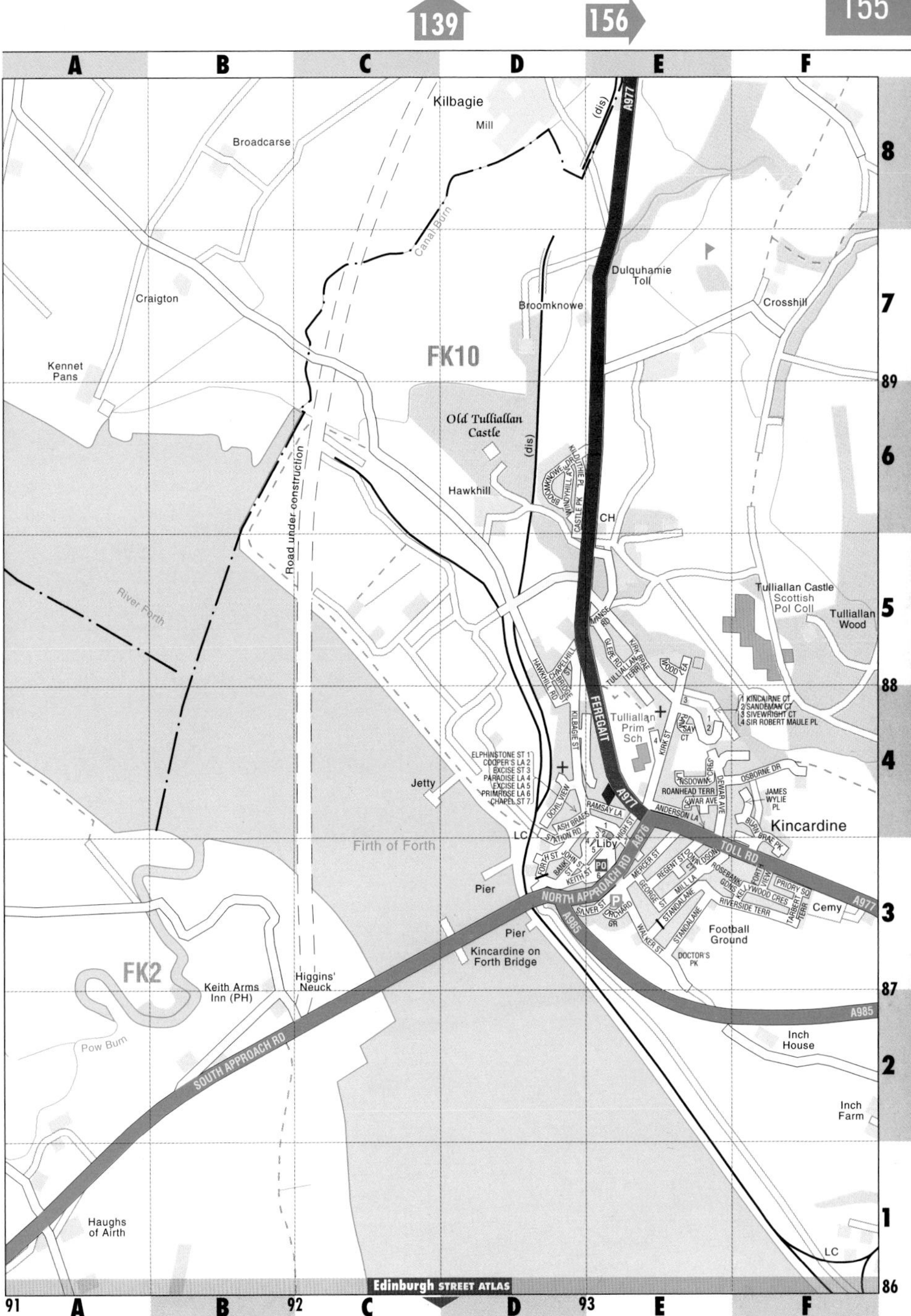
139
156
A
B
C
D
E
F
8
7
89
6
5
88
4
3
87
2
1
86
91
92
93
Kilbagie
Mill
Broadcarse
Canal Burn
Craigton
Kennet Pans
FK10
Old Tulliallan Castle
Broomknowe
Dulquhamie Toll
Crosshill
Hawkhill
CH
Road under construction
River Forth
Tulliallan Castle
Scottish Pol Coll
Tulliallan Wood
Tulliallan Prim Sch
1 KINCAIRNE CT
2 SANDEMAN CT
3 SIVEWRIGHT CT
4 SIR ROBERT MAULE PL
ELPHINSTONE ST 1
COOPER'S LA 2
EXCISE ST 3
PARADISE LA 4
EXCISE LA 5
PRIMROSE LA 6
CHAPEL ST 7
Jetty
FEREGAIT
A977
Kincardine
JAMES WYLIE PL
OSBORNE DR
ROANHEAD TERR
DEWAR AVE
ANDERSON LA
TOLL RD
Firth of Forth
LC
Liby
PO
Pier
NORTH APPROACH RD
A876
A985
Cemy
Football Ground
DOCTOR'S PK
Kincardine on Forth Bridge
FK2
Keith Arms Inn (PH)
Higgins' Neuck
Pow Burn
SOUTH APPROACH RD
Inch House
Inch Farm
Haughs of Airth
Edinburgh STREET ATLAS

156

155
140

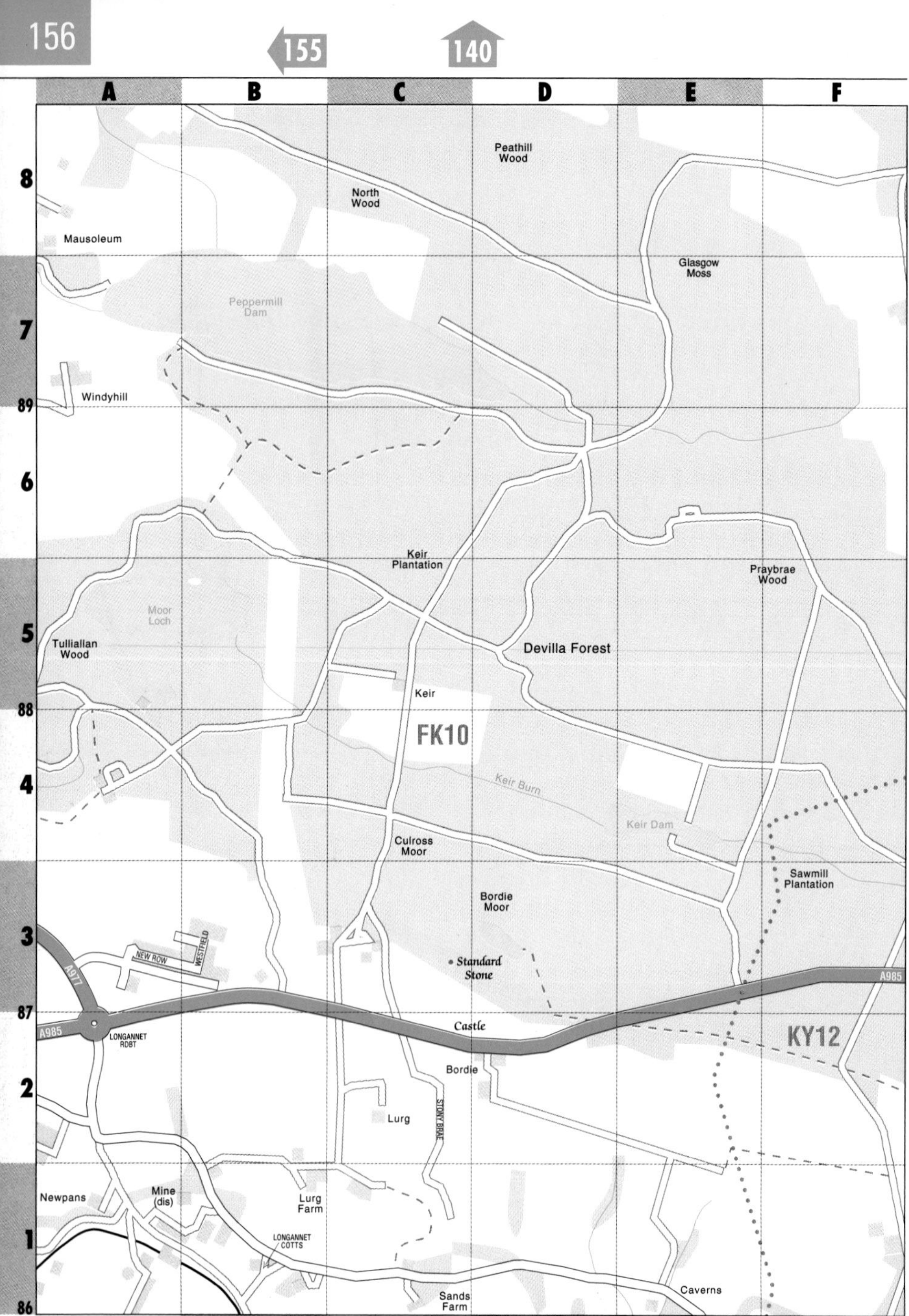
A
B
C
D
E
F
8
7
89
6
5
88
4
3
87
2
1
86
94
95
96
Peathill Wood
North Wood
Mausoleum
Glasgow Moss
Peppermill Dam
Windyhill
Keir Plantation
Praybrae Wood
Moor Loch
Tulliallan Wood
Devilla Forest
Keir
FK10
Keir Burn
Keir Dam
Culross Moor
Sawmill Plantation
Bordie Moor
NEW ROW
WESTFIELD
A977
Standard Stone
A985
Castle
KY12
LONGANNET RDBT
Bordie
Lurg
STONY BRAE
Newpans
Mine (dis)
Lurg Farm
LONGANNET COTTS
Sands Farm
Caverns

155
168

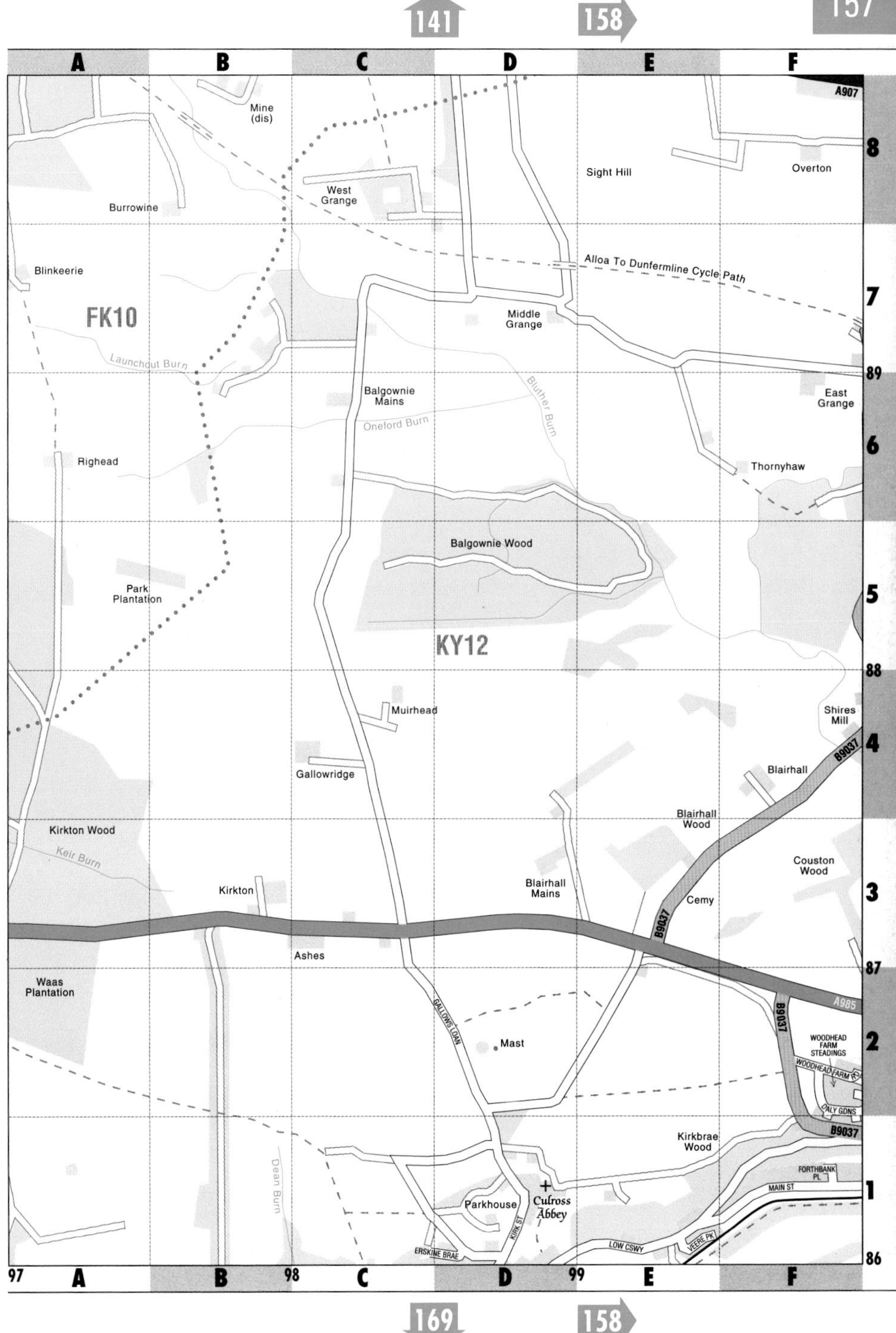

141
158

A907

8

Overton

Sight Hill

West
Grange

Mine
(dis)

Burrowine

Blinkeerie

FK10

Alloa To Dunfermline Cycle Path

7

Launchout Burn

Middle
Grange

89

Balgownie
Mains

East
Grange

Oneford Burn

Blubher Burn

Righead

Thornyhaw

6

Balgownie Wood

Park
Plantation

5

KY12

88

Muirhead

Shires
Mill

B9037

Gallowridge

Blairhall

4

Blairhall
Wood

Kirkton Wood

Couston
Wood

Keir Burn

Kirkton

Blairhall
Mains

Cemy

3

B9037

Ashes

A985

87

Waas
Plantation

Gallows Loan

B9037

WOODHEAD
FARM
STEADINGS

Mast

WOODHEAD FARM

2

DALY GDNS

Dean Burn

Kirkbrae
Wood

B9037

FORTHBANK
PL

Parkhouse

Culross
Abbey

MAIN ST

1

KIRK ST

ERSKINE BRAE

LOW CSWY

VERRE PK?

86

97

98

99

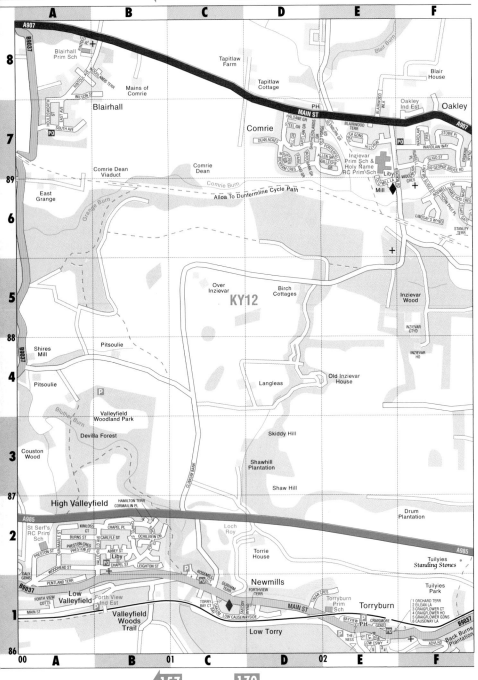
157
142

A B C D E F

8
7
89
6
5
88
4
3
87
2
1
86

A907
B9037
Blairhall Prim Sch
RINTOUL PL
RINTOUL AVE
WOODLANDS TERR
WILSON ST
Mains of Comrie
Blairhall
HOULDSWORTH ST
EAST AVE
SOUTH AVE
PO
Tapitlaw Farm
Tapitlaw Cottage
Blair Burn
Blair House
BLAIRWOOD WLK
Oakley Ind Est
Oakley
PH
MAIN ST
HALDANE GR
STEEL GR
HILL GR
TAPITLAW GR
SHEPHERDLANDS GR
OLD FORGE GR
GLENBURN GR
BLAIRWOOD TERR
FORTH GDNS
HILLVIEW
WARDLAW CRES
STOBIE PL
WARDLAW WAY
ERSKINE WYND
Comrie
DEAN ACRES
BOURTREE GR
PARKLAND GR
WOODBANK GR
PORTERFIELD
ALLEN GR
GILLESPIE GR
BICKRAM CRES
Inzievar Prim Sch & Holy Name RC Prim Sch
Liby
OLD MILL LA
STATION RD
Mill
RUSSELL PL
SLIGO ST
SIR GEORGE BRUCE RD
LINK RD
WOODBURN CRES
BOSWELL DR
JOHN
JAMES HOG CRES
THORN TREE PL
STUART GAIT
LINDSAY'S WYND
STANLEY TERR
Comrie Dean Viaduct
Comrie Dean
Comrie Burn
Alloa To Dunfermline Cycle Path
East Grange
Grange Burn
Over Inzievar
KY12
Birch Cottages
Inzievar Wood
INZIEVAR CTYD
INZIEVAR HO
Shires Mill
Pitsoulie
Pitsoulie
Langleas
Old Inzievar House
P
Valleyfield Woodland Park
Bluther Burn
Devilla Forest
Skiddy Hill
Couston Wood
Shawhill Plantation
CLINKUM BANK
Shaw Hill
High Valleyfield
HAMILTON TERR
CORMAILIN PL
A985
Drum Plantation
St Serf's RC Prim Sch
KINLOSS CT
CHAPEL PL
BURNS ST
CARLYLE ST
CHAPEL ST
OCHILVIEW DR
FORTH CRES
DUNIMARLE ST
PRESTON CRES
PRESTON ST
PRESTON ST
VALLEYFIELD AVE
ABBEY ST
Liby
PO
CHAPEL ST
LEIGHTON ST
Loch Roy
Torrie House
Tuilyies Standing Stones
DALY GDNS
WOODHEAD ST
PENTLAND TERR
P
ROSEMILL CT
PO
Newmills
Tuilyies Park
B9037
Low Valleyfield
Forth View Ind Est
FORTH VIEW COTTS
P
DURHAM TERR
FORTHVIEW TERR
TINIAN CRES
Torryburn Prim Sch
Torryburn
TORRY BAY CT
OAKUM BAY
SAWDOY
MAIN ST
1 ORCHARD TERR
2 EILEAN LA
3 CRAIGFLOWER CT
4 CRAIGFLOWER HO
5 CRAIGFLOWER GDNS
6 CAUSEWAY LA
MAIN ST
Valleyfield Woods Trail
LOW CAUSEWAYSIDE
BAYVIEW
P
PH
CRAIGMORE GDNS
PO
Low Torry
P
THE NESS
ROSE LA
LOW CSWY
ADIA RD
Back Burns Plantation

00 A B 01 C D 02 E F

157
170

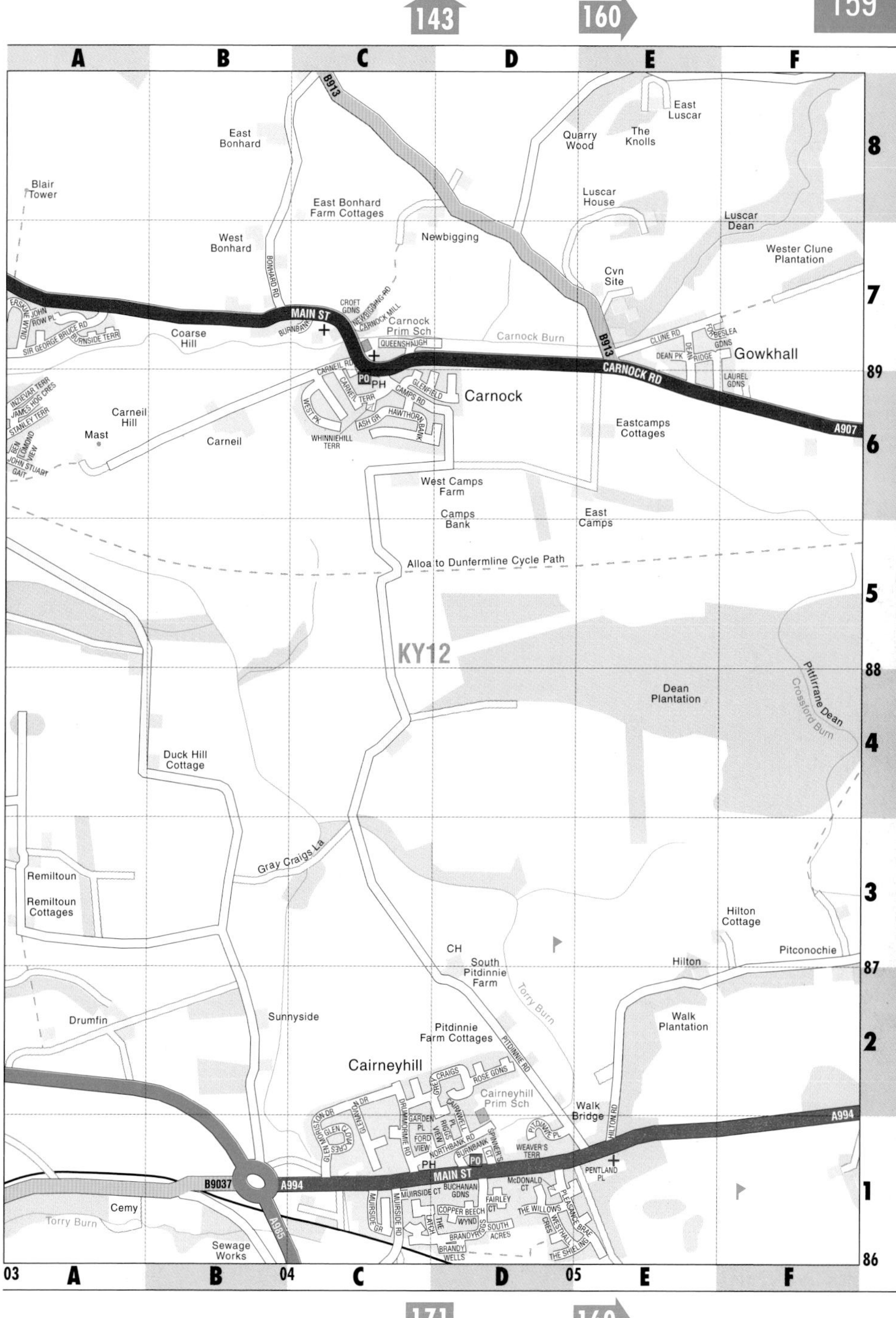

Map labels

Column headers (top): A B C D E F

Column headers (bottom): A B C D E F

Row numbers (right): 8 7 89 6 5 88 4 3 87 2 86

Blair Tower

East Bonhard

Quarry Wood

The Knolls

East Luscar

Luscar House

Luscar Dean

Wester Clune Plantation

East Bonhard Farm Cottages

West Bonhard

Newbigging

B913

Cvn Site

CLUNE RD

DEAN PK

BRIDGE

LAUREL GDNS

Gowkhall

CROFT GDNS

NICHOLSON RD

Carnock Mill

Carnock Prim Sch

MAIN ST

BURNS RD

Coarse Hill

DALY AR ROW PL

SIR GEORGE BRUCE RD

BURNSIDE TERR

Carnock Burn

CARNOCK RD

A907

QUEENSHAUGH

PO

PH

GLENFIELD

CAMPS RD

Carnock

Eastcamps Cottages

INGLEVAR TERR

JAMES STREET STONES

STANLEY TERR

BEN STUART VIEW

JOHN STUART GAIT

Carneil Hill

Mast

Carneil

CARNEIL RD

WEST PK

CARNEIL CT

ASH GR

HAWTHORN AV

WHINNIEHILL TERR

West Camps Farm

Camps Bank

East Camps

Alloa to Dunfermline Cycle Path

KY12

Dean Plantation

Pitfirrane Dean

Crossford Burn

Duck Hill Cottage

Remiltoun

Remiltoun Cottages

Gray Craigs La

Hilton Cottage

Pitconochie

CH

South Pitdinnie Farm

Hilton

Drumfin

Sunnyside

Pitdinnie Farm Cottages

Torry Burn

Walk Plantation

Cairneyhill

PITDINNIE RD

CRAIGS PL

GLEN CT

GLEN DR

GLEN CL

GARDEN PL

BRANDY ACRE RD

NORTHBANK

SOUTHBANK

FORD

Cairneyhill Prim Sch

WEAVER'S TERR

Walk Bridge

HILTON RD

A994

B9037

A994

A985

Cemy

Torry Burn

MUIRSIDE CT

MUIRSIDE RD

MAIN ST

PH

PO

BUCHANAN GDNS

COPPER BEECH WYND

FAIRLEY CT

McDONALD CT

PENTLAND PL

THE WILLOWS

BRANDY WELLS

BRANDYSIDE SOUTH ACRES

THE SHALLOWS

GREAT BURN

Sewage Works

03 04 05

86

159 144

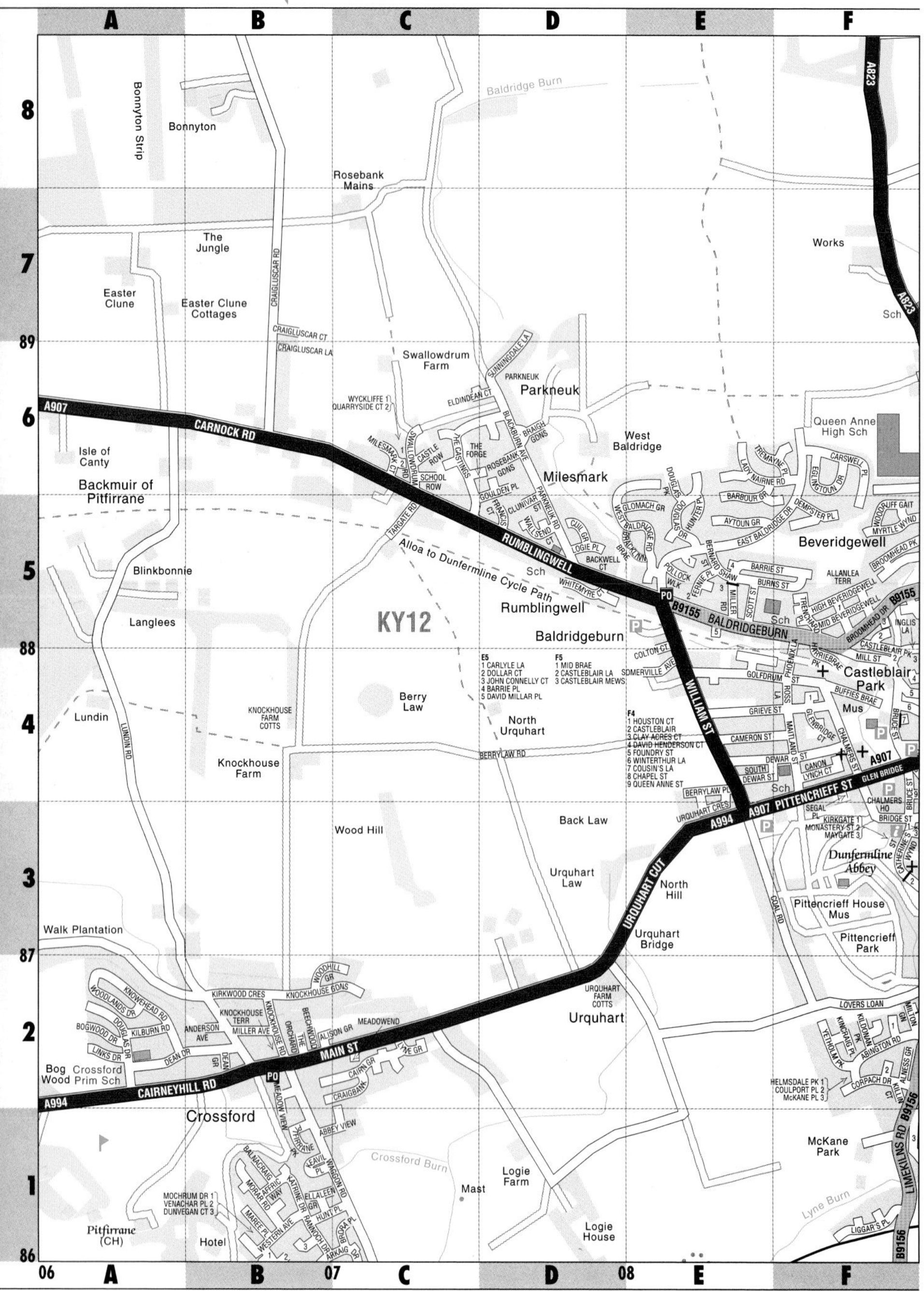

A
B
C
D
E
F
8
7
89
6
5
88
4
3
87
2
1
86
06
07
08
Bonnyton Strip
Bonnyton
Rosebank Mains
Baldridge Burn
A823
The Jungle
Easter Clune
Easter Clune Cottages
CRAIGLUSCAR RD
CRAIGLUSCAR CT
CRAIGLUSCAR LA
Works
Sch
Swallowdrum Farm
Parkneuk
A907
CARNOCK RD
West Baldridge
Queen Anne High Sch
Isle of Canty
Backmuir of Pitfirrane
Milesmark
Beveridgewell
Blinkbonnie
RUMBLINGWELL
Alloa to Dunfermline Cycle Path
Sch
Rumblingwell
Langlees
KY12
Baldridgeburn
B9155
BALDRIDGEBURN
Castleblair Park
WILLIAM ST
Berry Law
North Urquhart
Lundin
LUNDIN RD
KNOCKHOUSE FARM COTTS
Knockhouse Farm
BERRYLAW RD
A907 PITTENCRIEFF ST
A994
Wood Hill
Back Law
Dunfermline Abbey
Urquhart Law
URQUHART CUT
North Hill
Pittencrieff House Mus
Walk Plantation
Urquhart Bridge
Pittencrieff Park
URQUHART FARM COTTS
Urquhart
MAIN ST
CAIRNEYHILL RD
Bog Wood
Crossford Prim Sch
Crossford
McKane Park
Crossford Burn
Logie Farm
Mast
Lyne Burn
Pitfirrane (CH)
Hotel
Logie House
LIMEKILNS RD
B9156

159 172

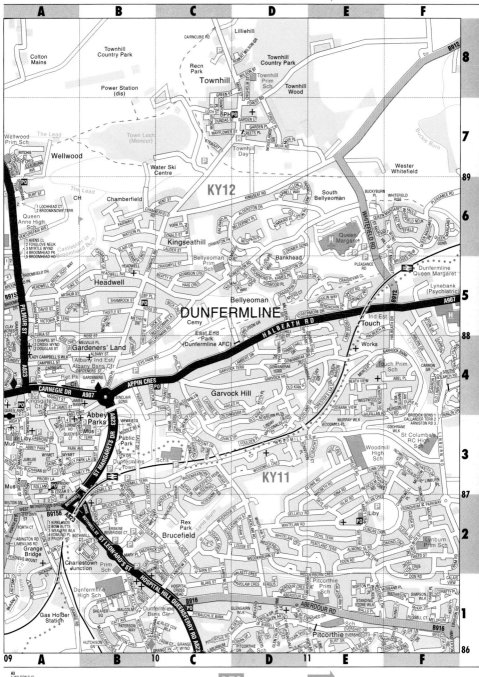

A   B   C   D   E   F

8

7

89

KY12

6

Townhill
Townhill Country Park
Colton Mains
Power Station (dis)
Recn Park
Lilliehill
CAIRNCUBIE RD
Townhill Country Park
Townhill Prim Sch
Townhill Wood

Wellwood Prim Sch
The Lead
Wellwood
Town Loch (Moncur)
Water Ski Centre
The Lead
Townhill Day
Wester Whitefield
Buckie Burn

Chamberfield
Kingseathill
KENT ST
YORK PL
Kingseathill
Chamberfield
FAIRWAYS
WATSON DR
DONALD ST
LAUDER DR
KINGSEAT RD
South Bellyeoman
WHITEFIELD RISE
Queen Margaret
WHITEFIELD RD
B912

Queen Anne High Sch

Headwell
HEADWELL RD
ARTHUR ST
SHAMROCK ST
THISTLE ST
METHVEN ST
Bellyeoman Prim Sch
Bankhead
CRAIGMYLE ST
HAIG CRES

B915
DUNFERMLINE
Cemy
East End Park (Dunfermline AFC)
HALBEATH RD
Ind Est Touch
Works
A907
H

Gardeners' Land
CARNEGIE DR   A907
APPIN CRES
Garvock Hill
GARVOCK TERR
Touch Prim Sch
CARRON GR

88

5

4

3

Abbey Parks
Mus
Public Park
Dunfermline Town
Schs
KY11
Woodmill High Sch
87

Rex Park
Brucefield
Lyne Burn
Liby
PO
Lynburn Prim Sch

2

B9156
Grange Bridge
Charlestown Junction
Gas Holder Station
Dunfermline High Sch
HOSPITAL HILL   QUEENSFERRY RD   A823
ST LEONARD'S ST
B916
ABERDOUR RD
Pitcorthie Prim Sch
Pitcorthie
B916

1

86

09   A   B   10   C   D   11   E   F

A3
1 WILSON S CL
2 MUSIC HALL LA
3 MAYGATE
4 COMMERCIAL SCHOOL LA

161 146

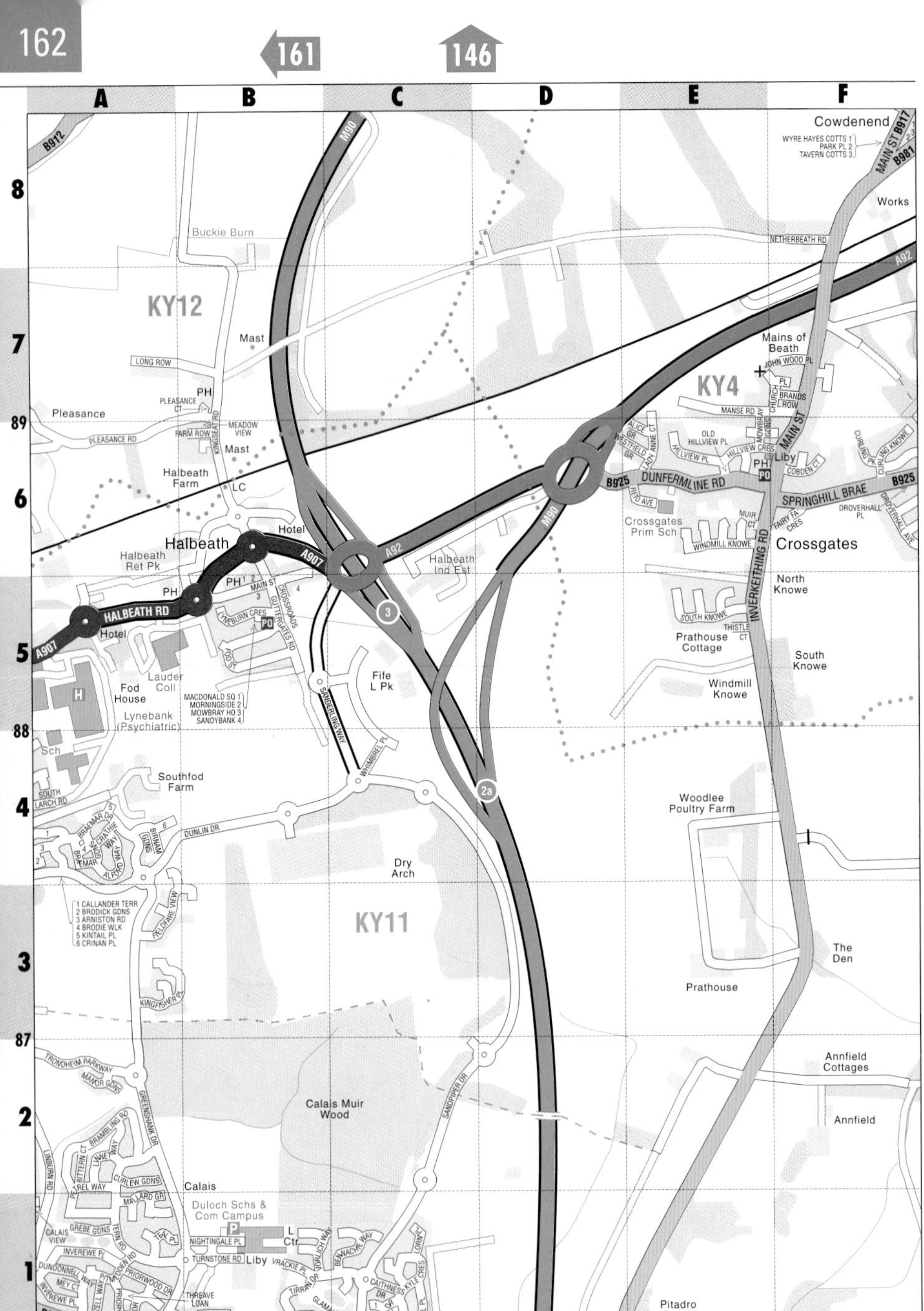

Cowdenend
WYRE HAYES COTTS 1
PARK PL 2
TAVERN COTTS 3
MAIN ST B917
B981
Works
NETHERBEATH RD
A92
Buckie Burn
KY12
Mast
LONG ROW
PH
PLEASANCE CT
Pleasance
PLEASANCE RD
FARM ROW
MEADOW VIEW
KINGSEAT RD
Mast
Halbeath Farm
LC
Hotel
Halbeath
Halbeath Ret Pk
A907
A92
Halbeath Ind Est
PH
MAIN ST
CROSSROADS
GUTTERGATES RD
LYNEBURN CRES
PO
HALBEATH RD
Hotel
A907
Lauder Coll
Fod House
H
Lynebank (Psychiatric)
MACDONALD SQ 1
MORNINGSIDE 2
MOWBRAY HO 3
SANDYBANK 4
Fife L Pk
SANDERLING WAY
WHIMBREL PL
M90
Mains of Beath
KY4
JOHN WOOD PL
PL
CHURCH
BRANDS
MANSE RD
L ROW
MOWBRAY GDNS
MAIN ST
ALICE GR
WESTFIELD GR
LADY ANNE CT
OLD HILLVIEW PL
HILLVIEW PL
HILLVIEW CRES
PH
Liby
COBDEN CT
CURLING PK
CURLING KNOWE
B925
DUNFERMLINE RD
B925
SPRINGHILL BRAE
DROVERHALL PL
DROVERHALL AVE
REID AVE
Crossgates Prim Sch
MUIR CT
FAIRY FA CRES
Crossgates
WINDMILL KNOWE
INVERKEITHING RD
North Knowe
SOUTH KNOWE
THISTLE CT
Prathouse Cottage
South Knowe
Windmill Knowe
Sch
Southfod Farm
SOUTH LARCH RD
BRAEMAR DR
CRATHIE WAY
ALFORD WAY
BIRNAM GDNS
DUNLIN DR
Dry Arch
Woodlee Poultry Farm
1 CALLANDER TERR
2 BRODICK GDNS
3 ARNISTON RD
4 BRODIE WLK
5 KINTAIL PL
6 CRINAN PL
FIELDFARE VIEW
KY11
The Den
Prathouse
KINGFISHER PL
TRONDHEIM PARKWAY
MAVOR GDNS
GREENSHANK DR
SANDPIPER DR
Annfield Cottages
Calais Muir Wood
Annfield
LINBURN RD
BRAMBLING RD
BITTERN CT
LINNET WAY
PETREL WAY
CURLEW GDNS
MALLARD GR
Calais
Duloch Schs & Com Campus
P
L Ctr
GREBE GDNS
CALAIS VIEW
TERN RD
NIGHTINGALE PL
TURNSTONE RD
Liby
VORLICH WAY
BENNACHIE WAY
LORNE
INVEREWE PL
DUNDONNELL WAY
MEY CT
EDZELL WAY
FEDDER RD
PRIORWOOD DR
PITMEDDEN
PRIORWOOD DR
THREAVE LOAN
PLOVER CRES
VRACKIE PL
TIRRAN DR
CAITHNESS DR
KYLE CRES
GLAMAING WAY
TARMACHEN RD
CROMAR DR
COWAL PL
1 NITHSDALE PL
2 DEESIDE PL
Pitadro Craigs
B981
M90
INVEREWE PL
B916
ABERDOUR RD
BRUCE GDNS
A B C D E F
8 7 89 6 5 88 4 3 87 2 1 86
12 13 14

161 174

147
164

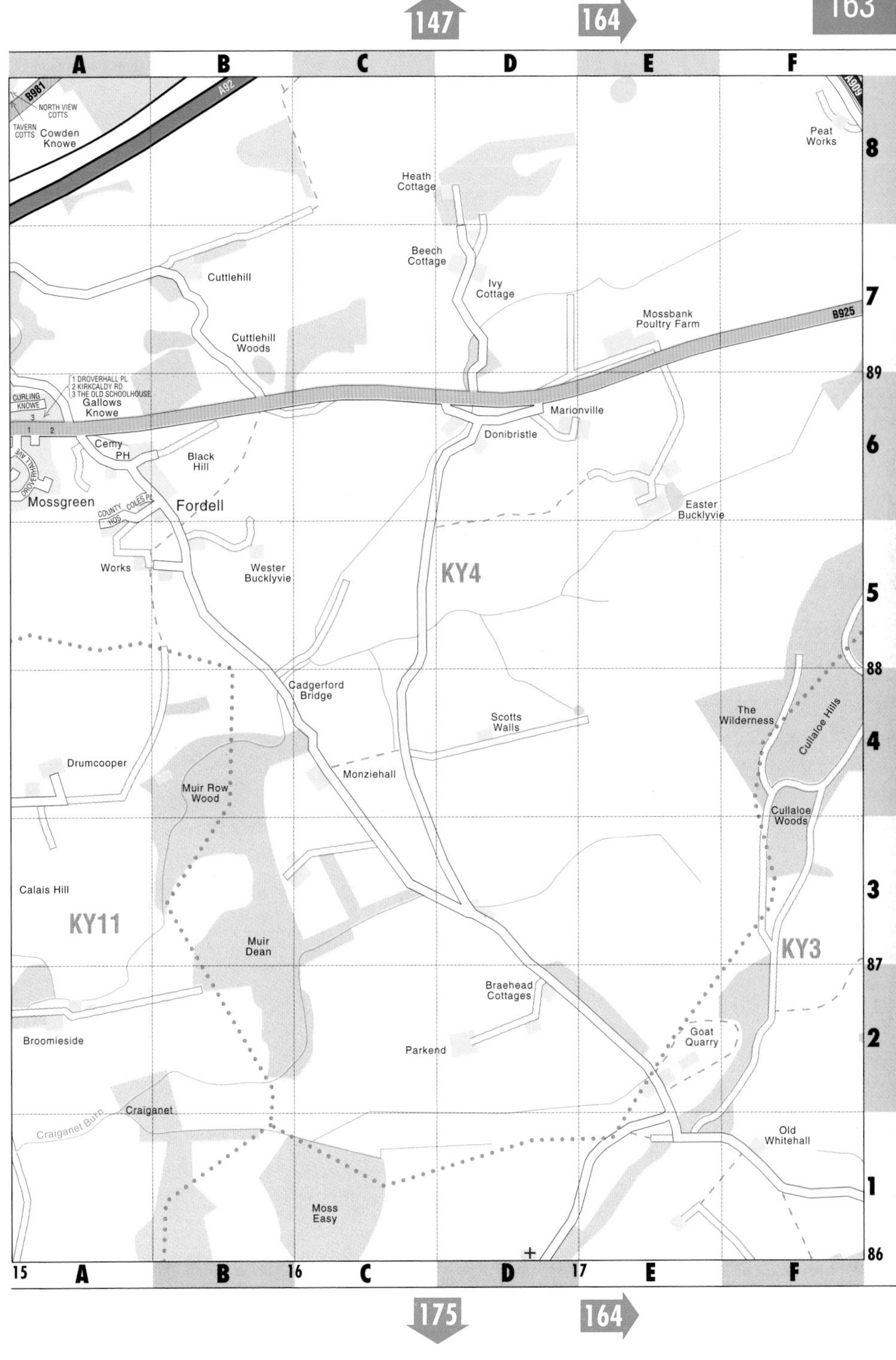
A
B
C
D
E
F
B981
NORTH VIEW COTTS
TAVERN COTTS
Cowden Knowe
A92
A909
Peat Works
8
Heath Cottage
Beech Cottage
Ivy Cottage
Cuttlehill
7
Cuttlehill Woods
Mossbank Poultry Farm
B925
89
1 DROVERHALL PL
2 KIRKCALDY RD
3 THE OLD SCHOOLHOUSE
CURLING KNOWE
Gallows Knowe
Marionville
Donibristle
Cemy
PH
Black Hill
6
DROVERHALL AVE
Mossgreen
COUNTY HOS
COLES PL
Fordell
Easter Bucklyvie
Works
Wester Bucklyvie
KY4
5
88
Cadgerford Bridge
The Wilderness
Cullaloe Hills
Scotts Walls
4
Drumcooper
Monziehall
Muir Row Wood
Cullaloe Woods
Calais Hill
3
KY11
Muir Dean
KY3
87
Braehead Cottages
Goat Quarry
2
Broomieside
Parkend
Craiganet
Craiganet Burn
Old Whitehall
1
Moss Easy
86
15
16
17

175
164

163
148

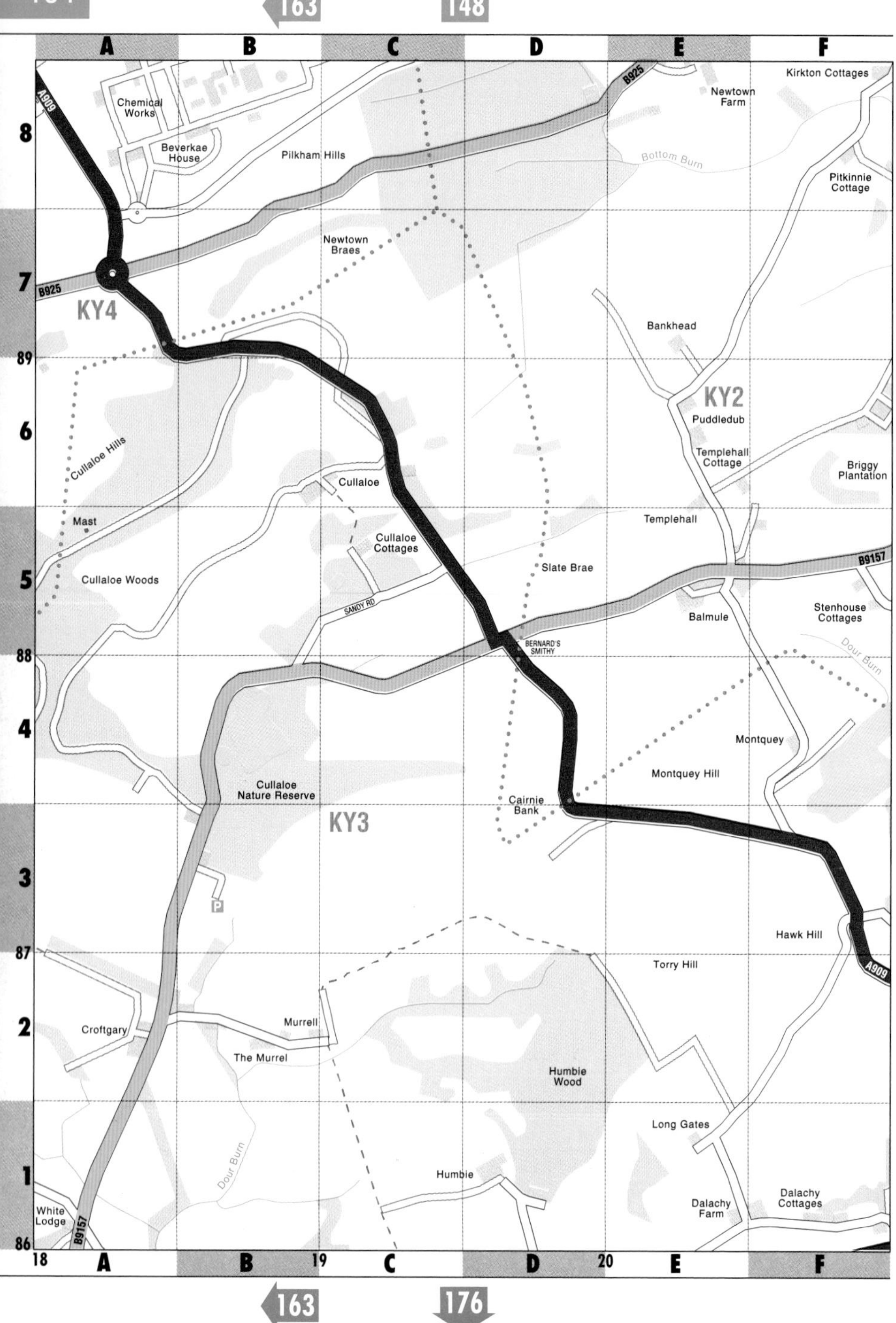
A
B
C
D
E
F
8
7
89
6
5
88
4
3
87
2
1
86
18
19
20
A909
B925
B9157
Chemical Works
Beverkae House
Pilkham Hills
Newtown Farm
Kirkton Cottages
Bottom Burn
Pitkinnie Cottage
Newtown Braes
KY4
Bankhead
KY2
Puddledub
Templehall Cottage
Briggy Plantation
Cullaloe Hills
Cullaloe
Mast
Templehall
Cullaloe Cottages
Slate Brae
Cullaloe Woods
SANDY RD
Stenhouse Cottages
Balmule
BERNARD'S SMITHY
Dour Burn
Montquey
Montquey Hill
Cullaloe Nature Reserve
Cairnie Bank
KY3
P
Hawk Hill
Torry Hill
Croftgary
Murrell
The Murrel
Humbie Wood
Long Gates
Dour Burn
Humbie
White Lodge
Dalachy Farm
Dalachy Cottages

163
176

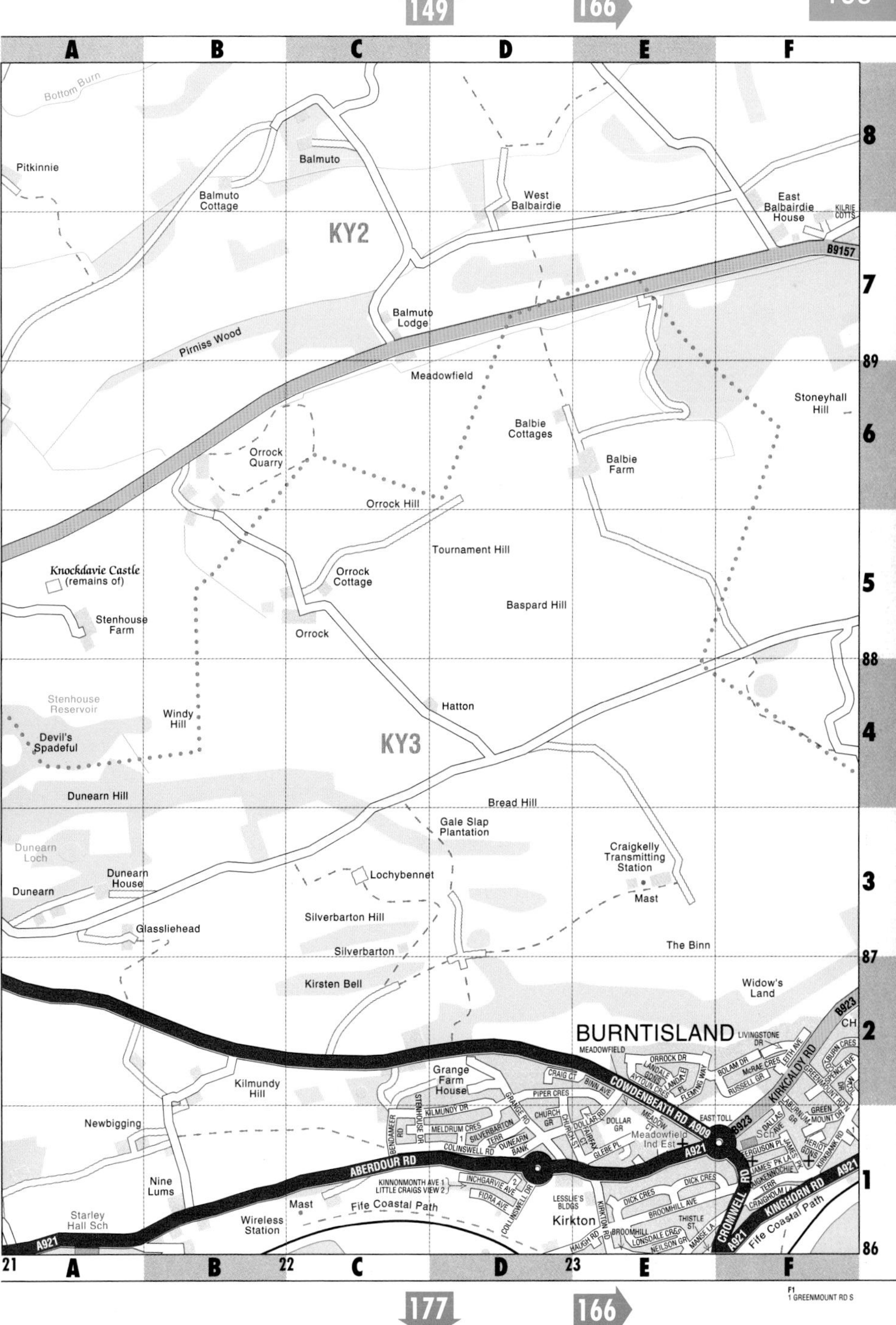

A B C D E F

8

Pitkinnie

Balmuto

Balmuto
Cottage

West
Balbairdie

East
Balbairdie
House

KILRIE
COTTS

KY2

B9157

7

Pirniss Wood

Balmuto
Lodge

89

Meadowfield

Stoneyhall
Hill

Balbie
Cottages

6

Orrock
Quarry

Balbie
Farm

Orrock Hill

Tournament Hill

Knockdavie Castle
(remains of)

Orrock
Cottage

5

Baspard Hill

Stenhouse
Farm

Orrock

88

Stenhouse
Reservoir

Windy
Hill

Hatton

KY3

4

Devil's
Spadeful

Dunearn Hill

Bread Hill

Gale Slap
Plantation

Craigkelly
Transmitting
Station

Dunearn
Loch

Dunearn
House

Lochybennet

3

Dunearn

Mast

Glassliehead

Silverbarton Hill

The Binn

87

Silverbarton

Kirsten Bell

Widow's
Land

BURNTISLAND

LIVINGSTONE
DR

B923

CH

2

MEADOWFIELD

ORROCK DR

BOLAM DR

KIRKCALDY RD

GREEN
MOUNT CT

Kilmundy
Hill

Grange
Farm
House

CRAIG OF

CHURCH
GR

COWDENBEATH RD A909

EAST TOLL

B923

Newbigging

KILMUNDY DR

MELDRUM CRES

SILVERBARTON

DOLLAR GR

DOLLAR RD

Meadowhill
Ind Est

FERGUSON ST

CROMWELL RD

KINGHORN RD A921

Nine
Lums

ABERDOUR RD

COLINSWELL RD

DUNEARN
BANK

GLEBE PL

A921

1

KINNONMONTH AVE 1
LITTLE CRAIGS VIEW 2

INCHGARVIE
AVE

DICK CRES

DICK CRES

Starley
Hall Sch

Mast

Wireless
Station

FIDRA AVE

Fife Coastal Path

LESSLIE'S
BLDGS

Kirkton

BROOMHILL

BROOMHILL AVE

LONSDALE CRES

NEILSON GR

THISTLE
ST

Fife Coastal Path

86

A921

21

A

B

22

C

D

23

E

F

F1
1 GREENMOUNT RD S

165 150

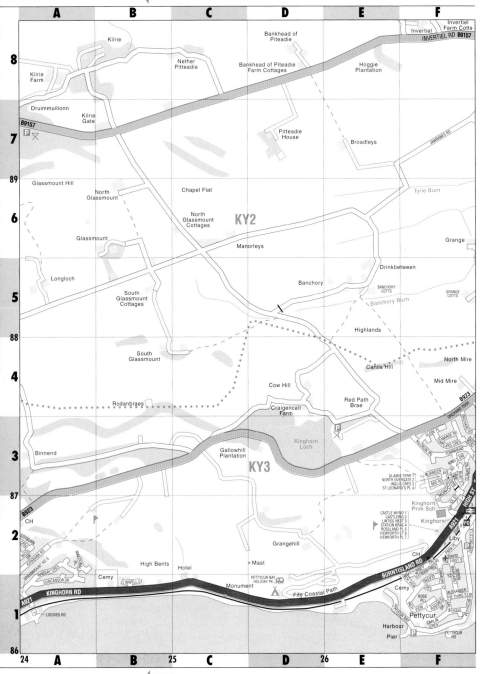

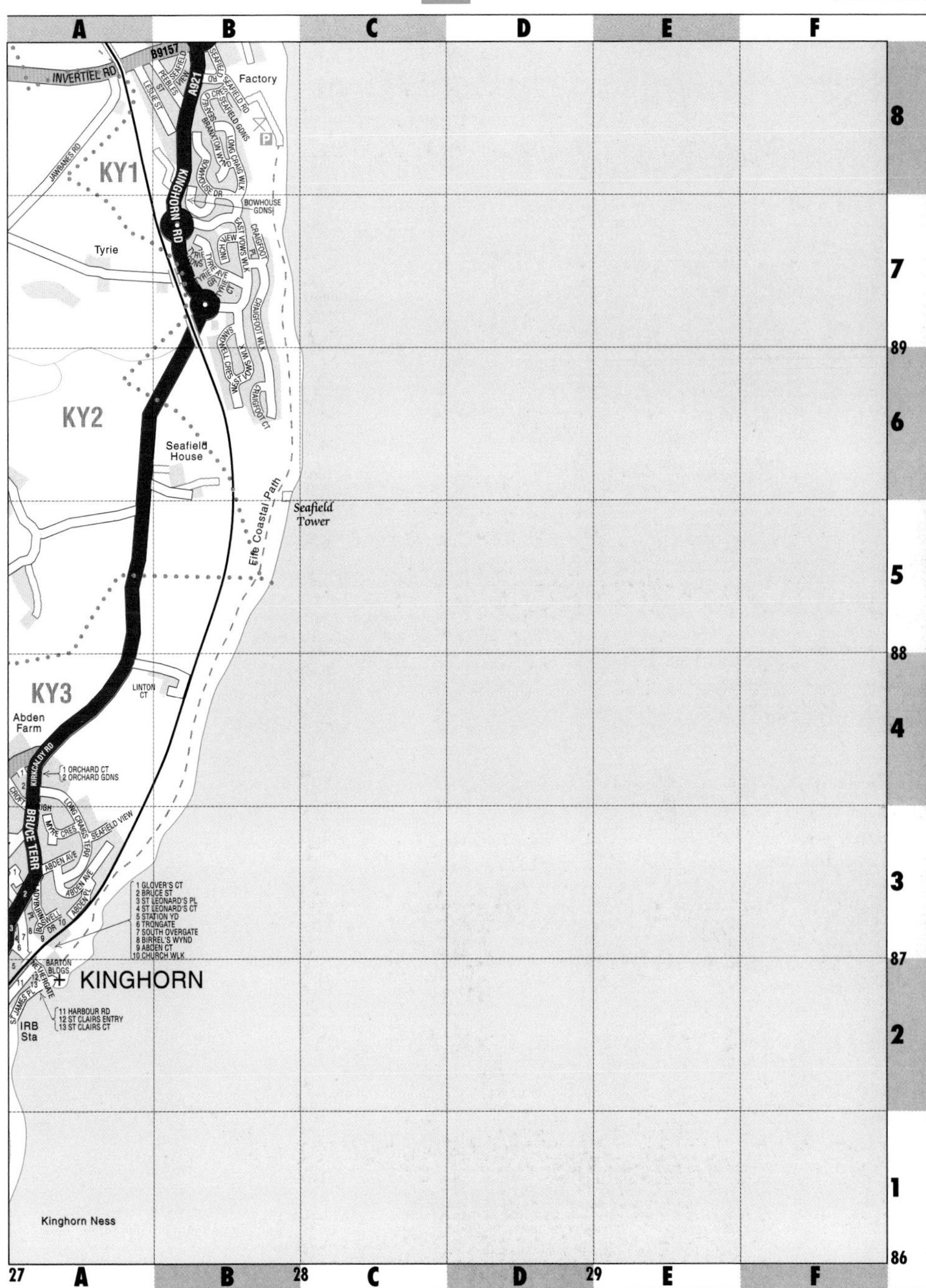

	A	**B**	**C**	**D**	**E**	**F**	

INVERTIEL RD

B9157

A921

Factory

KINGHORN RD

KY1

BOWHOUSE GDNS

Tyrie

KY2

Seafield House

Fife Coastal Path

Seafield Tower

KY3

LINTON CT

Abden Farm

1 ORCHARD CT
2 ORCHARD GDNS

BRUCE TERR

SEAFIELD VIEW

1 GLOVER'S CT
2 BRUCE ST
3 ST LEONARD'S PL
4 ST LEONARD'S CT
5 STATION YD
6 TRONGATE
7 SOUTH OVERGATE
8 BIRREL'S WYND
9 ABDEN CT
10 CHURCH WLK

BARTON BLDGS

KINGHORN

11 HARBOUR RD
12 ST CLAIRS ENTRY
13 ST CLAIRS CT

IRB Sta

Kinghorn Ness

27 A   B   28   C   D   29   E   F

156

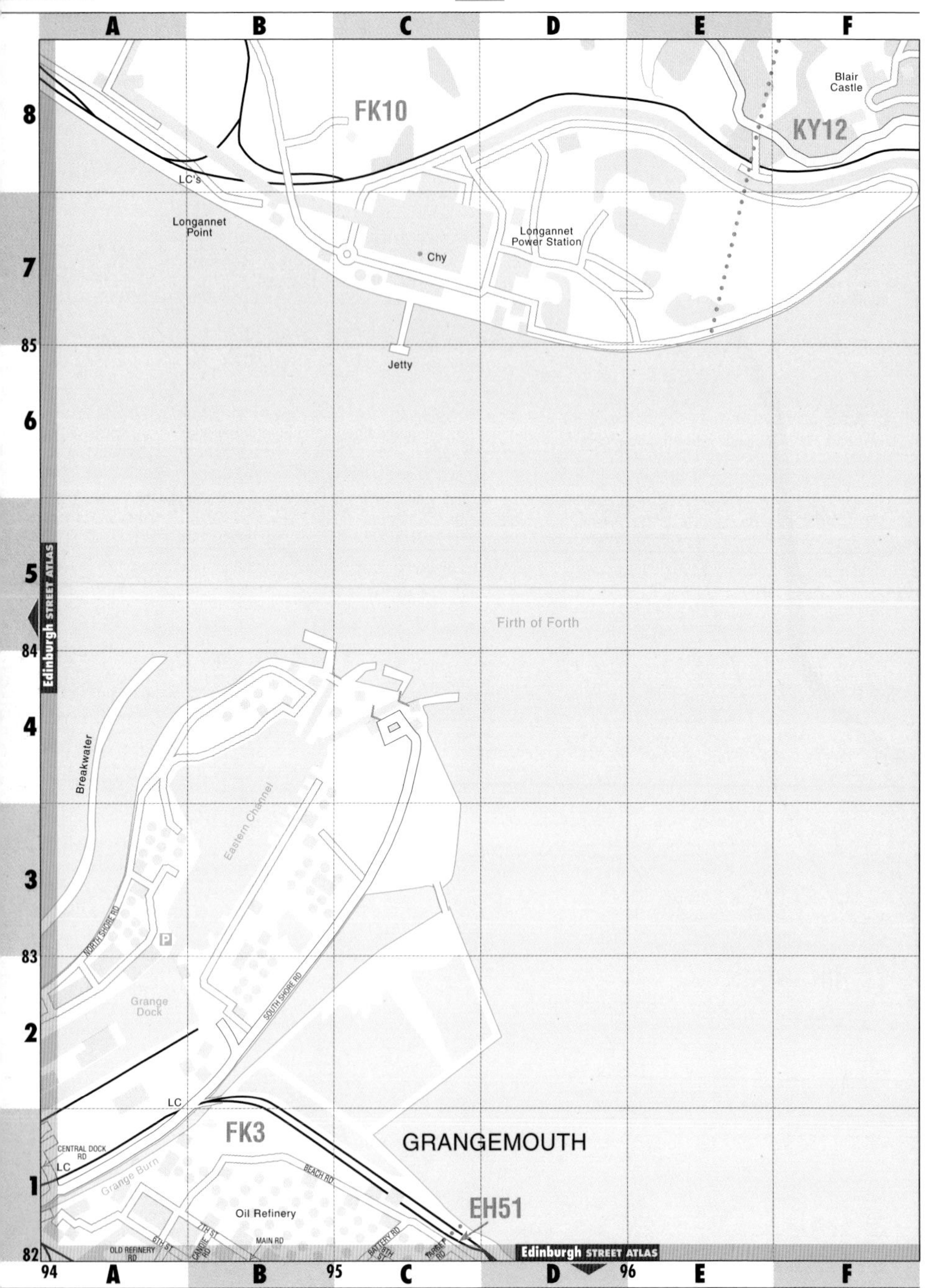
A
B
C
D
E
F
8
7
85
6
5
84
4
3
83
2
1
82
94
95
96
FK10
KY12
Blair Castle
LC's
Longannet Point
Longannet Power Station
Chy
Jetty
Firth of Forth
Edinburgh STREET ATLAS
Breakwater
Eastern Channel
NORTH SHORE RD
P
Grange Dock
SOUTH SHORE RD
LC
FK3
GRANGEMOUTH
CENTRAL DOCK RD
Grange Burn
BEACH RD
EH51
Oil Refinery
OLD REFINERY RD
6TH ST
7TH ST
CANDIE RD
MAIN RD
BATTERY RD
TARBET RD

157   170

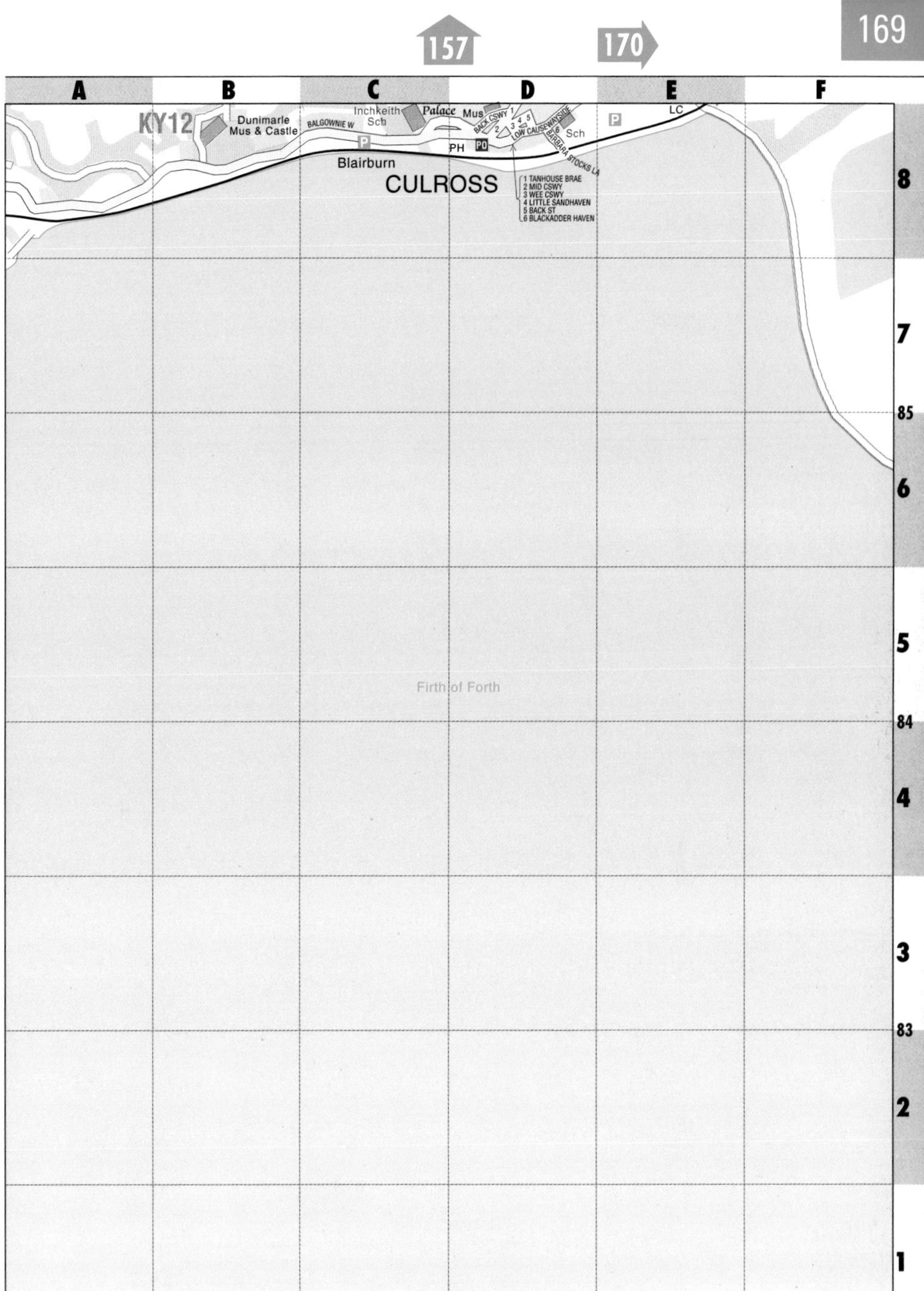

KY12

Dunimarle
Mus & Castle

Inchkeith
Sch
BALGOWNIE W

Palace Mus

Blairburn

CULROSS

PH PO

1 TANHOUSE BRAE
2 MID CSWY
3 WEE CSWY
4 LITTLE SANDHAVEN
5 BACK ST
6 BLACKADDER HAVEN

LC

Sch

Firth of Forth

West Pier

8
85
7
6
85
6
5
84
4
3
83
2
82
1

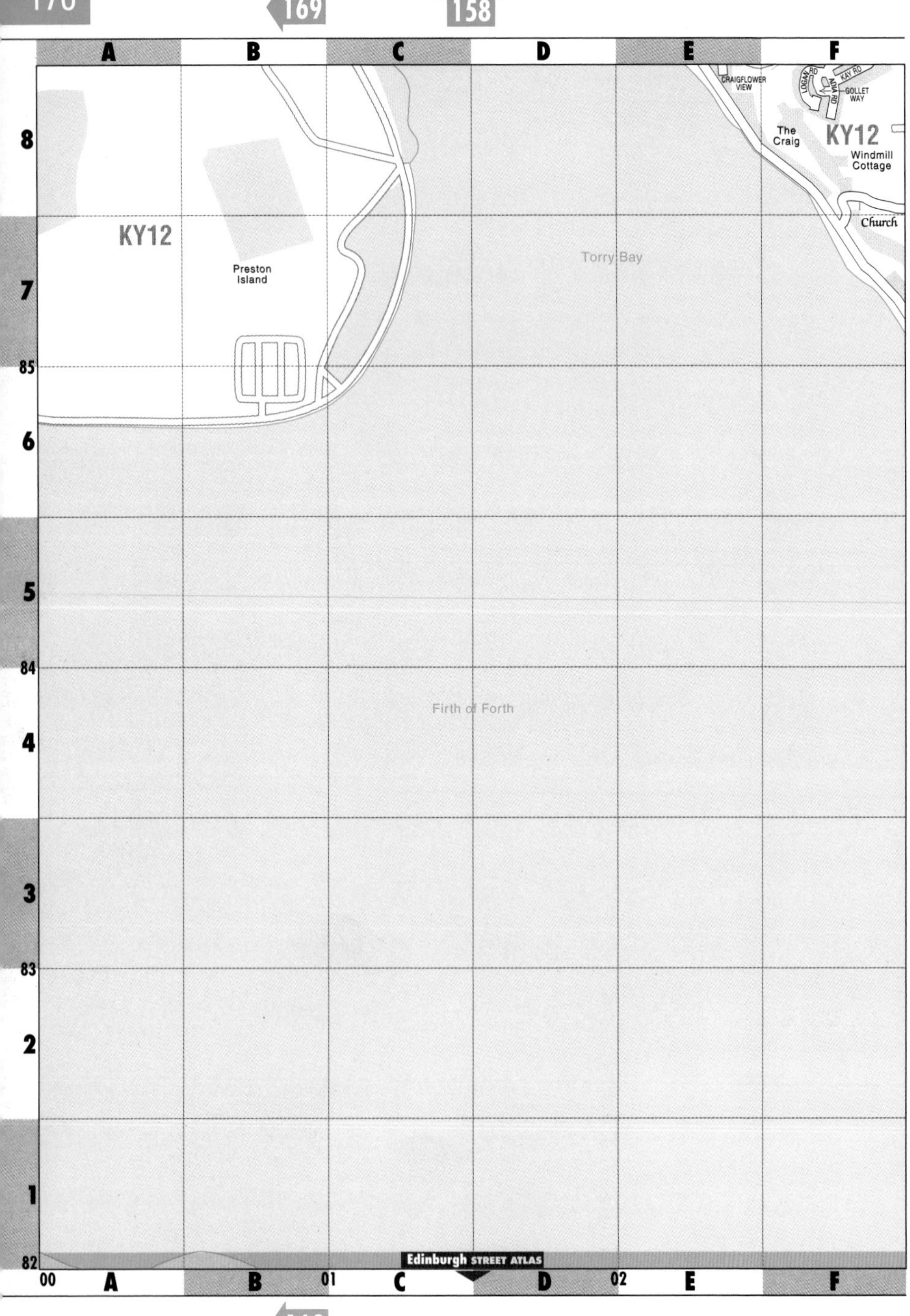

KY12

Preston
Island

Torry Bay

CRAIGFLOWER
VIEW

The
Craig

KY12

Windmill
Cottage

Church

Firth of Forth

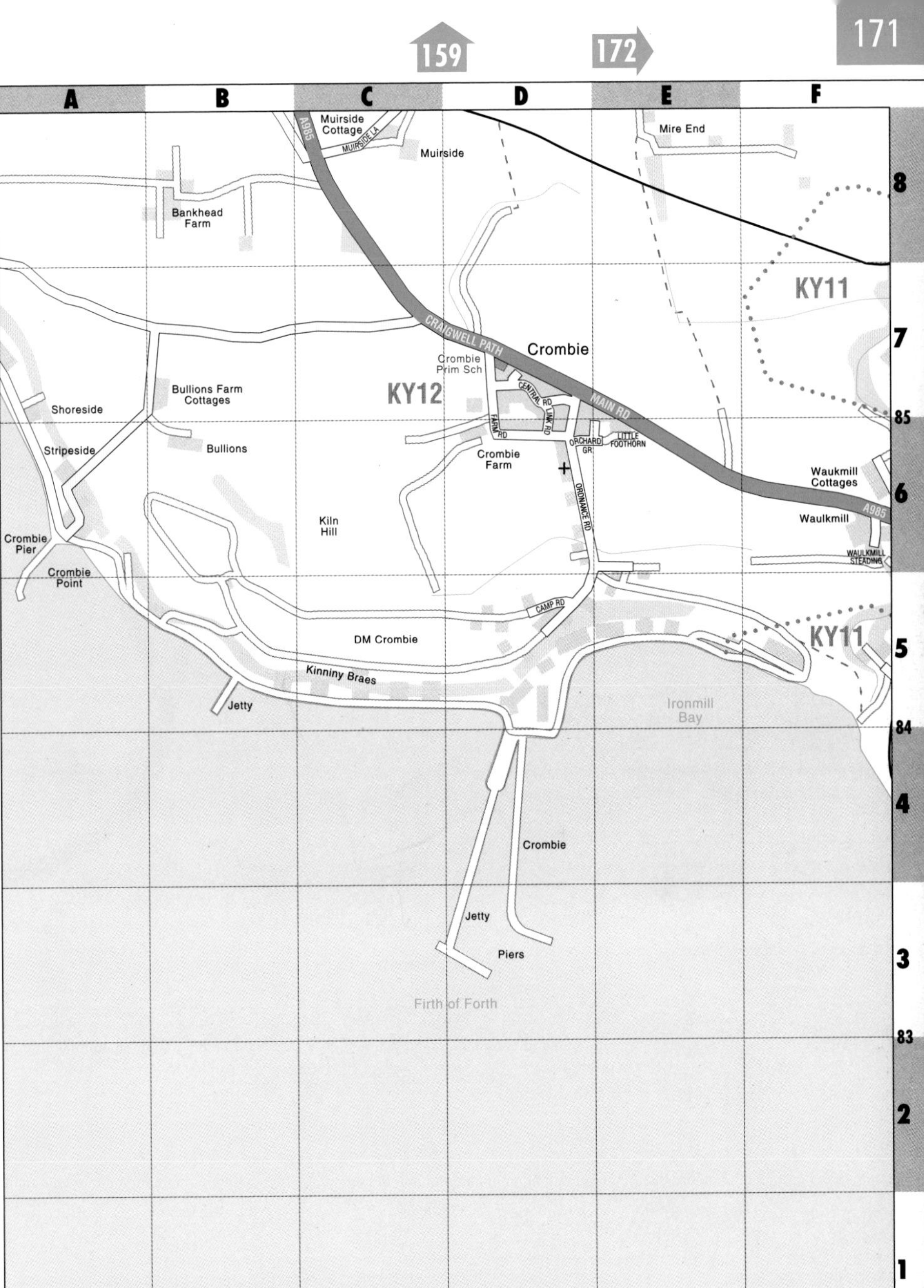

A   B   C   D   E   F

8

KY11

7

Muirside
Cottage
Muirside

Mire End

Bankhead
Farm

CRAIGWELL PATH

Crombie

Crombie
Prim Sch

KY12

Shoreside

Bullions Farm
Cottages

85

Stripeside

Bullions

CENTRAL RD

MAIN RD

ORCHARD
GR

LITTLE
FOOTHORN

Waukmill
Cottages

Crombie
Farm

FARM RD

LINK RD

6

Kiln
Hill

Waulkmill

A985

DRUMMANS RD

WAULKMILL
STEADING

Crombie
Pier

Crombie
Point

KY11

5

DM Crombie

CAMP RD

Kinniny Braes

84

Jetty

Ironmill
Bay

4

Crombie

Jetty

3

Piers

83

Firth of Forth

2

1

82

03   A   B   04   C   D   05   E   F

171
160

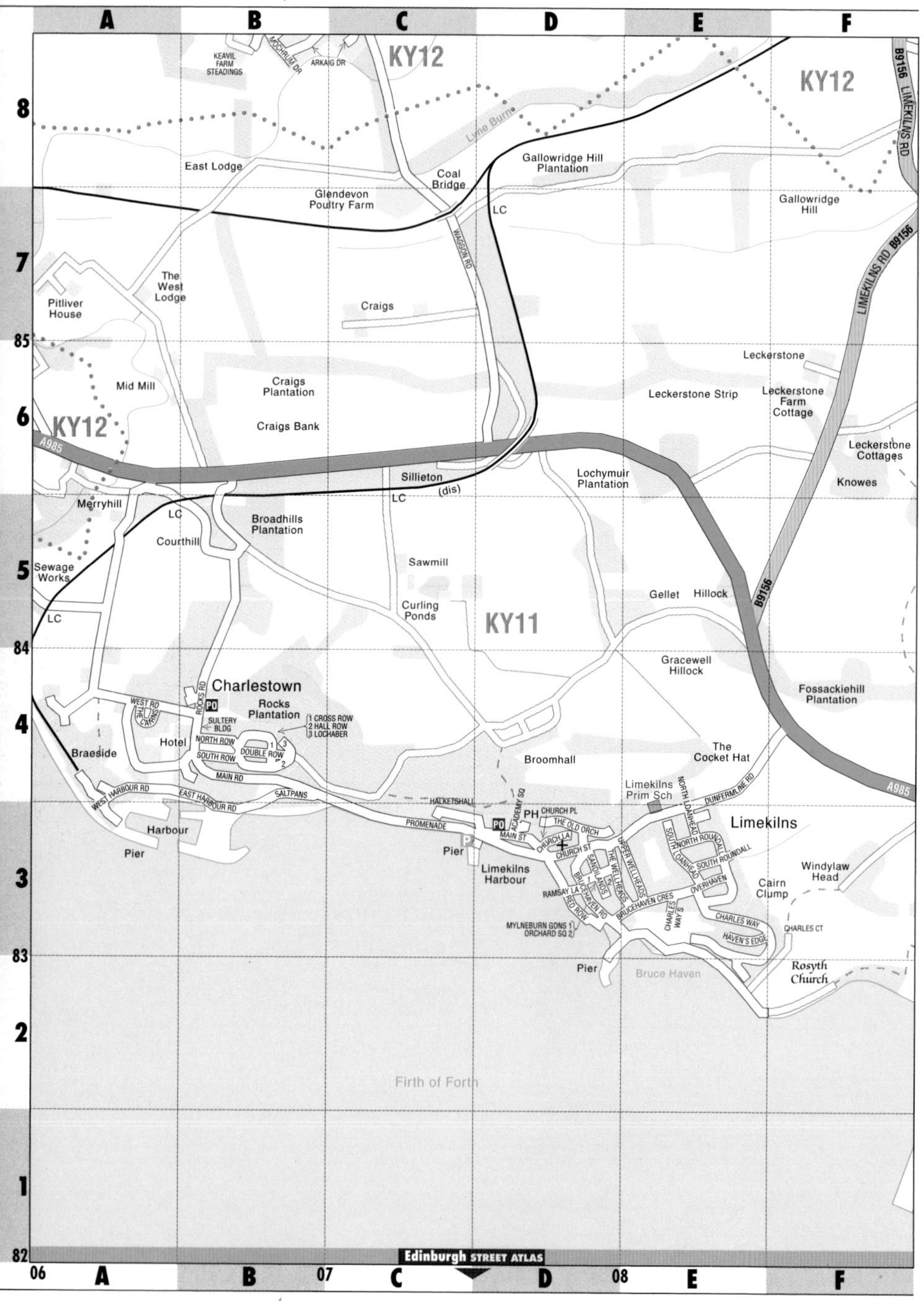
KY12
KY11
East Lodge
Glendevon Poultry Farm
Coal Bridge
Gallowridge Hill Plantation
Gallowridge Hill
Lyne Burn
The West Lodge
Pitliver House
Craigs
Mid Mill
Craigs Plantation
Craigs Bank
Leckerstone
Leckerstone Strip
Leckerstone Farm Cottage
Leckerstone Cottages
Knowes
Sillieton (dis)
Lochymuir Plantation
Merryhill
Broadhills Plantation
Courthill
Sewage Works
Sawmill
Curling Ponds
Gellet Hillock
Gracewell Hillock
Fossackiehill Plantation
Charlestown
Rocks Plantation
Hotel
Braeside
Harbour
Pier
Broomhall
The Cocket Hat
Limekilns Prim Sch
Limekilns
Limekilns Harbour
Windylaw Head
Cairn Clump
Rosyth Church
Bruce Haven
Firth of Forth
A985
B9156
LIMEKILNS RD
WAGGON RD
KEAVIL FARM STEADINGS
MOCHRUM DR
ARKAIG DR
ROCKS RD
WEST RD
THE CAIRNS
SULTERY BLDG
NORTH ROW
SOUTH ROW
DOUBLE ROW
1 CROSS ROW
2 HALL ROW
3 LOCHABER
MAIN RD
WEST HARBOUR RD
EAST HARBOUR RD
SALTPANS
HALKETSHALL
PROMENADE
ACADEMY SQ
CHURCH PL
THE OLD ORCH
MAIN ST
CHURCH LA
CHURCH ST
SANDILANDS
THE WELLHEADS
UPPER WELLHEADS
NORTH LOANHEAD
SOUTH LOANHEAD
NORTH ROUNDALL
SOUTH ROUNDALL
DUNFERMLINE RD
OVERHAVEN
BRUCEHAVEN CRES
BRUCEHAVEN RD
RAMSAY LA
RED ROW
CHARLES WAY
CHARLES WAYS
HAVEN'S EDGE
CHARLES CT
MYLNEBURN GDNS 1
ORCHARD SQ 2
LC
PO
PH
Edinburgh STREET ATLAS

171

161
174

Hill House
Grange Mount
KY12
Grange
Easter Gellet
Wester Gellet
Bellknowes
Bell Hills
Blackhall
Douglas Bank
Douglasbank Cemy
Pattiesmuir
Brucehaven Cottage
Hilton
HMS Caledonia
Rosyth Royal Dockyard
HM Naval Base
Cromarty Campus
Ferry Terminal
Rosyth Castle (remains of)
Rosyth Europarc
Forties Campus
Pitreavie Bsns Pk
Pitreavie Playing Fields
Carnegie Campus (Bsns Pk)
Pitreavie Ind Est
Pitreavie Castle
North Wood
Crem
Primrose Ind Est
Primrose
KY11
Camdean Prim Sch
Brankholm
Admiralty Park
Pease Hill
Playing Fields
St John's RC Prim Sch
ROSYTH
The Wilderness
Castlandhill Woods
QUEENSFERRY RD
ADMIRALTY RD
A823
A823 (M)
B980
A985
B9156

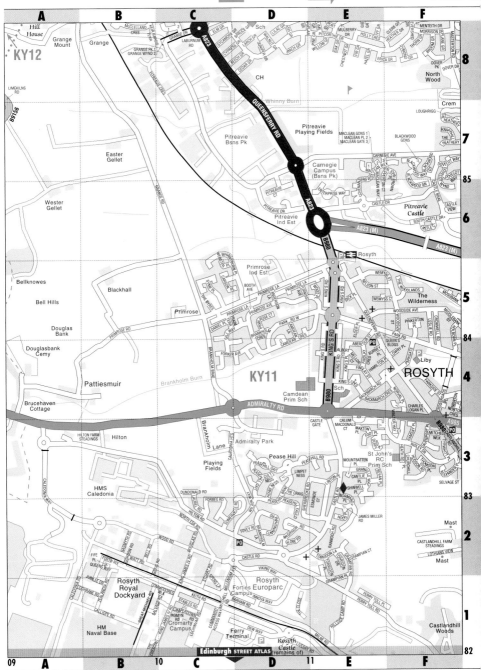

173
162

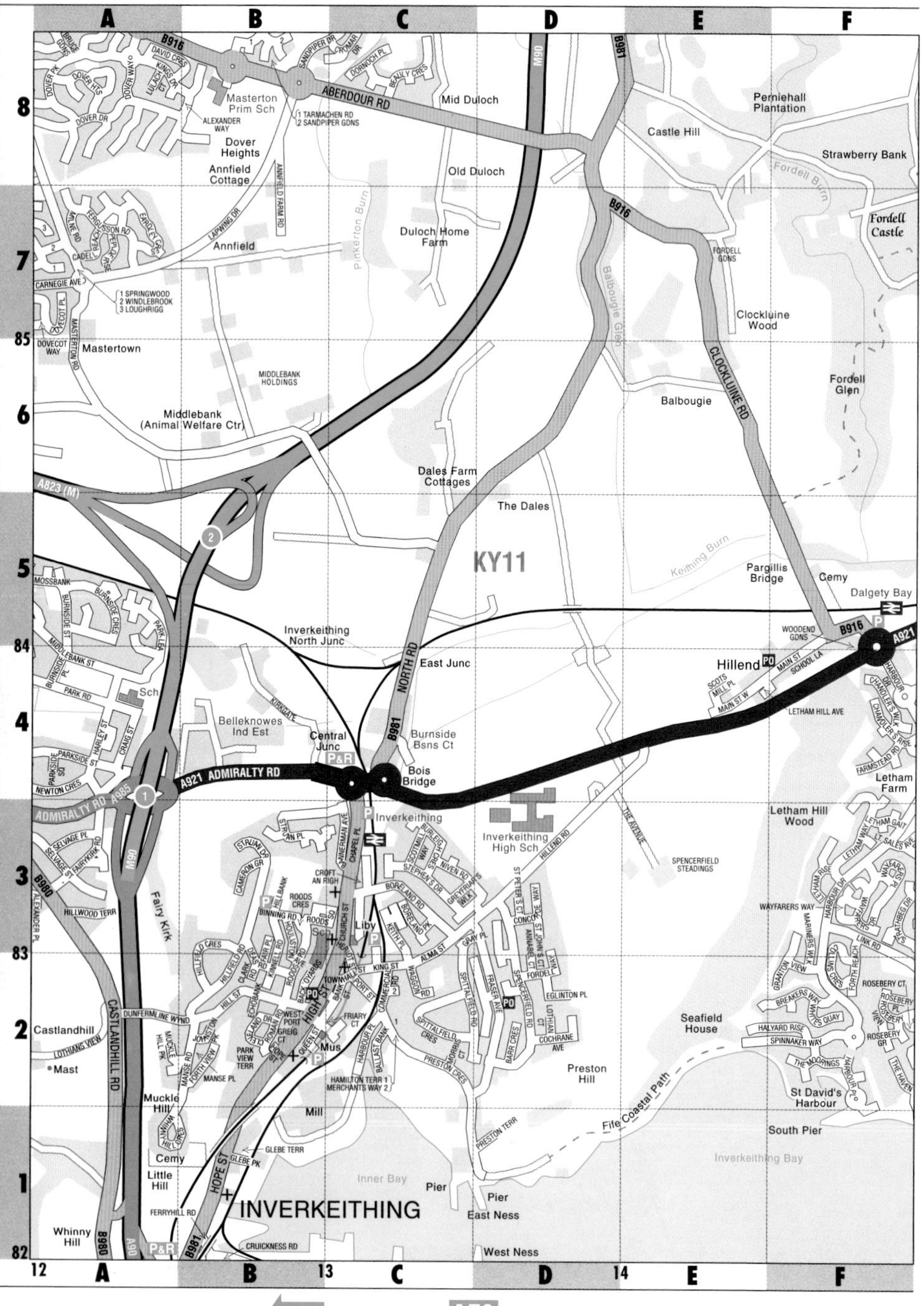
A
B
C
D
E
F
8
7
85
6
5
84
4
3
83
2
1
82
12
13
14
Aberdour Rd
Mid Duloch
Masterton Prim Sch
Dover Heights
Annfield Cottage
Old Duloch
Perniehall Plantation
Castle Hill
Strawberry Bank
Fordell Castle
Duloch Home Farm
Annfield
Pinkerton Burn
Clockluine Wood
Mastertown
Middlebank Holdings
Middlebank (Animal Welfare Ctr)
Balbougie
Fordell Glen
Dales Farm Cottages
The Dales
KY11
Keithing Burn
Pargillis Bridge
Cemy
Dalgety Bay
Inverkeithing North Junc
East Junc
Hillend
Belleknowes Ind Est
Central Junc
Burnside Bsns Ct
Bois Bridge
A921 Admiralty Rd
Letham Farm
Letham Hill Wood
Inverkeithing
Inverkeithing High Sch
Spencerfield Steadings
Fairy Kirk
Castlandhill
Mast
Seafield House
Preston Hill
Fife Coastal Path
St David's Harbour
South Pier
Inverkeithing Bay
Muckle Hill
Mill
Cemy
Little Hill
Inner Bay
Pier
Pier
East Ness
INVERKEITHING
Whinny Hill
West Ness
Castlandhill Rd
Hope St
High St
Cruickness Rd

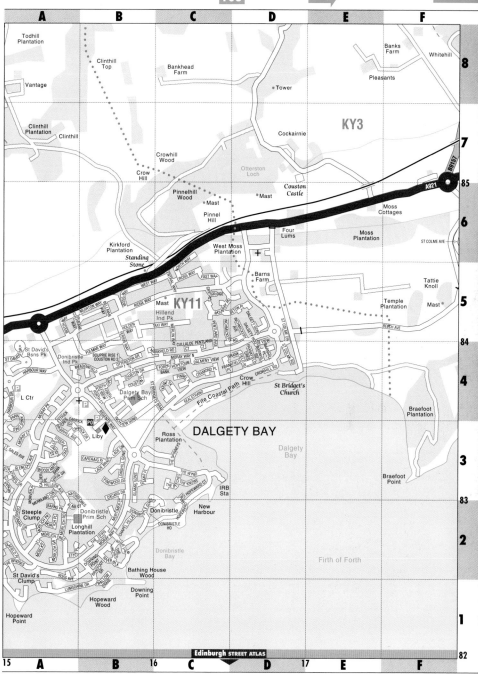

A | B | C | D | E | F

8

Todhill Plantation

Clinthill Top

Bankhead Farm

Banks Farm

Whitehill

Vantage

Tower

Pleasants

Clinthill Plantation

Clinthill

KY3

Cockairnie

7

Crowhill Wood

Otterston Loch

A921

B9157

85

Crow Hill

Couston Castle

Pinnelhill Wood

Mast

Mast

Moss Cottages

6

Kirkford Plantation

Pinnel Hill

West Moss Plantation

Four Lums

Moss Plantation

St COLME AVE

Standing Stone

WEST WAY

CENTRAL WAY

CROSS WAY

FAST WAY

NORTH WAY

Barns Farm

Temple Plantation

Tattie Knoll

Mast

5

Mast

KY11

RIDGE WAY

MURTON WAY

Hillend Ind Pk

TAXI WAY

HOLDEN WAY

MORAY WAY N

NICHOLSON WAY

ST COLME AVE

BEECH AVE

84

St David's Bsns Pk

ST DAVID'S

Donibristle Ind Pk

FULMAR WAY

MEADOWFIELD

BOUPRIE RISE
COUSTON RD

PRESTON DR

CULLALOE PENTLAND

MORAY WAY S

HOPE TOWN VIEW

PINKIE

DALMENY VIEW

ORMOND PL

FRANKFIELD

ST DAVID'S DR

HOLDEN VIEW

CROW VIEW

Crow Hill

CROWHILL RD

St Bridget's Church

Braefoot Plantation

4

HARBOUR WAY

L Ctr

FORTH

COUSTON

ST BRIDGET'S DR

Dalgety Bay Prim Sch

SEALSTRAND

Fife Coastal Path

3

PARK

CARRICK

VIEW SONS

P

Liby

Ross Plantation

DALGETY BAY

Dalgety Bay

Braefoot Point

CARCRAIG PL

JADE RIDGE

THE STANDS

THE WYND

THE KNOWE

THE WYND

THE KNOWS

HOPEWARD CT

IRB Sta

83

Steeple Clump

Donibristle Prim Sch

BARNS PK

Donibristle

Donibristle HO

New Harbour

2

Longhill Plantation

Donibristle Bay

Firth of Forth

THE BRIDGES

ROSS AVE

St David's Clump

LUMSDAINE DR

Bathing House Wood

Downing Point

1

Hopeward Point

Hopeward Wood

82

15 | A | B | 16 | C | D | 17 | E | F

175
164

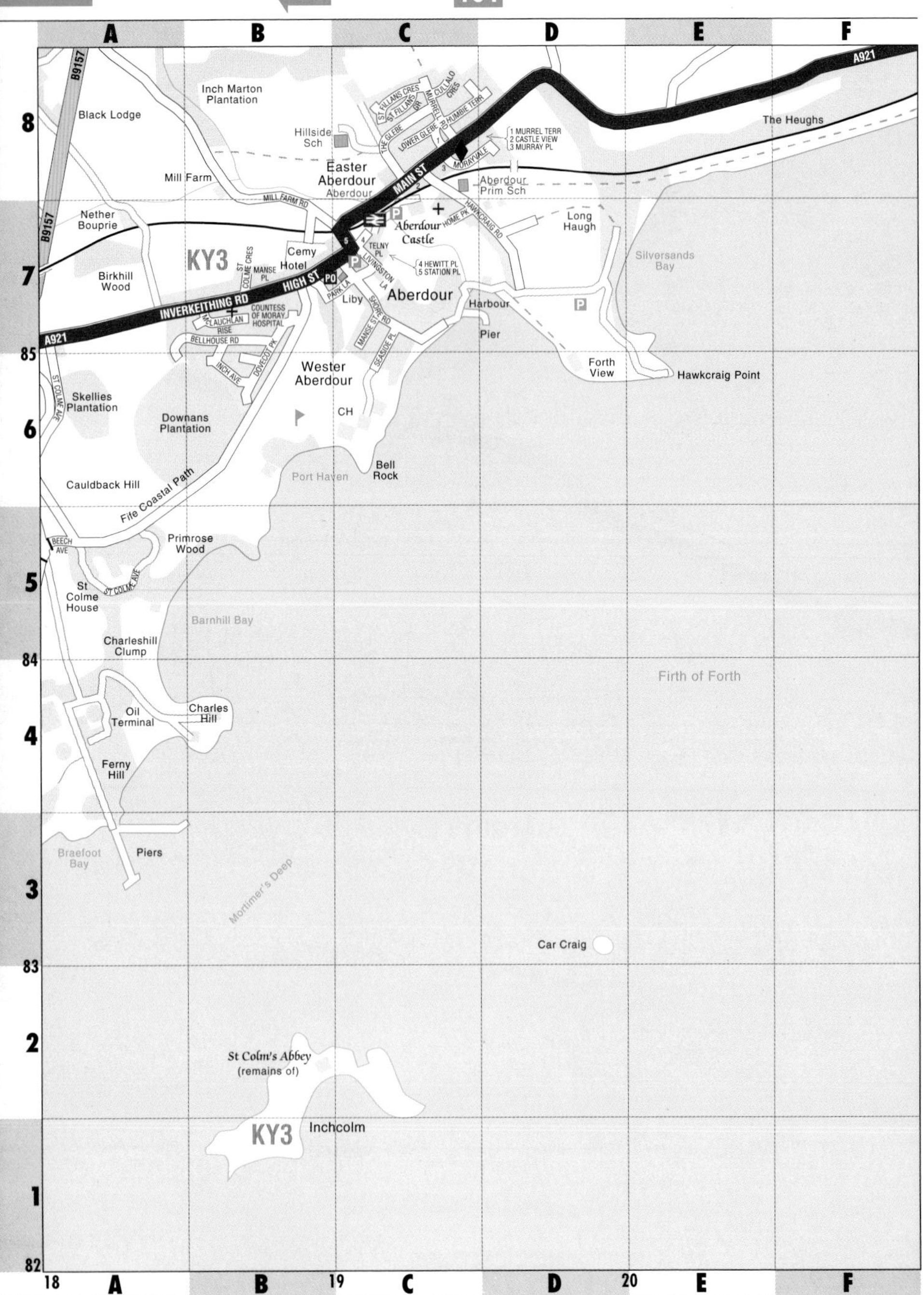
A
B
C
D
E
F
8
7
85
6
5
84
4
3
83
2
1
82
18
19
20
B9157
Black Lodge
Inch Marton Plantation
Hillside Sch
Mill Farm
Easter Aberdour
Aberdour
Nether Bouprie
MILL FARM RD
ST FILLANS CRES
ST FILLANS DR
MURRELL RD
CULLALO CRES
HUMBIE TERR
THE GLEBE
LOWER GLEBE
MAIN ST
MORAYVALE
1 MURREL TERR
2 CASTLE VIEW
3 MURRAY PL
Aberdour Prim Sch
A921
The Heughs
Aberdour Castle
HOME PK
HAWKCRAIG RD
Long Haugh
Silversands Bay
KY3
Cemy
Hotel
ST COLME CRES
MANSE PL
TELNY PL
LIVINGSTON LA
4 HEWITT PL
5 STATION PL
Birkhill Wood
HIGH ST
INVERKEITHING RD
PO
PARK LA
Liby
Aberdour
Harbour
COUNTESS OF MORAY HOSPITAL
McLAUCHLAN RISE
BELLHOUSE RD
SHORE RD
MANSE ST
SEASIDE PL
Pier
INCH AVE
DOVECOT PK
Wester Aberdour
Forth View
Hawkcraig Point
ST COLME AVE
Skellies Plantation
CH
Downans Plantation
Bell Rock
Port Haven
Cauldback Hill
Fife Coastal Path
Primrose Wood
BEECH AVE
St Colme House
ST COLME AVE
Barnhill Bay
Charleshill Clump
Firth of Forth
Oil Terminal
Charles Hill
Ferny Hill
Braefoot Bay
Piers
Mortimer's Deep
Car Craig
St Colm's Abbey
(remains of)
KY3
Inchcolm

175

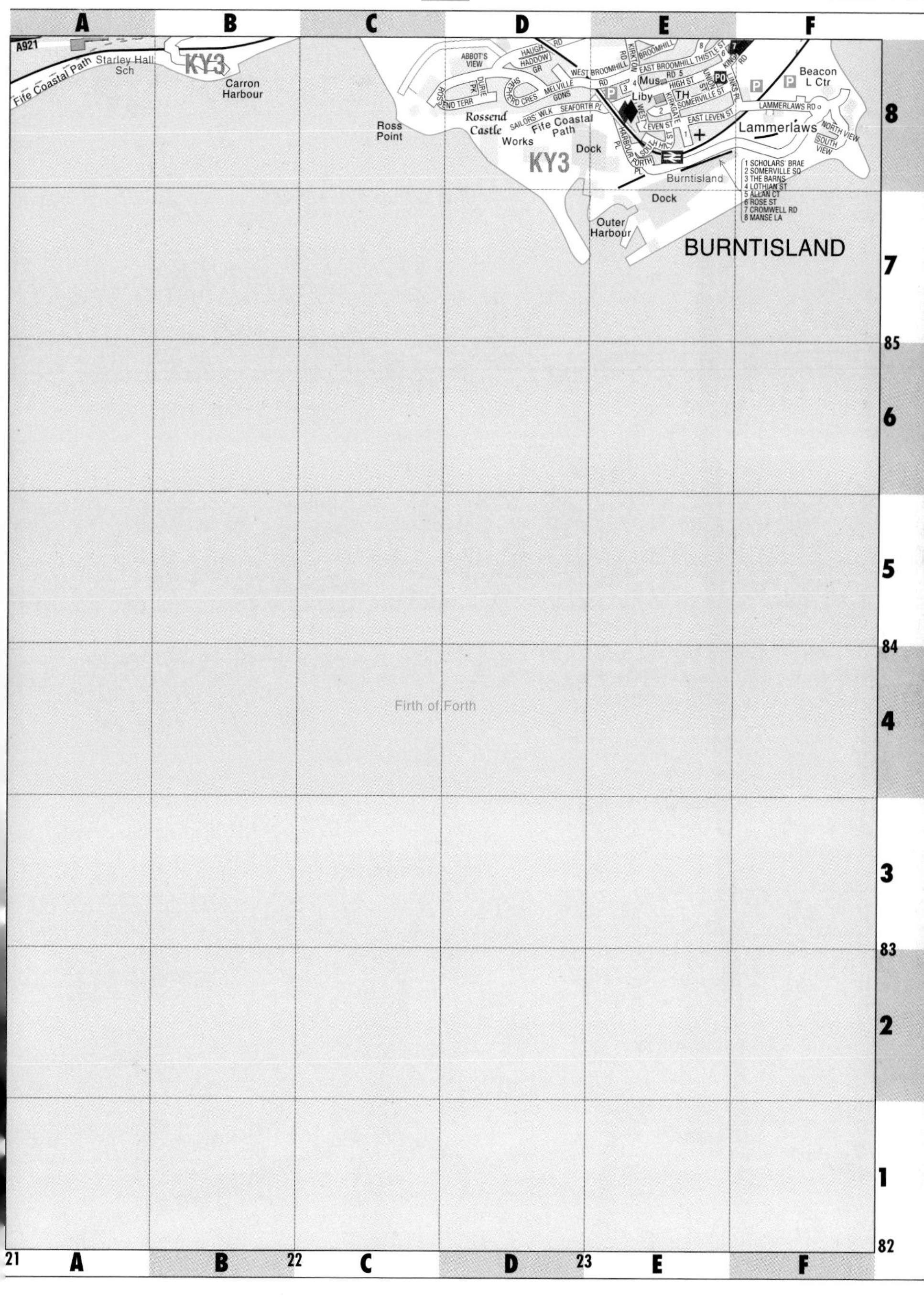

BURNTISLAND

Firth of Forth

1 SCHOLARS' BRAE
2 SOMERVILLE SQ
3 THE BARNS
4 LOTHIAN ST
5 ALLAN ST
6 ROSE ST
7 CROMWELL RD
8 MANSE LA

KY3

Carron Harbour

Fife Coastal Path

Starley Hall Sch

Ross Point

Rossend Castle

Works

Dock

Outer Harbour

Dock

Burntisland

Lammerlaws

Beacon L Ctr

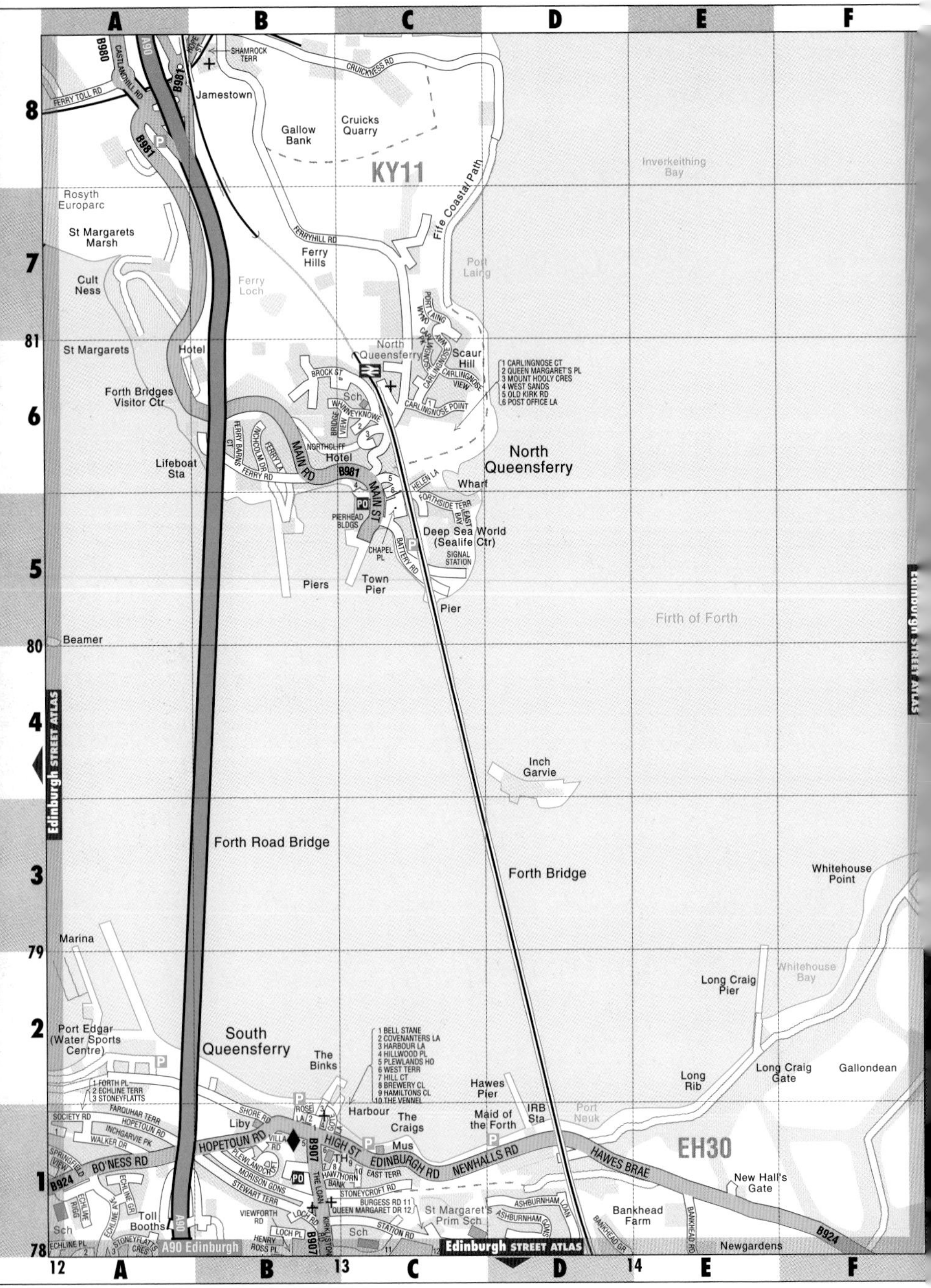

KY11

Inverkeithing
Bay

Rosyth
Europarc

St Margarets
Marsh

Cult
Ness

Port
Laing

St Margarets

Hotel

North
Queensferry

Scaur
Hill

1 CARLINGNOSE CT
2 QUEEN MARGARET S PL
3 MOUNT HOOLY CRES
4 WEST SANDS
5 OLD KIRK RD
6 POST OFFICE LA

Forth Bridges
Visitor Ctr

Lifeboat
Sta

North
Queensferry

Wharf

Deep Sea World
(Sealife Ctr)

Piers

Town
Pier

Pier

Firth of Forth

Beamer

Inch
Garvie

Forth Road Bridge

Forth Bridge

Whitehouse
Point

Marina

Whitehouse
Bay

Port Edgar
(Water Sports
Centre)

South
Queensferry

The
Binks

1 BELL STANE
2 COVENANTERS LA
3 HARBOUR LA
4 HILLWOOD PL
5 PLEWLANDS HO
6 WEST TERR
7 HILL CT
8 BREWERY CL
9 HAMILTONS CL
10 THE VENNEL

Long Craig
Pier

Long Craig
Gate

Gallondean

Long
Rib

1 FORTH PL
2 ECHLINE TERR
3 STONEYFLATTS

Harbour

The
Craigs

Hawes
Pier

Maid of
the Forth

IRB
Sta.

Port
Neuk

Liby

SOCIETY RD

HOPETOUN RD

HIGH ST

EDINBURGH RD

NEWHALLS RD

HAWES BRAE

New Hall's
Gate

EH30

BO'NESS RD

Mus

St Margaret's
Prim Sch

Bankhead
Farm

Sch

Toll
Booths

A90 Edinburgh

Sch

Newgardens

B924

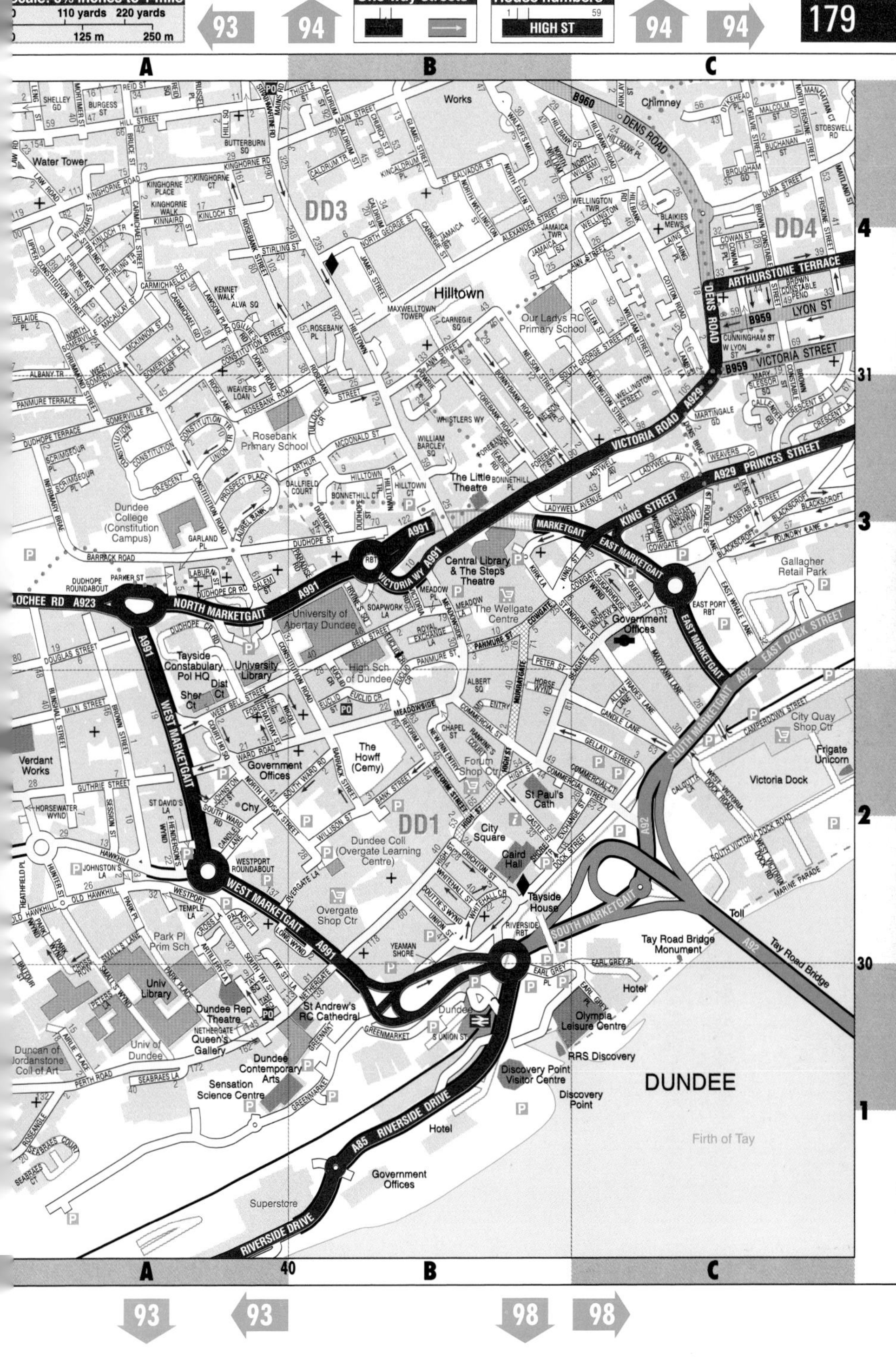

Index

Place name May be abbreviated on the map

Location number Present when a number indicates the place's position in a crowded area of mapping

Locality, town or village Shown when more than one place has the same name

Postcode district District for the indexed place

Page and grid square Page number and grid reference for the standard mapping

Church Rd 6 Beckenham BR2........53 C6

Cities, towns and villages are listed in CAPITAL LETTERS   Public and commercial buildings are highlighted in magenta
Places of interest are highlighted in blue with a star★

Abbreviations used in the index

Acad	**Academy**	Comm	**Common**	Gd	**Ground**	L	**Leisure**	Prom	**Promenade**
App	**Approach**	Cott	**Cottage**	Gdn	**Garden**	La	**Lane**	Rd	**Road**
Arc	**Arcade**	Cres	**Crescent**	Gn	**Green**	Liby	**Library**	Recn	**Recreation**
Ave	**Avenue**	Cswy	**Causeway**	Gr	**Grove**	Mdw	**Meadow**	Ret	**Retail**
Bglw	**Bungalow**	Ct	**Court**	H	**Hall**	Meml	**Memorial**	Sh	**Shopping**
Bldg	**Building**	Ctr	**Centre**	Ho	**House**	Mkt	**Market**	Sq	**Square**
Bsns, Bus	**Business**	Ctry	**Country**	Hospl	**Hospital**	Mus	**Museum**	St	**Street**
Bvd	**Boulevard**	Cty	**County**	HQ	**Headquarters**	Orch	**Orchard**	Sta	**Station**
Cath	**Cathedral**	Dr	**Drive**	Hts	**Heights**	Pal	**Palace**	Terr	**Terrace**
Cir	**Circus**	Dro	**Drove**	Ind	**Industrial**	Par	**Parade**	TH	**Town Hall**
Cl	**Close**	Ed	**Education**	Inst	**Institute**	Pas	**Passage**	Univ	**University**
Cnr	**Corner**	Emb	**Embankment**	Int	**International**	Pk	**Park**	Wk, Wlk	**Walk**
Coll	**College**	Est	**Estate**	Intc	**Interchange**	Pl	**Place**	Wr	**Water**
Com	**Community**	Ex	**Exhibition**	Junc	**Junction**	Prec	**Precinct**	Yd	**Yard**

Index of towns, villages, streets, hospitals, industrial estates, railway stations, schools, shopping centres, universities and places of interest

6th–Alb

6th St FK3. . . . . 168 A1
7th St FK3. . . . . 168 B1
8th St FK3. . . . . 168 C1

A

Abbey Craig Ct FK9. . . . . 115 D3
Abbeycraig Pk FK9 . . . . . 115 D4
Abbey Craig Rd FK10 . . . .118 B1
Abbey Cres PH2 . . . . 37 F5
Abbey Ct KY16. . . . . . . .106 E6
Abbey Gdns 8 PH13 . . . .16 A2
Abbey Kings Park Hospl
FK7. . . . . .134 F5
Abbey Mill FK8 . . . . . . 135 C8
Abbey Park Pl KY12. . . 161 A3
ABBEY PARKS. 161 B3
Abbey Path 12 DD11 . . . .89 D4
Abbey Pk
12 Arbroath DD11 . . . . . .89 D4
Auchterarder PH3 . . . . .104 F6
Abbey Rd
Auchterarder PH3 . . . . .104 F6
7 Coupar Angus PH13 . . .16 A2
Newburgh KY14. . . . . . . .50 E5
New Scone PH2. . . . . . .103 E8
Stirling FK8 . . . . 115 C1
Abbey Road Pl FK8 . . . 135 C8
Abbey St
4 Arbroath DD11. . . . . . .89 D4
High Valleyfield KY12 . . .158 B2
St Andrews KY16. . . . . .106 E6
Abbey Terr 22 PH2 . . . . . .37 F5
Abbey Theatre DD11 . . . .89 E4
Abbeyview KY9 . . . . . . .174 C4
Abbey View
Crossford KY12 . . . . . . 160 C1
Dunfermline KY11 . . . . .161 E2
Abbey Wall Rd 8 KY10. . .83 B5
Abbey Wlk KY16 . . . . . .106 E5
Abbie Gr KY8. . . . . 109 A6
Abbot Cres PH2 . . . . . .102 F2
Abbot Rd FK7 . . . . 135 D4
Abbotsfield Terr PH3. . . .104 E6
Abbotsford Cres
1 Dunfermline PH1. . . . .102 A3
3 St Andrews KY16. . . . .106 D6
Abbotsford Dr KY6. . . . .112 D6

Abbotsford Pl
Dundee DD2 . . . . .93 D3
9 St Andrews KY16 . . . .106 D6
Stirling FK8 . . . . 115 C1
Abbotsford Rd
Arbroath DD11 . . . . .89 F5
Lochore KY5 . . . . .127 F6
Abbotsford St DD2. . . . . .93 D3
Abbotshall Rd
Kirkcaldy KY1, KY2 . . . .151 B3
Kirkcaldy, Linktown KY1,
KY2. . . . . 151 A2
Abbots Mill KY2 . . . . . . 151 A3
Abbot St
Arbroath DD11 . . . . .89 D4
Dunfermline KY12 . . . . .161 A3
Perth PH2 . . . . 103 A2
Abbot's View KY3 . . . . . 177 D8
Abbots Wlk KY2 . . . . . .150 F3
Abbot's Wlk PH7 . . . . . .101 B4
Abbots Wynd KY4 . . . . 126 D3
Abbot's Wynd KY4 . . . .126 E3
Abbott Ho★ KY2 . . . . . 161 A3
Abden Ave KY3 . . . . . . 167 A3
Abden Ct KY3 . . . . 167 A3
Abden Pl KY3. . . . . 167 A3
Abel Pl KY11 . . . . 161 F4
ABERARGIE 49 C2
Abercairney Cl PH4 . . . . .57 B4
Abercairney Pl PH4 . . . . .57 B4
Abercorn St DD4 . . . . . . .94 D4
ABERCROMBIE 82 D5
Abercrombie Pl FK11 . . .116 F6
Abercromby Dr FK9. . . .115 B8
Abercromby Pl
Stirling FK8 . . . . 135 A7
Tullibody FK10 . . . . . . .117 B2
Abercromby Prim Sch
FK10. . . . . .117 B2
Abercromby St DD5. . . . .96 D4
ABERDALGIE 47 F6
ABERDOUR 176 C7
Aberdour Castle★
KY3 . . . . 176 C8
Aberdour Cres KY11 . . . 161 D1
Aberdour Pl
Broughty Ferry DD5. . . . .96 D4
Dunfermline KY11 . . . . .161 D1
Aberdour Prim Sch
KY3. . . . . 176 C8
Aberdour Rd
Burntisland KY3. . . . . . 165 C1
Dunfermline KY11 . . . . .162 A1

Aberdour Sta KY3. . . . . 176 C7
Aberfoyle Gdns DD5 . . . .96 A5
Aberhill Prim Sch
KY8. . . . . 109 C5
Aberlady Cres DD4. . . . . .95 C8
ABERLEMNO 3 B2
Aberlemno Prim Sch
DD8 . . . . .3 B2
Aberlour St KY11 . . . . . 173 E4
ABERNETHY 49 E3
Abernethy Prim Sch
PH2. . . . . .49 F3
Abernethy Rd
Broughty Ferry DD5. . . . .96 D5
Cupar KY14. . . . . .50 C4
Abernethy View 13 PH2 . .49 F7
ABERNYTE 27 B2
Abernyte Prim Sch
PH14 . . . . .27 B2
Abertay Cres DD5 . . . . . .96 C4
Abertay Gdns DD5 . . . . . .96 D3
Abertay St DD5 . . . . .96 C4
ABERUTHVEN 46 C2
Aberuthven Prim Sch
PH3 . . . . .46 B2
Abington Rd KY12 . . . . .160 F2
Aboyne Ave
Dundee DD4 . . . . .95 A4
Stirling FK9 . . . . 115 C4
Aboyne Gdns KY2 . . . . .150 E8
Aboyne Way KY7. . . . . .110 D3
Academy La DD11 . . . . . .89 D4
Academy Pl
Bannockburn FK7 . . . . .135 E1
22 Dollar FK14 . . . . . . .73 C1
Academy Rd
Crieff PH7 . . . . 101 C4
Stirling FK8 . . . . 135 A8
Academy Sq
Limekilns KY11 . . . . . . 172 D3
Montrose DD10 . . . . .85 D3
Academy St
Alloa FK10 . . . . 137 F8
10 Arbroath DD11. . . . . .89 D4
Forfar DD8. . . . . .87 D5
Accordian Way DD2. . . . . .90 B3
Acharn PH1 . . . . .102 B5
Achmore Pl 3 DD5 . . . . . .97 A6
Achray Ct FK10 . . . . . . 138 C5
Achray Dr FK9. . . . . . . 115 A4
Achray Pk KY7. . . . . . . 111 C2
Acorn Ct KY6. . . . . 113 B7
Acres The PH2. . . . . . . .103 F8

Active Kid Adventure Pk★
PH1. . . . . .24 E3
Adair Pl FK13. . . . . 119 D7
Adam Cargill Ct 12
DD11 . . . . .89 D3
Adam Hunter Ct KY4. . .126 E2
Adam Pl KY5. . . . . 148 A8
Adam Smith Cl KY1. . . . 151 C4
Adam Smith Coll
(Levenmouth Campus)
The KY8 . . . . .109 E6
Adam Smith Coll (Priory
Campus) KY1 . . . . . . .151 C5
Adam Smith Coll
(Southfield Campus) The
KY6. . . . . 112 C2
Adam Smith Coll (St
Brycedale Campus)
KY1. . . . . 151 B4
Adam Smith Coll (Stenton
Campus) The KY6 . . . .113 A4
Adam Smith Ct KY1. . . . 151 C4
Adamson KY15 . . . . . . .105 C6
Adamson Ave KY2 . . . . .151 B6
Adamson Cres KY12. . . . 161 C5
Adamson Ct KY15. . . . . .105 C5
Adamson Pl
Glenrothes KY6 . . . . . . 112 F6
Stirling FK9 . . . . 115 B3
Adamson Terr KY8 . . . . .109 D7
Adams Way 2 DD10 . . . . .85 D7
Adam's Way PH1 . . . . . . .88 B5
Adderley Cres DD5. . . . . .97 A6
Adderley Terr DD5 . . . . . .97 B6
Addison Cres
PH3 . . . . .46 A4
Addison Dr DD5 . . . . . . .96 C4
Addison Pl DD11. . . . . . .89 C3
Addison Rd DD5 . . . . . . .96 C4
Addison Terr PH1 . . . . . .102 A1
Adela Pl KY5. . . . . 113 A4
Adelaide Pl DD3 . . . . . .179 A4
Adelaide Terr DD3 . . . . . .93 E4
Adia Rd KY12 . . . . 158 F1
Admiral St DD7. . . . . . . 100 F3
Admirals La KY9 . . . . . . .82 B2
Admiralty Park KY11 . . .173 D3
Admiralty Rd
Inverkeithing KY11 . . . .174 B4
Rosyth KY11 . . . . .173 D4
Admiralty Wood PH1. . . . .36 E4
Adrian Rd DD5 . . . . . . .113 A6
Affleck Gdns DD5. . . . . . .20 D1

Affric Ave PH2. . . . . . . .103 E8
Affric Rd KY7. . . . . 111 C2
Affric Way KY12 . . . . . . 160 B1
Afton Ct FK7 . . . . 135 C5
Afton Gr KY11 . . . . 161 F5
Afton Pl DD4 . . . . .94 D7
Agnes Sq 7 DD5 . . . . . . .96 B2
Aikman Pl KY16. . . . . . .106 A3
Aikman Rd DD11. . . . . . .89 C6
Ailort Pl 8 KY6. . . . . . .112 E6
Ailsa Gr KY2. . . . . .150 F8
Aimer Sq 2 DD2 . . . . . . .93 B6
Ainslie Gdns PH1 . . . . . .102 F6
Ainslie Pl PH1 . . . . 103 A6
Ainslie St DD5 . . . . .95 C6
Airlie Cres DD8 . . . . .87 C3
Airlie Ct PH3 . . . . .57 E6
Airlie Dr DD5 . . . . .96 F6
Airlie Gdns DD9 . . . . .84 B3
Airlie Pl
Alyth PH11. . . . . .7 A3
Dundee DD1 . . . . 179 A1
Northmuir DD8 . . . . .86 D7
Airlie Prim Sch DD8 . . . . .8 B5
Airlie St
Alyth PH11. . . . . .7 A3
Brechin DD9 . . . . .84 B3
Airlie View 7 PH11 . . . . . .7 A3
AIRNTULLY. 24 D6
AIRTH 154 D3
Airth Dr FK7. . . . . 135 C4
Airth Prim Sch FK2 . . . .154 E4
Airthrey Ave FK9. . . . . . 115 B6
Airthrey Castle Yd
FK9. . . . . 115 E6
Airthrey Rd FK9 . . . . . . 115 C5
Aithernie Ct KY8. . . . . . 109 D7
Aithernie Dr 5 KY8. . . . . .81 A6
Aithernie Rd KY8 . . . . . 109 D7
Aitken Ave KY4 . . . . . . .126 F1
Aitken Cres FK7 . . . . . . 135 B2
Aitken Ct
Kirkcaldy KY1. . . . . . . 151 B2
Leven KY8 . . . . 109 E6
Aitken Pl 2 KY16. . . . . . .54 B8
Aitken Rd KY7 . . . . 111 A1
Aitken St
Kirkcaldy KY1. . . . . . . 151 E1
Leven KY8 . . . . 109 E6
Alastair Soutar Cres
DD2 . . . . .92 B4
Albany Bsns Ctr KY12 . . .161 B4

Albany Cres KY15 63 E1
Albany Dr 3 DD5 95 C3
Albany Gr 2 DD5 95 C3
Albany Ind Est KY12 161 B4
Albany Pk
Dundee DD5 95 D3
St Andrews KY16 106 F5
Albany Pl
1 Dundee DD5 95 C3
St Andrews KY16 106 D6
Albany Rd DD5 95 D3
Albany St KY12 161 B4
Albany Terr
Dundee DD3 179 A3
Perth PH1 102 F5
Albert Cres DD6 98 E4
Albert Gdns DD5 95 F3
Albert Pl
Brechin DD9 84 D2
Perth PH2 103 A3
Stirling FK8 135 A7
Albert Rd
Dundee DD5 95 F3
New Scone PH2 103 F8
Albert Sq DD1 179 B2
Albert St
Alyth PH11 7 A3
Arbroath DD11 89 C3
Dunblane FK15 107 C4
Dundee DD4 94 C3
2 Monifieth DD5 97 A5
Rosyth KY11 173 E4
Tayport DD6 99 E7
Albion Pl 8 DD8 87 D5
Alburne Cres KY7 113 D7
Alburne Ct KY7 113 D7
Alburne Pk KY7 113 D7
Alder Ave DD5 96 E6
Alder Cres FK11 116 F5
Alder Dr
Dundee DD5 96 E6
Perth PH1 102 B3
Alder Gr
Dunfermline KY11 161 D1
New Scone PH2 37 E5
Alder La KY6 112 F7
Alder Pl DD5 96 E6
Alderston Dr KY12 161 D6
Alder Terr KY8 109 A5
Aldie Castle* KY13 123 E8
Alexander Ct
Clackmannan FK10 139 A5
Stirling FK9 115 F6
Alexander Dr
Bridge of A FK9 115 A8
Kinross KY13 108 C3
Alexander Gordon Dr 6
DD5 97 B7
Alexander McLeod Pl
FK7 136 E3
Alexander Pl KY11 173 F3
Alexander Rd KY7 113 A6
Alexander St
Cowdenbeath KY4 147 D5
Dundee DD3 179 B4
Dysart KY1 152 A8
East Wemyss KY1 133 C7
Alexander The Third St
KY3 166 F1
Alexander Way KY11 174 B8
Alexandra Cres KY7 113 F7
Alexandra Ct 1 KY16 106 D6
Alexandra Dr FK10 137 F7
Alexandra Pl
Arbroath DD11 89 C3
Stirling FK8 115 C1
Alexandra St
24 Alyth PH11 7 A3
Dunfermline KY12 161 A5
Kirkcaldy KY1 151 C5
1 Perth PH2 103 A3
Tillicoultry FK13 119 A5
Alex Paterson La 6
KY16 54 E2
Alford Ave KY2 150 E7
Alford Dr KY6 112 D6
Alford Gdns
Dundee DD5 95 C4
Kirkcaldy KY2 150 E7
Alford Way KY11 162 A4
Alfred St DD10 85 D2
Alice Cox Wlk KY11 161 C1
Alice Gr KY4 162 E6
ALICHMORE 101 A2
Alichmore La PH7 101 A2
Aline Ct
Dalgety Bay KY11 175 A2
Glenrothes KY6 112 E5
Alison Gr KY12 160 B2
Alison Pl KY16 106 E5
Alison St
Kirkcaldy KY1 151 B2
3 Leven KY8 109 A1
Allanbank Rd FK15 70 D8
Allan Cres KY11 161 E2
Allan Ct KY3 177 E8
Allandale Cres FK15 56 B2
Allan La DD1 179 C2
Allanlea Terr KY12 160 F5
Allan Park Ho 10 FK8 135 B7
Allan Pk
Cowdenbeath KY4 147 A1
Cupar KY14 63 B5
Stirling FK8 135 A7
Allan Robertson Dr
KY16 106 D3
Allan's Prim Sch FK8 135 A7
Allan St
15 Arbroath DD11 89 D4
2 Blairgowrie PH10 88 C5
Glenrothes KY6 112 B8
Allan Terr PH1 102 D8
Allanvale Rd FK9 114 F7
Allanwater Apartments
FK9 115 A8
Allanwater Gdns FK9 115 A8
Allan Wlk
Bridge of A FK9 114 F8
Stirling FK9 70 C1
Allanwood Ct FK9 115 A8
Allardice Cres KY2 150 D5
Allen Gr KY12 158 E7
Alligan Cres PH7 101 D3
Alligan Rd PH7 101 D3
Allison Cres PH1 102 C7
ALLOA 138 C5
Alloa Acad FK10 137 E8
Alloa Bsns Ctr FK10 138 C7
ALLOA PARK 138 B5
Alloa Park Dr FK10 138 D5
Alloa Rd
Clackmannan FK10 139 B4
Fishcross FK10 118 D3
Menstrie FK9 116 B3
Stirling FK9 115 E3
Tullibody FK10 117 C3
Alloa Tower* FK10 138 B5
Alloa Trad Ctr FK10 138 C7
Alloa West Bsns Pk
FK10 137 E7
Alloway Dr KY2 151 A7
Alloway Pl DD4 94 D5
Alloway Pl E 2 DD4 94 D5
Alloway Pl W DD4 94 D5
Alloway Terr DD4 94 D5
Allsop Pl 18 FK14 73 C1
Alma Pl PH7 101 D4
Alma St KY11 174 C3
Alma Terr 5 DD6 98 C3
Almerie Cl 5 DD11 89 D4
ALMONDBANK 36 E5
Almond Bank KY7 113 D2
Almond Cres PH1 36 F5
Almond Ct
Perth PH1 102 A4
Stirling FK7 135 C5
Almond Gdns PH1 102 B4
Almond Gr PH1 36 F4
Almondgrove Pl PH1 37 B5
Almond Path KY6 112 F7
Almond Pl
Dundee DD2 92 F4
Kirkcaldy KY1 151 C7
Perth PH1 36 F4
Almond Rd KY11 161 E2
Almond View PH1 102 A4
Almond Way
Glenrothes KY6 112 F7
10 Whitfield DD4 94 F8
Alness Gr KY12 160 F2
Alpin Dr FK15 107 E7
Alpin Rd DD3 93 D6
Alpin Terr DD3 93 D5
Altamount PH10 88 D4
Altamount Rd PH10 88 C3
Altyre Ave KY7 113 C4
Altyre Ct KY7 113 C4
ALVA 118 A6
Alva Acad FK12 118 A7
Alva Glen Nature Trail*
FK12 118 A8
Alva Ind Est FK12 118 C6
Alva Prim Sch FK12 118 A6
Alva Sq DD3 179 A4
Alves Dr KY6 112 C5
Alveston Gdns 4 DD11 22 E4
Alwyn Gn KY7 110 F2
ALYTH 7 A3
Alyth Ct 14 KY7 111 C2
Alyth Golf Club PH11 7 C3
Alyth Mus* PH11 7 A3
Alyth Prim Sch PH11 7 A3
Alyth Rd
Blairgowrie PH10 88 F6
Meigle PH12 17 A7
Ambleside Ave DD3 91 F1
Ambleside Gdns 1
DD3 91 F1
Ambleside Gr 2 DD3 91 F1
Ambleside Terr DD3 91 F1
Ambrose St 2 DD5 96 A2
Amdoch Dr PH2 49 F7
Americanmuir Rd 4
DD3 91 D1
America St DD10 85 C2
Amond Gdns 11 DD4 94 F8
Amulree Rd PH1 102 C5
Ancaster Rd PH7 101 C5
Ancaster Way PH5 44 C3
Anchor La 6 DD1 93 E3
Anchorscross FK15 107 B5
Ancrum Ct
Glenrothes KY6 112 D8
Lochee DD2 93 C5
Ancrum Dr DD2 93 B5
Ancrum Gdns DD2 93 B5
Ancrum Pl DD2 93 B5
Ancrum Rd DD2 93 C5
Ancrum Rd Prim Sch
DD2 93 B5
Anderson Ave KY12 160 B2
Anderson Cres KY1 132 D4
Anderson Ct
Dunblane FK15 107 C5
Leven KY8 109 E6
Anderson Dr
Balmullo KY16 53 E7
Cowdenbeath KY4 147 B2
Glenrothes KY6 112 A8
Perth PH1 102 C4
Anderson La
Kincardine FK10 155 E4
Leven KY8 133 F8
Rosyth KY11 173 D5
Anderson Pl
Glenrothes KY6 112 F5
Stirling FK7 135 A4
Strathkinness KY16 54 B3
Andersons La DD2 93 A6
Anderson's La 3 DD2 93 A6
Anderson St
7 Arbroath DD11 89 C3
Carnoustie DD7 100 B2
Cupar KY14 50 D4
Dunblane FK15 107 C5
Dysart KY1 152 A7
Kirkcaldy KY1 151 E6
Leven KY8 109 E7
Anderson Terr 12 DD8 86 D5
Andover Prim Sch DD9 84 E3
Andownie Rd DD11 89 C7
Andrew Carnegie
Birthplace Mus*
KY12 161 A3
Andrew Hardie Dr
FK10 138 A8
Andrew Lang Cres 5
KY16 54 E2
Andrew Smyth Gdns
DD8 87 B4
Andrew St KY5 148 A6
Andrew Welsh Way 7
DD11 89 D5
Andson St DD11 12 F4
Angle Ind Est DD8 86 C6
Angle Pk Cres DD8 86 C7
Angle Rd DD8 86 C7
Angus Coll DD11 89 B4
Angus Cres PH7 101 B5
Angus Ct PH1 102 E6
Angus Dr DD10 85 C8
Angus Folk Mus* DD8 9 C1
Angus Rd
Leuchars KY16 54 B7
New Scone PH2 37 F5
Angus St 7 DD2 93 B6
Annabel Ct KY11 174 D2
Annandale Ave DD3 91 C1
Annandale Gdns KY6 112 C7
Annat Rd
Montrose DD10 85 D2
Perth PH2 103 D5
Anne Dr FK9 115 B6
Annesley Dr 3 DD11 89 A3
Anne St
Alloa FK10 137 F8
Dunblane FK15 107 C4
Annfield Dr
Arbroath DD11 89 A4
Stirling FK7 135 C5
Annfield Farm Rd
KY11 174 B7
Annfield Gdns FK8 135 B6
Annfield Gr FK8 135 B6
Annfield Rd DD1 93 D3
Annfield Row DD1 93 D3
Annfield St DD1 93 D3
Annsmuir Pl 6 KY2 130 F1
Ann St
Blairgowrie PH10 88 B4
Dundee DD1 179 B4
Tillicoultry FK13 119 B6
Ann Terr 11 DD9 84 C3
Anson Pl 3 KY16 54 B7
ANSTRUTHER EASTER 83 D6
Anstruther Golf Course
KY10 83 B5
Anstruther Prim Sch
KY10 83 C6
Anstruther Rd
Ceres KY15 65 E6
Crail KY10 69 A2
2 Dundee DD4 94 D4
ANSTRUTHER
WESTER 83 B6
Anthony Pl PH7 101 D5
Antiquary Gdns 3
DD11 22 E3
Antiquary Pl 11 DD11 22 E3
Anton Dr DD5 96 A3
Anvil Bank 11 DD8 11 E3
Apedaile Way 8 PH13 15 F3
Apollo Way DD2 92 C4
Appin Cres
Dunfermline KY12 161 B4
Kirkcaldy KY2 150 E7
Appin Terr PH1 102 D5
Appleby Pl DD3 91 C1
Applecross Gdns DD2 92 C5
Applegate 14 DD11 89 D4
Applehill Dr 5 DD5 30 F7
Applehill Gdns 7 DD5 30 F7
Applehill View 6 DD5 30 F7
Applehill Wlk 8 DD5 30 F7
Apple Wynd 3 DD10 85 C2
Approach Row KY1 133 B5
Approach Terr KY1 133 B6
Arbaile KY8 109 C8
ARBIRLOT 22 C3
Arbirlot Pl 4 DD11 89 A3
Arbirlot Prim Sch
DD11 22 A3
Arbirlot Rd DD11 89 A3
Arbirlot Rd W DD11 22 E4
ARBROATH 89 E3
Arbroath Abbey DD11 89 D4
Arbroath Artisan Golf Club
DD11 22 D1
Arbroath Cres FK9 115 B4
Arbroath High Sch
DD11 89 B4
Arbroath Infmy DD11 89 B2
Arbroath Rd
Carnoustie DD7 100 F3
Dundee DD4 94 F4
Forfar DD8 87 F5
Arbroath Signal Twr Mus*
DD11 89 D2
Arbroath Sta DD11 89 C4
Arbuthnott Loan DD5 96 B5
Archers Ave FK7 135 C4
Archer St DD5 96 A4
Archies Pk DD8 87 C4
Ardblair Rd PH10 88 B2
Ardblair Terr PH10 88 B2
Ardchoille Gdns PH2 103 C5
Ardchoille Pk PH2 103 C5
Ardeer Pl KY11 161 C2
Ardencaple Terr KY15 53 D4
Ardestie Pl DD5 96 F6
Ardestie Souterrain*
DD5 31 B5
Ardestie St DD5 96 F6
Ardgartan Ct 1 KY7 111 C2
Ardleighton Ct FK15 107 E5
ARDLER
Blairgowrie 16 E4
Dundee 91 B2
Ardler Complex DD2 91 B1
Ardler Prim Sch DD2 91 B1
Ardler Rd PH12 17 A7
Ardminish Pl DD4 95 E8
Ardmore Ave DD5 96 E4
ARDOCH 24 D8
Ardoch Cres FK15 107 C5
Ardoch Gr 3 FK15 56 B4
Ardoch Pk KY6 110 E2
Ardoch Way 2 FK15 56 B4
Ardovie Rd DD9 4 E1
Ardownie Pl 1 DD5 96 F6
Ardownie St DD5 96 F6
Ardross Castle (rems of)*
KY10 82 D3
Ardross Ct KY6 113 A5
Ardross Pl KY6 113 A5
Ardvreck Sch PH7 101 C6
Argyle Gr FK15 107 C4
Argyle Pk FK15 107 C4
Argyle St
Dundee DD4 94 C5
St Andrews KY16 106 C5
Argyle Terr FK15 107 C4
Argyle Way FK15 107 C3
Argyll Ave FK8 115 C1
Argyll Bsns Pk KY16 106 C3
Argyll Ct 3 KY13 108 B4
Argyll Pl
Alloa FK10 138 C7
Glenrothes KY6 110 F2
Saline KY12 142 D6
Argyll Rd
Kinross KY13 108 B4
Perth PH1 102 E8
Argyll's Lodging*
FK8 135 A8
Argyll St
Alloa FK10 138 C7
Brechin DD9 84 B4
19 Dollar FK14 73 C1
Ariel Cl 5 KY10 83 D7
Arisaig Gdns DD2 92 C4
Arkaig Dr KY12 160 C1
Arklay Ct DD3 94 B4
Arklay Pl DD3 94 B5
Arklay St DD3 179 C4
Arklay Terr DD3 94 B4
Arlick Rd KY4 126 F1
Armadale Cres PH2 38 D8
Armit Pl KY16 106 A3
Armour Pl
Dundee DD4 94 E6
Tillicoultry FK13 119 D7
Arnbeg KY8 109 D7
ARNCROACH 82 C8
Arngask Prim Sch PH2 61 B5
Arnhall Dr DD2 93 A2
Arnhall Gdns DD2 93 A3
Arniston Rd KY11 162 A4
Arnott Rd PH4 57 B4
Arnott St 6 KY14 62 F7
Arnot Twr & Gdns*
KY6 77 C4
Arns Gr FK10 137 E8
Arnswell FK10 118 C2
Arran Cres KY2 150 F7
Arran Ct FK10 138 B5
Arran Dr DD2 92 F6
Arran Rd PH1 102 E8
Arrighi Cres 7 KY10 69 B2
Arrol Cres FK10 138 C7
Arrol Rd DD2 92 C6
Artery Gall* KY16 106 E6
Arthur Bett Ct FK13 119 B6
Arthur Cl 10 PH10 88 C4
Arthur Ct KY4 147 D3
Arthurfield Gn 1 KY15 64 A3
Arthur Pl
Cowdenbeath KY4 147 D3
2 Cupar KY15 64 E6
Arthur St
Blairgowrie PH10 88 C4
Arthur St *continued*
Cowdenbeath KY4 147 D3
Dundee DD3 179 B3
Dunfermline KY12 161 B5
Arthurstone Terr DD4 179 C4
Artillery La DD1 179 A2
Ashbank Ct KY7 113 B2
Ashbank Gdns 4 KY15 64 E6
Ashbank Rd DD2 93 C3
Ashbrae Gdns FK7 135 B2
Ash Braes FK10 155 D4
Ashburnham Gdns
EH30 178 D1
Ashburnham Loan
EH30 178 D1
ASHFIELD 70 C6
Ash Gr
Alloa FK10 138 C6
Arbroath DD11 89 A4
Carnock KY12 159 C6
Cowdenbeath KY4 147 B4
Dunfermline KY11 173 D8
4 Glenfarg PH2 61 B5
Perth PH1 102 B3
Ashgrove
10 Leven KY8 79 F3
Monifieth DD5 97 B7
New Scone PH2 37 F5
Ashgrove Gdns 6
PH10 88 D5
Ashgrove Rd PH10 88 E4
Ashgrove Terr
Blairgowrie PH10 88 E4
8 Kinglassie KY5 77 E1
Ashkirk Gdns DD4 95 C7
Ashkirk Pl DD4 95 C7
Ash La 2 DD1 93 E4
Ashlar La KY15 105 C4
Ashlar Pk KY15 105 C4
Ashley Ave FK14 120 C8
Ashley Rd KY6 112 F3
Ashley Terr FK10 138 A8
Ashludie DD5 97 A7
Ashludie Mews 4 DD5 97 C6
Ashludie Pl 3 KY2 130 F2
Ashludie Steadings
DD5 97 C7
Ashludie Terr DD5 97 C6
Ashmore 3 PH2 48 F4
Ashmore St DD3 91 F1
Ash St DD1 93 E4
Ash Terr FK8 134 F5
Ashton Terr DD3 91 D4
Aspen Ave KY7 110 F1
Aspens The 7 DD4 95 A8
Asquith St KY1 151 B3
Athole Dr PH1 24 E4
Athole St 11 PH10 88 C4
Athollbank PH1 102 D3
Athollbank Dr PH1 102 E3
Atholl Cres 16 PH1 103 B4
Atholl Ct
Dunblane FK15 107 C5
Perth PH1 103 B5
Atholl Glen Yd 2 DD4 94 C8
Atholl Pl
Dunblane FK15 107 C5
Perth PH1 103 B4
Stirling FK8 114 F2
Atholl St
Dundee DD2 93 B5
Perth PH1 103 B4
Atholl Terr KY2 150 D7
Atholl Way KY6 110 E1
Athol Pl KY12 161 C4
Athol St PH10 88 C4
Auchavan Gdns KY7 113 A2
Auchencairn Pl 5 DD5 96 F6
Auchinbaird FK10 118 C2
Auchinblae Pl DD3 91 A3
AUCHMITHIE 23 D7
Auchmithie Pl KY7 113 A2
Auchmore Dr PH10 88 E1
AUCHMUIRBRIDGE 77 D4
AUCHMUTY 113 B6
Auchmuty Dr KY7 113 B7
Auchmuty High Sch
KY7 113 C6
Auchmuty Rd KY7 113 B7
Auchrannie Terr DD4 95 A3
AUCHTERARDER 104 C6
Auchterarder Golf Club
PH3 104 B4
Auchterarder Rd 6
PH2 46 F1
AUCHTERDERRAN 129 B5
Auchterderran Golf Course
KY5 128 F4
Auchterderran Rd
KY5 148 B8
Auchtergaven Prim Sch
PH1 24 A6
AUCHTERHOUSE 28 C8
Auchterhouse Prim Sch
DD3 18 A1
Auchterlonie Ct KY16 106 D4
AUCHTERMUCHTY 62 E6
Auchtermuchty Prim Sch
KY14 62 F7
Auchtermuchty Rd
KY14 63 A5
AUCHTERTOOL 149 A2
Auchtertool Prim Sch
KY2 149 B2
Auldbar Rd DD8 11 E4

Auld Bond Rd PH1 102 D8
Auld Brig Rd FK10 138 B6
Auld Burn Pk 5 KY16 106 D5
Auld Burn Rd KY16 106 D5
Auld House Wynd PH1 102 B5
Auld Kirk Rd FK10 117 C3
Auld Mart Bsns Pk KY13 108 C6
Auld Mart La KY13 108 C6
Auld Mart Rd KY13 108 C6
Auld Mart Wynd KY13 108 D6
Auld School Wynd FK7 134 D5
Aulton Way DD10 85 C6
Ava St KY1 151 A2
Avens Cl KY12 161 A5
Avenue Ind Est KY5 148 C7
Avenue Pk FK9 114 F7
Avenue Rd 6 KY13 108 C2
Avenue The
Bridge of A FK9 115 A7
Dundee DD2 40 E8
Inverkeithing KY11 174 E3
Lochgelly KY5 148 C7
2 Perth PH2 47 F2
8 Tillicoultry FK13 119 C7
Avon Cres DD5 96 D6
Avondale Terr DD5 95 F4
Avon Pl DD5 96 E6
Ayton Ct KY6 112 D8
Aytoun Cres KY3 165 E2
Aytoun Gr KY12 160 E5

B

Baberton Ct 5 DD3 91 B2
Back Brae PH10 88 D4
Back Braes DD9 84 C2
Back Causeway KY12 169 D8
Backcroft FK15 107 E6
Backdykes 7 KY10 83 C6
Back Dykes
3 Anstruther KY10 83 D7
16 Auchtermuchty KY14 62 F6
8 Crail KY10 69 B2
East Wemyss KY1 133 B6
8 Falkland KY15 63 B2
Perth PH2 49 E3
Back Dykes Pl 15 KY14 62 F6
Back Dykes Rd 1 KY13 76 F6
Backfaulds Pl KY4 126 E2
Backgate 14 KY10 83 A5
Backhill Rd DD2 93 A5
Back Latch 1 KY15 65 D6
Back Lebanon KY15 105 C5
Back Loan KY13 108 D7
Backmarch Cres KY11 173 E4
Backmarch Rd KY11 173 E4
Backmuir Dr DD2 90 C4
Back O' Hill Ind Est FK8 115 A2
Back O' Hill Rd FK8 114 F1
Back O' Yds KY11 174 B2
Back Pk KY15 64 A2
Back Rd
Alva FK12 117 E7
Dollar FK14 73 B1
Back Row
Crieff PH5 44 C3
5 Rattray PH10 88 E6
Back Row Croftouterly 1 KY6 112 B8
Back St
Bridge of Earn PH2 48 F5
Culross KY12 169 D8
4 Freuchie KY15 63 E1
Back Stile KY16 68 F6
Backwell Ct KY12 160 D5
Back Wlk 2 FK8 135 B7
Backwood Ct FK10 138 F5
Back Wynd
2 Blairgowrie PH10 88 E6
4 Falkland KY15 63 B2
Perth PH2 103 C4
Badenoch Pl 1 DD4 95 C7
Baden-Powell Rd DD11 89 A6
Bader Sq DD5 96 A3
Baffin St DD4 94 C3
Baffin Terr DD4 94 C3
Bailie Norrie Cres 3 DD10 85 C7
Bailies Wynd 3 KY7 113 F8
Bailie Wilson 1 DD10 85 D7
Baillie Waugh Rd FK7 135 C3
Baingle Brae FK10 117 B3
Baingle Cres FK10 117 B3
Bain St
Lochgelly KY5 148 B7
Tillicoultry FK13 119 B5
BAINTOWN 79 F6
Baird Ave DD2 93 B8
Baird Cres KY8 109 E7
Baird Ct KY5 148 A7
Baird Pl KY9 82 B3
Baird Rd KY7 113 D5
Baird Terr PH7 101 E5
Baird Way 6 DD10 85 D7
Baker La KY16 106 E6
Baker Pl 15 KY16 54 B8
Baker Rd DD5 95 F6
Baker St FK8 135 A8
Baker's Wynd 16 DD11 89 D4
BALADO 75 D5
Balado Wynd 2 KY13 75 D5
Balbedie Ave KY5 128 A6
Balbedie Ct KY5 128 A6
Balbedie Gdns KY5 128 A6
BALBEGGIE 38 D8
Balbeggie Ave KY1 131 C5
Balbeggie Pl DD4 95 C5
Balbeggie Prim Sch PH2 38 D8
Balbeggie St DD4 95 C5
Balbeggie Terr DD4 95 C5
Balbirnie Ave KY7 113 E8
Balbirnie Craft Ctr* KY7 111 E1
Balbirnie Ct KY7 113 F8
Balbirnie Pk Golf Club KY7 111 E2
Balbirnie Rd KY7 113 C6
Balbirnie St KY7 113 F8
Balbuthie Dr KY9 82 B5
Balbuthie Rd KY9 82 B5
Balcairn Pl DD4 95 C5
Balcarres St FK13 119 C6
Balcarres Terr DD4 95 C5
Balcomie Gn 6 KY10 69 B3
Balcomie Golf Links KY10 69 C5
Balcomie Rd
Crail KY10 69 B3
Kirkcaldy KY2 130 F2
Balcurvie Prim Sch KY8 79 F3
Balcurvie Rd KY8 79 E3
Balderran Dr KY5 129 B4
BALDINNIE 66 B6
Baldinnie Pl KY7 113 A3
Baldovan Rd DD3 91 D2
Baldovan St DD11 89 C5
Baldovan Terr DD4 94 C4
BALDOVIE 95 F6
Baldovie Gdns DD4 95 E5
Baldovie Ind Est DD4 95 C6
Baldovie Pl DD4 95 D5
Baldovie Rd DD5 95 E6
Baldovie Terr DD4 95 D5
Baldragon Acad DD3 91 E2
Baldragon Ct 6 DD3 91 D2
Baldragon View 3 DD3 91 C3
BALDRIDGEBURN 160 D5
Baldridgeburn KY12 160 E5
Baldwin Cres KY2 151 A5
Balerno Pl DD4 95 C5
Balerno St DD4 95 B5
BALFARG 111 C3
Balfield Rd DD3 93 D6
Balformo Rd 26 PH2 37 F5
Balfour Cres KY13 108 E7
Balfour Ct KY12 161 D5
Balfour Pl
Carnoustie DD7 100 D3
Glenrothes KY7 79 C3
St Andrews KY16 106 F5
Balfour St
Alloa FK10 138 C7
Bannockburn FK7 135 C1
Dundee DD1 179 A1
Kirkcaldy KY2 151 B5
Leven KY8 109 F7
Stirling FK8 114 F2
Balgarthno Pl DD2 92 E6
Balgarthno Rd DD2 92 E6
Balgarthno St DD2 92 D6
Balgarthno Terr DD2 92 D6
Balgarvie Cres KY15 105 B5
Balgarvie Ct 4 KY15 105 B5
Balgarvie Pl 29 PH2 37 F5
Balgarvie Rd KY15 105 B5
Balgavies Ave DD4 94 F4
Balgavies Loch Wildlife Reserve* DD8 11 F5
Balgavies Pl 2 DD4 95 A3
Balgay Ct DD2 92 E4
Balgay Rd DD2 93 C3
Balgayview Gdns DD3 93 D5
BALGEDDIE 110 D2
Balgeddie Cl KY6 110 E2
Balgeddie Ct KY6 110 D2
Balgeddie Gdns KY6 110 D2
Balgeddie Way KY6 110 D2
Balgillo Rd
Broughty Ferry DD5 96 B5
Dundee DD5 95 F4
Balgillo Rd E DD5 96 A5
BALGONAR 142 E8
Balgonie Ave KY7 113 D6
Balgonie Castle* KY7 79 A3
Balgonie Pl KY7 113 F8
Balgonie Rd KY7 113 F8
Balgove Ave DD6 41 F2
Balgove Links KY16 106 A8
Balgove Rd DD6 41 F2
BALGOWAN 35 D1
Balgowan Ave DD3 91 D2
Balgowan Dr DD3 91 E2
Balgowan Pl
Blairgowrie PH11 7 A2
Downfield DD3 91 F2
Balgowan Rd PH1 102 B5
Balgowan Sq 2 DD3 91 F2
Balgownie W KY12 169 C8
Balgray Pl 1 DD4 94 A5
Balgray St DD3 94 A5
Balgreggie Pk KY5 129 A5
Balgreggie Rd KY5 129 A5
BALHELVIE 51 E8
Balhousie Ave PH1 103 A5
Balhousie Prim Sch PH1 103 A5
Balhousie St PH1 103 A5
Baliol St KY3 166 F2
BALKEERIE 17 E7
Ballantine Pl PH1 103 A5
Ballantrae Gdns DD4 95 B6
Ballantrae Pl DD4 95 B6
Ballantrae Rd DD4 95 B5
Ballantrae Terr DD4 95 B5
Ballast Bank KY11 174 C2
Ballater Dr FK9 115 C4
Ballater Gn KY7 110 E2
Ballater Pl DD4 95 C5
BALLATHIE 25 C8
Ballengeich Pass FK8 115 A1
Ballengeich Rd FK8 114 F1
Ballinard Gdns DD5 95 F4
Ballinard Rd DD5 95 F4
Ballindean Cres DD4 95 B5
Ballindean Pl DD4 95 A5
Ballindean Rd DD4 95 B5
Ballindean Terr DD4 95 B5
Ballingall Dr KY6 110 E1
Ballingall Pk KY6 110 E1
BALLINGRY 127 E7
Ballingry Cres KY5 127 F7
Ballingry La KY5 148 B7
Ballingry Rd KY5 127 F7
Ballingry St KY5 148 A7
Ballo Braes 10 PH2 49 E3
Ballochmyle Dr DD4 94 D6
Balloch Pl DD4 95 D5
BALLUMBIE 95 C8
Ballumbie Braes DD4 95 C8
Ballumbie Dr DD4 95 C8
Ballumbie Gdns DD4 95 C8
Ballumbie Mdws DD4 95 C8
Ballumbie Pl DD4 95 C8
Ballumbie Rd DD4 95 C8
Ballumbie View DD4 95 C8
Balmachie Rd DD7 100 C4
Balmain Ct 7 DD10 85 C3
Balmain St 4 DD10 85 C3
Balmaise KY8 109 C8
BALMALCOLM 64 C3
Balmanno Gdns 2 PH2 48 F4
Balmanno Gn KY7 113 B2
Balmanno Pk PH2 48 E4
Balmashanner Pl DD8 87 C2
Balmashanner Rise DD8 87 C2
Balmedie Dr DD4 95 A5
BALMERINO 41 D3
Balmerino Abbey (rems of)* DD6 41 D3
Balmerino Prim Sch DD6 41 F2
Balmerino Rd DD4 95 B5
Balmoral Ave DD4 95 C5
Balmoral Ct
Auchterarder PH3 57 D6
Dunblane FK15 107 C4
Balmoral Dr KY2 150 D5
Balmoral Gdns DD4 95 D5
Balmoral Pl
Dundee DD4 95 C5
Leven KY8 109 E7
Perth PH2 102 F2
Stirling FK8 135 A7
Balmoral Rd
Blairgowrie PH10 88 B8
Glenrothes KY7 113 B3
Balmoral Terr
Dundee DD4 95 C5
Leven KY8 109 E7
Balmore St 3 DD4 94 C3
Balmossie Ave DD5 96 E4
Balmossie Bank DD5 96 C7
Balmossie Brae DD5 96 D7
Balmossie Mdw DD5 96 C7
Balmossie Pl 2 DD5 96 E5
Balmossie Sta DD5 96 F4
Balmuir Pl 3 DD3 91 F2
Balmuir Rd DD3 91 F2
BALMULLO 53 E7
Balmullo Pl DD4 95 B5
Balmullo Prim Sch KY16 53 E8
Balmullo Sq DD4 95 B5
BALMUNGO 55 C1
Balmyle Gr FK15 107 D6
Balmyle Rd DD5 95 E3
Balnacarron Ave KY16 106 A4
Balnacraig KY12 160 B1
Balnacraig Sch PH2 103 D2
Balnagowan Dr KY6 113 A5
Balquharn Cotts FK12 117 D7
Balquhidderock FK7 135 C4
Balrymonth Ct KY16 106 C3
Balshando Pl DD2 93 C7
Balsillie Ave KY6 110 B1
Balsusney Rd KY2 151 B5
Baltic Gdns DD2 93 D2
Baltic St DD10 85 D3
Baltimore Rd KY6 112 E4
Balunie Ave DD4 95 C5
Balunie Cres DD4 95 B6
Balunie Dr DD4 95 D5
Baluniefield Rd DD4 95 E5
Baluniefield Trad Est DD4 95 D6
Balunie Gdns DD4 95 D5
Balunie Pl DD4 95 D5
Balunie St DD4 95 D5
Balunie Terr DD4 95 D5
Balure Cres FK7 136 D4
Balvaird Castle* KY14 61 F6
Balvaird Pl
Dunfermline KY12 161 C6
Perth PH1 103 A6
Balwearie Cres KY2 151 A2
Balwearie Gdns KY2 150 F1
Balwearie High Sch KY2 151 A1
Balwearie Rd KY2 151 A2
Bamff Ct 19 PH11 7 A3
Bamff Rd PH11 7 A3
Bamff View PH11 7 A2
Bamff Wynd 4 PH11 7 A3
Banbeath Ind Est KY8 109 C8
Banbeath Pl KY8 109 C7
Banbeath Rd KY8 109 C7
Banchory Cotts KY2 166 E5
Banchory Gn KY7 110 E3
Banchory Pl FK10 117 C3
Banchory Prim Sch FK10 117 C3
Banchory Rd DD4 95 B5
Bandeath Ind Est FK7 137 A5
Bandeath Rd FK7 136 D4
Bandon Ave KY1 151 F8
Bank Ave DD3 93 E8
Bank Cl 6 DD8 86 C4
BANKFOOT 24 A6
Bankfoot Pk 4 KY13 77 A4
Bankhead PH10 88 C5
Bankhead Ave KY7 113 E3
Bankhead Cres 5 DD11 89 A3
Bankhead Gdns DD8 87 C6
Bankhead Gr EH30 178 D1
Bankhead Ind Est KY7 113 E3
Bankhead Moss* KY15 66 C5
Bankhead Pl 10 KY8 79 E3
Bankhead Rd
Arbroath DD11 89 A3
Fishcross FK10 118 D3
Forfar DD8 87 C6
South Queensferry EH30 178 E1
Bankhead Rise DD8 87 C6
Bankhead Terr DD8 87 C6
Bankhead W Ind Est KY7 113 D3
Banklands KY14 50 C4
Bank Mill Rd 3 DD1 93 D3
Banknowe Ave DD6 99 F5
Banknowe Dr 6 DD6 99 F5
Banknowe Gr DD6 99 E5
Banknowe Rd 1 DD6 99 F6
Banknowe Terr DD6 99 F5
Bank Pl
Crieff PH7 101 C4
Glenrothes KY6 112 A8
Banks Cres PH7 101 E4
Banks of Brechin DD9 84 A4
Bank St
Alloa FK10 138 B6
12 Alyth PH11 7 A3
Arbroath DD11 89 C3
4 Blairgowrie PH10 88 C5
Brechin DD9 84 C3
Crieff PH7 101 D3
Cupar KY15 105 C6
Dundee DD1 179 B2
Earlsferry/Elie KY9 82 A3
Inverkeithing KY11 174 C2
Kincardine FK10 155 D3
Kirkcaldy KY1 151 E7
2 Kirriemuir DD8 86 D4
Lochgelly KY5 148 B8
Newport-on-Tay DD6 98 E5
7 Stirling FK8 135 A8
Tillicoultry FK13 119 B6
Banks The DD9 84 A4
Banks View FK2 154 E4
Bankwell Cres 7 KY14 62 D5
Bankwell Rd 37 KY10 83 C6
Bannerman Ave KY11 174 C3
Bannerman St KY12 161 A5
Bannoch Brae KY12 161 C3
Bannoch Rise DD5 96 E6
BANNOCKBURN 135 E2
Bannockburn Cross FK7 135 E1
Bannockburn Heritage Ctr* FK7 135 B2
Bannockburn High Sch FK7 135 D3
Bannockburn Prim Sch FK7 135 E1
Bannockburn Rd FK7 135 C3
Bannockburn Station Rd FK7 136 A4
Bannock Rd FK7 136 C4
Barassie Ct 6 DD3 91 B2
Barassie Dr
Kirkcaldy KY2 130 F1
Kirkcaldy KY2 151 A8
Barbara Stocks La KY12 169 D8
Barber's Croft 5 DD11 89 E4
Barbour Ave FK7 135 C3
Barbour Gr KY12 160 E5
Barbush FK15 107 E8
Barclay Ct KY1 131 D1
Barclay Pl FK15 107 E8
Barclay Rd KY3 166 F3
Barclay St KY4 147 B3
Bards Way FK13 119 D7
Barham Rd KY11 173 D1
Barlow Ave DD5 95 E6
Barlow Pk DD5 95 E6
Barncraig St KY8 109 A2
Barnes Ave DD3 93 F7
Barnet Cres KY1 151 B1
Barnet's Brae 6 DD11 89 D5
Barn Gn DD11 89 D4
Barngreen 3 DD11 89 D4
BARNHILL
Broughty Ferry 96 C5
Perth 103 D2
Barnhill Dr FK10 117 C2
Barnhill Pl KY11 175 D4
Barnhill Prim Sch DD5 96 C5
Barnhill Rd KY11 175 D4
Barnhill Rock Gdn* DD5 96 E3
Barnkittoch PH7 101 C5
Barnpark Dr FK13 119 A6
Barn Rd FK8 135 A8
Barns Brae DD10 6 D2
Barnsdale Rd FK7 135 A3
Barns Neuk DD4 29 F5
Barns of Claverhouse DD3 29 F5
Barns of Claverhouse Rd
Claverhouse DD4 29 E5
Dundee DD4 94 B8
Barns Pk KY11 175 A2
Barns The KY3 177 E8
Barnton Pl KY6 112 B6
Barnton Rd KY2 130 F2
Barnton St FK8 135 B8
Barnwell Rd FK9 115 C4
Barnyards Marsh Wildlife Reserve* KY9 82 A5
Barony Ct FK7 134 D6
Barony Pk 6 PH11 7 A3
Barony Pl KY6 112 C8
Barony The KY1 133 B7
Barossa Pl PH1 103 B5
Barossa St PH1 103 B5
Barrack Rd
Dundee DD3 179 A3
Montrose DD10 85 D2
Barrack St
Dundee DD1 179 B2
Perth PH1 103 A5
Barra Terr DD4 94 C7
Barr Cres KY11 174 D2
Barrel Wynd 18 PH11 7 A3
Barrie Path KY6 112 F7
Barrie Pl
4 Dunfermline KY12 160 E5
4 Kirriemuir DD8 86 D5
Barrie's Birthplace* DD8 86 D5
Barrie's Pavilion & Camera Obscura* DD8 86 D6
Barrie St
Dunfermline KY12 160 E5
Leven KY8 109 B4
Barron Terr KY8 109 E8
BARRY 31 F5
BARRY BUDDON CAMP 31 E3
Barry Links Sta DD7 32 A4
Barry Prim Sch DD7 32 A5
Barry Rd
Carnoustie DD7 100 A2
Kirkcaldy KY2 130 F2
Barry Wr Mill* DD7 31 F6
Barton Bldgs KY3 167 A2
Basin View DD10 85 C4
Bassaguard Ind Est KY16 106 C5
Bastion Wynd 7 FK8 135 B7
Bathgate Ct KY15 105 C5
Bath St
3 Dundee DD5 96 A2
Kelty KY4 126 F1
Battenberg Rd DD11 22 D6
Batterflatts Gdns FK7 134 F6
Batterflatts Ho FK7 134 F6
Battery Rd
Grangemouth FK3 168 C1
North Queensferry KY11 178 C5
Bauk The PH2 49 F3
Baxter Pk Ct DD4 94 C3
Baxter Pk Glebe DD4 94 C3
Baxter Pk Terr DD4 94 C4
Baxter Rd KY7 113 B6
Baxter St
2 Dundee DD2 93 D4
Fallin FK7 136 D4
Bayfield Gdns DD5 95 F3
Bayfield Rd DD5 95 F3
Bayne St FK8 115 A1
Bay Rd DD6 42 B5
Bayview KY12 158 E1
Bayview Cres KY8 109 C4
Bayview Pl DD5 97 B7
Bayview Rd DD2 92 B3
Bayview Stadium (East Fife FC) KY8 109 E5
Beach Cres DD5 96 A2
Beach Rd
Grangemouth FK3 168 B1
Wormit DD6 98 A2
Beaconcroft FK9 115 C7
Beaconhurst Sch FK9 115 C6
Beacon Rd DD10 85 D2
Beacon Terr 6 DD10 85 D1
Bearehill Gdns DD9 84 B3
Bearside Rd FK7 135 A3
Beath High Sch KY4 147 B5
Beath View KY11 161 E4
Beath View Rd KY4 147 A2
Beaton Ave FK7 135 C1
Beatty Ave FK8 115 A2
Beatty Cres KY1 151 D7

Beatty Ct KY1 151 D7
Beatty Pl KY12 161 C5
Beauclerc St FK12 118 A7
Beaufort Cl KY16 54 C8
Beaufort Cres KY2 150 D5
Beaufort Dr KY7 113 C4
Beauly Ave DD3 91 F1
Beauly Cres
Dundee DD3 91 F1
Dunfermline KY11 174 C8
Beauly Ct KY6 112 E6
Beauly Pl KY2 150 F7
Beauly Sq 4 DD3 91 F1
Beaumont Cres DD5 95 F4
Beaumont Terr DD5 95 F4
Beck Cres KY12 161 C5
Beckman St KY6 112 F6
Beda Pl FK7 136 C5
Bedford Ct FK10 138 A6
Bedford Pl FK10 138 A6
Beech Ave
Dalgety Bay KY3, KY11 175 F5
Ladybank KY15 63 F5
Leven KY8 109 A5
Thornton KY1 131 E8
Beech Bank KY15 105 D4
Beechbank Cres KY4 126 C2
Beech Cres 1 FK15 56 B4
Beech Ct FK15 107 D5
Beech Dr PH7 101 E4
Beeches 2 KY15 64 A5
Beeches Rd PH10 88 C3
Beeches The
Dalgety Bay KY11 175 C3
2 Dundee DD4 95 A8
Glenrothes KY7 113 C6
Lochgelly KY5 128 A1
Beech Gdns FK7 134 F6
Beech Gr
Arbroath DD11 89 A4
Dunfermline KY11 173 D8
Beechgrove
Balbeggie PH2 38 D8
3 Monifieth DD5 97 B7
Beechgrove Dr PH1 102 C3
Beechgrove Gdns
PH1 102 B4
Beechgrove Pl PH1 102 B4
Beechgrove Rise
KY15 105 A3
Beechgrove Terr PH1 102 C3
Beech Hill Ct DD8 87 E4
Beech Hill Rd 1 PH13 16 A3
Beechill Pl 2 PH13 15 F3
Beech La FK9 115 B4
Beech Pk KY8 109 D8
Beech Rd FK15 107 D5
Beechtree Pl PH3 104 C6
Beech Way KY11 175 A5
Beech Wlk 3 KY10 69 B2
Beechwood
Alloa FK10 118 E1
Crossford KY12 160 B2
Sauchie FK10 118 D1
Beechwood Ave KY7 113 A8
Beechwood Cres DD8 86 D3
Beechwood Ct KY7 113 A8
Beechwood Dr KY7 113 A8
Beechwood Gdns
2 Arbroath DD11 89 B7
Stirling FK8 135 A5
5 Tillicoultry FK13 119 C7
Beechwood Pk
4 Carnoustie DD7 100 B3
Queensway KY7 113 A8
Beechwood Pl
Kirriemuir DD8 86 D3
Queensway KY7 113 A8
Beechwood Rd DD11 89 B7
Beechwood Terr DD2 93 B3
Beechwood Terr E 4
DD6 98 D3
Beechwood Terr W 3
DD6 98 D3
Beech Wynd 6 DD8 9 A7
Beehives The DD6 42 B4
Beldorney Pl KY12 161 D6
BELEYBRIDGE 68 A5
Belfield Gdns 4 KY15 105 C4
Bell Baxter High Sch
KY15 105 A4
Bellefield Ave DD1 93 E2
Belleisle Rd KY2 131 A2
Belleknowes Ind Est
KY11 174 B4
Bellenden Gr FK15 107 E8
Bellevue Gdns DD11 89 F5
Bellevue Pk FK10 137 E6
Bellevue Pl DD11 89 F5
Bellevue Rd FK10 137 F6
Bellevue Terr DD10 85 D1
Bellfield Ave PH1 102 C4
Bellfield Cres KY1 152 A8
Bellfield Pl KY7 79 B3
Bellfield Rd
Bannockburn FK7 135 E1
Stirling FK8 135 B5
Bellfield St 8 DD1 93 E3
Bellhouse Rd KY3 176 B7
Bellies Brae DD8 86 D4
Bellisle Dr DD4 94 F5
Bellisle Pl DD4 94 F5
Belliston Pl KY10 82 D8
Bellman Way KY11 175 B5
Bell Pl DD8 87 D5
Bell Rd KY11 173 B2
Bell Rock Sq DD5 95 F2
Bells Croft
Abernethy PH2 49 E3
12 Abernethy PH2 49 F4
Bell's La 4 DD5 96 A2
Bell's Sports Ctr PH1 103 B5
Bell St
Dundee DD1 179 B3
St Andrews KY16 106 D6
Tayport DD6 99 E7
Bell Stane EH30 178 B1
Bell's Wynd 5 KY16 68 F7
Belltree Gdns DD5 96 D6
Bellwood Pk PH2 103 C3
BELLYEOMAN 161 D5
Bellyeoman La KY12 161 C5
Bellyeoman Prim Sch
KY12 161 C5
Bellyeoman Rd KY12 161 C5
Belmont Dr FK13 119 C6
Belmont Pl 4 PH12 17 A7
Belmont St PH12 17 B4
Belsize Pl 5 DD5 95 C3
Belsize Rd DD5 95 B3
Belvidere La PH3 104 E5
Belvidere Pl PH3 104 D5
Benalder Ct 13 KY7 111 C2
Ben Alder Pl KY2 150 E5
Benarty Ave
Crosshill KY5 127 F5
Lochgelly KY5 128 B1
Benarty Ct KY5 127 F5
Benarty Prim Sch KY5 128 A7
Benarty Rd KY4 126 F4
Benarty Sq KY5 127 F8
Benarty St KY2 150 F5
Bendachin Dr KY12 161 E5
Bendameer Rd KY3 165 C1
Benedict Rd DD11 89 F5
Ben Hogan Pl DD7 100 A1
Benholm Gdns DD8 87 B4
Benholm Pl 5 DD3 91 A3
Ben Ledi Rd KY2 150 F5
Ben Lomond Dr FK9 115 A4
Ben Lomond View
KY12 159 A6
Ben More Ave DD10 85 C8
Bennachie Ct 2 KY7 111 C2
Bennachie Way KY11 162 C1
Bennan Gdns DD5 96 B3
Ben Nevis Pl KY2 150 F5
Bennochy Ave KY2 151 A5
Bennochy Ct KY2 151 A5
Bennochy Gdns KY2 151 A5
Bennochy Gr KY2 151 A5
Bennochy Rd
Kirkcaldy KY1 151 B4
Kirkcaldy, Templehall KY2 150 E6
Bennochy View KY2 151 A5
Bentham St PH12 16 E4
Bents Rd DD10 85 E3
Benvane Rd KY6 110 D3
Benvie Gdns 4 DD1 93 D4
Benvie Rd DD2 93 D4
Benview FK7 135 C2
Benview Terr FK10 118 E4
Berkeley St FK7 135 A4
Bernard Cres DD11 89 E5
Bernard Shaw St
KY12 160 E5
Bernard's Smithy KY3 164 D5
Berrydale Ave 2 PH10 88 C3
Berrydale Rd PH10 88 C3
Berryhill KY7 113 A3
Berrylaw Pl KY12 160 E4
Berrylaw Rd KY12 160 D4
Berry Pl 1 KY16 54 E2
Berry St KY5 148 B7
Berwick Dr DD4 95 A8
Berwick Pl
Dysart KY1 152 A8
Kirkcaldy KY1 151 C5
Beryl St DD4 95 D6
Bethune Pl KY7 79 C3
Bethune Rd KY7 113 A6
Betson St KY7 113 F8
Beufort Cres KY16 54 B8
Beulah Howe DD8 87 F6
Beurard KY8 109 C8
Bevan Ct KY6 112 F6
Bevan Dr FK12 118 C7
Bevan Pl KY11 173 E3
Beveridge Pl KY13 108 B3
Beveridge Rd KY1 151 B3
Beveridge St KY11 161 C2
BEVERIDGEWELL 160 F5
Bickram Cres KY12 158 D7
Biggin Wa's KY1 151 F7
Bighty Ave KY7 113 D6
Bighty Cres KY7 113 E6
Bighty Rd KY7 113 D6
Bilsland Path KY6 112 F6
Bilsland Path N 6
KY6 112 F6
Bilsland Path S 9
KY6 112 F6
Bilsland Rd KY6 112 E6
Bingham Terr DD4 94 D4
Binn Ave KY3 165 E2
Binney Wells KY1 151 E6
Binning Rd KY11 174 B3
Binsted Ave DD3 93 E8
Birch Ave
Blairgowrie PH10 88 C2
New Scone PH2 37 F5
Stirling FK8 134 F5
Birchbank KY4 147 B2
Birch Cres
Blairgowrie PH10 88 D3
12 New Scone PH2 37 F5
Birch Gr
Dunfermline KY11 173 D8
Kelty KY4 126 D1
1 Leven KY8 79 F3
Menstrie FK11 116 F6
Birch La 5 PH2 61 B5
Birch Path DD11 89 A4
Birch Pl PH1 102 B3
Birch Row 14 PH2 37 F5
Birch Terr 13 PH2 37 F5
Birchtree Pl KY1 131 E8
Birchtree Rd KY7 113 C5
Birchview Pl PH2 39 E2
Birchwood FK10 118 D2
Birchwood Pl 4 DD2 93 D3
Birkdale Pl DD2 91 B2
BIRKHILL 90 C3
Birkhill Ave DD6 98 A1
Birkhill Pl DD2 90 C3
Birkhill Prim Sch DD2 90 C3
Birkhill Rd FK7 134 E6
Birks Terr DD4 94 E6
Birnam Cres PH1 102 D5
Birnam Gdns KY11 162 A4
Birnam Pl DD2 93 A4
Birnam Rd KY2 150 E8
Birnam Wood Way
PH2 25 D4
Birnie Brae KY5 148 B7
Birnie & Gaddon Lochs Nature Reserve*
KY15 63 E7
Birnie St KY5 148 B7
Birrell Cl 6 KY1 151 D6
Birrell Dr KY11 161 D1
Birrell's La KY1 151 E7
Birrell Street Wynd 5
KY1 151 D6
Birrel's Wynd KY3 167 A3
Birsay Gdns DD5 96 B5
Bishop Ave KY5 128 B1
Bishopgate KY15 105 D6
Bishoploch Rd DD11 89 A3
Bishop's Cl 8 DD9 84 C3
Bishop's Ct KY8 79 F5
Bishops Gdns FK15 107 D6
Bishopshire Golf Course
KY13 77 A5
Bishop Terr KY13 76 F5
Bittern Ct KY11 162 A2
Blackadder Ct KY7 111 A3
Blackadder Haven
KY12 169 D8
Blackburn Ave KY12 160 D6
Blackburn Dr KY4 147 A3
Blackcraigs KY2 150 C7
Blackfaulds St FK13 119 B4
BLACKFORD 57 B4
Blackford Prim Sch
PH4 57 C4
Blackfriars Ct 10 DD10 85 C4
Blackfriars St
9 Montrose DD10 85 C4
4 Perth PH1 103 B4
Blackfriars Wynd 6
PH1 103 B4
Blackgrange Rdbt
FK9 116 D3
Blackhall Rd KY4 126 D1
Blackhall Sq KY4 126 D1
Blacklaw Dr DD2 90 B3
Blacklaw Rd KY11 161 D2
Blacklaws Cres KY10 83 D8
Blackloch Cres PH10 15 B5
Blacklock Cres DD4 94 E6
BLACKMUIR OF PITFIRRANE 160 A6
Blackmuir Pl FK10 117 D3
Blackness Ave DD2 93 C3
Blackness Prim Sch
DD2 93 D2
Blackness Rd DD1 93 E3
Blackness St 1 DD1 93 D3
Black Rd KY4 126 E3
Blackscroft DD4 179 C3
Black St 5 DD2 93 D4
Blacktorn Gr FK11 117 A5
Black Watch Cl 5
PH1 103 A4
Black Watch Gdns
PH1 103 A4
Black Watch Mus The*
PH1 103 A5
Blackwood Ct KY11 173 F7
Blackwood Dr KY7 113 E3
Blackwood Gdns KY11 173 F7
Blackwood Gn KY11 173 F6
Blackwood Rd KY7 113 E4
Blackwood Way
Dunfermline KY11 173 F7
Glenrothes KY7 113 E3
Blairadam Cres KY4 126 E2
Blairadam Ct KY7 111 C2
Blairadam Gr KY4 126 D3
Blair Ave KY7 113 B3
BLAIRBURN 169 C8
Blair Ct KY7 113 B3
Blairdenon Dr FK10 118 B2
Blairdenon Rd FK12 117 E6
Blair Dr
Dunfermline KY12 161 B6
Kelty KY4 126 D1
Kelty KY4 146 D8
Blairfield Rd DD2 90 C4
Blairfield Terr DD2 90 C2
Blairforkie Dr
Bridge of A FK9 114 F8
Stirling FK9 70 C1
Blair Gdns 3 DD5 96 B5
BLAIRGOWRIE 88 B5
Blairgowrie Cottage Hospl
PH10 88 B4
Blairgowrie Golf Course
PH10 88 C1
Blairgowrie High Sch
PH10 88 C3
Blairgowrie House Rd
PH10 88 D4
Blairgowrie Rd PH13 16 A3
BLAIRHALL 158 B7
Blairhall Prim Sch
KY12 158 A8
BLAIRINGONE 121 D6
Blairingone Prim Sch
FK14 121 D7
BLAIRLOGIE 116 B6
Blairmore Dr PH10 88 E1
Blairmore Rd KY2 150 D8
Blair Pl
Glenrothes KY6 112 B8
Kirkcaldy KY2 150 D5
Blair Rd 10 KY16 54 B7
Blairs Croft 12 DD8 11 E3
Blairs Rd DD8 11 E3
Blair St PH2 102 F3
Blairwood Terr KY12 158 E7
Blairwood Wlk KY12 158 E7
Blake Ave DD5 95 F4
Blakely Hill Ct KY9 66 F2
Blake Pl DD5 95 F4
Blake St
Dundee DD5 95 F4
Dunfermline KY11 161 C1
Blalowan Gdns KY15 105 C4
Blalowan Pk 6 KY15 105 C4
Blamey Cres KY4 147 B2
Blanche Path KY7 111 A1
Blantyre Pl DD3 91 D1
Bleachers' Way PH1 36 F4
Bleachfield Ct KY11 161 E3
BLEBOCRAIGS 53 F2
Blenheim Ct FK9 115 C3
Blenheim Pl 5 KY16 54 B7
Bliakie's Mews DD4 179 C4
Blindwells FK12 117 F6
Blinkbonny Rd KY10 82 D8
Blinshall St DD1 179 A2
BLOOMFIELD 54 D8
Bloomfield Cres 13
DD11 22 E4
Bloomfield Gdns 9
DD11 22 E4
Bloomfield Pl 10 DD11 22 E4
Bloomfield Rd 5 DD11 89 A4
Bluebell Gdns KY5 129 B2
Blyth Ct
21 Anstruther Easter KY10 83 D6
Newton on Tay DD6 98 E4
Blyth Pl DD2 93 D4
Blyth St
3 Dundee DD1 93 D4
Kirkcaldy KY1 151 E8
Newport-on-Tay DD6 98 E4
BOARHILLS 69 C9
Boase Ave KY16 106 E5
Boat Brae
Blairgowrie PH10 88 D5
Newport-on-Tay DD6 98 D3
Boat Rd DD6 98 D4
Bobber Wynd 1 KY15 105 D5
Bobbin Wynd FK7 134 D6
Bobby Jones Pl KY16 106 B3
Boe Ct FK15 107 D4
Bogies Wynd 10 KY1 151 D6
BOGINDOLLO 2 D2
Boglily Cotts KY2 150 D3
Boglily Rd KY2 150 D3
Bog Rd DD9 84 D3
Bogside FK15 107 E6
Bogside Rd 2 PH13 16 A3
Bogton Pl FK14 120 D8
Bogward Rd KY16 106 A3
Bogwood Dr KY12 160 A2
Bohun Ct FK7 135 D4
Bolam Dr KY3 165 F2
Bondgate 14 KY14 62 F6
Bond St FK10 117 A2
Bonella St DD7 100 D2
Bo'ness Rd EH30 178 A1
Bonfield Pk KY16 54 B3
Bonfield Rd KY16 54 B3
Bonhard Ave PH2 38 A4
Bonhard Rd
Carnock KY12 159 B7
New Scone PH2 103 F8
Boniface Gdns DD2 92 C3
Boniface Pl DD2 92 C3
Boniface Rd DD2 92 C3
Bonnar St KY12 161 A4
Bonnethill Ct DD3 179 B5
Bonnethill Pl DD1 179 B3
Bonnet Stane* KY14 62 A2
Bonnington Rd PH10 88 D8
BONNYBANK 79 F6
Bonnybank Rd DD1 179 B4
Bonnygate KY15 105 C5
Bonnyrigg Pl 3 DD4 94 D4
Bonnyton Ct KY7 113 A2
Bonnyton Pl KY11 161 D3
Bonnyton Rd
Arbroath DD11 21 F2
Dundee DD3 17 F1
Bonspiel Gdns DD5 96 C3
Bonvil Row 2 KY15 105 B5
Booth Ave KY11 173 D5
BORELAND 132 A2
Boreland Pk KY11 174 C3
Boreland Pl KY1 132 A1
Boreland Rd
Dysart KY1 152 A8
Inverkeithing KY11 174 C3
Kirkcaldy KY1 132 A2
BORESTONE 135 A2
Borestone Cres FK7 135 A4
Borestone Ct FK7 135 B2
Borestone Pl FK7 135 A2
Borestone Prim Sch
FK7 135 A2
BORROWFIELD 85 B6
Borrowfield Cres DD10 85 C6
Borrowfield Prim Sch
DD10 85 C7
Borrowfield Rd DD10 85 C6
Borrowlea Rd FK7 135 C7
Borrowmeadow Rd
FK7 135 E7
Borrows Gate FK9 114 F3
Borthwick Pl KY16 53 E7
Boston Rd KY6 112 F5
Boswell Dr
Kinghorn KY3 167 A3
Oakley KY12 158 F6
Boswell Rd KY5 148 B8
Bothwell Ct KY11 161 A2
Bothwell Gdns KY11, KY12 161 A2
Bothwell St KY11 161 B2
BOTTOMCRAIG 41 E3
Boulzie Hill Pl 1 DD11 89 F4
Bouprie Rise KY11 175 B4
Bourtree Bank KY8 109 A6
Bourtree Brae KY8 81 A5
Bourtree Gr KY12 158 D7
Bowbridge Ct DD3 94 A4
Bowbridge Ind Est DD3 94 A4
Bowbridge Pl DD3 94 A4
Bow Butts
2 Crail KY10 69 B2
Dunfermline KY12 161 A2
Markinch KY7 111 F1
6 Montrose DD10 85 D3
Bow Butts Rd KY10 69 B2
Bower Mill La 7 DD3 91 A3
Bower Pk KY14 62 A3
BOWERSHALL 145 B2
Bowerswell La PH2 103 D4
Bowerswell Rd PH2 103 C4
Bowery The KY6 112 C8
BOWHILL 129 C4
Bowhill Swimming Pool
KY5 129 A3
Bowhouse Dr KY1 167 B8
Bowhouse Gdns
Alloa FK10 138 B5
Kirkcaldy KY1 167 B7
Bowhouse Pl 2 KY8 79 F2
Bowhouse Rd FK10 138 B5
Bowhouse Terr KY5 129 D3
Bowiehill 9 KY14 62 F6
Bowling Gn Ave KY13 108 C7
Bowling Gn Cl 19 KY10 69 B2
Bowling Gn Pl
4 Crail KY10 69 B2
Cupar KY15 64 B3
Bowling Gn Rd
Cupar KY15 105 D6
Glenrothes KY7 113 F8
2 Kirriemuir DD8 86 D5
Bowling Gn St KY8 109 C4
Bowling Gn Terr KY1 132 E4
Bowling Green St KY4 147 C4
BOW OF FIFE 64 C7
Bow Rd 7 KY14 63 A6
BOWRIEFAULD 11 D3
Bow St
Leven KY8 109 A2
Stirling FK8 135 A8
Bowton Rd KY13 108 C2
Boyack Cres 2 DD5 97 C6
Boyd Ave PH7 101 E4
Boyd-orr Ave DD9 84 C4
Boyd Pl
6 Broughty Ferry DD5 96 B2
Lochgelly KY5 148 A8
Boyes Path KY6 112 F5
Boysack Gdns DD5 95 F5
Brackenbrae DD5 95 F3
Bracken La FK9 115 B3
BRACKENS 91 B3
Brackens Prim Sch
DD3 91 B1
Brackens Rd DD3 91 B3
Bracklinn Brae KY12 160 E5
BRACO 56 B4
Braco Prim Sch FK15 56 B4
Bractullo Gdns 14 DD8 11 E3
Bractullo Pl 13 DD8 11 E3
Bradbury St DD3 91 C3
Bradgate Gdns KY6 110 D1
Brady Cres KY8 109 A3
Brae Ct KY7 110 F2
Braefoot DD7 100 B3
Braefoot Gr KY11 175 B2
BRAEGRUM 35 E4
BRAEHEAD 135 C5
Braehead
Alloa FK10 117 D1

Braehead *continued*
Alva FK10 . . . 118 A7
Cupar KY15 . . . 105 D5
7 Monance KY10 . . . 82 E4
Tillicoultry FK13 . . . 119 A7
Braehead Ave FK10 . . . 117 C2
Braehead Dr DD7 . . . 100 C3
Braehead Ho KY1 . . . 151 D5
Brae Head Lodge KY1 . . . 151 D5
Braehead Prim Sch FK7 . . . 135 C4
Braehead Rd
Forfar DD8 . . . 11 E3
Kirkcaldy KY2 . . . 130 F2
6 Pittenweem KY10 . . . 83 B5
Stirling FK7 . . . 135 C3
Braehead Way KY6 . . . 110 E1
Braeheid DD11 . . . 89 C7
Braemar Ave FK15 . . . 107 B4
Braemar Ct KY6 . . . 112 F4
Braemar Dr KY11 . . . 162 A4
Braemar Gdns
Broughty Ferry DD5 . . . 96 C6
Halbeath KY11 . . . 162 A4
Viewfield KY6 . . . 112 F4
Braemar Gr FK15 . . . 107 B4
Braemar Pk FK15 . . . 107 B4
Braemount KY4 . . . 147 A2
Braeport FK15 . . . 107 D6
Braeside
Alloa FK10 . . . 118 C1
Dundee DD3 . . . 18 A1
8 Leven KY8 . . . 109 C4
Braeside Gdns PH1 . . . 102 E2
Braeside Rd 6 DD6 . . . 98 C3
Braes Rd PH10 . . . 88 D5
Braes The
Lochgelly KY5 . . . 148 A8
Tullibody FK10 . . . 117 D3
Brae The
Bannockburn FK7 . . . 135 D1
Cambusbarron FK7 . . . 134 D6
Dundee DD3 . . . 18 A1
Braeview Acad DD4 . . . 95 B8
Braeview Cres KY7 . . . 79 B6
Braeview Pl KY7 . . . 79 B6
Brahan Pk KY7 . . . 113 B5
Brahan Terr PH1 . . . 102 D5
Braid Cres KY16 . . . 106 F4
Braid Dr KY7 . . . 113 B5
Braid Rd DD6 . . . 99 E7
Braids Rd KY2 . . . 131 A2
Braigh Gdns KY12 . . . 160 D6
Bramblefield PH7 . . . 101 B5
Brambling Rd KY11 . . . 162 A2
Branch St 10 KY8 . . . 109 E6
Brand's Brae PH2 . . . 103 D6
Brands Row KY4 . . . 162 F7
Brandyhill FK10 . . . 118 E3
Brandyriggs KY12 . . . 159 D1
Brandywell Rd PH2 . . . 49 F3
Brandy Wells KY12 . . . 159 D1
Brankholm Brae KY11 . . . 173 C4
Brankholm Cres KY11 . . . 173 D5
Brankholm La KY11 . . . 173 D2
Branklyn Gdns* PH2 . . . 103 D2
Branning Ct 9 KY1 . . . 151 D6
BRANSHILL . . . 118 B1
Branshill Pk
Alloa FK10 . . . 138 B8
Sauchie FK10 . . . 118 B1
Branshill Rd FK10 . . . 138 B8
Brantwood Ave DD3 . . . 93 D6
Branxton Wynd KY1 . . . 167 B8
Braoch Pk DD10 . . . 85 B1
Braoch Rd DD10 . . . 85 B1
Breadalbane Cres KY6 . . . 110 E1
Breadalbane Terr 10 PH2 . . . 48 D8
Breahead Rd 2 DD8 . . . 9 C1
Breakers Way KY11 . . . 174 F2
BRECHIN . . . 84 B3
Brechin Bsns Pk DD9 . . . 4 B7
Brechin Castle* DD9 . . . 84 C2
Brechin Castle Ctr* DD9 . . . 4 B6
Brechin Cath DD9 . . . 84 C3
Brechin High Sch DD9 . . . 84 B4
Brechin Ind Est DD9 . . . 84 F2
Brechin Infmy DD9 . . . 84 D3
Brechin Leisure Ctr DD9 . . . 84 C2
Brechin Pl DD11 . . . 89 D6
Brechin Rd
Arbroath DD11 . . . 89 D6
Forfar DD8 . . . 87 C6
Kirriemuir DD8 . . . 86 D5
Montrose DD10 . . . 85 B6
Brechin Round Twr* DD9 . . . 84 C2
Brechin Sta DD9 . . . 84 D3
Brent Ave DD10 . . . 85 D8
Brentham Ave FK8 . . . 135 B5
Brentham Cres FK8 . . . 135 B5
Brent Pl KY7 . . . 110 F2
Brewery Cl EH30 . . . 178 B1
Brewery La
Dundee DD1 . . . 93 E3
8 Kinross KY13 . . . 108 C2
Brewhouse Ct 5 FK10 . . . 138 B6
Brewlands Ct 10 FK14 . . . 73 C1
Brewster Pl KY16 . . . 106 F4
Briarcliff St KY1 . . . 151 F6
Briar Gr DD8 . . . 87 B4
Briarhill Ave KY11 . . . 175 A3
Briar Lea KY4 . . . 126 F2
Briar Pl KY11 . . . 161 C3
Briar Rd FK10 . . . 117 E2
Briarwood Terr DD2 . . . 93 B3
Bridgefauld Rd KY13 . . . 108 C7
BRIDGEFOOT . . . 91 B5
Bridgehaugh Rd FK9 . . . 115 B2
Bridgehead Pl 9 DD6 . . . 42 B5
Bridge La
Broughty Ferry DD5 . . . 96 E3
9 Perth PH1 . . . 103 B4
BRIDGEND
Cupar . . . 65 D7
Perth . . . 103 D5
Bridgend
Dunblane FK15 . . . 107 D5
Kinross KY13 . . . 108 C1
Perth PH2 . . . 103 C5
Bridgend Gdns KY8 . . . 79 E3
Bridgend Ind Est KY13 . . . 108 C1
Bridgend St DD4 . . . 94 F6
BRIDGE OF ALLAN . . . 114 E8
Bridge of Allan Golf Club FK9 . . . 70 D1
Bridge of Allan Prim Sch FK9 . . . 115 B6
Bridge of Allan Sta FK9 . . . 114 E8
BRIDGE OF DUN . . . 5 E5
Bridge of Dun Sta DD10 . . . 5 E5
BRIDGE OF EARN . . . 48 E5
Bridge of Earn Rd PH2 . . . 47 A1
Bridge Rd PH1 . . . 24 D8
Bridge St
5 Arbroath DD11 . . . 89 C3
Brechin DD9 . . . 84 C2
Broughty Ferry DD5 . . . 96 D4
Cowdenbeath KY4 . . . 147 D3
Dollar FK14 . . . 120 E8
Dunfermline KY12 . . . 160 F3
Kincardine FK10 . . . 155 D5
Kirkcaldy KY1 . . . 151 B1
8 Leven KY8 . . . 109 E6
Montrose DD10 . . . 85 C2
5 Newport-on-Tay DD6 . . . 98 D3
Saline KY12 . . . 142 E6
St Andrews KY16 . . . 106 D6
Bridges The KY11 . . . 175 A2
Bridges View KY12 . . . 161 F6
Bridge Terr 12 FK10 . . . 138 B6
Bridgeton Brae PH1 . . . 36 E5
Bridgeton Cres PH1 . . . 36 E5
Bridgeton Pl PH1 . . . 36 E5
Bridge View KY11 . . . 178 C6
Bridgewater Ave PH3 . . . 104 F6
Bridieswell Gdns DD6 . . . 41 F2
Bridle Way PH7 . . . 101 B5
Brighton Rd KY15 . . . 105 B3
Bright St DD2 . . . 93 B6
Brighty Wood* DD4 . . . 30 C8
Brington Pl DD4 . . . 95 A3
Brington Rd DD4 . . . 95 A3
Brioch Ave PH7 . . . 101 B2
Britannia Dr 5 DD4 . . . 95 C7
British Golf Mus* KY16 . . . 106 D7
British Sch of Falconry* PH3 . . . 57 D6
Broadford Terr DD5 . . . 96 B4
Broadlands DD7 . . . 100 F3
Broadleys Rd FK7 . . . 135 D7
Broadleys Rdbt FK7 . . . 135 D6
Broad St
Alloa FK10 . . . 138 B5
Cowdenbeath KY4 . . . 147 C2
Stirling FK8 . . . 135 A8
Tayport DD6 . . . 99 F6
Broadwood View PH3 . . . 104 E5
Broad Wynd 8 KY1 . . . 151 D6
Brock Pl FK7 . . . 135 B2
Brock St KY11 . . . 178 B6
Brodick Gdns KY11 . . . 162 A4
Brodick Rd KY2 . . . 150 E7
Brodie Ct KY7 . . . 113 B2
Brodie's Yd 6 PH13 . . . 16 A2
Brodie Wlk KY11 . . . 162 A4
BROICH . . . 101 C1
Broich Rd PH7 . . . 101 C2
Broich Terr PH7 . . . 101 D3
Broich The FK12 . . . 117 E7
Brompton Terr PH2 . . . 103 C4
Brontonfield Dr 4 PH2 . . . 48 F4
Brookfield Pl FK12 . . . 118 A6
Brook St
Alva FK12 . . . 118 A6
Alva FK12 . . . 118 A7
Broughty Ferry DD5 . . . 96 B2
Dundee DD1 . . . 93 E3
Menstrie FK11 . . . 116 F6
Monifieth DD5 . . . 97 C6
BROOM . . . 109 D8
Broom Cres KY8 . . . 109 D8
Broom Ct
Kinross KY13 . . . 108 C4
Stirling FK7 . . . 135 C3
Broomfaulds Ave KY16 . . . 106 C4
Broomfield 11 KY8 . . . 79 F3
Broomfield Cres DD10 . . . 85 D6
Broomfield Dr KY12 . . . 161 A5
Broomfield Gdns DD10 . . . 85 D6
Broomfield Ind Est DD10 . . . 85 D6
Broomfield Pl 14 KY15 . . . 63 E1
Broomfield Rd
Cowdenbeath KY4 . . . 147 C5
Montrose DD10 . . . 85 D5
Broom Gr KY11 . . . 173 F8
Broomhead Dr KY12 . . . 160 F5
Broomhead Ho KY12 . . . 161 A5
Broomhead Pk KY12 . . . 160 F5
Broomhill KY3 . . . 177 E8
Broomhill Ave
Burntisland KY3 . . . 165 E1
Perth PH1 . . . 102 C3
Broomhill Ct
Cornton FK9 . . . 115 B3
7 Monifieth DD5 . . . 97 B7
Broomhill Dr DD5 . . . 97 B7
Broomhill Pl FK7 . . . 134 E6
Broomhill Rd
Dundee DD2 . . . 93 A7
Forfar DD8 . . . 2 D5
Broomieknowe
Dunfermline KY11 . . . 161 C3
Leven KY8 . . . 109 E6
Tullibody FK10 . . . 117 D3
Broomknowe Dr FK10 . . . 155 D6
Broomknowe Terr KY12 . . . 161 A6
Broomlee Rd DD2 . . . 92 F6
Broompark E FK11 . . . 117 A6
Broompark Rd 2 PH1 . . . 24 B6
Broompark W FK11 . . . 117 A6
Broom Pl KY2 . . . 150 C8
Broom Rd
Glenrothes KY6 . . . 112 E5
Kinross KY13 . . . 108 C4
Kirkcaldy KY2 . . . 150 C7
Leven KY8 . . . 109 D8
Stirling FK7 . . . 135 C4
BROOMRIDGE . . . 135 D3
Broomridge Rd FK7 . . . 135 B3
Broomside
Kirkcaldy KY2 . . . 150 C8
Perth PH1 . . . 102 E7
Broomwell Gdns DD5 . . . 20 D1
Brora Ct PH1 . . . 102 E8
Brora Pl KY12 . . . 160 C1
Brothock Bridge 2 DD11 . . . 89 D3
Brothock Gdns 1 DD4 . . . 94 D4
Brothock Mill Pl 11 DD11 . . . 89 D3
Brothock Way DD11 . . . 89 D7
Brougham Gdns DD4 . . . 179 C4
Brougham Sq DD10 . . . 85 D5
Brough Terr 3 KY13 . . . 76 F5
Broughty Castle* DD5 . . . 96 A1
Broughty Castle Mus* DD5 . . . 96 A1
BROUGHTY FERRY . . . 96 C2
Broughty Ferry Rd DD1 . . . 94 E3
Broughty Ferry Sta DD5 . . . 96 A2
Broughty Ferry Wlk DD4 . . . 95 E5
Brough Way PH1 . . . 102 A5
Brown Ave
Alloa FK10 . . . 117 F1
Stirling FK9 . . . 115 B2
Brown Constable Pend DD4 . . . 179 C4
Brown Constable St DD4 . . . 179 C3
Brown Cres
4 Leven KY8 . . . 79 F2
Thornton KY1 . . . 131 D8
Brownhill Pl DD2 . . . 92 E7
Brownhill Rd DD2 . . . 92 E7
Brownhills Steadings KY16 . . . 55 C2
Brownhill St DD2 . . . 92 E7
Brownlow Pl 1 DD10 . . . 85 D1
Brown's Cl 15 KY10 . . . 83 A5
Brown's La 10 DD8 . . . 86 D5
Brown St
Blairgowrie PH10 . . . 88 C5
Carnoustie DD7 . . . 100 B2
Dundee DD1 . . . 179 A2
11 Leven KY8 . . . 79 F1
Browns Wynd 8 DD6 . . . 99 F6
Broxden Ave PH2 . . . 102 B2
Broxden Bsns Pk PH2 . . . 102 B2
Bruce Ave FK15 . . . 107 B5
Bruce Brae FK15 . . . 107 E7
Bruce Cres PH1 . . . 102 D6
Bruce Dr
Carnoustie DD7 . . . 100 B3
Fallin FK7 . . . 136 C5
Bruce Emb KY16 . . . 106 C7
BRUCEFIELD . . . 161 C2
Brucefield Ave KY11 . . . 161 B2
Brucefield Cres FK10 . . . 139 B4
Brucefield Feus KY11 . . . 161 C3
Brucefield Rd PH10 . . . 88 E2
Brucefield Terr KY4 . . . 147 F6
Bruce Gate FK2 . . . 154 D2
Bruce Gdns KY11 . . . 174 A8
Brucehaven Cres KY11 . . . 172 E3
Brucehaven Rd KY11 . . . 172 D3
Bruce Rd
Arbroath DD11 . . . 89 D5
Dundee DD3 . . . 93 E8
Glenrothes KY7 . . . 113 B6
4 Kinross KY13 . . . 76 F5
Bruce Sq 3 KY9 . . . 82 A5
Bruce St
Alloa FK10 . . . 138 C7
Bannockburn FK7 . . . 135 E1
Clackmannan FK10 . . . 139 A4
Bruce St *continued*
Dundee DD3 . . . 179 A4
Dunfermline KY12 . . . 160 F4
Kinghorn KY3 . . . 167 A3
St Andrews KY16 . . . 106 D4
Stirling FK8 . . . 115 B1
Bruce Terr
Cambusbarron FK7 . . . 134 D5
Kinghorn KY3 . . . 167 A3
Bruce View FK7 . . . 135 B1
Brunel Rd DD2 . . . 92 C7
BRUNTHILL . . . 75 F3
Bruntley Pl 13 KY15 . . . 63 E1
BRUNTON . . . 52 A7
Brunton Ct 9 KY7 . . . 113 F8
Brunton Dr KY7 . . . 113 F8
Brunton Gdns KY7 . . . 113 F8
Brunton Pk KY7 . . . 113 F8
Brunton Pl 5 KY7 . . . 113 F8
Brunton Quadrant 4 KY7 . . . 113 B6
Brunton Rd KY7 . . . 113 F8
Brunton St 6 KY15 . . . 63 B2
Bryanston Dr FK14 . . . 120 C8
Bryony The FK10 . . . 117 B1
Buccaneer Way PH2 . . . 38 B6
Buccleuch Ct FK15 . . . 107 D6
Buchanan Ct KY1 . . . 151 B2
Buchanan Dr FK9 . . . 115 B3
Buchanan Gdns
Cairneyhill KY12 . . . 159 D1
St Andrews KY16 . . . 106 A5
Buchanan Pk 3 KY15 . . . 65 D6
Buchanan Rd KY7 . . . 113 A6
Buchanan St
Dundee DD4 . . . 179 C4
Dunfermline KY12 . . . 161 A3
Buchan Ave 1 KY13 . . . 76 F5
Buchan Dr
Dunblane FK15 . . . 107 B5
Perth PH1 . . . 102 D3
Buchan Gdns 5 KY8 . . . 79 F1
Buchan Path KY6 . . . 112 F7
Buchan Rd PH1 . . . 102 D3
BUCHANTY . . . 34 D7
BUCKHAVEN . . . 133 E8
Buckhaven High Sch KY8 . . . 79 F2
Buckhaven Mus* KY8 . . . 79 F1
Buckhaven Prim Sch KY8 . . . 109 A1
Buckhaven Theatre KY8 . . . 79 F1
Bucklemaker Ct DD3 . . . 93 F6
Bucklerscroft DD5 . . . 30 E7
Bucklers Wynd DD5 . . . 30 E6
Bucksburn Pk KY7 . . . 110 E2
Buckyburn Pl KY12 . . . 161 E6
Buddon Dr
Carnoustie DD7 . . . 100 A2
Monifieth DD5 . . . 97 B7
Buddon Pl DD7 . . . 100 A2
Buffies Brae KY12 . . . 160 F4
Bughties Rd DD5 . . . 96 B3
Buick Pl DD4 . . . 94 F6
Buick Rigg DD11 . . . 89 C4
Bulb Farm Rd PH12 . . . 17 B4
Bulb Pk PH12 . . . 17 B4
Buller St KY5 . . . 148 B7
Bunkerhill Cres DD8 . . . 10 F4
Buntine Cres FK7 . . . 135 A3
Burgess Rd EH30 . . . 178 C1
Burgess St DD3 . . . 179 A4
Burgh Ct KY5 . . . 148 A7
Burgh Mews 1 FK10 . . . 138 B6
BURGHMUIR . . . 102 C3
Burghmuir Ind Est FK8 . . . 135 B6
Burghmuir Rd
Perth PH1 . . . 102 C4
Stirling FK7 . . . 135 B6
Burgh Rd KY4 . . . 147 D4
Burial Brae 22 KY10 . . . 83 C6
Burial Rd KY13 . . . 76 C7
Burleigh Cres KY11 . . . 174 C3
Burleigh Ct KY7 . . . 113 C3
Burleigh Golf Course KY13 . . . 108 D6
Burleigh Rd KY13 . . . 108 D7
Burleigh Way FK10 . . . 138 C6
Burnbank
8 Bridge of Earn PH2 . . . 48 F5
Cairneyhill KY12 . . . 159 D1
Carnock KY12 . . . 159 C7
Leven KY8 . . . 79 E4
Burnbank Pl 6 KY5 . . . 77 E1
Burnbank Terr
Perth PH2 . . . 103 C5
Thornton KY1 . . . 113 D1
Burnbrae
Alloa FK10 . . . 138 C8
Sauchie FK10 . . . 118 C1
Burnbrae Gdns FK12 . . . 118 B6
Burn Brae Pk FK10 . . . 155 F4
Burn Dr FK7 . . . 135 C4
Burnee FK10 . . . 118 E3
Burney Pl KY11 . . . 173 E4
BURNFOOT . . . 73 E7
Burnhaven Gdns DD5 . . . 95 C4
Burnhead Rd PH10 . . . 88 A5
Burnhill La KY8 . . . 79 F5
Burnlea Terr 9 KY5 . . . 77 E1
Burnmill Rd KY8 . . . 109 D6
Burns Ave
6 Leven KY8 . . . 79 F1
Leven KY8 . . . 109 A1
Burns-Begg St 13 KY13 . . . 108 C2
Burns Begg St KY13 . . . 108 D2
BURNSIDE . . . 118 C7
Burnside
12 Auchtermuchty KY14 . . . 62 F6
8 Cupar KY15 . . . 64 D4
Kinglassie KY5 . . . 77 F1
8 Monance KY10 . . . 82 E4
New Scone PH2 . . . 103 E8
St Andrews KY16 . . . 53 E7
Burn Side PH2 . . . 103 C5
Burnside Ave KY3 . . . 166 F3
Burnside Bsns Ct KY11 . . . 174 C4
Burnside Cres
Clackmannan FK10 . . . 139 B5
Rosyth KY11 . . . 174 A5
Burnside Ct
Alva FK12 . . . 118 A7
27 Alyth PH11 . . . 7 A3
Lochee DD2 . . . 93 C5
Burnside Dr DD11 . . . 89 D4
Burnside Gdns
1 Carnoustie DD7 . . . 100 C2
5 Dundee DD2 . . . 93 C6
Burnside N KY15 . . . 105 C5
Burnside Pk PH1 . . . 36 E6
Burnside Pl
13 Anstruther Easter KY10 . . . 83 D6
1 Kelty KY4 . . . 126 E1
Montrose DD10 . . . 85 B1
Rosyth KY11 . . . 174 A4
Burnside Rd
Carnoustie DD7 . . . 32 A4
Invergowrie DD2 . . . 92 C3
1 Letham DD8 . . . 11 E3
Menstrie FK11 . . . 116 F6
Perth PH2 . . . 38 C8
Burnside St
Alloa FK10 . . . 118 D1
Carnoustie DD7 . . . 100 C2
Dundee DD2 . . . 93 B6
Rosyth KY11 . . . 174 A5
Stirling FK7 . . . 135 C6
Burnside Terr
12 Anstruther Easter KY10 . . . 83 D6
17 Auchtermuchty KY14 . . . 62 F6
Cowdenbeath KY4 . . . 147 A2
Oakley KY12 . . . 159 A7
Burnside Wlk 6 DD2 . . . 93 C6
Burns Rd KY6 . . . 112 F7
Burns St
Dunfermline KY12 . . . 160 E5
High Valleyfield KY12 . . . 158 A2
Stirling FK8 . . . 115 A2
Burn St DD3 . . . 91 D2
Burns Wynd KY1 . . . 132 F2
BURNTISLAND . . . 165 E2
Burntisland Mus* KY3 . . . 177 E8
Burntisland Prim Sch KY3 . . . 165 F1
Burntisland Rd KY3 . . . 166 F2
Burntisland Sta KY3 . . . 177 E8
Burnview DD3 . . . 91 F3
Burrell St PH7 . . . 101 B3
BURRELTON . . . 26 C8
Burrelton Ct KY7 . . . 113 D2
Burrelton Gdns DD3 . . . 91 B3
Burrelton Prim Sch PH13 . . . 26 B8
Burt Ave KY3 . . . 166 F3
Burt Gr KY11 . . . 161 E1
Burt St KY12 . . . 161 A6
Bute Cres KY11 . . . 161 E3
Bute Dr PH1 . . . 102 E8
Bute Pl KY7 . . . 111 A2
Bute Wynd KY1 . . . 151 B2
Buttar's Loan DD2 . . . 92 F6
Buttar's Pl DD2 . . . 92 F6
Buttar's Rd DD2 . . . 92 F6
Buttar's St DD2 . . . 92 E6
Buttar's Terr 1 DD2 . . . 92 F6
Butterburn Ct DD3 . . . 93 F6
Butterburn Sq DD3 . . . 179 A4
Butter Rd KY13 . . . 60 A1
Butterstone Pl PH2 . . . 103 E8
Butterstone Sch PH12 . . . 16 E5
Butter Wynd 5 DD6 . . . 99 F6
Butterybank 3 PH13 . . . 15 F3
Byres The KY11 . . . 173 C5
Byre Theatre of St Andrews The KY16 . . . 106 E6
Byron Cres DD3 . . . 93 D6
Byron Ct KY8 . . . 109 B4
Byron St
Dundee DD3 . . . 93 E6
Leven KY8 . . . 109 A4
Byron Terr DD3 . . . 93 E6

C

Cabbagehall Pl KY6 . . . 112 B7
Cabbagehall Rd KY6 . . . 112 B7
Cable Rd KY6 . . . 112 F4
Caddam Cres DD8 . . . 86 D7
Caddam Rd PH13 . . . 15 F2
Caddies Burn 12 KY10 . . . 83 C6
Cadell Reach KY11 . . . 174 A7
Cadgers Rd
Arbroath DD11 . . . 22 F8
Brechin DD9 . . . 4 E2
Cadgers' Rd KY9 . . . 66 F2
CADHAM . . . 111 B1
Cadham Cres KY7 . . . 111 B1

Cadham Ct 4 KY7 .... 111 B1
Cadham House KY7 ...... 113 B8
Cadham Rd KY7 .... 111 A1
Cadham Sq KY7 .... 111 C1
Cadham Terr KY7 .... 111 B1
Cadham Villas 3 KY7 .... 111 B1
Cadzow Pl 1 KY6 .... 112 F6
Caenlochan Gdns DD11 ... 89 B4
Caenlochan Pl DD5 .... 95 D4
Caenlochan Rd DD5 ...... 95 E4
Caesar Ave DD7 .... 100 E4
Caiplie Craig 22 KY10 .... 83 A5
Caird Ave
Dundee DD3 .... 93 F7
Montrose DD10 .... 85 B1
Caird Pk Golf Club DD4 ... 94 B7
Caird Terr DD3 .... 93 F7
Cairncubie Rd
Dunfermline KY12 .... 145 C1
Townhill KY12 .... 161 C8
CAIRNEYHILL 159 C2
Cairneyhill Prim Sch
KY12 .... 159 D2
Cairneyhill Rd
Crossford KY12 .... 160 B2
Perth PH1 .... 24 A6
Cairngorm Cres KY2 ..... 150 F5
Cairngorm Dr KY6 .... 110 E3
Cairn Gr KY12 .... 160 C2
Cairnhill Gdns KY16 ..... 106 A3
CAIRNIE 89 B6
Cairnie Braes PH3 .... 47 A5
Cairnie Cres
Arbroath DD11 .... 89 C5
Perth PH2 .... 49 F7
Cairniehill Gdns DD11 ..... 89 B5
Cairnie Loan DD11 .... 89 C5
Cairnie Mega Maze The*
KY15 .... 52 E4
Cairnie Pl DD11 .... 89 C5
Cairnie Rd
Arbroath DD11 .... 89 B5
Perth PH2 .... 49 F6
Cairnie St DD11 .... 89 C4
Cairnie Terr 5 PH2 .... 49 F7
Cairnleith Pl 30 PH11 ...... 7 A3
Cairnleith St 31 PH11 ...... 7 A3
Cairnoch Way FK7 .... 135 F1
Cairn O'Mohr Fruit Wines
Visitor Ctr* PH2 .... 39 E4
Cairnpark St 25 FK14 ..... 73 C1
Cairn Rd DD8 .... 86 D7
Cairns Cres PH1 .... 102 D6
Cairns Ct PH7 .... 101 E4
Cairnsden Gdns KY16 .... 106 B3
Cairns Pk PH11 .... 7 A2
Cairns Pl
2 Dollar FK14 .... 74 A3
Perth PH1 .... 102 D7
Cairns St E KY1 .... 151 E7
Cairns St W KY1 .... 151 D7
Cairns Terr 1 KY8 .... 79 F2
Cairns The
Charlestown KY11 .... 172 A4
Menstrie FK11 .... 117 A6
Cairnton Pl 2 FK13 ..... 119 B7
Cairnton St FK13 .... 119 B6
Cairnwell Cres DD10 ...... 85 C8
Cairnwell Pl
Cairneyhill KY12 .... 159 D1
Kirkcaldy KY2 .... 150 F7
Cairnwell View PH1 ..... 102 C4
Caithness Ct KY1 .... 151 E7
Caithness Dr KY11 ...... 162 C1
Caithness Glass Visitor
Ctr* PH1 .... 37 B5
Caithness Pl KY1 .... 151 E7
Calaisburn Pl KY11 ...... 161 E1
Calais View KY11 .... 161 F1
Calcutta La DD1 .... 179 C2
Calder Cres DD5 .... 96 A4
Calder Ct
6 Crail KY10 .... 69 B2
Glenrothes KY7 .... 111 A4
Stirling FK7 .... 135 C5
Calder Pl
Dalgety Bay KY11 .... 175 A3
Forfar DD8 .... 87 C3
Calderwood Cl 3 DD2 ..... 93 C6
Caldhame Gdns DD9 ...... 84 E3
Caldhame Pl DD9 .... 84 E2
Caldrum St DD3 .... 179 B4
Caldrum Terr DD3 .... 179 B4
Caldwell Acre KY15 .... 64 A3
Caledonia Hts KY11 ..... 173 C3
Caledonian Cres PH3 ..... 57 E6
Caledonian Pl
Alloa FK10 .... 138 A6
Dunblane FK15 .... 107 D5
Montrose DD10 .... 85 D2
Caledonian Rd
Alloa FK10 .... 137 F6
Brechin DD9 .... 84 C4
Perth PH2 .... 103 A3
Caledonian Rd Prim Sch
PH2 .... 103 A3
Caledonian Rly* DD9 ..... 84 F1
Caledonia Rd KY11 ...... 173 A1
Caledonia St DD10 .... 85 D2
Caledonia Way KY11 ..... 173 A3
Caledon St DD1 .... 94 D2
Calender Ave KY1 .... 151 C7
Calfford Brae PH2 .... 61 B4
California St 9 DD10 ..... 85 C2
Callander Pl 12 DD8 ...... 87 E5
Callander Terr KY11 ..... 162 A4
Callender Gdns DD4 .... 179 C3
Calliope Rd KY11 .... 173 B1
Callum's Hill PH7 .... 101 E5
Calsay Gdns 9 KY14 ..... 63 A6
Calton Cres FK7 .... 135 B4
Calton St 10 PH13 .... 16 A3
Caltrop Pl FK7 .... 135 E3
Calum Macdonald Ct
KY11 .... 173 E3
CAMBO 69 A6
Cambo Gdns* KY16 .... 69 A6
Cambridge Quad 34
PH11 .... 7 A3
Cambridge St
Alyth PH11 .... 7 A3
Dundee DD2 .... 93 A3
CAMBUS 137 B8
CAMBUSBARRON 134 C6
Cambusbarron Prim Sch
FK7 .... 134 D5
CAMBUSKENNETH 115 D1
Cambuskenneth Abbey*
FK9 .... 135 D8
Cambusmichael Rd
PH2 .... 37 C8
Cambus Pools Nature
Reserve* FK10 .... 136 F8
Cambustay Gdns 3
DD5 .... 96 D3
Camdean Cres KY11 .... 173 D5
Camdean La KY11 ...... 173 D5
Camdean Prim Sch
KY11 .... 173 D4
Cameron Ave 8 KY13 .... 108 B4
Cameron Bridge KY8 ...... 79 E2
Cameron Cres
Glenrothes KY6 .... 112 E7
Leven KY8 .... 79 E3
Cameron Dr 9 KY15 ...... 63 B2
Cameron Gr KY11 .... 174 B3
Cameronian St 9 FK8 .... 135 B7
Cameron Pk KY1 .... 131 D8
Cameron Pl PH7 .... 101 E3
Cameron Rd PH2 .... 38 B6
Cameron St KY12 .... 160 E4
Camilla Gr KY2 .... 149 C2
Campbell Cres
Arbroath DD11 .... 89 A7
Cupar KY15 .... 105 E3
Lochgelly KY5 .... 148 B8
Campbell Ct FK7 .... 134 F4
Campbell Pl KY6 .... 112 E7
Campbell St
6 Coupar Angus PH13 ..... 16 A3
Dollar FK14 .... 120 E8
Dundee DD3 .... 93 D5
Dunfermline KY12 .... 161 A4
Campbell Way 7 KY16 ..... 54 B7
Camperdown Dr DD11 .... 89 A5
Camperdown Golf Club
DD2 .... 92 D8
Camperdown Pl 1
KY2 .... 130 F1
Camperdown Rd
Dundee DD3 .... 91 D1
Rosyth KY11 .... 173 C1
Camperdown St
Dundee DD1 .... 179 C2
11 Dundee DD2 .... 93 B6
Camperdown Wildlife
Ctr* DD2 .... 92 D8
Campfield Gdns DD5 ..... 96 B4
Campfield Rd DD5 .... 96 C4
Campfield Sq 6 DD5 ...... 96 C4
Camphill Pl 4 DD5 .... 96 A3
Camphill Rd DD5 .... 96 B3
Camp Rd KY12 .... 171 D5
Campsie Cres KY2 .... 150 F7
Campsie Rd PH1 .... 102 C5
Camps Rd KY12 .... 159 C6
Camus Pl DD5 .... 20 F1
Camus Rd DD11 .... 89 E5
Camus St DD7 .... 100 C3
Canal Cres PH2 .... 103 B3
Canal St PH2 .... 103 B3
Canavan Ct FK7 .... 135 C3
Candie Rd FK3 .... 168 B1
Candlehouse La 4
PH13 .... 16 A2
Candle La DD1 .... 179 C2
Candleriggs FK10 .... 138 B6
Candleriggs Ct 7
FK10 .... 138 B6
Canisp Cres DD2 .... 92 C5
Canmore Gdns KY2 ...... 130 F2
Canmore Gr KY12 .... 161 B5
Canmore Path 6 KY7 .... 113 B6
Canmore Pl
Auchterarder PH3 .... 104 E6
1 Glenrothes KY7 .... 113 B6
Canmore Prim Sch
KY11 .... 161 E1
Canmore Rd 5 KY7 ...... 113 B6
Canmore St
Dunfermline KY12 .... 161 A3
Forfar DD8 .... 87 D5
Kinghorn KY3 .... 166 F1
Canmore Terr KY12 ..... 161 A7
Canning Pl 3 DD3 .... 93 F6
Canning St DD3 .... 93 F6
Canon Byrne Glebe
KY1 .... 151 C5
Canongate KY16 .... 106 B4
Canongate Prim Sch
KY16 .... 106 B5
Canon Lynch Ct KY12 .... 160 F4
Cant Cres 11 KY16 .... 54 E2
Cantlie Pl KY11 .... 173 E3
Cantsdam Rd KY4 .... 146 F7
Capledrae Ct
3 Ballingry KY5 .... 127 F7
Lochgelly KY5 .... 128 A7
Capshard Prim Sch
KY2 .... 131 A2
Cara Pl PH1 .... 102 E8
Carberry Cres 3 DD4 ..... 95 A8
Carberry Pk KY8 .... 109 F7
Carberry Pl KY1 .... 131 D1
Carberry Rd
Kirkcaldy KY1 .... 131 D1
Leven KY8 .... 109 E7
Carcraig Pl KY11 .... 175 B3
Cardean St 1 DD4 .... 94 C3
Cardean Way KY6 .... 110 E2
Carden Ave KY5 .... 129 C2
Cardenbarns Rd KY5 .... 129 C2
Carden Castle Ave
KY5 .... 129 C2
Carden Castle Pk KY5 ... 129 C3
Carden Cres KY5 .... 129 C3
CARDENDEN 129 C2
Cardenden Prim Sch
KY5 .... 129 B2
Cardenden Rd KY5 ...... 129 D3
Cardenden Sta KY5 ..... 129 B2
Cardowrie Loan KY7 ...... 79 B3
Cardross Pl DD3 .... 94 B5
Cardross St DD3 .... 94 B5
Cards Wynd 18 KY10 ...... 83 C6
CARESTON 3 D7
Carfrae Dr KY6 .... 112 D7
CARGILL 25 D7
Cargill Pl
Letham PH1 .... 102 D4
9 Rattray PH10 .... 88 D5
Carleton Ave KY7 .... 113 E5
Carleton Cres KY7 ...... 113 E6
Carleton Prim Sch
KY7 .... 113 D5
Carlie Ave FK9 .... 115 A6
Carlile Pl PH1 .... 102 F6
Carlin Craig KY3 .... 166 F1
Carlin Cres KY3 .... 166 F1
Carlingnose Ct KY11 .... 178 C6
Carlingnose Pk KY11 .... 178 C6
Carlingnose Point
KY11 .... 178 C6
Carlingnose View
KY11 .... 178 C6
Carlingnose Way
KY11 .... 178 C6
Carlochie Pl DD4 .... 94 F3
Carlogie Farm Rd
DD7 .... 100 C5
Carlogie Prim Sch
DD7 .... 100 E4
Carlogie Rd 1 DD7 ..... 100 E4
Carlow Ct KY8 .... 109 D6
Carlownie Pl PH3 .... 104 E6
Carlungie Earth House*
DD7 .... 31 D6
Carlunie Rd DD2 .... 93 B7
Carlunie St DD2 .... 93 B7
Carlyle Cres KY8 .... 79 F1
Carlyle La 1 KY12 ...... 160 E5
Carlyle Rd
Glenrothes KY6 .... 112 F6
Kirkcaldy KY1 .... 151 B4
Carlyle St KY12 .... 158 B2
Carmichael Ct
Bridge of A FK9 .... 115 A7
Dundee DD3 .... 179 A4
Carmichael Gdns DD3 ... 179 A4
Carmichael Pl FK14 ..... 119 C4
Carmichael St DD3 ..... 179 A4
CARMYLLIE 21 C5
Carmyllie Pl 2 DD5 ...... 97 A7
Carmyllie Prim Sch
DD11 .... 21 E7
Carnach FK10 .... 138 D6
Carnaughton Pl FK12 .... 117 F6
Carnbane Dr DD5 .... 96 B5
CARNBEE 67 F1
Carnbee Pl
Dunfermline KY12 .... 161 C4
Glenrothes KY7 .... 113 A2
CARNBO 74 F6
Carnegie Ave KY11 ..... 173 E7
Carnegie Campus (Bsns
Pk) KY11 .... 173 E7
Carnegie Ct
Dunfermline KY12 .... 161 A4
Montrose DD10 .... 85 D4
Muirton PH1 .... 103 A6
Carnegie Dr KY12 .... 161 A4
Carnegie Drive Ret Pk
KY12 .... 161 A4
Carnegie Pl
Glenrothes KY6 .... 112 F6
Perth PH1 .... 102 F7
Carnegie Sq DD3 .... 179 B3
Carnegie St
Arbroath DD11 .... 89 E5
Dundee DD3 .... 179 B4
Montrose DD10 .... 85 D4
Carneil Rd KY12 .... 159 C7
Carneil Terr KY12 ...... 159 C6
Carnethy Cres KY2 ..... 150 F7
CARNOCK 159 D6
Carnock Mill KY12 ...... 159 C7
Carnock Prim Sch
KY12 .... 159 C7
Carnock Rd KY12 .... 159 E7
CARNOUSTIE 100 D2
Carnoustie Ct 7 DD3 ..... 91 B2
Carnoustie Gdns KY6 ... 112 A5
Carnoustie Golf Links
DD7 .... 100 C1
Carnoustie High Sch
DD7 .... 100 B4
Carnoustie Sta DD7 ..... 100 E2
Carolina Ct DD1 .... 94 E2
Carolina St DD1 .... 94 E2
Caroline Cres FK12 ..... 117 F6
Caroline Pl PH2 .... 25 D4
Carpenter St 5 PH1 ..... 103 B4
Carpenters Wynd
FK10 .... 137 F6
Carradale Dr DD4 .... 95 D8
Carradale Gdns 2
KY2 .... 130 F1
Carr Cres 5 KY10 .... 69 A2
Carrick Ct FK7 .... 135 C5
Carrick Dr KY11 .... 175 A3
Carrick Gr KY11 .... 175 A3
Carrington Terr PH7 .... 101 C4
Carron Gr KY11 .... 161 F4
Carron La KY11 .... 161 F4
Carron Pl
Broughty Ferry DD5 ...... 96 B5
Dunnikier KY2 .... 130 D1
5 Glenrothes KY6 .... 112 E6
Kirkcaldy KY2 .... 150 D8
8 St Andrews KY16 .... 54 E2
Stirling FK7 .... 135 B2
Carsaig Ct FK9 .... 115 A5
Carsebridge Ct FK10 .... 138 C8
Carsebridge Rd FK10 ... 138 D8
Carsebridge Row
FK10 .... 138 D8
Carseburn Rd DD8 .... 87 D6
Carseburn Terr 3 DD8 .... 10 F7
Carseggie Cres KY7 ..... 113 D6
Carselea Rd DD2 .... 92 B3
Carse Pl DD2 .... 92 A2
Carse Terr FK10 .... 137 F8
Carseview
Bannockburn FK7 .... 135 E2
Dunblane FK15 .... 56 B4
Tullibody FK10 .... 117 A3
Carse View FK2 .... 154 E4
Carseview Gdns DD2 ..... 93 A2
Carseview Rd DD8 .... 87 D7
Carseview Terr 2 DD8 .... 10 F7
CARSIE 15 B5
Carslogie Rd KY15 ..... 105 A4
Carson Pl KY11 .... 173 C5
Carswell Pl KY12 .... 160 F6
Carswell Wynd 23 KY14 ... 62 F6
Cartmore Ind Est KY5 .... 128 A2
Cartmore Rd KY5 .... 148 A8
Cart Pl DD2 .... 92 E5
CARVENOM 83 A8
Carwhinny KY1 .... 131 E1
Casan KY8 .... 109 C8
Cash Feus 2 KY14 .... 62 D4
Cask Cres FK8 .... 135 C8
CASKIEBERRAN 112 D5
Caskieberran Dr KY6 .... 112 E5
Caskieberran Prim Sch
KY6 .... 112 D5
Caskieberran Rd KY6 ... 112 D5
Castings The KY12 ...... 160 D6
Castlandhill Farm
Steadings KY11 .... 173 F2
Castlandhill Rd KY11 ... 174 A2
Castle App DD5 .... 96 A2
Castle Ave
Airth FK2 .... 154 E3
Crosshill KY5 .... 127 F5
Castle Bank 1 DD6 .... 98 C3
Castlebank Gdns 5
KY15 .... 105 D5
Castlebank Rd KY15 .... 105 D5
Castleblair 2 KY12 ..... 160 F4
Castleblair La 2 KY12 ... 160 F5
Castleblair Mews 3
KY12 .... 160 F5
CASTLEBLAIR PARK 160 F4
Castleblair Pk KY12 .... 160 F5
Castle Brae
2 Auchterarder PH3 .... 104 D6
Dunfermline KY11 ...... 173 F6
4 Newport-on-Tay DD6 ... 98 C3
Perth PH1 .... 102 A7
Castle Bsns Pk The
FK9 .... 114 E2
Castle Campbell & Gdn*
FK14 .... 73 B2
Castlecary Gdns 4
DD4 .... 94 F8
Castle Ct
Dunfermline KY11 ...... 173 F6
Menstrie FK11 .... 116 F6
Stirling FK8 .... 135 A8
Castle Dr
Airth FK2 .... 154 E3
Dunfermline KY11 ...... 173 E6
Castle Driveway KY9 ..... 82 A5
Castlefield KY15 .... 105 D5
Castlegait 6 FK8 .... 135 B7
Castlegate 2 KY15 .... 65 E6
Castle Gate KY11 .... 173 E3
Castle Gr DD2 .... 40 E8
Castle Hill KY15 .... 105 D5
Castlehill Pl 2 KY15 .... 105 D5
Castlehill Prim Sch
KY15 .... 105 D3
Castle La DD5 .... 96 B2
Castlelaw Cres PH2 ...... 49 E2
Castlemount Terr KY2 ... 150 C8
Castle Pk
3 Ceres KY15 .... 65 E6
12 Falkland KY15 .... 63 B2
Castle Pk continued
Kincardine FK10 .... 155 D6
Castle Pl
3 Montrose DD10 .... 85 C3
Perth PH1 .... 102 C6
11 Perth PH2 .... 49 F7
Castle Rd
Dollar FK14 .... 73 C2
Dundee DD2 .... 40 E8
Menstrie FK11 .... 116 F6
Perth PH2 .... 25 D4
Rosyth KY11 .... 173 E2
Stirling FK9 .... 115 C3
3 Tayport DD6 .... 99 F7
Castlerig KY3 .... 166 F2
Castle Row KY12 .... 160 C6
Castleroy Cres DD5 ...... 96 B3
Castleroy Entry PH4 ...... 57 B3
Castleroy Rd DD5 .... 96 B3
Castle St Ind Est FK10 .. 138 A6
Castle St
Alloa FK10 .... 138 A5
Anstruther KY10 .... 82 D8
15 Anstruther Wester
KY10 .... 83 C6
8 Arbroath DD11 .... 12 F4
Blairgowrie PH10 .... 88 C4
Brechin DD9 .... 84 B3
Broughty Ferry DD5 ...... 96 B2
Clackmannan FK10 ..... 139 A4
Coalsnaughton FK13 .... 119 C4
14 Crail KY10 .... 69 B2
3 Cupar KY15 .... 105 D5
Dundee DD1 .... 179 B2
2 Forfar DD8 .... 87 D5
4 Monance KY10 .... 82 E4
Montrose DD10 .... 85 C3
Newtyle PH12 .... 17 B4
Tayport DD6 .... 99 F6
Castle Terr
8 Broughty Ferry DD5 .... 96 B2
Clackmannan FK10 ..... 139 A4
Dundee DD4 .... 94 C5
Leven KY8 .... 79 F4
4 Tayport DD6 .... 99 F7
CASTLETON 104 C7
Castleton Pk PH3 ...... 104 C6
Castleton Pl DD5 .... 95 F5
Castleton Rd PH3 ...... 104 C7
Castle Vale FK9 .... 115 A4
Castle View
Aberdour KY3 .... 176 C8
Airth FK2 .... 154 D2
Dunfermline KY11 ...... 173 F6
Fallin FK7 .... 136 D4
Perth PH1 .... 102 B6
Castleview Dr FK9 ..... 115 A7
Castle Way PH2 .... 49 F7
Castlewood Ave
Caird Park DD4 .... 94 B8
Claverhouse DD4 .... 29 E5
Castlewood Brae
Caird Park DD4 .... 94 B8
1 Claverhouse DD4 .... 29 E5
Castle Wynd
Auchterarder PH3 .... 104 E7
Kinghorn KY3 .... 166 F2
4 Stirling FK8 .... 135 A8
Castwell Wynd 3 KY9 .... 82 A2
Cathel Sq 2 KY15 .... 64 A3
Catherine Pl 9 DD6 ...... 99 F7
Catherine St
Arbroath DD11 .... 89 C3
Bannockburn FK7 .... 135 C1
6 Dundee DD4 .... 94 C4
Catherine Terr KY5 ..... 127 F5
Catmoor Ave PH2 .... 103 E8
Catmoor Rd 20 PH2 .... 37 F5
Catmoor Sq 15 PH2 .... 37 F5
Catterline Cres DD3 ...... 91 A3
Cattle Market FK10 ..... 139 A4
Cauldhame Cres FK7 .... 134 C5
Causeway Ct KY13 ...... 108 D2
Causewayend 7 PH13 ..... 15 F3
CAUSEWAYHEAD 115 B4
Causewayhead Rd
FK9 .... 115 C3
Causeway La KY12 ...... 158 E1
Causeway The
Bridge of A FK9 .... 115 D5
Kinross KY13 .... 77 A3
Leven KY8 .... 79 E5
Cavel Pl 1 KY9 .... 82 A3
Cavendish Ave PH2 ..... 102 F2
Cavendish Way KY6 ..... 112 D2
Cawder Gdns FK9 .... 114 F8
Cawder Rd FK9 .... 114 F7
Cawdor Cres
Dunblane FK15 .... 107 C5
Kirkcaldy KY2 .... 150 E6
Cawdor Dr KY6 .... 112 D6
Caxton Pl KY1 .... 131 E1
Cecil St FK7 .... 135 B6
Cedar Ave
Blairgowrie PH10 .... 88 D3
Kirkcaldy KY1 .... 151 C8
2 Leven KY8 .... 79 F3
Stirling FK8 .... 134 F5
Cedar Cres
Cowdenbeath KY4 ...... 147 D6
Thornton KY1 .... 131 D7
Cedar Dr
Glenrothes KY7 .... 110 F1
Perth PH1 .... 102 B3

Cedar Gr
Dundee DD5 96 A3
Dunfermline KY11 173 D8
Cedar Pl PH1 102 B3
Cedar Rd DD5 96 A4
Cedars The
6 Dundee DD4 95 A8
Tullibody FK10 117 B2
Cedarwood Dr DD2 93 C6
Cemetery Rd
Dunblane FK15 107 E7
1 Kirriemuir DD8 86 D5
Centenary Ct KY8 109 B6
Central Ave KY7 113 B7
Central Dock Rd FK3 168 A1
Central Pk (Cowdenbeath FC) KY4 147 C4
Central Rd KY12 171 D7
Central Way KY11 175 C5
Centre St KY4 126 D1
Ceramic Creations* DD7 100 D3
Ceramic Experience The* PH7 44 C5
CERES 65 E6
Ceres Cres DD5 96 C5
Ceres Prim Sch KY15 65 E6
Ceres Rd KY15 105 D3
Chaise Rd PH2 48 E5
Chalk Hill Ct DD4 95 B8
Challum Cres DD5 96 E6
Challum Pl DD5 96 E6
Chalmers Brae 9 KY10 83 C6
Chalmers Ho KY12 160 F3
Chalmers Pl FK13 119 D7
Chalmers St
6 Arbroath DD11 89 D3
3 Dundee DD4 94 C4
Dunfermline KY12 160 F4
4 Perth PH2 47 A1
Chalmerston Rd FK9 114 B2
Chalton Ct FK9 115 B7
Chalton Rd FK9 115 B7
Chamberfield Rd KY12 161 C6
Chamberlain St KY16 106 D4
Chambers Ct KY4 147 D4
Chambers Pl 12 KY16 54 E2
Chamfron Gdns FK7 135 E3
CHANCE INN 65 B5
Chandlers Rise KY11 174 F4
Chandler's Rise KY11 174 F4
Chandlers Wlk KY11 174 F4
Channonry Wynd DD9 84 C3
CHAPEL 150 C8
Chapelcroft FK7 134 D6
Chapelfauld Gn KY11 161 F3
Chapel Gn Rd KY9 82 A2
Chapel Gr KY2 150 C8
CHAPELHILL 50 A8
Chapelhill
Clackmannan FK10 139 A3
Kirkcaldy KY2 150 D8
Chapelhill St FK10 155 D5
Chapelle Cres FK13 119 B6
Chapel Level KY2 130 D1
Chapel Pk KY2 130 C1
Chapel Pl
26 Dollar FK14 73 C1
High Valleyfield KY12 158 B2
Inverkeithing KY11 174 C3
3 Kirkcaldy KY2 130 C1
1 Montrose DD10 85 D3
North Queensferry KY11 178 C5
Chapel Rd
Crieff PH7 101 B3
Cupar KY14 63 B5
Dundee DD5 19 F1
Kirkcaldy KY2 150 C8
Chapel St
11 Alyth PH11 7 A3
Cowdenbeath KY4 147 C3
Dundee DD1 179 B2
8 Dunfermline KY12 160 F4
Forfar DD8 87 D5
High Valleyfield KY12 158 B2
Kincardine FK10 155 E3
9 Leven KY8 79 F1
Lochgelly KY5 148 B8
Montrose DD10 85 D3
CHAPELTON 13 C2
Chapelton Dr KY2 130 C1
Chapel Villas KY11 175 B2
Chapelwell Pl KY11 161 F3
Chapel Wynd PH3 104 D7
Chapman Dr DD7 100 E4
Chapmans Pl 5 KY9 82 B3
Charles Ave
8 Arbroath DD11 89 A4
Bridge of A FK9 115 B6
Charles Bowman Ave DD4 29 F5
Charles Ct KY11 172 F3
Charles Jarvis Ct KY15 105 C4
Charles Logan Pl KY11 173 F4
Charles Pl 6 DD7 100 C2
Charles Rodger Pl FK9 115 A6
Charles St
Alloa FK10 137 F8
Carnoustie DD7 100 C2
Dunblane FK15 107 C4

Charles St *continued*
Dunfermline KY11 161 B2
3 Perth PH2 103 B3
4 Pittenweem KY10 83 A5
Stirling FK8 135 A5
CHARLESTON
Dundee 92 D7
Forfar 18 E8
Charleston Dr
Dundee DD2 92 E5
Glenrothes KY7 113 D2
Charleston Prim Sch DD2 92 D6
Charleston Rd
Dundee DD2 92 E6
3 Forfar DD8 9 C1
Charleston St 1 DD2 92 D6
CHARLESTOWN 172 B4
Charles Way KY11 172 E3
Charles Way S KY11 172 E3
Charleton Golf Course KY9 81 E6
Charleton Pk 3 DD10 85 D7
Charleton Pl DD10 85 D7
Charleton Rd DD10 85 D7
Charlotte Cl DD3 93 D8
Charlotte Pl
1 Dundee DD3 91 D1
8 Perth PH1 103 B4
Tillicoultry FK13 119 D7
Charlotte St
Dundee DD3 91 D1
Kirkcaldy KY1 151 B3
Perth PH1 103 B4
9 Stanley PH1 24 F4
CHARLOTTETOWN 63 E5
Charrier The FK11 116 F6
Charterhouse La 8 PH2 103 B3
CHARTERSHALL 135 A1
Chartershall Rd FK7 135 A1
Charter St FK7 135 A3
Chattan Ave FK9 115 B4
Chemiss Rd 6 KY8 79 F2
Cherry Ave KY6 112 E7
CHERRYBANK 102 E2
Cherry Bank KY12 161 D5
Cherrybank Gdns* PH2 102 D2
Cherrybank Gr PH1 102 D2
Cherrybank Specl Sch PH2 102 E2
Cherry Ct KY8 109 A4
Cherry Gr DD6 41 F2
Cherry La
Cupar KY15 105 D4
Newport-on-Tay DD6 41 F2
Cherrylea PH3 104 C6
Cherry Pl KY4 147 C3
Cherryton Dr FK10 139 A5
Chestnut Ave
Kirkcaldy KY1 151 C7
6 Leven KY8 79 F3
Chestnut Ct PH3 104 A5
Chestnut Gn DD5 95 E8
Chestnut Gr KY11 173 E8
Chestnut Pl PH1 102 B3
Chevaliers Pend 4 DD4 94 C8
Cheviot Cres DD4 94 E8
Cheviot Rd KY2 150 F7
Cheviot Rise DD4 94 E8
Chewton Rd KY1 131 D8
Chewton Way KY6 112 D5
Chief's Cl 7 KY1 151 D6
Chirnside Pl DD4 95 C8
Chisholm Ave
Dunblane FK15 107 E6
Stirling FK9 115 B4
Chisholm Cres KY5 148 A7
Chisholm Pl KY6 112 F7
Chisholm St KY12 161 D8
Christian Rd DD4 95 B3
Christie Ave KY8 109 C7
Christiegait 5 KY15 63 E1
Christie Pl
Kirkcaldy KY1 151 D7
7 Tulloch PH1 102 D8
Christies La DD10 85 D3
Christie St KY12 161 B5
Church Ave 3 PH2 39 F1
Church Brae PH2 61 B5
Church Ct
Alloa FK10 138 A6
Kirkcaldy KY1 151 C4
Church Gr
Alloa FK10 118 C1
Burntisland KY3 165 D1
Tillicoultry FK13 119 B7
Churchill Cres KY16 106 D4
Churchill Dr FK9 115 A6
Churchill Pl
1 Broughty Ferry DD5 96 B2
Rosyth KY11 173 F3
Churchill Rd 6 KY13 108 B3
Churchill St FK10 137 F8
Church La
5 Bankfoot PH1 24 A6
7 Brechin DD9 84 C3
6 Errol PH2 39 F1
1 Kinglassie KY5 77 E1
Kirkcaldy KY1 151 C4
3 Kirriemuir DD8 86 C4
2 Ladybank KY15 64 A4
Limekilns KY11 172 D3
Methven PH1 36 A5
Thornton KY1 131 E8

Church Pl
6 Auchterderran KY5 129 B4
6 Bankfoot PH1 24 A6
5 Coupar Angus PH13 15 F3
Crossgates KY4 162 F7
11 Freuchie KY15 63 E1
Letham PH1 102 F5
Limekilns KY11 172 D3
1 Upper Largo KY8 81 A6
Church Rd
Auchterarder PH3 104 A4
Blairgowrie PH13 26 C8
Dundee DD2 28 D4
Ferryden DD10 85 D1
Leven KY8 109 E7
Methven PH1 36 A5
Perth PH2 38 C1
St Andrews KY16 54 B3
Church Row KY4 126 D2
Church Sq 3 KY16 106 D6
Church St
Alloa FK10 138 A6
Arbroath DD11 89 D4
Blairgowrie PH12 16 E4
Brechin DD9 84 C3
Burntisland KY3 165 D1
Carnoustie DD7 100 E3
Cowdenbeath KY4 147 D3
Crieff PH7 101 D3
6 Dunblane FK15 56 B4
Dundee DD3 179 B4
Freuchie KY15 63 E1
Glenrothes KY7 113 B7
Inverkeithing KY11 174 C3
Kingseat KY12 146 B1
Kirkcaldy KY1 132 F2
Kirkcaldy KY1 151 E6
Ladybank KY15 64 A5
13 Leven KY8 79 F1
Limekilns KY11 172 D3
Lochgelly KY5 148 B7
Milnathort KY13 108 C7
Monifieth DD5 97 A5
Perth PH1 102 F5
4 St Andrews KY16 106 D6
Church Wlk KY3 167 A3
Church Wynd 5 KY15 64 A3
Circus St 3 PH2 46 F1
Citron Glebe 4 KY1 151 D6
City Quay Sh Ctr DD1 179 C2
City Rd
Brechin DD9 84 C3
Dundee DD2 93 C4
St Andrews KY16 106 C6
CLACKMANNAN 139 B3
Clackmannan Coll (Annexe) FK10 118 C1
Clackmannan Cty Hospl FK10 138 B8
Clackmannan Prim Sch FK10 139 A4
Clackmannan Rd FK10 138 D6
Clackmannan Tower* FK10 138 F4
Clair Wood Pl KY15 105 A4
Claredon Pl FK15 107 D4
Claremont FK10 137 F8
Claremont Dr FK9 115 C7
Claremont Ind Est FK10 138 A6
Claremont Prim Sch FK10 137 E8
Clarence Rd DD4 94 E4
Clarendon Dr 3 DD2 93 C2
Clarendon Pl FK8 135 A7
Clarendon Rd FK8 135 A7
Clark Pl KY2 151 A5
Clark Rd KY11 174 B2
Clark St FK7 135 B2
Clark Terr PH7 101 E3
Clashbenny Pl 4 PH2 49 F7
Clashburn Rd KY13 108 C1
Clashburn Way KY13 108 C1
CLATHY 46 D7
Clathymore Dr PH1 46 F8
Clatto Ctry Pk* DD3 90 F3
Clatto Gdns 3 DD3 91 A3
Clatto Pl KY16 106 C4
Clattowoods Dr DD2 90 F3
Clattowoods Pl DD2 91 A3
Clattowoods Rd 2 DD3 91 A3
Clattowoods Terr 1 DD2 91 A3
CLAVERHOUSE 29 E5
Claverhouse Old Rd DD4 94 B8
Claverhouse Rd DD4 94 B8
Claverhouse W Ind Pk DD4 94 C8
Clay Acres Ct KY12 161 A5
Claybraes KY16 106 C4
Claycrofts Pl FK7 135 B6
Clayhills Dr DD2 92 D3
Clayhills Gdns DD2 90 B3
Clayhills Gr DD2 92 D3
CLAYHOLES 100 C5
Claymore Dr
Glenrothes KY7 110 F2
Stirling FK7 135 D3
Claymore Path 4 KY7 110 F2
Claymore St DD4 95 D6
Claypotts Castle* DD5 95 E4
Claypotts Castle Gdns DD5 95 E4

Claypotts Castle Prim Sch DD4 95 C5
Claypotts Ct DD5 95 E4
Claypotts Pl DD5 95 E4
Claypotts Rd DD5 95 E4
Claypotts Terr DD5 95 E4
Clay Rd KY16 53 F7
Clayton Rd PH2 49 A4
Cleaves The FK10 117 B1
Cleeve Dr PH1 102 D2
Cleeve Pk PH1 102 D2
Cleghorn St DD2 93 D4
Cleikimin Cres KY5 127 E8
CLEISH 75 D1
Cleish Gdns KY2 150 F6
Cleish Pl KY11 161 F2
Cleish Prim Sch KY13 75 D1
Cleish Rd KY11 161 F2
Clement Pk Pl DD2 93 B6
Clement Pk Rd DD2 93 B7
Clement Pk Terr 13 DD2 93 B6
Clentry Cres KY4 126 C1
Clepington Ct DD3 94 B4
Clepington Prim Sch DD4 94 B4
Clepington Rd DD3 93 F7
Clepington St DD3 94 B4
Clerk Gr KY11 161 F1
Clerk St DD9 84 C3
Cleuch Ave FK10 117 B2
Cleuch Dr FK12 117 E7
Cleuch Rd FK9 115 C3
Cleveland Circ 9 DD4 94 F5
Cleveland Dr KY11 174 B2
Clifden Blue Ct DD4 95 B8
CLIFFBURN 89 F5
Cliffburn Gdns DD5 95 F5
Cliffburn Rd DD11 89 F4
Cliffburn Terr 6 DD11 89 F4
Clifford Pk FK11 117 A7
Clifford Rd FK8 135 B5
Clinkerheel Dr DD2 90 B3
Clinkum Bank KY12 158 C3
Clinton St 2 KY14 50 D5
Clinton Terr DD5 95 E4
Clive Rd DD3 91 E1
Clive St DD4 94 C5
Cloanden Pl KY2 151 A3
Cloan Dr PH3 104 E6
Cloan Gr 7 DD3 91 D2
Cloan Rd DD3 91 D2
Clockluine Rd KY11 174 E6
Clocktower Mews PH1 36 F4
Close The KY11 173 D1
Clova Ave
Arbroath DD11 89 E6
Blairgowrie PH10 88 C3
Clova Rd DD8 86 C4
Cloves The FK11 117 A5
Clovis Duveau Dr DD2 92 C3
Clow Sq 3 PH2 49 E3
Clune Rd KY12 159 E7
Clune Terr KY5 127 F3
Clunie Bank PH2 103 E8
Clunie Gdns DD3 91 B3
Clunie Rd KY11 161 E3
Clunie St 1 PH2 49 E3
Clunivar St KY12 160 D5
CLUNY 130 B4
Cluny Ct PH10 88 C4
Clunymore Dr PH10 88 E1
Cluny Pk KY5 129 C3
Cluny Pl KY7 113 B4
Cluny Terr PH1 102 C5
Clyde Cres KY11 161 F2
Clyde Ct KY6 112 E6
Clyde Pl
Dundee DD2 92 F4
Perth PH2 102 F2
Clydesdale Ct PH3 104 A5
Clyde St 2 KY8 109 A2
Coach House Ct PH1 102 F4
Coachman's Wlk KY9 82 B5
Coach Rd
4 Coupar Angus PH13 15 F3
11 Newburgh KY14 50 D5
Coalgate FK10 138 B6
Coalpots Way FK10 118 E3
Coal Rd
Cupar KY15 105 D5
Dunfermline KY12 160 F3
COALSNAUGHTON 119 B4
Coalsnaughton Prim Sch FK13 119 B4
COALTOWN OF BALGONIE 113 F3
COALTOWN OF BURNTURK 64 D2
COALTOWN OF WEMYSS 132 F4
Coaltown of Wemyss Prim Sch KY1 132 E4
Coaltown Rd KY7 113 F7
Coal Wynd
Bannockburn FK7 135 D1
Kirkcaldy KY1 151 C4
Coal Wynd Ind Est KY1 151 C4
Coarse Brae DD6 41 D2
Coats Cres FK10 117 E1
Coats Dr PH1 24 D1
Cobbles The KY13 76 F6
Cobden Ct
Crossgates KY4 162 F6
5 Dundee DD3 93 C5
Cobden Pl 6 DD2 93 C5

Cobden St
Alva FK12 118 A6
Alva FK12 118 A7
Dundee DD3 93 C5
Montrose DD10 85 D2
Coblecrook Gdns FK12 117 F6
Coblecrook La FK12 117 F6
Coblecrook Pl FK12 117 F6
Cochrane Ave KY11 174 D2
Cochrane Cres FK12 117 E7
Cochrane Rd KY11 173 B1
Cochranes The FK12 118 B7
Cochrane's Wynd 7 PH3 104 D6
Cochrane Way KY11 175 A5
Cochrane Wlk KY11 161 F4
Cochrie Pl FK10 117 C2
Cockburn Ave FK15 107 D7
Cocklaw St
Kelty KY4 126 D1
Kelty KY4 146 D8
Cockle Chairlies Way 1 KY9 82 A5
Coldingham Pl KY12 161 D4
Coldside Rd DD3 93 E6
Coldstream Ave
Dunblane FK15 107 B5
Leven KY8 109 E8
Perth PH1 102 A2
Coldstream Cres KY8 109 E8
Coldstream Dr DD4 95 D7
Coldstream Pk KY8 109 E8
Coldwells Rd PH7 101 C4
Coles Pl KY4 163 A6
Colin Gibson Dr DD5 96 F6
COLINSBURGH 81 F6
Colinsburgh Prim Sch KY9 81 F6
Colinswell Rd KY3 165 D1
Colinton Ct KY6 110 E1
Colinton Pl DD2 93 C4
COLLACE 26 C3
Collace Cres 1 DD3 91 C3
Collace Prim Sch PH2 26 C3
College Dr PH1 36 A4
College Mill Rd PH1 36 E5
College Pl PH1 36 A4
College Rd PH1 36 A5
College St
16 Leven KY8 79 F1
Leven KY8 109 A1
5 St Andrews KY16 106 D6
College Terr PH1 36 A5
COLLESSIE 63 E8
Colliers Ct FK13 119 B6
Colliers Rd FK7 136 D4
Collier St DD7 100 D3
Colliers Way FK7 135 C1
Collingwood Cres DD5 96 D3
Collingwood Pl 1 DD5 96 E4
Collingwood St DD5 96 E4
Collins Cres KY11 174 F2
Collinswell Dr KY3 165 D1
COLLISTON 22 C8
Colliston Ave KY7 113 B4
COLLISTON CASTLE 13 B1
Colliston Dr 2 DD5 96 C5
Colliston Prim Sch DD11 22 C8
Colliston Rd KY12 161 D6
Coll Pl PH1 102 F7
COLLYDEAN 110 F3
Collydean Prim Sch KY7 110 F2
Collydean Way KY7 110 F2
Collyland Rd FK10 118 D3
Collyland Rdbt FK10 118 A3
Colonsay Ct PH14 40 C7
Colonsay Gdns PH14 40 C7
Colonsay Pk KY7 111 E2
Colonsay St PH1 102 E8
Colonsay Terr DD4 94 C7
Colquhally Rd KY5 128 B2
Colquhoun Ave KY7 111 A3
Colquhoun St FK7 135 C6
Colquhoun Terr FK7 135 C6
Colsnaur FK11 117 A6
Colt Gdns PH3 104 A5
Colton Ct KY12 160 E4
Colville Gdns FK10 138 A6
Colvill Pl DD11 89 C3
Comelybank PH2 103 C6
Comelybank Gdns PH2 103 C5
Comely Park La KY12 161 A3
Comely Pk KY12 161 B3
Comerton Pl DD6 43 A4
Commander's Gr FK15 56 B4
Commando Access Way KY11 173 C1
Commerce St
Arbroath DD11 89 D3
Brechin DD9 84 D3
Cupar KY15 105 A2
8 Montrose DD10 85 C2
Commercial Ct DD1 179 C2
Commercial Prim Sch KY11 161 C3
Commercial Rd
Inverkeithing KY11 174 C2
21 Leven KY8 109 E6
Commercial School La 4 KY12 161 A3
Commercial St
36 Alyth PH11 7 A3
4 Blairgowrie PH10 88 D5
7 Coupar Angus PH13 16 A3

Commercial St *continued*
Dundee DD1 179 B2
Glenrothes KY7 111 F1
Kirkcaldy KY1 151 D6
Newtyle PH12 17 B4
Perth PH2 103 C4
Commissioner St PH7 101 C3
Commodores Wlk KY11 173 C1
Common Brae DD11 89 C2
Common Rd KY10 83 D8
Commonty Rd DD6 99 E7
Community Sch of Auchterarder PH3 104 D7
COMRIE 158 D7
Comrie Ct FK13 119 B6
Comrie Rd PH7 101 B6
Comrie St 1 PH7 101 C4
Conacher Ct 5 KY9 82 A5
Concorde Way KY11 174 D3
Condor Cres DD10 85 D7
Condor Dr DD11 89 A5
Coneyhill Rd FK9 115 B7
Coneypark FK7 134 E6
Conil Pl 8 DD8 11 E3
Coningsby Pl FK10 138 A6
Coniston Terr DD3 91 F1
Conland Ct KY6 110 D3
Connaught Terr PH7 101 D5
Connel Terr DD3 94 A8
Conon Terr DD11 89 E5
Constable Acre 1 KY15 105 B5
Constable La DD5 95 E3
Constable Rd FK7 135 B6
Constable St DD4 179 C3
Constitution Cres DD3 179 A3
Constitution Ct DD3 179 A3
Constitution Rd DD1 179 A3
Constitution St DD3 179 A4
Constitution Terr DD3 179 A3
Conveners Wynd DD9 84 B3
Convent St 4 DD11 89 E4
Cook Pl KY1 152 A8
Cook Sq KY5 148 B8
Cook St KY1 152 A8
COOKSTON 84 B5
Cookston Cres DD9 84 C4
Cookston Rd DD9 84 C5
Cooperage Quay FK8 135 C8
Cooperage Way FK10 138 D8
Cooper Dr PH1 102 D8
Cooper Ha' Ave KY5 128 B1
Cooper's La FK10 155 E4
Copeland Cres KY4 147 B2
Copland Pl FK12 117 F7
Copper Beech Row DD5 30 C5
Copper Beech Wynd KY12 159 D1
Coppice Dr PH2 37 E5
Coral Bank PH10 88 D6
Coralbank Cres 1 PH10 88 C7
Coralbank Terr PH10 88 D6
Corbett Pl KY11 161 F1
Corbie Dr DD7 32 A5
Cordiner Cl FK8 114 F2
Corlundy Cres PH7 101 C3
Cormailin Pl KY12 158 B2
Cornel La KY7 111 A1
Corn Exchange Rd 1 FK8 135 B7
Cornhill Cres FK7 135 B3
Cornhill Rd
Burghmuir PH1 102 D4
Glenrothes KY7 113 B2
Cornhill St 8 KY14 50 D5
Cornhill Way PH1 102 D4
CORNTON 115 B3
Cornton Cres FK9 115 A5
Cornton Pl 4 PH7 101 C4
Cornton Prim Sch FK9 115 A4
Cornton Rd FK9 115 A4
Cornton Vale Cotts FK9 115 A4
Coronation Ave DD10 85 C8
Coronation Cres KY8 109 C7
Coronation Pl KY1 132 F4
Coronation St KY7 79 A3
Coronation Way DD10 85 C7
Corpach Dr KY12 160 F2
Corran Gdns DD5 96 B4
Corrie Pl 23 PH2 37 F5
Corsar Croft DD11 89 B6
Corsie Ave PH2 103 E4
Corsie Dr PH2 103 E4
Corsie Hill PH2 103 F4
Corsie Hill Rd PH2 103 E3
Corsie Way PH2 103 E4
Corso St DD2 93 D3
CORTACHY 1 B6
Cortachy Circ 1 DD5 97 A6
Cortachy Cres
Broughty Ferry DD5 96 A5
Kirriemuir DD8 86 C7
Cortachy Dr DD8 86 C7
Cortachy Pl KY7 113 A2
Cortachy Prim Sch DD8 1 B6
Cortachy Rd DD8 86 C7
Corum Pl PH4 57 B3
Cos La KY7 113 C5
Cotburn Cres KY3 165 F2
Cottage Pl 3 DD5 96 B2
Cottarshade 9 PH10 88 C4
COTTON OF GUTHRIE 12 D5
COTTON OF OVENSTONE 20 C5
Cotton Rd DD3 179 C4
Cotton Yd PH1 24 F3
COTTOWN 50 A8
COUL 111 B3
Coulport Pl KY12 160 F2
Coul Steadings KY7 111 A1
COULTRA 41 D2
Countess Gdns PH7 101 D3
Countess of Moray Hospl KY3 176 B7
County Hos KY4 163 A6
County Pl PH1 103 A3
COUPAR ANGUS 16 B3
Coupar Angus Prim Sch PH13 16 A3
Coupar Angus Rd
Blairgowrie PH10 88 D4
Dundee DD2 90 D2
Kirkton PH12 17 B4
Coupar St DD3 93 C5
Couper Angus Rd DD2 93 B6
Couper Gr KY11 161 F1
Courcelles Ct KY13 108 B5
Courthill FK12 118 A7
Courthill Dr KY7 113 A2
Court Hillock Gdns 5 DD8 86 C5
Court House Sq DD1 179 A2
Court St N DD3 94 B4
Court St DD3 94 B4
Cousin's La 7 KY12 160 F4
Couston Dr KY11 175 B4
Couston Pl KY11 175 B4
Couston Rd KY11 175 B4
Couston St KY12 161 B4
Couttie's Wynd
Dundee DD1 179 B2
5 Forfar DD8 87 D5
Covenanters La EH30 178 B1
Covenanters Pend DD4 94 B8
Covenanters Rise KY11 173 E6
Coventry Pl KY13 108 D2
Coventry Way KY13 108 E7
Cowal Cres KY6 110 E1
Cowal Pl KY11 162 C1
Cowane St
Stirling FK8 115 B1
2 Stirling FK8 135 B8
Cowan Pl DD4 179 C4
Cowan St DD4 179 C4
Cowan Terr 11 FK14 73 C1
COWDENBEATH 147 E4
Cowdenbeath Bsns Ctr KY4 147 D3
Cowdenbeath Prim Sch KY4 147 D3
Cowdenbeath Rd KY3 165 E2
Cowdenbeath Sta KY4 147 D4
COWDENEND 162 F8
Cowgate
Dundee DD1 179 B3
3 Tayport DD6 43 C7
Cowgate Southbank PH2 39 F1
Cowie Rd
Bannockburn FK7 135 E1
Bannockburn FK7 135 F1
Cowley St KY8 109 A3
COWSTRANDBURN 143 B2
Coxburn Brae FK9 70 D1
COXET HILL 134 F4
Cox Gdns DD3 91 D2
Coxithill Rd FK7 135 A3
Coxland Cres PH1 24 A6
Cox St DD3 91 D2
Coxstool KY1 132 E2
Cragganmore FK10 117 A2
Cragganmore Pl PH1 102 C8
CRAICHIE 11 C2
Craigard Gdns DD2 92 E6
Craigard Rd
Crieff PH7 101 C5
Dundee DD2 92 E6
Perth PH2 103 C4
Craigbank
Alloa FK10 118 C1
Crossford KY12 160 C2
Craigbank Prim Sch FK10 118 C1
Craigbeath Ct KY4 147 B5
Craigclowan Prep Sch PH2 48 D7
Craig Cres FK9 115 D3
Craig Ct
Bridge of A FK9 115 A5
Burntisland KY3 165 D2
Craigdimas Gr KY11 175 A2
Craigearn Ave KY2 150 B7
Craigearn Pl KY2 150 C7
Craigellachie Ct 3 KY7 111 C2
Craigencalt Farm* KY3 166 D4
Craigend Rd FK7 135 A3
Craigflower Ct KY12 158 E1
Craigflower Gdns KY12 158 E1
Craigflower Ho KY12 158 E1
Craigflower View KY12 170 E8
Craigfoot Ct KY1 167 B6
Craigfoot Pl KY1 167 B7
Craigfoot Wlk KY1 167 B7
Craigford Dr FK7 135 D1
Craigforth Cres FK8 114 F1
Craighall Pl PH10 88 D6
Craighall St FK8 114 E1
Craighead Cres DD6 98 E5
Craighead Golf Links KY10 69 C4
Craighead Rd DD6 98 E5
Craighill Ct DD4 94 E5
Craigholm La KY3 165 F1
Craighorn FK11 117 A5
Craighorn Rd FK12 117 E6
Craighouse Pl KY12 142 E5
CRAIGIE
Dundee 94 F4
Perth 102 F2
Craigie Ave DD4 95 A3
Craigiebarn Rd DD4 95 B3
Craigiebarns Prim Sch DD4 95 B4
Craigie Dr DD4 95 B3
Craigie High Sch DD4 95 A4
Craigie Hill KY16 42 F3
Craigie Hill Golf Course PH2 48 C8
Craigieknowes Ave 1 PH2 102 F1
Craigie Knowes Rd PH2 102 F1
Craigielea Terr 8 DD4 94 F5
Craigiemalcolm Path 2 KY5 127 F7
Craigie Pl
4 Dundee DD4 95 A3
Kirkcaldy KY1 131 A2
Perth PH2 103 A2
Craigie Prim Sch PH2 103 A2
Craigie Rd PH2 103 A1
Craigie St
Ballingry KY5 127 F8
Dundee DD4 94 C3
Craigievar Cl KY12 161 E5
Craigievar Dr KY7 113 B5
Craigievar Gdns KY2 150 E5
Craigie View PH2 102 F1
Craiginnan Gdns FK14 120 D8
Craigkennochie Terr KY3 165 F1
Craig La DD6 99 E6
Craiglea FK9 115 C3
Craiglea Rd PH1 102 D4
Craigleith FK10 118 E3
Craig Leith Rd FK7 135 D6
Craigleith Terr FK12 118 A7
Craigleith View FK10 117 D3
Craigluscar Ct KY12 160 B7
Craigluscar La KY12 160 A6
Craigluscar Nature Reserve* KY12 144 A1
Craigluscar Rd
Dunfermline KY12 144 A1
Dunfermline KY12 160 B7
Craigmead Terr 4 KY5 129 B4
Craigmill Gdns DD7 100 E5
Craigmore Gdns KY12 158 E1
Craigmore St DD3 91 F2
Craigmount KY2 150 D7
Craigmount Ave 1 DD2 92 F6
Craigmount Pl 3 DD2 92 F6
Craigmount Rd DD2 92 E6
Craigmount Terr 2 DD2 92 F6
Craigmyle St KY12 161 C5
Craigneuk Rd PH1 36 E4
Craig O' Loch Rd DD8 87 C5
Craigomus Cres FK11 116 F6
Craigowan Rd DD2 92 E6
Craigowl Rd DD2 93 B8
Craigowl St DD2 93 B7
Craigowmill KY13 75 D8
Craig Pl
2 Carnoustie DD7 100 E4
Crieff PH7 45 E7
Craig Rd
East Haven DD7 32 E6
Montrose DD10 85 C1
Tayport DD6 99 F6
Craigridge Pl KY11 175 C5
Craigrie Rd FK10 138 F4
Craigrie Terr FK10 139 A4
CRAIGROTHIE 65 B5
Craigrothie Prim Sch KY15 65 B5
Craigroyston Cres PH2 103 F8
Craigroyston Rd PH2 103 F8
Craig's Cl 7 DD8 86 D5
Craigshannoch Rd 3 DD6 42 B5
Craigside Rd KY5 129 B4
Craigs Rdbt FK7 135 B7
Craig St KY11 174 A4
Craigs The FK13 119 B5
Craigston Dr KY12 161 D5
Craigston Pk KY12 161 D5
Craig Terr DD10 85 C1
Craig The KY11 173 D3
CRAIGTON 8 C5
Craigton Cres FK12 117 F6
Craigton Gdns 3 DD5 97 A7
Craigton Pl KY4 147 C2
Craigtoun Ctry Pk* KY16 54 E1
Craigview FK10 118 D2
Craigward FK10 138 A6
Craigwell Path KY12 171 D7
Craik Terr KY7 111 F1
CRAIL 69 B3
Crail Mus & Heritage Ctr* KY10 69 B3
Crail Pl DD5 96 D5
Crail Pottery* KY10 69 B2
Crail Prim Sch KY10 69 A2
Crail Rd KY10 83 D7
Crails La 11 KY16 106 D6
Crambeth Pl KY4 126 D2
Cramond Gdns KY2 150 F7
Cramond Pl
Dalgety Bay KY11 175 C4
5 Dundee DD4 94 F8
Perth PH1 102 F8
Cramond Way KY6 110 E1
Crathes Cl KY7 113 B2
Crathes Way DD5 96 B5
Crathie Pl DD4 95 B5
Crathie Way KY11 162 A4
Crawford Ave DD6 42 A2
Crawford Gdns KY16 106 B3
Crawford Pk 3 KY15 64 E6
Crawford Pl
Dundee DD5 95 C3
5 Glenrothes KY6 112 E7
Ladybank KY15 63 F5
Milnathort KY13 108 C6
Townhill KY12 161 C7
Crawford Sh Arc The 3 FK8 135 B7
Crawford Sq FK2 154 D4
Crawford Terr 1 KY15 64 E6
Crawley Cres KY15 64 E7
CREICH 52 A8
Creich Prim Sch KY15 52 A6
Crescent La DD4 179 C3
Crescent Rd
Dundee DD3 179 A3
15 Lower Largo KY8 80 F5
Crescent St DD4 179 C3
Crescent The
Dunblane FK15 107 E5
Luncarty PH1 24 D1
Rosyth KY11 173 B1
Crest Bsns Ctr FK7 135 D5
Crichton St
32 Anstruther Wester KY10 83 C6
Dundee DD1 179 B2
Crichton Way KY15 105 E3
CRIEFF 101 D3
Crieff Golf Club PH7 101 F6
Crieff High Sch PH7 101 D2
Crieff Hospl PH7 101 C3
Crieff Hydro Golf Ctr PH7 101 D8
Crieff Prim Sch PH7 101 D3
Crieff Rd PH1 102 F5
Crieff Visitor Ctr* PH7 101 B2
Crinan Pl
Glenrothes KY6 112 F6
Halbeath KY11 162 A4
Cringate Gdns FK7 135 F1
Crioch Pl PH7 101 C3
Croall Pl KY4 126 E1
Croall St KY4 126 D1
Croft 18 KY14 62 F6
Croftamorie KY1 132 F2
Croftangry Pl KY4 126 D1
Croftangry Rd KY4 126 D1
Croft An Righ
Inverkeithing KY11 174 C3
Kinghorn KY3 167 A4
Croft Ave 7 PH2 47 A1
Croft Bank PH2 103 A2
Croft Cres KY7 111 E1
Croft Ct 8 PH10 88 C5
Croft Gdns KY12 159 C7
Crofthead
5 Kirriemuir DD8 86 C4
7 Kirriemuir DD8 86 C4
Tillicoultry FK13 119 A7
Crofthead Ct FK8 115 A1
Crofthead Rd FK8 115 A1
Croft La PH10 88 C5
Croft Loan 4 KY15 65 E6
Crofton Pl 14 PH13 16 A3
CROFT OUTERLY 112 A8
Croftouterly 5 KY6 112 B8
Croft Pk PH2 103 A2
Croft Pl 6 PH2 47 A1
Croft Rd
Auchterarder PH3 104 D7
Glenrothes KY6 112 B8
Montrose DD10 85 B1
Croftshaw Rd FK12 118 A7
Croft's Rd FK10 117 B3
Croft Terr Gdns 8 DD8 86 C4
Croft The
Blairgowrie PH10 88 C5
10 Leuchars KY16 54 B8
Croft Wynd KY13 108 C7
Cromar Dr KY11 162 C1
Cromarty Campus KY11 173 C1
Cromarty Ct KY6 112 D6
Cromarty Dr 1 DD2 93 A5
Cromarty Pl KY1 151 E7
CROMBIE 171 D7
Crombie Ctry Pk* DD5 21 A3
Crombie Prim Sch KY12 171 D7
Crombie Terr DD4 94 F3
Cromdale Brae KY6 110 E3
Cromlix Cres FK15 107 B5
Cromlix Rd 13 PH2 48 D8
Crompton Rd KY6 112 C3
Cromwell Rd
Burntisland KY3 165 F1
Rosyth KY11 173 F5
CROOK OF DEVON 74 E3
Crophill FK10 118 C2
Crosbies Ct FK8 135 B7
CROSSFORD 160 B1
Crossford Prim Sch KY12 160 A2
Crossgate KY15 105 D4
CROSSGATES 162 F6
Crossgates Prim Sch KY4 162 E6
CROSSHILL 128 A5
Crosshills 21 KY14 62 F6
Crosshill Terr DD6 98 A1
Cross La DD1 179 A2
CROSSROADS 109 B4
Crossroads KY11 162 B5
Crossroads Pl KY11 173 F4
Cross Row
Charlestown KY11 172 B4
Dundee DD1 179 A1
Cross St
7 Bankfoot PH1 24 A6
Broughty Ferry DD5 96 B2
Dysart KY1 152 A7
7 Perth PH2 103 A3
Tayport DD6 99 F5
Cross The
8 Alloa FK10 138 B6
13 Auchtermuchty KY14 62 F6
Crieff PH5 44 C4
Cupar KY15 105 C5
Dunblane FK15 107 D5
9 Forfar DD8 87 D5
Lochgelly KY5 148 B7
Springfield KY15 64 E6
West Wemyss KY1 132 F2
CROSSTON 3 C3
Cross Way KY11 175 C5
Cross Wynd
Dunfermline KY12 161 A4
4 Earlsferry/Elie KY9 82 A2
3 Falkland KY15 63 B2
Crowhill Rd KY11 175 D4
Crowlin Ave KY7 111 A2
Crown Gdns FK10 137 F8
Crown Pl PH7 101 B2
Crown Sq 4 KY15 64 A3
Crown Wynd PH3 104 E6
Cruachan Ave FK9 115 B3
Cruckburn Wynd FK7 134 F4
Crudie Pl 1 DD11 89 A3
Cruickness Rd KY11 178 C8
Cruickshank Pk 7 DD10 6 C8
Crum Cres FK7 135 C2
Crusoe Gdns KY8 81 A5
Cuddyhouse Rd KY4, KY12 146 D3
Cuil Gr KY12 160 D5
Cuillin Terr PH14 40 C7
Culbin Ct KY7 111 C3
CULCRIEFF 101 C7
Culdees Ave KY6 110 E2
Culdeesland Rd PH1 36 B4
Cullalo Cres KY3 176 C8
Cullaloe Ct KY11 175 C4
Cullaloe Nature Reserve* KY3 164 B4
Cullaloe View KY4 147 C2
Cullen Cres KY2 150 E7
Cullen Dr KY6 112 C6
Cullen Pl DD4 95 B4
Culliven Ct PH1 102 D7
Culloden Cres 5 DD11 89 D5
Culloden Rd 4 DD11 89 D5
Culloden Terr DD11 89 D5
CULLOW 1 A8
CULROSS 169 C8
Culross Abbey* KY12 157 D1
Culross Palace* KY12 169 C8
Culross Prim Sch KY12 169 D8
Cultenhove Cres FK7 135 A3
Cultenhove Pl FK7 135 A3
Cultenhove Rd
Stirling, Coxet Hill FK7 135 A3
Stirling FK7 135 A4
Culteuchar Bank 1 PH2 47 F2
Culteuchar Rd PH2 47 F3
Cult Ness KY11 173 D3
CULTOQUHEY 33 F2
Cults Gdns DD5 95 C4
Culzean Cres KY2 150 C7
Culzean Pl KY7 113 B3
Cumberland Cl 5 DD8 86 D4
Cumbrae Ct KY2 151 A8
Cumbrae Pk KY7 111 A2
Cumbrae Pl PH1 102 E8
Cumbrae Terr KY2 151 A8
Cumnock Pl DD4 94 D6
Cunningham Pl 3 KY6 112 E6
Cunningham Rd
Rosyth KY11 173 D2
Stirling FK7 135 D7
Cunningham St DD4 179 C4
Cunninghar Dr FK13 119 C7
Cunzie St 17 KY10 83 C6

CUPAR 105 E4
Cupar Golf Club KY15 105 E2
Cupar Mills KY15 105 C3
CUPAR MUIR 105 A2
Cupar Rd
Auchtermuchty KY14 63 A6
Ceres KY15 65 D6
Cupar KY15 105 A2
Leven KY8 109 E8
Newburgh KY14 50 D5
Newport-on-Tay DD6 98 E4
St Andrews KY16 54 A5
Tayport DD6 99 F4
Cupar Sta KY15 105 D4
Cupar Swimming Pool KY15 105 A5
Cupar Trad Est KY15 105 F6
Curate Wynd 11 KY13 108 C2
Curlers Cres KY13 108 C7
Curlew Gdns KY11 162 A2
Curling Knowe KY4 162 F6
Curling Pk KY4 162 F6
Curling Pond Ct 1 KY15 105 E5
Curling Pond Rd 4 KY15 65 D6
Curlin' Ha' Gdns KY12 142 E6
Curran Ct 4 FK13 119 B7
Customs Rdbt FK8 115 B1
Cuthbert's Rd 10 DD6 98 C3
Cutlog Vennel 15 PH1 103 B4
Cynicus Pl KY16 53 E7
Cypress Gr KY11 173 C8
Cypress La 1 KY8 80 B5

D

Daiglen FK13 119 D7
Dairsie Bridge* KY15 53 D3
DAIRSIE OR OSNABURGH 53 D4
Dairsie Prim Sch KY15 53 C4
Daisyfield Terr KY5 129 B4
Daisy Gr KY8 79 F2
Dalbeath Cres KY4 147 A2
Dalbeath Gdns KY4 146 F1
Dalcraig Cres DD4 95 A4
Dalcross Way KY12 161 E5
Daleally Cres 9 PH2 39 F1
Dale Ct DD11 89 D5
Dale The 4 KY9 82 A5
Dalgairn Cres KY15 105 C5
Dalgarno Pk DD10 6 C4
Dalgetty Ct DD2 90 A4
DALGETY BAY 175 C3
Dalgety Bay Prim Sch KY11 175 B4
Dalgety Bay Sta KY11 174 F5
Dalgety Gdns KY11 175 D5
Dalgety House View KY11 175 D4
Dalgleish Ct FK8 135 B8
Dalgleish Rd DD4 94 E3
Dalgleish St DD6 99 F7
Dalhousie Gdns 2 DD5 97 B5
Dalhousie Pk 1 DD5 97 C6
Dalhousie Pl DD11 89 B3
Dalhousie Rd DD5 96 D3
Dalhousie St
Brechin DD9 84 D3
Carnoustie DD7 100 D3
Lucknow DD7 97 E7
Monifieth DD5 97 C6
Dalhousie Terr DD10 85 D7
Dalkeith Rd DD4 94 D4
Dallas Ave KY3 165 F1
Dallas Dr KY2 150 E7
Dallerie Rd PH7 101 B4
Dallfield Ct DD3 179 B3
Dall's La DD9 84 E2
Dalmahoy Cres KY2 131 A1
Dalmahoy Dr 4 DD3 91 A3
Dalmeny View KY11 175 C4
Dalmore Dr FK12 117 E6
Dalmorglen Pk FK7 134 F6
Dalreoch Pl PH1 102 C5
Dalrymple Pl DD2 92 F4
Dalrymple St DD2 92 F5
Dalrymple Terr DD2 93 A4
Dalton Rd KY6 112 F3
Dalwhinnie Pl 2 PH1 102 D8
Daly Gdns KY12 157 F2
Dalziel Ct DD4 29 F8
Dalziel Pl DD4 29 F8
Dalziel Rd DD4 29 F8
Damacre Rd DD9 84 C3
Danger Area DD7 32 A2
Daniel Ave 6 FK15 107 E7
Daniel Pl KY11 173 C5
Daniel St DD1 93 E3
Danskin Pl KY16 54 C3
Dargai Terr FK15 107 D6
Dargavel Gdns 3 DD4 94 F8
Dargie Rd DD2 92 B3
Dark Wlk 3 PH2 48 F5
Darnaway Dr 12 KY7 111 C2
Darney Terr KY3 166 F2
Darnhall Cres PH2 102 F2
Darnhall Dr PH2 102 F2
Darnley St FK8 135 A8
Darvel Pl DD4 94 D6
Davaar Dr KY2 150 E8
Davan Pl DD5 96 B4
Davenport Pl KY11 173 F3
David Cres KY11 174 A8
David Douglas Ave PH2 38 A5
David Henderson Ct KY12 161 A4
David Lawson Gdns DD8 9 A7
David Millar Pl 5 KY12 160 E5
David Rd 4 KY7 113 A6
David Robertson St DD3 94 B4
Davidson Cres 4 PH13 16 A3
Davidson Pl 2 KY6 112 E6
Davidson St
Bannockburn FK7 135 C1
Dundee DD5 95 F3
David St
Blairgowrie PH10 88 B5
Dundee DD5 96 A2
Dunfermline KY12 161 A5
Kirkcaldy KY1 151 B3
Lochgelly KY5 148 B8
2 Pittenweem KY10 83 A5
David The First St KY3 166 F2
David Wilson Pk 6 KY16 53 E8
Davie Pk Pl PH10 88 D5
Daviot Rd KY12 161 E5
Dawson Ave FK10 137 F8
Dawson Cres DD5 96 E5
Dawson Pl DD5 95 C3
Dawson Rd DD5 95 C4
Dawson's Ct 1 KY13 75 D5
Dayton Dr DD2 93 A8
Deads La PH2 49 F4
Dead Wynd 16 KY8 79 F5
Dean Acres KY12 158 D7
Dean Ave DD4 94 F3
Deanbank St DD2 93 A5
Dean Cres FK8 115 C1
Dean Dr KY12 160 A2
Dean Gr KY12 160 B2
Dean Pk KY12 159 E7
Dean Pk Brae 4 KY2 130 C1
Dean Pk Ct KY2 130 B1
Dean Pk Dr 1 KY2 130 B1
Dean Pk Gdns KY2 130 B1
Dean Pk Gr KY2 130 C1
Dean Pk Way KY2 130 C1
Dean Pl FK14 120 D8
Dean Rd KY2 151 A4
Dean Ridge KY12 159 E7
Deas Rd KY11 174 B2
Deas Wharf KY1 151 C4
Dee Gdns DD2 92 D5
Deepdale Pl DD5 95 F4
Dee Pl
Dundee DD2 92 D5
Dunfermline KY11 161 F2
Deep Sea World (Sealife Ctr)* KY11 178 C5
Deerpark FK10 118 E1
Deerpark Prim Sch FK10 118 F1
Deerpark Rd DD4 94 D4
Deer Pk PH1 36 E4
Deeside Pl KY11 162 C1
Dee St 1 KY8 109 A2
Delaney Ct FK10 138 A6
Delgatie Ave KY7 113 C4
Delgatie Ct KY7 113 C4
Delph Rd FK10 117 C2
Delphwood Cres FK10 117 D2
Delph Wynd FK10 117 C2
Demarco Dr KY7 111 A3
DEMONDALE 89 D5
Demondale Pl 1 DD11 89 D5
Demondale Rd DD11 89 D6
De Moray Ct FK9 115 A4
Dempster Ct 4 KY16 106 D5
Dempster Pl
Dunfermline KY12 160 F5
Letham DD8 11 F4
Dempster Terr KY16 106 D5
DENBEATH 109 A2
Denbeath Prim Sch KY8 109 A2
Denbecan FK10 138 E5
Denbert Gdns 13 KY8 79 F5
Denbert Pl 12 KY8 79 F5
Denburn Pl
5 Crail KY10 69 B3
Kirkcaldy KY2 151 C6
Denburn Rd KY1 151 D7
Denburn Way DD9 84 D2
Denend Cres KY2 151 B6
Denend Prim Sch KY5 129 B3
Denfield Ave KY5 129 B2
Denfield Ct 2 DD8 86 C4
Denfield Dr KY5 129 B2
Denfield Gdns
Arbroath DD11 89 A5
Cardenden KY5 129 B2
DENHEAD 66 E8
Denhead KY8 79 E5
Denhead Cres 6 DD2 92 D6
DENHEAD OF GRAY 92 B6
Denholm Ct KY6 112 C7
Denholm Gdns DD8 11 F3
Denholm Way KY5 127 F5
Denley Ct DD11 89 B4
Denley Gdns 9 DD11 89 A4
Dennison Rd DD4 94 D4
Denoon Terr DD2 93 A5
Den Pk PH2 49 E3
Den Rd
Kirkcaldy KY2, KY1 151 C6
Den Rd *continued*
New Scone PH2 103 F8
Dens Brae DD4 179 C3
Denside PH1 36 A5
Denside Cross Roads DD8 2 C7
Dens Pk (Dundee FC) DD3 94 A4
Dens Rd
Arbroath DD11 89 C5
Dundee DD3 179 C4
Dens Rd Ind Est DD11 89 C5
Dens Rd Prim Sch DD3 94 A4
Dens St DD4 179 C3
Den St KY8 109 A2
Den The DD8 11 F3
Denvale Gdns KY8 79 E5
Denwell Ct 38 PH11 7 A3
Den Wlk KY8 109 B3
Derby Pl FK13 119 C6
Derby St DD3 93 F6
Dermoche Dr FK15 107 B5
Deroran Pl FK8 134 F5
Derran Dr KY5 129 B4
Derwent Ave DD3 91 E1
Detroit Rd KY6 112 E4
Deveron Cres DD2 92 C5
Deveron Terr DD2 92 C5
Devlin Ct FK7 135 B2
Devonbank FK10 118 E3
Devon Ct FK10 117 B2
Devon Dr FK10 117 E4
Devonlea Rd 1 DD6 42 B5
Devon Pl
Auchterarder PH3 104 D6
Cambus FK10 117 A1
Saline KY12 142 E6
Devon Rd
Alloa FK10 138 C6
Dollar FK14 120 E6
DEVONSIDE 119 C5
Devon Terr KY11 161 E2
Devon Vale FK13 119 B6
Devonvale Cres FK13 119 B6
Devon Valley Dr FK10 118 D2
Devon Village FK10 118 E4
Devonway FK10 138 F5
Dewar Ave FK10 155 E4
Dewar Ct 7 PH1 103 A4
Dewar Dr KY8 109 D7
Dewars Ave KY4 126 F1
Dewars Ctr PH2 102 F3
Dewar St
Dollar FK14 120 E8
Dunfermline KY12 160 F4
Lochgelly KY5 148 A7
Dew Way KY11 173 D1
Diadem Pl 5 KY8 109 A1
Dick Cres KY3 165 E1
Dickies Wells FK12 118 C7
Dick McTaggart Sports Ctr DD3 91 F1
Dickmont Pl 5 DD11 89 F5
Dick Pl KY11 173 E5
Dickson Ave
Dundee DD2 92 E4
8 Hillside DD10 6 C8
Dickson Ct
Dunfermline KY12 161 A2
Lochgelly KY5 148 A7
Dickson La KY7 79 C3
Dickson St KY12 161 A1
Dick St
Broughty Ferry DD5 96 B3
Dunfermline KY12 161 C5
Monifieth DD5 97 C6
Dighty Gdns DD2 92 D5
Dighty Pl DD2 92 D5
Dirleton Gdns FK10 137 F7
Dirleton La FK10 137 F6
Dishlandtown St DD11 89 C3
Distillery Rd DD9 84 C4
Distillery St 3 KY14 62 F7
Diverswell FK10 118 D2
Dobson Dr DD7 100 D4
Dochart Terr DD2 92 E4
Docherty Gdns KY7 112 F8
Dock St DD1 179 B2
Doctor Lang Pl DD9 84 B5
Doctor's Pk FK10 155 E3
Dogton Stone Cross* KY5 129 F6
Dolan Gr KY12 142 D6
DOLLAR 120 F8
Dollar Acad FK14 73 C1
Dollarbeg Pk FK14 120 F6
Dollar Cres KY2 150 D7
Dollar Ct 2 KY12 160 E5
Dollar Golf Club FK14 73 B1
Dollar Gr KY3 165 E1
Dollar Mus* FK14 73 C1
Dollar Rd
Burntisland KY3 165 E1
Tillicoultry FK13 119 D7
Dollerie Cres PH7 101 D4
Dollerie Terr PH7 101 D4
Donald Cres KY1 131 D8
Donald Gdns DD2 93 A5
Donald's La DD2 92 F6
Donaldson Ave
Alloa FK10 117 E1
Forfar DD8 87 B3
Donaldson Ct FK10 155 E3
Donaldson Dr FK13 119 C7
Donaldson Gdns KY16 106 B5
Donaldson Pl FK7 134 D6
Donaldson Rd 14 KY8 79 F3
Donaldsons Acre 2 DD11 89 F4
Donaldson's Ct 4 KY8 80 F5
Donald St
Dundee DD2 93 A5
Dunfermline KY12 161 C6
Donibristle Gdns KY11 175 B2
Donibristle Ho KY11 175 B2
Donibristle Ind Pk KY11 175 A4
Donibristle Prim Sch KY11 175 B2
Don Rd KY11 161 F1
Don's Rd DD3 179 A4
Don St
Forfar DD8 87 D6
Leven KY8 109 A2
DoO'cot Brae FK10 138 A8
Doo'cot Hill FK10 118 D2
Doo'cot Pk 8 DD11 22 E3
Doocot Pl 4 DD11 22 E3
Doocot Rd KY16 106 A4
Doo'cot The PH3 104 E7
Doo Dells La KY3 166 F2
Doon Terr DD4 94 E6
Dora Ct KY4 147 D6
Dores Dr DD5 96 B5
Dornie Pl DD2 92 C5
Dornoch Cres KY2 130 E1
Dornoch Pl
Broughty Ferry DD5 96 C4
Dunfermline KY11 174 C8
Glenrothes KY6 112 D6
Dorothy Terr FK13 119 B7
Dorward Pl DD10 85 D5
Dorward Rd DD10 85 D4
Doubledikes Rd KY7 79 A1
Double Dykes DD9 84 A4
Doubledykes Rd KY16 106 C6
Double Row KY11 172 B4
Dougal Ct FK15 107 D7
Dougall St DD6 99 F6
DOUGLAS AND ANGUS 95 C6
Douglas Ave
Airth FK2 154 D3
Arbroath DD11 89 B6
Douglas Bader Com Gdn* KY15 105 B5
Douglas Cres KY13 108 B2
Douglas Ct PH1 102 E6
Douglas Dr
Crossford KY12 160 A2
Dunfermline KY12 160 E5
Stirling FK7 135 C4
Douglasfield Cres DD4 95 A5
Douglas Gdns 5 DD7 100 B3
Douglas Pk KY12 160 E6
Douglas Pl
Dunblane FK15 107 B3
1 Glenrothes KY6 112 E6
Douglas Rd
Blairgowrie PH10 88 D3
Dundee DD4 95 A4
Glenrothes KY6 112 B8
New Scone PH2 103 F8
Rosyth KY11 173 C2
Douglas Sports Ctr DD4 95 E5
Douglas St
Bannockburn FK7 135 E1
Dundee DD1 179 A3
Dunfermline KY12 161 A4
Kirkcaldy KY1 151 B3
2 Kirriemuir DD8 86 C5
Stirling FK8 115 B1
Douglas Terr
Dundee DD3 93 E4
New Scone PH2 103 F7
Stirling FK7 134 E6
DOUGLASTOWN 9 F2
Doune Pk KY11 175 C4
Doune Rd FK15 107 C5
Dovecot Cres KY1 152 B8
Dovecot La KY7 113 B6
Dovecot Pk
Aberdour KY3 176 B6
Glenrothes KY7 113 C6
Dovecot Pl
Dunfermline KY11 174 A7
Tullibody FK10 117 B3
Dovecot Rd
Glenrothes KY7 113 B6
Tullibody FK10 117 B3
Dovecot Recn Ctr KY7 113 C6
Dovecot Way KY11 174 A7
Dovecot Wynd KY11 173 F7
Dovehill FK10 138 B8
Dover Dr KY11 174 A8
Dover Hts KY11 174 A8
Dover Pk KY11 174 A8
Dover Way KY11 174 A8
Dove St 3 KY10 83 D6
Dovewells Dr DD9 84 B4
Dowan Pl FK7 134 E6
Dower Pl
Airth FK2 154 D4
Perth PH1 103 A5
Dowlas Ct 2 KY15 64 D4
DOWNFIELD 91 C2
Downfield KY4 147 C6
Downfield Golf Course DD2 90 F2
Downfield Pl KY1 131 A2
Downfield Prim Sch DD3 91 E1
Downiepark Pl DD3 94 A6
Downiepark Rd DD3 94 A6
Downie Pk DD3 94 A6
Downie Way 1 DD10 6 D8
Downing Point KY11 175 B2
Downs Cres FK10 137 F6
Dow St 10 DD1 93 E2
Doyle Pl 1 DD2 93 B5
Dreelside 33 KY10 83 C6
Dreel Terr KY10 82 F7
Drimmie Pl DD8 11 E4
Drimmie Rd DD8 11 E4
Drip Rd FK9 114 F2
Drive The DD2 40 E8
DRON 49 A3
Dronachy Rd KY2 150 F4
Dronley Ave DD2 90 A4
Dronley Rd
Dundee DD2 90 B4
Muirhead DD2 90 A5
Dronley Terr DD2 90 A4
Drony Rd KY16 68 F7
Drostan Terr DD11 89 E5
Droverhall Ave KY4 163 A6
Droverhall Pl KY4 163 A6
Dr Porter Gdns FK7 136 D4
Druid's Rd 17 PH2 37 F5
Druids Way 6 PH2 49 F7
DRUM 74 E3
Drumachlie Loan DD9 84 E2
Drumachlie Pk DD9 84 E2
Drumawhandie Rd 2 PH7 101 C4
Drumburn Rd FK14 74 A3
Drumcarrow Cres KY16 54 C3
Drumcarrow Rd KY16 106 C4
Drum Cl KY7 113 B2
Drum Ct 12 FK14 73 C1
Drumdryan Pl KY15 105 D2
DRUMELDRIE 81 C6
Drum Gate PH2 49 E3
Drumgeith Rd DD4 95 B7
Drumgrain Ave PH1 36 A5
Drumgrain Terr PH1 36 A4
Drumhar Ct 2 PH1 103 B4
Drumhead KY12 142 D6
Drumlanrig Pl DD4 94 F5
Drumlie Gdns KY7 113 A2
Drumlithie Pl DD3 91 B3
Drumlochie Gdns DD5 96 C6
Drummers Dell DD8 87 B4
Drummie Rd FK13 119 C5
Drummochy Rd KY8 80 F5
Drummond Ave PH3 104 A5
Drummond Castle Gdns* PH7 44 A4
Drummond Cres 11 PH2 48 D8
Drummond Ct KY15 105 B3
Drummond Grave PH10 88 C3
Drummond La FK8 135 A6
Drummond Pk KY13 74 D3
Drummond Pl
Dunfermline KY12 161 D5
Glenrothes KY6 112 E6
Stirling FK8 135 A6
Drummond Place La FK8 135 A6
Drummond Rd 1 PH10 88 C3
Drummond Rise FK15 107 D5
Drummond Sq KY5 148 B8
Drummond St
Crieff PH5 44 C4
Dundee DD3 179 A4
Drummond Terr PH7 101 C5
Drummormie Rd KY12 159 C1
Drumnagoil Gdns 3 KY4 126 E1
Drumoig Golf Club KY16 43 A3
Drumpark St FK7 135 B3
Drum Rd
Cupar KY15 105 A4
Dollar FK14 73 C1
Dunfermline KY11 161 F2
Kelty KY4 126 E1
DRUMSTURDY 31 A6
Drumsturdy Rd DD5 95 F8
Drum Well KY15 105 A2
Dryburgh Cres
Dundee DD2 93 A7
3 Perth PH1 102 A3
Dryburgh Gdns 3 DD2 93 A7
Dryburgh Ind Est DD2 93 B8
Dryburgh Pl 5 DD2 92 F7
Dryburgh St DD2 93 A7
Dryburgh Terr DD2 92 B3
Drylie Ct KY4 147 B4
Drylie St KY4 147 B4
Drysdale Gdns KY15 105 B4
Drysdale St FK10 138 B6
Dryside Rd KY13 76 F6
Duart Pl KY7 113 D4
Dubbieside 3 KY8 109 D5
Dubton Rd DD10 6 C7
Duchally Pl PH3 104 D5
Duchess St PH1 24 E3
DUCHLAGE 101 C2
Duchlage Ct PH7 101 C3
Duchlage Rd PH7 101 C3
Duchlage Terr PH7 101 C3
Duckburn Ind Est FK15 107 D3
Duddingston Dr KY2 130 F2
Dudhope Castle* DD3 93 E4
Dudhope Cres Rd DD3 179 A3

Dudhope Ct DD1 93 E4
Dudhope Gdns Stps 6 DD3 93 D4
Dudhope House Ypu Sch DD3 93 E4
Dudhope St DD3 179 B3
Dudhope Terr DD3 179 A3
Duff Cres FK8 114 F1
Duff St DD4 94 C5
Dufftown Pl 4 PH1 102 D8
Duffy Pl KY11 173 E3
Duich Pl 10 KY6 112 E6
Duke's Course The KY16 54 D1
Duke St
Alva FK12 118 A7
Arbroath DD11 89 C3
Bannockburn FK7 135 C1
Brechin DD9 84 B4
Clackmannan FK10 139 B4
West Wemyss KY1 132 F2
Dullomuir Dr KY4 126 C2
Duloch Schs & Com Campus KY11 162 B1
Dumbarnie Pl 4 KY8 81 A6
Dumbarton Rd
Cambusbarron FK8 134 E8
Stirling FK8 135 B7
Dumbreck Pk KY14 63 A5
Dumyat Ave FK10 117 B2
Dumyat Bsns Pk FK10 117 A2
Dumyat Rd
Alva FK12 117 E6
Menstrie FK11 116 F6
Stirling FK9 115 C3
Dumyat St FK10 117 F1
DUN 5 E6
Dunalastair Dr PH1 102 B5
Dunalistair Gdns 2 DD5 96 A3
Dunarn St PH12 17 B4
Dunarn Terr PH12 17 B4
Dunavon Gdns 2 DD3 91 C3
Dunbar Ct
Auchterarder PH3 57 D6
Glenrothes KY6 112 C7
Dunbarney Ave 17 PH2 48 F4
Dunbarney Prim Sch PH2 48 E5
Dunbar Pk DD4 95 B8
Dunbar Pl KY2 150 E5
Dunbeath Dr KY7 113 B4
DUNBLANE 107 D3
Dunblane Cath FK15 107 D5
Dunblane High Sch FK15 107 B4
Dunblane Mus* FK15 107 D5
Dunblane New Golf Club FK15 107 E4
Dunblane Prim Sch FK15 107 C5
Dunblane Sta FK15 107 D4
DUNBOG 51 C4
Dunbog Prim Sch KY14 51 C5
Duncan Ave DD11 89 A3
Duncan Buchanan Ct FK8 115 A2
Duncan Cres KY11 161 E2
Duncan of Jordanstone Coll of Art DD1 179 A1
Duncan Rd
Glenrothes KY7 113 A6
Letham DD8 11 E3
Duncansby Way PH1 102 F6
Duncanson Ave FK10 138 A8
Duncanson Dr KY3 166 A1
Duncan St
2 Dundee DD3 91 D2
Kirkcaldy KY2 151 A4
Duncan Terr DD3 91 D2
Duncan Way 8 KY16 54 B7
Duncarse Pl 4 DD2 92 D6
Duncarse Rd 3 DD2 92 D6
Duncraig Rd DD2 92 D6
DUNCRIEVIE 61 B4
Duncrievie Rd PH2 61 B4
Dundarroch Gdns 2 DD5 96 C3
Dundas Cres FK10 139 A4
Dundas Pk DD9 84 E3
Dundas Pl KY6 112 E6
Dundas Rd FK9 115 B4
Dundas St
1 Dundee DD5 95 F2
Lochgelly KY5 148 B7
Townhill KY12 161 C7
DUNDEE 179 C1
Dundee Airport DD2 92 F1
Dundee Coll (Constitution Campus) DD3 179 A3
Dundee Coll (Graham St Campus) DD1 94 A5
Dundee Coll (Kingsway Campus) DD1 94 A6
Dundee Coll (Melrose Campus) DD1 94 A5
Dundee Coll (Overgate Learning Ctr) DD1 179 B2
Dundee Ice Arena DD2 92 F8
Dundee Int Sports Complex DD4 94 B5
DUNDEE LAW 93 E5
Dundee Loan DD8 87 C4
Dundee Rd
2 Arbroath DD11 89 B2
Blairgowrie PH13 16 A2
Dundee DD5 95 D3
Forfar DD8 87 C2
Dundee Rd *continued*
Letham DD8 11 E3
Perth PH2 103 E1
Dundee Rd W DD4 95 A3
Dundee Repertory Theatre DD1 179 A1
Dundee St
Carnoustie DD7 100 C3
Letham DD8 11 E3
Dundee Sta DD1 179 B1
DUNDONALD 129 A2
Dundonald Cres KY5 129 B2
Dundonald Ct DD3 94 B4
Dundonald Pk KY5 129 B1
Dundonald Rd KY11 173 C3
Dundonald St DD3 94 B4
Dundonnell Way KY11 162 A1
Dunearn Bank KY3 165 D1
Dunearn Dr KY2 150 F6
Dunearn Prim Sch KY2 150 E7
Dunearn St DD5 96 B5
Dunecht Ct KY7 110 E3
Dunedin Pk 2 KY16 53 E7
Dunedin Pl KY7 113 E8
DUNFERMLINE 161 C5
Dunfermline Abbey* KY12 160 F3
Dunfermline Bsns Ctr KY11 161 B1
Dunfermline District Mus* KY12 161 B3
Dunfermline High Sch KY11 161 B1
Dunfermline Queen Margaret Sta KY12 161 F5
Dunfermline Rd
Crossgates KY4 162 E6
Limekilns KY11 172 E4
Dunfermline Town Sta KY12 161 B3
Dunfermline Wynd KY11 174 A2
Dunholm Pl 2 DD2 92 D6
Dunholm Rd DD2 92 D6
Dunholm St 5 DD2 92 D6
Dunholm Terr DD2 92 E6
Dunimarle Mus & Castle* KY12 169 B8
Dunimarle St KY12 158 A2
DUNINO 67 F5
Dunino Prim Sch KY16 67 F5
Dunipace Cres KY12 161 E5
Dunkeld Pl DD2 93 A4
Dunkeld Rd
Blairgowrie PH10 88 B4
Perth PH1 102 F6
Dunlin Ave KY7 110 F2
Dunlin Dr KY11 162 B4
Dunmar Cres FK10 117 E1
Dunmar Dr FK10 117 E1
DUNMORE 154 C7
Dunmore Dr DD2 92 F2
Dunmore Gdns DD2 92 F2
Dunmore Pl KY5 127 E8
Dunmore St DD3 91 F2
Dunn Cres KY11 161 E3
DUNNICHEN 11 C3
Dunnichen Rd DD8 87 F3
DUNNIKIER 130 E1
Dunnikier Golf Course KY1 131 B2
Dunnikier Prim Sch KY2 151 B5
Dunnikier Rd KY1 151 C5
Dunnikier Way
Kirkcaldy KY1 131 D1
Kirkcaldy KY1 151 B8
Dunninald House & Gdns* DD10 6 A4
DUNNING 46 F1
Dunning Pk PH2 47 A1
Dunning Prim Sch PH2 46 F1
Dunning Rd 6 PH3 46 B2
Dunning St 4 PH2 48 F5
Dunnottar Pl
Dundee DD5 95 D4
Kirkcaldy KY2 150 E4
Dunolly Gdns KY8 79 E3
Dunolly Pl KY16 106 E5
Dunrobin Rd
Glenrothes KY7 113 C3
Kirkcaldy KY2 150 E4
Dunrossie Cres DD10 85 A5
Dunrossie Terr DD10 85 A6
Duns Cres DD4 95 C7
DUNSHALT 63 B5
Dunshalt Prim Sch KY14 63 B5
Dunshelt Rd DD5 96 B5
Dunsinane Ave DD2 93 B7
Dunsinane Dr PH1 102 C5
Dunsinane Ind Est DD2 93 B7
Dunsinnan Rd PH2 25 D4
Dunsinnan View PH2 26 A3
Dunsire St
Kirkcaldy KY1 151 E8
5 Leven KY8 79 F2
Dunstaffnage Pl KY7 113 B4
Dunster Rd FK9 115 C3
Duntrune Terr DD5 95 E4
Dunure Pl KY2 150 E4
Dunvegan Ave KY2 150 D5
Dunvegan Ct
Alloa FK10 138 B6
Crossford KY12 160 B1
Glenrothes KY6 112 E5
Dunvegan Dr FK9 115 B3
Dunvegan Rd 1 DD5 96 B5
Dupplin Brae PH2 103 D6
Dupplin Rd PH2 103 C5
Dupplin Terr PH2 103 D4
Dura Cres KY7 113 D6
Dura Pk KY7 113 D6
Dura St DD4 179 C4
Dura View KY15 65 F8
Durham Cres 12 KY8 80 F5
Durham Gdns 5 KY8 80 F5
Durham Pl KY9 66 E2
Durham St DD5 97 A5
Durham Terr KY12 158 C1
Durham Wynd 6 KY8 80 F5
Durie Bank 2 KY8 79 E3
Durie Ct 3 KY8 109 C4
Durie Pk KY3 177 D8
Durie Pl
Dunfermline KY11 161 F4
Leven KY8 79 E3
Durie St KY8 109 E6
Durie Vale 3 KY8 79 E3
Durley Dene Cres PH2 48 E4
Durness Ct KY6 112 E5
Durness Terr DD2 92 C4
Durris Dr KY6 112 D6
Durris Loan DD5 96 B5
Durward Dr KY6 112 C5
Durward St
Leven KY8 109 E7
Lochore KY5 127 F6
Duthie St DD8 86 C3
Dyce Way KY7 110 E2
Dykedale FK15 107 F5
DYKEHEAD 1 A7
Dykehead Pl DD4 179 C4
Dyke Neuk KY8 109 C8
Dyke Side KY15 63 D1
Dymond Gr KY11 173 F8
DYSART 152 B7
Dysart Pl DD5 96 D5
Dysart Prim Sch KY1 152 A7
Dysart Rd KY1 151 F6

E

Eadie's Rd DD1 179 B3
Eagle Rd KY8 79 F1
Eardley Cres KY11 174 A7
Eardley Ct KY7 111 A3
Earl Grey Pl DD1 179 B1
Earl Haig Ave KY8 109 D7
Earl Of Mar Ct FK10 138 B6
Earlsburn Ave FK7 135 A3
Earls Ct FK10 138 B5
Earl's Dykes PH2 103 A3
EARLSFERRY 82 A2
Earlsferry Thistle Golf Club KY9 82 A3
Earlshall Castle* KY16 54 C8
Earlshall Rd KY16 54 B8
Earlshill Dr FK7 135 F1
Earls Row KY4 126 E2
Earl St 8 DD2 93 B6
Earlston Ave DD4 95 C7
Earlston Pl 3 DD7 100 E3
Earlston Way KY6 112 C7
Earnbank 5 PH2 48 F5
Earnbank Rd PH7 101 B3
Earn Cres DD2 92 D4
Earn Ct FK10 138 C6
Earn Dr PH1 35 D1
Earn Gr KY11 161 F4
Earngrove 15 PH2 48 F4
Earn Pl DD2 92 D4
Earn Rd
Kirkcaldy KY1 131 E1
Kirkcaldy KY1 151 D8
New Scone PH2 103 E8
Eassie Prim Sch DD8 17 F8
Eassie Terr DD2 93 A5
Easson's Angle 6 DD1 93 D3
East Abbey St DD11 89 D4
East Albert Rd KY1 151 C5
East Ave KY12 158 A7
East Back Dykes 4 KY14 62 D5
East Baldridge Dr KY12 160 E5
Eastbank DD9 84 C3
East Bank DD8 9 A7
Eastbank Pl DD2 28 B1
East Bay KY11 178 C5
East Blairs Rd DD8 11 F3
East Brae KY1 133 C6
East Bridge KY15 105 D5
East Bridge St PH2 103 C4
East Broomhill Rd KY3 177 E8
East Brougham St 5 PH1 24 E4
East Burn Ct KY1 151 D7
East Burnside
Cupar KY15 105 D5
Dollar FK14 120 E8
East Camperdown St DD1 94 C2
East Castle St FK10 138 B5
East Den Brae DD8 11 F3
East Dennison Rd 1 DD4 94 D5
East Dock St DD1 179 C3
East Dr
Dunfermline KY12 161 B3
Perth PH1 36 E4
Upper Largo KY8 81 A6
East End
Anstruther Easter KY10 83 D6
East Wemyss KY1 133 C6
East End Park (Dunfermline Athletic FC) KY12 161 C4
EASTER ABERDOUR 176 C8
EASTER BALGEDIE 76 E6
Easterbank DD8 87 E4
Easter Cornton Rd FK9 115 B4
Easter Craig Gdns KY12 142 E5
EASTER KNOX 22 B2
Easter Livilands FK7 135 C4
Eastern Access Rd FK7, FK8 135 C7
Eastern Prim Sch DD5 96 B3
Eastern Rd DD10 85 D3
Eastertoun 2 FK13 119 C7
East Fergus Pl KY1 151 B3
Eastfield KY7 113 E4
Eastfield Ind Est KY7 113 E5
East Forth St 4 KY10 83 D6
Eastgait Rise 1 DD6 43 C7
Eastgate
4 Arbroath DD11 12 F4
Kinghorn KY3 166 F3
East Gn 20 KY10 83 D6
East Goatmilk KY6 112 A4
East Grange St 3 DD5 96 F6
East Grimsby 8 DD11 89 D3
East Haddon Rd DD4 94 F3
East Harbour Rd KY11 172 B3
EAST HAVEN 32 E7
East Hemming St 5 DD8 11 E3
East Henderson's Wynd DD1 179 A2
East High St
Crieff PH7 101 D4
2 Forfar DD8 87 E5
Leven KY8 109 A1
East Hillbank 3 DD8 86 C5
Easthill Rd PH3 104 A5
East Hill Rd DD8 86 D7
East Home St 3 DD5 95 F2
East Kirkton Rd DD11 89 A7
East Leven St KY3 177 E8
East Link Rd FK9 115 D5
East Links KY8 109 F7
East Links Pl 2 DD5 96 B2
East Loan 10 KY15 63 B2
East Mains FK11 117 A6
EAST MAINS OF COLLISTON 22 D8
East March St KY1 151 E7
East Marketgait DD1 179 C3
East Mary St DD11 89 C3
Eastmill Brae DD9 84 E2
East Mill Ct 8 KY14 62 D5
East Mill Rd DD9 84 E1
East Muirlands Rd DD11 89 A5
East Murrayfield FK7 135 E1
East Navarre St DD5 96 E4
East Neuk Outdoors KY10 83 E7
East Newgate DD11 89 E3
Easton Ct FK8 115 B2
Easton Pl 6 KY6 112 E7
East Port
Dunfermline KY12 161 A4
2 Falkland KY15 63 B2
East Quality St KY1 152 A7
East Rd KY15 105 E5
East Row DD7 100 F3
East Sands Leisure Ctr KY16 106 F4
East Sch Rd DD3 91 D1
East Scores KY16 106 E6
East Scotscraig La 7 DD2 91 B1
East Shore
11 Anstruther Easter KY10 83 C6
18 Anstruther KY10 82 E4
10 Pittenweem KY10 83 B5
East Shore Rd 10 KY14 50 D5
East St 14 KY10 82 E4
East Station Pl DD6 98 E5
East Stirling St FK12 118 B7
East Terr EH30 178 C1
East Toll KY3 165 E1
East Vennel FK10 138 B6
East Vows Wlk KY1 167 B7
East Way KY11 175 C5
Eastwell Cl 1 DD2 93 C5
Eastwell Gdns 8 DD2 93 C6
Eastwell Rd DD2 93 C6
EAST WEMYSS 133 C6
East Wemyss Prim Sch KY1 133 B7
East Whale La DD4 179 C3
East Whitefield KY12 161 F6
Eccles Ct FK7 135 A4
Echline Gr EH30 178 A1
Echline Pl EH30 178 A1
Echline Prim Sch EH30 178 A1
Echline Rigg EH30 178 A1
Echline Terr EH30 178 A1
Echobank KY11 174 B2
Eddie Ave DD9 84 C5
Eddie Ct 8 KY16 106 D5
Edenbank Rd KY15 105 E5
Eden Course The KY16 54 F5
Eden Cres KY7 113 E6
Eden Estuary Ctr* KY16 54 B6
Eden Gr 5 KY14 62 D5
Eden Pk KY15 105 E5
Eden Rd
Alloa FK10 137 F8
Dunfermline KY11 161 E2
Edensmuir Ct KY7 111 B2
Eden Sq PH1 35 D1
Eden St DD4 94 C3
Eden Terr DD4 94 D2
Edenvale Terr KY15 64 D6
Eden Valley Bsns Pk KY15 105 F6
Eden Valley Gdns KY15 63 E2
Edgar St KY12 161 A3
Edinburgh Rd
Perth PH2 103 B2
South Queensferry EH30 178 C1
Edington Pl KY1 152 B8
Edison Pl DD2 93 A8
Edmund Pl KY12 161 A2
Ednam Dr KY6 112 D7
Edradour Gdns 4 DD11 89 F4
Edradour Pl 3 DD11 89 F4
Edradour Terr PH1 102 D8
Edward Ave FK8 115 C1
Edward Pl
Dunblane FK15 107 C4
Muirhead DD2 90 A3
Edward Rd FK8 115 B1
Edward St
Dunblane FK15 107 C4
2 Dundee DD1 93 E3
Dunfermline KY12 161 B5
Kirkcaldy KY2 151 B7
Edzell Pk 8 KY2 130 F1
Edzell St DD5 96 C5
Edzell Way KY11 162 A1
Eglingtoun Dr KY12 160 F6
Eglinton Pl KY11 174 D2
Eider Cl DD10 85 B6
Eighteenth St 7 KY5 129 B4
Eighth St FK3 168 C1
Eilean La KY12 158 E1
Elcho Castle* PH2 49 C8
Elcho Dr DD5 96 C6
Elcho La 8 PH2 49 F7
Elder Pl KY11 173 E5
Elder's Cl 11 DD8 86 C5
Elders Ct DD2 93 B5
Elders Knowe KY5 127 E7
Eldindean Ct KY12 160 D6
Elgin Ct KY12 161 A2
Elgin Dr
Glenrothes KY6 112 B6
Stirling FK7 135 C3
Elgin Gdns DD3 93 E8
Elgin Pl DD11 89 D4
Elgin Rd KY4 147 D4
Elgin St
Dundee DD3 93 F8
Dunfermline KY12 161 A2
Kirkcaldy KY2 151 B6
Elgin Terr DD3 93 F8
Elibank St PH1 103 A4
ELIE 82 A3
Elie Ave DD5 96 C5
Elie House Golf Course KY9 81 F2
Elie Pl DD5 96 C5
Elie Prim Sch KY9 82 A3
Elie Rd KY15 65 F7
Elie Sports Golf Course KY9 82 A3
Elistoun Dr FK13 119 C6
Elizabeth Cres
Carnoustie DD7 100 D4
Newport-on-Tay DD6 98 F5
Elizabeth Pl 30 KY10 83 C6
Elizabeth St
Dunfermline KY11 161 D2
Stirling FK8 135 A5
Tayport DD6 99 F5
Eliza St 5 DD4 94 C4
Ella Cargill Pl 6 DD11 89 A7
Ellaleen Gr KY12 160 B1
Ellengowan Dr DD4 94 D3
Ellen St DD1 179 C4
Ellice Pl 13 KY16 106 D6
Ellieslea Rd DD5 95 E3
ELLIOT 22 D2
Elliothill St KY11 161 B2
Elliot Ind Est DD11 22 E3
Elliot Pl
Arbroath DD11 89 B4
Glenrothes KY6 112 E7
Elliot Rd DD2 93 A3
Elliot St
Arbroath DD11 89 B4
Dunfermline KY11 161 B2
Ellisland Ave KY2 151 A7
Ellon Pk KY7 110 E2
Ellon Pl KY12 161 D6
Ellon Rd KY2 150 C7
Elmbank FK11 117 A6
Elmbank Cres DD11 89 A5
Elmbank Rd FK7 135 A3
Elm Brae DD11 89 B5
Elm Ct DD2 93 C3
Elm Dr PH10 88 D2
Elmfield Ave DD11 89 A5
Elm Gdns PH1 102 C3

Elm Gr
Arbroath DD11 .... 89 B5
2 Cupar KY15 .... 105 E5
Dunfermline KY11 .... 173 C8
Monance KY10 .... 82 E4
Elmgrove
2 Monifieth DD5 .... 97 B7
New Scone PH2 .... 37 F5
Elmgrove Pk DD5 .... 20 D1
Elm Hill DD11 .... 89 B5
Elm La
Glenrothes KY7 .... 112 F8
Perth PH1 .... 102 C3
Elm Path DD11 .... 89 A5
Elm Pk DD11 .... 89 B5
Elm Pl KY2 .... 150 F5
Elm Rd DD8 .... 86 D5
Elm Row PH2 .... 61 B5
Elm St
Dundee DD2 .... 93 C3
Errol PH2 .... 39 E2
Kirriemuir DD8 .... 86 D5
Stirling FK8 .... 114 E1
Elms The DD4 .... 95 A8
Elmvale PH3 .... 104 C6
Elmwood Ave 4 FK13 ... 119 C7
Elmwood Bsns Training KY15 .... 105 A5
Elmwood Coll KY15 ...... 105 A5
Elmwood Coll (Howe of Fife Learning Ctr) KY14 .... 62 F6
Elmwood Coll (Leng Ctr) DD6 .... 98 E5
Elmwood Coll (Newburgh Learning Ctr) KY14 ...... 50 D5
Elmwood Coll (St Andrews Learning Ctr) KY16 .... 106 C4
Elmwood Coll (Waid Ctr) KY10 .... 83 C6
Elmwood Dr 3 DD2 ...... 93 A5
Elmwood Golf Course KY15 .... 64 F7
Elmwood Rd
Dundee DD2 .... 93 A5
Leven KY8 .... 79 F3
Elmwood Terr KY4 ...... 126 D2
Elphinstone Cres FK2 .... 154 E4
Elphinstone St FK10 ..... 155 E4
Elrick Pk KY7 .... 110 E3
Elsinore Pl 4 DD5 .... 97 B7
Elvan Pl DD2 .... 93 B6
Emislaw Dr DD11 .... 89 A4
Emislaw Path DD11 .... 89 A4
Emma St 4 PH10 .... 88 C4
Emma Terr PH10 .... 88 B5
Emmoch Rd DD3 .... 91 F4
Emmock La DD4 .... 29 E5
Emmock Pl DD3 .... 91 E1
Emmock Rd DD4 .... 29 F5
Emmock View 2 DD4 ..... 29 E5
Emmock Wlk DD4 .... 29 E5
Emmock Woods Dr DD3 .... 29 F5
Emsdorf Cres 14 KY8 ...... 80 F5
Emsdorf Rd 16 KY8 .... 80 F5
Emsdorf St 13 KY8 .... 80 F5
Emslie Dr KY13 .... 108 C2
Endrick Pl FK7 .... 135 A4
Engelen Dr FK10 .... 138 B5
Enterprise Way KY11 ..... 173 E6
Erica Gr KY11 .... 173 E8
Ericht La 5 PH10 .... 88 C5
Ericht Pl DD2 .... 92 F4
Ericht Rd DD6 .... 98 A2
Eriskay Dr DD4 .... 94 C7
Eriskay Pl PH1 .... 37 C5
Eriskay Sq KY7 .... 111 A2
Ernest St DD11 .... 89 D4
Errochty Ct PH1 .... 102 B5
Errochty Gr PH1 .... 102 B5
Errochty Pl PH1 .... 102 B6
ERROL 39 F1
Errol Gdns KY6 .... 110 F2
Errol Prim Sch PH2 ...... 39 F2
Errol Rd DD2 .... 92 B2
ERROL STATION 39 F3
Erskine Beveridge Ct KY11 .... 161 B2
Erskine Brae KY12 .... 157 D1
Erskine La DD5 .... 96 A3
Erskine Pl
Clackmannan FK10 .... 138 F5
Glenrothes KY7 .... 113 A6
3 Montrose DD10 .... 85 D2
Erskine Rd
Leuchars KY16 .... 54 B7
6 Tayport DD6 .... 99 F6
Erskine Sq KY11 .... 161 C2
Erskine St
Alloa FK10 .... 138 B7
Alva FK12 .... 118 A7
Dundee DD4 .... 179 C4
1 Leven KY8 .... 109 A1
Lochgelly KY5 .... 148 A6
Montrose DD10 .... 85 D2
Erskine Terr DD5 .... 97 A7
Erskine Wynd KY12 ...... 159 A7
Esk Ct DD8 .... 87 D6
Eskdale Ave DD3 .... 91 C2
Esk Park DD9 .... 84 D2
Esk Park Terr DD9 .... 84 D2
Esk Rd DD10 .... 85 B1
Eskview Terr DD10 .... 85 C1
Esmonde Ct KY11 .... 173 E2
Esplanade
31 Anstruther Wester KY10 .... 83 C6
Kirkcaldy KY1 .... 151 C2
1 Stirling FK8 .... 135 A8
Esplanade The DD5 ...... 96 C2
Essendy Rd PH10 .... 88 B3
Ethiebeaton Pk DD5 ...... 96 F7
Ethiebeaton Terr DD5 .... 97 A6
Ethie Pl DD11 .... 89 E6
Ethie St DD11 .... 23 D7
Ethie Terr
Arbroath DD11 .... 89 E6
Barnhill DD5 .... 96 A5
Etive Gdns DD2 .... 92 D5
Etive Pl
Dalgety Bay KY11 .... 175 A2
Glenrothes KY6 .... 112 F6
Stirling FK9 .... 115 B3
Eton St DD2 .... 93 A3
Ettrick Cres
Dalgety Bay KY11 .... 175 A4
Dundee DD2 .... 93 A7
Ettrick Dr PH1 .... 102 A3
Ettrick Way KY6 .... 112 C7
Euclid Cres DD1 .... 179 B2
Euclid St DD1 .... 179 B2
Evandale Ct KY6 .... 112 D5
Evelyn Terr PH2 .... 103 A1
Evershed Ct KY11 .... 161 E1
Evershed Dr KY11 .... 161 E1
Ewanfield PH7 .... 101 D5
Ewan St PH10 .... 88 B4
Ewing Ct FK7 .... 135 C3
Ewing St
Cowdenbeath KY4 .... 147 B2
Lochgelly KY5 .... 148 A6
Exchange La 2 PH2 ..... 103 A3
Exchange St DD1 .... 179 B2
Excise La FK10 .... 155 E3
Excise St FK10 .... 155 E4
Explorer Rd DD2 .... 92 B4

F

Factory Rd
Cowdenbeath KY4 .... 147 D4
Kirkcaldy KY1 .... 151 D6
Leven KY8 .... 133 F8
Fairbairn St DD3 .... 94 A4
Fairfax Ct KY3 .... 165 E1
FAIRFIELD 118 B2
Fairfield 6 DD11 .... 89 A3
Fairfield Ave PH1 .... 102 E6
Fairfield Rd
Alloa FK10 .... 118 C1
Dundee DD3 .... 93 F7
Kelty KY4 .... 126 E1
Leven KY9 .... 81 F6
Fairfields FK2 .... 153 E5
Fairfield Sch FK10 ...... 118 B1
Fairfield St DD3 .... 93 F7
Fairhill Ave PH1 .... 102 C3
Fairhill Cres PH1 .... 102 C2
Fairhill Dr PH1 .... 102 C3
Fairhill Gr PH1 .... 102 C2
Fairhill Rd FK7 .... 135 B1
Fairhill View PH1 .... 102 C2
Fairhurst Wlk DD4 .... 94 E5
Fairies La PH1 .... 102 D4
Fairies Rd PH1 .... 102 D3
Fair Isle Prim Sch KY2 .... 150 E8
Fair Isle Rd KY2 .... 150 E8
Fairley Ct KY12 .... 159 D1
Fairlie Terr DD3 .... 91 B4
Fairmount Dr FK10 ...... 118 B2
Fairmount Rd PH2 .... 103 D2
Fairmount Terr PH2 ..... 103 D2
Fairmuir Rd DD3 .... 93 F7
Fairmuir St N DD3 .... 93 F8
Fairmuir Sq DD3 .... 93 F7
Fairmuir St DD3 .... 93 F7
Fairnsdale Terr KY5 ..... 127 E7
Fair Pl KY11 .... 174 B3
Fairport Rd 1 DD11 ...... 89 F5
Fairview PH1 .... 37 B8
Fairways KY12 .... 161 B6
Fairways Heavy Horse Ctr* PH2 .... 49 F8
Fairway The
Kirkcaldy KY1 .... 151 F8
Monifieth DD5 .... 97 B7
Fairyburn Rd FK10 .... 137 F8
Fairy Fa' Cres KY4 ...... 162 F6
Fairykirk Rd KY11 .... 174 A3
Fairy Knowe (Cairn)* FK9 .... 70 D1
Fa-Latch Rd KY8 .... 79 E4
Falcon Dr KY7 .... 113 C6
Falconer Ct FK7 .... 135 C3
Falcon Gdns KY7 .... 113 C6
Falcon Rd KY8 .... 79 F1
FALKLAND 63 B2
Falkland Cres DD5 .... 96 D5
Falkland Dr DD11 .... 89 A5
Falkland Gate KY7 .... 113 A7
Falkland House Sch KY15 .... 63 A2
Falkland Pal* KY15 .... 63 B2
Falkland Pl
1 Broughty Ferry DD5 .... 96 D5
Glenrothes KY7 .... 113 A7
4 Invergowrie DD2 ...... 41 B8
Falkland Prim Sch KY15 .... 63 B2
Falklands Golf Club KY15 .... 63 C2
Falkland View KY1 .... 131 F1
FALLIN
136 C3
136 C4
Fallin Prim Sch FK7 .... 136 D5
Fallodon Cres KY2 ...... 151 A3
Famous Grouse Experience The* PH7 .... 101 A7
Faraday Ct DD2 .... 93 B8
Faraday Rd KY6 .... 112 D3
Faraday St DD2 .... 93 A8
Farington Gdns DD2 ..... 93 B2
Farington St DD2 .... 93 A2
Farington Terr DD2 ..... 93 A2
Farm Ct 24 KY10 .... 83 C6
Farm Rd
25 Anstruther Easter KY10 .... 83 C6
Cowdenbeath KY4 .... 147 B3
Crombie KY12 .... 171 D6
Fallin FK7 .... 136 D4
Perth PH2 .... 103 D6
Farm Row KY12 .... 162 B6
Farmstead Rd KY11 ..... 174 F4
Farne Ct KY2 .... 150 F8
FARNELL 5 A2
Farnell Rd DD11 .... 13 A4
Farnell Way KY12 .... 161 D6
Farquhar Terr EH30 ..... 178 A1
Faulds Cres DD10 .... 85 E3
Faulds Rd DD10 .... 85 E3
Fechney Pk PH1 .... 102 F4
Feddal Rd FK15 .... 56 B4
Felkington Ave 4 KY10 .... 69 A2
Fenton Pl DD5 .... 97 A6
Fenton St FK10 .... 138 A7
Fenwick Pl DD4 .... 95 B7
Feregait FK10 .... 155 E4
Ferguson Ave DD9 .... 84 D4
Ferguson Dr PH1 .... 102 A5
Ferguson Pk Rd PH10 ..... 88 D6
Ferguson Pl
Burntisland KY3 .... 165 F1
Glenrothes KY6 .... 112 E6
Ferguson St FK8 .... 114 F2
Fergus Pl KY11 .... 161 D1
Fergusson Gall The* PH2 .... 103 C3
Fergusson Pl 3 KY16 ..... 54 E2
Fergusson Rd KY11 ..... 174 A7
Fergus Sq DD11 .... 89 C4
Fergus St DD11 .... 89 C4
Fergus Wynd KY11 ...... 151 B1
FERN 2 E8
Fernbank FK9 .... 115 B3
Fernbank Ave 5 KY8 ..... 79 E3
Fernbank Dr 6 KY8 ...... 79 E3
Fernbrae DD2 .... 93 B2
Ferndale Dr DD5 .... 95 F4
Fern Gr PH10 .... 88 E1
Fernhill Cres 8 KY8 ..... 79 E3
Fernhill Dr KY8 .... 79 E3
Fernhill Gdns 7 KY8 ..... 79 E3
Fernhill Rd PH2 .... 103 D3
Ferniebank Brae FK9 ..... 70 C1
Fernie Ct KY7 .... 113 C2
Fernie Gdns DD5 .... 96 C4
Fernie Pl KY12 .... 160 E5
Fern Pl KY16 .... 54 B8
Ferntower Pl 1 PH7 ..... 101 D4
Ferntower Rd PH7 ...... 101 C4
Ferrard Rd KY2 .... 151 A4
Ferrier St 2 DD7 .... 100 D2
Ferris Way KY11 .... 175 B4
Ferry Barns Ct KY11 .... 178 B6
Ferry Ct FK9 .... 115 A3
FERRYDEN 85 D1
Ferryden Pl KY7 .... 113 A2
Ferryden Prim Sch DD10 .... 6 C3
Ferryfield KY15 .... 105 B3
Ferryhill Rd
Inverkeithing KY11 ...... 174 B1
North Queensferry KY11 .... 178 B7
Ferry La KY11 .... 178 B6
Ferry Orch FK9 .... 115 D1
Ferry Rd
Broughty Ferry DD5 ...... 96 F4
5 Earlsferry/Elie KY9 .... 82 A2
Montrose DD10 .... 85 D2
North Queensferry KY11 .... 178 B6
South Alloa FK7 .... 137 F4
Stirling FK9 .... 115 D1
Ferry St DD10 .... 85 D2
Ferry Toll Pl KY11 ...... 173 E1
Ferry Toll Rd
Inverkeithing KY11 ...... 178 A8
Rosyth KY11 .... 173 E1
Fettercairn Dr DD5 ...... 96 C4
Fetterdale Fields 21 KY16 .... 54 B8
Fettes Way 7 DD10 ...... 85 D7
Fettykil Path KY6 .... 112 C8
Feus PH3 .... 104 F7
Feus Pl PH1 .... 102 F5
Feus Rd PH1 .... 102 F5
Feus The 9 KY15 .... 63 E1
Fidra Ave KY3 .... 165 D1
Fieldfare View KY11 ..... 162 A3
Fife Airport KY6 .... 112 A4
Fife Airport Ind Est KY6 .... 112 A3
Fife Animal Pk* KY15 ..... 63 E7
Fife Central Ret Pk KY2 .... 130 D1
Fife Folk Mus* KY15 ...... 65 D6
Fife Inst of Physical & Rec Ed KY6 .... 113 A4
Fife Ness Muir Wildlife Reserve* KY10 .... 69 E4
Fife Pl KY11 .... 173 B2
Fife Regional Pk* KY6 .... 77 F7
FINAVON 2 F4
Finavon Ct KY7 .... 113 B3
Finavon Doocot* DD8 ...... 2 E3
Finavon Pl DD4 .... 94 D8
Finavon St DD4 .... 94 D7
Finavon Terr DD4 .... 94 D7
Findale St DD4 .... 94 E7
Findcastle Pl DD4 ...... 94 E7
Findcastle St DD4 ...... 94 D8
Findcastle Terr DD4 ..... 94 D7
Findchapel Pl DD4 ...... 94 E8
Findhorn Pl
Dundee DD4 .... 94 D8
Kirkcaldy KY2 .... 150 E8
Findhorn St DD4 .... 94 D8
Findlay Cres KY11 ...... 173 E4
Findlays Land DD8 ...... 87 E6
Findlay St KY11 .... 173 E4
FINDO GASK 46 E7
Findon La KY7 .... 111 C2
Findowrie Pl DD4 .... 94 E8
Findowrie St DD4 .... 94 E8
Finedon Terr DD4 .... 94 E7
Finella Gdns DD4 .... 94 E8
Finella Pl DD4 .... 94 E8
Finella Terr DD4 .... 94 E8
Fingask Ave KY7 .... 113 C3
Fingask Ct PH2 .... 103 E8
Fingask Pl 10 PH2 .... 49 F7
Fingask St DD3 .... 93 E5
Finglassie KY7 .... 113 A2
Finlaggan Cres DD4 ..... 94 E7
Finlaggan Pl DD4 .... 94 E7
Finlaggan Terr DD4 ..... 94 E7
Finlarig Pl DD4 .... 94 E7
Finlarig Terr DD4 .... 94 E7
Finlathen Sports Ctr DD4 .... 94 E7
Finlow Pl DD4 .... 94 F8
Finlow Terr DD4 .... 94 F8
Finmore Pl DD4 .... 94 F7
Finmore St DD4 .... 94 F7
FINTRY 94 D7
Fintry Cres DD4 .... 94 E7
Fintry Dr DD4 .... 94 E7
Fintry Gdns DD4 .... 94 D7
Fintry Mains DD4 .... 94 E7
Fintry Pl DD5 .... 95 F4
Fintry Prim Sch DD4 .... 94 E8
Fintry Rd DD4 .... 94 E8
Fintryside DD4 .... 94 E7
Fintry Terr DD4 .... 94 F7
Firbank Rd PH1 .... 102 C4
Fir Gr KY11 .... 173 E8
Firpark Ski Ctr FK13 ... 119 C8
Firpark Terr FK7 .... 134 C5
Fir Pk FK13 .... 119 C7
Firs Cres FK7 .... 135 D2
Firs Entry FK7 .... 135 D2
Firs Rd FK10 .... 117 D2
Firs The
Bannockburn FK7 .... 135 D2
Dalgety Bay KY11 ...... 175 B2
First St KY5 .... 77 F1
FIRTH MUIR OF BOYSACK 22 B7
FISHCROSS 118 E3
Fishcross Prim Sch FK10 .... 118 D3
Fishdock Rd DD1 .... 94 F3
Fish Dock Rd DD1 .... 94 E2
Fisheracre DD11 .... 89 D5
Fishermans Wlk FK9 .... 115 A3
Fisher's Gn FK9 .... 70 C1
Fisher St
Broughty Ferry DD5 ..... 95 F2
Dundee DD5 .... 96 A2
Leven KY8 .... 109 C4
Fisher Studio & Gallery* KY10 .... 83 A5
Fittis Rd PH1 .... 102 A4
Fitzroy Sq KY1 .... 152 A7
Fitzroy St KY1 .... 152 A7
Fitzroy Terr PH2 .... 103 D6
Flairs Ave DD11 .... 89 F6
Flass Rd DD6 .... 98 A2
Flax Mill La KY7 .... 79 C3
Fleecefaulds Mdw Wildlife Reserve* KY15 .... 65 D3
Fleming Ct KY13 .... 108 C6
Fleming Dr KY2 .... 130 E1
Fleming Gdns E DD3 ..... 94 A5
Fleming Gdns N DD3 ..... 94 A5
Fleming Gdns S DD3 ..... 94 A4
Fleming Gdns W 4 DD3 .... 94 A5
Fleming Pl KY16 .... 106 D5
Flemington Rd KY7 ..... 113 B7
Fleming Way KY3 .... 165 E2
Fleshers' Vennel 1 PH1 .... 103 B3
Flesh Wynd 12 KY1 ..... 151 D6
Fletcher Pl PH7 .... 101 E3
Fleuchar St DD2 .... 93 D4
Fleurs Pk FK9 .... 114 F3
Fleurs The 5 KY15 .... 63 B2
FLISKMILLAN 51 E8
Flockhouse Ave KY5 .... 127 F7
Floors Ct KY7 .... 113 B2
Floors Pl KY2 .... 150 D5
Floors Rd KY7 .... 113 B2
Florence Pl PH1 .... 103 A6
Flower Pl KY4 .... 146 F8
Flutorum Ave KY1 ...... 131 D8
Fodbank View KY11 ..... 161 E4
Fod St KY11 .... 162 B5
Foggyley Gdns DD2 ...... 93 B7
Foggyley Pl 1 DD2 ...... 93 C6
Fontstane Cres DD5 ...... 96 F5
Fontstane Pl 3 DD5 ...... 97 A5
Fontstane Rd DD5 .... 97 A5
Fontstane St DD5 .... 96 F5
Fontstane Terr 4 DD5 .... 97 A5
Foote St KY5 .... 148 A6
Foot Pl KY11 .... 173 E3
Forbeslea Gdns KY12 .... 159 E7
Forbes of Kingennie Ctry Resort Visitor Ctr* DD5 .... 30 F7
Forbes of Kingennie Dr DD5 .... 30 F7
Forbes Pl
4 Arbroath DD11 .... 89 B7
2 St Andrews KY16 ...... 54 E3
St Andrews KY16 .... 106 A5
Forbes Rd KY11 .... 173 C2
Forbes St FK10 .... 137 F6
Forbes Terr KY2 .... 151 B5
Ford Cres KY1 .... 131 D7
FORDEL 61 B7
FORDELL 163 B6
Fordell Bank KY11 ...... 175 C4
Fordell Gdns
Dalgety Bay KY11 ...... 174 E7
Kirkcaldy KY2 .... 150 D5
Fordell Ind Est KY4 ..... 147 B1
Fordell Rd KY7 .... 111 A1
Fordell Way KY11 ...... 174 D2
Ford Rd PH7 .... 101 B3
Ford View KY12 .... 159 C1
Fordyce Ct KY16 .... 106 C3
Fordyce Way PH3 .... 104 D6
Forebank Rd
Blairgowrie PH10 .... 88 D5
Dundee DD1 .... 179 B3
Forebank St DD1 .... 179 B3
Forebank Terr DD1 ..... 179 B3
Forebraes FK10 .... 138 B7
Forester's Lea Cres KY12 .... 161 E4
Forester St DD1 .... 179 A2
FOREST MILL 140 C8
Forest Path
2 Broom KY8 .... 109 D8
Sillerhole KY8 .... 80 B5
Forest Pk Pl DD1 .... 93 D3
Forest Pk Rd DD1 .... 93 D3
Forest Pl KY12 .... 161 D7
Forest Rd
Cardenden KY5 .... 129 C3
Townhill KY12 .... 161 D7
Forestry Pl 13 PH1 ...... 24 A6
Forest Way PH10 .... 88 D3
FORFAR 87 E4
Forfar Acad DD8 .... 87 C6
Forfar Golf Course DD8 .... 11 A5
Forfar Infmy DD8 .... 87 E5
Forfar Loch Ctry Pk* DD8 .... 87 A5
Forfar Rd
Arbroath DD11 .... 89 A5
Blairgowrie PH12 .... 17 A7
Coupar Angus PH13 ..... 16 A3
Dundee DD4 .... 94 D6
Kirriemuir DD8 .... 86 D4
Forfar Swimming Pool DD8 .... 87 D5
FORGANDENNY 48 A5
Forgandenny Prim Sch PH2 .... 48 A5
Forgandenny Rd PH2 ..... 48 E4
Forgan Dr KY16 .... 42 F4
Forgan Pl KY16 .... 106 D4
Forgan St 2 DD6 .... 98 C3
Forgan Way DD6 .... 98 D3
Forge The KY12 .... 160 C6
Forglen Cres FK9 ...... 115 A6
Forglen Rd FK9 .... 115 B6
Forker Ave KY11 .... 173 D4
Forman Gr KY11 .... 161 E1
Forman Rd KY8 .... 109 E6
Formonthills Ct KY6 .... 110 D3
Formonthills La KY6 .... 110 D3
Formonthills Pk KY6 .... 110 D3
Formonthills Rd KY6 .... 110 E2
Forres Ave 3 DD3 .... 91 F1
Forres Cres DD3 .... 94 A7
Forres Dr
Glenrothes KY6 .... 112 C6
Kirkcaldy KY2 .... 150 C7
Forrester Gr FK10 ...... 117 F1
Forrester Pl FK2 .... 154 D3
Forresters Gait KY7 .... 113 F4
Forrest Rd FK8 .... 115 B1
Forrest St KY16 .... 106 D4
Forsyth La FK7 .... 135 C1
Fortar Way 2 DD5 .... 96 B5
FORTEVIOT 47 D4
Forteviot Prim Sch PH2 .... 47 D4
Fortharfield 15 KY15 ..... 63 E1
Forth Ave KY2 .... 151 A4
Forth Ave Ind Est KY2 ... 151 A3
Forthbank Ind Est FK10 .... 138 B4

Forthbank Pl KY12 157 F1
Forth Bridges Visitor Ctr* KY11 178 A6
Forth Cres
Alloa FK10 138 C5
Dalgety Bay KY11 175 B4
Dundee DD2 92 E5
High Valleyfield KY12 158 B2
Stirling FK8 135 B8
Forth Ct
Dalgety Bay KY11 175 B4
Dunfermline KY12 161 A2
Glenrothes KY6 112 E6
Stirling FK8 115 B1
Forth Gdns KY12 158 E7
Forthill Dr DD5 96 A4
Forthill Pl DD5 96 A4
Forthill Prim Sch DD5 96 A4
Forthill Rd DD5 96 A4
Forth Park Dr KY2 151 A5
Forth Park Gdns KY2 151 A5
Forth Park Maternity Hospl KY2 151 A5
Forth Pk
Bridge of A FK9 115 A5
Stirling FK9 114 F5
Forth Pl
Burntisland KY3 177 E8
Dundee DD2 92 E5
South Queensferry EH30 178 A1
Stirling FK8 135 B8
Forth Rd KY11 173 B2
Forth Reach KY11 174 F2
Forthside Terr KY11 178 C5
Forth St
Cambus FK10 137 A8
Dunfermline KY12 161 A2
Fallin FK7 136 C4
Kincardine FK10 155 D3
3 Leven KY8 109 A2
Monance KY10 82 E4
Stirling FK8 115 B1
Forthvale FK11 117 A6
Forthvale Ct FK9 115 B2
Forth Valley Coll Clackmannan Campus FK10 138 B8
Forth Valley Coll Hall Park (Annexe) FK10 138 C8
Forth Valley Coll Stirling FK7 135 C6
Forthview
Bannockburn FK7 135 E1
Leven KY8 79 E4
Forth View
Dalgety Bay KY11 175 B4
Inverkeithing KY11 174 B2
Kincardine FK10 155 F3
Stirling FK8 115 B1
Forth View Cotts KY12 158 A1
Forth View Ind Est KY12 158 B1
Forthview Terr KY12 158 D1
Forties Campus KY11 173 D1
Forties Rd
Dundee DD4 95 C7
Montrose DD10 85 D8
Forties Rd Ind Est DD10 85 D8
Fortingall Pl PH1 102 D5
Fort St DD2 93 C2
Forum Shop Ctr The DD1 179 B2
Fossoway Prim Sch KY13 74 D3
Foster Rd DD3 93 F8
Foswell PH3 104 D5
Fothringham Dr DD5 97 A7
Foula Terr DD4 94 C7
Foulden Pl KY12 161 D3
Foulford Pl KY4 147 B4
Foulford Prim Sch KY4 147 B5
Foulford Rd KY4 147 B4
Foulford St KY4 147 C4
Foundry La
Dundee DD4 179 C3
Perth PH1 103 B4
Foundry Pl DD5 97 B5
Foundry Rd DD5 97 B5
Foundry St KY12 161 A4
Fountainbleau Dr DD4 94 E6
Fountainbrae 1 DD5 97 B7
Fountain Pl KY4 147 D3
Fountain Rd FK9 115 A7
Fowler Pl 16 KY10 83 D6
Fowler Rd DD5 95 E7
Fowler St 15 KY10 83 D6
FOWLIS 28 B4
Fowlis Rd DD2 28 D4
FOWLIS WESTER 34 D2
Foxglove Neuk KY12 161 A5
Fox St DD7 100 D3
Foxton Dr KY7 113 C2
Frances Ind Pk KY1 152 C8
Frances View KY1 152 A8
Francis Ct KY12 160 D5
Francis Rd PH2 102 D2
Francis St
6 Dundee DD3 93 F6
Lochgelly KY5 148 B7
Frankfield Cres KY11 175 D4
Frankfield Pl KY11 175 C4
Frankfield Rd KY11 175 D4
Frank Wood Way DD10 85 E3
Fraser Ave
Blairgowrie PH10 15 B5
Inverkeithing KY11 174 D2
Perth PH2 25 D4
St Andrews KY16 106 D4
Fraser Dr KY5 148 B7
Fraser Path DD11 89 A4
Fraser Pl
15 Arbroath DD11 22 E4
Dysart KY1 152 A8
Glenrothes KY6 112 E6
Stirling FK9 115 B4
Fraser Rd KY16 54 B7
Fraser's La 4 DD10 85 C4
Fraser Terr PH1 102 E2
Freddie Tait St KY16 106 D4
Frederick Cres KY11 161 B2
Frederick St
Dundee DD3 91 D1
Tillicoultry FK13 119 B7
Frederick Wilson Pk KY2 151 A7
Freeman Gr 15 KY16 54 B8
FREUCHIE 63 F1
Freuchie Prim Sch KY15 63 E1
Frew Ct KY11 161 C1
Frew Pl KY12 146 A1
Friar Pl KY13 77 A4
Friars St FK8 135 B8
Friar St PH2 103 A2
FRIARTON 48 D8
Friarton Bsns Pk PH2 48 D8
Friarton Pl 12 PH2 48 D8
Friarton Rd PH2 103 B1
Friary Ct KY11 174 C2
Frigate Unicorn* DD1 179 C2
FRIOCKHEIM 12 F5
Friockheim Prim Sch DD11 12 F4
Front Lebanon KY15 105 C5
Front Row Croftouterly 3 KY6 112 B8
Front St FK15 56 B4
Fruithill DD8 87 C3
Fullarton St DD3 93 C5
Fullerton Rd KY7 113 A7
Fulmar Way KY11 175 B4
Fulton Rd DD2 92 C6
Furnace Pl KY4 147 E6
Furniss Ave KY11 173 D5
Fyfe-Jamieson St DD8 87 E6
Fyffe St DD1 93 D4
Fyne Ct KY7 111 A4
Fyne Rd DD5 96 B4
Fyvie Gn KY7 113 B3
Fyvie Loan DD5 95 D4

G

Gaberston Ave FK10 138 C7
Gagarin Way KY4 147 E6
Gagie Bank 4 DD5 30 F7
Gairloch Rd DD5 96 B4
GAIRNEY BANK 76 A2
Gairney Burn La KY13 74 B1
Gala Ave DD2 92 F4
Gallacher Ave KY8 109 D7
Gallacher Pl KY4 147 E6
Gallagher Ret Pk DD1 179 C3
GALLATOWN
151 E8
Kirkcaldy 131 F1
Galloway Cres PH7 101 B4
Gallowbank Rd PH10 88 B4
Gallowden Ave 4 DD11 89 A4
Gallowden Cres 3 DD11 89 A4
Gallowden Rd DD11 89 A4
GALLOWHILL 25 E6
Gallowhill
Brechin DD9 84 C4
Crieff PH7 101 B3
Gallowhill Gdns KY13 108 B4
Gallowhill Pl PH3 104 B6
Gallowhill Rd KY13 108 B5
Gallowhill Wynd KY13 108 B4
Gallowshade Rd DD8 87 C3
Gallows Loan
Culross KY12 157 D2
Dunfermline KY12 141 D1
Galvelmore St 7 PH7 101 C4
Gambeson Cres FK7 135 D3
Gamekeepers Rd KY13 76 F6
Gammie Pl KY5 129 B3
Gannochie Terr DD4 94 F3
GANNOCHY 103 D5
Gannochy Ave PH2 103 D6
Gannochy Cres DD10 85 C6
Gannochy Edge PH2 103 D6
Gannochy Gn PH2 103 D6
Gannochy Rd PH2 103 D5
Gannochy Terr PH2 103 E6
Gannochy Wlk PH2 103 E6
Garden Ct KY12 161 D7
Gardeners Ct KY12 161 B4
GARDENER'S LAND 161 B4
Gardeners' St KY12 161 B4
Garden Mill Pl 6 DD3 91 A3
Garden Pl
Cairneyhill KY12 159 C1
Clackmannan FK10 139 A4
Townhill KY12 161 D7
Gardens Rd KY14 50 D5
Garden St 2 DD11 89 C3
Garden Terr FK10 139 A4
Gardiner Pl KY4 147 B2
Gardiner Rd KY4 147 C2
Gardiner St KY5 148 B7
Gardner Ave 35 KY10 83 C6
Gardner Cres KY8 109 A6
Gardner La DD11 89 C6
Gardner's La 1 DD1 93 E4
Gardner St DD3 93 D5
Gardyne Pl DD4 95 B3
Gardyne Rd DD5 95 B3
Gardyne St
Arbroath DD11 12 F4
10 Letham DD8 11 E3
Montrose DD10 85 C6
Gare Pl 11 KY6 112 E6
Garland Pl
Dundee DD3 179 A3
1 Newport-on-Tay DD6 98 D3
Garliebank Cres KY15 105 D2
Garnet Terr DD4 95 A4
Garrison Rd DD10 85 D2
Garry Ct KY7 111 A3
Garry Pk KY5 127 E4
Garry Pl
9 Bankfoot PH1 24 A6
Dundee DD3 91 D1
8 Perth PH2 48 D8
Garry St KY5 148 B8
Garry Terr DD3 91 D1
Garry Wlk 21 PH2 37 F5
Garten St DD5 96 B4
Garth Ave PH1 102 C6
Garth Terr PH3 58 B8
Gartinny FK13 119 B4
Gartmorn Dam Ctry Pk* FK10 139 B8
Gartmorn Dam Visitor Ctr* FK10 139 A8
Gartmorn Rd FK10 118 D1
Gartwhinzean Loan FK14 122 C8
Gartwhinzean Rd KY13 74 B1
Garvald Way KY6 112 C7
Garvally Cres FK10 138 A8
Garvock Ave DD10 85 C8
Garvock Bank KY11 161 F4
GARVOCK HILL 161 C4
Garvock Hill KY12 161 D4
Garvock Pl DD3 91 B3
Garvock Terr KY12 161 D4
Gas Brae
Blairgowrie PH10 88 C5
Errol PH2 39 F1
Gas Wynd KY1 151 B2
GATESIDE 62 A4
Gateside Cotts KY7 111 C4
Gateside Ct KY4 147 A3
Gateside Ind Est KY4 147 A3
Gateside Prim Sch KY14 62 A4
Gateside Rd
Forfar DD8 19 E7
Stirling FK7 135 A3
Gauldie Cres DD3 91 C4
Gauldie Ct DD3 91 B4
Gauldie Pl DD3 91 B4
Gauldie Rd DD3 91 B4
Gauldie Terr DD3 91 B4
GAULDRY 41 F2
Gauldry Terr DD5 96 C4
GAULS 24 B5
Gavins Rd FK10 117 F1
Gayfield DD11 89 C2
Gayfield Pk (Arbroath FC) DD11 89 C2
Gean Gr PH10 88 D3
Gean Rd FK10 137 F8
Geddes Dr PH1 102 B4
Gedy Pl DD11 89 E5
Gellatly Pl DD9 84 C4
Gellatly Rd KY11 161 D2
Gellatly St DD1 179 C2
Gellyburn Rd PH1 36 E5
Gelvan Moor Rd KY13 74 F5
Gemini Cres DD2 92 C4
Gentlecroft 11 FK15 56 B4
George Buckman Dr DD2 91 A1
George Burn Wynd KY1 151 C3
George Dr 2 KY13 108 B4
George Govan Rd KY15 105 A4
George Inn La PH2 103 C4
George Pirie Way DD2 92 E3
George Pl DD2 92 B3
George St
Alva FK12 118 A6
Anstruther Easter KY10 83 D6
Arbroath DD11 89 C4
Blairgowrie PH10 88 C5
7 Coupar Angus PH13 15 F2
Cowdenbeath KY4 147 B4
Dunblane FK15 107 C4
Dundee DD2 93 A6
Dunfermline KY11 161 B2
Glenrothes KY7 113 F7
Kincardine FK10 155 E3
Kirkcaldy KY1 151 B3
Montrose DD10 85 C3
Perth PH1 103 B4
George Terr 15 KY10 82 E4
Georgina Pl 10 PH2 37 F5
Gerrard Pl 9 DD11 22 E3
Gibbs Cl 2 KY7 113 F8
Gibb's La DD2 93 B5
Gib Gdns KY15 105 E5
Gib Gr KY11 161 E1
Gibson Cl FK14 120 E8
Gibson Gr FK15 107 E4
Gibson Pl 2 DD10 85 D2
Gibson St DD7 100 A2
Gibson Terr DD4 94 C4
Gifford Ct KY6 112 D8
GIFFORDTOWN 63 E6
Gilfillan Rd KY11 161 E4
Gillburn Rd DD3 91 E1
Gillespie Cres PH1 102 D7
Gillespie Gr KY12 158 E7
Gillespie La 6 KY8 109 A1
Gillespie Pl
Perth PH1 102 D7
Stirling FK7 135 B1
Gillie Ct KY11 161 C2
Gillies' Ct 6 KY8 81 A6
Gillies Dr FK7 135 C4
Gillies Hill FK7 134 D5
Gillies Pl DD5 95 E4
Gillies Terr DD5 95 E4
Gill Way KY11 173 C5
GILMERTON 33 E2
Gilmour Ave KY8 109 D7
Gilmour Pl DD2 93 B5
Gilmours Ave PH4 57 B3
Gilmour St KY4 147 D6
Gilsay Pl PH1 37 C5
Gilston Pl DD5 96 B4
Gindera Rd DD10 85 D5
Girvan Gdns DD4 95 C7
Gladgate 19 KY14 62 F6
Gladney KY15 65 D6
Gladney Pl 2 KY15 65 D6
Gladney Sq KY1 151 B2
Gladstone Pl
Dunfermline KY12 161 A5
6 Kirriemuir DD8 86 C5
5 Ladybank KY15 64 A4
Stirling FK8 135 A6
Gladstone St KY8 109 E7
Gladstone Terr PH2 103 C4
Glaive Ave FK7 135 D3
Glamaig Way KY11 162 C1
GLAMIS 9 C1
Glamis Ave KY7 113 B4
Glamis Castle & Gdns* DD8 9 C3
Glamis Cres PH14 40 C7
Glamis Ct
Auchterarder PH3 57 D6
Glenrothes KY7 113 B3
Ninewells DD2 92 E4
Glamis Ctr KY7 113 B4
Glamis Dr DD2 92 F3
Glamis Gdns KY11 175 B3
Glamis Pl
Dalgety Bay KY11 175 B3
Dundee DD2 92 F3
Perth PH2 102 F2
Glamis Prim Sch DD8 9 B1
Glamis Rd
1 Arbroath DD11 22 D3
Dundee DD2 93 A3
Forfar DD8 87 B4
Kinghorn KY3 166 F3
Kirkcaldy KY2 150 D7
Kirriemuir DD8 86 D3
Glamis St DD3 179 B4
Glamis Terr
Dundee DD2 92 F3
Kinghorn KY3 166 F3
Glasclune Way 1 DD5 96 C5
Glasgow Rd
Perth PH2 102 F4
Stirling FK7 135 B2
Glassford Sq FK13 119 A7
Glasshouse Loan FK10 138 A6
Glass St KY7 113 F8
Glasswork St KY1 151 B3
Glebe Ave FK8 135 A7
Glebe Cres
Alva FK12 118 B7
Stirling FK8 135 A7
Tillicoultry FK13 119 C6
Glebe Ct 3 DD8 86 D5
Glebe Dr
3 Blairgowrie PH12 17 A7
Perth PH14 40 C7
Glebe Gdns 4 DD6 99 F5
Glebelands Prim Sch DD4 94 C3
Glebe Pk
East Wemyss KY1 133 C7
Inverkeithing KY11 174 B1
Kirkcaldy KY1 151 C5
7 Pittenweem KY10 83 B5
Glebe Pk (Brechin City FC) DD9 84 C4
Glebe Pl
Burntisland KY3 165 E1
Kinghorn KY3 166 F3
5 Tayport DD6 99 F5
Glebe Rd
Arbroath DD11 89 C7
Crieff PH5 44 C4
Kincardine FK10 155 E5
Kirriemuir DD8 86 D5
St Andrews KY16 106 E5
Glebe Specl Sch PH2 103 E8
Glebe St KY8 109 E7
Glebe Terr
Alloa FK10 138 A6
Inverkeithing KY11 174 B1
Perth PH2 103 D3
Glebe The
Aberdour KY3 176 C8
10 Abernethy PH2 49 E3
Alva FK12 118 B7
Clackmannan FK10 139 A4
1 Crail KY10 69 B3
17 Dollar FK14 73 C1
2 Perth PH2 46 F1
Saline KY12 142 E6
Glebeway 2 PH12 17 A7
Glenaffric Terr DD3 93 D6
Glenagnes Gdns 5 DD2 93 D3
Glenagnes Rd DD2 93 D3
Glenagnes St DD2 93 C3
Glen Albyn Dr KY2 130 B1
Glenalmond Coll PH1 35 B7
Glenalmond Ct PH1 36 A4
Glenalmond Rd PH10 88 D6
Glenalmond Terr 3 PH2 102 F1
Glenartney Ct 9 KY7 111 C2
Glen Artney Gr KY11 161 D1
Glenartney Terr 1 PH2 48 D8
Glenavon Dr KY12 159 C1
Glen Beasdale Ct KY11 161 D1
Glenbervie Gr KY11 161 D1
Glenbervie Rd KY2 130 F1
Glen Bridge KY12 160 F4
Glenbridge Ct KY12 160 F4
Glenbruar Cres 4 PH2 48 D8
Glen Bruar Pl KY2 150 B8
Glenburn Gr KY12 158 E7
Glenburn Rd
6 Anstruther Easter KY10 83 C6
Auchterarder PH3 104 D5
Glencadam Distillery Visitor Ctr* DD9 84 D4
Glencairn Cres KY8 109 D8
Glencairn Gdns KY8 109 D8
Glencairn St FK7 135 B3
GLENCARSE 49 F8
Glen Clova Cres KY12 159 C1
Glenclova Pl 1 DD10 85 C5
Glen Clova Pl 1 KY2 130 C1
Glenclova Terr
Dundee DD3 93 E6
Forfar DD8 87 C3
Glencoe Brae DD8 87 C1
Glencoe Rd FK8 115 A1
Glenconnor Dr DD4 94 D6
Glencoul Ave KY11 175 A3
Glen Ct FK15 107 E5
Glendale 3 KY8 109 D8
Glendale Pk 3 KY2 130 B1
Glendarvel Pl KY7 111 B2
GLENDEVON 73 F7
Glendevon Ct 1 PH10 88 E6
Glendevon Dr FK8 114 F2
Glendevon Pl 7 KY2 130 F1
Glendevon Rd
Glenrothes KY7 113 C3
Perth PH2 48 C8
Glendevon Way DD5 96 C6
Glendoick Gdns* PH2 39 A2
GLENDUCKIE 51 C5
Gleneagles Ave
Dundee DD2 91 B2
Glenrothes KY6 112 A5
Gleneagles Gdns KY1 131 A1
Gleneagles Golf Course PH3 57 D5
Gleneagles La DD2 91 C1
Gleneagles Rd
Dundee DD2 91 B1
Perth PH2 48 D8
Gleneagles St DD2 91 B1
Gleneagles Sta PH3 104 A2
Glenearn Pk PH2 48 A4
Glenearn Pl
Bridge of Earn PH2 48 E4
2 Perth PH2 103 A1
Glenearn Rd PH2 103 A1
Glenesk Ave
Arbroath DD11 89 E6
Dundee DD3 93 D6
Montrose DD10 85 C5
Glenesk Pl DD11 89 E6
Glen Esk Pl 2 KY2 130 B1
GLENFARG 61 B5
Glenfarg Cres KY4 147 D5
Glenfarg Terr 6 PH2 48 D8
Glenfield KY12 159 C6
Glenfield Ave KY4 147 C6
Glenfield Cres KY4 147 C5
Glenfield Ct
Cowdenbeath KY4 147 C5
5 Leven KY8 109 C4
Glenfield Gdns KY4 147 C5
Glenfield Ind Est KY4 147 C6
Glenfield Rd KY4 147 C5
GLENFOOT 49 D2
Glen Fruin Gr KY11 161 D1
Glengairn Wlk KY11 161 D1
Glengarry Ct KY7 111 C3
Glengarry Rd PH2 48 D8
Glengate 4 DD8 86 C4
Glen Gr KY8 109 D8
Glenhead Ave FK14 119 C4
Glenisla Ct PH10 88 D6
Glenisla Dr DD11 89 E6

Glenisla Golf Course PH11 7 B3
Glenisla Gr KY11 161 D1
Glenisla Rd DD10 85 C5
Glen Isla Rd 2 KY2 130 C1
Glenisla Terr DD3 93 D6
Glenisla View 8 PH11 7 A3
Glen Kinchie FK10 117 A2
Glenlaw Pl 7 PH2 49 E3
Glenlethnot Pl 2 DD10 85 C5
Glenleven Dr 2 DD6 42 B5
Glenleven Ind Est KY6 112 A7
Glenlochay Rd 2 PH2 102 F1
GLENLOMOND 76 F7
Glenlyon Pl KY8 109 D6
Glenlyon Rd
Leven KY8 109 C7
Perth PH2 103 A1
Glen Lyon Rd KY2 130 B1
Glenmarkie Terr DD3 93 D7
Glenmore Ct KY6 110 E1
Glen More Gdns 5 KY2 130 B1
Glen Moriston Dr KY12 159 C1
Glenmoy Ave DD3 93 D7
Glenmoy Pl DD11 89 E6
Glenmoy Terr DD8 87 C3
Glen Nevis Dr KY11 161 D1
Glenochil Pk FK10 117 E4
Glenochil Terr FK10 117 E4
Glenogil Ave DD3 93 D7
Glenogil Dr DD11 89 E6
Glenogil Gdns 5 KY10 83 C6
Glenogil St DD10 85 C5
Glenogil Terr DD8 87 C3
Glenogle Cres 2 PH2 48 D8
Glenogle Ct PH7 101 B4
Glenorchil Cres PH3 104 C5
Glenorchill Pl PH3 104 B5
Glenorchill View PH3 104 B5
Glenorchil Terr PH3 104 B5
Glenorchy Ct 5 KY7 111 C2
Glenprosen Dr DD3 93 E7
Glenprosen St 4 DD10 85 C5
Glenprosen Terr DD3 93 E6
Glen Rd FK9 70 D1
Glenree 3 PH11 7 A3
GLENROTHES 112 D8
Glenrothes Ed Ctr KY6 112 F6
Glenrothes Golf Club KY6 112 B5
Glenrothes High Sch KY6 112 E7
Glenrothes Hospl KY7 110 F1
Glenrothes with Thornton Sta KY1 131 E7
Glenshee Cres 7 PH2 48 D8
Glenshee Dr PH10 88 D6
Glen Shiel Gr KY11 161 D1
Glenshieling Dr 2 PH10 88 C7
Glen The
Tillicoultry FK14 119 C4
Tullibody FK10 117 C3
Glenthorne Rd 2 KY8 109 D5
Glentilt Terr 3 PH2 48 D8
Glentress Gdns KY7 111 C3
Glentruim Terr DD3 93 D7
Glenturret Pl PH1 102 D8
Glenturret Terr 5 PH2 48 D8
Glentye Dr FK10 117 D4
Glen Tye Rd FK7 135 D5
Glenurquhart Ct 4 KY7 111 C2
Glenview FK11 117 A6
Glenwinnel Rd FK12 117 E7
Glenwood Ctr KY6 112 D6
Glenwood High Sch KY6 112 C7
Glenwood Rd KY6 112 B6
Globe Rd KY11 173 D2
Glomach Gr KY12 160 E5
Glover Ct 4 PH2 102 F3
Glover Rd KY7 113 D2
Glover's Ct KY3 167 A3
Glover St PH2 102 F3
Glovers Wynd 2 KY9 82 A2
Gogar Loan FK9 116 D5
Gogar Pl FK7 135 C2
Golf Ave DD5 97 C6
Golf Course Rd
Blairgowrie PH10 88 D1
Cowdenbeath KY4 147 C6
Glenrothes KY6 112 D3
Golf Cres 8 DD6 43 C7
Golfdrum St KY12 160 E4
Golf Pl
Northmuir DD8 86 D8
St Andrews KY16 106 D7
Golf Rd
Kirriemuir DD8 86 D8
Lower Largo KY8 80 E5
7 Tayport DD6 43 C7
Golf Rd Pk DD9 84 C5
Golf St
3 Carnoustie DD7 100 C2
Ladybank KY15 64 A5
Golf View
Auchterderran KY5 128 F4
Tillicoultry FK13 119 A7
Gollet Way KY12 170 F8
Golspie Terr 2 DD5 96 C4
Goodlyburn Pl PH1 102 E4
Goodlyburn Prim Sch PH1 102 E5
Goodlyburn Terr PH1 102 E5
Goose Croft DD8 87 D5
Goosecroft Rd FK8 135 B8
Gordon Cres
Bridge of A FK9 115 A8
Stirling FK8 114 F2
Gordon Dr FK10 138 C7
Gordon Pk DD8 86 C5
Gordon Pl DD11 12 F4
Gordon Rd
Crieff PH7 101 C5
Leuchars KY16 54 C7
Rosyth KY11 173 B2
Gordon Sq DD3 93 C5
Gordon St
Broughty Ferry DD5 96 D4
Cowdenbeath KY4 147 D6
4 Dundee DD2 93 C5
5 Forfar DD8 87 E5
Lochgelly KY5 148 A8
Gordon Terr KY11 161 B1
Gorrie St KY11 161 C2
Gorrie Terr DD3 91 C4
Gorse Loan PH1 102 E7
Gosford Rd KY2 150 C7
Goshen Cres PH2 103 F8
Goshen Rd PH2 103 F8
Goshen Terr PH2 103 F8
Gote La EH30 178 B1
Gotterstone Ave 3 DD5 95 C4
Gotterstone Dr 5 DD5 95 C4
Goulden Pl KY12 160 D6
Gourdie Cres DD2 92 E6
Gourdie Ind Est DD2 92 D7
Gourdie Pl DD2 92 E7
Gourdie Rd DD2 92 D6
Gourdie St DD2 92 E6
Gourdie Terr DD2 92 E6
Gourlay Cres 1 KY10 82 E4
Gourlay St KY2 151 A4
Gourlay Wynd KY16 106 D4
GOWANBANK 10 F5
Gowanbrae 10 PH10 88 C5
Gowanbrae Dr KY12 161 D4
Gowanbrae Pl KY12 161 D4
Gowanbrae Terr KY12 161 D4
Gowanhill Gdns FK8 114 F1
Gowan Pk KY15 105 D6
Gowan Pl
1 Arbroath DD11 89 E4
Whitehills DD8 87 F5
Gowan Rigg DD8 87 F5
Gowan St DD11 89 C3
Gowans Terr PH1 102 F7
Gow Cres KY1 151 B4
GOWKHALL 159 F7
Gowrie Cres DD2 92 B3
Gowrie Ct DD2 92 E5
Gowriehill Prim Sch DD2 92 D5
Gowrie Pk DD2 92 C5
Gowrie Rd PH2 39 F2
Gowrie St
8 Dundee DD2 93 D2
Newport-on-Tay DD6 98 E4
Perth PH2 103 C4
Grace St KY5 148 C8
Gracie Cres FK7 136 D4
Graham Ave
Dunblane FK15 107 D7
Leven KY8 109 B7
Stirling FK9 115 C4
Graham Cres
Forfar DD8 87 B4
Leven KY8 109 B7
Montrose DD10 85 C6
Graham Ct
4 Bankfoot PH1 24 A6
Caird Park DD4 94 B8
Lochore KY5 128 A6
Grahame Terr PH7 33 E2
Graham Pl
Dollar FK14 120 D8
2 Dundee DD4 94 C2
Graham St
Bridge of A FK9 115 B7
Dundee DD4 94 A5
Montrose DD10 85 D6
Grahamstone Ave KY13 76 F4
Graham Terr
Airth FK2 154 D4
3 Dundee DD4 94 A5
Graham Wynd 2 DD3 94 A5
Graigmill Rd DD3 91 B5
Grainger St KY5 148 B8
Grampian Ave PH3 104 A5
Grampian Cl DD4 94 E8
Grampian Cres DD8 86 D6
Grampian Ct
Perth PH1 102 E6
Rosyth KY11 173 E2
Grampian Dr DD8 86 D6
Grampian Gdns
Arbroath DD11 89 E7
Dundee DD4 94 F8
Kirkcaldy KY2 150 F5
Grampian Pk DD8 87 C4
Grampian Pl KY11 173 E1
Grampian Rd
Rosyth KY11 173 E2
Stirling FK7 134 E6
Grampian View
6 Coupar Angus PH13 15 F3
Montrose DD10 6 D2
Granary La DD6 98 D4
Granary Terr DD5 20 E1
GRANGE 40 A4
Grange Ave DD5 96 F5
Grange Cotts KY2 166 F5
Grange Dr KY11 173 C8
Grange Gait DD5 96 F6
Grange Gdns
Bridge of A FK9 115 C7
Monifieth DD5 96 F7
Grangehill Dr DD5 97 A6
Grange La DD5 96 F6
GRANGEMOUTH 168 C1
GRANGE OF LINDORES 50 F3
Grange Path DD11 89 C6
Grange Pk
Dunfermline KY11 161 C1
Dunfermline KY11 173 C8
Grange Pl
Arbroath DD11 89 C5
Monifieth DD5 96 F5
Grange Prim Sch DD5 96 F5
Grange Rd
Alloa FK10 137 F6
Arbroath DD11 89 C5
Bridge of A FK9 115 C6
Burntisland KY3 165 D1
Dunfermline KY11 173 C6
Earlsferry/Elie KY9 82 A3
Leven KY9 81 F3
Monifieth DD5 96 F6
St Andrews KY16 106 F4
Grange Terr PH1 102 B6
Grange Wynd KY11 173 C8
Grannie Clark's Wynd KY16 106 C7
Grant Cres 6 PH10 88 C4
Grant Dr FK15 107 B6
Granton Ct KY6 110 D1
Granton Pl DD4 94 B6
Granton Terr DD4 94 A6
Granton View KY11 174 F2
Grant Pl FK9 115 B4
Grant Rd
Arbroath DD11 89 D4
5 Blairgowrie PH10 88 C4
Grants Bank KY12 161 A4
Grant St FK10 137 F6
Grants Wynd DD3 91 B5
Granville Way KY11 173 E3
Gravesend DD11 89 D4
Graybank Rd PH2 102 F3
Gray Den DD2 28 C3
Gray Pk KY4 147 C6
Gray Pk Rd PH13 26 C7
Gray Pl KY11 174 C3
Gray's La DD2 93 C5
Grays' Rd KY5 128 B1
Gray St
2 Coupar Angus PH13 16 A2
Dundee DD2 93 A6
Dundee DD5 96 A2
Perth PH2 102 F3
Graystale Rd FK7 135 A3
Great Michael Rd
Arbroath DD11 89 F6
Rosyth KY11 173 B1
Great N Rd KY4 126 F3
Grebe Gdns KY11 162 A1
Greenacre 7 KY16 53 E8
Greenacre Ct FK7 135 E1
Greenacre Pl FK7 135 E1
Greenacres KY12 146 B1
Greenbank Cres 1 PH2 61 B5
Greenbank Dr KY4 147 A2
Greenbank Pl DD2 93 C4
Greenbank Rd 2 PH2 61 B5
Greenbank St PH10 88 B4
Green Beeches
Chapelton DD11 13 C1
East Mains of Colliston DD11 22 E8
Greenbourne Gdns 1 DD5 97 B6
Greenbrig Rd KY9 82 A5
Green Crofts 1 PH3 104 D6
Greendykes Rd DD4 94 F3
Greenfield La FK13 119 A6
Greenfield Pl 4 DD1 93 E2
Greenfield St FK10 138 B7
Greenfield View KY8 109 A7
Green Gates KY8 109 D8
Greenhaugh Ct 4 FK15 56 B4
Greenhaugh Way FK15 56 B4
Greenhead FK12 118 B6
Green La
Carnoustie DD7 100 D3
Monifieth DD5 97 C7
Greenlaw Cres KY6 112 C7
Greenlee Dr DD2 92 F6
Greenloan 3 FK14 74 A3
GREENLOANING 56 B2
Greenloaning Prim Sch FK15 56 B2
Greenloanings KY2 150 D8
Greenmantle Pl KY6 110 D1
Greenmantle Way KY6 110 D1
Greenmarket DD1 179 B1
Greenmount KY4 147 A2
Greenmount Dr KY3 165 F1
Greenmount Rd N KY3 165 F2
Greenmount Rd S KY3 166 A1
Greenpark 5 KY13 108 B3
Green Rd
Blairgowrie PH13 26 C8
3 Blairgowrie PH10 88 E2
Kinross KY13 108 B3
Perth PH2 38 C8
Greenshank Dr KY11 162 A2
Greenside
Balgeddie KY6 110 D1
Glenrothes KY6 112 C8
Greenside Ct
Balgeddie KY6 110 D1
St Andrews KY16 106 E5
Greenside Pl
Glenrothes KY6 110 C1
St Andrews KY16 106 E5
Greenside St FK10 138 B6
Green St
Forfar DD8 87 D5
Townhill KY12 161 C8
Greenstone Pl DD2 92 C5
Greenstone Terr DD2 92 C5
Green The
Alva FK12 118 A7
Coaltown of Balgonie KY7 79 A2
Findo Gask PH1 46 F8
Peat Inn KY15 66 D4
Greenwell Pk KY6 110 D1
Green Wood KY13 108 C3
Greenwood Ave FK8 135 A8
Gregory Ct 3 DD6 99 F5
Gregory La KY16 106 E6
Gregory Pl KY16 106 E6
Greig Cres DD11 89 F6
Greig Ct KY11 174 B2
Greig Pl KY5 148 A7
Greig Rd KY11 173 B2
Grenada Brae DD6 98 E6
Grendon Ct FK8 135 A6
Grendon Gdns FK8 135 A6
Grey Craigs KY12 159 D2
Greyfriars Gdn KY16 106 D6
Greyfriars RC Prim Sch KY16 106 E5
Greyfriar's Wlk KY11 174 C3
Greygoran FK10 118 C2
Grey St DD6 99 F6
Greystane DD2 92 B4
Grey Stanes 11 PH2 37 F5
Greystane Terr DD2 92 B4
GREYSTONE 21 C6
Greystone Pk KY7 113 D2
Grierson Cres FK7 134 D6
Grieve Gr KY1 133 B6
Grieve St
Dunfermline KY12 160 E4
Kirkcaldy KY2 151 A6
11 Leven KY8 79 F2
Grimond La 3 DD3 91 A2
Grimsby Pl 7 DD11 89 D3
Grinnan Rd FK15 56 B4
Griselda Hill Pottery* KY15 65 D6
Groban KY8 109 C8
Grodwell Dr FK12 117 E7
Grosvenor Rd 1 DD2 93 C2
Grove Acad DD5 95 F3
Grove La 16 PH2 48 F4
Grove Rd DD5 95 E3
Grove The
Auchterarder PH3 104 E7
Kelty KY4 126 C2
Gruinard Terr DD4 94 C7
Grunnan KY8 109 C8
GUARDBRIDGE 54 B6
Guardbridge Prim Sch KY16 54 A6
Guards Way PH1 102 E7
Guildhall St KY12 161 A3
Guildry Gr KY12 161 E4
GUILDTOWN 25 B2
Guildtown Prim Sch PH2 25 B2
Gullane Ave 6 DD2 91 B1
Gullane Pl
Ardler DD2 91 B1
2 Kirkcaldy KY2 130 F2
Gullane Rd DD2 91 C1
Gullane Terr 1 DD2 91 B1
GUTHRIE 12 C5
Guthrie Cres
Arbroath DD11 12 F5
Glenrothes KY7 113 E7
Guthrie Ct
Auchterarder PH3 57 D6
Glenrothes KY7 111 A3
14 Newburgh KY14 50 D5
Guthrie Gdns 15 KY14 50 D5
Guthrie Hill 2 DD11 89 D4
Guthrie Pk DD9 84 D2
Guthrie Port 6 DD11 89 D4
Guthrie St
Arbroath DD11 12 F5
Carnoustie DD7 100 E3
Dundee DD1 179 A2
Forfar DD8 11 E3
Guthrie Terr DD5 96 D4
Guttergates Rd KY11 162 B5
Gwendoline Row PH2 61 C3
Gwydyr Rd PH7 101 B5

H

Hackston Pl 5 KY15 105 C4
Haddfoot Wynd 10 KY10 83 C6
Haddington Ave DD4 95 B7
Haddington Cres
4 Dundee DD4 95 B7
Glenrothes KY6 112 D7
Haddington Gdns DD4 95 B8
Haddington Pl DD4 95 B8
Haddon Rd PH2 103 D6
Haddow Gr KY3 177 D8
Ha'en The 7 DD8 87 E5
Haggis Ha' KY5 128 B1
Haig Ave
Kirkcaldy KY1 151 D7
Stirling FK8 115 A2
Haig Bsns Pk KY7 113 F7
Haig Cres KY12 161 C5
Haig Pl 9 KY8 79 E3
Hailes Pl KY12 161 D4
Haining FK15 107 D6
HALBEATH 162 B6
Halbeath Dr KY11 161 F5
Halbeath Ind Est KY11 162 C6
Halbeath Pl KY11 161 E5
Halbeath Rd
Dunfermline KY11 161 D5
Halbeath KY11 162 A5
Halbeath Ret Pk KY11 162 A6
Halberts Cres FK7 135 B2
Haldane Ave
Bridge of A FK9 115 A6
Dundee DD3 91 E2
Haldane Cres DD3 91 D2
Haldane Gr KY12 158 D7
Haldane La 6 DD5 96 A2
Haldane Pl DD3 91 E2
Haldane St DD3 91 D2
Haldane Terr 3 DD3 91 D2
Halfields KY8 79 F5
Halfield's Ct 4 KY8 79 F5
Halfield's Gdns 3 KY8 79 F5
Halford Ct 3 KY15 105 C5
Halketshall KY11 172 C4
Halkett Cres KY11 161 D2
Hall Cres PH13 26 C8
Halley Pl 8 DD3 91 D3
Halley's Ct KY1 151 B2
Halley Terr 7 DD3 91 D3
Hallfields Pl KY8 79 F6
Hall La KY5 148 B8
Hallowhill KY16 106 A4
Hallows The KY1 151 F8
Hallpark FK10 138 C8
Hall Pk
Leven KY9 66 E2
5 Perth PH2 49 E3
Hall Pl DD4 29 F7
Hall Rd
3 Auchterarder PH3 46 B2
Dundee DD4 29 F8
Perth PH2 25 B2
Hall Row KY11 172 B4
Hall St
Cowdenbeath KY4 147 C4
4 Kingskettle KY15 64 A2
Lochgelly KY5 148 B8
Hall Wynd 5 PH2 39 F1
Halyard Rise KY11 174 F2
Halyard Terr KY2 149 B2
Halyburton Pl KY15 105 B3
Hamilton Ave
St Andrews KY16 106 D4
Tayport DD6 99 E7
Hamilton Dr FK9 115 C4
Hamilton Gdns PH2 102 E3
Hamilton Gn
20 Arbroath DD11 89 D4
7 Arbroath DD11 89 D4
Hamilton La PH1 102 E3
Hamilton Pl
2 Glenrothes KY6 112 F6
Perth PH1 102 E3
Rosyth KY11 173 E4
Hamiltons Cl EH30 178 C1
Hamilton St
Arbroath DD11 89 E6
Broughty Ferry DD5 96 D4
Lochgelly KY5 148 B6
Tillicoultry FK13 119 B7
Hamilton Terr
Broughty Ferry DD5 96 C4
High Valleyfield KY12 158 B2
Inverkeithing KY11 174 C2
Hampden Cl 19 KY16 54 B8
Hanick Terr DD8 87 C6
Hannah St 10 DD11 89 C3
Hanover Ct
Dunblane FK15 107 D4
Stirling FK9 115 D4
Hanover Gdns
3 Auchterarder PH3 104 D6
2 New Scone PH2 37 F5
Happer Cres KY7 113 D5
Happies Cl KY1 132 F2
Happyhillock Rd DD4 94 F6
Happyhillock Wlk DD4 95 A6
Harbour Dr KY11 174 F3
Harbourhead 1 KY10 83 D6
Harbour La EH30 178 B1
Harbour Pl
Burntisland KY3 177 E8
Dalgety Bay KY11 174 F2
Inverkeithing KY11 174 C2
Harbour Rd
Kinghorn KY3 167 A2
16 Perth PH2 48 D8
Perth PH2 103 B1
1 Tayport DD6 99 F7
Harbour View KY8 109 D4
Harbour Way KY11 175 A4

Harbour Wynd
7 Leven KY8 109 C4
Lower Largo KY8 80 F5
Harcourt Rd KY2 151 B5
Harcourt St 5 DD3 93 F6
Hardie Cres FK7 136 C4
Hardie Ct FK7 135 C3
Hareburn Rd FK13 119 A6
Harefield Ave DD3 93 D6
Harefield Gr DD3 93 D6
Harefield Mews DD2 93 C6
Harefield Rd DD3 93 D6
Harestane Cres 6 DD3 91 D3
Harestane Gr DD3 91 E3
Harestane Pl 5 DD3 91 C3
Harestane Rd DD3 91 E3
Harestane Terr 7 DD3 91 F2
Harlands The FK10 137 E7
Harley Pl PH1 103 A6
Harley St
Dundee DD5 96 A3
12 Leuchars KY16 54 B8
Rosyth KY11 174 A4
Harley Terr PH1 103 A6
Harlow Pl DD3 93 D6
Harper Way PH2 37 E5
Harriebrae Pk KY12 160 F4
HARRIETFIELD 35 C8
Harriet Row 3 PH10 88 C4
Harriet St
4 Dundee DD4 94 C3
Kirkcaldy KY1 151 E6
Harris Acad DD2 93 B2
Harris Ct
Alloa FK10 138 B5
Perth PH1 37 C5
Harris Dr KY2 150 F8
Harrison Ave DD2 91 B1
Harrison Rd DD2 91 A1
Harris Pl KY11 161 C1
Harris Rd DD7 100 A2
Harris Terr DD4 94 C8
Harris Way KY7 111 A2
Harrow St DD2 93 A3
Harry Farmer Ct DD11 89 D5
Harry Nicoll Gdns DD11 89 F4
Hart Wynd FK7 135 F1
Harvard Pl PH12 38 B6
Harvest St FK9 115 A4
Harvey Wynd FK8 115 A1
Harviestoun Gr FK13 119 D7
Harviestoun La 1 FK14 73 B1
Harviestoun Rd FK14 120 D8
Hastings Pl DD3 93 F6
Haston Cres PH2 103 E4
Hatchbank La KY13 76 A2
Hatchbank Rd KY13 76 A2
Hatton Gn KY7 113 B3
Hatton Mews PH2 103 D3
Hatton Pl
Dundee DD2 93 C7
8 Luncarty PH1 37 B8
Rattray PH10 88 D6
Hatton Rd
Blairgowrie PH10 88 D6
Luncarty PH1 37 B8
Perth PH2 103 E3
Hatton View PH2 103 D3
Hatton Way PH2 103 E3
Haughfield Terr 1
KY15 64 A2
Haughgate Ave KY8 109 E7
Haughgate St KY8 109 E7
Haughgate Terr KY8 109 E7
Haughmill La 4 KY8 79 E3
Haugh Rd
Blairgowrie PH10 88 D5
Burntisland KY3 177 D8
Stirling FK9 115 B2
Haugh The KY1 133 B6
Haven Ct 4 KY8 109 C4
Haven's Edge KY11 172 E3
Haven The
Dalgety Bay KY11 174 F2
South Alloa FK7 137 F3
Hawarden Terr PH1 102 E4
Hawes Brae EH30 178 D1
Hawick Dr DD4 95 D7
Hawkcraig Rd KY3 176 D7
Hawkhill DD1 179 A2
Hawkhill Pl DD1 93 E2
Hawkhill Rd
Alloa FK10 138 C6
Kincardine FK10 155 D5
Hawkslaw Gdns KY8 109 D6
Hawkslaw Rd KY8 109 D6
Hawkslaw St KY8 109 D6
Hawkslaw Trad Est
KY8 109 D6
Hawksmuir 3 KY1 151 D6
Hawthorn Ave FK13 119 B4
Hawthorn Bank
Carnock KY12 159 C6
Perth PH2 25 D4
South Queensferry
EH30 178 B1
Hawthorn Cres
Cowdenbeath KY4 146 F1
Fallin FK7 136 D4
Stirling FK8 114 F2
Hawthorn Dr FK7 136 C4
Hawthorne Ave FK13 119 B4
Hawthorne Pl 5 PH10 88 C4
Hawthorn Gr
Dundee DD5 30 D5
Lammerton DD5 95 E8
Hawthorn Pl
7 Arbroath DD11 89 A4
Hawthorn Pl *continued*
Perth PH1 102 B3
Hawthorn St KY8 109 E7
Hawthorns The 8 DD4 95 A8
Hawthorn Terr KY1 131 D7
Hay Ave DD5 97 A6
HAYFIELD 151 B6
Hayfield 5 KY13 77 A4
Hayfield Ind Est KY2 151 A7
Hayfield Pl KY2 151 A7
Hayfield Rd
Kirkcaldy KY1, KY2 151 C7
Perth PH2 61 A5
Hay Fleming Ave 4
KY16 54 E2
Hayford Mills FK7 134 D6
Hayford Pl FK7 134 D6
Hay Gr KY11 161 F1
Haymount Pk 3 KY15 105 B5
Hays Ct KY13 108 C6
HAYSHEAD 89 E6
Hayshead Prim Sch
DD11 89 E5
Hayshead Rd DD11 89 E5
Hays Rd DD6 41 F2
Hay St
5 Alyth PH11 7 A3
3 Coupar Angus PH13 16 A3
Monifieth DD5 97 A6
Perth PH1 103 A5
Hayston Pk KY16 53 E8
Hayston Terr DD2 93 A5
Hayswell Rd DD11 89 E5
Hay Terr DD11 89 D5
Haywood Pl DD4 94 B5
Hazel Ave
Crieff PH7 101 E4
Dundee DD2 92 F2
Kirkcaldy KY2 151 B6
Menstrie FK11 116 F6
Hazelbank Gdns FK8 115 A2
Hazelbank Terr KY4 126 D3
Hazel Dene KY8 79 F3
Hazel Dr DD2 92 F2
Hazel Gdns DD2 92 F3
Hazel Gr KY11 173 E8
Hazelhead Dr 2 DD2 91 B1
Hazelhead Pl 5 DD2 91 B1
Hazel Hill KY6 112 F7
Hazel Pl
Blairgowrie PH10 88 C3
Glenrothes KY6 112 A7
Hazels The 10 DD4 95 A8
Hazelton Way 1 DD5 96 C4
Hazelwood Cl 2 DD2 93 C7
Hazelwood Rd PH10 88 B2
Hazlehead Ave 4 DD2 91 B1
Hazlehead La 9 DD2 91 B1
Hazlehead St DD2 91 B1
Hazlehead Terr 3 DD2 91 B1
Headingstone Pl DD8 87 E6
HEADWELL 161 B5
Headwell Ave KY12 161 B5
Headwell Ct KY12 161 B5
Headwell Rd KY12 161 A5
Heathcote Rd PH7 101 C4
Heather Croft 2 DD8 11 E3
Heather Ct KY7 110 F2
Heather Dr PH10 88 F1
Heather Gdns 6 DD3 91 F2
Heather Gr KY11 173 F8
Heatherlea Dr 18 PH2 48 F4
Heather Path 3 KY7 110 F2
Heathery The KY11 173 F7
Heathfield Pl DD1 179 A2
Heathfield Wynd 2
DD3 91 A2
Heath Rd KY11 173 F3
Heathwood Cres FK13 119 C8
Hebridean Gdns PH7 101 D2
Hebrides Dr DD4 94 C8
Hedges Loan FK7 135 E1
Heggie's Wynd KY1 151 B1
Heimdal Gdns KY7 110 F3
Helen La KY11 178 C6
HELENSFIELD 139 A5
Helen St
Arbroath DD11 89 C4
Forfar DD8 87 E5
Helmsdale Ave DD3 91 F2
Helmsdale Cres DD3 91 F2
Helmsdale Dr DD3 91 E2
Helmsdale Pk KY12 160 F2
Helmsdale Pl DD3 91 F2
Henderson Ave FK10 138 A8
Henderson Pk KY8 79 E3
Henderson Pl
Alva FK12 118 A7
Dunfermline KY12 142 D6
Henderson Rd DD11 22 D6
Henderson St
Bridge of A FK9 115 B7
Kingseat KY12 146 B1
Lochgelly KY5 148 A8
Henderson Terr 8
KY16 54 B8
Hendrie Cres KY1 133 A6
Hendrie Ct KY1 133 A6
Hendrie La 2 KY1 133 A6
Hendrie Pl KY1 133 A6
Hendry Cres KY2 151 A6
Hendry Rd KY2 151 A7
Hendry's Wynd KY1 151 B2
Henge Gdns KY7 111 C3
Henge The KY7 111 C3
Hennings The FK10 118 C1
Henry Ross Pl EH30 178 B1
Henryson Rd KY11 161 E4
Henry St
Alva FK12 118 A6
Kirriemuir DD8 86 C3
Hepburn Cres DD11 89 E5
Hepburn Ct FK15 107 D7
Hepburn Gdns KY16 106 C5
Hepburn Pl 2 DD11 89 E5
Hepburn St DD3 93 F7
Herald Ave DD11 89 A6
Hercules Pl 1 DD11 89 B7
Hercules Rd DD11 89 B5
Herd Cres KY8 79 F2
Heriot Ct KY6 112 C7
Heriot Gdns KY3 165 F1
Heriot St KY11 174 C2
Hermitage Dr PH1 102 B5
Hermitage Gn KY7 113 C2
Hermitage Rd
Broughty Ferry DD5 96 A2
Stirling FK9 115 E6
Heron Pl 13 DD5 30 F7
Heron Rise DD4 94 B8
Heron's La DD2 93 A6
Herriot Cres KY8 109 C4
Hervey St FK10 138 A8
Hetherington Dr FK10 139 B4
Heughfield Pl 1 PH2 48 F4
Heughfield Rd PH2 48 E4
Hewat Pl PH1 102 C7
Hewitt Pl KY3 176 C7
Higham Loan KY15 66 E4
High Beveridgewell
KY12 160 F5
Highfield Ave DD6 98 A2
Highfield Circ KY13 108 B5
Highfield La 7 PH2 37 F5
Highfield Pl
Dundee DD2 90 C3
3 Perth PH1 24 B6
Highfield Rd
New Scone PH2 37 F5
Perth PH2 38 A5
Highfields FK15 107 B4
Highland Chief Way
DD4 94 C8
Highland Cres PH7 101 A4
Highlander Way FK10 117 D2
Highlandman Loan
PH7 33 E1
Highland Rd PH7 101 A4
Highmill Ct 9 DD2 93 D2
High Mill Ct 3 DD2 93 D2
High Rd
Auchtermuchty KY14 62 F6
East Wemyss KY1 133 C7
Newport-on-Tay DD6 98 D4
St Andrews KY16 54 B3
High Rigg DD8 11 C2
High St E 21 KY10 83 C6
High Sch of Dundee
DD1 179 B2
High St
Aberdour KY3 176 B7
Airth FK2 154 D3
Alloa FK10 138 B6
Alyth PH11 7 A3
29 Anstruther Wester
KY10 83 C6
Arbroath DD11 89 D3
Auchterarder PH3 104 E6
Auchtermuchty KY14 62 F6
Blairgowrie PH10 88 E6
Brechin DD9 84 C3
Burntisland KY3 177 E8
Burrelton PH13 26 C7
Carnoustie DD7 100 D3
Clackmannan FK10 138 F4
Cowdenbeath KY4 147 D4
Crail KY10 69 B2
Crieff PH7 101 C4
4 Cupar KY15 64 D4
Dollar FK14 73 C1
Dunblane FK15 107 D5
Dundee DD1 179 B2
Dunfermline KY12 161 A3
Dysart KY1 152 A7
Earlsferry/Elie KY9 82 B3
Errol PH2 39 F1
Falkland KY15 63 B2
Freuchie KY15 63 E1
Glenrothes KY6 112 C8
Inverkeithing KY11 174 B2
Kincardine FK10 155 E4
Kinghorn KY3 166 F2
2 Kinross KY13 108 C2
Kirkcaldy KY1 151 C3
Kirkcaldy KY1 151 C5
6 Kirriemuir DD8 86 D4
Leven KY8 109 D4
Lochgelly KY5 148 B7
Monifieth DD5 97 B5
Montrose DD10 85 C3
Newburgh KY14 50 D5
Newport-on-Tay DD6 98 E4
Perth PH1 103 A4
Pittenweem KY10 83 A5
South Queensferry
EH30 178 C1
Strathmiglo KY14 62 D5
Tillicoultry FK13 119 A7
High Terr 27 KY10 83 C6
HIGH VALLEYFIELD 158 A2
Hillbank KY11 174 B3
Hillbank Gdns DD3 179 B4
Hillbank Pl DD3 179 C4
Hillbank Rd DD3 179 C4
Hillbank Terr DD8 86 C5
Hill Cres KY15 105 C5
Hillcrest KY4 147 B3
Hillcrest Ave
Kirkcaldy KY2 150 E6
Perth PH1 102 F5
Hillcrest Dr FK10 138 C6
Hillcrest Rd DD2 93 C3
Hill Ct
Dunfermline KY12 161 D5
South Queensferry
EH30 178 B1
HILLEND 174 E4
HILL END 123 B4
Hillend Ind Pk KY11 175 C5
Hillend Rd
Arbroath DD11 89 B3
Inverkeithing KY11 174 D3
Perth PH1 102 B4
HILLERAYE 68 D4
Hillfield Cres KY11 174 B3
Hillfield Rd
10 Balmutto KY16 53 E8
Inverkeithing KY11 174 B2
Hillfoots Rd
9 Dollar FK14 73 C1
Menstrie FK9 116 C6
Stirling FK9 115 E4
Hill Gr KY12 158 D7
Hillhead La 8 KY8 80 F5
Hillhead Rd DD5 20 D1
Hillhead St 9 KY8 80 F5
Hillhead Terr DD8 86 C5
Hill O' Blair PH10 88 C6
HILL OF BEATH 147 A1
Hill of Beath Prim Sch
KY4 146 F1
Hill of St Margaret
KY12 161 F5
Hill of Tarvit
Mansionhouse & Gdns*
KY15 65 C6
Hillpark Cres FK7 135 C2
Hillpark Dr
Bannockburn FK7 135 D2
Dundee DD2 90 C3
Hillpark Pl DD2 90 C4
Hillpark Rd 8 DD6 42 B5
Hillpark Terr 5 DD6 42 B5
Hill Pk FK10 138 B7
Hill Pl
Alloa FK10 138 A8
Arbroath DD11 89 D3
9 Coupar Angus PH13 16 A3
Glenrothes KY7 111 E1
Kirkcaldy KY1 151 C4
Montrose DD10 85 C2
Hill Prim Sch PH10 88 C6
Hill Rd
Arbroath DD11 89 E3
Ballingry KY5 127 F8
Dundee DD5 96 A3
Hillside DD10 6 C8
Leven KY8 79 E6
5 Newburgh KY14 50 D5
Hill Rise DD8 86 D6
HILLSIDE 6 C8
Hillside FK10 118 C2
Hillside Ave
Dalgety Bay KY11 175 A3
Dunblane FK15 107 C4
Hillside Camp Rd
KY11 173 E1
Hillside Ct DD2 92 E5
Hillside Dr DD2 92 F4
Hillside Pl
Dundee DD2 92 F3
7 Newport-on-Tay DD6 98 E4
Hillside Prim Sch DD2 92 F5
Hillside Rd
Dundee DD2 92 F3
Forfar DD8 87 D4
Hillside Sch KY3 176 C8
Hillside Terr
Alloa FK10 138 B7
Dundee DD2 92 F3
2 Kinglassie KY5 77 F1
Hill Sq DD3 179 A4
Hill St
Alloa FK10 138 B7
Alyth PH11 7 A3
Arbroath DD11 89 D3
Blairgowrie PH10 88 B5
8 Coupar Angus PH13 16 A3
Cowdenbeath KY4 147 C4
Crieff PH7 101 C4
Cupar KY15 105 B5
Dundee DD3 179 A4
Dunfermline KY12 161 A4
Dysart KY1 152 A7
Inverkeithing KY11 174 B2
Kirkcaldy KY1 151 B3
Ladybank KY15 64 A4
Lochgelly KY5 128 B1
Monifieth DD5 97 B6
6 Montrose DD10 85 C2
Newport-on-Tay DD6 98 C3
Stirling FK7 135 B3
Tillicoultry FK13 119 B7
Hill Terr
Arbroath DD11 89 E3
Dundee DD2 90 C3
Glenrothes KY7 111 F1
HILLTOWN 179 B4
Hilltown DD3 179 B4
Hilltown Ct DD3 179 B3
Hilltown Terr DD3 179 B3
Hillview
Bechin DD9 84 E2
Hillview *continued*
Cowdenbeath, Hill of Beath
KY4 147 A1
Cowdenbeath KY4 147 B3
Oakley KY12 158 E7
Hill View
Glenrothes KY7 113 C5
3 Kinglassie KY5 77 F1
Hillview Cres
Crossgates KY4 162 E6
Montrose DD10 85 D1
Hillview Dr FK9 115 A6
Hillview Pl
Crossgates KY4 162 E6
13 Dollar FK14 73 C1
Fallin FK7 136 C4
Hillview Terr
Alloa FK10 138 C6
Dundee DD3 91 A5
Tillicoultry FK13 119 B7
Hillwood Pl EH30 178 B1
Hillwood Terr KY11 174 A3
HILLYLAND 102 B6
Hilton Cres FK10 138 D7
Hilton Farm Steadings
KY11 173 B3
Hilton Rd
Alloa FK10 138 D7
Cairneyhill KY12 159 E1
Rosyth KY11 173 C2
Hilton Terr FK7 136 C4
Hilton View KY4 147 E6
Hindmarsh Ave DD3 94 A4
Hirst Cres FK7 136 D4
Hirst Ct FK7 136 D4
Hobart St DD8 86 D3
Hogarth Dr KY15 105 E3
Hoggan Cres KY11 161 C2
Hoggan Way FK12 117 F6
Holborn Pl KY11 173 F5
Holbourne Pl FK11 117 A7
Holden Way KY11 175 B5
Hollybank
Kirkland KY8 109 A5
3 Leven KY8 79 F3
Hollybush Cres PH7 101 E4
Hollybush Dr PH7 101 E4
Hollybush Rd PH7 101 E4
Holly Cres
Blairgowrie PH10 88 D3
Broughty Ferry DD5 96 B3
Dunfermline KY11 173 E8
Holly Gr
Leven KY8 109 D8
Menstrie FK11 116 F6
Holly Pk KY15 105 D4
Holly Pl
Crieff PH7 101 E4
Kirkcaldy KY1 151 C7
Holly Rd
Broughty Ferry DD5 96 B3
Leven KY8 109 D8
Holly Terr PH1 102 B3
Hollytree Rd KY7 113 D5
Holme Hill Ct FK15 107 D5
Holm Rd KY15 63 C2
Holm Sq KY7 111 A2
Holton Cotts FK10 118 C1
Holton Cres FK10 118 C1
Holton Ct FK10 118 C1
Holton Sq FK10 118 C1
Holy Name RC Prim Sch
KY12 158 E7
Holyrood Ave KY6 110 E1
Holyrood Pl KY12 161 B4
Holyrood St DD7 100 D4
Home Pk KY3 176 C7
Home St DD5 95 F2
Homesteads The FK8 134 D7
Honeyberry Cres PH10 88 E6
Honeyberry Dr PH10 88 E6
Honeygreen Rd DD4 94 D7
Hood Pl KY11 173 E2
Hope Pl
Crieff PH7 101 E5
Monance KY10 82 E4
Hope St
Cowdenbeath KY4 147 E6
Inverkeithing KY11 174 B1
St Andrews KY16 106 D6
Stirling FK8 114 F1
Hopetoun Dr FK9 115 A8
Hopetoun Pl KY2 150 C6
Hopetoun Rd EH30 178 A1
Hopetoun View KY11 175 C4
Hopeward Ct KY11 175 C3
Hopeward Mews
KY11 175 C2
Horologe Hill DD11 89 E5
Horse Cross 10 PH1 103 B4
Horseleys Pk KY16 106 C4
Horse Mkt 7 KY15 63 B2
Horseshoe Dr PH7 101 B5
Horsewater Wynd
DD1 179 A2
Horse Wynd DD1 179 B2
HOSH 101 A8
Hospital Cross Head
KY11 161 C1
HOSPITALFIELD 89 A2
Hospitalfield Gdns 10
DD11 22 E3
Hospitalfield Rd DD11 22 E3
Hospital Hill KY11 161 B1
Hospital Rd DD10 6 C8

Hospital St
Dundee DD3 ... 93 E6
5 Perth PH2 ... 103 A3
Hot Pot Wynd KY1 ... 152 A6
Houghton Dr 2 DD10 ... 6 D8
Houldsworth St KY12 ... 158 A7
Houliston Ave KY11 ... 174 B3
House of Dun* DD10 ... 5 E6
Houston Ave KY7 ... 111 A3
Houston Ct
2 Cupar KY15 ... 105 C5
1 Dunfermline KY12 ... 160 F4
Howard Cres KY11 ... 161 C2
Howard Pl
Dysart KY1 ... 152 A7
6 St Andrews KY16 ... 106 D6
Howard St Cotts 1
DD11 ... 89 C5
Howard St DD11 ... 89 C5
Howe Ness KY11 ... 173 D3
Howe The 7 DD8 ... 11 E3
Howetown FK10 ... 118 D4
Howiegate Gdns 7
KY7 ... 113 F8
Howlands Rd FK7 ... 135 A3
Hudson Pl KY16 ... 54 B8
Hudson Rd KY11 ... 173 F3
Hugh Ave KY5 ... 128 B1
Hugh Pl KY5 ... 148 B8
Hugo Ave KY1 ... 132 E4
Humbie Terr KY3 ... 176 C8
Hume Cres FK9 ... 115 A6
Hume Ct FK9 ... 115 A6
Hume St
Arbroath DD11 ... 89 C4
Montrose DD10 ... 85 C3
Hunter Cres
Invergowrie DD2 ... 92 B3
Leuchars KY16 ... 54 B8
Hunterhall Pl PH2 ... 49 F7
Hunter Pl
Dunfermline KY12 ... 160 E5
Kirkcaldy KY1 ... 151 B3
Hunter Rd
2 Arbroath DD11 ... 22 E5
Leuchars KY16 ... 54 B7
Hunter St
Auchterarder PH3 ... 104 E7
Dundee DD1 ... 179 A2
Kirkcaldy KY1 ... 151 B4
Huntingfaulds Rd DD4 ... 19 A2
HUNTINGTOWER ... 36 F3
Huntingtower Castle*
PH1 ... 102 A7
Huntingtower Cres
PH1 ... 102 B5
Huntingtower Pk KY6 ... 110 D1
Huntingtower Rd PH1 ... 102 B6
Huntly Cres
Kirkcaldy KY2 ... 150 C8
Stirling FK8 ... 114 F2
Huntly Dr KY6 ... 112 C6
Huntly Pl
Dundee DD4 ... 95 A4
St Andrews KY16 ... 106 B4
Huntly Rd DD4 ... 95 B4
Hunt Pl KY12 ... 160 B1
Huntsmans Ct KY7 ... 111 B1
Huntsman's Rd KY7 ... 111 B1
Hurlburn Rd KY1 ... 131 C5
Husband Pl KY11 ... 161 F1
HUSBANDTOWN ... 20 C2
Hutchison Ct KY16 ... 106 D4
Hutchison Gn KY11 ... 161 B1
Hutchison Way 10
KY2 ... 130 E1
Hutton Browne Gr 8
KY8 ... 79 F6
Hutton Pk FK10 ... 138 C7
Hutton Pl 5 DD5 ... 96 B2
Hyndford Pl DD2 ... 93 C3
Hyndford St DD2 ... 93 C3
Hyndhead Sch KY8 ... 109 A2
Hyndloup Terr KY5 ... 129 B3

I

Ian Rankin Ct KY5 ... 129 B2
Imrie Pl PH1 ... 102 D8
Inchaffray St PH1 ... 103 A5
Inch Ave KY3 ... 176 B6
Inchbrakie Dr PH7 ... 101 E3
Inchbrakie Gdns PH7 ... 101 E4
Inchbrayock Rd DD10 ... 6 D3
Inchcape Pl
7 Broughty Ferry DD5 ... 96 D5
Perth PH1 ... 37 C5
Inchcape Rd
Arbroath DD11 ... 89 A3
Broughty Ferry DD5 ... 96 D5
Inchcape Terr 8 DD5 ... 96 D5
INCHCOLM ... 176 B1
Inchcolm Dr
Broughty Ferry DD5 ... 96 E5
North Queensferry
KY11 ... 178 B6
Inchcolm Gdns 5 DD5 ... 96 D5
Inchcolm Rd KY11 ... 161 E3
Inchcolm Terr 1 DD5 ... 96 E5
Inches The KY11 ... 175 B2
Inchgall Ave KY5 ... 127 F5
Inchgarth Ave DD8 ... 87 B5
Inchgarth St DD8 ... 87 B5
Inchgarvie Ave KY3 ... 165 D1
Inchgarvie Cres KY11 ... 161 E3
Inchgarvie Pk EH30 ... 178 A1
Inchgarvie Rd KY2 ... 150 F8
Inch Head Terr PH2 ... 103 B1
Inchkeith Ave DD5 ... 96 D5
Inchkeith Ct KY11 ... 161 F3
Inchkeith Dr KY11 ... 161 F3
Inchkeith Pl 6 DD5 ... 96 D5
Inchkeith Sch KY12 ... 169 C8
Inchkeith Terr 4 DD5 ... 96 D5
Inchlaw KY16 ... 53 E7
Inchmacoble Pk
(Strathmore RFC)
DD8 ... 87 B4
Inchmickery Ave
KY11 ... 175 D5
Inchmickery Rd KY11 ... 175 C5
Inchna FK11 ... 117 A6
Inch Terr DD10 ... 85 B1
INCHTURE ... 40 C7
Inchture Prim Sch
PH14 ... 40 C7
Inch View
Kinghorn KY3 ... 166 F1
Kirkcaldy KY1 ... 167 B7
Inchview Gdns KY11 ... 175 B3
Inchyra Pl 4 DD3 ... 91 C3
India La DD10 ... 85 D3
India St DD10 ... 85 D3
Infirmary Brae
3 Arbroath DD11 ... 89 B2
Dundee DD3 ... 179 A3
Infirmary Rd DD9 ... 84 D3
Infirmary St DD9 ... 84 D3
Inglefield St DD4 ... 94 F5
Inglewood Gdns FK10 ... 138 A8
Inglewood Ho FK10 ... 117 F1
Inglewood Rd FK10 ... 137 F8
Inglis Cres KY3 ... 166 F3
Inglis La KY12 ... 160 F5
Inglis St
Dundee DD1 ... 94 E2
Dunfermline KY12 ... 161 A4
Ingram Dr FK15 ... 107 D7
Ingrie Ave KY6 ... 77 F4
Innerbridge St KY16 ... 54 A6
Innerdownie Pl 2
FK14 ... 73 C1
INNERLEITH ... 63 E6
Innerleithen Way PH1 ... 102 B2
INNERLEVEN ... 109 D4
Innes Rd
Glenrothes KY6 ... 112 E6
Leuchars KY16 ... 54 B8
Innewan Gdns PH1 ... 24 B6
Innewan Pl PH1 ... 24 B6
Innovation Pk FK9 ... 115 D5
Innova Way KY11 ... 173 D1
Inn St DD6 ... 99 F7
Inshewan Ave DD8 ... 2 A3
Institute Row KY8 ... 79 F2
Institution St
Kirkcaldy KY1 ... 151 E7
Leven KY8 ... 109 A2
INVERALDIE ... 29 F8
Inveraldie Cres DD4 ... 29 F7
Inveraldie Terr DD4 ... 29 F8
Inverallan Ct FK9 ... 114 F8
Inverallan Dr FK9 ... 114 F7
Inverallan Rd FK9 ... 114 F7
Inveralmond Cl PH1 ... 37 B5
Inveralmond Gr PH1 ... 102 C8
Inveralmond Ind Est
PH1 ... 102 B8
Inveralmond Pl PH1 ... 102 C8
Inveralmond Rd PH1 ... 102 B8
Inveralmond Way PH1 ... 102 B8
Inveraray Ave KY7 ... 113 B4
INVERARITY ... 19 F7
Inverarity Cres 5 DD10 ... 6 C8
Inverarity Gdns 4 DD5 ... 97 A7
Inverarity Prim Sch
DD8 ... 19 E7
Inverary Terr DD3 ... 93 D5
Inverbay DD2 ... 92 B2
Inverbrothock Prim Sch
DD11 ... 89 B7
Invercraig Pl DD2 ... 92 E6
Inveresk Cres 7 DD4 ... 94 F8
Inverewe Pl KY11 ... 162 A1
INVERGOWRIE ... 92 A3
Invergowrie Dr DD2 ... 92 F3
Invergowrie Prim Sch
DD2 ... 92 B3
Invergowrie Sta DD2 ... 92 B2
Inverie St KY10 ... 82 E4
Inverkeillor Gdns KY7 ... 113 D2
INVERKEILOR ... 14 B4
Inverkeilor Prim Sch
DD11 ... 14 B4
INVERKEITHING ... 174 B1
Inverkeithing High Sch
KY11 ... 174 D3
Inverkeithing Mus*
KY11 ... 174 B2
Inverkeithing Prim Sch
KY11 ... 174 B3
Inverkeithing Rd
Aberdour KY3 ... 176 B7
Crossgates KY4 ... 162 E6
Inverkeithing Sta
KY11 ... 174 C3
Inverlaw Pl DD3 ... 93 E4
Invermark Terr DD5 ... 96 D4
Inver Pl KY6 ... 112 F6
Inver Terr DD2 ... 90 A3
Invertiel Bank KY1 ... 151 B1
Invertiel Rd KY1 ... 167 A8
Invertiel Terr KY1 ... 151 B1
Inzievar Ctyd KY12 ... 158 F5
Inzievar Ho KY12 ... 158 F4
Inzievar Prim Sch
KY12 ... 158 E7
Inzievar Terr KY12 ... 159 A6
Iona Ct PH1 ... 102 E7
Iona Pk KY7 ... 111 A1
Iona Rd KY11 ... 161 E3
Ireland St DD7 ... 100 E3
Irvine Cres KY16 ... 106 E4
Irvine Pl FK8 ... 135 A8
Irvine's Sq DD1 ... 179 B3
Isabella Pl PH2 ... 37 E5
Isla Ave DD7 ... 100 C4
Isla Cres 2 PH1 ... 37 B8
Isla Ct PH11 ... 7 B3
Isla Gr PH11 ... 7 B3
Island View PH2 ... 103 C2
Isla Pl
Forfar DD8 ... 87 E6
5 Tayport DD6 ... 99 F7
Isla Rd
Alyth PH11 ... 7 A3
Blairgowrie PH10 ... 88 C3
Kirriemuir DD8 ... 86 C4
Luncarty PH1 ... 37 B8
Perth PH2 ... 103 B6
Islay Rd KY11 ... 161 E2
Ivanhoe Ave KY5 ... 127 F6
Ivanhoe Dr KY6 ... 112 C5
Ivanhoe Pl
Dundee DD4 ... 94 D3
Stirling FK8 ... 115 A2
Ivory Pl DD5 ... 95 E6
Ivy Gr KY11 ... 173 E8
Ivygrove 9 KY8 ... 79 F2
Ivy La KY1 ... 152 A7
Ivy Pl KY14 ... 63 B5
Ivy Rd DD8 ... 87 E7
Ivy Terr DD8 ... 87 E7
Ivy Wlk KY15 ... 63 C2
Izatt Ave KY11 ... 161 B1
Izatt St FK10 ... 138 B7
Izatt Terr FK10 ... 139 A4

J

Jack Martin Way DD4 ... 29 F5
Jack Smith Rd DD10 ... 85 D1
Jacobson Gdns 3 DD3 ... 91 D3
Jacobson Pl 4 DD3 ... 91 D3
Jacobson Terr 5 DD3 ... 91 D3
Jail Wynd 6 FK8 ... 135 A8
Jamaica Sq DD3 ... 179 B4
Jamaica St DD3 ... 179 B4
Jamaica Twr DD3 ... 179 B4
James Arrott Dr DD2 ... 92 E4
James Bank KY12 ... 161 A4
James Bell Wynd DD5 ... 96 F7
James Black Pl DD2 ... 92 D4
James Chalmers Rd
Arbroath DD11 ... 89 A6
Cairnie DD11 ... 22 E5
James Cowie Cl DD5 ... 96 F7
James Ct
13 Bridge of Earn PH2 ... 48 E4
Cowdenbeath KY4 ... 147 C2
Jamesfield 3 KY13 ... 77 A4
James Foulis Ct KY16 ... 106 B3
James Gr KY1 ... 151 B2
James Herald Terr DD5 ... 96 F7
James Hog Cres KY12 ... 158 F6
James Ingles Cres
KY15 ... 105 C4
James Miller Rd KY11 ... 173 E2
James' Park La KY3 ... 165 F1
James' Pk KY3 ... 165 F1
James Pl
Broughty Ferry DD5 ... 95 F2
1 Stanley PH1 ... 24 E4
Tillicoultry FK14 ... 119 C4
James Robb Ave
KY16 ... 106 D4
James Sq 3 PH7 ... 101 C4
James St
Alva FK12 ... 118 A6
25 Alyth PH11 ... 7 A3
9 Anstruther KY10 ... 83 D6
9 Arbroath DD11 ... 89 D4
Bannockburn FK7 ... 135 C1
Blairgowrie PH10 ... 88 C5
Carnoustie DD7 ... 100 A2
Cowdenbeath KY4 ... 147 C2
Dundee DD3 ... 179 B4
Dunfermline KY12 ... 161 A4
Methven PH1 ... 36 A4
Newport-on-Tay DD6 ... 98 E5
4 Perth PH2 ... 103 B3
Pittenweem KY10 ... 83 A5
10 St Andrews KY16 ... 106 D5
2 Stanley PH1 ... 24 E4
Stirling FK8 ... 115 B1
James Wylie Pl FK10 ... 155 F4
Jamie Anderson Pl
KY16 ... 106 D3
Jamieson Cl PH1 ... 102 A5
Jamieson Gdns FK13 ... 119 B7
Jamiesons Cl 9 DD8 ... 86 C4
Jamieson St
Arbroath DD11 ... 89 C3
Forfar DD8 ... 87 E5
JAMPHLARS ... 128 F4
Jamphlars Rd KY5 ... 129 A4
Janefield Pl DD4 ... 94 C4
Janet Forbes Ave DD2 ... 40 E8
Jannetta Terr 19 KY8 ... 109 E6
Jarvie Pl KY6 ... 112 C5
Jarvis Pl DD7 ... 100 C3
Jasmine Ct KY7 ... 113 C5
Jawbanes Rd KY2 ... 167 A8
Jean Armour Gdns
KY2 ... 151 A7
Jeanfield Cres DD8 ... 87 B3
Jeanfield Rd
Forfar DD8 ... 87 B3
Perth PH1 ... 102 E4
Jedburgh Ct KY6 ... 112 D7
Jedburgh Pl PH1 ... 102 B3
Jedburgh Rd DD2 ... 93 B3
Jellyholm Rd FK10 ... 138 E8
Jenner Pl DD9 ... 84 C5
Jennie Lee La KY7 ... 112 F8
Jennie Rennie's Rd
KY11 ... 161 B1
Jenny Gray Path 2
KY7 ... 111 B1
Jerdan Gall The* KY10 ... 69 B2
JERICHO ... 9 E1
Jessie St PH10 ... 88 C4
Jetty La 5 DD5 ... 96 A2
John Allan Pl 5 DD11 ... 89 A7
John Connelly Ct 3
KY12 ... 160 E5
John Coupar Ct 9
KY16 ... 106 D5
John Cowane Row
FK9 ... 115 A4
John Fergus Specl Sch
KY7 ... 113 A6
John Grahame Ave 5
DD4 ... 94 C8
John Huband Dr DD2 ... 90 B3
John Hunter Ct KY1 ... 151 B4
John Knox Gdns KY7 ... 111 A3
John Knox Rd KY16 ... 106 B3
John McDouall Stuart
Mus* KY1 ... 152 A7
John Mckay Pl 6
DD10 ... 85 C3
John Murray Dr FK9 ... 115 A8
Johnny Marshalls Loan
KY1 ... 131 B4
Johnny Marshall's Loan
KY2 ... 131 A1
John Paul Jones Ct
KY2 ... 130 E2
John R Gray Rd FK15 ... 107 C4
John Ross Pl KY7 ... 79 A2
John Row Pl KY12 ... 159 A7
John Rushforth Pl
FK8 ... 114 F3
John St W DD11 ... 89 C4
Johnshill Rd PH11 ... 7 A3
John Smith Bsns Pk
KY2 ... 130 C1
John Smith Pl KY4 ... 126 F2
John St
7 Anstruther Easter
KY10 ... 83 D6
Arbroath DD11 ... 89 D3
Blairgowrie PH10 ... 88 C5
Dunfermline KY11 ... 161 B2
Forfar DD8 ... 87 D6
Kincardine FK10 ... 155 D3
Kirkcaldy KY2 ... 151 B5
Montrose DD10 ... 85 D4
Johnston Ave
Dundee DD3 ... 93 D7
Invergowrie DD2 ... 92 B3
Stirling FK9 ... 115 B3
Johnston Cres
Dunfermline KY11 ... 161 B1
Lochgelly KY5 ... 148 B7
Tillicoultry FK13 ... 119 C7
Johnstone Ct FK12 ... 118 A6
Johnstone Path
Balgeddie KY6 ... 110 E1
Glenrothes KY7 ... 112 E8
Johnstone St
Alva FK12 ... 118 A6
Menstrie FK11 ... 116 F6
Johnston Path KY7 ... 112 E8
Johnston Pk
Cowdenbeath KY4 ... 147 C5
Inverkeithing KY11 ... 174 B2
Johnston's La DD1 ... 179 A2
Johnston St
Bannockburn FK7 ... 135 C1
Dundee DD1 ... 179 A2
Johnston Terr KY8 ... 79 E3
John Stuart Gait KY12 ... 158 F6
John Wood Pl KY4 ... 162 F7
Joiners Cl PH4 ... 57 B4
Jones St KY12 ... 146 A1
Jordan La 17 KY8 ... 79 F5
Jubilee Bldgs 8 DD6 ... 99 F7
Jubilee Course The
KY16 ... 54 F5
Jubilee Cres KY15 ... 63 C2
Jubilee Ct
Dunfermline KY12 ... 161 A3
Lochgelly KY5 ... 128 B1
Jubilee Dr KY11 ... 173 B1
Jubilee Gdns KY7 ... 79 C3
Jubilee Gr KY6 ... 112 F7
Jubilee Pk DD8 ... 11 E3
Julian Ct KY7 ... 111 B1
Julian Rd KY7 ... 111 B1
Junction Pl 11 FK10 ... 138 B6
Junction Rd KY1 ... 151 D7
Juniper Gr KY11 ... 173 D8
Juniper Hill KY7 ... 110 F1
Juniper Pl PH1 ... 102 B3
Jura St PH1 ... 102 E7
Jute Pl KY1 ... 151 C7

K

Kaims' Croft DD11 ... 89 B4
Kames Pl KY12 ... 161 D5
Katarine St DD8 ... 87 D7
Katherine Pk KY2 ... 151 B6
Katherine St KY2 ... 151 B6
Katrine Ave DD5 ... 96 A4
Katrine Cres KY2 ... 150 E8
Katrine Ct
Alloa FK10 ... 138 C5
16 Perth PH2 ... 37 F5
Katrine Dr KY12 ... 160 B1
Katrine Pl KY13 ... 108 B3
Kaye Dr PH12 ... 38 B6
Kay Rd KY12 ... 170 F8
Keats Pl DD3 ... 93 E6
Keavil Farm Steadings
KY12 ... 172 B8
Keavil Pl KY12 ... 160 B1
Keay St PH10 ... 88 B5
Keddie Pl KY15 ... 105 B4
KEILARSBRAE ... 138 D8
Keilarsbrae FK10 ... 138 C8
Keilburn KY8 ... 80 F5
Keillor Croft DD5 ... 30 E7
Keir Ave FK8 ... 115 A2
Keir Ct FK9 ... 115 A7
Keirfold Ave FK10 ... 117 D3
Keir Gdns FK9 ... 115 A7
Keir Hardie Rd FK12 ... 118 C7
Keir Hardie St KY8 ... 109 B3
Keir Hardie Terr KY11 ... 161 B1
Keirsbeath Ct KY12 ... 146 B2
Keirsbeath Rise KY12 ... 146 B1
Keirs Brae KY5 ... 129 D2
Keir St
Bridge of A FK9 ... 115 A7
Cowdenbeath KY4 ... 147 B4
Dunblane FK15 ... 107 C5
Perth PH2 ... 103 C5
Keithall Gdns DD2 ... 90 C3
Keith Ave
Carnoustie DD7 ... 100 D4
Stirling FK7 ... 135 C4
Keith Cres 14 KY16 ... 54 B8
Keith Dr KY6 ... 112 C6
Keith Pl
Dundee DD4 ... 95 B5
Dunfermline KY12 ... 161 D4
Inverkeithing KY11 ... 174 C3
Keith Rd KY11 ... 173 C1
Keith Rigg 6 DD11 ... 89 B7
Keith St FK10 ... 155 D3
KELLAS ... 30 D6
Kellas Rd DD5 ... 95 E8
Kelliebank FK10 ... 137 E6
Kellie Castle* KY10 ... 82 E8
Kellie Castle & Gdn*
DD11 ... 22 C3
Kellie Ct KY7 ... 113 C2
Kellie Pl FK10 ... 138 A7
Kellie Wynd FK15 ... 107 F7
Kellock La KY16 ... 54 B3
Kellyburn Pk FK14 ... 120 F8
Kelly Ct FK8 ... 135 A8
Kelly Rd DD11 ... 22 D6
Kellywood Cres FK10 ... 155 F3
Kelso Ct KY6 ... 112 C7
Kelso Pl
Dundee DD2 ... 93 B3
Kirkcaldy KY2 ... 151 B6
4 Perth PH1 ... 102 A3
Kelso St DD2 ... 93 B3
KELTY ... 126 E2
KELTYBRIDGE ... 126 E3
Keltyhill Ave KY4 ... 126 C1
Keltyhill Cres KY4 ... 126 C1
Keltyhill Rd KY4 ... 126 C1
Kelty Prim Sch KY4 ... 126 E2
KEMBACK ... 53 D2
Kemback Prim Sch
KY15 ... 53 E2
Kemback St DD4 ... 94 C3
Kemnay Dr KY7 ... 110 E2
Kemnay Gdns DD4 ... 95 A4
Kemnay Pl DD4 ... 95 A4
Kemsley Pk DD8 ... 87 B3
Kemsley Pl DD8 ... 87 B3
Kenilworth Ave DD4 ... 94 D3
Kenilworth Ct FK9 ... 115 B7
Kenilworth Dr KY6 ... 112 D5
Kenilworth Rd FK9 ... 115 B7
Kenilworth Terr 4
KY5 ... 127 F6
Kenmore Terr
Dundee DD3 ... 93 D5
Kirkcaldy KY2 ... 150 E7
Perth PH1 ... 102 C5
Kenmount Dr 15 KY8 ... 79 F5
Kenmount Pl KY8 ... 79 F5
Kenmure Pl KY12 ... 161 C5
Kennard St KY5 ... 148 B8
Kennedy Ave DD10 ... 85 C7
Kennedy Cres
Dunfermline KY12 ... 161 B5
Kirkcaldy KY2 ... 151 B6
Kennedy Gdns KY16 ... 106 C5
Kennedy Rd 1 KY7 ... 113 A6
Kennedy Way FK2 ... 154 E3
KENNET ... 139 C2
Kennet Village FK10 ... 139 D3
Kennet Wlk DD3 ... 179 A4
Kenningknowes Rd
FK7 ... 134 E5

KENNOWAY 79 F5
Kennoway Pl DD5 96 B5
Kennoway Prim Sch KY8 79 F6
Kennoway Rd KY8 109 C7
Kent Rd
  Alloa FK10 137 F8
  Stirling FK7 135 B5
Kent St KY12 161 C6
Kenworthy Ave PH2 37 E5
Keptie Rd 2 DD11 89 A4
Keptie St 4 DD11 89 C3
Kerbet Pl DD8 9 F2
Kerrera Pl KY7 111 A1
Kerrington Cres DD5 96 E4
Kerrisk Dr KY11 161 F1
Kerr Pl KY11 161 F1
Kerr's La DD2 93 A6
Kerrs Miniature Rly* DD11 89 A1
Kerr St
  1 Dundee DD2 93 B6
  Newport-on-Tay DD6 98 E5
Kerrsview Terr DD4 94 B6
Kerrystone Ct DD4 94 E5
Kersebonny Rd FK7 134 C7
Kersegreen Rd FK10 138 F5
Kerse Rd
  Stirling FK7 135 C6
  Stirling, Loanhead FK7 135 E5
Kersie Rd FK7 137 A3
Kersie Terr FK7 137 E3
Kestrel Gr KY8 79 F2
Keswick Terr DD3 91 F1
KETTINS 16 B1
Kettins Prim Sch PH13 16 B1
Kettins Terr DD3 91 B3
KETTLEBRIDGE 64 B2
Kettle Prim Sch KY15 64 B3
Keverkae FK10 137 F6
Kidd St KY1 151 D7
Kidlaw Cres FK10 117 D3
Kier Ct FK9 115 B7
KILBAGIE 155 D8
Kilbagie St FK10 155 D4
Kilberry St DD3 93 C5
Kilbride Ct FK15 107 C5
Kilbride Pl 3 DD4 95 B7
Kilbryde Cres FK15 107 C6
Kilbryde Gr FK15 107 C6
Kilburn Rd KY12 160 A2
KILCONQUHAR 82 B5
Kilcruik Rd KY3 166 F3
Kilda Pl PH1 37 C5
Kilda Rd PH1 37 C5
Kildean Hospl FK8 114 F2
Kildean Sch FK8 114 F2
Kildinny Yards 1 KY16 68 F7
Kildonan Pk KY12 160 F2
Kildownie Cres KY5 127 E7
Kilduthie Pl FK10 155 D6
Kilgask St DD6 98 E5
Kilgour Ave KY1 151 D7
Kilgraston Sch PH2 48 E4
Kilgraston Terr 12 PH2 48 F4
Killacky's Cnr 3 DD8 87 D5
Killiebone Rd KY12 145 D2
Killin Ave DD3 93 D5
Killin Ct KY12 160 F2
Killochan Way KY12 161 D5
KILMANY 53 B8
Kilmany Rd DD6 42 B4
Kilmaron Cres KY15 105 B6
Kilmaron Loan DD5 96 C5
Kilmaron Sch KY15 105 B6
Kilmartin Way KY12 161 C5
Kilmichael Rd KY7 111 C3
Kilminning Coast Wildlife Reserve* KY10 69 D3
Kilmore Terr DD4 94 A8
Kilmundy Dr KY3 165 D1
Kilmun Rd KY2 150 D7
Kilmux Pk 4 KY8 79 F6
Kilnbank La 7 DD8 86 C5
Kilnburn 5 DD6 98 E4
Kilncraigs Ct FK10 138 C5
Kilncraigs Rd FK10 138 C6
Kilndales Terr KY14 50 F3
Kilnheugh 11 KY14 62 F6
Kilravock Gdns 1 DD4 94 F8
KILRENNY 83 E7
Kilrenny Lea 4 KY10 83 D7
Kilrie Cotts KY2 165 F7
Kilrymont Cres KY16 106 E3
Kilrymont Pl KY16 106 E4
Kilrymont Rd KY16 106 E4
KILSPINDIE 39 B4
Kilspindie Cres KY2 131 A1
Kilspindie Pl DD2 93 C7
Kilspindie Rd 2 DD2 93 A7
Kilspindie St DD2 93 B7
Kilwinning Pl 2 DD4 95 B7
Kinaldy Mdws KY16 67 C5
Kinbrae Ct DD6 98 D3
Kinbrae Pk 6 DD6 98 D3
Kinbrae Pk Gdns DD6 98 E4
KINBUCK 70 D7
Kinburn Pl KY16 106 C6
Kincairne Ct FK10 155 E4
Kincaldrum Pl DD3 179 B4
KINCAPLE 54 C5
KINCARDINE 155 F4
Kincardine Rd
  Auchterarder PH3 104 E5
  Crieff PH7 101 D3
Kincardine St
  9 Dundee DD1 93 E3
  Montrose DD10 85 D4
Kincarrathie Cres PH2 103 C5
Kinclaven Dr DD3 91 B3
Kinclaven Gdns
  Finglassie KY7 113 B2
  Perth PH2 49 F3
Kincraig Pl KY12 160 F2
KINFAUNS 38 C1
Kingarth Dr PH10 88 E1
King David St 2 KY10 82 E4
Kingdom Ave KY7 113 A7
Kingdom Ct 4 KY15 105 C5
Kingdon Sh Ctr KY7 113 A7
King Edward St
  Glenrothes KY7 113 F7
  Perth PH1 103 B4
King Edward Wlk FK15 107 E8
Kingennie Ct DD4 94 E5
Kingennie Rd 10 DD5 30 F7
Kingfisher Pl
  2 Dundee DD4 95 C7
  Dunfermline KY11 162 A3
King George V Wharf Rd DD1 94 D2
KINGHORN 167 A2
Kinghorne Ct DD3 179 A4
Kinghorne Pl DD3 179 A4
Kinghorne Rd DD3 179 A4
Kinghorne St DD11 22 D3
Kinghorne Terr DD3 93 D4
Kinghorne Wlk DD3 179 A4
Kinghorn Pl DD9 84 C5
Kinghorn Prim Sch KY3 166 F2
Kinghorn Rd
  Burntisland KY3 166 A1
  Kirkcaldy KY1, KY2 167 B7
Kinghorn Sta KY3 166 F2
King James Dr FK10 117 C2
King James IV Rd KY11 173 C1
King James Pl PH2 103 B3
King James VI Golf Couse PH2 103 C1
King James VI Hospl PH2 103 B3
KINGLASSIE 77 E1
Kinglassie Prim Sch KY5 77 F1
Kinglassie Rd
  Glenrothes KY6 112 B3
  4 Lochgelly KY5 77 F1
King O' Muirs Ave FK10 117 E4
King O'Muirs Dr FK10 117 D4
King O' Muirs Farm Steading FK10 117 F4
King O' Muirs Rd FK10 117 E4
KINGOODIE 41 B8
King Robert Ct FK8 114 E1
King St Wynd PH7 101 C4
KINGSBARNS 68 E7
Kingsbarns Golf Links KY16 69 A7
Kingsbarns Prim Sch KY16 68 F6
Kingsburn Gdns 3 DD2 92 F7
King's Cres KY11 173 E4
Kings Cross DD3 93 E7
King's Cross Pl DD2 93 C7
King's Cross Rd DD2 93 C6
Kings Ct
  Alloa FK10 138 A7
  Stirling FK7 135 D5
Kingsdale Gdns KY8 79 E6
Kings Dr KY11 174 A8
King's Dr
  Arbroath DD11 89 F4
  Kinghorn KY3 166 F3
KINGSEAT 146 B1
Kingseat Dr FK13 119 C7
KINGSEATHILL 161 C6
Kingseat Rd
  Dunfermline KY12 161 D6
  Halbeath KY11, KY12 162 B6
Kingsgate Ctr KY12 161 A4
Kings Highway KY9 66 E2
KINGSKETTLE 64 A3
King's Knot* FK8 134 F8
Kingsland Terr 2 KY4 126 E1
Kingslaw KY1 133 C6
Kingsloan Ct KY9 66 E2
King's Mason 2 DD2 41 B8
Kingsmill Dr KY8 79 E4
KINGSMUIR 10 F4
Kingsmuir Gdns KY7 113 D2
Kingsmuir Pk DD3 91 B3
Kings Neuk PH2 38 D8
King's Park Rd FK8 135 A7
Kingspark Sch DD3 91 F1
King's Pl
  Perth PH2 103 A3
  Rosyth KY11 173 E4
King's Pl Mews 5 PH2 103 B3
Kings Rd DD8 87 E4
King's Rd
  5 Coupar Angus PH13 15 F2
  Rosyth KY11 173 E5
King's Road Prim Sch KY11 173 E4
King St
  18 Anstruther KY10 69 B2
  Broughty Ferry DD5 96 A2
  Cowdenbeath KY4 147 B4
King St *continued*
  Crieff PH7 101 C3
  Dundee DD1 179 C3
  Fallin FK7 136 C4
  6 Freuchie KY15 63 E1
  Inverkeithing KY11 174 C2
  Kirkcaldy KY2 151 B6
  3 Montrose DD10 85 D1
  Newport-on-Tay DD6 98 E5
  Perth PH2 103 B3
  St Andrews KY16 106 D4
  Stanley PH1 24 F3
  Stirling FK8 135 B7
  Tayport DD6 99 F6
Kingstables La 3 FK8 135 A8
Kingston Pl DD8 10 F4
Kingston Rd DD8 87 F2
Kingsway DD3 93 E8
Kingsway E 1 DD4 94 F5
Kingsway Pl DD3 93 F8
Kingsway Rest Pk DD3 93 D8
Kingsway Terr DD3 93 F8
Kingsway W DD2 92 B5
Kingswell Pk FK10 138 C7
Kingswell Pl PH1 102 D5
Kingswell Terr PH1 102 E5
Kininmonth St KY1 151 B2
Kinkell Ave KY7 113 A5
Kinkell Terr KY16 106 F4
Kinloch Ct PH10 88 C4
Kinloch Dr KY7 113 C2
Kinloch Pk
  4 Carnoustie DD7 100 D2
  Findo Gask PH1 46 F8
  Ninewells DD2 92 F4
Kinloch Pl 1 PH12 17 A7
Kinloch Prim Sch DD7 100 C2
Kinloch St
  2 Carnoustie DD7 100 C2
  Dundee DD3 179 A4
  8 Ladybank KY15 64 A4
Kinloch Terr
  Dundee DD3 179 A4
  Perth PH1 102 D5
Kinloss Cres KY15 105 B5
Kinloss Ct KY12 158 A2
Kinloss Dr KY15 105 B6
Kinloss Pk KY15 105 B5
Kinmond Ct PH2 103 D6
Kinnaber Rd DD10 6 D8
KINNAIRD 39 E7
Kinnaird Bank PH2 103 A1
Kinnaird Cl KY7 113 A2
Kinnaird Cres 10 DD11 12 F4
Kinnaird Pl
  2 Brechin DD9 84 D2
  Dunfermline KY12 161 D6
  Kirkcaldy KY2 150 D4
  Perth PH2 48 A4
Kinnaird Rd PH2 48 A4
Kinnaird St
  Arbroath DD11 89 C5
  Dundee DD3 179 A4
Kinnarchie Cres KY8 109 D5
Kinnarchie Pk 1 KY8 109 D5
Kinnear Ct KY16 54 A6
Kinnear St 8 KY8 79 F1
Kinneddar Pk KY12 142 E2
Kinneff Cres DD3 91 B3
KINNELL 13 A5
Kinnell Gdns 1 DD11 12 F4
Kinnell Pl DD11 12 F4
Kinnell Rd KY11 174 B2
Kinnell St 2 DD11 12 F4
Kinnessburn Rd KY16 106 D5
Kinnessburn Terr 6 KY16 106 D5
KINNESSWOOD 76 F5
Kinnettles Terr DD3 91 B3
Kinnis Ct KY11 161 F1
Kinnonmonth Ave KY3 165 D1
Kinnordy Ave DD8 86 B5
Kinnordy Pl
  Glenrothes KY7 113 B2
  1 Kirriemuir DD8 86 C5
Kinnordy Rd DD8 86 B6
Kinnordy Terr DD4 95 A3
Kinnoull Ave FK15 107 B5
Kinnoull Causeway PH2 103 A3
Kinnoull Hill Pl PH2 103 D3
Kinnoull Prim Sch PH2 103 C3
Kinnoull Rd DD2 93 C8
Kinnoull St
  Dundee DD2 93 B8
  Perth PH1 103 B4
Kinnoull Terr PH2 103 C4
Kinpurnie Dr 20 PH11 7 A3
Kinpurnie Pl DD3 93 E5
KINROSS 108 C3
Kinross Golf Club KY13 108 D3
Kinross High Sch KY13 108 C2
Kinross House & Gdns* KY13 108 E2
KINROSSIE 26 B3
Kinrossie Terr DD3 91 C3
Kinross Mus* KY13 108 C1
Kinross Prim Sch KY13 108 B2
Kintail Ct KY6 110 E1
Kintail Pl
  Broughty Ferry DD5 96 A5
  Halbeath KY11 162 A4
Kintail Wlk PH14 40 C7
KINTILLO 48 F4
Kintillo Gdns 14 PH2 48 F4
Kintillo Pl 9 PH2 48 F4
Kintillo Rd PH2 48 F4
Kintore Pk KY7 110 E2
Kintore Pl 4 DD5 95 C4
Kippendavie Ave 1 FK15 107 E7
Kippendavie Rd FK15 107 E7
Kippford St 6 DD5 96 F6
Kirkaldy Ct KY16 106 D3
Kirkbank DD11 23 D7
Kirkbank Rd KY3 165 F1
Kirkbrae
  7 Ceres KY15 65 D6
  Clackmannan FK10 138 F4
Kirk Brae
  10 Alyth PH11 7 A3
  4 Glenrothes KY7 113 F8
  Kincardine FK10 155 E5
Kirkbuddo Pl 5 DD5 97 A7
Kirkburn Dr KY5 129 B4
KIRKCALDY 151 C3
Kirkcaldy Campus Support Ctr KY1 132 A1
Kirkcaldy High Sch KY1 151 B8
Kirkcaldy Mus & Art Gallery* KY1 151 B4
Kirkcaldy North Prim Sch KY2 151 B6
Kirkcaldy Rd
  Burntisland KY3 165 F2
  Crossgates KY4 163 A6
  Kinghorn KY3 167 A4
Kirkcaldy Sta KY1 151 A4
Kirkcaldy West Prim Sch KY1 151 B2
Kirkconnel Terr 1 DD4 95 B7
Kirkcroft Brae DD2 28 D3
Kirk Ct FK13 119 C6
Kirkden St DD11 12 F5
Kirk Dr KY6 112 A8
Kirke Pk 15 KY8 79 F3
Kirkford Ct KY4 147 A4
KIRKFORTHAR FEUS 111 D6
Kirkgate
  Alloa FK10 138 B6
  Burntisland KY3 177 E8
  Cupar KY15 105 C4
  Dunfermline KY12 160 F3
  Inverkeithing KY11 174 B4
  Kinross KY13 108 D1
  9 Letham DD8 11 E3
  13 Perth PH1 103 B4
  12 Pittenweem KY10 83 A5
Kirkgate Prim Ed Ctr KY15 105 C4
Kirkhall Rd PH1 36 E5
KIRKHILL 6 A7
Kirkhill
  1 Dollar FK14 74 A3
  St Andrews KY16 106 E6
Kirkhill Dr PH1 37 B8
Kirkhill Terr 6 FK13 119 C7
KIRKINCH 17 D7
Kirkinch Rd KY7 113 B2
Kirk La DD1 179 B3
KIRKLAND 109 B5
Kirkland Ave KY5 127 F8
Kirkland Dr KY8 109 B4
Kirkland Gdns
  Ballingry KY5 127 F7
  Leven KY8 109 B5
Kirkland High Sch & Com Coll KY8 109 B4
Kirkland Pk KY5 127 E8
Kirkland Rd KY8 109 C4
Kirklands KY12 161 A2
Kirklands Pk KY15 105 B6
Kirkland Wlk KY8 109 C5
Kirklatch Ct 3 KY10 83 B5
Kirkliston Rd EH30 178 B1
Kirkmay Rd KY10 69 A2
Kirkpark Rd 3 KY9 82 B3
Kirk Rd
  Dundee DD2 28 C4
  Newport-on-Tay DD6 98 D3
Kirkriggs DD8 87 D4
Kirk Riggs DD8 87 D4
Kirkriggs Ct DD8 87 D4
Kirkshotts Terr 3 KY5 129 B4
Kirkside 13 PH1 103 B4
Kirkside Cres FK7 135 B5
Kirkside Ct 20 KY8 109 E6
Kirk Sq 18 DD11 89 D4
Kirk St
  Culross KY12 157 D1
  Dunblane FK15 107 D5
  Dundee DD2 93 B5
  Glenrothes KY7 111 F1
  Kincardine FK10 155 E4
Kirkstyle
  15 Dollar FK14 73 C1
  St Vigeans DD11 89 C7
Kirkstyle Sq 8 PH2 46 F1
Kirkstyle Terr 16 FK14 73 C1
KIRKTON
  165 E1
  Arbroath 89 B6
  Auchterarder 46 A5
  Blairgownie 17 B3
  Dundee 29 E8
  Forfar 10 A1
  Newport-on-tay 41 E4
Kirkton Ave DD3 91 E2
Kirkton Cres DD3 91 E1
Kirkton Ct DD8 86 C5
Kirktonhill Rd DD8 86 C5
Kirkton Ind Est DD11 89 A6
KIRKTON OF AIRLIE 8 B6
KIRKTON OF AUCHTERHOUSE 18 A1
KIRKTON OF COLLACE 26 C3
KIRKTON OF CRAIG 6 C2
KIRKTON OF LARGO OR UPPER LARGO 81 A7
Kirkton of Largo Prim Sch KY8 81 A6
Kirkton of Liff DD2 28 D3
KIRKTON OF MONIKIE 20 F1
KIRKTON OF NEVAY 17 E6
Kirkton Pk PH10 88 E5
Kirkton Pl
  3 Arbroath DD11 89 B7
  Cowdenbeath KY4 147 B5
  Dundee DD3 91 E1
Kirkton Rd
  Arbroath DD11 89 C7
  Blairgowrie PH10 88 E6
  Burntisland KY3 165 E1
  Dundee DD3 91 D1
  Kirkton PH12 17 B4
  Kirriemuir DD8 8 B5
  Newtyle PH12 17 C4
Kirkton Rd E DD3 91 E1
Kirkton Terr DD7 100 C3
Kirktoun Gdns
  Ballingry KY5 127 F8
  Tillicoultry FK13 119 C6
Kirktoun Pk KY5 127 E8
Kirktoun St KY5 127 F8
Kirkway FK2 154 D4
Kirk Wlk DD7 100 E4
Kirkwood Cres KY12 160 B2
Kirk Wynd
  20 Anstruther Easter KY10 83 C6
  2 Anstruther KY10 83 D7
  Blairgowrie PH10 88 C6
  Clackmannan FK10 139 A5
  2 Crail KY10 69 B2
  Cupar KY15 105 C4
  4 Dunning PH2 46 F1
  1 Forfar DD8 9 C1
  Glenrothes KY7 113 F8
  Kirkcaldy KY1 151 C4
  Kirriemuir DD8 86 D4
  2 Leven KY9 82 A5
  Perth PH2 49 F3
  Stirling FK7 135 B4
KIRRIEMUIR 86 E4
Kirriemuir Aviation Mus* DD8 86 D4
Kirriemuir Gateway to the Glens Mus* DD8 86 D4
Kirriemuir Rd DD8 87 B7
Kirsty Semple Way DD2 92 D4
Kirton Pk 6 DD8 87 E5
Kishorn Ct KY7 110 F4
Knapdale Pl DD4 95 D8
KNAPP 27 E2
Knapphill KY11 173 F7
Knockhill Cl KY5 148 B7
Knockhill View KY12 143 B5
Knockhouse Farm Cotts KY12 160 B4
Knockhouse Gdns KY12 160 B2
Knockhouse Rd KY12 160 B2
Knockhouse Terr KY12 160 B2
Knock Rd PH7 101 D5
Knowehead DD8 86 C4
Knowehead Cres DD8 86 C4
Knowehead Rd KY12 160 A2
Knowehead Terr PH2 103 E8
Knowelea Pl PH2 102 F2
Knowelea Terr PH2 102 F2
Knowes Loan DD7 31 F5
Knowe The
  Alloa FK10 118 C2
  Dalgety Bay KY11 175 C3
Knowfaulds Rd FK10 117 B3
Knox Cl PH12 17 C4
Knox Gdns KY15 105 D3
Kyle Cres KY11 162 C1
Kyle Gdns 3 KY16 54 E3
Kyles The KY1 151 E6

L

Laburn St DD3 179 A3
Laburnum Dr KY1 151 C8
Laburnum Gr
  Burntisland KY3 165 F2
  Stirling FK8 134 F5
Laburnum Rd
  Dunfermline KY11 161 C1
  Leven KY8 109 A5
Lade Braes
  Dalgety Bay KY11 175 B3
  St Andrews KY16 106 C5
Lade Gn KY11 175 B3
Lade Mill FK7 135 C1
Ladeside
  Kinross KY13 108 A5
  3 Perth PH2 61 B5

Ladeside Bsns Ctr
PH1 .... 102 F5
Ladeside Ct PH1 .... 102 E6
Ladeside Rd DD9 .... 84 C2
Lade Wlk PH1 .... 102 F5
Lady Anne Ct KY4 .... 162 E6
Lady Ann Gr FK13 .... 119 C7
LADYBANK 64 B4
Ladybank Golf Course
KY15 .... 64 A6
Ladybank Pl 7 DD5 .... 96 C5
Ladybank Prim Sch
KY15 .... 64 A4
Ladybank Rd KY14 .... 63 A5
Ladybank Sta KY15 .... 64 A4
Ladybridge St DD11 .... 89 D3
Ladyburn Pl KY3 .... 167 A3
Lady Campbell's Wlk
KY12 .... 161 A4
Lady Helen Cotts KY5 .... 149 B8
Lady Helen St KY1 .... 151 B2
Ladyloan DD11 .... 89 C2
Ladyloan Prim Sch
DD11 .... 89 C3
Lady Macbeth Wlk PH2 .... 25 D4
Lady Nairn Ave KY1 .... 151 F6
Lady Nairne Dr PH1 .... 102 B5
Lady Nairne Rd KY12 .... 160 E6
Lady Nina Cotts KY7 .... 113 F4
Lady Nina Sq KY7 .... 79 A3
Ladysmill Ct KY12 .... 161 A1
Ladysneuk Rd FK9 .... 115 D2
Ladywalk 4 KY10 .... 83 C6
Ladywell Ave DD1 .... 179 C3
Ladywell Dr FK10 .... 117 B3
Ladywell Gr FK10 .... 139 A4
Ladywell Pk PH3 .... 104 C6
Ladywell Pl FK10 .... 117 B3
Ladywood FK10 .... 139 C4
Lady Wynd
Cupar KY15 .... 105 C5
4 Leven KY8 .... 109 A1
8 Pittenweem KY10 .... 83 A5
7 St Andrews KY16 .... 68 F7
Lagavulin Pl 3 PH1 .... 102 D8
LAGGAN 33 A1
Laggan Cres KY7 .... 111 A3
Laggan Ct PH2 .... 103 E8
Laggan Rd PH7 .... 101 A5
Laidon Terr DD3 .... 93 D8
Laighill Ct FK15 .... 107 D6
Laighill Pl FK15 .... 107 D6
Laing Cres 15 PH13 .... 16 A3
Laing Mus* KY14 .... 50 D5
Laing Pl DD4 .... 179 C4
Laing St DD3 .... 179 C4
Laird Ave KY8 .... 109 C4
Laird's Dr FK10 .... 139 B3
Laird St
Dundee DD3 .... 91 C3
2 Monifieth DD5 .... 97 B6
Lakeside Rd KY2 .... 150 F4
Lamberkine Dr PH1 .... 102 A2
Lambert Dr KY12 .... 161 D4
Lamberton Ave FK7 .... 135 C3
Lamberton Pl KY16 .... 106 C3
Lambert Terr FK10 .... 138 C7
Lambourn PH2 .... 25 D4
Lamb's La DD4 .... 179 C3
Lamb Terr DD11 .... 89 C6
Lamb Way 5 DD10 .... 85 D7
Lamley Terr DD11 .... 89 E5
LAMMERLAWS 177 F8
Lammerlaws Rd KY3 .... 177 F8
Lammermoor Ct KY6 .... 112 E5
Lammermuir Gdns
PH1 .... 102 A4
Lammermuir Pl KY2 .... 150 F5
LAMMERTON 95 F8
Lammerton Terr DD4 .... 94 C5
Lamond Dr KY16 .... 106 D4
Lamondfauld La 6
DD10 .... 6 C8
Lamondfauld Rd DD10 .... 6 C8
Lamont Cres FK7 .... 136 D5
Lamont Terr 3 KY10 .... 69 A2
Landale Gdns
Burntisland KY3 .... 165 E2
Cupar KY15 .... 105 E5
Landale Pl KY3 .... 165 E2
Landale St KY5 .... 148 B8
Landel St KY7 .... 113 F7
Landrick Ave 3 FK15 .... 107 E7
Landrick Terr 2 FK15 .... 107 E7
Lane The DD2 .... 90 C3
Langholm Cres KY6 .... 112 D7
Langholm Gdns DD5 .... 95 E4
Langhouse Gn 4 KY10 .... 69 B3
Langlands Prim Sch
Forfar DD8 .... 87 C4
St Andrews KY16 .... 106 E4
Langlands Rd
Forfar DD8 .... 87 C3
St Andrews KY16 .... 106 E5
Langland's St 5 DD4 .... 94 C3
Langlea Pl 3 DD5 .... 96 C5
Langley Ave DD10 .... 85 D6
Langley Dr PH2 .... 103 E4
Langley Pl PH2 .... 103 E4
Langour FK13 .... 119 B5
Langshaw Rd 1 DD2 .... 93 A7
Langside Ave KY8 .... 79 E5
Langside Cres KY8 .... 79 E5
Langside Dr KY8 .... 79 E5
Langside Pl PH1 .... 102 B6
Langside Rd
Leven KY8 .... 79 E6
Perth PH1 .... 102 C6
Lansbury St KY1 .... 151 E7
Lansdowne Cres FK10 .... 155 E4
Lansdowne Ct DD2 .... 93 B7
Lansdowne Gdns DD2 .... 93 A7
Lansdowne Pl DD2 .... 93 B7
Lansdowne Sq DD2 .... 93 B7
Lapwing Dr KY11 .... 174 B7
Larach Ct KY2 .... 150 C8
Larch Ave
Blairgowrie PH10 .... 88 C3
Glenrothes KY7 .... 110 F1
Larch Ct DD2 .... 92 C7
Larches The 5 DD4 .... 95 A8
Larchfield KY8 .... 109 A5
Larchfield Gdns 1
DD3 .... 91 A2
Larch Gr KY11 .... 173 D8
Larch Pl PH1 .... 102 B3
Larch St DD1 .... 93 E3
Largo Dr KY9 .... 82 B5
Largo Pl DD5 .... 96 C5
Largo Rd
Leven KY8 .... 109 E8
Lower Largo KY8 .... 80 F5
St Andrews KY16 .... 106 C4
Largo St DD11 .... 89 F6
LARGOWARD 66 F2
Largoward Prim Sch
KY9 .... 66 F2
Latchburn Wynd 1
PH2 .... 46 F1
Latch Gdns DD9 .... 84 B4
Latch Rd DD9 .... 84 B4
Latch The KY12 .... 159 C1
Lathallan Rise KY9 .... 82 B5
LATHONES 66 F3
Lathro Ct KY13 .... 108 C5
Lathro La KY13 .... 108 B5
Lathro Pk KY13 .... 108 B5
Lauder Coll KY11 .... 162 A5
Lauder Cres PH1 .... 102 A3
Lauder Ct KY6 .... 112 D7
Lauderdale Ave DD3 .... 91 C2
Lauderdale Pl 1 DD3 .... 91 D2
Lauder Rd
5 Arbroath DD11 .... 89 B7
Kirkcaldy KY2 .... 151 C6
Lauder St KY12 .... 161 C6
Launcherhead Rd KY5 .... 128 A1
Laurel Ave
Crieff PH7 .... 101 E4
Kelty KY4 .... 126 C2
9 Leven KY8 .... 79 F3
Laurel Bank
Dundee DD3 .... 179 A3
Forfar DD8 .... 87 C4
Laurel Bank Dr KY7 .... 113 F8
Laurel Cres KY2 .... 151 B7
Laurel Gdns
Glenrothes KY7 .... 113 D5
Gowkhall KY12 .... 159 F6
Laurelhill Bsns Pk
FK7 .... 134 F6
Laurelhill Gdns FK8 .... 134 F5
Laurelhill Pl FK8 .... 135 A5
Laurel Rd KY11 .... 173 C2
Laurels The
Tullibody FK10 .... 117 B1
9 Whitfield DD4 .... 95 A8
Laurencecroft Rd FK8 .... 115 B2
Laurence Pk KY5 .... 77 F1
Laurieston Pk KY7 .... 111 C3
Lauriston Dr KY12 .... 161 D5
Lavender St DD4 .... 95 A3
Laverock Ave KY7 .... 113 C6
Laverock Path KY7 .... 113 C6
Laverock Terr KY7 .... 113 C6
Law Cres DD3 .... 93 D5
Lawder Pl 5 FK15 .... 107 E7
Lawers Dr DD5 .... 96 D6
Lawers Pl PH1 .... 102 D4
Lawers Rd DD5 .... 96 E6
Lawgrove Pl PH1 .... 37 B5
Lawhead Prim Sch
KY16 .... 106 A4
Lawhead Rd E KY16 .... 106 A5
Lawhead Rd W KY16 .... 106 A5
Law Hill Rd 8 FK14 .... 73 C1
Lawmill Gdns KY16 .... 106 A4
LAW OF BRIGTON 7 E3
Law Rd
Dundee DD3 .... 179 A4
Dunfermline KY11 .... 161 F4
Lawrence Ct KY8 .... 133 F8
Lawrence Dr KY8 .... 109 C7
Lawrence St
Broughty Ferry DD5 .... 95 F2
4 Dundee DD1 .... 93 E4
Kelty KY4 .... 126 E1
10 Leven KY8 .... 79 F1
Lawrie Terr KY8 .... 109 D7
Lawside Ave DD3 .... 93 D5
Lawside RC Acad DD3 .... 91 C1
Lawside Rd DD3 .... 93 D5
Lawside Terr DD3 .... 93 D5
Lawson Gdns KY1 .... 151 E8
Lawson La KY8 .... 133 F8
Lawson Pl DD3 .... 179 A4
Lawson St KY1 .... 151 E8
Laws Pl 2 DD5 .... 97 A6
Law St DD3 .... 93 E5
Lawswell FK10 .... 118 E3
Lawton Rd DD3 .... 93 E6
Lawton Terr DD3 .... 93 E6
Law View Gdns KY8 .... 79 F6
Laxford Cres KY11 .... 175 A3
Laxford La DD5 .... 96 A4
Laxford Rd KY6 .... 112 F6
Leach Cl 1 DD11 .... 22 E5
Leadburn Ave KY12 .... 161 A7
Leadenflower Ct PH7 .... 101 D3
Leadenflower Pl PH7 .... 101 D4
Leadenflower Rd PH7 .... 101 D3
Leadenflower St 6
PH7 .... 101 D4
Leadside Cres KY12 .... 161 A7
Leargan 4 KY8 .... 109 D8
Learmonth Pl KY16 .... 106 B4
Lebanon Terr 1 KY15 .... 105 C5
Leckiebank Rd KY14 .... 62 F6
LEDCAMEROCH 107 F6
Ledcameroch Gdns
FK15 .... 107 E6
Leden Urquhart Rd
KY14 .... 61 F5
Ledi Ave FK10 .... 117 B2
Ledi View FK9 .... 115 B3
Ledmore Terr DD2 .... 92 C4
Lee Mar DD10 .... 6 B6
Leemount La DD5 .... 95 E4
LEETOWN 50 B8
Leewood Pk FK15 .... 107 E4
Leewood Rd FK15 .... 107 E4
Legion Ct KY2 .... 151 A5
Leighton Ave FK15 .... 107 F6
Leighton Ct FK15 .... 107 F5
Leighton's Sq 39 PH11 .... 7 A3
Leighton St KY12 .... 158 B2
Leitfie Links Strathmore
Golf Course PH11 .... 16 C8
Leitfie Terr PH11 .... 7 A2
Leith Ave KY3 .... 165 F2
Leith Gdns DD2 .... 92 E5
Leith Wlk DD2 .... 92 D5
Lemon Terr KY8 .... 109 E7
Leng St DD3 .... 179 A4
Lennox Ave FK7 .... 135 A4
Lennox Ct KY6 .... 110 F1
Lennox Gdns DD2 .... 92 F4
Lennox Way 9 KY16 .... 54 B7
Lentlands Rd DD8 .... 87 C3
Leny Pl KY12 .... 161 B5
Leny Rd PH1 .... 102 B5
Leonard Gdns KY16 .... 106 A3
Leonard Pl 9 PH2 .... 103 A3
Leonard St
Arbroath DD11 .... 89 D4
Perth PH2 .... 103 A3
LESLIE 112 B7
Leslie Ct PH1 .... 102 E6
Leslie Golf Club KY6 .... 110 B1
Leslie Mains KY6 .... 110 E1
Leslie Prim Sch KY6 .... 112 A7
Leslie Rd
Glenrothes KY7 .... 112 E8
Kinross KY13 .... 77 A4
Rosyth KY11 .... 173 F5
Leslie St
6 Blairgowrie PH10 .... 88 C5
Kirkcaldy KY1 .... 167 B8
Lesslie's Bldgs KY3 .... 165 E1
Lestrange Ave FK12 .... 118 B7
LETHAM
Cupar 51 E1
Forfar 11 E3
Perth 102 D5
Letham Ave KY8 .... 109 E7
Letham Com Leisure Ctr
PH1 .... 102 C5
Letham Ct 1 KY8 .... 109 E7
Letham Gait KY11 .... 174 F3
Letham Glen* KY8 .... 109 E8
Letham Grange Golf
Course DD11 .... 22 E7
Letham Hill Ave KY11 .... 174 E4
Letham Pl 7 KY16 .... 54 E2
Letham Prim Sch
Cupar KY15 .... 51 E1
Letham DD8 .... 11 F3
Perth PH1 .... 102 C5
Letham Rd PH1 .... 102 D5
Letham Rise KY11 .... 174 F3
Letham Terr KY8 .... 109 E7
Letham Terrs FK2 .... 154 C1
Letham Way KY11 .... 174 F3
Lethen View FK10 .... 117 C3
Lethnot Gdns
4 Broughty Ferry DD5 .... 96 D3
Carnoustie DD7 .... 100 C4
Forfar DD8 .... 87 E6
Lethnot Gn DD7 .... 100 C4
Lethnot Pl DD7 .... 100 C4
Lethnot Rd DD11 .... 89 F6
Lethnot St DD5 .... 96 D3
LEUCHARS 54 A8
Leuchars Airfield KY16 .... 54 C7
Leuchars Prim Sch
KY16 .... 54 B8
Leuchars Sta KY16 .... 54 A7
Leuchatsbeath Dr KY4 .... 147 B6
LEVEN 109 E6
Leven Ct FK10 .... 138 C5
Leven Pl
Glenrothes KY7 .... 113 E6
2 Kinross KY13 .... 108 B3
Leven Rd
Leven KY8 .... 79 E3
8 Leven KY8 .... 79 F5
Lower Largo KY8 .... 80 E5
Leven Sh Ctr KY8 .... 109 C8
Leven St DD5 .... 96 B4
Leven Thistle Golf Course
KY8 .... 109 F7
Leven Vale KY8 .... 109 D6
Leven Valley Gdns
KY7 .... 113 E8
Lewis Ct FK10 .... 138 B5
Lewis Pl PH1 .... 102 F7
Lewis Terr 6 DD4 .... 94 C8
Leyshade Ct DD4 .... 94 E5
LEYSMILL 13 A2
Leys Park Rd KY12 .... 161 B4
Liberton Dr KY6 .... 110 E1
Liberton Rd 9 KY2 .... 130 F1
Liberty KY9 .... 82 A3
Lickley Ct PH1 .... 103 A4
Lickley St PH1 .... 103 A4
Liddel Rd DD2 .... 92 F4
Liddles Cl 6 DD9 .... 84 C3
LIFF 28 D4
Liff Cres DD2 .... 92 F7
Liff Pk DD2 .... 28 D4
Liff Pl 2 DD2 .... 92 F7
Liff Prim Sch DD2 .... 28 D4
Liff Rd 6 DD2 .... 93 B6
Liff Terr DD2 .... 92 F7
Liggar's Pl KY12 .... 160 F1
Lilac Bank KY8 .... 109 A5
Lilac Cres KY1 .... 151 C8
Lilac Gr KY11 .... 173 D8
Lilly's La KY11 .... 161 B1
Lilybank 11 DD8 .... 86 D5
Lilybank Cres DD8 .... 87 F5
Lilybank Ct FK10 .... 118 D1
Lilybank Rd
Dundee DD4 .... 94 C2
Forfar DD8 .... 87 F5
Lilybank St 11 DD11 .... 12 F4
Lilybank Terr 1 DD4 .... 94 C2
Lily Wynd DD8 .... 87 F5
Lime Gr
Ballumbie DD5 .... 30 C5
Dunfermline KY11 .... 161 E1
5 Leven KY8 .... 79 F3
Limegrove 3 PH2 .... 37 F5
LIMEKILNS 172 E3
Limekilns Prim Sch
KY11 .... 172 E3
Limekilns Rd KY12 .... 160 F1
Limekilns The KY6 .... 110 C2
Limelands Ave KY16 .... 67 F4
Limepark Cres KY4 .... 126 F2
Lime St DD2 .... 93 C3
Limpet Ness KY11 .... 173 D3
Lina St KY2 .... 151 B5
Linburn Gr KY11 .... 161 F4
Linburn Pl KY11 .... 161 F3
Linburn Rd KY11 .... 161 F3
Linden Ave
Newport-on-Tay DD6 .... 98 E4
Stirling FK7 .... 135 C6
Linden Pk KY13 .... 108 D8
Linden Pk Rd KY13 .... 108 D8
Linden Pk Terr KY13 .... 108 D7
LINDORES 51 A3
Lindores Dr KY2 .... 150 E8
Lindores Pl 8 DD5 .... 96 C5
Lindsay Berwick Pl
KY10 .... 83 C7
Lindsay Brae FK15 .... 107 B3
Lindsay Ct 5 KY4 .... 126 E1
Lindsay Dr FK9 .... 115 B4
Lindsay Gdns KY16 .... 106 B4
Lindsay Pl
Glenrothes KY7 .... 113 A5
Lochgelly KY5 .... 148 A8
Perth PH1 .... 103 A7
Lindsay St
Arbroath DD11 .... 89 C4
Dundee DD5 .... 96 A3
Kirriemuir DD8 .... 86 C3
Lindsay's Wynd KY12 .... 158 F6
Linefield Rd DD7 .... 100 E4
Linen Mill Ct 1 KY15 .... 63 E1
Linfield St DD4 .... 95 A5
Lingard St DD7 .... 100 B3
Lingay Ct PH1 .... 102 F8
Lininghills La DD8 .... 87 C4
Link Rd
Crombie KY12 .... 171 D6
Dalgety Bay KY11 .... 174 F3
Oakley KY12 .... 158 F7
Links Ave
Carnoustie DD7 .... 100 C2
Montrose DD10 .... 85 E4
Links Cres 4 DD6 .... 43 C6
Links Ct 5 DD6 .... 43 C6
Links Dr KY12 .... 160 A2
Linksfield DD6 .... 99 F5
Linksfield St KY8 .... 109 E6
Links Par 1 DD7 .... 100 D2
Links Pk (Montrose FC)
DD10 .... 85 E4
Links Pl
Burntisland KY3 .... 177 E8
4 Earlsferry/Elie KY9 .... 82 A3
Monifieth DD5 .... 97 C7
Links Rd
Earlsferry/Elie KY9 .... 82 A2
Leven KY8 .... 109 F6
Lower Largo KY8 .... 80 E5
3 Tayport DD6 .... 43 C6
Links Rd N DD6 .... 43 C7
Links St KY1 .... 151 B2
Links The KY16 .... 106 C7
LINKTOWN 151 B2
Linlathen DD4 .... 94 D5
Linlithgow Pl 3 DD2 .... 41 B8
Linnet Way KY11 .... 162 A2
Linn Mill FK10 .... 139 D6
Linn Pl
Airth FK2 .... 154 E3
Kirkcaldy KY2 .... 131 A2
Linn Rd PH1 .... 24 F4
Linnwood Dr KY8 .... 109 C8
Linnwood Gdns KY8 .... 109 C8
Linsay Macdonald Ct
KY12 .... 161 D3
Lintibert Rd PH5 .... 44 C3
Lintibert Terr PH5 .... 44 C3
Lintie Croft DD8 .... 87 C3
Linties Nest KY3 .... 166 F2
Linton Ct
Glenrothes KY6 .... 112 C7
Kinghorn KY3 .... 167 A4
Linton La KY2 .... 150 E6
Linton Pl KY11 .... 173 E3
Linton Rd
Arbroath DD11 .... 89 E5
Dundee DD2 .... 92 F7
Linton Terr PH1 .... 102 C4
Lintrathen Ct DD3 .... 93 E7
Lintrathen Gdns DD3 .... 93 E7
Lintrathen St DD3 .... 93 E7
Linum Gr KY1 .... 151 C7
Linwell Ct KY3 .... 166 B1
Lipney FK11 .... 117 A6
Liquorstane Rd 16
KY15 .... 63 B2
Lisden Gdns DD8 .... 86 E5
Lismore Ave KY2 .... 150 F8
Lismore Ct
Glenrothes KY7 .... 111 A1
Perth PH1 .... 102 E8
Lismore Pl KY2 .... 150 F7
Lismore St 1 DD3 .... 91 F2
Lismore Terr DD4 .... 94 C7
Lister Ct
Bridge of A FK9 .... 115 A6
Dundee DD2 .... 92 E3
Lister Pl
7 Cupar KY15 .... 64 D4
Dundee DD2 .... 92 E3
Littleblair Dr 2 PH10 .... 88 E2
Little Cairnie DD11 .... 89 A6
Little Carron Gdns 2
KY16 .... 54 E2
Little Causeway DD8 .... 87 D5
Little Craigs View
KY3 .... 165 D1
Little Foothorn KY12 .... 171 E6
Little Nursery DD10 .... 85 C5
Little Sales Ave KY11 .... 174 F3
Little Sandhaven
KY12 .... 169 D8
Little Theatre The
DD1 .... 179 B3
Littleton Gdns DD2 .... 90 C3
Littlewood Gdns
1 Blairgowrie PH10 .... 88 E2
Borrowfield DD10 .... 85 B5
Livesay Rd KY11 .... 173 D1
Livilands Ct FK8 .... 135 B5
Livilands Gate FK8 .... 135 B5
Livilands La FK8 .... 135 B5
Livingstone Cres
KY16 .... 106 D5
Livingstone Dr KY3 .... 165 F2
Livingstone Pl
Dundee DD3 .... 91 C1
1 St Andrews KY16 .... 106 D5
Livingstone St KY14 .... 50 D5
Livingstone Terr DD3 .... 91 D1
Livingstone Way FK10 .... 139 A5
Livingston La KY3 .... 176 C7
Loan Brae PH2 .... 39 E2
Loan Dykes DD10 .... 6 D7
Loanfoot Pk 1 PH3 .... 46 B2
LOANHEAD 135 E6
Loanhead Ave KY5 .... 128 A6
Loanhead Pl KY2 .... 151 A5
Loanhead Rd KY12 .... 143 E1
Loan The
28 Anstruther Wester
KY10 .... 83 C6
South Queensferry
EH30 .... 178 B1
Lochaber KY11 .... 172 B4
Lochaber Ct KY6 .... 110 E1
Lochalsh St DD5 .... 96 B4
Lochay Pl DD2 .... 92 D4
Lochbank Gdns DD8 .... 87 B6
Lochbank Rd DD8 .... 87 B6
Lochbrae FK10 .... 118 D2
Lochcraig Ct KY5 .... 127 F4
LOCHEE 93 A6
Lochee Prim Sch DD2 .... 93 A5
Lochee Rd DD1 .... 179 A3
Locheil Ct KY7 .... 111 B2
Locheil Gdns KY7 .... 111 B2
LOCHELBANK 61 A7
Lochend Rd DD7 .... 100 B3
LOCHGELLY
148 C7
Lochgelly 128 B1
Lochgelly High Sch
KY5 .... 128 A2
Lochgelly Ind Est KY5 .... 128 C1
Lochgelly Ind Pk KY5 .... 148 D7
Lochgelly North Sch
KY5 .... 148 B8
Lochgelly Rd KY4 .... 147 D5
Lochgelly South Prim Sch
KY5 .... 148 B7
Lochgelly Sta KY5 .... 128 B1
Lochgelly West Prim Sch
KY5 .... 148 A7
Lochhead Cres KY1 .... 132 E4

Lochhead Ct KY12 161 A6
Lochhead Row KY1 132 E4
Lochiebank Cres 4 KY14 62 F6
Lochiebank Pl 7 KY14 62 F6
Lochie Brae PH2 103 C4
Lochiel Pl KY8 109 A4
Lochies Rd
Burntisland KY3 166 A1
Clackmannan FK10 139 A4
Lochies Sch FK10 118 F1
Lochinblair Gdns PH10 88 B4
Lochinvar Rd KY11 173 C1
Lochinver Cres DD2 92 C5
LOCHLANDS 89 B4
Lochlands Dr DD11 89 B4
Lochlands Gdns DD11 89 B4
Lochlands Pk DD11 89 B4
Lochlands St DD11 89 C4
Lochlea Gr KY2 151 A7
Lochlea Terr KY2 151 A7
Lochlee Terr DD4 94 F3
Lochleven Castle (remains of)* KY13 76 B4
Lochleven Ct
Kinross KY13 76 E7
Lochore KY5 128 A7
Loch Leven Gdns 4 KY5 127 F7
Loch Leven Leisure Ctr KY13 108 C5
Loch Leven National Nature Reserve* KY13 76 C4
Loch Leven Pl KY5 127 F7
Lochleven Rd KY5 128 A7
Loch Leven Terr
8 Ballingry KY5 127 F6
Kelty KY4 126 D1
5 Lochore KY5 127 F6
Lochmill DD8 86 B5
Lochnagar Ct KY6 110 E3
Loch of Liff Rd DD2 28 D4
LOCHORE 127 F6
Lochore Mdws Ctry Pk* KY4 127 D5
Loch Pl EH30 178 B1
Loch Rd
Saline KY12 142 D6
South Queensferry EH30 178 B1
Lochside DD11 22 D2
Lochside Cres DD10 85 C6
Lochside Gdns DD6 43 C7
Lochside Leisure Ctr DD8 87 C5
Lochside Prim Sch DD10 85 C5
Lochside Rd DD8 87 C6
Loch St KY12 161 C7
LOCHTY 36 E4
Lochty Ave KY5 77 F1
Lochty Pk PH1 36 E4
Lochty Rd KY5 77 F1
Lochty St DD7 100 D3
Loch Venachar Gdns KY6 112 E5
Lochview Terr DD8 87 B4
Lochwood Pk KY12 146 B1
Lochy St PH10 88 B4
Lochy Terr PH10 88 B5
Lodge Rise KY7 110 F1
Lodge St PH7 101 C4
Lodge Wlk 7 KY9 82 B3
Loftus Pl 4 DD3 91 D2
Loftus Rd DD3 91 D3
Loftus St 9 DD3 91 D2
Loganlee Terr DD2 93 C4
Logan Rd KY12 170 F8
Logan The DD2 28 D4
LOGIE
Cupar 53 C7
Kirriemuir 86 E1
Logiealmond Prim Sch PH1 35 D8
Logie Ave DD2 93 C3
Logie Cres PH1 102 C5
Logie Gdns DD2 93 D3
Logie La
Bridge of A FK9 115 C7
Stirling FK9 115 D4
Logie Pl KY12 160 D5
Logie Rd FK9 115 D4
Logie's La 2 KY16 106 D6
Logie St
Dundee DD2 93 C5
Leven KY8 109 C4
Lomond Bank 6 PH2 61 B5
Lomond Cres
Cupar KY15 63 B2
Dunfermline KY11 161 F2
Lochgelly KY5 128 B1
Stirling FK9 115 B4
Lomond Ct
Alloa FK10 138 C5
8 Cupar KY14 63 A6
Lomond Dr
Bannockburn FK7 135 E1
Carnoustie DD7 100 E3
Lomond Gdns
Kirkcaldy KY2 150 F5
Leven KY8 109 A4
Lomond Mews 3 KY13 108 C2
Lomond Pl
5 Balmutto KY16 53 E8
Dundee DD4 94 D6
Kinross KY13 108 B4
Lomond Rd 7 KY15 63 E1
Lomond St FK10 117 E1
Lomond View KY6 112 A8
Longannet Cotts FK10 156 B1
Longannet Rdbt FK10 156 A2
Longbraes Gdns KY2 150 D6
Long Causeway PH1 102 F4
Long Craigs Terr KY3 167 A3
Long Craig Wlk KY1 167 B8
Longcroft Rd 6 DD4 94 F5
LONGFORGAN 28 B1
Longforgan Prim Sch DD2 40 F8
Longhaugh Prim Sch DD4 94 F7
Longhaugh Rd DD4 94 F7
Longhaugh Terr DD4 94 F7
Longhill Gdns KY11 175 B3
Long La
Broughty Ferry DD5 96 B2
Dundee DD5 95 F2
Long Row
Carnoustie DD7 100 F3
Halbeath KY12 162 A7
Menstrie FK11 117 A7
Longtown Pl 2 DD4 94 F5
Longtown Rd DD4 95 A5
Longtown St DD4 95 A5
Longtown Terr 3 DD4 94 F5
Long Wynd DD1 179 A2
Lonsdale Cres KY3 165 E1
Lookaboutye Brae FK10 139 A3
Loom Rd KY2 151 B6
Loon's Rd DD3 93 C5
Loraine Rd DD4 94 D4
Lordburn DD11 89 D4
Lordburn Pl DD8 87 E5
Lord Gambier Wharf KY1 151 C5
Lorimer Gdns KY12 161 D6
Lorimer St DD3 93 E6
Lorne Ave DD5 97 B7
Lorne Cres DD5 97 B6
Lorne Ct KY6 112 E5
Lorne Ho KY12 161 A4
Lorne La 14 FK14 73 C1
Lorne St
Dundee DD2 93 A6
Kirkcaldy KY1 151 E7
3 Ladybank KY15 64 A5
Monifieth DD5 97 B6
Lorne Terr 4 KY15 64 A4
Lorn Pl KY11 162 C1
Lornshill Acad FK10 117 E2
Lornshill Cres FK10 137 F8
Lorraine Dr KY15 105 B3
Losset Pk 37 PH11 7 A3
Losset Rd PH11 7 B3
Losshill FK11 117 A6
Lossie Pl DD2 92 D5
Lossley Pk PH2 61 B4
Lothian Cres
Dundee DD4 94 F7
Stirling FK9 115 C3
Lothian Ct
Glenrothes KY6 112 D8
Inverkeithing KY11 174 D2
Lothian St KY3 177 E8
Lothians View KY11 174 A2
Lothian Terr KY2 151 A7
Loughborough Rd KY1 151 F7
Loughrigg KY11 174 A7
Louise St KY11 161 D2
LOUR 10 F1
Lour Rd DD8 87 E3
Lousen Pk 3 DD7 100 D2
Lovat Rd KY7 113 D3
Lovers La
Cupar KY15 105 C4
New Scone PH2 37 F5
Lovers Loan
Alva FK12 118 B7
Dollar FK14 120 E8
Dunfermline KY12 160 F2
Lovers' Loan FK14 120 F8
Lovers Wlk FK8 115 B1
Low Causeway
Culross KY12 157 E1
Torryburn KY12 158 E1
Low Causewayside
Culross KY12 169 D8
Newmills KY12 158 C1
Lowe Pl DD11 89 B6
LOWER AUCHINLAY 107 B8
Lower Balmain St 4 DD10 85 C2
Lower Bank St 13 PH11 7 A3
Lower Bridge St FK8 115 A1
Lower Castlehill FK8 115 A1
Lower Craigo St 1 DD10 85 C2
Lower Glebe KY3 176 C8
Lower Granco St 5 PH2 46 F1
Lowerhall St DD10 85 C4
LOWER LARGO 80 F6
LOWER MAINS 120 D7
Lower Methil Heritage Ctr* KY8 109 C4
Lower Mill St
1 Blairgowrie PH10 88 D5
Tillicoultry FK13 119 A6
Lower Pleasance DD1 93 E4
Lowfield Cres PH1 37 C8
Lownie Rd
Carnoustie DD7 100 E3
Lownie Rd *continued*
Forfar DD8 10 F3
Low Rd
Auchtermuchty KY14 62 F6
Kirriemuir DD8 86 A2
Perth PH2 102 E2
Thornton KY1 131 E7
Lowry Pl KY11 173 F4
Lowson Ave
Carnoustie DD7 100 E3
Forfar DD8 87 C4
Lowson Cotts DD8 87 F5
Lowson Terr DD8 87 C4
Low St PH1 103 A5
LOW TORRY 158 D1
LOW VALLEYFIELD 158 A1
Loyal Rd PH11 7 A3
Loyne Ct KY7 110 F3
Lubbock Pk Gdns DD9 84 B4
LUCKLAWHILL 53 E8
Lucklawhill KY16 42 E1
Lucklaw Rd 4 KY16 53 E7
LUCKNOW 97 F7
Ludgate FK10 138 A6
Luke Pl DD5 96 A4
Lulach Ct KY11 174 A8
Lulworth Ct DD4 95 B8
Lumgig Loan 18 KY8 79 F5
LUMPHINNANS 147 E6
Lumphinnans Prim & Com Sch KY4 147 D5
Lumphinnans Rd KY5 148 A7
Lumsdaine Dr KY11 175 A1
Lumsden Cres
Almondbank PH1 36 E5
5 St Andrews KY16 54 E3
Lumsden Pk KY15 105 D3
Lumsden Rd 10 KY7 112 F6
LUNAN 14 C6
Lunan Ave
Arbroath DD11 14 A4
Montrose DD10 85 C7
Lunan St DD11 12 F5
Lunan Terr DD4 94 F3
Luna Pl DD2 92 B4
Lunardi Pl KY15 105 E4
LUNCARTY 37 C8
Luncarty Prim Sch PH1 37 C8
LUNDIE 27 E7
Lundie Ave DD2 93 C7
Lundie Pl DD2 93 C7
Lundies Ct PH3 104 E6
Lundies Wlk PH3 104 E6
Lundin Cres
Glenrothes KY7 113 A5
2 Tayport DD6 43 C6
Lundin Golf Club KY8 80 E5
LUNDIN LINKS 80 E5
Lundin Mill Prim Sch KY8 80 F6
Lundin Pl 3 KY7 113 A6
Lundin Rd KY12 160 A4
Lundin Sq KY8 80 F5
Lundin View KY8 80 C5
Luther Pl DD2 92 D5
LUTHRIE 52 B6
Lyall Pl 13 KY14 50 D5
Lychgate Rd FK10 117 B2
Lyle Ave KY7 113 B6
Lyle Cres KY7 113 B6
Lynburn Prim Sch KY11 161 F2
Lynch Sports Ctr DD2 92 D5
Lyndhurst Ave DD2 93 B7
Lyndhurst Pl DD2 93 B7
Lyndhurst Terr DD2 93 B7
Lyndoch Rd PH1 36 A5
Lyndsay Ct 5 KY15 105 C5
Lynebank (Psychiatric) Hospl KY11 162 A5
Lyneburn Cres KY11 162 B5
Lynedoch Rd PH2 37 F5
Lyne Gr KY12 160 C2
Lyning Hills DD8 87 C4
Lynnewood Pl 4 DD4 94 C4
Lyon Cres FK9 115 A6
Lyon Sq KY7 113 A7
Lyon St DD4 179 C4
Lytton St DD2 93 D2

M

MacAdam Pl DD2 93 C8
MacAllister Ct FK7 135 D1
MacAlpine Ct FK10 117 D3
MacAlpine Prim Sch DD3 91 C2
MacAlpine Rd DD3 91 C3
MacAlpine Sq DD3 91 C1
MacAulay St DD3 179 A4
McBain Pl KY13 108 B3
Macbeth Rd KY11 161 E3
McCallum Ct PH1 102 F6
McClelland Cres KY11 161 B1
McCormack Pl PH1 102 C7
McCulloch Dr DD8 10 F5
MacDiarmid Dr 1 DD10 6 C8
McDiarmid Pk (St Johnstone FC) PH1 102 B7
MacDonald Ave 2 KY13 108 C3
MacDonald Cres 8 PH10 88 D5
McDonald Ct
Cairneyhill KY12 159 D1
Perth PH1 102 E6
MacDonald Dr FK7 135 A4
MacDonald Pk PH2 38 D8
MacDonald Pl KY3 166 A2
McDonald Rd DD2 28 B1
MacDonald Smith Dr DD7 100 A1
MacDonald Sq KY11 162 B5
McDonald St
Dundee DD3 179 B3
Leven KY8 109 C4
McDonald Terr 11 KY8 109 C4
McDouall Stuart Pl KY1 152 A7
Macduff Cres KY3 166 F2
Macduff Dr 7 DD6 99 F6
Macduff Gdns KY7 113 B6
Macduff Pl 3 KY14 62 F6
Macduff Rd KY7 113 B6
MacDuff's Castle* KY1 133 D7
McDuff St KY1 133 C8
Mace Ct FK7 135 D3
MACEDONIA 112 D7
McFarlane Croft 15 DD8 11 E3
McGill Rd DD7 100 F3
McGill St 7 DD4 94 C3
McGinlay Terr 1 KY5 127 F6
McGonagall Sq 7 DD1 93 E2
McGregor Ave KY5 148 A8
McGregor's Land 12 DD8 86 C5
MacGregor St 1 DD9 84 C3
McGregors Wlk 2 DD11 89 D5
McGrigor Rd
Rosyth KY11 173 D2
Stirling FK7 135 A4
McHaney Ct PH7 101 B2
Machrie Pl DD4 95 D8
Macindoe Cres KY1 151 D7
McInnes Gdns KY15 105 D6
McInnes Rd KY7 113 E7
McIntosh Cres KY8 109 C7
McIntosh Ct 8 KY2 130 E1
McIntosh Gdns 6 KY2 130 E1
McIntosh Par KY2 130 E1
McIntosh Patrick Pl 7 DD5 96 F6
McIntosh Pk 7 KY2 130 E1
McIntosh Pl 9 KY2 130 E1
McKane Pl KY12 160 F1
McKay Dr KY11 161 F1
McKenzie Cres KY5 148 C7
McKenzie Ct PH1 102 E6
Mackenzie Ct FK15 107 B4
Mackenzie Dr PH1 36 E4
Mackenzie Gdns DD9 84 B4
McKenzie St KY1 151 E7
Mackenzie St DD7 100 D4
Mackie Ave KY8 109 D7
Mackie Cres KY7 113 E7
Mackie Gdns
2 Anstruther KY10 69 A2
Glenrothes KY7 113 E7
Mackie Pl KY11 161 F2
McKinlay Cres FK10 138 C7
McKinnon St DD3 179 A4
Mackintosh Way PH1 102 A4
McLachlan Ave FK7 135 B2
MacLagan Rd DD7 100 A2
MacLaren Gdns 12 DD2 93 C6
McLaren Terr FK7 135 B3
MacLaren Wlk 7 DD2 93 C6
McLauchlan Rise KY3 176 B7
Maclean Cres FK12 118 C7
Maclean Ct FK7 135 C3
Maclean Gate KY11 173 F7
Maclean Gdns KY11 173 E7
McLean Pl 6 DD3 91 C3
Maclean Pl
Crieff PH7 101 E3
Dunfermline KY11 173 E7
McLean Prim Sch KY12 160 E5
McLean St DD3 91 C3
Maclean Way KY11 173 E7
Maclean Wlk KY11 173 E7
McLeish Pl PH1 102 C7
McLellan Ct 12 DD11 12 F4
McLennan Dr PH12 38 B6
McLennan Rd PH1 102 F7
McLeod Ct PH1 102 E6
MacNab Ave DD10 85 C6
MacNabb Pl DD4 94 D5
McNabb St FK14 120 E8
McNabb St DD4 94 D5
McNee Pl PH7 101 B2
McOwan Ave PH7 101 E3
Macpherson Dr FK8 115 A2
McRae Cres KY3 165 F2
Macrosty Gdns PH7 101 B5
Macrosty Pk* PH7 101 B5
McTaggart Sports Ctr DD3 94 A7
MacTaggart Way KY7 111 A2
Mc Vicar's La 3 DD1 93 E2
McWalters Fields 11 KY16 53 E8
McWilliam Pl 4 KY13 108 B3
MADDERTY 45 F8
Madderty Prim Sch PH7 45 F8
Madeira St DD4 94 C4
Madoch Rd 1 PH2 49 F7
Madoch Sq 12 PH2 49 F7
Madras Coll Kirymont KY16 106 E4
Madras Coll South St KY16 106 D5
Madras Rd 8 KY14 62 F6
Magdalen Pl DD1 93 E1
Magdalen Yd Rd DD2 93 D1
Magnus Dr KY7 110 F2
Maidenplain Pl PH3 46 C2
Maid of the Forth* EH30 178 D1
Main Ave KY1 133 C7
Main Rd
Arbroath DD11 14 A4
Auchterarder PH3 46 B2
Blairgowrie PH13 26 C8
Cardenden KY5 129 B2
Charlestown KY11 172 B4
Crombie KY12 171 E7
Crosshill KY5 127 F4
Cupar KY14 62 A4
Dunfermline KY12 143 B5
East Wemyss KY1 133 B6
Grangemouth FK3 168 B1
Hillside DD10 6 C8
Kirriemuir DD8 9 A7
Luncarty PH1 37 B8
Newport-on-Tay DD6 41 F2
North Queensferry KY11 178 B6
Perth PH2 25 B2
Main St E FK11 117 A6
Main St W
Dalgety Bay KY11 174 E4
Menstrie FK11 116 F6
Mains Castle* DD4 94 C6
Mains Dr DD4 94 B5
Mains Loan DD4 94 C6
MAINS OF HALLYBURTON 16 D1
Mains Rd DD3 179 A4
Main St
Aberdour KY3 176 C8
Abernethy PH2 49 E3
Airth FK2 154 D4
Alloa FK10 118 D1
Almondbank PH1 36 E4
Anstruther KY10 83 D7
Auchterderran KY5 129 A4
Auchtertool KY2 149 B2
Balmutto KY16 53 E7
Bankfoot PH1 24 A6
Bannockburn FK7 135 D1
Blairgowrie PH12 16 E4
Blairingone FK14 121 D6
Bridge of Earn PH2 48 F5
Cairneyhill KY12 159 D1
Cambusbarron FK7 134 D5
Cambus FK10 137 B8
Carnock KY12 159 C7
Ceres KY15 65 D6
Clackmannan FK10 139 A4
Coaltown of Wemyss KY1 132 E4
Comrie KY12 158 D7
Cowdenbeath, Hill of Beath KY4 147 A1
Cowdenbeath, Lumphinnans KY4 147 E6
Crossford KY12 160 C2
Crossgates KY4 162 F6
Crosshill KY5 127 F5
Dairsie or Osnaburgh KY15 53 D4
Dalgety Bay KY11 174 F4
Dundee DD3 179 B4
East Wemyss KY1 133 C6
Fallin FK7 136 E3
Forfar DD8 9 C1
Glanfarg PH2 61 B5
Glenrothes KY7 113 F4
Guardbridge KY16 54 A6
Halbeath KY11 162 B5
High Valleyfield KY12 157 F1
Hill Of Beath KY4 162 F8
Invergowrie DD2 92 B3
Kelty KY4 126 E2
Kinglassie KY5 77 F1
Kingsbarn KY16 68 F7
Kingseat KY12 146 B1
6 Kingskettle KY15 64 A3
2 Kinross KY13 77 A4
Kirkcaldy KY1 132 F2
Leuchars KY16 54 B7
Leven KY8 109 C3
Limekilns KY11 172 D3
Lochgelly KY5 148 B7
Lower Largo KY8 81 A5
Methven PH1 36 B4
Newton of Falkland KY15 63 C2
North Queensferry KY11 178 C5
Perth PH2 103 C5
Saline KY12 142 E5
Stirling FK7 135 B4
Strathkinness KY16 54 B2
Thornton KY1 113 D1
Tillicoultry FK14 119 C4
Torryburn KY12 158 D1
Townhill KY12 161 D8
Tullibody FK10 117 B2
Upper Largo KY8 81 A6
Mains Terr DD4 94 C5
Maisondieu La 2 DD9 84 C3

Maisondieu Prim Sch DD9 84 C3
Maitland Ave FK7 135 D1
Maitland Cres FK7 135 B3
Maitland Dr KY15 105 C4
Maitland St
Dundee DD4 179 C4
Dunfermline KY12 160 F4
Leven KY8 109 F7
Tayport DD6 99 F6
Makgill Row 7 KY15 64 E6
Malcolm Cres DD5 97 A6
Malcolm Ct
Dollar FK14 120 D8
Dunfermline KY11 161 B1
Perth PH1 102 E6
Malcolm Rd KY7 113 A6
Malcolm's Mdw 1 KY2 130 E1
Malcolm St
Ballingry KY5 127 F8
Dundee DD4 179 C4
Dunfermline KY11 161 B2
Dunfermline KY11 161 C2
Malcolms Wynd KY1 151 C5
Mallaig Ave DD2 92 C4
Mallard Dr DD10 85 B6
Mallard Gr KY11 162 A1
Mallard Rd 1 KY8 79 F1
Malloch Ave 5 PH1 102 D8
Mall Pk Rd DD10 85 D5
Mall The DD10 85 D5
Maltings The
Auchtertool KY2 149 B2
7 Cupar KY15 64 A4
Montrose DD10 85 E4
Malt Row KY15 64 D4
Malvern Terr PH1 102 D4
Malvina Ct PH1 103 A6
Malvina Pl PH1 103 A6
Mamore Rd KY7 111 C2
Manhattan Ct DD4 179 C4
Mannan Dr FK10 139 B4
Mannering Ct KY6 112 C5
Mannering St KY5 127 F6
Manor Bsns Pk FK9 116 B3
Manor Cres FK10 117 B2
Manor Croft DD8 87 C5
Manor Ct
Blairgowrie PH10 88 D4
Forfar DD8 87 C5
Manor Gdns
Blairgowrie PH10 88 D3
Carnoustie DD7 100 E5
Dunfermline KY11 162 A2
Manor House Rd 24 FK14 73 C1
Manor Loan FK9 116 B5
Manor Pl DD5 96 A2
MANOR POWIS 116 B3
Manor Powis Cotts FK9 116 B3
Manor St DD8 87 C5
Manor Steps FK9 116 C3
Manse Cres
Stanley PH1 24 E4
Stirling FK7 135 B4
Manse Ct PH10 88 C5
Manse La
Almondbank PH1 36 E5
Burntisland KY3 165 E1
Forfar DD8 2 D5
10 Kirriemuir DD8 86 D4
Manse Pk 7 KY8 79 F5
Manse Pl
Aberdour KY3 176 B7
Bannockburn FK7 135 E1
Inverkeithing KY11 174 B2
2 Leven KY8 109 E6
Monifieth DD5 97 A5
Manse Rd
Blairgowrie PH13 26 C8
Crossgates KY4 162 E7
Crosshill KY5 127 F4
Cupar KY15 64 E6
Dollar FK14 120 F8
5 Dunblane FK15 56 B4
Glenrothes KY7 111 F1
4 Hillside DD10 6 C8
Inverkeithing KY11 174 B2
Kincardine FK10 155 E5
Kinghorn KY3 166 F3
Milnathort KY13 108 C8
Perth PH2 103 D3
Manse St KY3 176 C7
Manse Terr FK10 139 A4
Mansfield KY6 112 A8
Mansfield Ave
Alloa FK10 118 D1
Kinross KY13 108 D7
Mansfield Pk 10 PH1 24 A6
Mansfield Rd
2 Balmutto KY16 53 E8
24 New Scone PH2 37 F5
Mansion Dr DD4 94 B8
Manson Ave PH2 103 B1
Manson Cres PH2 103 B1
Manson Rd PH2 103 B1
Manson Terr PH2 103 B1
Maple Ct 10 FK10 138 B6
Mapledene Pl 4 PH2 37 F5
Mapledene Rd 6 PH2 37 F5
Maple Gdns
Arbroath DD11 89 A4
Leven KY8 109 A4
Maple Pl
Blairgowrie PH10 88 C2
Glenrothes KY6 112 E7
Perth PH1 102 B3
Maple Rd PH1 102 B2
Maple St KY2 151 B7
Maples The 4 DD4 95 A8
Maple Terr KY4 126 C2
Maplewood Dr DD2 93 C6
March Cres 18 KY10 83 D6
Marches The 8 FK8 135 B7
Marchfield Cres DD2 93 C3
Marchfield Rd DD2 93 C3
Marchfield Terr DD2 93 C3
Marchglen FK13 118 F5
Marchmont Cres KY6 112 D8
March Pl 19 KY10 83 D6
March Rd KY10 83 D6
Marchside Ct FK10 118 C1
Mar Dr KY7 113 B2
Maree Ct FK10 138 C6
Maree Pl
Crossford KY12 160 B1
1 Kinross KY13 108 B3
Kirkcaldy KY2 150 E8
Maree Way KY7 111 B4
Mare Pk PH3 104 A5
Margaret Cres DD5 95 B3
Margaret Rd FK7 135 C2
Maria St KY1 151 C5
Marindin Pk PH2 61 B5
Marine Ave DD10 85 D3
Marine Dr DD5 97 B5
Marine Par DD1 179 C2
Marine Pl KY16 106 E6
Mariner Dr DD2 92 C4
Mariners St KY2 151 B6
Mariner St 3 DD7 100 F3
Mariners Wlk KY11 174 F3
Marionfield Pl KY15 105 D3
Marion St KY1 151 B2
Marjory's Ave KY2 130 D1
Market Ct PH1 103 A4
Marketgate
5 Arbroath DD11 89 D3
Crail KY10 69 B2
Market Pl
10 Arbroath DD11 89 D3
Forfar DD8 87 D6
Market St
Brechin DD9 84 C4
Dundee DD1 94 D2
Dunfermline KY12 161 A4
Forfar DD8 87 D6
Montrose DD10 85 D4
4 Perth PH1 103 A4
St Andrews KY16 106 D6
Markfield Rd KY11 175 C4
MARKINCH 113 F7
Markinch Prim Sch KY7 113 F8
Markinch Sta KY7 113 F7
Marlborough Dr FK9 115 C3
Marlee Pl
Broughty Ferry DD5 96 B4
New Scone PH2 103 E8
Marlee Rd
Dundee DD5 96 A4
Perth PH1 102 C5
Marlefield Gr PH1 36 D2
Marmion Dr KY6 112 D5
Marmion Rd KY5 127 F6
Marnie Pk DD8 86 C7
Mar Pl
Alloa FK10 138 A7
Saline KY12 142 E5
Sauchie FK10 118 C1
Stirling FK8 135 A8
Marquis Dr FK10 139 B4
Marryat St DD3 93 F6
Marryat Terr 4 DD3 93 F6
Marschal Ct FK7 135 D3
Marsden Ct FK9 115 D4
Mars Gdns DD6 98 B2
Marshall Cres 4 PH1 37 B8
Marshall Gdns PH1 37 B8
Marshall Mews 7 PH2 103 B3
Marshall Pl
1 Ballingry KY5 127 F7
Dunfermline KY11 161 B1
5 Luncarty PH1 37 B8
Milnathort KY13 108 C7
Perth PH2 103 B3
Marshall Rd 13 PH1 37 B8
Marshall St
Cowdenbeath KY4 147 D3
2 Dundee DD2 93 B5
Marshall Way
7 Luncarty PH1 37 B8
Tullibody FK10 117 C4
Marshill FK10 138 A6
Mar St FK10 138 B6
Mar Terr FK10 139 A4
Martin Cres KY5 127 E7
Martingale Gdns DD4 179 C3
Martin Gdns PH5 44 C3
Martin's La 3 DD9 84 C3
Martin St
Dundee DD4 94 D5
Leven KY8 79 F1
Mart La DD8 86 D6
Mart St 33 PH11 7 A3
Mary Ann La DD1 179 C3
Marybank La 2 DD2 93 A6
Maryburgh KY4 126 D4
MARYFIELD 94 C5
Maryfield Cres KY6 112 B8
Maryfield Gdns 4 KY6 112 B8
Maryfield Rd DD5 96 A3
Maryfield Terr DD4 94 C4
Mary Findlay Dr DD2 40 E8
Marygate 10 KY10 83 A5
Maryhall St KY1 151 C5
Marykirk Rd DD10 6 D8
Maryknowe DD6 41 F2
Mary Pl
Clackmannan FK10 139 A5
Dunfermline KY11 161 B2
Mary Slessor Sq DD4 179 C3
Mary Stevenson Dr FK10 138 A8
MARYTON
Kirriemuir 86 E3
Montrose 6 A3
Maryton DD6 98 E5
MARYWELL 23 A7
Marywell KY1 151 C5
Marywell Brae DD8 86 D4
Marywell Gdns DD8 86 D4
Mason's La 2 DD6 99 F7
Mason St 3 KY14 50 D5
Massereene Rd KY2 150 F5
Masterton Prim Sch KY11 174 B8
Masterton Rd KY11 174 A7
Mathers Pk 9 DD9 84 C3
Matheson Pl 4 KY6 112 F7
Mathieson Ct 5 KY14 63 A6
Mathieson Dr PH1 102 D7
Mathieson Gdns 6 KY14 63 A6
Mathieson Pl
Dunfermline KY11 161 F1
Leven KY8 79 F2
Matthews Dr PH1 102 C8
Matthew St KY2 151 B6
Mattocks Prim Sch DD5 30 F7
Mattocks Rd DD5 30 F7
Mauchline Ave DD4 94 F5
Mauchline Gr KY2 151 A8
Mauchline Pl E 4 DD4 94 F5
Mauchline Pl W 5 DD4 94 F5
Maule St
11 Arbroath DD11 89 D4
2 Broughty Ferry DD5 96 E4
Carnoustie DD7 100 E3
Monifieth DD5 97 A5
Maurice Ave FK7 135 D4
Mavis Bank KY8 79 F1
Mavisbank Gdns PH1 102 C4
Mavisbank Pl PH1 102 C4
Maviscroft DD8 87 B2
Mavis Haugh KY16 106 A4
Maxton Cres FK12 118 C7
Maxtone Ct 12 PH1 37 B8
Maxtone Terr PH7 33 E2
Maxton Pl
Perth PH1 102 D7
Rosyth KY11 173 E3
Maxton Rd PH7 101 D3
Maxwell Cres KY4 147 A2
Maxwell Pl
Glenrothes KY6 112 E7
6 Stirling FK8 135 B8
Maxwelltown Twr DD3 179 B4
Maybole Pl 4 DD4 95 C7
Mayfield Ave FK13 119 C7
Mayfield Cres FK10 139 A5
Mayfield Ct FK7 135 B3
Mayfield Gdns KY13 108 E7
Mayfield Gr DD4 94 E3
Mayfield La 4 DD7 100 C2
Mayfield Rd PH2 103 F8
Mayfield St FK7 135 B4
Mayfield Terr
4 Arbroath DD11 89 F5
Leven KY9 81 F6
New Scone PH2 103 F7
Mayflower St KY12 161 C7
Maygate 3 KY12 161 A3
Maynard Rd KY16 106 B4
Mayne Ave FK9 115 B6
Mayo Ave DD2 93 A2
May Pl PH1 102 F8
Mayview 5 KY10 83 B5
Mayview Ave 3 KY10 83 C6
Mayview Ct 2 KY10 83 C6
Mayview Rd 17 KY10 83 C6
Meadowbank Dr 3 DD5 30 F7
Meadowbank Gdns 1 DD5 30 F7
Meadowbank View 2 DD5 30 F7
Meadow Ct KY3 165 E1
Meadowend KY12 160 C2
Meadow Entry DD1 179 B2
Meadowfield
Burntisland KY3 165 E2
Cowdenbeath KY4 147 C6
Dalgety Bay KY11 175 B4
Meadowfield Ind Est KY3 165 E1
Meadowforth Rd FK7 135 C7
Meadow Gn FK10 118 B1
Meadow Gr FK10 139 D3
Meadow La DD1 179 B3
Meadowland Rd FK9 115 A6
Meadow Pk
Alva FK12 118 A6
2 Leven KY8 79 F5
Meadow Pl
Crieff PH7 101 C4
Dundee DD1 179 B3
Dunfermline KY11 161 F3
Stirling FK8 115 C1
Meadow Rd
1 Leuchars KY16 54 B8
Leven KY9 82 A5
Meadows Ct KY5 127 F5
Meadowside DD1 179 B2
Meadowside Rd KY15 105 D4
Meadows The
Bridge of Earn PH2 48 F4
Dollar FK14 119 C4
Stirling FK9 115 B3
Meadow View
Crossford KY12 160 B2
Halbeath KY12 162 B6
Kelty KY4 126 E2
Meadowview Dr PH14 40 C7
Meadowview Pl PH14 40 C7
Meal Vennel 9 PH1 103 B3
Mearns Ct KY7 111 C2
Mearns Dr DD10 85 C7
Mears Ct 5 KY16 54 B8
Medicine Well Dr DD10 85 C5
Medwyn Pl FK10 137 F6
Meethill Rd PH11 7 A3
Meffan Mus & Gall The* DD8 87 C5
Megginch Castle* PH2 39 E3
Megginch Gdns 12 DD4 94 F8
Megginch Pl KY7 113 C4
MEIGLE 17 A7
Meigle Dr PH11 7 B2
Meigle Prim Sch PH12 17 B7
Meigle Rd PH11 7 B2
Meigle Sculptured Stone Mus* PH12 17 A7
Meikle Mill 3 DD9 84 D2
Meikle Sq KY1 152 A7
Melbourne Pl DD8 87 D4
Meldrum Cres KY3 165 D1
Meldrum Ct
Dunfermline KY11 161 F1
Glenrothes KY2 110 E3
Meldrum Rd KY2 151 B5
Melford Pl 7 KY6 112 E6
Melfort Dr FK7 135 C4
Melfort Pl DD3 94 A8
Melginch Steading PH2 38 D8
Melgund Pl KY5 148 B8
Mellerstain Rd KY2 150 C6
Melloch Cres FK13 119 C6
Mellor Ct KY11 173 E4
Melrose Cres
Kirkcaldy KY2 151 C6
Perth PH1 102 A3
Melrose Ct KY6 112 D8
Melrose Gdns 7 KY5 127 F6
Melrose Terr DD3 94 B4
Melvich Pl KY6 112 E5
Melville Cl KY7 113 C3
Melville Ct 2 DD6 99 F6
Melville Gdns
Burntisland KY3 177 D8
Montrose DD10 85 D3
Melville La DD1 94 C2
Melville Pl
Bridge of A FK9 115 A7
Dunfermline KY12 161 B4
Kirkcaldy KY2 150 D5
2 Newburgh KY14 50 E5
Melville Rd
Ladybank KY15 64 A5
Montrose DD10 85 D3
Melville St
Lochgelly KY5 148 B8
Perth PH1 103 A5
Melville Terr
Dundee DD2 93 B2
Stirling FK8 135 B6
Memorial Ct KY8 109 C3
Memorial Rd KY8 109 B3
Memorial Sq KY1 132 E4
MEMUS 1 E6
Mennieburn Rd PH3 46 A2
MENSTRIE 116 E6
Menstrie Bsns Ctr FK11 116 F6
Menstrie Castle* FK11 116 F6
Menstrie Pl FK11 117 A6
Menstrie Prim Sch FK11 117 A6
Menstrie Rd FK10 117 C3
Menteith Ct FK10 138 C6
Menteith Dr KY11 161 F1
Menteith Rd FK9 115 A3
Menteith St DD5 96 A5
Menteith View FK15 107 F6
Menzies Cres KY2 150 F5
Menzies Ct PH1 102 F6
Menzies Dr FK8 115 A2
MENZIESHILL 92 E5
Menzieshill High Sch DD2 92 F5
Menzieshill Rd DD2 92 E3
Mercat Gn PH2 26 A3
Mercat Pl FK10 139 B4
Mercat The KY1 151 C3
Mercat Wynd
2 Alloa FK10 138 B6
Kinrossie PH2 26 A3
Mercer Pl KY11 161 E4
Mercer St FK10 155 E3
Mercer Terr PH1 102 D5
Merchant Pl KY1 131 E2
Merchants Way KY11 174 C2
Mercury Way DD2 93 B2
Mericmuir Gdns DD3 91 C1
Mericmuir Pl DD3 91 C2
Meridian St 5 DD10 85 D2
Merkland Cres KY11 175 A3
Merlin Cres KY8 79 F1
Merlin Pk 1 FK14 73 C1
Merlin Way KY11 175 C5
Merton Ave DD2 93 B7
Meteor Row 12 KY16 54 B7
METHIL 109 D3
Methil Brae KY8 109 B4
Methilhaven Rd
3 Leven KY8 79 F1
Leven KY8 109 C5
METHILHILL 79 F3
Methilhill Prim Sch 16 KY8 79 F3
Methil Ind Est KY8 109 D5
Methill Brae KY8 109 C4
Methlick Brae KY7 110 E2
METHVEN 36 B5
Methven Dr KY12 161 B5
Methven Pl KY1 151 B2
Methven Prim Sch PH1 36 A4
Methven Rd KY1 151 B2
Methven St DD2 93 B6
Methven Wlk DD2 93 C6
Mey Ct KY11 162 A1
Mey Gn KY7 113 B2
Michael Bruce Ct FK10 140 C8
Michael Nairn Gdns 2 KY2 130 E1
Michael Nairn Gr 4 KY2 130 E1
Michael Nairn Par KY2 130 E1
Michael Nairn Pk 3 KY2 130 E1
Michael Nairn Pl 5 KY2 130 E1
Michael Path 1 KY7 111 B1
Michael Pl KY1 133 B6
Michael St
14 Leven KY8 79 F1
2 Leven KY8 109 A1
Michelin Athletic Club DD4 95 D7
Midbank St KY14 62 D4
Mid Beveridgewell KY12 160 F5
Mid Bonvil KY15 105 B5
Mid Brae 1 KY12 160 F5
Mid Causeway KY12 169 D8
Mid Craigie Prim Sch DD4 94 F5
Mid Craigie Rd DD4 94 F4
Middlebank Cres DD2 93 C3
Middlebank Holdings KY11 174 B6
Middlebank St KY11 174 A4
Middlefield Ave 1 DD8 86 C4
Middlefield Brae KY15 105 D6
Middlefield Rd 3 KY10 69 B3
Middleflat 4 KY14 63 A6
Middleflat Ct 3 KY14 63 A6
Middlegate Cres 5 DD11 12 F4
Middlehills 1 PH13 15 F3
Middlemuir Rd FK7 135 C6
Middle Rd PH10 88 D6
Middleshade Rd KY16 106 B5
Middleton FK11 117 A5
Middleton Cres
7 Caird Park DD4 94 C8
Claverhouse DD4 29 E5
Middleton Pk
Brechin DD9 84 D2
Keltybridge KY4 126 D4
Middleton Pl KY8 109 C7
Middle Wlk KY12 161 B3
Midfield Rd KY1 131 D2
Midfield Terr KY12 143 B5
Mid La 10 FK15 56 B4
Mid La Cl 7 FK15 56 B4
Midlaw Cres KY8 109 C7
Midmill Rd DD4 94 E6
Mid Rd
Dundee DD3 93 F6
Kinghorn KY3 166 F3
Kirriemuir DD8 86 C7
Mid Row
6 Forfar DD8 10 F7
Kirriemuir DD8 86 E3
Mid Row Croftouterly 2 KY6 112 B8
Mid Shore
21 Anstruther KY10 83 A5
Monance KY10 82 E4
Mid Shore Rd 9 KY14 50 D5
Mid St
28 Alyth PH11 7 A3
5 Kingskettle KY15 64 A2
Kirkcaldy KY1 151 D6
Leven KY9 66 E2
Lochgelly KY5 148 B7
Midtown FK11 116 F6
Mid Wynd DD1 93 E2
MILESMARK 160 D6
Milesmark Ct KY12 160 C6
Milesmark Prim Sch KY12 160 D5
Millar Pl FK8 115 C1

Millar St
Carnoustie DD7 100 C3
Crieff PH7 101 C4
Millars Wynd FK10 118 C2
Millbank
Cupar KY15 105 B4
Stanley PH1 24 F3
Millbank Cres FK10 139 A5
Millbank Pk KY15 105 C3
Millbank Rd FK15 70 D8
Millbay Gdns DD2 92 D3
Millbay Terr DD2 92 D3
Mill Brae 1 DD5 97 B5
Mill Bridge 14 KY13 108 C2
Millbrook Pl FK11 116 F6
Millburn Ave KY7 79 A2
Millburn Gdns DD3 94 A8
Mill Ct
6 Bridge of Earn PH2 48 F5
Tayport DD6 43 C7
Milldean Gr KY12 161 D5
Millden Rd KY14 61 E6
MILLDENS 12 A5
Millenium Ave KY11 173 C1
Miller Ave
Crossford KY12 160 B2
Perth PH1 102 D2
Miller Pl FK2 154 E4
Miller Rd
Dunfermline KY12 160 E5
6 Luncarty PH1 37 B8
Miller St
2 Kirkcaldy KY1 131 F1
Kirkcaldy KY1 151 F8
Millers Wynd DD1 93 E2
Miller's Wynd DD1 93 E2
Miller Terr KY10 82 E4
Mill Farm Rd KY3 176 B7
Millfield KY15 105 B3
Millfield Pl DD11 89 B7
Millfield Rd DD11 89 B7
Millflat 5 KY14 62 F6
Millgate
1 Arbroath DD11 89 D3
Cupar KY15 105 C4
Millgate Loan DD11 89 C3
Mill Gdns FK14 74 B1
Millglen Dr PH1 35 D1
Millhall Cres DD2 92 F2
Millhall Rd FK7 135 D5
Millhill DD5 96 F5
Mill Hill FK7 134 D6
Millhill Cl FK15 56 B2
Millhill Cres FK15 56 B2
Millhill Dr FK15 56 B2
Millhill Rd FK15 56 B2
Millhill St KY11 161 B2
Millhill Way FK15 56 B2
Millie St KY1 151 D6
Mill La
Kincardine FK10 155 E3
Montrose DD10 85 C2
2 Tayport DD6 43 C7
Mill Lade KY13 108 C7
Mill Lade Ct PH3 104 E6
Mill Of Airthrey Ct
FK9 114 F8
Mill of Mains Prim Sch
DD4 94 C8
Mill Rd
Alloa FK10 138 B6
Cambusbarron FK7 134 D6
Carnoustie DD7 31 E6
Clackmannan FK10 139 A5
Crieff PH7 101 B4
Cupar KY14 63 A5
Dunfermline KY11 161 B2
Invergowrie DD2 92 B4
2 Montrose DD10 85 C3
Stanley PH1 24 F3
Millrow FK15 107 D5
Mills Obsy* DD2 93 B4
Mill Sq
Montrose DD10 85 D4
Stanley PH1 24 F3
Mill St
Alloa FK10 138 B6
22 Alyth PH11 7 A3
3 Blairgowrie PH10 88 D5
Broughty Ferry DD5 96 B2
Dunfermline KY12 160 F4
9 Kinross KY13 108 C2
Kirkcaldy KY1 151 B1
Kirriemuir DD8 86 C3
Montrose DD10 85 D4
Perth PH1 103 B4
Stanley PH1 24 F4
MILLTOWN OF
ABERDALGIE 47 F7
Mill Wynd
1 Falkland KY15 63 B2
7 Lower Largo KY8 80 F5
3 Perth PH1 103 A4
Milnab St PH7 101 C4
Milnab Terr PH7 101 B5
Milnamair 1 DD10 85 C3
MILNATHORT 108 E7
Milnathort Prim Sch
KY13 108 C7
Milnbank Gdns DD1 93 D3
Milnbank Rd DD1 93 D3
Milne Cres KY4 147 C3
Milne Ct PH1 103 A4
Milne Gdns 5 KY10 69 B2
Milne Rd
Dunfermline KY11 174 A7
Rosyth KY11 173 E1
Milner St DD4 94 D5
Milne's E Wynd 5 DD1 93 E3
Milne's Land 4 DD8 86 C5
Milne St PH1 103 A4
Milne's W Wynd 1
DD1 93 E3
Miln St DD1 179 A2
Milnwood Ct KY6 112 D5
MILTON 104 F7
Miltonbank Cres KY16 54 A7
Milton Brae
Glenrothes KY7 79 B3
Stirling FK7 135 B2
Milton Cres
Anstruther Wester
KY10 83 B6
Auchterarder PH3 104 F6
Bannockburn FK7 135 C1
Milton Ct 2 KY10 83 B5
Milton Gdns FK7 135 B1
Milton Gn KY12 161 A2
Milton Gr FK7 135 C1
Milton La DD8 2 F3
MILTON OF BALGONIE 79 C3
Milton of Balgonie Prim
Sch KY7 79 C3
Milton of Craigie Rd N
DD4 94 F5
Milton of Craigie Rd S
DD4 95 A4
MILTON OF
CULTOQUHEY 33 F1
MILTON OF OGILVIE 18 E6
Milton Pk
Auchtertool KY2 149 B2
Glenrothes KY7 79 B3
Monifieth DD5 96 F4
Milton Pl
1 Monifieth DD5 96 F5
Pittenweem KY10 83 B5
Milton Rd
Bannockburn FK7 135 C1
Kirkcaldy KY1 151 B2
Leven KY8 79 E3
Perth PH1 102 C6
1 Pittenweem KY10 83 B5
Milton St
Broughty Ferry DD5 96 E4
Dundee DD3 93 F6
Milton Terr FK7 135 B1
Mina Cres KY5 77 F1
Minard Cres DD3 93 E5
Mine Rd FK9 115 A8
Mintlaw Pk 2 DD5 95 C4
Minto Cres KY6 112 D7
Minto Ct FK12 118 B6
Minto Gdns FK12 118 B6
Minto Pl
Dundee DD2 93 D2
Glenrothes KY6 112 D6
Kirkcaldy KY2 150 F4
Minto St KY5 148 B8
Mitchell Cres
Alloa FK10 137 F7
Cowdenbeath KY4 147 A1
Mitchell Ct FK14 120 E8
Mitchell Dr DD9 84 D1
Mitchell Pl
34 Anstruther Wester
KY10 83 C6
2 Kirkcaldy KY1 151 D6
Mitchell Rd KY11 173 C1
Mitchell Sq PH10 88 C5
Mitchell St
Crieff PH7 101 D4
Dundee DD1 93 D4
Kirkcaldy KY1 151 C4
Leven KY8 109 E6
16 Newburgh KY14 50 D5
Mitchell Terr 10 KY7 113 F8
Mitchell Wlk KY11 173 F3
Mitchelston Dr KY1 131 E2
Mitchelston Ind Est
KY1 131 E2
Moathill E KY15 105 C5
Moathill Rd KY15 105 B5
Mochrum Dr KY12 172 B8
Modan Rd FK7 135 A3
Moffat Cres KY5 148 A7
Moffat Ct KY6 112 D8
Moffat Rd DD4 94 F5
Moidart Dr KY7 110 F3
Moir Cres KY16 106 A3
Moir Ct
4 Kelty KY4 126 E1
Kelty KY4 146 E8
Moir Pl
Cairnie DD11 89 C6
3 Glenrothes KY6 112 E7
Moir St FK10 138 A8
Moirs Well 7 FK14 73 C1
Molison St DD4 94 C4
Monar Ct KY11 175 A3
Monastery St KY12 161 A3
MONCREIFFE 48 C8
Moncreiffe Terr PH2 103 A1
Moncreiffe Sch PH2 48 D8
Moncrieff Way 17 KY14 50 D5
Moncur Cres DD3 93 F6
Moncur Rd PH14 40 C8
Moncur St KY12 161 C7
Monenna Cres PH2 103 F8
MONEYDIE 36 E8
MONIFIETH 97 C5
Monifieth High Sch
DD5 96 E5
Monifieth Sta DD5 97 B5
MONIKIE 20 D1
Monikie Ctry Pk* DD5 20 E1
Monikie Prim Sch DD5 20 F1
MONIMAIL 51 D1
Monimail Rd KY15 51 E1
Monkbarns Ave 1
DD11 89 B2
Monkbarns Dr DD11 89 B2
Monks Moss 5 KY15 64 A5
Monkswell Rd KY14 50 D4
Monk's Wlk KY6 112 C8
Montague St DD5 96 D4
Monteath St PH7 101 D3
Monteith Pl PH12 17 B4
Montgomerie Ave DD4 94 F4
Montgomerie Cres DD4 94 F4
Montgomerie Rd DD4 94 F4
Montgomery Cres
FK15 107 B4
Montgomery Ct KY13 108 C2
Montgomery Dr KY8 109 C6
Montgomery Rd 10
KY13 108 C2
Montgomery St
Kinross KY13 108 C2
Kirkcaldy KY2 151 B5
Montgomery Way
Kinross KY13 108 B2
Stirling FK9 115 B3
Montifieth Rd DD5 96 B3
Montpelier Gdns DD4 95 D7
Montrave Ave KY15 105 B4
Montrave Cres KY8 109 D7
Montrave Pl DD5 96 B4
MONTROSE 85 E5
Montrose Acad DD10 85 D3
Montrose Air Sta Heritage
Ctr* DD10 85 D6
Montrose Ave PH7 101 E5
Montrose Basin Nature
Reserve* DD10 85 A3
Montrose Basin Wildlife
Ctr* DD10 6 B3
Montrose Cres KY5 127 F6
Montrose Gn KY7 110 F3
Montrose Mus* DD10 85 D3
Montrose Rd
Arbroath DD11 89 E6
Auchterarder PH3 104 E6
Bechin DD9 84 E2
Forfar DD8 87 E5
Stirling FK9 115 C4
Montrose Royal Infmy
DD10 85 B2
Montrose Sports Ctr
DD10 85 E3
Montrose St DD9 84 D2
Montrose Sta DD10 85 C4
Montrose Way FK15 107 B6
Monument View FK8 115 B2
Monymusk Rd DD11 89 A3
MONZIE 33 E4
Moodie St KY12 161 A3
Moon The 8 DD8 86 D4
MOONZIE 52 C4
Moonzie Bank KY15 105 B3
Moorfields Gdns KY15 64 D7
Moorings The KY11 174 F2
Moor Rd KY15 65 D7
Morar Ct KY6 112 E5
Morar Pl
Broughty Ferry DD5 96 B5
Kinross KY13 108 B3
Morar Rd KY12 160 B1
Morar St KY8 109 A4
Moray Ct
Auchtertool KY2 149 B2
Dalgety Bay KY11 175 A3
Moray La 5 PH13 16 A2
Moray Pk KY11 175 A4
Moray Pl
Auchterarder PH4 57 B4
Glenrothes KY6 112 E6
Moray St PH4 57 B3
Morays The PH4 57 B4
Morayvale KY3 176 C8
Moray Way N KY11 175 C4
Moray Way S KY11 175 B2
Moredun Sq PH2 102 F1
Moredun Terr PH2 103 A1
Morgan Acad DD3 94 C4
Morgan Ct FK7 135 C3
Morgan Pl 2 DD4 94 C3
Morgan St DD4 94 C3
Morison Gdns EH30 178 B1
Morley Cres FK7 135 A3
Morlich Cres KY11 175 A2
Morlich Ct KY11 175 A2
Morlich Gdns
Broughty Ferry DD5 96 B4
Glenrothes KY7 110 F3
Morlich Gr KY11 175 A2
Morlich Mews PH2 103 E8
Morlich Pk KY11 175 A2
Morlich Pl
Dalgety Bay KY11 175 A2
Kinross KY13 108 B4
Morlich Rd KY11 175 A2
Morningside KY11 162 B5
Morris Ave KY5 128 B1
Morris Ct KY11 174 C2
Morrison Dr
Bannockburn FK7 135 C2
Dunfermline KY11 173 F8
Morrison Pl
Dunblane FK15 107 D7
2 Glenrothes KY6 112 E7
Morrison's Acad PH7 101 C4
Morrison St DD8 86 D3
Morrison Terr 16 PH11 7 A3
Morris Pl
Invergowrie DD2 92 B2
1 Newburgh KY14 50 E5
Morris Terr FK8 135 A8
Mortimer Ct KY11 175 B2
Mortimer St DD3 179 A4
Mortlach Pl PH1 102 D8
Morton Cres KY16 106 A4
Morven Ave DD10 85 C8
Morven Gr KY2 150 F7
Morven Pk KY6 110 F1
Morven Pl KY11 175 A3
Morven Terr DD2 93 C5
Mosquito Dr 4 KY16 54 B7
Mossbank
Cowdenbeath KY4 147 B2
Rosyth KY11 173 F5
Mossburn Pl 3 DD8 11 E3
Mossend Gn FK14 74 C1
Mossend Terr KY4 147 B2
Mossgiel Ave FK8 115 A2
Mossgiel Cres DD4 94 E5
Mossgiel Pl DD4 94 E6
Mossgiel Prim Sch
DD4 94 D6
MOSSGREEN 163 A6
Mossgreen St KY4 126 E1
Mosshouse FK7 134 F4
Mosside View DD8 87 E6
Moss Rd
Airth FK2 153 E5
Fallin FK7 136 C4
Tillicoultry FK13 119 C6
Moss-Side Rd KY4 147 B3
Moss Way KY11 175 B5
Motion St KY5 148 A7
Motray Cres KY16 54 A7
Moubray Gdns FK10 117 B1
Moubray La KY13 74 D3
Moubray Rd KY11 175 C5
Moulin Cres PH1 102 B4
Moulin Way KY12 161 E5
Mountains Animal
Sanctuary Visitor Ctr*
DD8 2 B8
Mount Ave DD10 85 D4
Mountbatten Pl KY11 173 E3
Mount Blair View PH1 102 B4
Mount Ericht Rd PH10 88 D5
Mount Feredith DD8 87 D4
MOUNTFLEURIE 109 C6
Mountfleurie Cres
KY8 109 C7
Mountfleurie Prim Sch
KY8 109 C7
Mountfleurie St KY8 109 C7
Mount Frost KY7 113 D8
Mount Frost Dr KY7 113 D8
Mount Frost Gdns
KY7 113 D8
Mount Frost Pl KY7 113 D8
Mount Hooly Cres
KY11 178 C6
Mount Hope FK9 115 B7
Mount Melville Cres
KY16 54 C3
Mount Pleasant
1 Dundee DD1 93 E2
Glenrothes KY6 112 A7
Mount Rd DD10 85 D4
Mountskip Cres DD9 84 B4
Mountskip Rd DD9 84 B4
Mount Stewart Rd 6
DD6 42 B5
Mount Tabor Ave PH2 103 E4
Mount Tabor Rd PH2 103 D4
Mount The 9 KY16 53 E8
Mountview Rd PH1 102 C4
Mount William FK10 118 E1
Mount Zion Brae 9
DD11 89 C3
Mournipea KY14 62 F7
Mowbray Gdns KY4 162 E6
Mowbray Ho KY11 162 B5
Mowbrey Ct FK7 135 D4
Moyness Pk Cres PH10 88 E3
Moyness Pk Dr PH10 88 E3
Muckhart Golf Course
FK14 74 A2
Muckhart Prim Sch
FK14 73 F3
Muckhart Rd FK14 73 C1
Muckle Hill Pk KY11 174 A2
Mugdrum Pl 4 KY14 50 D5
Muir Bank PH2 37 E5
Muircot Pl FK14 119 C4
Muircroft Dr PH1 102 C3
Muircroft Terr PH1 102 B3
Muircroft W Terr PH1 102 B4
Muir Ct KY4 162 E6
MUIRDRUM 100 D8
Muirdrum Gdns KY7 113 D2
MUIREDGE 79 E1
Muiredge Ind Est KY8 79 F1
Muirend Ave PH1 102 D3
Muirend Gdns PH1 102 C3
Muirend Gr PH1 102 D3
Muirend Rd
Perth PH1 102 C4
Stirling FK7 135 B5
Muirfield PH1 102 D4
Muirfield Cres DD3 93 E8
Muirfield Ct
Anstruther KY10 83 B6
Gallatown KY1 131 D2
Perth PH1 102 D4
Muirfield Dr KY6 112 B6
Muirfield Gr 1 KY13 108 C3
Muirfield Pl
7 Arbroath DD11 22 E4
3 Dundee DD3 93 E8
Muirfield Prim Sch
DD11 22 E3
Muirfield Rd DD3 93 E8
Muirfield St
Dundee DD3 93 E7
Kirkcaldy KY2 131 A1
Muirfield Terr 2 DD3 93 E8
Muir Gdns 1 KY16 54 E3
Muir Gr KY13 108 C3
Muirhall Rd PH2 103 D4
Muirhall Terr PH2 103 C5
MUIRHEAD
Cupar 111 D7
Dundee 90 B3
Muirhead KY1 131 D2
Muirhead Ind Est DD8 86 D3
Muirhead Pl DD8 86 D3
Muirlands Cresent 6
DD11 22 E4
Muirlands Ct 4 DD8 10 F7
Muirmont Cres 6 PH2 48 F4
Muirmont Ct 8 PH2 48 F4
Muirmont Pl 7 PH2 48 F4
Muirnwood Pl 3 DD5 97 B6
MUIR OF PERT 29 E7
Muirpark Gdns FK10 117 E4
Muirpark Rd KY13 108 C3
Muir Pl
Dunfermline KY12 161 D7
Forfar DD8 87 D6
Muir Rd
6 Cupar KY15 64 E6
Forfar DD8 87 D6
Kirriemuir DD8 86 D6
Leuchars KY16 54 B7
Townhill KY12 161 D7
Muirs KY13 108 C4
Muirside Ave FK10 117 C3
Muirside Ct KY12 159 C1
Muirside Gr KY12 159 C1
Muirside La KY12 171 C8
Muirside Rd
Cairneyhill KY12 159 C1
Tullibody FK10 117 C3
Muirside Terr DD5 95 F5
Muir St
Forfar DD8 87 D6
Kirriemuir DD8 86 C3
Muirs The FK10 117 C4
MUIRTON
Auchterarder 57 E6
Perth 102 F7
Stirling 135 E6
Muirton Bank PH1 103 A6
Muirtonhill Rd KY5 128 F5
MUIRTON OF
ARDBLAIR 88 A2
Muirton Pl
Blairgowrie PH11 7 A2
Perth PH1 103 A5
Muirton Rd
8 Arbroath DD11 22 E4
2 Dundee DD2 93 C5
Stirling FK7 135 E6
Muirton Rdbt FK7 135 F7
Muirton Terr KY4 126 F1
Muirton Way KY11 175 B5
Mulberry Cres KY8 109 A6
Mulberry Dr KY11 161 E1
Mull Ct FK10 138 B5
Mullion Way PH10 88 E2
Mull Pl PH1 102 E8
Mull Terr DD4 94 C7
Munduff Dr 6 KY7 113 F8
Munro Ave FK9 115 B4
Munro Ct KY7 112 F8
Munroe Ave PH1 35 D1
Munro Gate FK9 115 A5
Munro Pl
Alloa FK10 137 F6
Dundee DD2 93 A7
Glenrothes KY6 112 F7
Munro Rd FK7 135 E6
Munro St KY1 151 B2
Murchison Ct 2 KY7 110 F2
Murchison Path 1
KY7 110 F2
Murdoch Pl 1 KY6 112 E7
Murdoch Terr FK15 107 B5
Murnin Ct FK7 135 C3
Murray Cres PH2 102 E2
Murray Ct 4 KY16 53 E8
Murray Dr PH7 101 D5
Murrayfield Dr 4 DD4 95 A7
Murrayfield Gdns 1
DD4 95 A7
Murrayfield Loan PH7 101 E3
Murrayfield Pl
Bannockburn FK7 135 D1
2 Dundee DD4 95 A7
Murrayfield Rd KY16 106 A5
Murrayfield Terr
Bannockburn FK7 135 D1
3 Dundee DD4 95 A7
Murrayfield Wlk 6
DD4 95 A7
Murraygate DD1 179 B2
Murrayknowe 1 KY5 129 B4
Murray La
4 Crieff PH7 101 D4
3 Montrose DD10 85 C4
Murray Pk KY16 106 D6

Murray Pl
Aberdour KY3 176 C8
Cambusbarron FK7 134 D5
Crieff PH7 101 D5
Cupar KY14 62 F7
Dollar FK14 120 D8
Glenrothes KY6 112 B8
Perth PH1 102 E2
8 St Andrews KY16 106 D6
6 Stanley PH1 24 F4
Stirling FK8 135 B7
Murray Rd 8 PH2 37 F5
Murray Row 3 KY16 53 E8
Murray Royal PH2 103 D5
Murrayshall Rd
28 New Scone PH2 37 F5
Perth PH2 38 B5
Stirling FK7 135 B3
Murray Sq FK13 119 C6
Murray St
Dundee DD4 94 E3
Montrose DD10 85 C4
Perth PH1 103 B4
Murray Terr
Kirkcaldy KY2 151 B5
Perth PH1 102 E3
Murray Wlk KY11 161 E4
Murrell Rd KY3 176 C8
Murrel Terr KY3 176 C8
Murroes Pl DD5 97 A7
Murroes Prim Sch DD4 30 C7
Murthly Prim Sch PH1 24 D8
Museum of Abernethy* PH2 49 F3
Museum of Communication* KY3 177 E8
Museum St 3 DD10 85 D3
Music Hall La 2 KY12 161 A3
MUTHILL 44 D4
Muthill Golf Course PH5 44 B3
Muthill Mus* PH5 44 C4
Muthill Prim Sch PH5 44 D4
Muthill Rd PH7 101 B1
Muttoes La KY16 106 D6
Myers Ct KY12 161 D5
Myers Dr KY7 113 C3
Myles Ho FK8 135 A8
Mylne Ave FK14 73 B1
Mylneburn Gdns KY11 172 D3
Mylnefield Cotts DD2 92 A2
Mylnefield Rd DD2 92 B3
Myre Cres KY3 167 A3
Myregormie Pl KY1 131 E1
Myrekirk Rd DD2 92 C6
Myrekirk Terr DD2 92 C6
Myre Rd DD8 87 C5
Myreriggs Rd PH13 15 E5
Myreside Ave KY8 79 F5
Myreside Dr DD11 14 A4
Myreside Gdns KY8 79 F5
Myreside Pl 14 KY8 79 F5
Myres View 6 KY14 62 F6
Myre Terr KY13 108 C1
Myreton FK11 117 A6
Myretoungate FK12 117 E6
Myrtle Ave KY6 112 F7
Myrtle Cres KY2 151 B7
Myrtlehall Gdns DD4 95 D8
Myrtle Pk 2 PH10 88 C4
Myrtle Rd 27 PH2 37 F5
Myrtle Terr
1 Newport-on-Tay DD6 98 E4
7 Tayport DD6 99 F7
Myrtle Wynd KY12 160 F5

N

Naemoor Rd KY13 74 C3
Nagle Rd KY12 146 A1
Nailer Rd FK7 135 B2
Nairn Path 5 KY6 112 F6
Nairn St
Dundee DD4 94 D5
Kirkcaldy KY1 151 D6
5 Leven KY8 109 E6
Nan Walker Wynd KY13 108 D1
Napier Dr DD2 92 F7
Napier Pl
4 Dundee DD2 92 F7
Glenrothes KY6 112 F7
Napier Rd
Glenrothes KY6 112 E7
11 Leuchars KY16 54 B7
Napier St KY1 151 E8
Napier Terr DD2 93 A7
Nasmyth Pl KY4 126 F1
Nasmyth Rd
Glenrothes KY6 112 C3
Rosyth KY11 173 B2
Nason Ave FK15 107 E8
Natal Pl KY4 147 D3
National Ct KY8 109 C3
Naughton Pl DD2 93 A4
Naughton Rd DD6 42 B5
Navarre St DD5 96 E4
Navitie Dr
Kinross KY13 77 A1
Lochgelly KY5 128 A8
Navitie Pk
Ballingry KY5 127 F8
Navitie Pk *continued*
Lochgelly KY5 128 A8
Neave Ct PH1 102 E8
Nebit The FK12 117 E6
Necessity Brae PH2 102 D1
Nechtan Pl 6 DD8 11 E3
Nectan Terr 1 DD11 89 E5
Neddertoun View DD2 28 D4
Needless Rd PH2 102 E2
Needle St 3 KY15 64 A2
Neidpath Pl KY12 161 D6
Neilson Gr KY3 165 E1
Neish St DD3 94 A4
Nellfield Gdns 2 PH7 101 D4
Nellfield La 3 PH7 101 D4
Nellfield Pl PH7 101 D4
Nellfield Rd PH7 101 D4
Nelson La 4 DD6 43 C7
Nelson Pl FK7 135 C6
Nelson St
Dundee DD1 179 B4
Kirkcaldy KY2 151 B6
6 Perth PH2 103 B3
Rosyth KY11 173 E5
St Andrews KY16 106 D5
Tayport DD6 43 C7
Nelson Terr DD1 179 B3
Nesbitt St DD4 94 D3
Ness Dr DD11 89 F6
Ness The
Dollar FK14 73 C1
Torryburn KY12 158 E1
Netherbeath Rd KY4 162 F8
Netherby Pk KY6 110 E2
Netherby Rd FK2 154 D4
Nether Caldhame DD9 84 E3
Nethergate
11 Crail KY10 69 B2
Dundee DD1 179 B1
Kinghorn KY3 167 A2
Nethergate The FK12 117 E6
Netherlea DD6 98 C3
Netherlea PH2 38 A4
Netherlea Pl 2 DD6 98 C3
Nethermill Pl PH2 49 C3
Nether St
Dysart KY1 152 B7
Kirkcaldy KY1 151 D6
NETHERTON
Forfar 3 E4
Perth 49 C3
Netherton Gdns
Kelty KY4 126 F1
8 Kirriemuir DD8 9 A7
Netherton Ind Est KY10 82 E5
Netherton Pl 7 DD8 9 A7
Netherton Terr DD2 92 F5
Nethertown Broad St KY12 161 A2
Nethy Pl PH2 49 F3
Neuk The DD2 92 A1
Nevay Terr DD2 93 A5
Neville St DD11 89 C5
Nevill St DD3 93 E8
Nevis Cres FK10 138 B8
Nevis Pl
Broughty Ferry DD5 96 A5
12 Glenrothes KY6 112 E6
NEW ALYTH 7 A2
New Alyth Rd PH11 7 A2
Newark Castle (rems of)* KY10 82 D4
Newark Pl KY7 113 E4
Newark Rd N KY7 113 D4
Newark Rd S KY7 113 E4
Newark St 5 KY10 82 E4
Newbiggin Cres FK10 117 C2
NEWBIGGING 149 C2
Blairgownie 17 A5
Dundee 30 A8
Newbigging KY2 149 C2
Newbigging Dr DD11 89 A3
Newbigging Prim Sch DD5 31 B7
Newbigging Rd KY12 159 C7
Newbigging Terr KY2 149 C2
NEWBURGH 50 C5
Newburgh Prim Sch KY14 50 D5
Newburgh Rd
4 Auchtermuchty KY14 62 F7
Perth PH2 49 F3
Newburn Pl KY12 161 D3
Newcastle Prim Sch KY6 112 B6
New Course KY16 106 C7
Newfields Prim Sch DD4 95 C7
New Flockhouse KY5 128 A7
NEW FOWLIS 34 C1
NEW GILSTON 66 B3
New Gilston Prim Sch KY8 66 B3
New Grange Cres 6 KY10 83 A5
New Grange Pk 7 KY10 83 A5
Newhall Gdns DD2 92 F2
Newhalls Rd EH30 178 C1
Newhall St 8 PH1 24 A6
Newhame Rd DD10 85 C7
Newhouse FK8 135 A5
Newhouse Pl PH1 102 B5
Newhouse Rd PH1 102 B4
Newington Gdns 5 DD9 84 D2
New Inn Entry DD1 179 B2
Newlands Pk KY12 161 B5
Newlands Pl FK10 117 C3
New Line Rd FK7 135 B1
NEWLISTON 150 C6
Newliston Dr KY2 150 C7
Newmanswalls Ave DD10 85 C6
Newmarket FK7 135 E1
Newmill Gdns KY16 106 B4
NEWMILLS 158 D1
Newmills FK10 117 B3
Newmiln Rd PH1 102 B4
Newmonthill 7 DD8 87 D5
Newpark Cres FK7 135 A2
Newpark Rd FK7 135 B2
NEWPORT-ON-TAY 98 C4
Newport Prim Sch DD6 98 E3
Newport Rd DD6 99 D7
New Rd
Bannockburn FK7 135 D2
Blairgowrie PH10 88 E6
Broughty Ferry DD5 96 B2
Cupar KY15 63 B2
Forfar DD8 87 D4
Leven KY8 79 E5
Milnathort KY13 108 D7
New Row
Dunfermline KY12 161 A3
Kincardine FK10 156 A3
4 Perth PH2 103 A3
New Sch La PH3 104 D7
New St
Bridge of A FK9 114 F8
1 Tayport DD6 99 F5
Newstead Pl 5 PH1 102 A3
New Struan Sch FK10 137 E7
Newton Ave 14 DD11 22 E4
Newton Cres
16 Arbroath DD11 22 E4
Carnoustie DD7 100 D4
Dunblane FK15 107 E5
Rosyth KY11 174 A4
Newton La 9 PH10 88 C5
Newton Loan FK15 107 E5
NEWTON OF BALCORMO 82 D7
NEWTON OF FALKLAND 63 C2
Newton Pl
6 Arbroath DD11 89 A4
Perth PH1 102 D7
Rosyth KY11 173 F4
Newton Prim Sch FK15 107 F6
Newton Rd
Carnoustie DD7 100 D4
Dundee DD3 91 F3
Falkland KY15 63 B2
Newtonshaw FK10 118 C1
Newton St PH10 88 B5
Newton Terr PH10 88 B5
Newtown KY15 105 C5
New Town KY15 65 D6
NEWTYLE 17 C4
Newtyle Prim Sch PH12 17 C4
Newtyle Rd DD2 90 A4
New Wynd DD10 85 C3
Nicholls Ave KY16 54 B8
Nicol Dr KY3 166 A2
Nicoll Dr 14 PH1 24 A6
Nicoll Pl
15 Bankfoot PH1 24 A6
Carnoustie DD7 100 D4
Nicoll's La 10 DD2 93 B6
Nicoll St DD1 179 A2
Nicol St KY1 151 B3
Nightingale Pl KY11 162 B1
Nile St KY2 151 B6
Nimmo Ave PH1 102 D7
Nimmo Pl PH1 102 D7
NINEWELLS 92 D3
Ninewells Ave DD2 92 F4
Ninewells Ct DD2 92 E4
Ninewells Dr DD2 92 E4
Ninewells Hospl & Medical Sch DD2 92 E3
Ninian Fields 1 KY10 83 A5
Ninian Quadrant KY7 113 A6
Nithsdale Ave DD3 91 C2
Nithsdale Pl KY11 162 C1
Nith St KY11 161 F2
Niven Rd KY11 174 C3
No 7 Pit Rd KY4 147 C4
Nobel Rd DD2 92 C7
Noble Ave DD2 92 B2
Nolt Loan Rd DD11 89 B3
Noran Ave
Arbroath DD11 89 D5
Dundee DD4 94 F3
NORANSIDE 2 C7
Norie Terr PH1 102 D2
Norlands PH2 39 E1
Normand Brae KY1 152 A7
Normand Rd KY1 152 A8
Normandy Pl KY11 173 E2
Norman Pl KY6 112 B8
Norman View 6 KY16 54 B8
Norrie's Law (Cairn)* KY8 65 F2
Norries Rd 2 DD7 100 F3
Norrie St DD5 96 B3
Northampton Pl DD8 87 C2
Northampton Rd DD8 87 C2
North Approach Rd FK10 155 E3
North Balmossie St
4 Barnhill DD5 96 D6
1 Broughty Ferry DD5 96 D6
Northbank 2 PH2 39 F1
North Bank Dykes 1 PH2 39 F1
Northbank Rd KY12 159 D1
North Bank St DD5 96 F5
North Bridge St PH7 101 B2
North Brown St 2 DD7 100 B3
North Burnside 6 KY15 105 C5
North Burnside St DD7 100 B3
North Carr View 8 KY16 68 F7
North Castle St
Alloa FK10 138 A5
St Andrews KY16 106 E6
Northcliff KY11 178 B6
NORTH CORSTON 16 B1
North Croftdyke 6 KY15 65 D6
North Crofts PH3 104 D6
North Dronley Rd DD3 28 D7
North Drum St KY4 126 E2
North Ellen St DD3 179 B4
North End FK7 134 D6
Northern Coll DD4 95 B4
North Erskine St DD4 179 C4
North Esk Rd
Montrose DD10 85 D4
Rosyth KY11 173 C2
North Feus KY8 81 A6
Northfield KY4 147 C6
Northfield Gdns FK10 139 B4
Northfield Rd
Newport-on-Tay DD6 98 E5
Perth PH2 25 B3
North George St DD3 179 B4
North Green Dr FK2 154 D4
North Grimsby 4 DD11 89 D3
Northhall Rd KY7 111 F1
North Haugh KY17 106 C6
North Hill St FK13 119 B7
NORTH INCH 103 B5
North Isla St DD3 94 A4
North Larches KY11 161 F4
North Latch Rd DD9 84 A4
North Lindsay St DD1 179 A2
North Links KY8 109 F7
North Loanhead KY11 172 E3
North Loch Rd DD8 87 B5
North Mains Rd DD8 86 C3
North March KY10 83 C7
North Marketgait DD1 179 B3
North Methven St PH1 103 B4
NORTHMUIR 86 C7
Northmuir Pl KY7 113 C2
Northmuir Prim Sch DD8 86 D6
North Muirton Ind Est PH1 102 E8
North Muirton Prim Sch PH1 102 F8
North Overgate KY3 166 F3
North Pk 1 KY14 63 A6
North Port
4 Arbroath DD11 89 D4
7 Perth PH1 103 B4
North Quarter Steading 2 KY16 68 F7
NORTH QUEENSFERRY 178 D6
North Queensferry Prim Sch KY11 178 C6
North Queensferry Sta KY11 178 C6
North Rd
Inverkeithing KY11 174 C4
Saline KY12 142 E6
North Roundall KY11 172 E3
North Row KY11 172 B4
North Shore Rd FK3 168 A3
North Somerville Pl DD3 179 A4
North St
Alloa FK10 138 A7
Burrelton PH13 26 B8
Clackmannan FK10 139 A4
Dundee DD3 93 F6
6 Earlsferry/Elie KY9 82 B3
Forfar DD8 87 D6
2 Freuchie KY15 63 E1
Glenrothes KY6 112 B8
Kingskettle KY15 64 A2
Leven KY8 109 E6
Lochgelly KY5 148 A7
Milnathort KY13 108 D7
Montrose DD10 85 D4
Newtyle PH12 17 B4
St Andrews KY16 106 D6
Stirling FK9 115 D1
North Union St
Cupar KY15 105 C5
Monifieth DD5 97 B5
North Vennel FK10 139 A4
North View KY3 177 F8
North View Cotts KY4 163 A8
North Watson St DD8 11 F4
North Way KY11 175 C5
North Wellington St DD3 179 B4
North William St
Dundee DD3 179 B4
North William St *continued*
1 Perth PH1 103 B4
Northwood Rd FK10 117 D2
North Wynd KY9 81 F6
Norton Pl KY11 161 E1
Norton St FK12 118 B7
Norval Pl KY11 173 F4
Norwell Dr PH2 38 B6
Norwood DD6 98 E5
Norwood Ave FK10 137 F7
Norwood Cres
Alloa FK10 137 F7
Dundee DD2 93 A3
Norwood Gr FK10 137 F7
Norwood La DD6 98 E5
Norwood Terr DD2 93 B3
Novar Cres KY1 151 B2
Nugent Dr PH2 38 B6
Nurseries The
3 Kinross KY13 75 D5
1 Perth PH2 49 F8
Nursery Cres 5 DD10 85 C5
Nursery La
Brechin DD9 84 D1
Montrose DD10 85 C5
Nursery Pk DD9 84 D2
Nursery Rd
Broughty Ferry DD5 96 B4
Montrose DD10 85 C5
Nursery St 4 DD8 87 E5

O

Oakbank Cres PH1 102 D2
Oakbank Pl
Crieff PH7 101 B5
Guildtown PH2 25 B3
Perth PH1 102 D2
Oakbank Prim Sch PH1 102 D3
Oakbank Rd PH2 25 B3
Oakdene Cres PH2 37 E5
Oakdene Pl 1 PH2 37 F5
Oakdene Rd PH2 37 F5
Oak Dr FK7 136 D4
Oakfield Ct 6 KY4 126 E1
Oakfield St KY4 146 F8
Oak Gr KY11 173 E8
Oaklea KY12 142 F5
OAKLEY 158 F7
Oakley Ind Est KY12 158 F7
Oakley Pl DD5 96 B2
Oakley Rd KY12 142 E5
Oak Loan DD5 30 C5
Oak St
Kelty KY4 126 E2
Stirling FK8 114 F1
Oaktree Ct KY1 151 C8
Oaktree Sq KY1 151 C8
Oakum Bay KY12 158 C1
Oak Vale 3 KY15 105 E5
Oakvale Rd KY8 109 A5
Oak Wynd 5 DD8 9 A7
Oathlaw Pottery & Gall* DD8 2 D3
OATHLAW 2 D3
Oban Pl PH1 102 C8
Oban Terr DD3 94 A8
Oberon FK10 137 F8
Ochil Ave KY2 150 F5
Ochil Cres FK8 115 B2
Ochil Ct FK10 117 C3
Ochil Gdns 9 PH2 47 A1
Ochilmount FK7 135 F1
Ochil Pl PH7 101 D3
Ochil Rd
Alva FK12 118 B7
Menstrie FK11 117 A7
Stirling FK9 115 C4
Ochil St
Alloa FK10 138 A7
Fallin FK7 136 C4
Tillicoultry FK13 119 B7
Tullibody FK10 117 B3
Ochil Terr KY11 161 E2
Ochiltree FK15 107 E5
Ochiltree Ct
Dunblane FK15 107 F5
Glenrothes KY6 112 D5
Ochil Twr (Rudolph Steiner) Sch PH3 104 D6
Ochilvale Terr FK10 118 D3
Ochilview
Alva FK12 118 A7
Tillicoultry FK13 119 B5
Ochil View
Cowdenbeath KY4 147 E6
Kincardine FK10 155 D4
Kinross KY13 108 B3
9 Perth PH2 49 F7
Ochilview Dr KY12 158 B2
Ochilview Gdns PH7 101 E4
Ochil View Gdns PH7 101 E4
Ochilview Rd FK13 119 B7
Ochlochy Pk FK15 107 E4
Octavia St KY2 151 B5
Ogilivie Ct DD5 95 E3
Ogilvie Pl
Auchterarder PH4 57 B3
Bridge of A FK9 115 A6
Ogilvie Rd
Dundee DD5 95 D3
Stirling FK8 135 A5
Ogilvie's Rd DD3 179 A4
Ogilvie St DD4 179 C4
Ogilvie Terr DD10 85 C1
Ogilvy Pl DD11 89 C5

Ogilvy Pl Cotts 2 DD11 89 C5
Ogilvys Cl 11 DD8 86 D4
Ogilvy St DD6 99 F5
O'Hanlon Way FK8 114 F2
Oldany Rd KY7 111 A2
Old Brechin Rd DD8 87 F6
Old Brewery La FK10 138 B7
Old Bridge Wynd FK9 115 A4
Old Buchanty Rd PH1 36 A5
Old Causeway KY13 108 C1
Old Church Rd PH2 25 D4
Old Course The KY16 106 B8
Old Craigie Rd DD4 94 E4
Old Dairy The
Auchterarder PH3 104 C6
1 Dundee DD5 96 A3
Old Doune Rd FK15 107 C5
Old Dronley Rd DD2 90 A4
Old Drove Rd
1 Blairgownie PH11 7 A3
Cambusbarron FK7 134 C5
Old Edinburgh Pl 10 PH2 48 F5
Old Edinburgh Rd
9 Bridge of Earn PH2 48 F5
1 Bridge of Earn PH2 48 F5
Old Forge Gr KY12 158 E7
Old Gallows Rd PH1 102 A4
Old Glamis Rd DD3 93 F7
Old Halkerton Rd DD8 87 B2
Old Hawkhill DD1 179 A2
Old Hillview Pl KY4 162 E6
Old King's Cross Rd DD3 93 C5
Old Kirk La 1 DD11 22 D6
Old Kirk Pl KY12 161 D4
Old Kirk Rd
Dunfermline KY12 161 D4
North Queensferry KY11 178 C6
Old Linburn Rd KY11 161 F4
Old Market Pl PH1 103 A4
Old Mart Pl DD9 84 D3
Old Military Rd
Blairgownie PH10 88 B7
Couper Angus PH2 15 B2
Old Mill Ct KY8 109 D7
Old Mill Ctyd The KY11 161 B2
Old Mill La KY12 158 E6
Old Mill Pl DD11 12 F4
Old Mill Rd PH10 88 E5
OLD MONTROSE 5 F3
Old Muirton Rd 3 DD2 93 C5
Old Orchard The KY11 172 D3
Old Perth Rd
Cowdenbeath KY4 147 A4
Milnathort KY13 108 D7
Old Quarry Rd DD4 95 C8
Old Refinery Rd FK3 168 A1
Old St Andrews Rd KY16 54 B5
Old School Ct FK10 117 B2
Old Schoolhouse The KY4 163 A6
Old School La 7 PH3 46 B2
Old School Pl KY1 131 D7
Old School Rd 3 DD8 9 A7
Old School Way DD10 6 C7
OLD SCONE 37 E5
Old Sheriffmuir Rd FK9 115 C6
Oldshorehead DD11 89 D3
Old Station Rd
Leven KY8 79 F4
St Andrews KY16 106 B7
Old Toll Loan DD5 95 E8
Old Town FK7 135 D1
Old Whisky Rd DD3 18 A1
Oliphant Ct FK8 115 B1
Oliver Ave DD8 2 D7
Oliver St KY5 127 F6
Oliver Wynd DD11 89 B6
Ollerton Ct KY1 151 B5
Olympia Arc KY1 151 B3
Olympia Leisure Ctr DD1 179 C1
Omachie Pl 11 DD5 30 F7
Omar Ave DD10 85 B5
Omar Cres KY8 79 F1
O'Neill Terr DD4 94 F6
Orange La DD10 85 D4
ORCHARDBANK 87 A4
Orchardbank Ind Est DD8 87 A4
Orchard Brae DD8 86 C5
Orchardcroft 5 FK8 135 B7
Orchard Ct
Dundee DD4 94 B8
Kinghorn KY3 167 A4
Orchard Dr KY7 113 D7
Orchard Flat 24 KY14 62 F6
Orchardgate 1 KY15 105 C4
Orchard Gdns KY3 167 A4
Orchard Gr
Broom KY8 109 C8
Crombie KY12 171 D6
Kincardine FK10 155 E3
Orchard House Hospl FK8 115 A1
Orchard La
Dunfermline KY11 161 D1
Dysart KY1 152 A7
Orchard Loan DD8 87 A4
Orchard Pk
Crieff PH7 101 E4
Orchard Pk *continued*
Cupar KY15 53 D4
Orchard Pl
Dysart KY1 152 A7
Perth PH2 102 F2
Thornton KY1 131 D7
Orchard Rd
Bridge of A FK9 115 A6
Kinghorn KY3 166 F3
Thornton KY1 131 D7
Orchard Sq KY11 172 D3
Orchard St DD11 89 C4
Orchard Terr
Kinghorn KY3 166 F4
Torryburn KY12 158 F1
Orchard The
Blairgownie PH13 26 C8
Bridge of Earn PH2 48 E5
Crossford KY12 160 B2
Glenrothes KY6 112 C8
1 Leven KY8 79 E3
Tullibody FK10 117 B2
Orchard Way
Inchture PH14 40 C7
Longforgan DD2 40 D8
Orchil Cres PH3 104 B5
Orchil Rd PH3 104 B5
Ordie Pl 8 PH1 37 B8
Ordie Rd 9 PH1 37 B8
Ordnance Rd KY12 171 D6
Orebank Rd KY5 129 B4
Orebank Terr KY1 131 D7
Oriel Cres KY2 151 A4
Oriel Rd KY2 150 E5
Oriel Road Rdbt KY2 151 A4
Orkney Ct FK10 138 B5
Orkney Pl KY1 151 E7
Orleans Pl DD2 92 D5
Orme's La 5 KY8 79 F5
Ormiston Cres DD4 94 F8
Ormiston Dr FK10 117 E2
Ormiston Pk KY12 161 C6
Oronsay Ct PH1 102 E7
Orrin Gr KY11 175 A3
Orrin Pl DD2 92 E5
Orrock Dr KY3 165 E2
Orwell Pl KY12 161 C4
Osborne Dr FK10 155 F4
Osborne Ho KY1 151 B4
Osborne Pl
1 Dundee DD2 93 D2
10 Dundee DD2 93 D2
Osborne Terr DD11 89 C3
Osnaburgh Ct KY15 53 D4
Osnaburg St 4 DD8 87 D5
Osprey Ave DD2 28 A6
Osprey Bank DD2 27 F6
Osprey Pl 12 DD5 30 F7
Osprey Rd KY6 112 A3
Osprey View DD2 28 A6
Ossian Cres KY8 109 B4
Oswald Ct 1 KY1 131 F1
Oswald Pl 9 KY8 109 E6
Oswald Rd KY1 131 E1
Oswalds Wynd KY1 151 C4
Otterston Gr KY11 175 B4
Otterston Pl KY2 150 E8
Our Ladys RC Prim Sch PH1 102 C6
Our Lady's RC Prim Sch DD1 179 C4
Overgate La DD1 179 B2
Overgate Sh Ctr DD1 179 B2
Overhaven KY11 172 E3
Overton Ct
Dunfermline KY11 173 F7
Kirkcaldy KY1 151 E8
Overton Gdns DD2 92 F6
Overton Mains
Gallatown KY1 131 E1
Kirkcaldy KY1 151 E8
Overton Rd KY1 151 D8
Oxcars Dr KY11 175 B3
Oxford St DD2 93 A3

P

PADANARAM 10 A6
Paddock The
Auchterarder PH3 104 A5
Cupar KY15 64 B3
Page Rd 12 KY8 79 F3
Page St KY5 128 B1
Pakenham Rd DD11 22 D6
Palais Ct DD1 179 A2
Palmer Pl
Dundee DD2 90 B3
Kingseat KY12 146 A1
Palmer St DD11 89 D4
Palmerston St 4 DD10 85 D2
Palnackie Rd 4 DD5 96 E6
PANBRIDE 100 F5
Panbride Pl 1 DD7 100 E3
Panbride Prim Sch DD7 100 F5
Panbride Rd DD7 100 E5
Panbride St DD7 100 E3
Panbride View DD7 100 E5
Panda La DD7 100 B2
Pan Ha' KY1 152 A6
PANHALL 152 A6
Panmurefield Den 6 DD5 96 E6
Panmurefield Rd
3 Broughty Ferry DD5 96 E5
3 Dundee DD5 96 D6
Panmurefield Terr DD5 96 E4
Panmure Golf Course DD7 31 E4
Panmure Ind Est DD7 100 B2
Panmure Pl
4 Kirkcaldy KY2 130 F2
Montrose DD10 85 D3
Panmure Rd DD5 20 D1
Panmure Row 5 DD10 85 D3
Panmure St
Brechin DD9 84 C3
Broughty Ferry DD5 96 B3
Carnoustie DD7 100 B2
Dundee DD1 179 B3
Monifieth DD5 97 C6
2 Montrose DD10 85 D3
Panmure Terr
Broughty Ferry DD5 96 D4
Dundee DD3 179 A3
9 Montrose DD10 85 D3
Pannie Rd KY1 151 D7
Panter Cres DD10 85 C6
Paradise Ave 11 PH2 48 F4
Paradise La FK10 155 E3
Paradise Pl
10 Bridge of Earn PH2 48 F4
8 Perth PH2 103 A3
Paradise Rd
Dundee DD3 179 B3
2 Monifieth DD5 96 F5
Parbroath Rd
Finglassie KY7 113 A3
Glenrothes KY7 113 B2
Park Ave
Carnoustie DD7 100 D2
Cowdenbeath KY4 147 C3
Dundee DD4 94 C3
Dunfermline KY12 161 A3
Leven KY8 109 D8
Stirling FK8 135 A6
Tillicoultry FK13 119 A6
Park Circ KY7 113 E8
Park Cres
Alloa FK10 118 C1
Bannockburn FK7 135 D2
New Scone PH2 37 F5
Park Dr
Bannockburn FK7 135 D2
8 Blairgownie PH10 88 C4
Leven KY8 109 D8
Parkdyke FK7 134 E6
Parker St DD3 179 A3
Parker Terr 3 KY8 109 E6
Parkgate
Alva FK12 117 F6
Rosyth KY11 173 F4
Park Gdns FK7 135 D2
Park Gr
Brechin DD9 84 E3
Letham DD8 11 E4
Parkhead Ct FK10 138 C8
Parkhead Gdns PH1 102 C4
Parkhead Pl DD4 94 F6
Parkhead Rd FK10 138 C8
PARKHILL 50 E5
Parkhill 1 KY8 109 E6
Parkhill Pl
Broughty Ferry DD5 96 A5
Kirriemuir DD8 86 D7
Parkhill Prim Sch KY8 109 D6
Parkhill Rd PH10 88 E7
Park La
Aberdour KY3 176 C7
Blairgownie PH10 88 B4
Glenrothes KY7 111 A3
Stirling FK8 135 B8
Parkland Ct 6 KY8 109 A2
Parkland Gr KY12 158 D7
Parklands Cres KY11 175 A3
Parklands Pl FK10 140 C8
Park Lea KY11 174 A5
Park Manor PH7 101 B5
PARKNEUK 160 D6
Parkneuk KY12 160 D6
Park Neuk PH10 88 C4
Parkneuk Rd KY12 160 D5
Park Pl
Alloa FK10 138 C7
5 Auchterarder PH3 46 B2
Brechin DD9 84 D3
Clackmannan FK10 139 B4
Cowdenbeath KY4 162 F8
Dollar FK14 120 E8
Dundee DD1 179 A1
Dunfermline KY12 161 B4
1 Forfar DD8 10 F7
Kinghorn KY3 166 F2
Kirkcaldy KY1 151 B3
Kirriemuir DD8 86 C5
Leven KY9 82 A3
Perth PH2 102 F2
Stirling FK7 134 F6
Thornton KY1 131 D8
Park Pl Prim Sch DD1 179 A2
Park Prim Sch FK10 138 B5
Park Rd
Bechin DD9 84 E3
Cowdenbeath KY4 147 B3
Dundee DD3 93 F8
Invergowrie DD2 92 B2
Kirkcaldy KY1 131 E1
Kirkcaldy KY1 151 E8
Letham DD8 11 E4
Menstrie FK11 117 A6
Rosyth KY11 173 F5
Park Rd W KY11 173 D5
Park Road Prim Sch KY11 174 A4
Parkside DD3 18 A1
Parkside Rd 15 PH11 7 A3
Parkside Sq KY11 174 A4
Parkside St KY11 173 F4
Park St
Alva FK12 118 A7
17 Arbroath DD11 89 D4
Cowdenbeath KY4 147 C3
Crosshill KY5 127 F4
Dundee DD1 93 E4
Lochgelly KY5 148 B7
3 St Andrews KY16 106 D5
Tillicoultry FK13 119 B7
Park Terr
4 Auchterarder PH3 46 B2
Glenrothes KY7 113 E8
8 Kirriemuir DD8 86 C5
Stirling FK8 135 A6
Tillicoultry FK13 119 A7
Tullibody FK10 117 B1
Park Terr W 18 PH2 37 F5
Park View
14 Alyth PH11 7 A3
Arbroath DD11 89 C6
Balmutto KY16 53 E7
Brechin DD9 84 E4
Glenrothes KY7 113 E8
Kirkcaldy KY2 150 F6
Monifieth DD5 97 A7
Park View Gdns DD11 89 B6
Parkview Sch DD2 93 B3
Park View Terr KY11 174 B2
Park Village PH7 101 B6
Parkway FK10 138 B7
Parkway Ct FK10 138 A7
Park Wynd DD1 179 A2
Parliament Pl
10 Auchtermuchty KY14 62 F6
4 Kinglassie KY5 77 E1
Parliament Sq
7 Cupar KY15 105 C4
12 Kinross KY13 108 C2
Parmelia Ct PH1 103 A4
Pasteur La DD2 92 E3
Paterson Dr PH10 88 D3
Paterson La KY4 147 D3
Paterson Pk KY6 112 A8
Paterson Pl
Bridge of A FK9 115 A6
Dundee DD2 28 B1
1 Montrose DD10 85 C7
Paterson St DD3 93 F6
Paterson Way KY11 161 B1
Pathfoot Ave FK9 115 C7
Pathfoot Dr FK9 115 C7
Pathfoot Rd FK9 115 C6
PATHHEAD 151 D6
Pathhead Ct 1 KY1 151 D6
Pathhead Prim Sch KY1 151 D7
PATH OF CONDIE 60 B6
PATHSTRUIE 60 B7
Path The
Airth FK2 154 D4
Bannockburn FK7 135 D2
Kirkcaldy KY1 151 D5
Paton Ct FK10 138 B7
Patons La DD10 85 E3
Paton's La DD1 93 E2
Paton St
Alloa FK10 138 A7
Dunfermline KY12 161 C6
Patrick Allan-Fraser St 2 DD11 22 D3
Patrick Pl 4 DD2 93 D2
Patterson Pl KY2 151 B6
Patterson St
Kirkcaldy KY2 151 B6
Leven KY8 109 C5
PATTIESMUIR 173 B4
Paul Dr FK2 154 E4
Paul Pl KY4 147 D4
Paul St
Lochgelly KY5 148 A6
1 Perth PH1 103 A4
Pavilions Bsns Pk FK10 137 E7
Pavilions The FK10 137 E7
Pavilion View FK10 137 F8
Paxton Cres KY5 128 A1
Paxton Pl KY5 148 B8
Pearce Ave DD5 95 E6
Pearse St DD9 84 B3
Pearson View FK10 138 C8
Peasehill Brae KY11 173 D3
Peasehill Fauld KY11 173 D2
Peasehill Gait KY11 173 D3
Peasehill Rd KY11 173 E3
Peasiehill Rd DD11 22 E3
Peat Gate KY13 74 E2
PEAT INN 66 D4
Peddie St DD2 93 D3
Peebles Dr DD4 95 D8
Peebles St KY1 167 B8
Peel St DD2 93 B5
Peep O'Day La DD4 94 C2
Peffer's Pl 1 DD8 87 D5
Peirson Rd KY11 161 F4
Pelstream Ave FK7 135 B4
Pendreich Rd FK9 70 D1
Pendreich Way FK9 115 D6
Pends The KY16 106 E6
Pennan Gr 1 DD5 95 C4
Pennan Pl KY7 110 E2
Pennyacre Ct 5 KY15 64 E6
Pennycook La 6 DD1 93 D2
Pennyschool Pl FK10 139 A5
Penrice Pk 1 KY8 80 F5
Pentland Ave DD2 93 C4
Pentland Cres DD2 93 C4
Pentland Ct
Dalgety Bay KY11 175 C4
Glenrothes KY6 112 F5
Pentland Dr 3 KY8 79 F6
Pentland Pk
Glenrothes KY6 112 F5
2 Leven KY8 79 F6
Pentland Pl
Cairneyhill KY12 159 E1
Kirkcaldy KY2 150 F6
Pentland Rd KY6 112 E5
Pentland Rise KY11 175 C5
Pentland Terr
Dunfermline KY11 161 E2
High Valleyfield KY12 158 A1
Pentland View 1 KY8 79 F5
Peploe Dr
Glenrothes KY7 111 A3
Pitcairn KY7 110 F3
Peploe Rise KY11 174 A7
Percival St KY2 151 A5
Percy St 8 PH1 24 E4
Perdieus Mount KY12 161 A2
Perrie St DD2 93 A6
PERTH 103 D3
Perth Acad PH1 102 E3
Perth Airport PH2 38 B7
Perth Airport Bsns Pk PH2 38 B7
Perth Artisan Golf Club PH1 103 B6
Perth Bsns Pk PH1 103 A4
Perth Coll
Blairgowrie PH10 88 C3
Perth PH1 102 D6
Perth Gram Sch PH1 102 F7
Perth High Sch PH1 102 C3
Perth Mart Visitor Ctr The* PH1 102 A6
Perth Mus & Art Gall* PH1 103 B4
Perth Rd
Abernethy PH2 49 D2
Bankfoot PH1 24 B5
Blairgowrie PH10 88 B3
Cowdenbeath KY4 147 D6
Crieff PH7 101 E5
Dunblane FK15 107 E6
Dundee DD1 179 A1
Dunning PH2 47 A1
Milnathort KY13 108 D7
Perth PH2 103 D7
Stanley PH1 24 E4
Perth Royal Infmy PH1 102 E4
Perth Sailing Club PH2 48 F8
Perthshire Visitor Ctr* PH1 24 B5
Perth St PH10 88 C4
Perth Sta PH2 103 A3
Perth Theatre PH1 103 B4
Perth Wr Ski Club PH2 103 C1
Peter Arbuckle Pl DD2 92 B3
Peterburn Terr DD2 92 C5
Peter Howling Pl 1 KY10 83 C6
Petersgarth La PH10 88 B5
Peters La DD1 179 A1
Peter St DD1 179 B3
Peterswell Brae FK7 135 E1
Peth Coll KY13 108 D6
Petrel Way KY11 162 A2
Petrie Way 1 DD11 89 A7
PETTYCUR 166 F1
Pettycur Bay KY3 166 E1
Pettycur Bay Holiday Pk KY3 166 D1
Pettycur Ho KY3 166 F1
Pettycur Rd KY3 166 F1
Pheasantry The FK10 138 E5
Philip St DD7 100 D3
Phoenix Ind Est FK7 135 C7
Phoenix La KY12 160 F4
Piccadilly DD10 85 C5
Pickford Cres 7 KY10 83 D7
PICKLETILLEM 42 F3
Pickletullum Gdns 1 PH2 102 F3
Pickletullum Rd PH2 102 F3
Pictavia Ex* DD9 4 B6
Pie Ann Pl 3 KY15 64 A4
Pier Cottage PH2 49 C8
Pierhead 4 DD8 86 D4
Pierhead Bldgs KY11 178 C5
Pier Rd KY13 108 D2
Pike Rd FK7 135 D4
Pilkham Ct KY4 147 C3
Pilmour Links KY18 106 C6
Pilmour Pl KY19 106 D6
Pilmuir Rd KY8 80 E5
Pilmuir St KY12 161 A5
Pineapple The* FK2 154 B6
Pine Cres FK11 116 F6
Pinedale Terr PH2 37 E5
Pine Gr
Alloa FK10 138 C6
Blairgowrie PH10 15 B5
Dunfermline KY11 173 E8
6 Ladybank KY15 64 A5
Pine La KY7 112 F8
Pines The 8 DD4 94 F8

Pine Way PH1 102 B3
Pinewood Dr KY11 175 B3
Pinewood Gdns 1 DD2 93 C7
Pinkerton Pl KY11 173 F5
Pinkerton Rd
- Crail KY10 69 B3
- Glenrothes KY7 113 A6

Pinnel Pl KY11 175 C4
Pipeland Rd KY16 106 D4
Pipeland Wlk KY20 106 D4
Piper Cres KY3 165 D2
Piperdam Ctry Pk* DD2 28 A5
Piperdam Dr DD2 28 A6
Piperdam Golf Club* DD2 28 A5
Piper Dr KY7 110 F2
Piper Row 5 KY13 108 C2
Piper St DD4 95 C6
Piper's Way DD3 18 A1
Pirnie Mill DD8 87 E6
Pirnie St 10 KY8 79 F2
PISGAH 107 E4
Pitairlie Rd
- 7 Dundee DD4 94 F5
- Newbigging DD5 31 B6

Pitalpin Ct DD2 93 B7
Pitalpin St DD2 92 F7
Pitbauchlie Bank KY11 161 C1
PITCAIRN 110 F3
Pitcairn Ave KY7 110 E3
Pitcairn Dr 1 KY16 53 E7
Pitcairnfield Pl PH1 36 E5
PITCAIRNGREEN 36 E6
Pitcairn Pk
- Glenrothes KY6 110 E3
- 4 Leuchars KY16 54 B8

Pitcairn Pl KY2 130 E2
Pitcairn Prim Sch PH1 36 E5
Pitcairn Rd
- Dundee DD3 91 D3
- Lochgelly KY5 128 E3

Pitcairn St KY11 161 C2
PITCORTHIE 161 E1
Pitcorthie Dr KY11 173 E8
Pitcorthie Prim Sch KY11 161 E1
Pitcorthie Rd KY11 161 C1
PITCOUDIE 111 B2
Pitcoudie Ave KY7 111 A1
Pitcoudie Prim Sch KY7 111 A1
Pitcruvie Pk 10 KY8 80 F5
Pitcullen Cres PH2 103 C6
Pitcullen Gdns PH2 103 C5
Pitcullen Terr PH2 103 C5
Pitcur St 1 DD3 91 D3
Pitdinnie Pl KY12 159 D1
Pitdinnie Rd KY12 159 D2
Pitempton Rd DD3 91 C4
Pitfairn Rd FK10 118 E3
Pitfirrane Pk KY12 160 B1
Pitforthie Pl DD9 84 E4
Pitfour PH2 49 F8
Pitfour Pl KY2 150 C7
Pitfour St DD2 93 D4
Pitheavlis Castle Gdns PH2 102 F2
Pitheavlis Cres PH2 102 F3
Pitheavlis Terr PH2 102 F2
Pitkellony St PH5 44 C3
Pitkerro Dr DD4 94 D5
Pitkerro Rd DD4 94 E5
Pitkevy Ct KY6 110 D3
Pitkevy Gdns KY6 110 C3
Pitlair Pk KY15 64 B6
PITLESSIE 64 D4
Pitlessie Gdns 2 DD3 91 D3
Pitlessie Mill Rd KY15 64 D4
Pitlessie Prim Sch KY15 64 D4
Pitlessie Rd KY15 64 B5
Pitlethie Rd KY16 54 B8
Pitlochie Terr KY5 77 F1
Pitmedden Loan KY7 110 E2
Pitmedden Rd KY11 162 A1
Pitmedden Wynd 20 KY14 62 F6
Pitmuies Gdn* DD8 12 C4
Pitnacree St 17 PH11 7 A3
Pit Rd KY4 147 E6
Pitreavie Bsns Pk KY11 173 C7
Pitreavie Cres KY11 173 C8
Pitreavie Ct KY11 173 D6
Pitreavie Dr KY11 173 D6
Pitreavie Ind Est KY11 173 D6
Pitreavie Pl
- Dundee DD3 91 D3
- 1 Kirkcaldy KY2 130 F2

Pitreavie Prim Sch KY11 173 D8
PITREUCHIE 87 F4
Pitreuchie Pl DD8 87 F5
Pitroddie Gdns 7 DD3 91 C3
Pitscandly Pk 5 DD8 10 F7
PITSCOTTIE 65 F8
Pitscottie Rd KY15 105 D5
Pitskelly Rd DD7 100 A3
PITTACHAR 101 E1
Pittencrieff House Mus* KY12 160 F3
Pittencrieff Prim Sch KY12 160 F4
Pittencrieff St KY12 160 F4
Pittendriech Rd DD9 84 A4
PITTENWEEM 83 A6
Pittenweem Prim Sch KY10 83 B6
Pittenweem Rd KY10 83 B5
Pittenzie Rd PH7 101 D3
Pittenzie St PH7 101 D3
PITTEUCHAR 113 B4
Pitteuchar Dr KY6 113 A4
Pitteuchar E Prim Sch KY7 113 C3
Pitteuchar W Prim Sch KY7 113 B5
Pitt Terr FK8 135 B6
PLAINS 60 D5
Plane Gr KY11 173 F8
Plantation Row KY1 132 E4
Plantation St KY5 148 B7
Planton Sq 3 PH1 37 B8
Player Dr KY12 146 A1
Players Rd FK7 135 C7
Playfair Dr
- Dundee DD3 93 D8
- 17 Leuchars KY16 54 C8

Playfair Terr
- Dundee DD3 93 D8
- 12 St Andrews KY21 106 D6

Playfield Ct KY15 64 F8
Pleasance KY15 63 B2
Pleasance Brae KY12 159 D1
Pleasance Ct
- Dundee DD1 93 E3
- Halbeath KY12 162 B7

Pleasance Rd
- Coupar Angus PH13 16 A2
- Dunfermline KY12 161 F6
- Halbeath KY12 162 A6

Pleasance The KY4 126 D3
Pleasures The FK10 137 E7
Plewlandcroft EH30 178 B1
Plewlands Ho EH30 178 B1
Plockton Terr DD2 92 C5
Plover Cres KY11 162 B1
Poet's Pl DD9 84 E2
Pole Pk Rd DD1 93 E4
Pollock Terr PH7 101 E5
Pollock Wlk KY12 160 E5
Polmaise Ave FK7 135 B3
Polmaise Cres FK7 136 C5
Polmaise Ct FK7 135 B3
Polmaise Rd
- Cambusbarron FK7 134 E3
- Stirling FK7 134 F5

Polworth Pl KY4 147 D4
Pomarium St 6 PH2 103 A3
Pompee Rd FK10 118 B1
Ponderlaw La 6 DD11 89 E4
Ponderlaw St DD11 89 E4
Pond La 2 DD6 99 F5
Pont Cres FK15 107 D7
Pool La KY1 131 F1
POOL OF MUCKHART 74 A3
Poplar Ave PH10 88 C3
Poplar Cres
- Kirkcaldy KY2 151 B7
- Perth PH1 102 B3

Poplar Gdns KY2 151 A7
Poplar Gr KY11 173 E8
Poplar Grey Ct DD4 95 B8
Poplar Pl PH1 102 B3
Poplar Rd
- Glenrothes KY7 113 C5
- Leven KY8 79 F3
- St Andrews KY16 53 F5

Poplars The
- 1 Dundee DD4 95 A8
- Tullibody FK10 117 B1

PORT ALLEN 50 E8
PORT BRAE 151 C4
Porterfield KY12 158 E7
Porter's Brae KY7 79 D7
Port Laing Wynd KY11 178 C7
Portland Gdns 3 KY2 130 F1
Portmoak Prim Sch KY13 76 F6
Portmore Pl DD2 92 F6
Portpatrick Terr 1 DD5 96 E6
Portree Ave DD5 96 B4
Port St
- Clackmannan FK10 139 A4
- Inverkeithing KY11 174 C2
- Stirling FK8 135 B7

Post Box Rd DD2 90 C3
Postgate KY7 113 A6
Posthill FK10 118 D1
Postings The KY1 151 B3
Post Office La KY11 178 C6
Potterhill PH2 103 C4
Potterhill Gdns PH2 103 C4
Potters Pk DD8 87 C3
Potters Pk Cres DD8 87 C2
Pottery St
- Kirkcaldy KY1 131 E1
- Kirkcaldy KY1 151 E8

Pottis Rd FK7 135 D3
Powfoot Rd KY2 130 F2
POWMILL
- Dollar 122 E8
- Kinross 74 C1

Powrie Pl DD1 179 B4
Powrie Prim Sch DD4 95 D4
Powside Pl PH14 40 B7
Prains Ct PH7 101 E4
Pratt St KY1 151 A1
PRAYTIS 65 C1
Praytis Farm Pk* KY8 65 C1
Preston Cres
- High Valleyfield KY12 158 A2
- Inverkeithing KY11 174 C2

Prestonfield KY12 142 E6
Prestonfield Dr KY2 130 F1
Prestonhall Ave KY7 113 D8
Prestonhall Dr KY7 113 D8
Prestonhall Ind Est KY15 53 B2
Prestonhall Rd KY7 113 D8
Preston St KY12 158 A2
Preston Terr
- Inverkeithing KY11 174 D1
- Sauchie FK10 118 D1

Prestwick Pl 5 KY2 130 F1
Pretoria Pl KY4 147 B4
Priestden Pk KY16 106 E4
Priestden Pl KY16 106 E4
Priestden Rd KY16 106 E4
Priestfield Maltings 6 KY15 64 D4
Prieston Rd
- Bankfoot PH1 24 A6
- Dundee DD3 91 F2

Prime Gilt Box St KY2 151 B6
Primmer Pl KY4 147 D3
Primrose Ave KY11 173 D5
Primrose Bank DD4 95 B3
Primrose Bsns Pk KY11 173 D5
Primrose Cres PH1 102 D8
Primrose Ct
- Alloa FK10 138 B6
- Rosyth KY11 173 D5
- Tillicoultry FK13 119 A7

Primrose La
- Cowdenbeath KY4 147 C5
- Kincardine FK10 155 E3
- Rosyth KY11 173 D5

Primrose Pl
- Alloa FK10 138 B6
- Perth PH1 102 D7
- Tillicoultry FK13 119 A7

Primrose Rd KY11 173 B5
Primrose St
- Alloa FK10 138 B7
- Carnoustie DD7 100 B3

Primrose Terr PH1 102 D8
Princes Cres 5 FK14 73 C1
Princes Cres E 4 FK14 73 C1
Princes Cres N 3 FK14 73 C1
Princes Croft 6 PH13 15 F2
Princess Cres 10 KY15 63 E1
Princes St
- 11 Arbroath DD11 89 C3
- Dundee DD4 179 C3
- Monifieth DD5 97 C6
- Perth PH2 103 B3
- Stirling FK8 135 B8

Pringle Ct PH1 102 C7
Prinlaws Rd KY6 112 A7
Priorland 15 PH2 49 F7
PRIOR MUIR 67 E8
Prior Rd DD8 87 E5
Priorwood Dr KY11 162 A1
Priory Cres DD11 89 D6
Priory Ct
- Dunfermline KY12 161 A3
- 11 Pittenweem KY10 83 A5
- 9 Whitehills DD8 87 E5

Priory Gdns KY16 106 B4
Priory Ho KY12 161 A3
Priory La
- Dunfermline KY12 161 A3
- Newport-on-Tay DD6 42 A2

Priory Pl PH2 103 A2
Priory Rd DD6 42 A2
Priory Sq FK10 155 F3
Priory Way DD8 87 F5
Promenade
- Leven KY8 109 F6
- Limekilns KY11 172 C3

Prosen Bank DD7 100 D4
Prosen Dr 2 DD11 89 F5
Prosen Pl DD8 87 E6
Prosen Rd
- Carnoustie DD7 100 D4
- Kirriemuir DD8 86 C4

Prospect Bsns Ctr DD2 92 C3
Prospect Pl DD3 179 A3
Prospect Row KY16 54 E1
Prospect St KY4 147 B4
Prospect Terr DD6 98 E5
Proudfoot Ct 2 KY5 77 E1
Proudfoot Way 3 KY5 77 E1
Provost Black Dr DD6 99 D7
Provost Buchan Rd DD9 84 B5
Provost Chapel Rd DD11 89 C6
Provost Hunter Ave FK12 118 C7
Provost Johnston Rd 2 DD10 85 C2
Provost Jones Ct 3 FK13 119 B7
Provost Kay Pk KY1 151 C6
Provost McGowan Pl DD1 93 E2
Provost Mains PH2 49 E3
Provost Millar Ave DD9 84 B4
Provost Mitchell Rd 2 DD10 85 C7
Provost Niven Cl KY22 106 C6
Provost Pk 1 KY14 62 F7
Provost Rd
- Blairgowrie PH10 88 C4
- Brechin DD9 84 B4
- Dundee DD3 94 A4
- Tayport DD6 99 F6

Provost Reids Rd DD10 85 D2
Provost Scott Ct 3 KY15 105 C4
Provost Scott's Rd DD10 85 D4
Provost Sq DD9 84 B4
Provost's Wlk DD5 97 A6
Provost Wynd KY15 105 C5
Pullar Ave FK9 115 A6
Pullar Ct FK9 115 A6
Pullar Terr PH1 102 C7
Purves Ct KY1 151 B2
Pyetree Rd KY7 79 A2

Q

Quakerfield FK7 135 E1
Quality St
- Dysart KY1 152 A7
- Newport-on-Tay DD6 41 F2

Quarry Brae KY1 151 F8
Quarry Ct KY4 147 B3
Quarry Gdns DD2 93 A7
Quarry Knowe 1 DD2 93 A6
Quarryknowe Cres PH14 40 C7
QUARRYMILL 103 C7
Quarrymill Woodland Pk* PH2 103 C7
Quarry Pk DD8 86 E5
Quarry Pl FK10 138 C8
Quarry Rd
- Cambusbarron FK7 134 C5
- Dundee DD2 90 A3
- 2 Dunning PH2 47 A1
- 4 Perth PH2 103 A1
- Tayport DD6 99 D7

Quarry Side DD2 93 A6
Quarryside Ct KY12 160 C6
QUARTERBANK 45 C8
Queen Anne High Sch KY12 160 F6
Queen Anne St KY12 161 A4
Queen Elizabeth Rd 18 KY10 83 A5
Queen Margaret Dr
- Glenrothes KY7 113 A6
- South Queensferry EH30 178 C1

Queen Margaret Fauld KY12 161 F6
Queen Margaret Gdns KY12 161 F6
Queen Margaret Hospl KY12 161 E6
Queen Margaret Pk KY12 161 F6
Queen Margaret's Gait DD8 87 C5
Queen Margaret's Pl KY11 178 C6
Queen Margaret St
- Kinghorn KY3 166 F1
- 3 Monance KY10 82 E4

Queen St E DD6 98 E5
Queens Ave
- Blairgowrie PH10 88 C4
- 3 Leven KY8 79 F2

Queen's Ave
- Bridge of A FK9 115 B6
- Perth PH2 102 F1

Queens Bldgs 6 DD6 99 F7
Queen's Bldgs KY11 173 E5
Queen's Cl DD10 85 D3
Queens Cres
- Glenrothes KY7 113 F7
- Kinghorn KY3 166 F1
- Kinross KY13 108 C2
- 1 Ladybank KY15 64 A5

Queens Ct PH2 102 F1
Queen's Ct FK9 114 F7
Queen's Ct KY12 161 A3
Queen's Dr
- Arbroath DD11 89 B2
- Perth PH2 103 B8

Queensferry Mus* EH30 178 C1
Queensferry Prim Sch EH30 178 C1
Queensferry Rd
- Crieff PH5 44 C3
- Dunfermline KY11 173 D7
- Rosyth KY11 173 E5

Queen's Gall* DD1 179 A1
Queensgate KY7 113 B7
Queens Gdns
- 38 Anstruther Easter KY10 83 C6
- Bridge of A FK9 114 F7

Queen's Gdns KY16 106 D6
Queenshaugh KY12 159 C7
Queenshaugh Dr FK8 115 C1
Queen's La 1 FK9 115 A7
Queens Mdw KY7 113 F4
Queens Mews 8 FK9 115 A7
Queen's Pend 12 PH10 88 C5
Queen's Rd
- New Scone PH2 103 F8
- Stirling FK8 134 F7

Queen St
- Alloa FK10 138 B7
- Alva FK12 118 A7

Queen St *continued*
- 8 Arbroath DD11 89 C3
- Bannockburn FK7 135 C2
- Carnoustie DD7 100 D3
- Coupar Angus PH13 16 A2
- Cupar KY14 63 B5
- Dundee DD1 179 C3
- Fallin FK7 136 C4
- Forfar DD8 87 D5
- 3 Freuchie KY15 63 E1
- Inverkeithing KY11 174 B2
- Monifieth DD5 97 A6
- Montrose DD10 85 D4
- Newport-on-Tay DD6 98 E5
- Perth PH2 103 A2
- Stirling FK8 135 A8
- 3 Tayport DD6 99 F6

Queens Terr
- Auchterarder PH3 104 E6
- 2 Bridge of A FK9 115 A7

Queen's Terr KY16 106 D5
Queens View KY13 76 E6
QUEENSWAY 113 B7
Queensway KY7 113 B7
Queens Way KY11 173 B2
Queensway Ind Est KY7 113 B7
Queensway Rdbt KY7 113 B7
Queenswell Rd DD8 87 C5
Queen Victoria Sch FK15 107 F8
Queich Pl KY13 108 C1

R

RADERNIE 66 E4
Radernie Pl KY16 54 E2
Raeburn Cres KY2 151 A4
Raeburn Hts KY6 112 F6
Raeburn Path KY7 112 F6
Raeburn Pk PH2 103 A3
Raeburn Pl PH2 103 A2
Rae Pl PH1 102 F6
Rae St KY4 147 C2
Raglan St DD4 94 C3
Railway Pl
- 2 Cupar KY15 105 D4
- Montrose DD10 85 D2

Railway Rd PH10 88 D4
RAIT 39 C5
Raith Ave KY4 147 C3
Raith Cres KY2 151 A4
Raith Ctr KY4 147 D4
Raith Dr KY2 151 A3
Raith Gdns KY2 151 A3
RAITH PARK 150 D5
Ralston Ct KY6 112 B6
Ralston Dr KY2 130 F2
Ralston Mount DD5 95 C3
Ralston Pl 4 DD5 95 C3
Ralston Rd DD5 95 C3
Ramornie Pl 3 KY15 64 A3
Ramoyle FK15 107 D6
Ramsay Cres KY3 166 A2
Ramsay Ct FK10 155 E4
Ramsay Dr FK15 107 F7
Ramsay Gdns KY6 112 A8
Ramsay La
- Kincardine FK10 155 E4
- Limekilns KY11 172 D3

Ramsay Pl
- Glenrothes KY6 112 F7
- Rosyth KY11 173 F3
- Stirling FK8 115 A2

Ramsay Rd KY1 151 B1
Ramsay St N 5 DD5 97 C6
Ramsay St S 3 DD5 97 C6
Ramsay St
- Broughty Ferry DD5 96 B2
- 5 Crieff PH7 101 D4
- Monifieth DD5 97 C6
- 1 Montrose DD10 85 D2
- Tillicoultry FK14 119 C4

Ramsay Terr FK13 119 B7
Ramsden Rd KY6 112 D2
Ramsey Tullis Dr FK10 117 C1
Randolph Cres FK7 135 C1
Randolph Ct
- Kirkcaldy KY1 132 A1
- Kirkcaldy KY1 152 A8
- Leven KY8 133 F8
- Stirling FK8 135 A5

Randolph Ind Est
- Kirkcaldy KY1 132 A1
- Kirkcaldy KY1 152 A8

Randolph Pl
- Bannockburn FK7 135 C2
- Kirkcaldy KY1 132 A1
- Kirkcaldy KY1 151 F8
- Kirkcaldy KY1 152 A8

Randolph Rd
- Kirkcaldy KY1 131 F1
- Stirling FK8 135 B4

Randolph St
- Cowdenbeath KY4 147 D3
- East Wemyss KY1 133 B5
- Leven KY8 133 F8

Randolph Terr FK7 135 A4
Randolph Wemyss Meml KY8 109 A2
Ranfurly Gdns 4 KY2 130 F1
Rankeillor St 9 KY9 82 B3
Rankine Ct DD6 98 B3
Rankine's Ct DD1 179 B2
Rankine St DD3 93 D4
Rankine Wynd FK10 117 C2

Rannaleroch Strathmore Golf Course PH11 7 B1
Rannoch Ct FK10 138 C5
Rannoch Dr KY12 160 B1
Rannochmoor Gdns [8] DD3 91 C3
Rannoch Pl
Dundee DD2 91 C1
Kinross KY13 108 B4
Rannoch Rd
Dundee DD3 91 C1
Glenrothes KY7 111 C2
Kirkcaldy KY2 150 E8
Leven KY8 109 B4
Perth PH1 102 E5
Rosyth KY11 173 E2
RAPLOCH 114 F2
Raploch Prim Sch FK8 114 E2
Raploch Rd FK8 114 F1
Rashleigh Ct KY6 112 D5
Ratagan Ct [6] KY7 111 C2
RATHILLET 52 E8
Rathillet Prim Sch KY15 52 E7
Ratho Cl KY6 112 B6
Ratho Pl
Dunfermline KY11 161 C3
Kirkcaldy KY2 130 F2
RATTRAY 88 E5
Rattray Pl [5] DD5 97 A5
Rattray Prim Sch PH10 88 E6
Rattray St
Dundee DD1 179 A2
Monifieth DD5 97 A5
Rattray Terr KY5 148 A7
Raven Cres KY8 79 F2
Ravensby Pk Gdns DD7 32 A5
Ravensby Rd DD7 100 A2
Ravens Craig [11] KY1 151 D6
Ravenscraig Castle* KY1 151 E5
Ravenscraig Gdns DD5 95 D3
Ravenscraig Park Nature Trail* KY1 151 F6
Ravenscraig Pl DD2 92 E6
Ravenscraig Rd DD2 92 E6
Ravenscraig St KY1 151 E6
Ravenscraig Terr KY12 143 A5
Ravenswood [3] FK13 119 C7
Ravenswood Dr KY6 112 D5
Recreation Pk (Alloa Athletic FC) FK10 138 C6
Rectory La KY1 152 A7
Rectory Rd PH7 101 D4
Red Admiral Ct DD4 95 B8
Redburn Wynd KY1 151 C4
Redcastle Cres DD5 95 F5
Red Cliffs [1] DD2 41 B8
Redcraigs KY2 150 C7
Redfield Cres DD10 85 C4
Redfield Rd DD10 85 C4
REDFORD 21 E7
Redford Pl [1] DD5 97 A7
Redford Rd DD8 10 B6
REDGORTON 37 A7
Redhall FK7 136 A4
Redlands Rd FK10 117 A3
Redmyre Gdns [3] DD4 95 A3
Redpath Loan KY7 110 F3
Red Row KY11 172 D3
Redwell Pl FK10 137 F7
Redwells Rd KY5 77 E2
Redwood Ave [4] DD2 93 C6
Reform St
Blairgowrie PH10 88 C5
Dundee DD1 179 B2
[5] Kirriemuir DD8 86 D5
Monifieth DD5 97 B5
Montrose DD10 85 D4
Tayport DD6 99 E6
Regent Pl DD5 95 E3
Regent St FK10 155 E3
Regents Way KY11 175 B3
Regent Terr KY14 63 B5
Reid Ave KY4 162 E6
Reid Cres KY13 108 E7
Reid Gdns KY16 106 A3
Reid Pk Rd DD8 87 D4
Reid Pl
Balbeggie PH2 38 B6
Glenrothes KY6 112 F6
Reid's La DD2 93 A6
Reid Sq DD3 179 A4
Reid St
Dundee DD3 179 A4
Dunfermline KY12 161 A3
Lochgelly KY5 148 B8
Renfrew Dr PH1 102 C7
Rennell Rd DD4 94 D5
Renny Cres DD10 85 C6
Rennyhill Gdns KY10 83 D7
Renton Dr [1] KY13 108 B4
Reres Gdns [5] DD5 96 C4
Reresmount Pl [1] DD5 96 C3
Reres Rd DD5 96 C3
RESCOBIE 11 C7
Rescobie Ave DD4 95 A3
Reservoir Rd [4] DD6 42 B5
Restenneth Dr DD8 87 E5
Restenneth Pl [8] DD8 10 F7
Retinue Row PH1 36 A5
Rev. Shirra St KY2 130 E1
Rhodders Gr FK12 118 B7
Rhodes St KY11 161 B2
RHYND 49 B7
Rhynd La PH2 48 E7
Rhynd Public Sch PH2 49 B6
Rhynd Rd PH2 48 E7
Rhynie Rd
Dundee DD4 95 C4
Glenrothes KY7 110 E2
RICCARTON 139 B5
Richmond Ct [4] DD2 93 C2
Richmond Pl KY5 148 B7
Richmond Terr DD2 93 C2
Riddell Terr DD4 94 E6
Ridge Way KY11 175 B5
Ridley Dr KY11 173 F3
Riggend Rd DD11 89 A3
Rigg's Pl [3] KY15 105 D4
Riggs Rd PH1 102 F4
Riggs The
[2] Auchtermuchty KY14 62 F6
[17] Falkland KY15 63 B2
Riggs View KY12 159 D1
Rimble Loan [4] KY6 112 F6
Rimble Path [7] KY6 112 F6
Rimble Sq [8] KY6 112 F6
RIMBLETON 112 F6
Rimbleton Ave KY6 112 F5
Rimbleton Pk [12] KY6 112 F6
Rimbleton Prim Sch KY6 112 E6
Rimsdale Cres KY7 111 A3
Rintoul Ave
Blairhall KY12 158 A8
Crieff PH7 101 E4
Rintoul Pl KY12 158 A8
Rires Rd [20] KY16 54 B8
Rising Sun Rd KY8 109 A1
Ritchie Ave DD5 97 B6
Ritchie Ct KY12 161 A7
Ritchie Pl
Crieff PH7 101 E4
Perth PH1 102 D7
Riverbahk View FK8 115 C1
Riverbank View FK8 135 C8
River Cres DD2 92 E2
RIVERSIDE 115 B1
Riverside
[2] Bridge of Earn PH2 48 F5
Perth PH2 103 C4
Thornton KY1 131 D6
River Side KY8 109 D6
Riverside App DD2 93 E1
Riverside Ave DD2 92 E2
Riverside Ct
[6] Cupar KY15 105 D5
Rattray PH10 88 D5
Riverside Dr
Blairgowrie PH10 88 C6
Dundee DD1 179 A1
Stirling FK8 115 C1
Riverside La DD6 98 C3
Riverside Pk [13] PH10 88 C5
Riverside Pl DD2 92 E2
Riverside Prim Sch FK8 115 B1
Riverside Rd
Blairgowrie PH10 88 C6
Leven KY8 109 D6
Montrose DD10 85 B2
Woodhaven DD6 98 B2
Riverside Terr FK10 155 F3
Riverside View FK10 138 B4
Riverside Way KY8 109 A6
River St
Brechin DD9 84 D2
Montrose DD10 85 D1
River Terr KY16 54 A6
Riverview FK10 138 A7
River View KY11 175 B2
Riverview Bsns Pk PH2 48 D8
Riverview Dr DD5 97 B5
River Wlk KY11 175 B2
River Wynd FK9 115 A4
Roanhead Terr FK10 155 E4
Robert Adam Dr KY2 130 D1
Robert Dick Ct FK10 117 C2
Robert Douglas Memoral Prim Sch PH2 37 F6
Robert Dow Ct KY5 148 B8
Robert Henryson Sch KY11 162 A4
Robert Hutchison Gdns [7] KY8 79 F6
Robert Kinmond Ave FK10 117 C2
Robert Knox Ave FK10 117 C2
Robert Lindsay Pl [2] DD11 89 A7
Robert Philp Rd [11] KY2 130 E1
Robert Smith Ct KY4 147 E6
Robertson Ave KY8 109 C7
Robertson Cres KY14 50 D5
Robertson Pl FK7 135 B3
Robertson Rd
Cupar KY15 105 E3
Dunblane FK15 107 F6
Dunfermline KY12 161 D5
Perth PH1 102 A5
Robertson St
Alva FK12 118 B7
[9] Dundee DD4 94 C3
Robertson Terr DD8 87 C6
Roberts St N DD8 87 E6
Roberts St
Forfar DD8 87 D6
Kirkcaldy KY1 151 E8
Robert St
Arbroath DD11 89 C4
Robert St *continued*
Newport-on-Tay DD6 98 E5
Robert Wilson Gr KY12 161 D8
Robin Cres KY8 79 F1
Robson St DD4 94 D3
Rockfield Cres DD2 93 C3
Rockfield Gdns KY7 110 E3
Rockfield St DD2 93 C3
Rocks Rd KY11 172 B4
Rockwell Gdns DD3 93 E6
Rockwell Pl DD3 93 E6
Rodd Rd DD4 94 D4
Rodger Pl KY1 132 E4
Rodgers Pl KY15 63 E8
Rodger St [14] KY10 83 D6
Roger's Cl [12] DD8 86 D4
Rolland Ave KY1 133 C7
Rolland St
Dunfermline KY12 161 A3
[6] Monance KY10 82 E4
Romangate [8] PH2 47 A1
Roman Rd
Almondbank PH1 36 E5
Inverkeithing KY11 174 B2
Kirriemuir DD8 9 A7
Roman Way FK15 107 C4
Romyn Rd KY11 173 C1
Rona Ct PH1 102 F8
Ronald Pl FK8 135 B8
Ronaldson Gr KY12 161 D5
Rona Pl KY7 111 A2
Roods DD8 86 C5
Roods Cres KY11 174 B3
Roods Pl DD8 86 C6
Roods Rd KY11 174 B2
Roods Sq KY11 174 C3
Roodyards Rd DD1 94 D2
Roomebay Ave [1] KY10 69 B2
Roomebay Cres KY10 69 B2
Roomlin Gdns KY1 151 F7
Rorrie Terr PH1 36 A5
Rosabelle St KY1 151 E7
Rosamonde Pilcher Dr DD2 40 F8
Roseangle DD1 179 A1
ROSEBANK 16 E1
Rosebank
Alloa FK10 118 D1
Cowdenbeath KY4 147 D4
Dunfermline KY11 161 C2
Perth PH1 102 E3
Rosebank Gdns
Alloa FK10 138 C8
Dunfermline KY12 160 D6
Kincardine FK10 155 F3
Rosebank La DD8 87 D4
Rosebank Pl DD3 179 B4
Rosebank Prim Sch DD3 179 A3
Rosebank Rd
[4] Blairgowrie PH10 88 E6
Dundee DD3 179 A3
Rosebank St DD3 179 A4
Roseberry Pl DD11 89 B2
Roseberry St [1] DD2 93 D4
Roseberry Terr [17] KY8 109 E6
Rosebery Ct
Dalgety Bay KY11 174 F2
Kirkcaldy KY1 151 B5
Rosebery Gr KY11 174 F2
Rosebery Pl
Dalgety Bay KY11 174 F2
Stirling FK8 115 B1
Rosebery Terr KY1 151 B5
Rosebery View KY11 174 F2
Rosebine Gdns KY7 79 A2
Roseburn Gdns [2] DD4 94 F8
Rosebush Cres KY11 161 C3
Rose Cres
Dunfermline KY12 161 A4
Perth PH1 102 E4
Rosedale Cres [2] DD5 96 D5
Rosefield Gdns [6] DD8 86 D5
Rosefield Pl
[1] Arbroath DD11 22 E3
[2] Dundee DD1 93 D3
Rosefield Rd DD8 86 D5
Rosefield St DD1 93 D3
Rose Gdns KY12 159 D2
Rosehall Gdns DD2 92 C4
Rose Hemming Pl [16] DD8 11 E3
Rose Hill DD10 85 D5
Rosehill Cres KY4 147 B3
Rosehill Ct DD10 85 D5
Rosehill Rd DD10 85 D5
Rose La
Dundee DD3 179 A3
Lochgelly KY5 148 B7
South Queensferry EH30 178 B1
St Andrews KY16 106 D6
Torryburn KY12 158 E1
Roselea Gdns [1] KY15 64 A4
Rosemalen Pl KY12 161 C4
Rosemarkie Cres DD5 96 D4
Rosemarkie Pl [3] DD5 96 D5
Rosemill Ct KY12 158 C1
Rosemill Rd DD3 91 A5
ROSEMOUNT 88 F1
Rosemount DD8 87 D4
Rosemount Ave
Dunnikier KY2 131 A1
Kirkcaldy KY2 151 A8
Rosemount Cres
Dundee DD2 90 C3
Rosemount Cres *continued*
Glenrothes KY6 112 B6
Rosemount Gdns PH10 88 E1
Rosemount Pk PH10 88 D3
Rosemount Pk Gdns PH10 88 D4
Rosemount Pl
[3] Hillside DD10 6 C8
Perth PH2 103 C5
Rosemount Prim Sch DD10 6 C8
Rosemount Rd
Arbroath DD11 89 B2
Dundee DD2 90 C3
Glenrothes KY6 112 A6
Montrose DD10 6 C8
Rose St
Alloa FK10 117 E1
Arbroath DD11 89 B3
Burntisland KY3 177 E8
Carnoustie DD7 100 C3
Cowdenbeath KY4 147 C3
Dunfermline KY12 161 B4
Leven KY8 109 C4
[17] Monance KY10 82 E4
Tayport DD6 99 F6
Tullibody FK10 117 D4
Rosetay Ct KY12 161 C4
Rose Terr
Leven KY8 109 E7
Perth PH1 103 B5
Rosethorn Wynd KY12 161 C3
Roseville Pl [5] DD11 22 E4
Rosewell Dr KY5 128 A6
Rosewell Rd DD8 86 E2
Rosewood Terr DD2 93 B2
Rose Wynd [9] KY10 69 B2
Rosie The KY1 133 D8
Rosin Ct KY1 151 C7
Roslin Gdns DD4 94 D4
Ross Ave
Dalgety Bay KY11 175 A2
Woodlands PH1 102 D2
Ross Ct
Stirling FK7 135 B3
Tillicoultry FK13 119 C7
Rossend Terr KY3 177 D8
Ross Gdns
Dundee DD2 93 A5
Kirkcaldy KY1 151 E7
Rossie Ave
Broughty Ferry DD5 96 A5
Dundee DD5 95 F5
Rossiebank Cres [4] DD8 9 A7
ROSSIE ISLAND OR INCHBRAOCH 85 A1
Rossie Island Rd DD10 85 B1
ROSSIE MILLS 6 B3
Rossie Pk Dr PH14 40 B7
Rossie Pl
Auchterarder PH3 104 D5
Perth PH2 48 A5
Rossie Sch DD10 14 A8
Rossie Sq [2] DD10 85 D1
Rossie St DD11 89 C4
Rossie Terr DD10 85 D1
Ross La KY12 160 F4
Rossland Pl KY3 166 F2
Rosslyn Ave [3] PH2 102 F3
Rosslyn Gdns KY1 131 F1
Rosslyn Sch KY1 151 F8
Rosslyn St
Kirkcaldy KY1 131 F1
Kirkcaldy KY1 151 F8
Rossness Dr KY3 166 F1
Ross Pl KY3 166 F1
Ross Rd [11] KY16 54 B8
Ross St
Dunfermline KY12 161 B5
Kinross KY13 108 C2
Ross Terr DD5 97 B6
ROSYTH 173 F4
Rosyth Europarc
North Queensferry KY11 178 A7
Rosyth KY11 173 D1
ROSYTH ROYAL DOCKYARD 173 B1
Rosyth Sta KY11 173 E6
Rothesay Path KY7 113 B6
Rothesay Pl KY7 113 A7
Rothes Pk
Dundee DD5 95 C4
Glenrothes KY6 112 A7
Rothes Pl KY6 112 A8
Rothes Rd KY6 112 F6
Rothes Rdbt KY7 113 A7
Rotten Row [2] KY9 82 A3
Roughburn Rd FK9 115 A6
Roundel The
Auchterarder PH3 104 E7
[3] Lower Largo KY8 80 F5
Roundelwood
Alloa FK10 118 B1
[9] Tillicoultry FK13 119 C7
Roundel Wood [1] FK13 119 C7
Roundhill Rd KY16 106 E4
Round The KY12 161 C3
Roundyhill DD5 96 F6
Routine Row [13] KY10 83 A5
Rowallan Gn KY7 113 B2
Rowan Ave
Blairgowrie PH10 88 C2
Kirriemuir DD8 86 C6
Rowan Bank PH2 37 F5
Rowanbank Gdns DD5 96 B3
Rowan Cres
[8] Leven KY8 79 F2
Leven KY8 109 A4
Menstrie FK11 116 F5
Rowan Ct FK7 135 E1
Rowan Gr KY11 161 D1
Rowan Lea KY4 126 F2
Rowan Pl [5] PH2 48 F4
Rowans The
Alloa FK10 118 C2
Dundee DD4 95 A8
Rowan Terr
Cowdenbeath KY4 147 C3
Perth PH1 102 B3
Thornton KY1 131 D7
Rowantree Cres DD4 94 E6
Row The KY15 51 E1
Roxburgh Rd KY6 112 D7
Roxburgh Terr DD2 93 B3
Royal & Ancient Golf Club KY16 106 C7
Royal Bldgs DD6 98 E5
Royal Dundee Liff Hospl DD2 92 A8
Royal Exchange La DD1 179 B3
Royal Gdns FK8 135 A8
Royal Scot Way KY12 161 A5
Royal Stuart Way FK7 135 E8
Royal Tat Yatching Club DD5 95 E3
Royal Terr [14] KY15 63 B2
Royal Victoria DD2 93 B4
Roy St PH7 101 C3
RRS Discovery* DD1 179 B1
Ruby Pl [2] PH10 88 D5
Rugby Terr DD5 96 C2
RUMBLING BRIDGE 74 B2
RUMBLINGWELL 160 D5
Rumblingwell KY12 160 D5
Rumdewan Cres [2] KY15 64 A2
Rumdewan Terr KY15 64 A2
Rumford [12] KY10 69 B2
Ruskie Rd FK9 115 B3
Ruskin Cres [2] KY8 79 F1
Russel Ct KY5 148 B8
Russell Cres DD4 94 E6
Russell Ct KY11 161 F1
Russell Dr KY7 113 B6
Russell Gdns [9] KY15 64 A4
Russell Gr KY3 165 F2
Russell Pl
[1] Dundee DD3 93 F6
Dundee DD3 179 A4
[1] Kirkcaldy KY1 151 C5
Oakley KY12 158 F7
Russell Sq DD11 89 C4
Russell St
Arbroath DD11 89 C4
Cowdenbeath KY4 147 B4
Lochgelly KY5 148 B8
Montrose DD10 85 D3
[4] Stanley PH1 24 E4
Russel St [3] KY14 62 D4
Rutherford Ct
Bridge of A FK9 115 A8
Kirkcaldy KY1 151 E7
Rutherford Rd
Dundee DD2 93 B8
Glenrothes KY6 112 D3
RUTHVEN 7 E3
Ruthven Ave PH1 102 E6
Ruthvenfield Ave PH1 102 B8
Ruthvenfield Gr PH1 102 C8
Ruthvenfield Pl PH1 37 A5
Ruthvenfield Prim Sch PH1 36 F4
Ruthvenfield Rd PH1 102 A8
Ruthvenfield Way PH1 102 B8
Ruthven Gn KY7 113 C3
Ruthven Pk PH3 58 B8
Ruthven Pl KY16 106 B4
Ruthven Rd DD4 95 B4
Ruthven St PH3 104 E6
Ruthvenvale Terr PH3 104 F6
Ruthven Wr [2] PH3 46 B2
Rutland Cres DD10 85 C5
Ruxton Pl [4] DD7 100 C2
Ryan Pl PH7 101 B4
Ryan Rd KY6 112 E6
Ryehill La [8] DD1 93 E2
Rylands Ave FK15 107 E7
Rylands Rd FK15 107 F7
Rymalton KY1 151 D6

S

Saddlers Ct PH3 104 A5
Saggar St DD2 93 C4
Sahara Pk [5] KY9 82 A3
Sailors' Wlk KY3 177 D8
St Abbs Cres [4] KY10 83 B5
St Abb's Rd DD11 89 E5
St Adrian's Pl KY10 83 C6
St Adrian's Rd [9] KY10 83 B5
St Agathas RC Prim Sch KY8 109 D8
St Albans Terr DD3 91 B3
ST ANDREWS 106 E7
St Andrews Aquarium* KY16 106 D7

St Andrews Bay Golf Resort* KY16 ... 55 F1
St Andrews Botanic Gdn* KY16 ... 106 C5
St Andrews Castle* KY16 ... 106 E6
St Andrews Cres DD11 ... 89 F5
St Andrew's Dr
  Airth FK2 ... 154 B7
  Leven KY9 ... 82 B5
St Andrew's La DD1 ... 179 C3
St Andrews Meml KY16 ... 106 E5
St Andrews Mus* KY16 ... 106 C6
St Andrews Preservation Trust Mus & Gdn* KY16 ... 106 E6
St Andrew Sq 9 KY8 ... 109 C4
St Andrew's RC Cath DD1 ... 179 B1
St Andrew's RC High Sch KY2 ... 151 D8
St Andrews Rd
  Anstruther KY10 ... 69 A3
  13 Anstruther Wester KY10 ... 83 C6
  Leven KY9 ... 82 A5
  2 Upper Largo KY8 ... 81 A6
St Andrew's St DD1 ... 179 B3
St Andrew St
  26 Alyth PH11 ... 7 A3
  Brechin DD9 ... 84 B4
  Dunfermline KY11 ... 161 C2
  3 Perth PH2 ... 103 A3
St Anne's Cres FK7 ... 135 E1
St Ann's La 2 PH1 ... 103 B3
St Ann St DD2 ... 93 B5
St Ayles Cres 8 KY10 ... 83 C6
St Bean Ct PH3 ... 104 F7
St Bernadette's Prim Sch FK10 ... 117 A2
St Blane's Rd FK15 ... 107 D5
St Boswells Pl PH1 ... 102 A3
St Boswells Terr DD3 ... 91 B3
St Bride's RC Prim Sch KY4 ... 147 C3
St Bridgets Brae KY11 ... 175 C4
St Brioc Way DD10 ... 85 B1
St Brycedale Ave KY1 ... 151 B4
St Brycedale Ct KY1 ... 151 B4
St Brycedale Rd KY1 ... 151 B4
St Bunyans Pl 3 KY16 ... 54 B8
St Catherine's Rd PH1 ... 103 A4
St Catherines Ret Pk PH1 ... 103 A4
St Catherine St KY15 ... 105 D5
St Catherine's Wynd KY12 ... 160 F3
St Clairs Ct KY3 ... 167 A2
St Clairs Entry KY3 ... 167 A2
St Clair St KY1 ... 151 E7
St Clair's Wynd 13 KY10 ... 69 B2
St Clement Ave FK15 ... 107 C4
St Clement Pl DD3 ... 91 A3
St Clement's RC Prim Sch DD2 ... 92 E6
St Clement Terr DD3 ... 91 A3
St Colme Ave
  Aberdour KY3 ... 176 A5
  Aberdour KY3 ... 176 A6
St Colme Cres KY3 ... 176 B7
St Colme Dr KY11 ... 175 D5
St Colme Rd KY11 ... 175 D4
St Colme's Cl 1 DD8 ... 86 D4
St Colm's Abbey* KY3 ... 176 B2
St Columba Gdns DD3 ... 91 B3
St Columbas High Sch PH1 ... 103 A7
St Columba's RC High Sch KY11 ... 161 F3
St Columba's RC Prim Sch
  Cupar KY15 ... 105 C4
  Dundee DD3 ... 91 E1
St Columba's Rdbt KY6 ... 112 F6
ST DAVID'S ... 45 F7
St David's Bsns Pk KY11 ... 175 A4
St David's Ct KY11 ... 175 A3
St David's Dr KY11 ... 175 A4
St David's La DD1 ... 179 A2
St David St 5 DD9 ... 84 C3
St Dennis Pl 9 DD3 ... 91 A3
St Dennis Terr DD3 ... 91 A3
St Dominic's Prim Sch PH7 ... 101 C2
St Drostan Rd KY7 ... 113 B6
St Drostan's Ct KY7 ... 111 F1
St Edmund Pl DD3 ... 91 A2
St Edmund Terr 8 DD3 ... 91 A3
St Fergus RC Prim Sch DD2 ... 91 B1
St Fillans Cres KY3 ... 176 C8
St Fillans Gr KY3 ... 176 C8
St Fillans Pl
  Dundee DD3 ... 91 B2
  Kirkcaldy KY2 ... 150 D7
St Fillans Rd
  Dundee DD3 ... 91 A2
  Kirkcaldy KY2 ... 150 D7
St Fillans Terr DD2 ... 91 B2
St Fort Rd DD6 ... 98 B2
St Giles Pl DD3 ... 91 B2
St Giles Terr DD3 ... 91 B2
St James' Orch FK9 ... 115 D1
St James Pl
  10 Bechin DD9 ... 84 C3
  Kinghorn KY3 ... 167 A2
St James Rd DD8 ... 87 C4
St John's Cotts 5 DD10 ... 85 C4
St John's Ct KY11 ... 174 D3
St John's Dr KY12 ... 161 C3
St John's Pl
  Auchterarder PH3 ... 104 D6
  Dunfermline KY12 ... 161 D3
  6 Montrose DD10 ... 85 C4
  Perth PH1 ... 103 B4
St John's Prim Sch FK10 ... 137 F6
St John's RC High Sch DD3 ... 93 D7
St Johns RC Prim Sch PH1 ... 103 B5
St John's RC Prim Sch KY11 ... 173 F3
St Johns Sh Ctr PH1 ... 103 B4
St John St
  Perth PH1 ... 103 B3
  Stirling FK8 ... 135 A8
St Johnswood Terr DD2 ... 93 B2
St Josephs Cath Prim Sch 10 DD1 ... 93 E3
St Josephs RC Prim Sch KY4 ... 126 E1
St Kattan Pl PH3 ... 104 F7
St Kenneths Prim Sch KY5 ... 127 E8
St Kessog's Pl 5 PH3 ... 104 D6
St Kessogs Wynd 6 PH3 ... 104 D6
St Kilda Cres KY2 ... 150 F8
St Kilda Pl DD3 ... 91 B2
St Kilda Rd DD3 ... 91 B2
St Kilda Terr DD3 ... 91 B2
St Laurence Ave FK15 ... 107 C5
St Lawrence St KY11 ... 161 C1
St Leonard Pl DD3 ... 91 C2
St Leonard Rd DD3 ... 91 C3
St Leonards FK13 ... 119 D7
St Leonard's Bank PH2 ... 103 A2
St Leonard's Bridge PH2 ... 103 A2
St Leonard's Ct KY3 ... 167 A3
St Leonards - New Pk KY16 ... 106 E5
St Leonard's Pl
  Dunfermline KY11 ... 161 B1
  Kinghorn KY3 ... 166 F3
St Leonard's Prim Sch KY11 ... 161 B2
St Leonard's Rd KY16 ... 106 B5
St Leonard's Sch KY16 ... 106 E6
St Leonard's St KY11 ... 161 B2
St Leonard Terr DD3 ... 91 C2
St Luke's Prim Sch DD4 ... 94 F8
St Luke's Rd DD3 ... 91 D3
ST MADOES ... 49 F7
St Madoes Prim Sch PH2 ... 49 F8
St Madoes Rd PH2 ... 39 E1
St Magdalene's La 1 PH2 ... 103 A1
St Magdalene's Rd PH2 ... 103 A1
St Malcolm's Wynd 9 DD8 ... 86 C5
St Margarets PH3 ... 104 C6
St Margaret's Cave Mus* KY12 ... 160 F4
St Margaret's Cres PH3 ... 104 C5
St Margarets Dr KY12 ... 161 B3
St Margaret's Dr FK15 ... 107 E5
St Margaret's Loan FK15 ... 107 E5
St Margaret's Pk DD8 ... 87 F7
St Margaret's Pl DD8 ... 87 F7
St Margaret's Prim Sch EH30 ... 178 C1
St Margarets RC Prim Sch DD10 ... 85 C4
St Margaret's RC Prim Sch
  Dundee DD3 ... 91 D2
  Dunfermline KY11 ... 161 C3
St Margaret St KY12 ... 161 A3
St Margaret Wynd KY12 ... 161 F6
St Marie's RC Prim Sch KY2 ... 151 D8
St Martin Ave DD3 ... 91 B4
St Martin Dr DD3 ... 91 B4
ST MARTINS ... 25 D1
St Martins Rd PH2 ... 38 B8
St Mary Pl DD3 ... 93 E4
ST MARY'S ... 91 B3
St Marys Ct 11 PH10 ... 88 C5
St Marys Dr PH2 ... 103 E4
St Mary's Dr FK15 ... 107 E5
St Mary's Episcopal Prim Sch FK15 ... 107 E5
St Mary's Glebe KY1 ... 151 C5
St Mary's La
  3 Dundee DD2 ... 93 B5
  8 Newport-on-Tay DD6 ... 98 E4
St Marys Pl KY25 ... 106 D6
St Mary's Pl
  7 Kinross KY13 ... 108 B4
  Kirkcaldy KY1 ... 151 C5
  6 Mavisbank KY13 ... 108 B4
St Mary's RC Prim Sch
  Bannockburn FK7 ... 135 D2
  4 Dundee DD2 ... 93 B5
  Stirling FK8 ... 114 E2
St Mary's Rd
  Dundee DD3 ... 91 C2
  Kirkcaldy KY1 ... 151 C5
  4 Montrose DD10 ... 85 D3
St Mary St
  Arbroath DD11 ... 89 C4
  4 Brechin DD9 ... 84 C3
  Dundee DD3 ... 93 E4
  St Andrews KY16 ... 106 F5
St Mary's Terr KY1 ... 133 B5
St Mary's Wynd 5 FK8 ... 135 A8
St Matthews La 4 DD4 ... 94 C2
ST MICHAELS ... 43 A1
St Michaels Dr KY15 ... 105 D4
St Michaels Golf Club KY16 ... 54 A8
St Modan's High Sch FK7 ... 135 A3
St Monance Pl 5 DD3 ... 91 A2
ST MONANS ... 82 E4
St Monans Prim Sch KY10 ... 82 E5
St Monans Windmill* KY10 ... 82 F4
St Mungo's RC Prim Sch FK10 ... 138 C5
St Mungo's Wynd FK10 ... 138 A6
St Mungo Terr DD3 ... 91 B3
St Murdoch's Cres 6 DD11 ... 89 F5
St Nicholas Pl DD3 ... 91 A3
St Nicholas St KY16 ... 106 E5
St Ninian Pl 4 DD3 ... 91 A2
ST NINIANS ... 135 B4
St Ninian's Cath PH1 ... 103 A4
St Ninians Ct 32 PH11 ... 7 A3
St Ninians Pl DD9 ... 84 D3
St Ninians Prim Sch
  Perth PH1 ... 103 A5
  Stirling FK7 ... 135 A4
St Ninians RC Prim Sch KY5 ... 129 C4
St Ninian's RC Prim Sch DD2 ... 92 E5
St Ninians Rd
  Arbroath DD11 ... 89 F5
  Cambusbarron FK7 ... 134 E5
  Forfar DD8 ... 10 A6
  Stirling FK8 ... 135 B6
St Ninian's Rd
  Alyth PH11 ... 7 A3
  Blairgowrie PH11 ... 7 A3
St Ninian Terr DD3 ... 91 A2
St Patricks RC Prim Sch KY5 ... 128 B1
St Paul's Cath DD1 ... 179 B2
St Pauls RC Prim Sch KY6 ... 112 F6
St Paul's Sq 3 PH1 ... 103 B4
St Peter's Ct KY11 ... 174 D3
St Peters & Pauls RC Prim Sch 7 DD3 ... 93 F6
St Peters Pl DD10 ... 85 D3
St Peter's Rd DD10 ... 85 D3
St Peter St 9 DD1 ... 93 E2
St Phillan's La 6 DD6 ... 98 E4
St Pius RC Prim Sch DD4 ... 95 B5
St Regulu's Gdns KY7 ... 113 B6
St Regulus Rd DD5 ... 97 A6
St Ronan's Ave DD4 ... 94 D3
St Ronan's Cres KY5 ... 127 F5
St Ronan's Ct KY6 ... 112 C5
St Roque's La DD4 ... 179 C3
St Rule Pl 3 KY7 ... 113 B6
St Rule Rd 2 KY7 ... 113 B6
St Rule's Twr* KY16 ... 106 E6
St Salvador St DD3 ... 179 B4
St Sarf's Pl KY1 ... 152 A7
St Saviours RC High Sch DD4 ... 95 B6
St Serf Rd KY7 ... 113 B6
St Serfs Gr FK10 ... 139 B4
St Serf's Pl
  Kinross KY13 ... 74 D3
  Tullibody FK10 ... 117 B3
St Serf's Prim Sch FK10 ... 117 B3
St Serf's RC Prim Sch KY12 ... 158 A2
St Serf's Rd
  Kinross KY13 ... 74 D3
  7 Tillicoultry FK13 ... 119 C7
  Tullibody FK10 ... 117 B3
St Serf's Wlk FK12 ... 117 E6
St Stephen's Pl PH1 ... 103 A6
St Stephen's RC Prim Sch PH10 ... 88 B5
St Thomas Cres DD11 ... 89 D5
St Thomas RC Prim Sch DD11 ... 89 E4
St Thomas's Pl FK7 ... 134 E6
St Thomas's Well FK7 ... 134 D7
St Valery Ct FK7 ... 135 A4
St Valery Dr FK7 ... 135 A4
ST VIGEANS ... 89 C8
St Vigeans Brae DD11 ... 89 D7
St Vigeans Rd DD11 ... 89 C5
St Vincent Ct 1 DD5 ... 96 A2
St Vincents RC Prim Sch DD4 ... 94 E6
St Vincent St DD5 ... 96 A2
Salem St DD3 ... 179 A3
SALINE ... 142 E5
Saline Golf Club KY12 ... 143 A5
Saline Prim Sch KY12 ... 142 E5
Salisbury Pl DD11 ... 89 B3
Salisbury St KY2 ... 151 B5
Saltire Leisure Ctr DD11 ... 89 D6
Saltire Ret Pk KY6 ... 112 F5
Salton Cres DD4 ... 95 A8
Saltpans KY11 ... 172 B4
Salvage Rd KY11 ... 173 C1
Samson Pl 3 DD7 ... 100 B3
Sanda Ct PH1 ... 102 F8
Sandeman Ct
  Kincardine FK10 ... 155 E4
  Perth PH1 ... 102 D8
Sandeman Pl
  Dundee DD3 ... 94 B4
  10 Luncarty PH1 ... 37 B8
Sandeman St DD3 ... 94 A4
Sanderling Way KY11 ... 162 B5
Sanderson Pl DD5 ... 31 B7
Sanderson Terr KY2 ... 149 B2
Sandford Gate KY1 ... 151 B3
Sandhaven Gdns DD4 ... 95 B5
Sandilands KY11 ... 172 D3
Sandpiper Dr KY11 ... 162 C2
Sandpiper Gdns KY11 ... 174 B8
Sandpiper Mdw FK10 ... 138 D5
Sandport KY13 ... 108 C1
Sandport Cl KY13 ... 108 D1
Sandport Gait KY13 ... 108 D1
Sandray Pk KY7 ... 111 A2
Sandwell Cres KY1 ... 167 B6
Sandwell St 5 KY8 ... 109 A2
Sandwood Pl 5 KY13 ... 108 B4
Sandybank KY11 ... 162 B5
Sandy Brae KY8 ... 79 E4
Sandy Brae Ind Est KY8 ... 79 F4
Sandycraig Rd 20 KY10 ... 83 A5
Sandygates KY14 ... 62 E5
Sandy Herd Ct KY16 ... 106 D4
Sandyhill Cres KY16 ... 106 D5
Sandyhill Ct KY23 ... 106 D4
Sandyhill Rd
  St Andrews KY16 ... 106 D4
  Tayport DD6 ... 99 F5
Sandy Knowe FK13 ... 119 C7
Sandylands Rd KY15 ... 105 D2
Sandy Rd
  Aberdour KY3 ... 164 C5
  New Scone PH2 ... 37 F5
Sang Pl KY1 ... 151 B4
Sang Rd KY1 ... 151 B4
Sauchenbush Rd KY2 ... 150 F5
SAUCHIE ... 118 E1
Sauchie Ct FK7 ... 135 F1
Sauchie Pl PH7 ... 101 B3
Sauchie Rd PH7 ... 101 B4
Sauchie St
  Kinglassie KY5 ... 77 F1
  Stirling FK7 ... 135 A2
Sauchie Terr PH7 ... 101 B3
Sauchob Cres PH1 ... 36 A5
Sauchob Pl PH1 ... 36 A5
Sauchob Rd PH1 ... 36 A5
Sauchob Terr PH1 ... 36 A5
Sauchope Cres KY10 ... 69 B3
Saunders Ct KY1 ... 151 B2
Saunders St KY1 ... 151 B2
Scaraben Cres KY6 ... 110 E3
Scarth Rd 1 PH1 ... 37 B8
Schaw Ct FK10 ... 118 D1
Schawpark Ave FK10 ... 118 D1
Schiltron Way FK7 ... 135 D3
Scholars' Brae KY3 ... 177 E8
School Brae
  Cupar KY15 ... 51 E1
  Dysart KY1 ... 152 A7
School Cl PH1 ... 102 D7
School Dr DD3 ... 93 D8
School Gn 19 KY10 ... 83 C6
Schoolhill 1 KY15 ... 65 E6
School Hill 7 KY16 ... 54 B8
School La
  Cardenden KY5 ... 129 B3
  Dalgety Bay KY11 ... 174 F4
  Forfar DD8 ... 3 C2
  3 Kirkcaldy KY1 ... 131 F1
  4 Leven KY8 ... 109 E6
  Menstrie FK11 ... 117 A7
School Mews FK11 ... 117 A7
School Rd
  5 Arbroath DD11 ... 22 E3
  Balmutto KY16 ... 53 E8
  Blairgowrie PH13 ... 26 B8
  Coupar Angus PH13 ... 16 A3
  Dollar FK14 ... 73 F3
  Dundee DD4 ... 19 A1
  Glenrothes KY7 ... 79 A2
  13 Leven KY8 ... 79 F3
  Perth PH2 ... 25 B2
  Tullibody FK10 ... 117 B2
School Row KY12 ... 160 C6
School St
  Cowdenbeath KY4 ... 147 D3
  Glenrothes KY7 ... 111 F1
  16 Leven KY8 ... 109 E6
  2 Methil KY8 ... 109 C4
School Terr
  Arbroath DD11 ... 13 A5
  Tillicoultry FK13 ... 119 B5
School View 3 KY15 ... 64 D4
School Wynd
  Crieff PH7 ... 101 B2
  10 Earlsferry/Elie KY9 ... 82 B3
  1 East Wemyss KY1 ... 133 B6
  4 Errol PH2 ... 39 F1
  7 Kinross KY13 ... 108 C2
  Kirkcaldy KY1 ... 151 B2
  3 Kirriemuir DD8 ... 86 D4
  15 Leven KY8 ... 109 E6
  Muirhead DD2 ... 90 A3
  Perth PH2 ... 49 E3
Scobie Pl KY12 ... 161 D4
SCONE ... 38 A5
Scone Pal* PH2 ... 37 D5
Scone Rd PH2 ... 103 D6
Scone Recn Pk Sports Club PH2 ... 37 F5
SCOONIE ... 109 E8
Scoonie Brae KY8 ... 109 E8
SCOONIEBURN ... 48 D7
Scoonieburn Hill PH2 ... 48 E8
Scoonie Cres 2 KY8 ... 109 E7
Scoonie Ct KY8 ... 109 E8
Scoonie Dr KY8 ... 109 E7
Scoonie Golf Course KY8 ... 109 F8
Scooniehill Rd KY16 ... 106 C3
Scoonie Pk KY8 ... 109 E8
Scoonie Rd KY8 ... 109 E7
Scoonie Terr KY8 ... 109 E8
Scores The KY16 ... 106 D7
Scotland Dr KY12 ... 161 E4
Scotland Pl FK13 ... 119 A7
Scotland's Secret Bunker* KY16 ... 68 D3
Scotland Terr KY14 ... 50 D5
SCOTLANDWELL ... 77 A4
Scotmill Way KY11 ... 174 C3
Scotscraig Cres 7 DD2 ... 91 A2
Scotscraig Ct 4 DD2 ... 91 B2
Scotscraig Dr DD6 ... 99 D7
Scotscraig Golf Course DD6 ... 43 C6
Scotscraig Gr 1 DD2 ... 91 B2
Scotscraig La 9 DD2 ... 91 A2
Scotscraig Pl
  5 Broughty Ferry DD5 ... 96 C5
  5 Kirkcaldy KY2 ... 130 F2
Scotscraig Rd 3 DD2 ... 91 B2
Scotscraig St 2 DD2 ... 91 B2
Scots Mill Pl KY11 ... 174 E4
Scots Tarvit Pl KY7 ... 113 A3
Scotstarvit Twr* KY15 ... 65 B6
Scotstarvit View KY15 ... 105 B3
Scotston Gdns DD4 ... 95 A3
Scots Wood Cres DD6 ... 98 A1
Scotswood Terr DD2 ... 93 B3
Scott Cres
  Alloa FK10 ... 138 B5
  Hillside DD10 ... 6 C8
  Tayport DD6 ... 99 D7
Scott Ct FK12 ... 118 B6
Scott Dr FK15 ... 107 B5
Scottish Deer Ctr* KY15 ... 64 C7
Scottish Fisheries Mus* KY10 ... 83 D6
Scottish Liqueur Ctr* PH1 ... 24 B5
Scottish National Golf Acad* DD6 ... 42 F4
Scottish Off Rd Driving Ctr* KY14 ... 62 B6
Scottish Pol Coll FK10 ... 155 F5
Scottish Raptor Ctr The* KY13 ... 108 A3
Scottish Vintage Bus Mus* KY12 ... 145 A4
Scott Path KY6 ... 112 F6
Scott Path N 11 KY6 ... 112 F6
Scott Path S 3 KY6 ... 112 F6
Scott Pl 3 KY5 ... 127 F6
Scott Rd KY6 ... 112 F6
Scott St
  Blairgownie PH13 ... 26 B8
  Brechin DD9 ... 84 D2
  Dundee DD2 ... 93 C4
  Dunfermline KY12 ... 160 E5
  Kirkcaldy KY1 ... 151 B2
  Newport-on-Tay DD6 ... 98 E4
  Perth PH1 ... 103 B4
  Stirling FK8 ... 115 A2
Scott Way
  Dundee DD5 ... 95 E6
  6 Leuchars KY16 ... 54 B7
Scrimgeour Pl DD3 ... 179 A3
Scroggiehill PH1 ... 36 E5
Seabourne Gdns 4 DD5 ... 96 C3
Seabrae DD7 ... 100 E3
Seabraes Ct DD1 ... 179 A1
Seabraes La DD1 ... 179 A1
Seacraig Ct DD6 ... 98 E5
Seafar Dr KY4 ... 126 E2
Seafield Cl 5 DD1 ... 93 E2
Seafield Cres KY1 ... 167 B8
Seafield Gdns KY1 ... 167 B8
Seafield La 6 DD1 ... 93 E2
Seafield Pl KY11 ... 175 A2
Seafield Rd
  Arbroath DD11 ... 89 F5
  Broughty Ferry DD5 ... 95 F4
  Dundee DD1 ... 93 E2
  Kirkcaldy KY1 ... 167 B8
Seafield Terr DD5 ... 95 F4
Seafield View
  Kinghorn KY3 ... 167 A3

Seafield View *continued*
Kirkcaldy KY1 167 B8
Seaforth Cres DD5 95 C4
Seaforth Dr KY13 108 B3
Seaforth Pl
Burntisland KY3 177 D8
Kirkcaldy KY1 151 F8
5 Stirling FK8 135 B8
Seaforth Rd DD5 95 C4
Seagate
Arbroath DD11 89 D3
Dundee DD1 179 C2
9 Kingsbarns KY16 68 F7
14 Leven KY8 109 E6
Montrose DD10 85 C2
St Andrews KY16 68 F7
Sealstrand KY11 175 C4
Seamark Pl KY5 127 E8
Sea Rd KY8 109 A3
Seaside Pl KY3 176 C7
Sea Tangle Rd 1 KY9 82 A2
Seath Ct KY6 112 B8
Seaton Cliffs Nature Reserve* DD11 23 C5
Seaton Pl 3 DD11 89 E5
Seaton Rd DD11 89 F6
Seatoun Pl 18 KY8 80 F5
Seaview Pl DD10 85 B1
Seaview Prim Sch DD5 97 A6
Seco Pl KY4 147 D4
Secret Gdn The KY6 110 D2
Segal Pl KY12 160 F4
Seggieden Pl 3 PH2 49 F7
Selkirk Ave KY4 147 C2
Selkirk Gdns DD4 95 D8
Selkirk Pk KY8 81 A5
Selkirk Pl
2 Glenrothes KY7 113 A6
1 Markinch KY7 113 F8
2 Perth PH1 102 A3
Selkirk St
Glenrothes KY7 113 F7
Leven KY8 109 B5
Selvage Pl KY11 174 A3
Selvage St KY11 174 A3
Sensation Science Ctr* DD1 179 A1
Serpentine Ave
Newport-on-Tay DD6 99 C6
Tayport DD6 99 C4
Service Rd DD8 87 E6
Session La 5 KY10 83 A5
Session St
Dundee DD1 179 A2
3 Pittenweem KY10 83 A5
Seton Cl PH10 88 D4
Seton Ct 6 KY8 79 F5
Seton Dr FK7 135 C4
Seton Pl
Dalgety Bay KY11 175 D5
Kirkcaldy KY2 150 D7
Seton Rd KY7 113 B6
Seton Terr KY8 79 F5
Seventh St FK3 168 B1
Seymour Ave DD2 93 D2
Seymour St DD2 93 C3
Shaftesbury Pk DD2 93 C2
Shaftesbury Pl 2 DD2 93 C2
Shaftesbury Rd DD2 93 C2
Shaftesbury St FK10 138 A7
Shaftesbury Terr 7 DD2 93 D2
Shakespeare Ave 4 KY8 79 F1
Shamrock St
Carnoustie DD7 100 C3
Dundee DD4 94 C4
Dunfermline KY12 161 B5
Shamrock Terr KY11 178 B8
Shanks Rigg DD11 89 B6
Shanwell Rd
Carnoustie DD7 100 C4
Tayport DD6 43 C7
Shanwell Rd S 1 DD6 43 C6
Sharp Gr KY5 128 B1
Sharp's La 2 DD2 93 A5
Shaw Cres KY5 148 B7
Shawfield La PH10 88 E2
Shaw's Sweet Factory* DD4 94 C6
Shaw St
Blairgowrie PH10 88 B4
Dunfermline KY11 161 D2
Sheardale Dr FK14 119 C4
Shearer Sq KY11 161 B1
Sheila Rd PH10 88 C4
Sheilings The FK10 117 B1
Shelley Gdns DD3 179 A4
Shepherd Ave KY8 109 B7
Shepherd Cres KY3 177 D8
Shepherd La 3 DD11 89 A7
Shepherdlands Gr KY12 158 D7
Shepherd's Loan DD2 93 D2
Shepherds Pk KY8 109 B3
Shepherd's Rd DD6 98 D3
Shepherd St KY2 130 D1
Shepherd's Wynd 4 PH3 104 D6
Sherbrook Cres DD3 91 E1
Sherbrooke Rd KY11 173 D3
Sherbrook Gdns 1 DD3 93 E8
Sherbrook Pl DD3 91 E1
Sherbrook St DD3 91 E1
Sheriffmuirlands FK9 115 C3
Sheriffmuir Rd
Bridge of A FK9 115 D7
Sheriffmuir Rd *continued*
Stirling FK9 70 F2
Sheriff Pk Gdns DD8 87 B4
Sheriff Pk Rise DD8 87 B4
Shetland Ct FK10 138 B5
Shetland Pl KY1 151 E7
Shiel Ct KY6 112 E5
Shields Ave KY16 106 E5
Shields Rd KY11 161 E3
Shielhill Pk PH1 24 F4
Shielhill Pl PH1 24 F4
Shielhill Rd DD8 86 C6
Shielinghill Pl PH7 101 B3
Shielinghill Rd PH7 101 B3
Shieling The KY12 159 E1
Shiell Ct DD5 96 D3
Shiells Ave KY15 63 E4
Shiell St DD5 96 D3
Shiels Ave 16 KY15 63 E1
Shierlaw Gdns FK2 154 D4
Shillinghill
Alloa FK10 138 B6
Tillicoultry FK13 119 A7
Shin Ct KY7 111 C2
Shinwell Pl KY11 173 E3
Shiphaugh Pl FK8 115 C1
Shire Way FK10 137 F6
Shirra's Brae Rd FK7 135 B4
Shoolbraids KY16 106 D4
SHORE 135 C8
Shore 9 DD11 89 D3
Shoregate 17 KY10 69 B2
Shorehead
Newburgh KY14 50 D5
St Andrews KY16 106 F6
Shore Head 12 KY8 109 E6
Shore Rd
Aberdour KY3 176 C7
Airth FK2 154 D4
36 Anstruther Wester KY10 83 C6
Dysart KY1 152 A6
Perth PH2 103 C2
South Queensferry EH30 178 B1
Stirling FK8 135 C8
Shore St
2 Anstruther Easter KY10 83 D6
11 Anstruther Easter KY10 83 D6
Leven KY8 109 A1
Shore Terr DD1 179 B2
Shore The
Alloa FK10 138 A5
Dundee DD2 41 B8
Invergowrie DD2 92 A1
St Andrews KY16 106 F5
Shore Wynd 5 DD10 85 C2
Short La 2 KY15 105 C4
Shotburn Cres KY8 109 D7
Shuna Ct PH1 102 E8
Shuna Sq KY7 111 A1
Shuttlefield St KY14 50 C5
Sibbald St DD3 94 A4
Side St 7 PH2 48 F5
Sidey Pl PH1 102 C7
Sidlaw Ave
Arbroath DD11 89 D7
Dundee DD3 91 B4
Sidlaw Cres
21 Alyth PH11 7 A3
3 Coupar Angus PH13 15 F2
Sidlaw Ct DD3 91 C4
Sidlaw Gdns
2 Coupar Angus PH13 15 F2
Dundee DD2 90 B3
Sidlaw Pk 2 PH2 49 F8
Sidlaw Pl 1 PH13 15 F2
Sidlaw Range DD8 86 C3
Sidlaw Rd PH10 88 D6
Sidlaw St KY2 150 F7
Sidlaw Terr
Dundee DD2 90 B3
7 Perth PH2 49 F7
Sidlaw View Prim Sch DD3 91 E3
Sidney St DD11 89 D5
Signal Box Rd PH10 88 D4
Signal Station KY11 178 C5
SILLERHOLE 109 E8
Sillerhole Rd KY8 109 E8
Silport Pl DD7 100 A2
Silverbank KY13 77 A4
Silverbarton Terr KY3 165 D1
Silver Birch Dr DD5 30 C5
Silverburn Est* KY8 80 D5
Silverburn Gdns FK12 118 C7
Silver Button Yd 1 DD4 94 C8
Silver Link Ave 3 DD4 95 C7
Silver St FK10 155 E3
Silverton Dr KY5 129 B4
Silver Way DD10 85 C7
Simon Cres KY8 79 F3
Simpson Ave
Dundee DD2 92 E3
Tillicoultry FK13 119 D7
Simpson Ct
Crail KY10 69 A2
Dundee DD2 92 E3
Tillicoultry FK13 119 D7
Simpson Dr FK13 119 B5
Simpson Pl
Carnoustie DD7 100 C3
Perth PH1 102 C7
Simpson Wlk KY11 161 F1
Sinclair Ave KY6 112 E6
Sinclair Ct FK7 135 E1
Sinclair Dr
Cowdenbeath KY4 147 B2
Fallin FK7 136 D4
Sinclair Gdns
Dunfermline KY12 161 B4
Montrose DD10 6 D8
Sinclairs St FK15 107 D5
Sinclair St 3 DD2 93 B6
SINCLAIRTOWN 151 F7
Sinclairtown Prim Sch KY1 151 F7
Sir George Bruce Rd KY12 158 F7
Sir George Sharp Ct KY1 131 E8
Sir James Black Gait KY5 148 A8
Sir Jimmy Shand Ct 2 KY1 133 B6
Sir John Brown Pl KY11 173 F7
Sir Robert Maule Pl FK10 155 E4
Sir Thomas Elder Ct KY2 130 D2
Sir Thomas Elder Way KY2 130 E2
Sir William Smith Rd DD11 89 A6
Sivewright Ct FK10 155 E4
Siward La 7 KY9 82 A2
Sixth St FK3 168 A1
Skelton Pl PH1 36 A5
Skelton Rd PH1 36 A5
Skene Ct KY7 110 E2
Skene St
Broughty Ferry DD5 96 B5
Cupar KY14 62 D4
Skibo Ave KY7 113 C5
Skibo Ct
Dunfermline KY12 161 A3
Glenrothes KY7 113 C5
Skibo Pl KY2 150 D5
Skinnergate 11 PH1 103 B4
Skinners Stps KY15 105 C5
Skirmie Pk PH10 88 E4
Skye Cres PH7 101 D2
Skye Rd KY11 161 E2
Slade Gdns DD8 86 B5
Slade Rd DD8 86 B4
Slap o' the Gask DD8 11 E2
SLATEFIELD 87 C2
Slatefield Gdns DD8 87 B2
Slatefield Pl DD8 87 C2
Slatefield Rise DD8 87 C2
Sligo St KY12 158 F7
Sloan St KY16 106 C5
Small Mdw Ct DD4 95 B8
Small's La DD1 179 A2
Smalls Sq DD9 84 E2
Small St KY5 148 A6
Small's Wynd DD1 179 A1
SMEATON 151 C8
Smeaton Gdns KY2 151 C6
Smeaton Ind Site KY1 151 C7
Smeaton Rd
Dundee DD2 92 D7
Kirkcaldy KY1 151 D6
Smellies La 3 DD1 93 E4
Smiddy Brae
8 Dunblane FK15 56 B4
Fowlis DD2 28 C4
Smiddy Burn 4 KY16 68 F7
Smiddy Rd PH12 17 B4
Smiddy View FK7 134 D6
Smiddy Wynd
Alva FK12 118 A6
Newmills KY12 158 C1
Smieton Ct DD7 100 B2
Smieton St DD7 100 B2
Smith Art Gallery & Mus* FK8 135 A8
Smith Ave KY4 147 B3
Smithbank Rd DD9 84 C4
Smith Dr PH2 38 B6
Smithfield Ave 4 PH10 88 C3
Smithfield Cres PH10 88 C3
Smithfield Loan FK10 137 E6
Smithfield Mdws FK10 137 E6
Smithfield Way 3 PH10 88 C3
Smith La PH11 7 A2
Smith Rd KY8 79 F3
Smith's Brae 1 PH1 24 A6
Smith St
Dundee DD3 93 F7
Kinross KY13 108 C1
Smith's Terr 3 KY1 151 C5
Smithy Croft 1 DD11 89 D4
Smithygreen Prim Sch KY8 80 B8
Smithy La
12 Balmullo KY16 53 E8
Blairgowrie PH12 17 A7
Smithy Loan FK15 107 D5
Smithy Rd 1 KY16 53 E8
Smythe St 23 PH11 7 A3
Sneddon Ct KY4 126 E1
Sneddon Pl FK2 154 D3
Snowdon Pl FK8 135 A6
Snowdon Place La FK7 135 A6
Snowdon Sch FK8 135 A7
Soapwork La DD1 179 B3
Society Rd EH30 178 A1
Solway Gdns 4 DD5 96 F6
Solway Pl KY6 112 D6
Somerville Ave KY12 160 E4
Somerville Pl DD3 179 A3
Somerville Pl E DD3 179 A4
Somerville Rd
Leven KY8 109 D7
Rosyth KY11 173 C2
Somerville Sq KY3 177 E8
Somerville St KY3 177 E8
Somerville Way
Balgeddie KY7 110 F1
Glenrothes KY7 112 F8
Sorley's Brae 20 FK14 73 C1
Sorn Gn KY7 113 B2
Soutar Cres PH1 102 A4
Soutar St DD3 93 E7
South Acres KY12 159 D1
SOUTH ALLOA 137 F3
Southampton Pl DD4 95 B3
Southampton Rd 5 DD4 95 A3
South Approach Rd FK2 155 B2
South Ave KY12 158 A7
South Baffin St 5 DD4 94 C2
South Balmossie St DD5 96 E4
South Bank Dykes 8 PH2 39 F1
South Bridge KY15 105 D4
South Bridgend PH7 101 B2
South Castle Dr KY11 173 F6
South Castle St
7 Blairgowrie PH10 88 C4
St Andrews KY16 106 E6
Southcroft FK12 117 F6
South Croftdyke 8 KY15 65 D6
South Dewar St KY12 160 E4
South Dr KY12 161 B3
Southend KY1 131 E7
Southern Cl 3 DD11 22 E5
Southerton Cres KY2 150 F3
Southerton Gdns KY2 150 F3
Southerton Rd KY2 150 F3
Southesk Ct DD10 85 D1
Southesk Pl DD10 85 C1
Southesk Prim Sch DD10 85 C2
South Esk Rd DD8 2 D5
Southesk St
Brechin DD9 84 C3
Montrose DD10 85 C2
Southesk Terr 1 DD9 84 D2
South Fergus Pl KY1 151 B3
South Feus KY8 81 A6
SOUTHFIELD 112 D3
Southfield
Cowdenbeath KY4 147 C5
15 Falkland KY15 63 B2
2 St Andrews KY16 106 D5
Southfield Ave KY5 127 F7
Southfield Cres FK8 135 A6
Southfield Ind Est KY6 112 E3
Southgait Cl 10 KY24 106 D6
South George St DD1 179 B3
South Gr KY8 109 C3
South Green Dr FK2 154 E3
South Hill St KY3 177 E8
SOUTH INCH 103 B2
South Inch Ct PH2 103 B2
South Inch Pk PH2 103 A2
South Inch Pl PH2 103 B2
South Inch Terr PH2 103 B2
South Inch View PH2 103 A2
South Kersebonny Steading FK8 134 C7
South Kinloch St DD7 100 C2
South Knowe KY4 162 E5
Southlands Rd PH3 104 D5
South Larch Rd KY11 161 F4
South Loan KY10 83 A5
South Loanhead KY11 172 E3
South Mains FK7 137 B1
South Marketgait DD1 179 B2
South Methven St PH1 103 B4
SOUTHMUIR 86 D3
Southmuir Prim Sch DD8 86 D4
South Muirton Cotts PH1 103 A7
South Overgate KY3 167 A3
SOUTH PARKS 112 E7
South Parks Prim Sch KY6 112 F7
South Parks Rd KY6 112 E6
South Pilmuir Rd FK10 139 A4
South Quay DD10 85 C1
SOUTH QUEENSFERRY 178 B2
South Rd
Cupar KY15 105 D3
Dundee DD2 92 F6
South Roundall KY11 172 E3
South Row
Charlestown KY11 172 B4
Coaltown of Wemyss KY1 132 E4
Kirkcaldy KY1 151 E8
South St E KY6 112 B8
South St John's Pl PH1 103 B4
South St W
18 Falkland KY15 63 B2
South St W *continued*
Glenrothes KY6 112 B8
South Shore Rd FK3 168 B2
South St
Arbroath DD11 89 E3
Blairgowrie PH10 88 D5
Burrelton PH13 26 C8
Cambus FK10 137 B8
Cowdenbeath KY4 147 C2
Earlsferry/Elie KY9 82 B2
Falkland KY15 63 B2
3 Forfar DD8 87 E5
Glenrothes KY7 112 F6
8 Kingskettle KY15 64 A3
Kirriemuir DD8 86 C3
Leven KY8 109 E6
Lochgelly KY5 148 B6
Milnathort KY13 108 C6
Monifieth DD5 97 B5
Newtyle PH12 17 B4
Perth PH1 103 B3
St Andrews KY16 106 D6
Stirling FK9 115 D1
South Taymouth St 5 DD7 100 C2
South Tay St DD1 179 A2
South Union St
Cupar KY15 105 C4
Dundee DD1 179 B1
Monifieth DD5 97 B5
South Victoria Dock Rd DD1 179 C2
South View KY3 177 F8
South Ward Rd DD1 179 A2
South William St PH2 103 B3
Southwood Prim Sch KY6 112 D7
South Wynd KY9 81 F6
Sou'wester Ct 6 KY10 83 D6
Sowerby Pl 2 DD3 91 D1
Soyaux Ave 5 DD5 97 B7
SPALEFIELD 68 B1
Sparrow Croft 6 DD8 87 D5
Spartleton Pl DD4 95 D8
Spearshill Rd DD6 99 E7
Speckled Wood Ct DD4 95 B7
Speed St DD2 93 C2
Spence Ave KY3 165 F2
Spence Dr KY6 112 A8
Spence Gdns 4 DD5 95 F2
Spence Pl 6 DD5 95 F2
Spencer Cres DD7 100 E4
Spencerfield Rd KY11 174 D2
Spencerfield Steadings KY11 174 E3
Spencer Pl KY1 151 F6
Spens Cres PH1 102 F4
Spens La KY11 173 C1
Spey Ct FK7 135 C5
Spey Dr DD2 92 D5
Speygate PH2 103 C3
Spey St KY8 109 A3
Spinkie Cres KY16 106 B3
Spink Path DD11 89 C6
Spink St DD11 89 C4
Spinnaker Way KY11 174 F2
Spinners Ct FK13 119 B6
Spinner's Ct KY12 159 D1
Spinners Wynd
5 Dundee DD2 93 D2
Tillicoultry FK13 119 B6
Spinneys The KY11 175 C3
Spitalfield Pl 2 DD11 89 A3
Spitfire Ave PH2 38 B6
Spitfire Pl 2 KY16 54 B7
Spittalfield Cres KY11 174 C2
Spittalfield Rd KY11 174 C2
Spittal Hill FK9 115 C4
Spittal St FK8 135 A8
Spottiswoode Gdns KY16 106 C4
Spoutwells Ave PH2 37 F5
Spoutwells Dr PH2 37 F5
Spoutwells Pl PH2 37 F5
Spoutwells Rd PH2 37 F5
Springbank PH14 40 C7
Springbank Cres FK15 107 C5
Springbank Gdns FK15 107 C6
Springbank La KY13 108 D7
Springbank Rd
Alyth PH11 7 A3
Leven KY8 79 F6
Stirling FK7 135 C6
Springbank Terr KY12 161 A6
SPRINGFIELD 64 E7
Springfield DD8 87 C4
Springfield Ct FK15 107 C5
Springfield Pk KY13 108 B3
Springfield Prim Sch KY15 64 E7
Springfield Rd
Alloa FK10 138 C7
Kinross KY13 108 B3
Stirling FK7 135 C5
Springfield Sch DD4 95 A7
Springfield Sta KY15 64 F6
Springfield Terr
Arbroath DD11 89 E4
Dunblane FK15 107 C5
Springfield View EH30 178 A1
Springhill 3 DD4 94 D3
Springhill Brae KY4 162 F6

Springhill Gdns 4 DD4 94 D3
Springkerse Bsns Pk FK7 135 E7
Springkerse Ind Est FK7 135 D6
Springkerse Rd FK7 135 D6
Springkerse Rdbt FK7 135 E7
Springkerse Ret Pk FK7 135 E6
Springwood
Dunfermline KY11 174 A7
Stirling FK7 134 F5
Springwood Ave FK8 134 F5
Sprotwell Terr FK10 118 D1
Spruce Gdns KY15 64 F8
Spruce Gr KY11 173 D8
Spruces The 9 DD4 94 F8
Square The
Cupar KY15 51 E1
Fallin FK7 136 D4
4 Letham DD8 11 E3
Methven PH1 36 A4
6 St Andrews KY16 68 F7
Stables Rd KY11 173 C1
Stables The PH1 102 F5
Stackyard The KY13 108 F7
Staffa Ct PH1 102 E7
Staffa Pl DD2 91 C1
Stalker Ave FK13 119 C7
Stalkers Entry PH4 57 B3
Standalane FK10 155 E3
Standing Stane Rd
Kirkcaldy KY1 132 C5
Leven KY8 79 E2
Standing Stone Wlk KY11 161 E1
STANLEY 24 E4
Stanley Cres PH1 102 F6
Stanley Dr FK9 115 B7
Stanley Gdns KY7 113 C2
Stanley Junc PH1 24 F4
Stanley Pk KY1 151 B5
Stanley Prim Sch PH1 24 E3
Stanley Rd DD5 96 A3
Stanley St DD11 89 D4
Stanley Terr
Alva FK12 118 A6
Oakley KY12 159 A6
Stanma La KY13 76 E6
Stanmore Pl KY8 109 D6
STANNERGATE 95 B2
Stannergate Rd DD1 94 E2
Stanton Ave FK10 137 F6
STAR 79 B6
Stark's Cl DD8 87 C4
Stark's Park (Raith Rovers FC) KY1 151 A1
Stark St KY8 79 F2
Starley Hall Sch KY3 177 A8
Star Prim Sch KY7 79 B6
Station Brae
Kinghorn KY3 166 F2
Newport-on-Tay DD6 98 E4
Station Cres DD2 92 B2
Station Ct
Anstruther KY10 83 A6
10 Kingkettle KY15 64 A3
Leven KY8 109 D6
Stationhead Rd KY5 128 B1
Station House Rd PH2 47 C4
Station Pk
East Wemyss KY1 133 B6
20 Lower Largo KY8 80 F5
11 Lower Largo KY8 80 F5
Station Pk (Forfar Athletic FC) DD8 87 D6
Station Pl
Aberdour KY3 176 C7
Forfar DD8 87 E6
7 Leven KY8 79 F1
Station Rd
Abernethy PH2 49 E3
26 Anstruther KY10 83 C6
Auchterderran KY5 129 B3
Bannockburn FK7 135 E1
Barry DD7 31 F5
Blairgowrie PH13 26 C8
Bridge of A FK9 114 F8
Bridge of Earn PH2 48 E5
Cambus FK10 117 B1
Cardenden KY5 129 B3
Carnoustie DD7 100 E3
Cowdenbeath KY4 147 D4
Crieff PH5 44 C3
Crook of Devon KY13 74 D3
Cupar KY15 105 D4
Daisie or Osnaburgh KY15 53 D4
Dollar FK14 120 E8
Dunblane FK15 107 D5
Dunning PH2 46 F1
Dysart KY1 152 A7
Errol PH2 39 F2
Forfar DD8 87 F6
Frockheim DD11 12 E4
Invergowrie DD2 92 B2
Inverkeilor DD11 14 A4
Kelty KY4 126 E1
Kincardine FK10 155 D4
Kingsbarns KY16 68 E6
7 Kingskettle KY15 64 A3
Kinross KY13 108 B2
Leuchars KY16 54 A7
Leven KY8 109 D7
Lochgelly KY5 128 A1
Station Rd *continued*
Longforgan DD2 40 F8
Methven PH1 36 A4
Monance KY10 82 E4
Oakley KY12 158 F6
South Queensferry EH30 178 C1
St Andrews KY16 106 C6
Stanley PH1 24 F4
Stirling FK8 135 B8
1 Strathmiglo KY14 62 D5
Thornton KY1 131 E8
Station Terr DD2 92 B2
Station Wynd 19 KY8 80 F5
Station Yd KY3 167 A2
Steadfast La DD8 87 E6
Steading Pl 6 DD11 22 E3
Steadings The
Airth FK2 153 E5
Collessie KY15 63 E8
Fallin FK7 136 A4
Steading The
7 Arbroath DD11 22 E3
St Andrews KY16 68 F6
STEELEND 143 B5
Steel Gr KY12 158 D7
Steeple Cres KY11 175 A3
Stein's Pl KY4 147 C3
Stein Sq FK7 135 F1
Stenhouse Dr KY3 165 C1
Stenhouse St KY4 147 B4
STENTON 113 C2
Stenton Rd KY6 112 F3
Stenton Row 8 KY9 82 B3
Stephen Pl KY5 148 B8
Stephen's Dr KY11 174 C3
Stephens Yd 2 DD2 93 E2
Stephen Terr PH1 102 D2
Step Row DD2 93 D2
Sterling Mill Outlet Village FK13 119 B6
Steuart Rd FK9 114 F7
Stevenson Ave KY6 112 F7
Stevenson Ct FK9 115 A5
Stevens Yd 2 DD2 93 D2
Stewart Cres KY5 148 A8
Stewart Rd KY4 126 E2
Stewart's La DD2 93 A6
Stewart Sq FK8 115 A2
Stewart St
Cambusbarron FK7 134 D6
5 Dundee DD2 93 B6
Dundee DD5 96 A4
Dysart KY1 152 B8
Townhill KY12 161 C7
Stewart Terr
Monifieth DD5 97 B6
South Queensferry EH30 178 B1
STIRLING 135 C8
Stirling Ave DD3 179 A4
Stirling Br* FK8 115 B2
Stirling Bsns Ctr FK8 135 B6
Stirling Castle* FK8 114 F1
Stirling Ct 5 FK13 119 B7
Stirling Ent Pk FK7 135 C7
Stirling High Sch FK8 135 A5
Stirling Rd
Alloa FK10 137 E8
Alva FK12 117 F7
Dunblane FK15 107 D5
Fallin FK7 136 C4
Glenrothes KY6 112 C2
Milnathort KY13 108 C7
Tullibody FK10 117 B3
Stirling Royal Infmy FK8 135 B5
Stirling St
Alva FK12 118 A7
Auchterarder PH4 57 B3
Dundee DD3 179 A4
Tillicoultry FK13 119 B7
Stirling Sta FK8 135 B8
Stirling Terr DD3 179 A4
Stiven Cres DD8 86 C5
Stobcross DD11 89 C4
Stob Cross Rd KY7 111 F1
Stobie Pl KY12 158 F7
Stobsmuir Rd DD4 94 D5
Stobs Pl KY2 150 C7
Stobswell Rd 8 DD4 94 C3
Stocks Wynd 3 KY14 62 D5
Stoneyacre FK13 119 B6
Stoneycroft La 12 DD11 89 C3
Stoneycroft Rd EH30 178 C1
Stoneyflatts EH30 178 A1
Stoneyflatts Cres EH30 178 A1
Stony Brae FK10 156 C2
Store La DD8 86 D3
Store St PH1 24 F4
STORMONTFIELD 37 C8
Stormontfield Rd PH2 37 D6
Stormont Pk PH2 37 F5
Stormont Pl PH2 37 E5
Stormont Rd PH2 37 F5
Stormont St PH1 103 B5
Stormont Way PH2 37 E5
Stracathro Terr 4 DD5 96 C4
Strachan Ave DD5 95 C4
Strachan Cres 2 FK14 73 B1
Strachans Pk DD9 84 D3
Strachan St DD11 89 D5
Straiton Terr 3 KY16 53 E7
Straiton Wynd KY26 106 D4
Strand Ct PH3 58 B8
Strang's Ley DD8 10 F5
Strang St DD8 87 E5
Strathaird Pl DD2 92 C4
Strathairlie Ave DD11 89 D5
Strathallan Airfield PH3 45 C3
Strathallan Cl KY7 113 C2
Strathallan Ct FK9 115 A6
Strathallan Dr KY2 150 E5
Strathallan Prim Sch KY2 150 E4
Strathallan Rd FK9 115 A6
Strathallan Sch PH2 48 B5
Strathardle Cres PH10 88 D6
Strathaven Terr DD4 95 B7
Strathbeg Dr KY11 174 F3
Strathbeg Pl DD5 96 B5
Strathblair Ave 10 DD6 42 B5
Strathburn Dr KY7 113 A2
Strathcarron Pl DD2 92 D4
Strathconon Cl 7 KY7 111 C2
Strathdee Terr DD5 95 C4
Strathdevon Pl FK14 120 E8
Strathdevon Prim Sch FK14 120 E8
Strathdon Pk KY6 110 E3
Strathdon Pl DD5 95 C4
Strathearn Ct
Auchterarder PH3 104 E6
Crieff PH7 101 D4
Strathearn Gall* PH7 101 C4
Strathearn Leisure Ctr PH7 101 D2
Strathearn Pl PH2 102 F3
Strathearn Terr
Crieff PH7 101 D4
Perth PH2 102 F3
Stratheden Ct KY15 64 E8
Stratheden Hospl KY15 64 F7
Stratheden Pl 22 KY14 62 F6
Stratheden Rd DD5 95 C4
Strathenry Ave KY6 77 E5
Strathenry Pl KY6 112 A7
Strathern Rd DD5 95 D3
Strathisla Rd DD5 95 C4
Strathkinnes Rd KY2 151 A4
STRATHKINNESS 54 C3
Strathkinness High Rd KY16 106 A5
Strathkinness Low Rd KY16 106 A5
Strathkinness Prim Sch KY16 54 B3
Strathmartine DD3 91 D5
Strathmartine Prim Sch DD3 91 B5
Strathmartine Rd
5 Downfield DD3 91 D2
Dundee DD3 179 A4
STRATHMIGLO 62 C5
Strathmiglo Prim Sch KY14 62 D5
Strathmore Ave
4 Coupar Angus PH13 15 F2
Dunblane FK15 107 B6
Dundee DD3 93 D6
Forfar DD8 87 C3
Kirriemuir DD8 86 D5
Strathmore Cres FK9 115 A3
Strathmore Dr
Dunfermline KY12 161 D5
Stirling FK9 115 A3
Strathmore Pl
Broughty Ferry DD5 96 D5
2 Montrose DD10 85 C4
Strathmore Prim Sch DD8 87 D4
Strathmore Rd 4 DD8 9 C1
Strathmore St
Broughty Ferry DD5 96 C4
Dundee DD3 94 B4
Kinghorn KY3 166 F3
Perth PH2 103 C5
Strathmore Terr
Alyth PH11 7 A3
5 Forfar DD8 9 C1
Strathmore View 2 PH11 7 A3
Strathnairn Ct 11 KY7 111 C2
Strathord Terr PH1 102 C5
STRATHORE 130 F7
Strathore Rd KY2 130 D7
Strathspey Pl 7 DD5 95 C4
Strathtay Rd
6 Dundee DD5 95 C4
Perth PH1 102 C6
Strathview DD8 87 C1
Strathview Pl PH1 36 A5
Strathview Rd DD8 86 D3
Strathview Terr PH2 103 D6
Strathyre Ave PH1 102 D5
Strathyre Pl KY7 111 C3
Strathyrum Course The KY16 54 E5
STRAVITHIE 67 F6
Strawberry Bank DD2 93 D2
Streets Pl KY12 161 D7
Stripehead 3 FK10 138 B6
Strips of Craigie Pl 1 DD4 95 A3
Strips of Craigie Rd DD4 95 A3
Striven Pl
Broughty Ferry DD5 96 B4
4 Glenrothes KY6 112 E6
Kirkcaldy KY2 150 E8
Stroma Ct PH1 102 F8
Stroma Way KY7 111 A1
Strome Terr 3 DD5 96 C4
STRONACHIE 60 A3
Stronsay Ct PH1 102 F8
Struan Dr KY11 174 B3
Struan Pl
Inverkeithing KY11 174 B3
2 Newport-on-Tay DD6 98 E4
Struan Rd PH1 102 B6
Struan St 3 DD6 98 E4
Strude Howe FK12 118 B7
Strude Mill FK12 118 B7
Strude St FK12 118 B7
Stuart Ave PH2 102 F3
Stuart Pl KY4 147 D5
Stuart Rd
Glenrothes KY7 113 A6
Rosyth KY11 173 C2
Stuart St 2 DD11 89 E4
Sturdee Rd 2 DD11 22 D6
Sugarhouse Wynd DD1 179 C3
Sultery Bldg KY11 172 B4
Summerfield Ave DD4 95 B7
Summerfield Gdns DD4 95 B7
Summerfield Terr DD4 95 B7
Summerhill 8 KY16 53 E8
Summer Rd KY8 79 E1
Sunadale Ct DD4 95 E8
Sunart Pl
Broughty Ferry DD5 96 B4
6 Glenrothes KY6 112 E6
Sunart St DD5 96 B4
Sunningdale La KY12 160 D6
Sunnybank Rd FK7 135 B3
Sunnybraes Terr KY12 143 B5
Sunnybrae Terr 3 DD3 91 D1
SUNNYLAW 70 C1
Sunnylaw Rd
Bridge of A FK9 115 A8
Stirling FK9 70 C1
Sunnypark KY13 108 C4
Sunnyside
Dunblane FK15 107 D4
Kirriemuir DD8 86 C3
St Andrews KY16 54 B3
Stirling FK7 135 A4
Sunnyside Ct
Alloa FK10 138 B7
Cowdenbeath KY4 147 D4
Sunnyside Eastern DD8 87 C4
Sunnyside Pl
Lochgelly KY5 148 A6
Stirling FK9 115 A4
Sunnyside Prim Sch FK10 138 B7
Sunnyside Rd
Alloa FK10 138 B7
Cardenden KY5 129 D3
Sunnyside Royal DD10 6 C8
Surcoat Loan FK7 135 E3
Sutherland Ave
Alloa FK10 138 C7
Stirling FK8 115 C1
Sutherland Cres DD2 93 A5
Sutherland Cresent 9 PH2 49 E3
Sutherland Dr KY13 108 B4
Sutherland Pl
Dundee DD2 93 A5
Kirkcaldy KY1 151 F7
Sutherland St DD2 93 B5
SUTTIESIDE 87 D7
Suttieside Rd DD8 87 E7
Suttie St KY8 109 D4
Suttie Way FK9 114 F8
Suttie Wynd DD8 11 E4
Swallow Craig KY11 175 B1
Swallow Cres KY8 79 F1
Swallowcroft DD8 87 E4
Swallowdrum Rd KY12 160 C6
Swallowtail Ct DD4 95 B7
Swan Ave KY8 79 E5
Swan Ct KY8 109 B3
Swan Pl KY6 112 F7
Swan Rd KY1 151 B3
Swansacre 4 KY13 108 C2
Swan St
Brechin DD9 84 C3
Leven KY8 109 A2
Swards Pl 5 KY8 79 F6
Sweetbank Cres KY7 113 E7
Sweetbank Dr KY7 113 E8
Sweetbank Terr KY7 113 E8
Swinburne Dr FK10 118 B2
Swintons Pl KY4 146 F1
Sycamore Ave
Kirkcaldy KY1 151 C8
7 Leven KY8 79 F3
Sycamore Cres KY4 147 D6
Sycamore Gr KY11 173 C8
Sycamore Path DD11 89 A4
Sycamore Pl
Dundee DD2 93 C3
Kirriemuir DD8 86 C6
Stirling FK8 134 F5
Sycamores The FK10 117 B1
Sydney Cres PH3 104 D5
Syme Pl KY11 173 C5
Symers St DD3 91 C3
Symon Field FK15 107 F5
Sythrum Cres KY7 113 D6

T

Taeping Cl 8 KY10 83 D7
TAIL 34 D3
Tailyour Cres DD10 85 C6
Tait Pl FK13 119 D8
Tait's La DD2 93 D3
Talisker FK10 117 B2
Talisker Pl PH1 102 C8
Talisman Pl KY6 112 C5
Tallapark KY13 108 C2
Tanhouse Brae KY12 169 D8
TANNADICE 2 D5
Tannadice Ct DD3 94 B4
Tannadice Pk (Dundee United FC) DD3 94 A4
Tannadice Prim Sch DD8 2 D5
Tannadice St DD3 94 A4
Tanna Dr KY7 111 A3
Tannage Brae DD8 86 C4
Tannage St 5 PH10 88 D5
Tannahill Terr FK15 107 D6
Tannery Ct KY15 105 C5
Tannery La FK8 115 A1
TANSHALL 112 D6
Tanshall Prim Sch KY6 112 C6
Tanshall Rd E KY6 112 C5
Tanshall Rd W KY6 112 C5
Tantallon Ave KY7 113 C4
Tantallon Ct KY7 113 C4
Tapitlaw Gr KY12 158 D7
Taransay Pk KY7 111 A2
Taransay Rd KY7 111 A1
Taranty Pl DD8 87 C4
Taranty Rd DD8 87 B3
Tarbert Pl
Dundee DD2 92 F4
13 Glenrothes KY6 112 E6
Tarbert Terr FK10 155 F3
Tarbolton Ct KY2 151 A7
Targate Rd KY12 160 C5
Target Rd EH51 168 C1
Targe Wynd FK7 135 E3
Tarland Knowe KY7 110 E2
Tarmachen Rd KY11 162 B1
Tarmangie Dr FK14 73 C1
Tarriebank Gdns DD11 23 A7
Tarry Dykes DD11 89 D7
Tarry Rd DD11 89 D7
Tarry Row PH1 102 A7
Tarves Pk DD5 95 C4
Tarves Pl KY7 110 E2
Tarvie Pl PH1 102 C6
Tarvit Ave KY15 105 E4
Tarvit Ct KY15 105 E4
Tarvit Dr KY15 105 E4
Tarvit Gdns KY15 105 E4
Tarvit Gn KY7 113 C3
Tarvit Terr KY15 64 E6
Tavern Cotts KY4 162 F8
Ta-Verne La KY11 161 D1
Taxi Way KY11 175 C5
Taybank Pl PH2 39 F2
Tay Ct
Alloa FK10 138 C6
Glenrothes KY6 112 E6
Monifieth DD5 97 B6
Tayfield Ave DD6 98 D4
Tayfield Pl 11 DD2 93 E2
Taylor Ave KY4 147 C4
Taylor Dr KY7 113 B5
Taylor Gdns KY7 113 B5
Taylor St Gdns DD8 87 C6
Taylor's La DD2 93 D2
Taylor St
Dundee DD2 93 B6
Forfar DD8 87 B6
Leven KY8 109 D5
Taymount Terr PH1 102 E3
Taymouth Pl 4 DD5 96 B2
Taymouth St DD7 100 C2
Taymouth Terr DD7 100 A2
Tayock Ave 3 DD10 85 C5
Taypark Rd 11 PH1 37 B8
Taypark Terr 7 DD6 99 F5
TAYPORT 99 F7
Tayport Prim Sch DD6 99 F6
Tayport Rd DD6 99 A6
Tay Rd 35 PH11 7 A3
Tay St La DD1 179 A2
Tayside Pl 10 PH2 49 F7
Tayside St DD7 100 E3
Tay Sq DD1 179 A1
Tay St
Leven KY8 109 A2
Monifieth DD5 97 B6
12 Newburgh KY14 50 D5
Newport-on-Tay DD6 98 E5
Perth PH2 103 C3
Tayport DD6 99 F6
Tay Terr
Dunfermline KY11 161 E2
Newport-on-Tay DD6 98 E5
Tayview Dr DD2 92 A8
Tayview Rd DD2 92 A8
Tayview Terr DD6 98 E5
TEALING 19 B1
Tealing Prim Sch DD4 19 A1
Tealing Rd DD3 18 A1
Teal Pl KY11 162 A1
Telfer Wynd 3 KY9 82 A3
Telford Ct FK7 135 D1
Telford Rd
Dundee DD2 93 B8
Glenrothes KY7 113 D5

Telny Pl KY3 176 C7
Templars Cres KY3 166 F3
Temple Cres 6 KY10 69 A2
TEMPLEHALL 150 F7
Templehall Ave KY2 150 F7
Templehall Pl DD5 31 B7
Templehall Rd KY6 112 C5
Temple La DD1 179 A2
Temple The KY8 81 A5
TEMPLETON 17 D5
Templeton Rd DD3 90 D2
Ten Acres FK10 118 B1
Tennis Rd DD7 100 D3
Tentsmuir Pl 4 DD5 96 C5
Terminus St 7 PH10 88 D5
Tern Ct KY7 110 F2
Tern Path KY7 110 F3
Tern Rd KY11 162 A1
Terrace Rd DD7 100 C3
Terrace St KY1 152 A7
Terris Pl KY4 147 D3
Terr The KY9 82 B2
Teuchatcroft DD8 87 C3
Teviotdale Ave DD3 91 D2
Teviot Pl DD10 85 E3
Thane Pl KY11 161 F1
Thane Rd KY7 113 B6
Thane Terr KY1 133 C7
THE BALLOCH 44 A6
Thimblehall Dr KY12 161 D4
Thimblehall Pl KY12 161 D4
Thimblehall Rd KY12 161 E4
Thimblerow 3 PH2 47 A1
Third Row DD8 86 E3
Thirlstane Pl DD4 95 D8
Thistle Chambers 4
FK8 135 B7
Thistle Ct KY4 162 E5
Thistle Ctr The FK8 135 B7
Thistle Dr KY7 110 F2
Thistle Ind Est
Cowdenbeath KY4 147 E4
Stirling FK7 135 C6
Thistle La KY16 106 D6
Thistle Pl
9 New Scone PH2 37 F5
Stirling FK8 115 A2
Thistle St
Alloa FK10 138 C6
Burntisland KY3 177 E8
Carnoustie DD7 100 C3
Cowdenbeath KY4 147 D3
Dundee DD3 179 B4
Dunfermline KY12 161 B5
Kirkcaldy KY1 151 C3
Thistle Terr KY8 109 D6
Thomas Ct DD7 100 A2
Thomas Maclagan Way
DD2 92 E4
Thomas St DD7 100 A2
Thomastoun Dr KY15 105 E5
Thomas Wise Pl DD2 92 E4
Thompson Ave DD7 100 A2
Thompson Pl 4 KY13 108 B4
Thoms Cl DD3 91 B4
Thomson Ct KY5 129 A4
Thomson Pl
Cambusbarron FK7 134 D5
Rosyth KY11 173 F3
Tillicoultry FK13 119 B5
Thomson St DD1 93 E2
Thomson Terr DD10 85 B1
Thornbank Ct 2 DD4 94 D3
Thornbank Pk 5 DD4 94 D3
Thornbank Rd FK14 120 D8
Thornbank St 1 DD4 94 D3
Thornbank Terr DD1 94 D2
Thorne Rd FK10 117 E1
Thorney Shade PH2 48 B5
Thorn Gr KY11 173 F8
Thorngreen Rd PH2 26 A3
Thornhill Ct KY6 112 D8
Thornhill Dr KY2 151 B6
Thornhill Rd KY2 151 C6
Thornhill St PH5 44 C2
THORNTON 131 D8
Thornton Gdns DD11 89 B5
Thornton Golf Club
KY1 132 A8
Thornton Pk DD8 87 B3
Thornton Pl DD8 87 B3
Thornton Prim Sch
KY1 131 E8
Thornton Rd
4 Dundee DD3 91 F2
Thornton KY1 131 E4
Thorn Tree Pl KY12 158 F6
Thorntree Sq 7 PH2 46 F1
Thorter Neuk DD1 94 C1
Thorter Row DD1 94 C1
Threave Loan KY11 162 A1
Threewells Dr DD8 87 B3
Threewells Pl DD8 87 B3
Thriepland Wynd PH1 102 B5
THROSK 137 A3
Thrum's Gdns DD8 86 C4
Thrush Ave KY8 79 F1
Thurso Cres DD2 92 C4
Thurso Gdns DD2 92 D4
TIBBERMORE 36 D2
Tibbermore Gdns PH1 102 E5
Tibbertreoch 5 PH7 101 C4
Tiel Path KY7 113 D7
Tiger Beach Dr DD7 100 A1
Tighnduin Gdns 1
DD5 97 A5
Tillibardine Distillery
Visitor Ctr PH4 57 B3
TILLICOULTRY 119 B8
Tillicoultry Golf Club
FK13 119 A7
Tillicoultry Prim Sch
FK13 119 C7
Tillycairn Pl 6 DD4 94 F8
TILLYLOSS 86 D5
Tillyloss
Dykehead DD8 1 A7
8 Kirriemuir DD8 86 D5
Timbergreens 2 DD11 22 E3
Timmergreens Prim Sch
DD11 89 A4
Timmons Pk KY5 148 A8
Tinian Cres KY12 158 D1
Tinnisburn Cl 10 KY7 111 C2
Tinto Pl KY11 161 F2
Tircarra Bank 1 DD5 96 D3
Tircarra Gdns DD5 96 C3
Tircarra Pl DD5 96 C3
Tiree Pl
Kirkcaldy KY2 150 F8
Perth PH1 102 E7
Tirran Dr KY11 162 B1
Titania FK10 138 A8
Toboggan Rd 4 KY8 109 D5
Tod's Gn 1 KY10 69 A2
Toft Ct 19 KY10 83 A5
Tofthill
Dundee DD2 93 B6
Glenrothes KY7 111 D2
Tofthill Pl
9 Dundee DD2 93 B6
2 Perth PH2 49 F7
Toft The KY9 82 B2
Tolbooth St KY1 151 C3
Tolbooth Wynd
16 Anstruther Easter
KY10 83 C6
8 Anstruther KY10 83 D6
10 Crail KY10 69 B2
Toll Ave 12 KY8 79 F2
Toll Cres DD8 87 F5
Toll Ct 2 KY8 80 F5
Tollgate KY11 161 B2
Toll Rd
Anstruther Easter KY10 83 D7
Kincardine FK10 155 F3
St Andrews KY16 53 F7
Tolmount Cres
Dunfermline KY12 161 C3
Montrose DD10 85 C7
Tolmount Dr KY12 161 C3
TOMAKNOCK 101 F4
Tom Johnstone Rd
DD5 95 E5
Tom Mcdonald Ave
DD2 92 D4
Tom Morris Dr KY16 106 D4
Tommy Armour Pl
DD7 100 A1
Tom Stewart La KY16 106 C4
Torbain KY2 150 D8
Torbain Prim Sch
KY2 150 D8
Torbain Rd KY2 150 B6
Torbeith Gdns
Cowdenbeath KY4 146 F1
Hill Of Beath KY4 147 A1
TORBREX 134 F5
Torbrex Farm Rd FK7 135 A4
Torbrex La FK7, FK8 135 A5
Torbrex Rd FK7 134 F4
Torphin Pl KY2 131 A2
Torphins Ave KY7 110 E2
Torres Loan KY5 128 D6
Torridon Ct FK10 138 C5
Torridon Dr KY11 173 E2
Torridon La KY11 173 E2
Torridon Pl
9 Glenrothes KY6 112 E6
Kinross KY13 108 B4
Kirkcaldy KY2 150 E8
Rosyth KY11 173 E2
Torridon Rd DD5 96 B4
Torrie Wynd 3 KY16 68 F7
Torry Bay Ct KY12 158 C1
TORRYBURN 158 E1
Torryburn Prim Sch
KY12 158 E1
Torry Dr FK12 117 E7
Torvean Pl KY11 161 C2
Torwoodlee PH1 102 A4
Torwood Pl
Dundee DD4 94 F8
Dunfermline KY12 161 D5
Torwood Way 8 KY7 111 C2
TOUCH 161 E5
Touch Prim Sch KY11 161 E4
Touch Rd FK7, FK8 134 B6
Touch Wards KY12 161 E4
Tovey Rd KY11 173 D2
Tower Ct DD5 95 C3
Tower Pl FK10 138 F5
Towers Pl FK9 115 D4
Tower Sq FK10 138 B5
Tower St FK10 138 A7
Tower Terr KY1 151 F8
Tower View FK10 118 E1
Tower View Ct 2 KY14 63 A6
Tower Wynd PH1 46 F8
Town Burn FK7 134 F4
Townhall St KY11 174 C2
Townhead
Auchterarder PH3 104 C6
Coupar Angus PH13 16 A3
Dysart KY1 152 A7
Kinghorn KY3 166 F3
Townhead Apartments 9
FK10 138 B6
Town Head Mus*
KY12 169 D8
Townhead Rd DD11 89 D5
TOWNHILL 161 C8
Townhill Ctry Pk*
KY12 161 D8
Townhill Day Hospl
KY12 161 D7
Townhill Prim Sch
KY12 161 D8
Townhill Rd KY12 161 B5
Townsend Cres KY1 151 C4
Townsend Pl KY1 151 C4
Trades La
1 Coupar Angus PH13 16 A2
Dundee DD1 179 C2
Trades St 1 KY10 83 D7
Traill Dr DD10 85 E3
Traill St DD5 96 A4
Traill Terr DD10 85 E2
Train Terr KY11 173 C5
Tranent Cres DD4 95 A8
Tranent Gdns DD4 95 A8
Tranent Gr DD4 95 A8
Tranent Wlk DD4 95 A8
Transy Gr KY12 161 C4
Transy Pl KY12 161 C4
Traquair Gdns
Dundee DD4 95 D8
Perth PH1 102 A4
Travebank Gdns 4
DD5 97 B6
Tree Back PH12 17 A7
Tremayne Pl KY12 160 F6
Trenchard Pl KY12 160 F5
Triangle The PH1 102 D8
Trident Dr PH2 38 B6
Trinafour PH1 102 B5
TRINITY 84 E7
Trinity Fields Cres DD9 84 C5
TRINITY GASK 45 F4
Trinity Gr PH1 46 F8
Trinity Pl
13 Leven KY8 109 E6
St Andrews KY16 106 A4
Trinity Rd DD9 84 C4
Tron Ct FK10 117 B2
Trondheim Parkway
Dunfermline KY11 161 F2
Dunfermline KY11 162 A2
Trondheim Pl KY11 161 F2
Trongate KY3 167 A3
Tron Sq 9 PH2 46 F1
Troon Ave DD2 91 A2
Troon Cres 6 DD2 91 A2
Troon Ct 8 DD2 91 A2
Troon Gdns DD2 91 A2
Troon Pl DD2 91 B2
Troon Rd DD2 91 A2
Troon Terr DD2 91 A2
TROTTICK 94 A8
Trottick Mains DD4 94 A8
Trynlaw Gdns KY15 105 A2
Tuke St KY12 161 A5
Tulliallan Prim Sch
FK10 155 E4
Tulliallan Terr FK10 155 E5
TULLIBARDINE 45 C1
Tullibardine Cres PH3 104 B5
Tullibardine Rd PH3 104 B5
TULLIBODY 117 C3
Tullibody Rd FK10 137 F8
Tullich Terr FK13 119 C7
Tullideph Pl DD2 93 C5
Tullideph Rd DD2 93 C5
Tullideph St DD2 93 D4
Tulliebelton Cres 11
PH1 24 A6
Tulliebelton Pl 12 PH1 24 A6
Tulliebelton Rd PH1 24 A5
Tulligarth Pk FK10 138 A7
TULLOCH 102 C7
Tulloch Cres DD3 179 B3
Tulloch Ct KY4 147 C5
Tulloch Hill PH1 102 D7
Tulloch Pl
St Andrews KY16 106 A3
Tulloch PH1 102 D7
Tulloch Prim Sch
PH1 102 D7
Tulloch Rd
Path of Condie PH2 60 D4
Perth PH1 102 D6
Tulloch Sq PH1 102 D7
Tulloch Terr PH1 102 D7
Tulloch Wynd DD8 1 A7
Tullylumb Farm La
PH2 102 F3
Tullylumb Terr PH1 102 E3
Tummel Dr KY2 150 D8
Tummel Pl
Dundee DD2 92 F4
Kinross KY13 108 B4
Tummel Rd
Glenrothes KY7 111 C2
Perth PH1 102 D5
TURFBEG 87 B6
Turfbeg Ave DD8 87 B6
Turfbeg Cres DD8 87 B6
Turfbeg Dr DD8 87 B6
Turfbeg Pl DD8 87 B6
Turfbeg Rd DD8 87 B6
Turfbeg Rise DD8 87 B6
Turleum Rd PH7 101 E3
Turnberry Ave DD2 91 A1
Turnberry Dr KY2 131 A1
Turnbull Gr KY11 161 F1
Turner Cres KY8 109 B3
Turniehill Gdns DD2 90 B3
Turnstiles The 10 KY8 109 C4
Turnstone Rd KY11 162 B1
Turpie Rd KY8 109 A6
Turretbank Dr PH7 101 A6
Turretbank Pl PH7 101 B6
Turretbank Rd PH7 101 B6
Turret Ct FK10 138 C6
Turriff Brae KY7 110 E2
Turriff Pl
Dundee DD3 91 C1
Kirkcaldy KY2 150 E8
Turriff St DD3 91 C1
Tutor Cl 13 KY16 54 B8
Tuttle Cl 16 KY16 54 B8
Tweed Ave KY1 151 E8
Tweed Cres DD2 92 E5
Tweeddale Dr KY11 161 E1
Tweed Mill Brae DD8 87 D6
Tweedsmuir Ct KY6 110 D2
Tweedsmuir Rd PH1 102 C5
Tweed St
Dunfermline KY11 161 F2
Leven KY8 109 A2
Twynholm Gdns 3
DD5 96 E6
Tyndall Cres DD5 96 E4
Tyndall Pl DD5 96 F4
Tyndrum Pl KY2 150 E7
Tyrie Ave KY1 167 B7
Tyrie Cres KY7 113 D6
Tyrie Ct KY1 167 B7
Tyrie Gdns KY1 167 B7
Tyrie Gr KY1 167 B7
Tyrwhitt Pl KY11 173 F3

U

Uist Pl PH1 102 F8
Uist Rd KY7 111 A1
Uist Terr DD4 94 C7
Ullapool Cres DD2 92 C5
Ulva Way PH1 102 E8
Ulverston Terr DD3 91 F1
Underwood Cotts FK7 134 D5
Underwood Rd FK7 134 D5
Unicorn Way KY7 113 A6
Unionbank DD2 93 B6
Union Cres 3 DD11 12 F4
Union La PH1 103 B4
Union Pl
Dundee DD2 93 D2
6 Ladybank KY15 64 A4
Montrose DD10 85 D4
Union Rd
Montrose DD10 85 D4
New Scone PH2 37 F5
Union Row DD10 85 E4
Union St E DD11 89 E3
Union St
4 Alloa FK10 138 B6
9 Arbroath DD11 12 F4
13 Arbroath DD11 89 D3
1 Blairgowrie PH10 88 C4
Brechin DD9 84 C2
Bridge of A FK9 115 A7
Burntisland KY3 177 E8
13 Coupar Angus PH13 16 A3
Cowdenbeath KY4 147 D4
Dundee DD1 179 B2
8 Glenrothes KY7 113 F8
Kelty KY4 126 D1
Kirkcaldy KY1 151 F7
11 Leven KY8 109 E6
Lochgelly KY5 148 B8
Monifieth DD5 97 B5
Montrose DD10 85 D4
Newport-on-Tay DD6 98 E5
14 Perth PH1 103 B4
St Andrews KY16 106 E6
Stirling FK8 115 B1
Tillicoultry FK13 119 B7
Union Terr
Crieff PH7 101 C3
Dundee DD3 179 A3
Unity Cres PH1 102 F5
Unity Terr PH1 102 E5
University Ave 17 KY10 83 A5
University of Abertay
Dundee DD1 179 B3
University of Dundee
Dundee DD1 179 A1
Dundee DD2 93 A2
University of Dundee
Botanic Gdns* DD2 93 A2
University of St Andrews
KY16 106 B6
University of Stirling
FK9 115 D6
University Rd W FK9 115 C6
University Terr 16 KY10 83 A5
Univ of Dundee Sch of
Nursing & Midwifery
Kirkcaldy Campus
KY2 151 A4
Upper Allan St PH10 88 C6
Upper Andover Hill 4
DD9 84 D2
Upper Bridge St FK8 115 A1
Upper Castlehill 2
FK8 135 A8
Upper Constitution St
DD3 179 A4
Upper Craigo St 5
DD10 85 C3
Upper Craigs FK8 135 B7
Upper Dalgairn KY15 105 C6
Upper Glen Rd FK9 70 D1
Upper Granco St 5
PH2 47 A1
Upper Greens 5 KY14 62 F7
Upper Hall St 8 DD10 85 C4
Upper Hillfoot Rd FK14 73 C1
Upper Kinnedar Gdns
KY12 142 F4
Upper Kinneddar
KY12 142 F5
Upper Millhill St KY11 161 B3
Upper Mill St
1 Blairgowrie PH10 88 C5
Tillicoultry FK13 119 A7
Upper Wellheads
KY11 172 E3
Upper Woodlands
PH1 102 C3
Ure St DD1 93 E3
URQUHART 160 D2
Urquhart Cres KY12 160 E3
Urquhart Ct KY2 150 D5
Urquhart Cut KY12 160 E3
Urquhart Farm Cotts
KY12 160 D2
Urquhart Gn KY7 113 C2
Urquhart St 4 DD1 93 E3
Urquhart Wynd 5
KY10 83 D6
USAN 6 E1
Usan Rd DD10 85 D1

V

Vale Gr FK9 114 F5
Valgreen Ct DD4 94 E5
Valley Dr KY6 112 A7
Valleyfield Ave KY12 158 B2
Valleyfield Pl
Cowdenbeath KY4 147 D5
Stirling FK7 135 C6
Valleyfield Woodland Pk*
KY12 158 B3
Valleyfield Woods Trail*
KY12 158 B1
Valley Gdns
Kirkcaldy KY2 150 F6
Leslie KY6 112 B7
Valley Gdns S KY2 150 F6
Valley Gr KY6 112 B7
Valley Prim Sch KY2 151 A7
Valley View KY2 150 F6
Vane Farm RSPB
Reserve* KY13 76 D2
Vardon Dr KY7 113 B5
Vasart Ct PH1 103 A4
Vaynes Pk DD9 84 B3
Veere Pk KY12 157 E1
Venachar Pl KY12 160 B1
Vennel The
2 Earlsferry/Elie KY9 82 B3
Forfar DD8 87 D5
South Queensferry
EH30 178 C1
Venturefair Ave KY12 161 A6
Verdant Works* DD1 179 A2
Verena Terr 3 PH2 103 A1
Vernonholme DD2 93 A2
Veronica Cres KY1 151 C8
Vettriano Vale KY8 109 B7
Vicar's Bridge Rd
FK14 121 D6
Viceroy St KY2 151 B6
Victoria Ave
East Wemyss KY1 133 A5
Milnathort KY13 108 D7
Victoria Gdns
Dundee DD5 95 F4
Kirkcaldy KY1 151 B4
Victoria Gn FK15 107 F7
Victoria Hospl KY2 151 B7
Victoria Pl
Blairgowrie PH10 88 D6
Brechin DD9 84 D2
Dundee DD5 20 E1
13 Falkland KY15 63 B2
Stirling FK8 135 A7
Victoria Rd
7 Arbroath DD11 12 F4
Auchterarder PH3 104 D6
Buckhaven KY8 133 F8
Dundee DD1 179 B3
Glenrothes KY7 113 F7
Kirkcaldy KY1 151 C5
Leven KY8 109 E6
Lower Largo KY8 80 E5
25 New Scone PH2 37 F5
Stirling FK8 135 A8
Tayport DD6 99 F6
Victoria Sq
5 Montrose DD10 85 D1
Stirling FK8 135 A7
Victoria St
Alloa FK10 138 A7
23 Alyth PH11 7 A3
Arbroath DD11 89 C3
Blairgowrie PH10 88 D6
Carnoustie DD7 100 B2
11 Coupar Angus PH13 16 A3
Dundee DD4 179 C4
Dunfermline KY12 161 A5
Dysart KY1 152 A7

Victoria St *continued*
Forfar DD8 87 D5
Kirriemuir DD8 86 C3
10 Ladybank KY15 64 A4
Monifieth DD5 97 A7
7 Montrose DD10 85 C4
Newport-on-Tay DD6 98 E4
Perth PH2 103 B3
Victoria Terr
Crieff PH7 101 C4
Dunfermline KY12 161 A5
Markinch KY7 113 F7
Menstrie FK11 117 B7
Viewbank KY6 112 B7
Viewbank Pl DD9 84 E3
Viewbank Terr 10 DD8 86 C5
Viewfar Rd KY13 108 D7
VIEWFIELD 112 F5
Viewfield KY6 112 E4
Viewfield Dr FK12 117 F6
Viewfield Ho KY12 161 B3
Viewfield Ind Est KY6 112 F4
Viewfield Pl
Blairgowrie PH13 26 C7
Perth PH1 102 F5
3 Stirling FK8 135 B8
Viewfield Rd DD11 89 B3
Viewfield St 4 FK8 135 B8
Viewfield Terr
Cowdenbeath KY4 147 F6
Dunfermline KY12 161 B3
Viewforth
Glenrothes KY7 111 C2
Leven KY8 133 E8
Stirling FK8 135 B6
View Forth 7 KY8 109 E6
Viewforth Ave KY1 151 F7
Viewforth Ct KY3 166 F2
Viewforth Gdns KY1 151 F7
Viewforth High Sch
KY1 151 F7
Viewforth Pl
Kinghorn KY3 166 F2
Leven KY8 109 E6
Pittenweem KY10 83 A5
Viewforth Rd EH30 178 B1
Viewforth Sq 25 KY8 109 E6
Viewforth St KY1 151 F7
Viewforth Terr KY1 151 F8
Viewlands PH2 39 F2
Viewlands Ct PH1 102 E3
Viewlands Pl PH1 102 E2
Viewlands Prim Sch
PH1 102 D2
Viewlands Rd PH1 102 E3
Viewlands Rd W PH1 102 C3
Viewlands Terr PH1 102 E2
View Mount DD8 87 D4
Viewmount Rd 7 DD6 42 B5
Viking Way KY11 173 D2
Villa Pl FK10 139 A5
Villa Rd EH30 178 B1
Vinny Den DD8 11 F3
Virgin Sq 13 KY10 82 E4
Viscounts Pend 3 DD4 94 C8
Voil Rd FK9 115 A3
Volunteer's Gn KY1 151 C3
Vorlich Ave DD5 96 D6
Vorlich Dr DD5 96 D6
Vorlich Pl FK9 115 A3
Vorlich Way KY11 162 B1
Vrackie Pl KY11 162 B1

W

Wadeslea KY9 82 B3
Wade St DD2 92 C7
Waggon Rd
Crossford KY11 172 C7
Inverkeithing KY11 174 C2
Leven KY8 109 E7
9 Pittenweem KY10 83 A5
Waid Acad KY10 83 C7
Waid Terr 23 KY10 83 C6
Waldron Rd DD10 85 D7
Walker Dr EH30 178 A1
Walker Pl
8 Arbroath DD11 89 D4
Dunfermline KY11 161 E1
10 St Andrews KY16 54 E2
Walker's Mill DD3 179 B4
Walker St
Cowdenbeath KY4 147 B3
Kincardine FK10 155 E3
Kirkcaldy KY2 151 B6
Lochgelly KY5 148 A6
Walker Terr FK13 119 B7
Walkerton Dr KY6 112 A7
Walk The
Alloa FK10 138 A5
Dysart KY1 152 B7
Wallace Ave KY16 106 C5
Wallace Cres PH1 102 D6
Wallace Ct FK8 115 B1
Wallace Gait PH1 102 D6
Wallace Gate FK8 135 B8
Wallace Gdns FK9 115 D3
Wallace High Sch FK9 115 B3
Wallace Monument*
FK9 115 E4
Wallace Pl
Cambusbarron FK7 134 D5
Dundee DD2 28 B1
Fallin FK7 136 C4
Wallace Pl *continued*
Kingseat KY12 146 A1
Perth PH1 102 D6
Wallace Rd FK15 107 B5
Wallace St
Alloa FK10 138 C7
Arbroath DD11 89 C2
Bannockburn FK7 135 E1
Blairgowrie PH12 16 E4
Carnoustie DD7 100 B3
Cowdenbeath KY4 147 C3
3 Dundee DD4 94 C2
Dunfermline KY11 161 C2
7 St Andrews KY16 106 D5
Stirling FK8 115 B1
Wallace View FK10 117 D3
Wallgate Ctr The DD1 179 B3
Wallsend Ct KY12 160 D5
Wallsgreen Gdns KY5 129 A4
Wallsgreen Rd 5 KY5 129 B4
Walls Pl KY11 161 E1
Wall St 4 KY8 109 A2
Wallstale Rd FK7 135 A3
Walmer Dr KY12 161 A3
Walnut Cres 8 KY8 79 F3
Walnut Gr
Blairgowrie PH10 88 D3
1 Broom KY8 109 D8
Dunfermline KY11 173 D8
Perth PH2 103 F1
3 Sillerhole KY8 80 F5
WALNUT GROVE 103 F1
Walnut Pk FK13 119 D7
Walrond St 2 DD4 94 C4
Walter Hay Ct KY11 173 F3
Walton Cres FK14 120 D8
Walton Pk KY15 65 B5
Walton St 3 DD1 93 E3
WARDDYKES 89 D7
Warddykes Ave DD11 89 D6
Warddykes Path DD11 89 D7
Warddykes Prim Sch
DD11 89 D6
Warddykes Rd DD11 89 D7
Wardhouse Rd DD10 85 D7
Wardlaw Cres
Dunfermline KY11 161 D1
Oakley KY12 158 F7
Wardlaw Gdns KY16 106 C6
Wardlaw St
Cowdenbeath KY4 147 C3
Tillicoultry FK13 119 B4
Wardlaw Way KY12 158 F7
Wardmill Ind Est DD11 89 C5
Wardmill Rd DD11 89 C5
Ward Rd
Crieff PH5 44 D4
Dundee DD1 179 A2
Wards Ave 1 DD7 100 B3
Wardside PH5 44 C4
Wards Rd DD9 84 E4
Ward St
Alloa FK10 138 A5
Leven KY8 109 A2
Ward The 5 KY5 77 E1
Warout Brae KY7 113 B6
Warout Gdns KY7 113 A6
Warout Prim Sch KY7 113 A6
Warout Rd KY7 113 B5
Warout Wlk KY7 113 A5
Warrack St KY16 106 E4
Warrack Terr DD10 85 D4
Warren Pl DD2 90 C3
Warslap Ave DD11 89 A2
Warwick Cl 9 KY16 54 B8
Waterend Rd 1 KY15 105 D4
Waterford & Stuart Crystal Factory Shop PH7 101 B2
Waterfront Way FK9 115 A3
WATERGATE 125 C8
Watergate PH1 103 C3
WATERLOO 24 A7
Waterside
9 Dunblane FK15 56 B4
Monifieth DD5 96 F5
Waterside Rd DD10 85 E2
Waterside View 4
DD7 100 F3
Water Ski Ctr* KY12 161 C7
Waterson Crook Sports Ctr
DD6 98 C2
Waterson Dr DD9 84 C4
Waterston Crook 3
DD6 98 C3
Waterston Rd DD8 3 C5
Water Vennel PH1 103 C3
Watson Ave KY16 106 D5
Watson Pl KY12 161 B6
Watson St
Cowdenbeath KY4 147 D3
Dundee DD4 94 C2
Letham DD8 11 F3
Watson Watt Pl DD9 84 C4
Watson Way DD7 100 D8
Watters Cres KY5 148 B6
Watt Rd KY11 173 B2
Watt's Gdns KY15 105 E5
Watt St KY1 152 A7
Waulker Ave FK8 114 F2
Waulkmill Dr PH4 57 B3
Waulkmill Steading
KY12 171 F6
Waverley Cres FK8 115 C1
Waverley Dr KY6 112 C5
Waverley Pl 6 KY5 127 F6
Waverley Rd KY1 131 E1
Waverley Terr DD4 94 D3
Waverly Terr DD11 89 F5
Wayfarers Dr KY11 174 F3
Wayfarers Pl KY11 174 F3
Wayfarers Way KY11 174 F3
Weaver Row FK7 135 A4
Weavers Cl 6 DD11 89 C3
Weavers Cres KY2 151 B6
Weavers Ct
1 Cupar KY14 62 D4
East Wemyss KY1 133 C6
Weavers Loan DD3 179 A3
Weaver's Terr KY12 159 D1
Weavers Way FK13 119 A6
Weavers Wlk
Dunfermline KY12 161 A2
Forfar DD8 87 E6
Weavers Yd DD4 179 C3
Webster Ct DD11 89 C6
Webster Pl KY11 173 C5
Websters High Sch
DD8 86 C4
Webster's Sports Ctr
DD7 86 C4
Webster Theatre DD11 89 D3
Wedderburn Cres
KY11 161 E1
Wedderburn Pl
8 Dundee Law DD3 93 F6
Dunfermline KY11 161 D2
Wedderburn Rd
Dunblane FK15 107 D7
Kirkcaldy KY2 150 C7
Wedderburn St
Dundee DD3 93 F6
Dunfermline KY11 161 D2
Wee Causeway KY12 169 D8
Wee Course La PH10 88 B1
Weir Ave KY4 147 B2
Weir Dr FK7 136 D4
Weir Pl 1 PH1 102 D8
Weir St FK8 114 F2
Well Acre Cald 9 KY15 64 A3
WELLBANK 30 F7
Wellbank 9 DD8 86 D5
Well Bank 4 KY14 62 D4
Wellbank Gdns KY7 113 B2
Wellbank La DD2 93 C5
Wellbank Pl DD5 97 B6
Well Brae 11 KY15 63 B2
Wellbraehead DD8 87 D5
Wellburn St DD2 93 A6
Well Cres KY7 113 D5
Wellesley Path KY7 111 B1
Wellesley Rd KY8 109 D5
Wellfield KY13 108 C8
Wellgate
Arbroath DD11 89 C4
Kirriemuir DD8 86 C5
Wellgate Dr FK9 115 C7
Wellgate St 9 DD6 98 C3
Well Gdns KY7 113 D5
Wellgreen La 11 FK8 135 B7
Wellgreen Pl FK8 135 B6
Wellgreen Rd FK8 135 B7
Wellgrove St DD2 93 A6
Wellheads The KY11 172 D3
Wellington Cl DD10 85 D4
Wellington Gdns DD10 85 D4
Wellington Pk DD10 85 D4
Wellington Pl DD10 85 D4
Wellington Sq DD3 179 C4
Wellington St
Dundee DD1 179 C4
Montrose DD10 85 D4
Wellington Twr DD3 179 C4
Wellmeadow 3 PH10 88 C5
Wellmyre FK10 139 A3
Wellpark Cres FK7 134 F4
Wellpark Pl KY15 64 C2
Wellpark Terr E 8
DD6 98 C3
Wellpark Terr W 7
DD6 98 C3
Well Pl
4 Cupar KY15 105 D5
Dunblane FK15 107 C5
Well Rd
Bridge of A FK9 115 A8
Dundee DD1 93 E3
7 Forfar DD8 10 F7
Glenrothes KY7 113 C5
4 Ladybank KY15 64 A4
Lochgelly KY5 148 B7
1 Perth PH2 47 A1
Wellshill Terr PH1 102 F4
Wellshot 11 KY8 79 F5
Wellshot Cres KY8 79 F5
Wellshot Pl 10 KY8 79 F5
Well St
Cupar KY15 105 D5
Monifieth DD5 97 C6
WELLWOOD 161 A7
Wellwood Prim Sch
KY12 161 A7
Welsh Gdns FK9 115 A8
Welton Ind Est PH10 88 D4
Welton Rd PH10 88 D4
Wemyss Castle* KY1 132 F3
Wemyss Cres DD5 96 E5
Wemyss Ct
Glenrothes KY7 113 C3
Rosyth KY11 173 E5
Wemyssfield KY1 151 B3
Wemyss Gdns 4 DD5 96 B5
Wemysshall Rd KY15 65 C6
Wemysshaven Gdns
KY1 133 C7
Wemyss Pl 6 KY8 109 C4
Wemyss Rd KY1 152 B8
Wemyss St
Cowdenbeath KY4 147 D3
Rosyth KY11 173 F5
Wentworth Ave DD2 91 A1
Wentworth Cres DD2 91 A1
Wentworth Ct 4 DD2 91 A1
Wentworth Dr DD2 91 A1
Wentworth Gdns 3
DD2 91 A1
Wentworth La 2 DD2 91 A1
Wentworth Pl 5 DD2 91 A1
Wentworth Rd DD2 91 A1
Wentworth St 1 DD2 91 A1
Wentworth Terr DD2 91 A1
Wesley Gdns 3 DD11 89 E4
West Abbey St DD11 89 D4
West Acres 4 KY16 54 E3
West Acres Dr DD6 98 B2
West Albert Rd KY1 151 B4
West Altamount La
PH10 88 B3
West Back Dykes 2
KY14 62 D5
West Baldridge Rd
KY12 160 E5
Westbank 1 KY14 62 F6
West Bank DD8 9 A7
Westbank Gdns 1 DD8 9 A7
Westbank Rd DD2 40 F8
Westbank Terr 2 DD8 9 A7
Westbarn Rd 2 DD5 96 D3
West Bell St DD1 179 A2
Westbourne Ave FK13 119 C7
West Brae KY1 133 B6
West Braes
Anstruther KY10 83 A5
Crail KY10 69 A2
West Braes Cres 7
KY10 69 A2
West Bridge St PH1 103 B4
West Broomhill Rd
KY3 177 E8
West Brougham St 3
PH1 24 E4
Westburn Ave KY4 147 B2
West Burn La KY16 106 E6
West Burnside 22 FK14 73 C1
Westcroft Pl DD4 94 F6
Westcroft Rd DD4 94 F6
Westcroft Way KY4 126 D2
West Crook Way KY13 74 D2
West Dr KY12 161 B3
Westend PH2 39 C5
West End
7 Kinglassie KY5 77 E1
9 Monance KY10 82 E4
West End Gdns FK10 138 A6
WESTER ABERDOUR 176 B6
WESTER BALGEDIE 76 E7
Wester Bogie Rd KY2 150 B7
Wester Gourdie Ind Est
DD2 92 C7
Westerhill PH1 102 C2
Westerlands Dr FK8 135 B5
Westerlea KY6 112 A8
Westerlea Ct FK9 115 A5
Westerlea Dr FK9 115 A5
Wester Loan KY13 108 D7
Western Ave
Crossford KY12 160 B1
Glenrothes KY7 110 F1
Perth PH1 102 E4
Western Rd
Auchterarder PH3 104 C5
Montrose DD10 85 C3
Western Rd N DD10 85 C4
Western Wharf Rd DD1 94 C1
Wester Restenneth
DD8 87 F6
Westerton Ave DD5 96 A5
Westerton Dr FK9 115 A7
West Fergus Pl KY1 151 B3
WEST FERRY 95 D4
WESTFIELD 87 A3
Westfield
Kincardine FK10 156 B3
Kirriemuir DD8 86 C4
Luncarty PH1 37 B8
Westfield Ave KY15 105 B4
Westfield Brae 2 KY5 129 B4
Westfield Cres DD8 87 B3
Westfield Dr DD8 87 B4
Westfield Gdns DD8 87 B2
Westfield Gr KY4 162 E6
Westfield La DD1 93 E2
Westfield Loan DD8 87 B3
Westfield Pk DD8 87 B3
Westfield Pl
Carnoustie DD7 100 A2
Dundee DD1 93 E2
Forfar DD8 87 B3
Westfield Rd
Cupar KY15 105 B4
Dundee DD5 95 F2
Westfield St DD7 100 A2
Westfield Terr
Auchterderran KY5 129 B4
Newport-on-Tay DD6 98 C3
West Forth St 10 KY10 83 D6
Westgate
6 Arbroath DD11 12 F4
15 Crail KY10 69 B2
Glenrothes KY6 112 A8
West George St PH10 88 C4
West Gn 16 KY10 69 B2
West Grange Rd DD5 96 F6
West Grange St 2 DD5 96 F6
West Grange Wlk 5
DD5 96 E6
West Gr Ave DD2 93 A3
Westgreen Wynd DD2 28 D3
West Grimsby 3 DD11 89 D3
Westhall Cres KY12 159 D1
Westhall Ct DD4 94 E5
Westhall Terr DD4 30 C7
West Harbour Rd
KY11 172 A4
Westhaugh Cvn Site
FK10 118 A4
Westhaugh Rd FK9 114 F4
WEST HAVEN 100 F4
Westhaven Gdns 5
DD11 89 D5
West Haven Pk DD7 100 F4
West Hemming St DD8 11 E3
West Henderson's Wynd 7
DD1 93 E3
West High St
6 Crieff PH7 101 C4
Forfar DD8 87 C4
Leven KY8 133 F8
West Hillbank DD8 86 C5
West Hillhead Rd DD5 20 E1
West Hill Rd DD8 86 D6
WEST INGLISTON 9 F3
West James St FK12 118 A6
West Johnstone St
FK12 118 A6
West Keptie St 1
DD11 89 C3
West La KY4 147 B2
Westland Pk 2 KY14 62 F7
Westlaw Pl KY6 112 C3
Westlaw Rd KY6 112 C3
West Leven St KY3 177 E8
West Lights DD6 99 D7
West Link Rd FK9 115 D5
West Lodge Gdns
FK10 137 F8
West Lyon St DD3 179 C4
West Mains Ave PH1 102 B5
West March St KY1 151 D7
West Marketgait DD1 179 A2
West Mill St 2 PH1 103 A4
WESTMUIR 9 A7
Westmuir Rd DD8 86 B2
West Murrayfield FK7 135 D1
West Netherton KY13 61 B1
West Nethertown St
KY12 161 A2
West Newgate DD11 89 E3
West Park
Carnock KY12 159 C6
Lochgelly KY5 148 A7
6 Perth PH2 49 E3
7 Stanley PH1 24 E4
West Park Ave KY6 112 A7
Westpark Gate KY12 142 D6
Westpark Gdns DD2 93 B3
Westpark Rd PH10 88 B3
West Park Rd
Cupar KY15 105 B4
Dundee DD2 93 B3
Newport-on-Tay DD6 98 C2
West Path DD7 100 C3
West Pitkerro Ind Est
DD5 95 E7
Westport DD1 179 A2
West Port
3 Arbroath DD11 89 C3
Cupar KY15 105 B4
Dysart KY1 152 A7
Falkland KY15 63 A2
Inverkeithing KY11 174 B2
Westport Pl KY15 105 B4
West Port Rd 1 KY14 50 D5
West Quality St KY1 152 A7
West Queen St DD5 95 F3
Westray Ct PH1 102 F8
West Rd
Charlestown KY11 172 A4
Cupar KY14 62 D5
Denhead of Gray DD2 92 A8
Newport-on-Tay DD6 98 C3
Saline KY12 142 D5
Westreton Ho FK9 115 A8
West Sands KY11 178 C6
West Sands Rd KY16 106 C8
West Sch Rd DD3 91 D1
West Shore
Anstruther KY10 83 A5
10 Monance KY10 82 E4
West Shore Rd 6
KY14 50 D5
West Smieton St DD7 100 B2
West Somerville Pl
DD3 179 A3
West St
Dundee DD3 93 F6
11 Monance KY10 82 E4
West Stirling St FK12 117 F7
West Terr
Montrose DD10 85 C1
South Queensferry
EH30 178 B1
WEST TOFTS 24 E5
West Torbain KY2 150 D8
West Vennel 6 FK10 138 B6
West Victoria Dock Rd
DD1 179 C2
Westview KY16 106 D5
West View PH1 46 E8
Westview Cres FK10 117 C2
Westview Pk (Kirrie Thistle FC) DD8 86 B4

West Vows Wlk KY1 167 B6
Westwater Pl DD6 98 A2
Westwater St KY5 148 B8
Westway [1] DD11 89 A4
West Way KY11 175 B5
Westway Ret Pk DD11 22 E3
WEST WEMYSS 132 F2
Westwood DD9 84 B3
Westwood Ave KY1 151 E8
Westwood Cres KY5 127 F7
Westwood Ct KY7 113 E6
Westwood Pk KY7 113 D3
Westwood Pl KY11 161 E4
Westwood Rd KY7 113 E6
Westwood Wlk DD10 85 C7
West Wynd
Dundee DD1 93 E2
[13] Kirkcaldy KY1 151 D6
Leven KY8 133 F8
Wetherby Pl DD3 93 E6
Whalers' Cl [6] DD4 94 C3
Wharf St DD10 85 C2
Wharry Rd FK12 117 E7
Wheatfield Ave PH14 40 C7
Wheatfield Rd KY1 131 D1
Wheatley St KY8 109 B3
Wheatstone Pl KY6 112 C3
Whig St DD8 2 C4
WHIGSTREET 20 B6
Whimbrel Pl KY11 162 C4
Whinfield Dr KY13 108 B4
Whinfield Gdns KY13 108 B4
Whinfield Pl DD6 98 E5
Whinfield Rd DD10 85 E4
Whinfield Way DD10 85 E4
Whinhill KY11 161 C3
Whinneyknowe KY11 178 C6
Whinnie KY7 79 C4
Whinniehill Terr KY12 159 C6
Whinny Brae DD5 96 B2
Whinnyburn Pl KY11 173 D5
Whinnyhill Cres KY11 174 A1
Whinnyknowe KY6 110 D1
WHINS OF MILTON 135 B2
Whins of Milton Sch FK7 135 B1
Whins Rd
Alloa FK10 138 C7
Stirling FK7 135 B2
Whinwell Rd FK8 115 A1
Whirlbut Cres KY11 161 B2
Whirlbut St KY11 161 B2
Whirlwind Pl [1] KY16 54 B7
Whistlers Way DD1 179 B3
Whitburn Pl DD3 91 E3
White Ave KY8 109 D7
Whitecraig Rd KY14 50 D5
Whitecraigs [5] KY13 76 F5
Whitecraigs Rd KY6 112 C3
Whitecross Ave [4] FK15 107 E7
Whitefauld Rd DD2 92 E3
Whitefield Neuk KY12 161 F6
Whitefield Rd KY12 161 E6
Whitefield Rise KY12 161 F6
Whitefriars Cres PH1 102 F4
Whitefriars St PH1 102 F4
White Gates Terr KY4 126 E2
Whitehall Ave KY5 129 D2
Whitehall Cres
Cardenden KY5 129 D3
Dundee DD1 179 B2
Whitehall Dr KY5 129 D2
Whitehall St DD1 179 B2
Whitehall Theatre DD1 93 E2
WHITEHILL 112 C4
Whitehill Ind Est KY6 112 C3
Whitehill Pl FK8 135 A5
Whitehill Rd KY6 112 C4
WHITEHILLS 87 F6
Whitehills DD8 87 F6
Whitehills KY12 142 D6
Whitehills Cres DD8 87 F7
Whitehills Prim Sch DD8 87 E5
Whitehouse Rd FK7 135 D7
Whitelaw Cres KY11 161 D2
Whitelaw Pl KY11 161 D2
Whitelaw Rd KY11 161 D2
Whitelea Rd PH13 26 B7
Whiteloch Ave PH10 15 A5
Whitemyre Ct KY12 160 D5
Whitenhill [4] DD6 99 F6
Whiteside DD8 86 C5
Whites Pl DD10 85 D4
Whites Quay KY11 174 F2
White Wisp Gdns [6] FK14 73 C1
Whiteyetts Cres FK10 118 D2
Whiteyetts Dr FK10 118 D2
Whiteyetts Pl FK10 118 D2
WHITFIELD 95 A7
Whitfield Ave DD4 95 A7
Whitfield Dr DD4 95 A7
Whitfield Gdns DD4 95 A7
Whitfield Loan DD4 95 A7
Whitfield Prim Sch DD4 95 A7
Whitfield Rise DD4 95 A7
Whitfield Sq DD4 95 A7
Whitfield Terr [5] DD4 95 A7
Whithorn Pl [2] DD5 96 E6
Whitson Way [4] DD10 85 D7
Whittle Pl DD2 92 D7
Whitworth Rd KY6 112 E3
Whorterbank DD2 93 C5
Whytebank Gdns KY2 151 B5
Whyte Ct KY13 108 C2
Whytehouse Ave KY1 151 B3
Whyteman's Brae KY1 151 C8
Whytemans Brae Hospl KY1 151 B7
Whyte Melville Rd KY2 151 A4
Whyte Pl KY13 108 C7
Whyte Rose Terr KY8 109 D4
Whytescauseway KY1 151 B3
Whyte St KY5 148 B8
Whyte Wlk KY11 161 F4
Wicks O'Baiglie Rd PH2 48 F4
Wilderness The FK2 154 D4
Wilkie Ct [1] KY15 64 D4
Wilkie's La DD1 93 E3
William Barcley Sq DD1 179 B3
William Booth Pl FK7 135 A3
Williamfield Ave FK7 135 A4
William Fitzgerald Way DD4 29 E5
William Laing Cres [18] KY8 109 E6
William Lammond Cres [8] DD5 96 F6
William Path KY7 111 B1
William Philips Dr [7] DD10 85 D3
William Pl
[2] Carnoustie DD7 100 E3
Perth PH2 37 E5
William Rodger Dr [8] DD10 85 D3
Williamsburgh [6] KY9 82 A2
William Sharp Pl KY4 147 D4
William Sinclair St KY2 130 D1
Williamson's Quay KY1 151 C4
William St
Blairgowrie PH10 88 C5
Carnoustie DD7 100 E3
Dundee DD1 179 C4
Dunfermline KY12 160 E4
East Wemyss KY1 133 C7
[1] Forfar DD8 87 E5
Kirkcaldy KY1 151 B2
[7] Kirriemuir DD8 86 D4
[4] Montrose DD10 85 D1
Newport-on-Tay DD6 98 E5
Tayport DD6 99 F6
Willison Cres FK13 119 C7
Willison St DD1 179 B2
Willoughby St PH5 44 C3
Willow Bank [4] KY8 79 F3
Willow Cres KY6 112 E7
Willow Dr KY1 151 B8
Willow Glade [2] KY8 80 F5
Willow Gr
Dunfermline KY11 173 E8
Menstrie FK11 116 E6
Willow Pl
Blairgowrie PH10 88 D2
[5] New Scone PH2 37 F5
Willows The
Cairneyhill KY12 159 D1
Dundee DD4 94 F8
Kelty KY4 126 F2
Tullibody FK10 117 B1
Wilmington Dr KY7 110 F3
Wilson Ave KY2 151 B6
Wilson Bruce Ct KY5 148 C8
Wilson Ct KY13 108 B3
Wilson Dr FK7 135 C2
Wilson's Cl [1] KY12 161 A3
Wilson's Pk DD9 84 C3
Wilsons Pl KY16 54 C3
Wilson Sq [7] KY8 79 F2
Wilson St
Blairhall KY12 158 A8
Cowdenbeath KY4 147 C4
Lochgelly KY5 128 A1
Perth PH2 102 F2
Townhill KY12 161 D8
Wilson Way KY11 173 D2
Wimberley Ct [12] PH13 16 A3
Windlebrook KY11 174 A7
Windmill Ct [6] KY10 83 D7
Windmill Gn KY1 151 F8
Windmill Knowe KY4 162 E6
Windmill Pl KY1 152 A8
Windmill Rd
Anstruther KY10 83 D7
Kirkcaldy KY1 151 F8
St Andrews KY16 106 C6
Windmill View FK10 118 D2
Windsole PH3 104 F7
Windsor Ct
Craigie PH2 103 A2
Dundee DD2 93 D2
[2] Dundee DD5 95 F2
Windsor Gdns
Alloa FK10 137 F8
Auchterarder PH3 57 C6
St Andrews KY16 106 A3
Windsor Pl
Dundee DD2 93 D2
Stirling FK8 135 A7
Windsor St
Dundee DD2 93 D2
Menstrie FK11 116 F6
Windsor Terr PH2 103 A2
Windyedge Pl DD8 87 C4
Windyedge Terr DD8 87 C4
Windygate KY2 150 F1
WINDYGATES 79 D3
Windygates Rd KY8 109 D7
Windyghoul Rd DD8 86 B7
Windyhill Ave FK10 155 D6
Winifred Cres KY2 151 A6
Winifred St KY2 151 A6
Winram Pl KY16 106 B3
Winter Pl [1] DD7 100 F3
Winterthur La KY12 161 A4
Winthank Ct [7] KY15 105 C5
Wishart Ave DD10 85 D5
Wishart Dr FK7 135 D3
Wishart Gdns
Montrose DD10 85 D5
St Andrews KY16 106 D3
Wishart Pl
Dundee DD1 179 C4
Kirkcaldy KY1 151 F6
Wishart St DD3 179 A4
Wiston Pl [2] DD2 93 C6
Witchbrae KY12 161 B4
Witchden Rd DD9 84 D2
Witches Craig Cvn Pk FK9 116 A6
WOLFHILL 25 D4
Wolfhill Rd PH2 25 B3
Wolseley St DD3 94 B4
Wood Avens FK10 117 B1
Woodbank KY4 147 B2
Woodbank Gr KY12 158 D7
Woodbine Terr DD6 98 E5
Woodburn Cres KY12 158 F7
Woodburn Dr FK10 117 F1
Woodburne [5] KY15 65 D6
Woodburne St DD4 94 E3
Woodburn Pl KY16 106 F5
Woodburn Rd
Ceres KY15 65 D6
Glenrothes KY7 113 E7
Woodburn Terr KY16 106 F5
Woodburn Way FK12 118 A6
WOODEND 129 A5
Woodend Bsns Ctr KY4 147 B1
Woodend Dr DD8 86 C6
Woodend Gdns KY11 174 F5
Woodend Ind Est KY4 147 B1
Woodend Pk KY5 128 F5
Woodend Pl
Cowdenbeath KY4 147 B1
Kelty KY4 126 D3
[19] New Scone PH2 37 F5
Woodend Rd
Auchterderran KY5 129 A5
Gauldry DD6 41 F2
Woodgate Dr KY7 113 D4
Woodgate Way N KY7 113 D4
Woodgate Way S KY7 113 D4
WOODHAVEN 98 C1
Woodhaven Ave DD6 98 B2
Woodhaven Pl [6] DD5 96 C5
Woodhaven Terr DD6 98 B2
Woodhead Farm Rd KY12 157 F2
Woodhead Farm Steadings KY12 157 F2
Woodhead Pl FK13 119 B3
Woodhead St KY12 158 A2
Woodhill Gr KY12 160 B2
Woodielea Rd KY8 80 E5
Wood La DD5 97 A6
Woodland Entrance KY9 82 A5
Woodland Gait KY2 130 A4
Woodland Park Nature Reserve* FK12 118 D8
Woodland Pk* PH2 38 A2
WOODLANDS 102 C2
Woodlands
Chapelton DD11 13 C1
Croof of Devon KY13 74 C3
Sauchie FK10 118 E1
Woodlands Ave DD8 2 C7
Woodlands Bank KY11 175 A3
Woodlands Cres KY8 109 C8
Woodlands Dr KY12 160 A2
Woodlands Est PH2 26 A3
Woodlands Gr
Blairgowrie PH10 88 D1
Townhill KY12 161 D7
Woodlands Mdw PH10 88 E1
Woodlands Pk PH10 88 D2
Woodlands Rd
Blairgowrie PH10 88 D2
Kirkcaldy KY2 150 D6
[17] Lower Largo KY8 80 F5
Woodlands Terr
Blairhall KY12 158 B8
Dundee DD4 94 A5
Woodlands The
Rosyth KY11 173 F5
Stirling FK8 135 B6
Woodland Way DD2 92 A1
Woodlaw Pk [3] KY8 81 A6
Wood Lea FK10 155 E5
Woodlea Gdns
Alloa FK10 118 A1
Carnoustie DD7 100 C3
Woodlea Pk
Alloa FK10 138 B8
Sauchie FK10 118 A1
Woodmill Cres KY11 161 D3
Woodmill High Sch KY11 161 E3
Woodmill Pl KY11 161 E3
Woodmill Rd KY11 161 D3
Woodmill St KY11 161 B3
Woodmill Terr KY11 161 B3
Woodmuir Cres DD6 98 C3
Wood Muir Terr DD6 98 D3
Wood Pl KY11 173 E5
Wood Rd
Dundee DD2 90 C3
Rosyth KY11 173 C2
Woodriffe Rd KY14 50 C4
Woodruff Gait KY12 160 F5
Woods Cvn Site FK10 118 C4
Woods Dr KY6 113 A4
WOODSIDE
Blairgownie 26 B8
Leven 66 A3
Woodside
Cowdenbeath KY4 147 C3
Glenrothes KY7 113 E6
[10] Northmuir DD8 86 C7
Woodside Ave
Dundee DD4 94 B5
Rosyth KY11 173 F5
Woodside Cres
[1] Earlsferry/Elie KY9 82 B3
Perth PH2 102 F2
Woodside Ct FK7 134 D5
Woodside Pl
[4] Earlsferry/Elie KY9 82 B3
Fallin FK7 136 C4
Woodside Rd
Alloa FK10 117 F1
Dundee DD2 28 D4
Earlsferry/Elie KY9 82 B3
Glenrothes KY7 113 C5
Letham DD8 11 E3
Stirling FK8 115 A3
Tullibody FK10 117 A1
Woodside St KY11 173 F5
Woodside Terr
Auchterderran KY5 129 B4
Carnoustie DD7 100 B3
Clackmannan FK10 138 F4
Woodside Terr *continued*
Dundee DD4 94 A5
Woodside Way KY7 113 D5
Woodside Wlk KY7 113 D5
Woods Pl KY6 113 A4
Woodstock Pl [2] KY5 127 F6
WOODVILLE FEUS 22 C6
Woodville Gdns [5] DD11 22 D6
Woodville Pk KY15 53 D4
Woodville Pl [1] DD4 94 C4
Woolcarders Ct FK7 134 D6
Woollcombe Sqare PH2 37 E5
Woolmill Rd KY7 113 D7
Worbey Pl DD2 28 B1
Wordie Rd FK7 134 F4
WORMIT 98 A1
Wormit Prim Sch DD6 98 B2
Wortley Pl DD4 94 D4
Wren St KY8 79 F1
Wright Ave DD2 92 E2
Wright Pl
Kirkcaldy KY1 151 D7
Lochgelly KY5 148 A8
Wurzburg Ct DD2 92 D4
Wyckliffe KY12 160 C6
Wylie's Brae [9] PH11 7 A3
Wyllie St DD8 87 E6
Wymet Ct KY12 161 A3
Wymet Ho KY12 161 A3
Wynd The
Alva FK12 118 A7
Cupar KY14 63 A5
Dalgety Bay KY11 175 C3
Glenrothes KY7 79 B3
Leven KY8 66 B3
Muthill PH5 44 C4
Wyre Hayes Cotts KY4 162 F8
Wyvis Ave DD5 96 D6
Wyvis Pl [2] DD5 96 D6
Wyvis Rd DD5 96 D6

Y

Yard Rd PH10 88 D5
Yarrow Pl PH1 102 A3
Yarrow Terr DD2 92 F4
Yeamans Alley DD2 93 B6
Yeaman's Alley [4] DD2 93 B6
Yeaman Shore DD1 179 B2
Yeaman's La DD2 93 A5
Yeaman St
[3] Blairgowrie PH10 88 E6
Carnoustie DD7 100 C3
Forfar DD8 87 E5
Yellowhill Rd
Cupar KY14 61 D4
Perth PH2 61 C5
Yetholm Pk KY12 160 F2
YETTS O' MUCKHART 74 A4
Yetts The FK7 134 C5
Yewbank Ave [3] DD5 96 C3
Yew Gdns PH1 37 B8
Yew La [3] PH2 47 F2
York Pl
Dunfermline KY12 161 C6
[4] Kirkcaldy KY1 131 F1
Kirkcaldy KY1 151 F8
[1] Montrose DD10 85 C4
[7] Newburgh KY14 50 D5
Perth PH1 103 A3
York Terr DD10 85 C4
Young Ave DD2 90 B3
Young Ct
Cowdenbeath KY4 147 C3
Tayport DD6 99 D7
Younger Gdns KY16 54 E2
Younger Pl KY16 54 B2
Youngs Ct PH7 101 E4
Youngsdale Pl [4] DD6 98 E4
Young St PH2 103 A2
Young's Terr [2] KY1 151 C5
Young Terr KY4 147 B3

Z

Zealandia Rd KY11 173 B1
Zetland Pl KY5 148 A7
Zetland St FK10 139 B4

Notes

Name and Address	Telephone	Page	Grid reference

Addresses

Name and Address	Telephone	Page	Grid reference

Any feature in this atlas can be given a unique reference to help you find the same feature on other Ordnance Survey maps of the area, or to help someone else locate you if they do not have a Street Atlas.

The grid squares in this atlas match the Ordnance Survey National Grid and are at 500 metre intervals. The small figures at the bottom and sides of every other grid line are the National Grid kilometre values (**00** to **99** km) and are repeated across the country every 100 km (see left).

To give a unique National Grid reference you need to locate where in the country you are. The country is divided into 100 km squares with each square given a unique two-letter reference. Use the administrative map to determine in which 100 km square a particular page of this atlas falls.

The bold letters and numbers between each grid line (**A** to **F**, **1** to **8**) are for use within a specific Street Atlas only, and when used with the page number, are a convenient way of referencing these grid squares.

Example *The railway bridge over DARLEY GREEN RD in grid square B1*

Step 1: Identify the two-letter reference, in this example the page is in **SP**

Step 2: Identify the 1 km square in which the railway bridge falls. Use the figures in the southwest corner of this square: Eastings **17**, Northings **74**. This gives a unique reference: **SP 17 74**, accurate to 1 km.

Step 3: To give a more precise reference accurate to 100 m you need to estimate how many tenths along and how many tenths up this 1 km square the feature is (to help with this the 1 km square is divided into four 500 m squares). This makes the bridge about **8** tenths along and about **1** tenth up from the southwest corner.

This gives a unique reference: **SP 178 741**, accurate to 100 m.

Eastings (read from left to right along the bottom) come before Northings (read from bottom to top). If you have trouble remembering say to yourself "Along the hall, THEN up the stairs"!

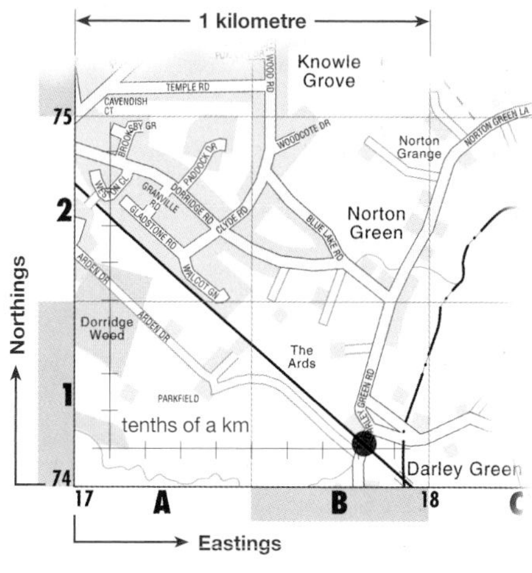

PHILIP'S MAPS
the Gold Standard for drivers

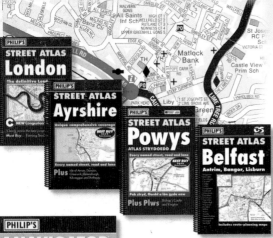